TRIPS and Access to Medicines

TRIPS and Access to Medicines

Pharmaceutical Patents and the Experience of Brazil

Renata Curzel

Wolters Kluwer

Published by:
Kluwer Law International B.V.
PO Box 316
2400 AH Alphen aan den Rijn
The Netherlands
E-mail: international-sales@wolterskluwer.com
Website: lrus.wolterskluwer.com

Sold and distributed by:
Wolters Kluwer Legal & Regulatory U.S.
7201 McKinney Circle
Frederick, MD 21704
United States of America
Email: customer.service@wolterskluwer.com

ISBN 978-94-035-2882-3

e-Book: ISBN 978-94-035-2874-8
web-PDF: ISBN 978-94-035-2880-9

This study was accepted as a doctoral thesis by the University of Oldenburg (Germany) in the winter semester 2019/2020 under the title "The TRIPS Agreement's Balancing of Incentives for Research and Access to Medicines: The Participation of the Brazilian National Health Surveillance Agency (Agência Nacional de Vigilância Sanitária—ANVISA) in the Patent Proceedings: A Model for Controlling Pharmaceutical Patents?" The thesis was defended on January 22, 2020. This version was slightly changed to provide an update on developments that occurred until August 2020.

Table of Contents

List of Abbreviations

ABIFINA	Associação Brasileira das Indústrias de Química Fina, Biotecnologia e suas Especificidades (Brazilian Association of the Fine Chemical and Biotechnology Industry and Their Specialties)
ABPI	Associação Brasileira de Propriedade Intelectual (Brazilian Association of Intellectual Property)
ABIFARMA	Associação Brasileira da Indústria Farmacêutica (Brazilian Association of the Pharmaceutical Industry), INTERFARMA's Predecessor
AGU	Advocacia Geral da União (Brazilian Federal Attorney General)
AL 94	Brazilian former Antitrust Law, Lei No. 8.884 of June 11, 1994
AL 2011	Brazilian Antitrust Law, Lei No. 12.529 of November 30, 2011
ALANAC	Associação dos Laboratórios Farmacêuticos Nacionais (Brazilian National Association of National Pharmaceutical Laboratories)
Am. J. L. & Med.	American Journal of Law and Medicine
ANVISA	Agência Nacional de Vigilância Sanitária (Brazilian National Health Surveillance Agency)
API	Active Pharmaceutical Ingredient
ARV Drugs	Antiretroviral Drugs
AZT	Zidovudine
BC	Brazilian Constitution

BGH	German Federal Court of Justice (Bundesgerichtshof)
BPatG	German Federal Court of Patents (Bundespatentgericht)
CADE	Conselho Administrativo de Defesa Econômica (Administrative Counsel for the Economic Defense, Brazilian Antitrust Authority)
CAE	Comissão de Assuntos Econômicos (Commission for Economic Topics of the Brazilian Parliament)
CCJ	Comissão de Constituição e Justiça (Commission for Constitutional and Justice Topics of the Brazilian Parliament)
CD	Câmara dos Deputados (Lower House at the Brazilian Federal Parliament)
CEME	Central de Medicamentos (Former Brazilian Federal Agency for Development and Procurement of Medicines)
CEPR	Centre for Economic Policy Research
COOPI	Coordenação de Propriedade Intelectual da ANVISA (ANVISA's Unit of Intellectual Property)
CUP	Cambridge University Press
DCL	Federal Decree about Compulsory Licenses Based on Public Interest (Decreto No. 3.201, of October 6, 1999)
DCN	*Diário do Congresso Nacional* (Brazilian Gazette of the Federal Parliament)
DJ	*Diário da Justiça* (Brazilian Official Journal of the Federal Judiciary)
Dje	*Diário da Justiça Eletrônico* (Brazilian Eletronic Official Journal of the Federal Judiciary)
DOU	*Diário Oficial da União* (Brazilian Federal Official Gazette)
DPMA	*Deutsches Patent-und Markenamt* (German Patent and Trademark Office)
DSU	(WTO) Dispute Settlement Understanding
Duke L. J.	Duke Law Journal
EBA	Enlarged Board of Appeal of the European Patent Office
EC	European Communities
EEC	European Economic Community
EPC	European Patent Convention

EPO	European Patent Office
EU	European Union
fn.	Footnote
FTA	Free Trade Agreement
FDI	Foreign Direct Investment
GATT	General Agreement on Tariffs and Trade
GRUR Int.	*Gewerblicher Rechtschutz and Urheberrecht—Internationaler Teil* (German Journal of International Intellectual Property Law)
GTI	Grupo de Trabalho Interministerial (Brazilian Interministerial Working Group)
HAART	Highly Active Antiretroviral Therapy
ICTSD	International Centre for Trade and Sustainable Development
IFPMA	International Federation of Pharmaceutical Manufacturers & Associations
IIC	International Review of Intellectual Property and Competition Law
IMF	International Monetary Fund
IJIPM	International Journal of Intellectual Property Management
INPI	Instituto Nacional da Propriedade Industrial (Brazilian Patent Office)
INTERFARMA	Associação da Indústria Farmacêutica de Pesquisa (Brazilian Research-based Pharmaceutical Association), formerly ABIFARMA
IP	Intellectual Property
I.P.Q.	Intellectual Property Quarterly
ITO	International Trade Organization
J. Generic Med.	Journal of Generic Medicines
JIEL	Journal of International Economic Law
JIPR	Journal of Intellectual Property Rights
JWIP	The Journal of World Intellectual Property
JWLT	Journal of World Trade
LB	Live Beings
LDC	Least Developed Countries
LoIS	Lack of Inventive Step
LoN	Lack of Novelty
LoSD	Lack of Sufficient Description
LPI 71	Brazilian Former Law of Industrial Property, Lei No. 5.772 21 December 21, 1971

LPI 96	Lei de Propriedade Industrial (Brazilian Current Law of Industrial Property), Lei No. 9279 of May 14, 1996
MERCOSUL	Southern Common Market
MERCOSUR	Southern Common Market (MERCOSUL)
MDIC	Brazilian Ministry of Industry and Trade
MoH	Brazilian Ministry of Health
MP	Medida Provisória (Provisional Measure, a Brazilian Presidential Decree with Force of Law)
NAFTA	North American Free Trade Agreement
NBER	National Bureau of Academic Research
NCoAR	Non-compliance with ANVISA's Requests
OJ	*Official Journal of the European Union*
OUP	Oxford University Press
PC	Paris Convention for Industrial Property of 1883
PhRMA	Pharmaceutical Research and Manufacturers of America, Formerly known as PMA
PMA	American Pharmaceutical Manufacturers Association
PoI	Presentation of Information
PSDB	Partido da Social Democracia Brasileira (Brazilian Conservative Party)
RDC	Administrative Norm Issued by ANVISA (Resolução da Diretoria Colegiada)
RDISAN	*Revista de Direito Sanitário*
RENAME	List of Essential Drugs Made by the Brazilian Ministry of Health (Relação Nacional de Medicamentos Essenciais)
REVEL	*Revista Eletrônica do IBPI*
RtH	Risk to Health
RPI	*Revista de Propriedade Industrial* (INPI's Official Gazette)
RT	*Revista dos Tribunais*
R & D	Research and Development
SF	Senado Federal (Higher House at the Brazilian Federal Parliament)
SoPtB	Scope of Patent Too Broad
SPLT	Substantive Patent Law Treaty
STF	Supremo Tribunal Federal (Brazilian Supreme Court of Justice, Constitutional Court)

STJ	Superior Tribunal de Justiça (Brazilian Superior Court of Justice)
SUS	Sistema Universal de Saúde (Brazilian Public Healthcare System)
TM	Therapeutic Method
TRF-2	Tribunal Regional Federal da Segunda Região (Federal Court of Second Instance, 2nd District)
TRIPS	Agreement on Trade-Related Aspects of Intellectual Property Rights
UNAIDS	Joint United Nations Programme on HIV/AIDS
UNCTAD	United Nations Conference on Trade and Development
UNDP	United Nations Development Programme
UNTC	United Nations Treaty Collection
USPTO	United States Patent and Trademark Office
USTR	Office of the United States Trade Representative
VCLT	Vienna Convention on the Law of the Treaties
WB	World Bank
WHO	World Health Organization
WIPO	World Intellectual Property Organization
WTO	World Trade Organization

List of Tables

Acknowledgments

This work would have never come into being without the constant support of my Ph.D. supervisor, Prof. Dr. Christine Godt. It was Prof. Godt who encouraged me both to start this work and to persist in it when I thought about giving up. Moreover, I will never forget how dedicated she was to me and to all the other Ph.D. students, especially at the annual colloquium she used to organize at the University of Oldenburg and Bremen. I am very grateful to her.

I also would like to thank my co-supervisor, Prof. Dr. Josef Falke. His active participation and frequent interventions at the Ph.D. colloquium organized by Prof. Godt were always very helpful.

I would like to give my sincere thanks to the Max Planck Institute (MPI) for Innovation and Competition from Munich, which awarded me with a scholarship from 2008 to 2010. The MPI also financed my trip to Brazil in 2009, which gave me the opportunity to look for research material at the Brazilian Patent Office (Instituto Nacional da Propriedade Industrial–INPI) and to interview a large number of people with the Brazilian National Health Surveillance Agency (Agência Nacional de Vigilância Sanitária—ANVISA's) prior consent. I would also like to thank both the staff at the MPI for the interest they showed in my research, in particular, Prof. Dr. Josef Drexl and Dr. Henning Grosse Ruse-Khan, as well to other scholarship holders, such as Viviane Yumy Mitsuuchi Kunisawa and Enzo Baiocchi.

I am also especially thankful to the people I interviewed in Brazil in March 2009. In particular, I would like to thank Erika Mattos Veiga, a pharmacist and jurist I met at ANVISA. When I arrived in Brasilia, she provided me with a warm welcome and put me in touch with other people there. I am also thankful to Antonio Luiz Figueira Barbosa, Prof. Denis Borges Barbosa (in memoriam), Gonzalo Vecina, who were kind enough to receive me at their offices and with whom I had long and productive conversations.

I am also very thankful to my mother, Benedita, and my sister Rosana for their belief in me, which helped me to finish this work.

Last but not least, I am deeply thankful to my beloved husband Andreas and his family, Christine, Dorothea and Bernward, who have supported me in countless ways during the years I have spent working on this project.

CHAPTER 1

Introduction

Brazilian patent law incorporates a unique legal instrument that became central to the discussion on the conflicts between the international patent system and access to medicines. It integrates the participation of the ANVISA in the patent grant proceedings led by the Brazilian Patent Office (Instituto Nacional da Propriedade Industrial—INPI). The provision of the Brazilian patent law (LPI) reads:

> Article 229-C—The granting of patents on pharmaceutical products or processes shall depend on the prior consent of the National Health Surveillance Agency (ANVISA).

The legal provision described above has become the focal point of a contentious debate—both domestically in Brazil and internationally. While some praise the system as a prime example for modern horizontal policy integration, incorporating public health policy into industrial policy decisions,[1] others[2] view the system as violating the Trade-Related Aspects of Intellectual Property Rights Agreement (TRIPS Agreement[3]).

The present thesis focuses on this dispute and localizes it both in the Brazilian and the international dispute on the right balance between patent policy and access to medicines.

Under Article 27.1 of the TRIPS Agreement, patents must be available for inventions in all fields of technology, provided that they are new, involve an inventive step, and are suitable for industrial applications. Usually, the responsible authority for checking these three conditions is a patent office, but this is not a requirement, as another body can carry out the examination as well. As a rule, if the three conditions are met, the patent must be granted. Brazil, however, is a unique case when it comes to dealing with pharmaceutical patents. According to Brazilian law, if the object of the

1. Drahos (2008), "'Trust me': Patent Offices in Developing Countries," 34 *AMJLM* 151, 169-171.
2. Mitsuuchi Kunisawa (2015), *The TRIPS Agreement Implementation in Brazil—Patents in the Pharmaceutical Area*, Nomos, Baden, p. 118.
3. The TRIPS Agreement is the Annex 1C of the *Marrakesh Agreement Establishing the World Trade Organization*, April 15, 1994, United Nations Treaty Collection (UNTC) I-31874, 1867-1869.

patent application is a drug, the INPI is only allowed to grant the patent if approval is granted by ANVISA.

Thus, ANVISA has a veto power in the granting of pharmaceutical patents. From 2001 to 2017, ANVISA's prior consent took the form of a binding opinion (*parecer*). The criteria that ANVISA is allowed to use to form its opinion is a matter of controversy because the Brazilian law is not clear on how this decision of prior consent should be carried out and which criteria ANVISA should take into consideration. One of the objectives of this work was to investigate, concretely, what ANVISA checks in its reports and how this is carried out: is it truly only duplication,[4] or does it base on its expertise, discarding "bad" or "evergreening" patents?

The participation of the Health Authority in the patent granting proceedings was introduced by the Brazilian legislator in December 1999 to dealing with conflicts between patent rights and the right of access to medicines. Such a legal mechanism is unknown in other national patent law systems around the world. However, because of the recent internationalization of patent law, this field has become much more homogeneous worldwide, making it necessary to examine whether ANVISA's system of prior consent is in accordance with the applicable international patent rules.

Bearing in mind the three conditions of patentability as set by Article 27.1 of the TRIPS Agreement, the central question is whether ANVISA's participation is a "fourth hurdle" to the grant of pharmaceutical patents. If ANVISA checks the three conditions of patentability in an *identical* way to the INPI, its work would be superfluous. If ANVISA checks criteria other than the three conditions set by Article 27.1 of the TRIPS Agreement, it would be examining *more* than TRIPS allows. If, however, ANVISA makes its examination under the framework of flexibilities allowed by the TRIPS Agreement, its participation would not violate this agreement.

With the foundation of the World Trade Organization (WTO) in 1994, it was recognized worldwide that a lack of patent protection in any technical field could be an obstacle to commerce. After a lengthy negotiation period, industrialized countries and developing nations—category to which Brazil, as an emerging economy,[5] also belongs to—signed the TRIPS-Agreement).[6] As background to the development of this agreement, it should be noted that prior to 1994, many countries had excluded pharmaceuticals from patentability. Some developing countries took economic advantage of this situation since the production of imitative pharmaceutical products is generally not considered to be technically difficult. Hence, these developing countries were able to produce medicines without having to negotiate licenses with the patent owner. Because the production of these so-called generic medicines requires little investment

4. Borges Barbosa (2013a), "Patents and the Emerging Markets of Latin America." in: Abbott/Correa /Drahos (eds.), *Emerging Markets and the World Patent Order*, Edward Elgar, Cheltenham (UK), Northampton—MA (USA), p. 140.
5. In the WTO linguistic usage, one speaks of three categories of nations, divided according to their economic development, namely: "developed," "developing" and "least-developed" countries. Each member announces to the WTO Secretariat to which category it belongs.
6. Reichman (1996), "From Free Riders to Fair Followers: Global Competition under the TRIPS Agreement," 29 *N.Y. U. J. L. & Pol.*, 423-456.

in research and development (R & D), they could be marketed more cheaply in the developing world than the original products.

Because such "free-riding" in the post-TRIPS era is no longer allowed internationally, we might expect one effect of the TRIPS Agreement to be a shrinkage in the global availability of cheaper drugs. This would have negative consequences for access to medicines in developing countries since the majority of people living in these countries cannot afford to pay the high prices of patented drugs. Due to the lack of monetary resources in these countries, they would not be able to satisfy their duty of guaranteeing healthcare for their populations. Since the beginning, and in order to correct this problem, the TRIPS Agreement has called for so-called flexibilities or instruments of flexibilization of patent rights, taking into consideration the underlying public policy objectives of national systems for the protection of intellectual property, including developmental and technological objectives.[7]

The problem of access to life-saving medicines has been at the center of public discussion at least since the year 2000 when South Africa, aiming to provide AIDS treatment to sick people, changed its patent law in order to facilitate parallel imports and compulsory licenses of patent rights.[8] This measure triggered an offensive reaction from patent owners, who subsequently sued the government of South Africa, as well from the U.S. administration, which threatened South Africa with trade sanctions.[9] The South African case encouraged a global discussion on the relationship between patent protection and public health. Since then, many works have been published discussing the difficulties encountered by developing countries in complying with their duties under the TRIPS Agreement as well as their duties concerning healthcare.[10] Thus in

7. *See* TRIPS Agreement, Preamble.
8. *See*, for instance, Bartelt (2003), "Compulsory Licenses Pursuant to TRIPS Article 31 in the Light of the Doha Declaration on the TRIPS Agreement and Public Health," 6 *JWIP*, 291-294; Halbert (2005), "South Africa's Intellectual Property Fight for Access to AIDS Medication," in: Halbert (ed.), *Resisting Intellectual Property*, Routledge, Taylor and Francis Group, London et al., pp. 87-111; Liebig (2006), *Auswirkungen des internationalen Patentregimes auf die Medikamentenproduktion und den Zugang zu Medikamenten in LDCs, Deutsche Instituto für Entwicklungspolitik*, Bonn; Scherer/Watal (2002), "Post-TRIPS Options for Access to Patented Medicines in Developing Nations," 5(4) *JIEL*, 913-939.
9. *See*, for instance, Bartsch/Kohlmorgen (2007), "The Role of Southern Actors in Global Governance: The Fight Against HIV/AIDS," 46 *GIGA Research Program, Working Paper*, 18; Pretorius (2002), "TRIPS and Developing Countries: How Level Is the Playing Field?," in: Drahos/Mayne, *Global Intellectual Property Rights—Knowledge, Access and Development*, Pallgrave Macmillan, Chippenham, Wiltshire, pp. 0189-193.
10. *See*, for instance, Abbott (2002a), *WTO TRIPS Agreement and Its Implications for Access to Medicines in Developing Countries*—Study Paper 2a; United Kingdom Commission on Intellectual Property Rights;

    Abbott (2005a), "Managing the Hydra: The Herculean Task of Ensuring Access to Essential Medicines," in: Maskus/Reichman (eds.), *International Public Goods and Transfer of Technology under a Globalized Intellectual Property Regime*, CUP, Cambridge et al., pp. 393-424; Abbott (2006a), "TRIPS and Human Rights: Preliminary Reflections," in: Abbott/Breining-Kaufmann/Cottier (eds.), *International Trade and Human Rights—Foundations and Conceptual Issues* (World Trade Forum, Vol. 5), University of Michigan Press, Michigan, pp. 145-169; *Correa, Carlos M.* (2015), *Intellectual Property: How Much Room is Left for Industrial Policy?*, UNCTAD Discussion Papers No. 233; Correa (2000a), *Integrating Public Health Concerns into Patent Legislation in Developing Countries*, Geneva, South Centre; Guise Rosina/de Oliveira Novaes (2014), "Brazil and the Case of Patents and Access to Medicines. A Material Condition?,"

2001, the WTO launched the Doha Round with a Declaration of Principles on the topic of "patent protection and public health," which recognized that patent rights can be flexibilized through flexibility instruments, as, for example, compulsory licenses.[11]

The topic gains momentum in 2020, given the challenges faced under the coronavirus pandemic, declared by the World Health Organization (WHO) as a "public health emergency of international concern."[12] Unlike other global public health crisis, the COVID-19 pandemic illustrates the urgent need for both developing innovative medicines and making these available for the emerging economies and the poorest countries. It will be impossible to curb the COVID-19 pandemic without developing an innovative vaccine to which people living in developing countries will have access.

With the global discussion on the problems of patent law as it relates to access to medicines, old problems of patent law, such as "evergreening" and "trivial patents," became more visible to the wider public. Formerly, such problems had only been discussed by a community of legal and technical experts. "Trivial patents" are characterized by the fact that they are not based on an original innovation. They predominantly serve to strengthen a company's dominant position in the market, but they do not bring the advantages of innovation. The latter issue, however, is the only social advantage that theoretically justifies the patent monopoly. On the one hand, the granting of such patents in the field of pharmaceuticals jeopardizes public health since the price of certain drugs remains extremely high for a much longer period. On the other hand, the granting of such patents questions the efficacy of the patent system since an ideal patent system should predominantly serve to incentivize research into the development of new medicines.

Bearing in mind the question of access to medicines and the abovementioned problem of evergreening trivial patents, the requirement of drug agency approval for the granting of pharmaceutical patents could contribute to their solution. Access to medicines could be enhanced, and the granting of trivial patents could be avoided through monitoring by the drug agency. I begin with the premise that the Brazilian model could be an example for other countries to follow in dealing with tensions between patent protection and the right to healthcare.

---

in: Dreyfuss, Rochelle C. / Rodríguez-Garavito, César (eds.), *Balancing Wealth and Health. The Battle over Intellectual Property and Access to Medicines in Latin America*, OUP, Oxford University Press, pp. 89-110; Knoblich, Ruth (2017), *Die globale Regulierung geistiger Eigentumsrechte. Interessen, Strategien und Einfluss Brasiliens, Indiens und Chinas*, Springer, Baden-Baden; Reichman (2009a), "Compulsory Licensing of Patented Pharmaceutical Inventions: Evaluating the Options," 37 *J. L., Med. & Ethics*, 247-263.; Reichman (2009b), "Intellectual Property in the Twenty-First Century: Will the Developing Countries Lead or Follow?," 46 *Hous. L. Rev.*, 1115-1185; Shadlen (2012), "The Politics of Pharmaceutical Patent Examination in Brazil," in: Burlamaqui/ Castro/ Kattel (eds.), *Knowledge Governance. Reasserting the Public Interest*, Anthem Press, London, pp. 139-162.

11. *See* Abbott (2005b), "The WTO Medicines Decision World Pharmaceutical Trade and the Protection of Public Health," 99 *Am. J. Int'l L.*, 317-358; Abbott (2004), *The Doha Declaration on the TRIPS Agreement and Public Health and the Contradictory Trend in Bilateral and Regional Free Trade Agreements*, Quaker United Nations Office, Occasional Paper No. 14.
12. WHO (2020), Statement on the second meeting of the International Health Regulations (2005) Emergency Committee regarding the outbreak of novel coronavirus (2019-nCoV) of January 30, 2020.

This study is divided into the introduction (Chapter 1) and three main parts, namely Chapters 2, 3 and 4, as well the conclusion (Chapter 5).

Chapter 2 deals with the relationship between patents and drugs, introduces the Brazilian prior consent and analyzes it within the law of the WTO. Its Part A deals with basic questions of patent law, as well as with straightforward questions regarding public health and the development of drugs. Its first section reviews the literature about theoretical justifications of patents and discusses the economic consequences of patent monopoly, giving special attention to pharmaceutical patents and their legal treatment from the nineteenth century up to the present day. Afterward, it discusses the importance of patent protection for pharmaceutical products. The second section presents basic concepts of public health, stressing the relationship between patent protection and public health. The third section discusses how distortions of the patent system may affect public health and access to medicines, putting in context the problem of "evergreening" and "trivial patents." The last section of Part A reviews the methods offered by patent systems for the correction of abuses and to control patent quality. Its Part B is subdivided into three sections. Its first section offers a short account of the development of the right to health as a human right, while its second section reviews the development of the international patent law. Its third section examines the flexibilities of patent rights under the TRIPS Agreement. Part C offers a short economic overview of Brazil and presents the Brazilian National Health Innovation System. Finally, Part D examines the compatibility between ANVISA's prior consent mechanism and the TRIPS Agreement.

Chapter 3 deals with the relationship between patents and medicines in Brazil, delineates how ANVISA's prior consent was implemented and presents the empirical study regarding the content of ANVISA's reports. Its Part A investigates the reasons why the system of prior consent was created in Brazil. In its Section I, I offer a review of the development of Brazilian patent law. In Section II, I describe ordinary patent grant proceedings in Brazil. Section III evaluates Brazilian patent law post-TRIPS, while Section IV describes Brazilian policy on access to medicines. Finally, Section V presents the reasons for the creation of prior consent by ANVISA in Brazil. Its Part B examines the contents of the amendment, which introduced prior consent and is subdivided into four sections. Part C describes how it has been implemented in Brazil, presenting its historical development and the controversy around the prior consent mechanism in the Brazilian case law. Part D is dedicated to empirical study. In its Section I, I analyze 147 ANVISA's reports concerning prior consent, while in its Section II, I present the number and the grounds of ANVISA's past denials of prior consent, according to the information provided by ANVISA itself. In Section III, I analyze how effectively ANVISA has influenced the granting of patents for medicines in Brazil, while in Section IV, I relate how the dispute between ANVISA and INPI was solved.

Chapter 4 deals with the integration of pharmacology superior expertise in the patent examination for public health purposes. Its first section critiques the 2017 agreement between ANVISA and INPI concerning the application of Article 229-C LPI, which introduced the need for ANVISA's prior consent to the patent grant of pharmaceuticals in Brazil. The second section delineates how Article 229-C LPI has been interpreted in Brazil. The third section presents the author's viewpoint and classifies the Brazilian prior consent mechanism within the patent theory.

Chapter 5 concludes with a reflection on the modern theory of the interface between regulation and patents, regulatory agencies and patent offices.

This thesis intends to contribute to the discussion on the balance of patent rights and the right of access to medicines. The basic problem of access to medicines in the developing world has been the subject of many legal, political and economic publications.[13] In Germany,[14] several works dealing with the flexibilities of patent rights in developing countries have been published, as well as some concentrating on the theoretical questions concerning the conflict between social rights and patent rights.

The thesis distinguishes itself from the existing literature in the following way: it is the first legal study to analyze the concrete problem of the required prior consent of ANVISA. Unlike many works on Brazilian law, it is not limited to a literature-based legal analysis of Brazilian law. Based on an empirical study, I analyzed how ANVISA contributes to patent examination. This was done by examining 147 reports ANVISA issued as a basis for its decisions, as well as both by interviewing Brazilian experts and analyzing the Brazilian case law on Article 229-C LPI. In so doing, the work deals with the central question of the interface of regulation and innovation in the patent system.

---

13. *See*, for instance, Abbott/Reichman (2007), "The Doha Rounds Public Health Legacy: Strategies for the Production and Diffusion of Patented under the Amended TRIPS Provisions," 10 *JIEL*, 921-987; Correa (2003), "Recent International Developments in the Area of Intellectual Property Rights," *ICTSD-UNCTAD Dialogue, 2. Bellagio Series on Development and Intellectual Property*, pp. 18-21; Forman (2007), "Trade Rules, Intellectual Property, and the Right to Health," 21 *Ethics & Int'l Aff.*, 337-357; Godt (2007a), "The So-Called 'Waiver Compromise' of Doha and Hong Kong: About Contested Concepts of the Nature of the International Intellectual Property System—A Comment," in: Govaere/Ullrich (eds.), *Intellectual Property, Public Policy and International Trade*, Schriftenreihe College of Brugge, Peter Lang, Frankfurt et al., pp. 201-228; Mercurio (2006), "Resolving the Public Health Crisis in the Developing World: Problems and Barriers of Access to Essential Medicines," 5 *Nw. U. J. Int'l Hum. Rts.* 1-40.
14. *See*, for instance, Harnisch (2006), *Die Zwangslizenz im südafrikanischen und deutschen Patentrecht—ein Rechtsvergleich unter besonderer Berücksichtigung der Arzneimittelerfindungen*, BWV, Berlin; Herrmann (2002), "TRIPS, Patentschutz für Medikamente und staatliche Gesundheitspolitik: Hinreichende Flexibilität?," *Europäische Zeitschrift für Wirtschaftsrecht*, 37-43; Herrlich (2005), *Internationale Menschenrechte als Korrektiv des Welthandelsrechts—Eine Vertragskonkurrenz im Spannungsfeld von Pharmapatentschutz und dem Zugang zu Medikamenten*, LIT-Verlag, Berlin et al.; Hestermeyer (2007), *Human Rights and the WTO—The Case of Patents and Access to Medicines*, OUP, Oxford; Kramer (2007), *Patentschutz und Zugang zu Medikamenten. Rechtliche und ökonomische Implikation*, Carl Heymanns, Köln; Ridder (2004), *Die Bedeutung von Zwangslizenzen im Rahmen des TRIPS-Abkommens unter besonderer Berücksichtigung des Spannungsverhältnisses zwischen patentrechtlichen Vorgaben und gesundheitlichen Erfordernissen*, Verlag Recht und Wirtschaft, Düsseldorf; Rott (2002), *Patentrecht und Sozialpolitik unter dem TRIPS-Abkommen*, Nomos, Baden-Baden; Von Kraack (2006), *TRIPs oder Patentschutz weltweit—Zwangslizenzen, Erschöpfung, Parallelimporte*, Duncker & Humblot, Berlin.

CHAPTER 2

The Case of Patents and Drugs

A PATENT PROTECTION AND DRUG DEVELOPMENT

I Why Patent Protection?

1 Background Information

1.1 Introduction

Physically speaking, a patent is no more than a piece of paper. A patent, in a purely physical sense, is similar to a government bond. However, the rights that a patent confers on its owner and the rights that a government bond gives to its owner are very distinct. While the latter confers on the title's owner the right to be paid by the government the amount of money written in the bond by a certain date, a patent gives its owner a monopoly power to do the thing described in his patent. This thing should be an invention, that is, something useful created by a human engineer. What a patent confers on its owner is not the right to exploit his invention, which he has anyway, but rather a right to forbid others to exploit the same invention. The patent owner has a piece of paper that gives him exclusive rights concerning a way of doing something, thereby not only prohibiting other people from deliberately imitating the idea protected by the patent but also prohibiting those who learn how to do that thing independently from doing it. This thing might be concrete, such as the invention of a machine, chemical or drug, as in the case of product patents, or it could be abstract, such as the knowledge of how to create that machine, chemical or drug, as in the case of process patents.

Essentially, a patent guarantees its possessor a temporary monopoly on the commercial exploration of something. Currently, the monopoly power guaranteed through patents is only applied to "inventions," but this has not always been so. According to *Machlup*, during the early years of the patent system, "many of the privileges served 'just to grant profitable monopoly rights to favorites of the court or to supporters of the royal coffers'."[1] In essence, a patent is a privilege conceded by the state, and this is how it was regarded and described in its earliest times. He who has a patent—or "the patentee"—has an exclusive right to use the object of the patent. Therefore, the patentee has the power to impede anyone from imitating the patented thing, which currently must be an invention.

As a matter of principle, the act of imitation is not by itself something censurable that *must* be forbidden by law. In fact, there are more indications that imitating is something inherent to the human being: we learn a language, for instance, by imitating what we heard from others. Psychologists often stress that children tend to imitate their parent's behavior. In reality, imitation is the rule, and the prohibition of imitation is an exception. *Dutfield and Suthersanen*, for instance, discuss whether learning to innovate may require the freedom to imitate.[2] In an imaginary world where patents were not available, the right to imitate would be absolute: everyone would have the right to imitate whatever he wanted. By guaranteeing the patent owner the monopoly right to exploit his invention, the state is restricting, for a limited period of time, the natural right of others to imitate the patented invention.

States confer monopoly rights on inventors not because they like monopolies or because imitation is a bad thing, but rather do so moved by the belief and *hope* that they are encouraging innovation.[3] *Boldrin* and *Levine* ironically observe that we currently live in the "era of Universal Intellectual Property," which "has acquired the status of a public religion, at the core of which stands the shockingly profound revelation that anything that can be monopolized ought to, by whoever lays claim to it first."[4] As *Stiglitz* puts it, the patent system must be seen within the major context of the broader system of innovation, with the patent incentive as just one of a multitude of strategies that supposedly incentivize innovation.[5]

How patents are perceived varies from time to time, according to the moods of the moment: sometimes the negative effects of having a patent system tend to be stressed, as the nineteenth-century anti-patent movement did;[6] sometimes, its positive effects are rather highlighted, as the contemporary pro-patent movement has been doing since the 1990s.

1. Machlup (1958), *An Economic Review of the Patent System—Study of the Subcommittee on Patents, Trademarks and Copyrights of the Committee on the Judiciary*, United States Government Printing Office, Washington, p. 2.
2. Dutfield/Suthersanen (2007), "Innovation and Development" in Suthersanen et. al. (eds.), *Innovation Without Patents—Harnessing the Creative Spirit in a Diverse World*, Cheltenham, Edward Elgar, pp. 10-11.
3. De Wit (2014), "Challenges in Public and Private Domains will Shape the Future of Intellectual Property," 3 *National Taipei U. Tech. J. Intell. Prop. L. & Mgmt.*, 21-33.
4. Boldrin/Levine (2007), "Intellectual Property and the Efficient Allocation of Social Surplus from Innovations," in: Porrini/Ramello (eds.), *Property Rights Dynamics: A Law and Economic Perspective*, Routledge, London, pp. 93-94. *See also* Lemley (2015), "Faith-Based Intellectual Property," 62 *UCLA L. Rev.*, 1328-1346.
5. Stiglitz (2008), "Economic Foundations of Intellectual Property Rights," 57 *Duke L. J.*, 1697.
6. *See* Machlup/Penrose (1950), "The Patent Controversy in the Nineteenth Century," 10 *The J. Econ. Hist.*, 1-29.

In the next section, a short review of the history and rationales of the patent system will be summarized.

1.2 Short History of Patent Protection

The oldest privileges given by princes to innovators are found during the fourteenth century. *Penrose* identifies "the first patent law" as the rules of the Republic of Venice, which, as early as 1474, included a systematic use of monopoly privileges for inventions, which "generally promised privileges of ten years to inventors of new arts and machines."[7] She also mentions the cases of some German princes, who made wide use of patents in the sixteenth century. Both *Penrose* and *Machlup* highlight that, in their early days, patents for inventions were not easy to distinguish from other privileges granted by the Crown and that in view of that, there are many histories of abuses. *Penrose* tells us that in seventeenth-century England, for instance, the monopoly grant was so often used as an easy way to reward favorites that it caused a revolt in the Commons. According to her, it was this abuse that moved the Parliament to pass the famous Statute of Monopolies of 1623,[8] which was the first general law to guarantee that monopoly patents were only to be given to "the first and true inventor" of a new manufacture.[9]

With the edition of the English Statute of Monopolies of 1623, patent laws began to spread around the world. At first, the statute worked as a model for the patent laws of the British colonies in America, such as Massachusetts and South Carolina, which passed patent laws in 1641 and 1691, respectively.[10] Much time later, France established a patent law by means of an edict of King Louis XV from 1762. After attaining its status as an independent country, the United States of America passed its first patent law in 1790.[11]

In 1809, a time when many European countries did not have yet a patent law, the Portuguese colony of Brazil also passed a patent law per royal decree. As explained by *Pires de Carvalho*, the introduction of a patent law to the South American colony had been part of a political bargain made between Great Britain and Portugal.[12] In fact, one year earlier, the Portuguese royal family had escaped from Napoleon's troops by leaving Portugal and transferring the capital of the Portuguese kingdom from Lisbon to Rio de Janeiro. The British Navy protected the Portuguese royal family during these exceptional times. Under the bargain, Portugal paid its debt to Great Britain by opening Brazilian harbors to English products and, at the same time, guaranteeing patent

7. Penrose (1951), *The Economics of the International Patent System*, Baltimore, The John Hopkins Press, p. 2.
8. United Kingdom (1623), Statute of Monopolies 1623, Acts of the English Parliament, available at https://www.legislation.gov.uk/aep/Ja1/21/3 (last visited on August 14, 2020).
9. *Ibid.*, p. 6.
10. Machlup (1958), *An Economic Review of the Patent System*, p. 3.
11. *Ibid.*
12. Pires de Carvalho (2009), *200 anos do Sistema Brasileiro de Patentes: O Alvará de 28 de abril de 1809—Técnica e Vida*, Lumen Juris, Rio de Janeiro, pp. 5-7.

privileges to English machines—considering that the British Crown planned to introduce and to produce such machines in Brazil—by passing a law following the model of the British Statute of Monopolies of 1623.[13]

According to *Machlup*, patent laws continued to spread in other European countries,[14] but from 1850, the patent system began to suffer its first serious crisis in Europe, with the rise of an anti-patent movement, which was in line with the free-trade movement of the period.[15] *Penrose* wrote that the anti-patent movement, particularly strong in Germany, England and the Netherlands, was in favor of the complete abolition of the patent system, but only the Netherlands actually repealed the patent law in 1869.[16] *Lang*, when examining the anti-patent movement in Germany, explains that in that country, a pro-patent movement emerged as a reaction to it, and, at the end of the day, the pro-patent movement won the battle.[17] But the anti-patents also lost the battle elsewhere in Europe, after a compromise concerning the acceptance of compulsory licensing was reached during the international patent conference of 1873 in Vienna. *Machlup* writes that the anti-patent movement "suddenly collapsed in 1873" so that the patent system could begin to spread again.[18] With the victory of the pro-patent movement, claims for the necessity for uniform patent rules worldwide gained momentum. In 1883, the first international convention for the protection of industrial property was approved in Paris. This convention, however, did not rule substantive requirements of patentability. This topic was seen as a matter of domestic law, so patent laws still continued to vary from country to country. A common point, however, was the exclusion of many kinds of inventions from the patentable subject matter, for instance: scientific theories; inventions that contravened public law, morals or safety; pharmaceutical compounds; foodstuffs; and chemical products.[19]

In the course of the first half of the twentieth century, the patent system gained more prestige, at least in the industrialized countries. In the developing world, however, the resistance against the patent system did not disappear. As put by *Penrose*, "non-industrialized countries and countries in the early stages of industrialization gain nothing from granting patents since they themselves do little if any, patenting abroad. These countries receive nothing in return for the price they pay for the use of foreign inventions or for the monopoly they grant to foreign patents."[20]

In the late 1950s, the industrialized countries started making efforts to convince developing countries that stronger intellectual property laws would also benefit them.

13. *Ibid.*, pp. 40-43.
14. Machlup (1958), *An Economic Review of the Patent System*, pp. 3-4 mentions that patent laws were enacted in Russia in 1812; Prussia, 1815; Belgium and the Netherlands, 1817; Spain, 1820; Bavaria, 1825; Sardinia, 1826; the Vatican State, 1833; Sweden, 1834; Wurttemberg, 1836; Portugal, 1837; Saxonia, 1843.
15. Machlup (1958), *An Economic Review of the Patent System*, p. 4.
16. Penrose (1951), *The Economics of the International Patent System*, Baltimore, p. 15. The Netherlands reintroduced a patent system in 1910.
17. Lang (2014), "The Anti-Patent Movement Revisited: Politics and Professionalism in Nineteenth-Century Germany," in: Müller/Siegrist (eds.), *Professionen, Eigentum und Staat: Europäische Entwicklungen in Vergleich—19. und 20. Jahrhundert*, Wallstein Verlag, Göttingen, pp. 230-249.
18. Machlup (1958), *An Economic Review of the Patent System*, p. 5.
19. Penrose (1951), *The Economics of the International Patent System*, Baltimore, p. 17.
20. *Ibid.*, p. 220.

With the explicit goal of extending intellectual property worldwide and combating poor countries' lack of interest in recognizing monopoly rights for imported goods, in 1967, the World Intellectual Property Organization (WIPO) was created as an agency pertaining to the United Nations.[21] The WIPO assumed the administration of the Paris Convention for Industrial Property of 1883 (PC) and the Berne Convention for the Protection of Literary and Artistic Works. However, to achieve its primordial goal of extending the protection of intellectual property worldwide was not an easy thing. In the 1970s and 1980s, the developing world resisted the idea and insisted in the WIPO arena that stronger patent protection would in no way benefit them. Developing countries believed that by accepting the duty of paying royalties to rich countries, they would restrict their own right to imitate, and, consequently, this would rather hinder their access to technological development. Developing countries resisted as long as they could.

However, it was not within the context of the WIPO negotiations that developing countries eventually came to agree with the view that stronger patent protection would benefit them. This objective was reached in the early 1990s, during the negotiations for the creation of the WTO. At that time, a broad treaty concerning the protection of intellectual property rights—which would later be officially named TRIPS (Trade-Related Intellectual Property Rights Treaty)—was brought to the agenda by a lobby led by pharmaceutical and agricultural chemical producers. The treaty's objective was to require all WTO members to adopt and enforce high levels of patent protection.[22] During the so-called Uruguay Round, industrialized countries succeeded in obtaining greater patent protection for their products by propagating the idea that more and stronger intellectual property protection brings with it increased investment and, therefore, more economic development. Concretely, industrialized countries promised more access to their agrarian and textile markets to developing countries. Developing countries accepted the offer, even though the relationship between intellectual property protection and economic development is doubtful. According to *Stiglitz*, "the contention that stronger intellectual property rights always boost economic performance is not in general correct. It is an example of how special interests—those who do benefit from stronger intellectual property rights—use simplistic ideology to advance their causes."[23]

The TRIPS Agreement is a milestone in the history of patents worldwide. The agreement not only succeeded in obliging developing countries to establish a patent system—a longstanding demand from industrialized countries—but also introduced uniform standards of patentability, the latter longstanding demand of the pharmaceutical and chemical sectors of the richest countries.

21. For a detailed history of the WIPO, *see* Halbert (2006), *The World Intellectual Property Organization: Changing Narratives on Intellectual Property*, Paper presented at the International Studies Association Conference, San Diego, California.
22. Abbott (2008), "Intellectual Property Rights in World Trade," in: Abbott/Cottier/Gurry (eds.), *International Intellectual Property in an Integrated World Economy*, Wolters Kluwer, Gaithersburg, pp. 186-187.
23. Stiglitz (2006), *Making Globalization Work*, London, Penguin Books, p. 106.

Currently, the debate concerning the role and the effects of patents in the economy seems to be as lively as it was in the nineteenth century. At that time, however, the central question was the very existence of a patent system, while nowadays, its existence is no longer seriously questioned. On the contrary, its importance is often exaggerated.[24] Now, the central point of the discussion is whether and how patent protection promotes technological innovation, as well as the possible counterproductive effects patents might have, and how these can be avoided in order to improve the patent system as a whole.[25] Furthermore, the global expansion of a stronger patent system has introduced new elements into the discussion, such as the relationship between patents and public health, between patents and access to technological and economic development, or between patents and traditional knowledge.[26]

1.3 Rationales of Patent Protection

The question of the reasons for and the need for a country to have a patent system is not new. As explained by *Machlup,*[27] the question occupied jurists and economists during the so-called patent controversy of the nineteenth century, when most Western countries had already established a patent system and were discussing whether it was worth having one. In his famous study, *Machlup* speaks of four different "legal philosophies" for justifying patents: "the French, recognizing a property right of the inventor in his invention and deriving from it its right to obtain a patent; the American, silent on the property question, but stressing the inventor's legal right to a patent; the English, recognizing the monopoly character of the patent, and regarding it in theory as a grant of royal favor, but in practice regularly allowing the inventor's claim to receive a patent on his invention; the Austrian, insisting that the inventor has no right to protection, but may, as a matter of policy, be granted a privilege if in the public interest."[28]

Essentially, the four approaches, as outlined by *Machlup* 64 years ago, have not changed. Nowadays, patent protection tends to be justified by "economic" and

24. *See*, for instance, Straus (2006), "The Impact of the New World Order on Economic Development: The Role of Intellectual Property Rights System," 6 *John Marshall Revue Intell. Prop. L.* 1-16 and Straus (2008) "Is There a Global Warming of Patents?," 11 *JWIP*, 58-62.
25. *See*, for instance, Lewis/Reichman (2005), "Using Liability Rules to Stimulate Local Innovation in Developing Countries: Application to Traditional Knowledge," in: Maskus/Reichman (eds.), *International Public Goods and Transfer of a Technology under a Globalized Intellectual Property Regime,* Cambridge University Press, Cambridge et al., pp. 337-366; Peritz (2008), *Patents and Progress: The Incentive Conundrum,* Paper presented at the *ATRIP Conference Session: Free Access to Use, What We Learned in the Past Fifty Years?;* Grimes (2005), "Counterproductive Incentives for Innovation?—Exclusionary Conduct in the Sale of an IP Product," 36 *IIC*, 214-225.
26. *See*, for instance, Dose/Stiglitz (2013), *The Role of Intellectual Property Rights in the Development Process, with Some Lessons from Developed Countries: An Introduction,* LEM Working Papers Series, No. 2013/23.
27. Machlup (1958), *An Economic Review of the Patent System*, pp. 4-5.
28. *Ibid.*, p. 3.

"noneconomic" approaches.[29] The economic justifications for the existence of patents are more widely accepted than the noneconomic ones. All theories have been discussed and criticized, but none of them, in fact, justify patents in a satisfactory manner, as I will show in the following.

1.3.1 Noneconomic Justifications for the Patent System

1.3.1.1 The "Natural-Law" or "Property" Thesis

The "natural-law" thesis adopted by the French Assembly of 1791 was very popular in the nineteenth century, especially in France.[30] The base of this theory is constructed in the following dogma: if a person has some new idea—and this idea results in something industrially applicable—the result of this idea belongs to him; that is, it is his property. If the dogma is accepted, there are certain logical consequences of this. First, if you use my intellectual property, you will first need to have my authorization before you use it, and second, you will have to pay me money, in the same way that you would have to pay me rental fees if you used a house of mine. Another logical consequence is that there is no difference between imitation and stealing.

The problem of the "natural-law" approach lies in the difficulty of accepting its dogmatic starting point. In fact, the premise that everyone is the owner of his ideas is questionable from a conceptual, moral, economic and legal point of view.

From a conceptual point of view, it is problematic to accept that immaterial and material goods can both be owned by someone in the same way. The first essential difference between them is that material goods are single things, in the sense that they have clear boundaries. That is: if I have a house, I have only a house; if I then obtain two houses, I have three houses, and so on. However, if I invent a machine and I have a patent granted for the process of manufacturing it, I do not *necessarily possess* a machine. I might only know how to create the machine. Then, if I build the machine I invented, I am only the owner of that particular machine. If someone else builds an identical machine, this person continues to be the owner of his own machine, even if he is violating my exclusive right to build this machine. All I can do as a patent owner is to make the imitator stop producing the machine I invented. Thus, I do not lose my ownership of the machine I built myself, and neither does he over his. But, as a proprietor of a house, I cannot hinder anyone from building a house identical to mine. My ownership of the house does not give me the exclusive right to build such a house. Everyone who has the resources for it might build an identical house, and I cannot do anything to prevent his act of imitation. My house is not being "stolen" because my neighbor built a house identical to mine.

Moreover, as *Machlup* asks, if patent rights are similar to property rights, why should be the first be limited to a certain period of time, while the latter are perpetual?

29. Towse/Holzhauer (eds.) (2002), *The Economics of Intellectual Property, Vol. I: Introduction and Copyright*, Edward Elgar, Cheltenham (UK).p. XXI.
30. Penrose (1951), *The Economics of the International Patent System*, Baltimore, p. 21.

From a moral perspective, it is difficult to justify why only the first to obtain a patent for his idea should be the owner of that idea since two or more people can develop the same idea simultaneously. Why should the owner be only the first to have that idea or the first to file it in the patent office? This is as unequal a system as that of the ancient right of primogeniture, which gives the firstborn child the exclusive right to inherit land, for instance. This idea might have been accepted in former times, but it is not adequate in the modern democracies of the twenty-first century.

From an economic perspective, it is difficult to accept that patent rights are similar to property rights. According to *Machlup*, "this notion of French lawyers that an 'idea' could be subject to the same kind of property right that applied to material objects was criticized, rejected and ridiculed in many quarters."[31] He explains that "in contrast to property in material things, so-called intellectual property is neither control of a thing nor of an idea but rather 'control of a market' for things embodying an idea."[32]

From a legal point of view as well, patent and property rights are so intrinsically different that the inclusion of both in the same category is difficult to accept. The first obvious difference between them is regarding their objects: while the object of a tangible property is clearly delimited or easy to delimit, the object of an intangible property does not have any defined boundaries. I come back to the given example of the house I possess and the machine I invented. While my rights over the house are clearly limited, my patent rights over the machine I invented are not: if I rent the house, I get the contracted rent fees paid by one renter. My patent rights over the machine, however, are unlimited and indeterminate, that is: if no one uses or copies my machine, I cannot have any royalties paid, whereas if hundreds or thousands of people imitate it, I have the right to receive royalties proportionate to the number of people who use it. The second difference is in the duration of a property right, which is, as a rule, perpetual. A patent right, however, is, in its essence, limited to 20 years.

Justifying the existence of patents with the theory of property was common in the nineteenth century. Currently, the idea that intellectual property should be governed by property rules is supported, for instance, by *Merges*.[33]

1.3.1.2 The "Reward-by-Monopoly" Thesis

The "reward-by-monopoly" thesis advocates that the monopoly conferred by patents are no more than the just reward given by society to remunerate the inventor's efforts,

31. Machlup (1958), *An Economic Review of the Patent System*, p. 22.
32. *Ibid.*
33. *See* Merges (1994), "Of Property Rules, Coase and Intellectual Property," 94 *Columbia L. Rev.*, 2655-2673; Merges (2005), "A Transactional View of Property Rights," 20 *Berkeley Tech. L. J.*, 1477-1520. In opposition to *Merges*' view, *see*, for instance, Reichman (1994), "Legal Hybrids Between the Patent and Copyright Paradigm," 94 *Columbia L. Rev.*, 2432 and Lewis/Reichman (2005), "Using Liability Rules to Stimulate Local Innovation in Developing Countries: Application to Traditional Knowledge," in: Maskus/Reichman (eds.), *International Public Goods and Transfer of a Technology under a Globalized Intellectual Property Regime*, Cambridge, pp. 337-366.

which are important to society. As *Penrose* puts it, this point is also based on a concept of natural rights, although it rests on an economic hypothesis.[34]

The most common critiques of this theory are the following: first of all, if a patent monopoly rewards the work of its inventor, what about the work of the inventor whose efforts lead to the same result, but who arrived at the Patent Office a few minutes later? This inventor does not reap any right to a reward for his efforts. As in the case of the "natural-law theory" also, here, it is difficult to justify why only the first person to file the idea at the Patent Office deserves a reward for his work. The idea that only the person who attains a first place in a race deserves a reward—as was the case for the Olympic Games in Ancient Greece, which did not give a prize for second or third places—is also no longer defensible in our times. At the modern Olympic Games, those who attain second or third place receive the silver and bronze medals, respectively.

According to *Pires de Carvalho*, a critic of the reward theory, patents do not perform a rewarding function for the following three reasons: for him, patents are, first, a technical evaluation without any judgment as to the economic relevance of the invention; second, they are subject to identical standards, regardless of the field of technology; and third because "the laws of some countries expressly establish that patents further social goals, rather than rewarding individuals."[35]

That the inventor should be awarded a prize is widely accepted. The question, however, is whether granting patents—which reward all inventions in the same arbitrary way, without considering their usefulness or importance[36]—is an adequate prize for the inventor's efforts. As explained by *Machlup*, some economists regarded patents as the worst form of reward and propose that inventors should be rewarded with prizes or bonuses according to the social value of the invention.[37]

Because there are, in theory, other methods of rewarding an inventor, the idea that society has the moral duty to grant a patent of monopoly for the inventor is difficult to support.

1.3.2 Economic Justifications for the Patent System

Currently, patents are basically justified by the expected benefits they supposedly bring to the economy. As *Cornish* puts it, "the main purpose of a modern patent system is unquestionably economic," so the system should be judged on whether it produces newer and advanced technologies.[38]

For economists, the basic idea of the "intellectual property" category, to which patents belong, is that knowledge is a public good. According to *Stiglitz*, a public good is a technical term: "a public good is a good whose consumption is non-rivalrous. By contrast, private goods can only be consumed by one person. For instance, only a person can sit in a chair. The same goes for food: if I eat my ice cream cup, you cannot

34. Penrose (1951), *The Economics of the International Patent System*, Baltimore, p. 26.
35. Pires de Carvalho (2001), "The Primary Function of Patents," *U. Ill. J. L., Tech. & Pol'y*, 29, 2001
36. Penrose (1951), *The Economics of the International Patent System*, Baltimore, p. 26.
37. Machlup (1958), *An Economic Review of the Patent System*, p. 23.
38. Cornish (2003), *Intellectual Property—Omnipresent, Distracting, Irrelevant?*, OUP,Oxford, p. 9.

eat it. Knowledge, however, is different. I have just shared with you some of the things I know, but sharing this knowledge with you has not taken away from what I know. Thus, knowledge has the quality of a non-rivalrous consumption."[39]

Penrose proposed that by limiting the use of an invention, the patent system creates an artificial scarcity in order to make the good useful to society. In terms of price, scarcity is the basis of the price mechanism. In other words, for her, the patent system "is an attempt to include the production of inventions in the same framework of pricing as the production of other things."[40]

According to the classical economic approach, the use of public goods—such as patentable inventions, trademarks or copyrights—must be rationally ruled in order to improve their efficiency and distribution in society.[41] Intellectual property rights are seen as one of the instruments for reaching this goal.

1.3.2.1 The "Exchange for Secret" Thesis

This theory assumes that if inventors had no protection against imitators, they would keep their inventions secret forever, and, therefore, they would die without disclosing them to society. Because inventors are interested in obtaining monopoly rights in order to protect their inventions against imitation, they publicly disclose them by filing a patent request. On the grounds of this exchange element, this theory is also called the "social contract" theory.

According to *Penrose*, opponents of this theory argue that, in reality, it is not possible to keep important inventions secret for a long time, and even if secrecy is maintained, other people will make the same discovery or create the same invention.[42] *Machlup* thinks that an inventor only files a patent application when he has no hope that his invention will remain secret; additionally, *Machlup* points out that "the patent system might promote rather than reduce secrecy; since patents are granted only on inventions developed to a stage at which they can be reduced to practical use, the system encouraged secrecy in the developmental stage of inventions whereas, if there are no patents to be obtained, earlier publications of ideas might hasten technological advance on all fronts."[43]

1.3.2.2 The "Incentive to Invent/Innovate" Thesis

The fourth general argument for patents assumes that the hope of gaining high profits through a patent monopoly incentivizes inventors to develop innovations that are useful to society. Because society desires useful inventions, it agrees to award the inventor the prize of giving him a temporary monopoly with which to explore his

39. Stiglitz (2008), "Economic Foundations of Intellectual Property Rights," 57 *Duke L. J.*, 1700.
40. Penrose (1951), *The Economics of the International Patent System*, Baltimore, p. 28.
41. Davi (2001), *A Tragedy of the Public Knowledge "Commons"? Global Science, Intellectual Property and the Digital Technology Boomerang*, UNU-MERIT Research Memoranda. UNU-MERIT.
42. Penrose (1951), *The Economics of the International Patent System*, Baltimore, p. 32.
43. Machlup (1958), *An Economic Review of the Patent System*, pp. 24-25.

invention. The thesis that the patent system may produce effective profit incentives for inventive activity and thereby encourage invention is widely accepted. According to *Machlup*, this thesis is regarded as the fundamental economic justification of patents.[44]

Penrose points out that in modern times an inventor is no longer a person who develops something alone. Most inventors are paid salaries for developing desired inventions—which means that they invent not because of the patent system, but because they are paid monthly for their efforts to create new inventions—therefore, what patents nowadays incentivize is rather an investment of capital in the development of inventions than inventions itself. Currently, the benefits of the patent system are justified by the belief that, in its absence, capitalists would not risk their money in the R & D of inventions.[45] Since then, patents have been justified as a necessary incentive to investments, that is, the whole process of innovation.[46]

1.3.3 Do Patents Really Promote Innovation?

Supporters of patents commonly argue that patents are necessary to promote innovation. This assumption has never been confirmed, but some empirical studies have been carried out by economists in order to test how important patents really are and to which extent it is true that some inventions might not have been invented without the patent's incentive. In these studies, a sample of firms was asked if they considered patent protection essential to making an investment. Even though such studies must be evaluated with caution—considering that what is declared by the company may not necessarily coincide with the truth—many of them showed similar results to one another. In the 1950s, *Scherer* studied firms in the United States and in the 1970s, *Taylor and Silberston* studied firms in the United Kingdom.[47] Both studies concluded that patent protection was neither effective nor necessary, except in the case of pharmaceuticals. A more recent study, conducted by *Mansfield*, came to a similar conclusion. After examining a random sample of 100 firms in the United States in the 1980s, his results show that only in the pharmaceutical and chemical sector was patent protection judged to be essential for the development of 30 percent or more of inventions.[48] *Peritz* mentions three studies that evaluated the importance of patents to inventive activity by measuring the amount of spending in R & D and the resulting number of inventions:

> The Japanese study found no empirical support for the hypothesis that R & D responds to changes in patent scope. An investigation of the US semiconductor industry found a mix of some positive and some negative effects of greater patent protection over the period 1979–1995. The third study of 29 countries found strong

44. *Ibid.*, p. 36.
45. Penrose (1951), *The Economics of the International Patent System*, Baltimore, p. 35.
46. Scherer (2005), "The Economics of the Patent System", in: Scherer (ed.), *Patents—Economics, Policy and Measurement*, Edward Elgar, Cheltenham (UK), Northampton—MA (USA), p. 5.
47. Mazzoleni/Nelson (1998), "The Benefits and Costs of Strong Patent Protection: A Contribution to the Current Debate," 27 *Res. Pol'y*, p. 275.
48. Mansfield (1996), "Patents and Innovation: An Empirical Study," 32 *Mgmt. Sci.*, 174.

positive correlations between the strength of patent protection and R & D expenditures in the period 1981–1990. In sum, the results are inconclusive.[49]

Given such inconclusiveness, one should not overestimate the possible benefits of patent protection for society. As suggested by *Stiglitz*, patents are important, but that importance should not be exaggerated since they are just one among many instruments that finance R & D. The other instruments for financing research are directly financed by the state, such as research carried out in universities or in other state institutions and prizes.[50]

A relevant point for the discussion regarding the supposed positive impact of patents on innovation is whether this assumption can be applied in the case of developing countries, where the majority of patent applications are made by foreign companies. *Branstetter*, for instance, carried out an empirical economic study to discover whether or not there was a correlation between the number of patents and increased research in Japan; he found that this was not the case, although "firms in the United States and in Western European countries have a comparative advantage in the sort of research that is enabled by strong IPRs."[51] These findings are surprising, considering that Japan is not a developing country, but only a "latecomer." In the case of the classical developing countries, it seems to be that the impact of patents on the economy is negative. *McCalman*, in a study published in 2001, found that harmonization of patent rights brought a net benefit to the United States while developing countries suffered losses from the strengthening of patent rights.[52] Later, *Akers* and *Ecers*, in a more comprehensive study, came to a conclusion that corroborated the views of both TRIPS supporters and TRIPS critics, finding that stronger protection of intellectual property rights, on the one hand, helped developing countries to obtain greater access to technology transfer from more advanced countries. On the other hand, this study also found that, in the case of pharmaceutical patents, the benefits gained by industrial nations were greater than the returns provided to developing countries.[53]

Last but not least, the history of economic development confirms that the importance of patents is related to the stage of economic development:[54] the more economically advanced a country is, the greater the importance of patents for that country will be. As put by *Odagiri et al.*, "the channels for developing countries to acquire advanced technologies are diverse and these countries frequently do so by imitating advanced technologies, reverse-engineering advanced products, or applying

49. Peritz (2008), *Patents and Progress: The Incentive Conundrum,* Paper presented at the *ATRIP Conference Session: Free Access to Use, What We Learned in the Past Fifty Years?* p. 13.
50. Stiglitz (2008), "Economic Foundations of Intellectual Property," 57 *Duke L. J.*, 1719-1721; Odermatt (2009), "Investigating New Models of Pharmaceutical Innovation to Protect the Human Right to Health," 40 *IIC*, 173-181.
51. Branstetter (2004), "Do Stronger Patents Induce More Local Innovation?," 7 *JIEL*, 365.
52. McCalman (2001), "Reaping What You Sow: An Empirical Analysis of International Patent Harmonization," 55 *J. Int'l Econ.*, 178.
53. Akers/Ecers (2009), "The TRIPS Agreement and its Effects on the R & D Spending of US-Owned Multinational Countries in Developing Countries," 43 *JWLT*, 1173-1192.
54. Correa (2015), "Intellectual Property: How Much Room is Left for Industrial Policy?," *UNCTAD Discussion Papers No. 233,* October.

knowledge and technologies disclosed in patents, papers, and elsewhere. A stronger patent system that limits these activities can be detrimental to catch-up efforts."[55] This shows a clear tension between intellectual property and the right to development,[56] as recognized by the United Nations in 1986 in its "Declaration on the Right to Development."[57]

2 *Economic Consequences of the Patent Monopoly*

2.1 *The So-Called Paradox of Patents*

The intrinsic problem of the patent system is that its fundamental principles do not seem to be logical.[58] As put by *Robinson*, in her explanation of what she calls "the paradox of patents," "a patent is a device to prevent the diffusion of new methods before the original investor has recovered profit adequate to induce the requisite investment. The justification of the patent system is that by slowing down the diffusion of technical progress it ensures there will be more progress to diffuse."[59]

The great question concerning the patents system is whether its benefits outweigh its costs. Innovation is, of course, desired by society, but the price charged by the patent system is the monopoly rights conferred on the patentee. Whether society has a net gain in this bargain will be dependent on the answer one gives to the following question: would inventions exist if there were no patent protection available? As *Machlup* puts it, some economists answer "yes" to this question, while another group of economists points out that many inventions for which patents are granted would have been created anyway; and even if we consider that only a certain number of inventions would come into being without the promise of patents, society pays for all patented inventions so that, at the end of the day, society loses by paying the monopoly prices for inventions for which no payment was necessary.[60]

Peritz, in his paper revisiting *Machlup* and *Penrose's* analysis, called the lack of correspondence between the ideas behind of the existing patent incentive for investors and the actual lack of social results of patent protection, as the patents policy's "Incentive Conundrum" which he explains as follows:

55. Odagiri/Goto/Sunami/Nelson (2010), "Introduction" in: Odagiri/Goto/Sunami/Nelson (ed.), *Intellectual Property, Rights, Development, and Catch-Up—An International Comparative Study*, Oxford, p. 10.
56. Drahos (1999), "Intellectual Property and Human Rights," *I.P.Q.*, 3, 349-371.
57. UN Office of the High Commissioner (1986), United Nations General Assembly, Document A/RES/41/128, December 4, 1986.
58. For a discussion of the irrationality of the theories justifying the existence of patents, *see* Figueira Barbosa (2005a), who denies the validity of all of them and concludes that "patents are the form of private appropriation of production techniques, now called technology. For this reason, the concept of property cannot be renounced in order to unveil its economic and social essence," in: *Patentes: Crítica à racionalidade, em busca da racionalidade*, Caderno de Estudos Avançados, Instituto Oswaldo Cruz, No. 1, p. 34.
59. Robinson (1956), *The Accumulation of Capital*, Macmillan, London, p. 87.
60. Machlup (1958), *An Economic Review of the Patent System*, p. 44.

> It turns out that the widespread belief in the patent regime as a means to promote progress is not a simple matter of faith because belief in patents as incentives to invent is not entirely unfounded. Our attitudes toward incentive theory are complicated by widespread experience with the effectiveness of patents as incentives. (...)
>
> Still, incentives *can* be effective in channeling *individual* behavior. Patent protection can attract inventors and investors to apply their scarce resources to the production of patentable inventions and then to the subsequent innovation needed to bring them to market. (...)
>
> (...) While we can be confident that patent incentives attract resources to the production of patentable inventions, we cannot be confident that society will be better off because of it. There is no doubt that patent protection produces *private* benefits for successful inventors and investors but a great deal of doubt whether patents promote progress in the *public* interest. In short, there is no correspondence between the means and the ends, the private and public effects of patents as incentives for encouraging innovation, no correspondence between individual impacts and social results of patent protection. I call this patents policy's Incentive Conundrum.[61]

2.2 Benefits of Patent Protection

For society, the most important benefit *expected* from patents is that they stimulate the development of inventions which, it is believed, would not have come into existence if patent protection were not available. For *Scherer*, under the patent system, society gains not only the direct benefits of innovation but also saves on the R & D costs, which are funded by the capitalist's investment.[62] According to him, society also directly benefits when the patent expires. Another benefit of the patent system is the element of disclosure since the invention is made public, making its improvement possible.

2.3 Social Costs of Patent Protection

The most evident cost of the patent system is the monopoly power given to patentees, who, during the time in which patent protection is enjoyed, can charge higher or prohibitive prices for their products without being afraid of competition and loss of markets. The pricing of patented pharmaceuticals is, for instance, an extreme case where very high prices are charged by the patentees.

Another social cost of the patent system is that it produces a waste of resources since it foments what economists call "competitive research." Many different firms engage in finding solutions to the same problems in order to win the race to be the first to file the application at the patent office. The rivals who are not lucky enough to be the first go on with the research by "inventing around," which is defined by *Machlup* in the

61. Peritz (2008), "Patents and Progress: The Incentive Conundrum," Paper presented at the *ATRIP Conference Session: Free Access to Use, What We Learned in the Past Fifty Years?* p.2.
62. Scherer (2005), "The Economics of the Patent System", in: Scherer (ed.), *Patents—Economics, Policy and Measurement*, Cheltenham (UK), Northampton—MA (USA), p. 6.

following words: "After a competitor has found such a solution and has obtained exclusive patent rights in its exploitation, to find an alternative solution to the same problem in order to be able to compete with him in the same market."[63] He points out that the strategy of "inventing around" can also be used by the patent holder in order to block rivals from competing in the same market.

Moreover, some companies make use of strategies for extended patent protection. *Scherer* illustrates this strategy with the case of Du Pont, referring to the invention of nylon. According to him, the firm's scientists "did not rest content with patenting the basic super polymer's composition and processes for producing it. They systematically investigated the whole array of molecular variations with properties potentially similar to nylon, blanketing their findings with hundreds of patent applications to prevent other firms from developing an effective substitute."[64]

Another common strategy is the extension of monopoly power by prolonging the effective life of a basic patent after its expiry. According to *Scherer*, applicants used to drag their heels on the Patent Office while the application was still pending.[65] In addition, one must also take into consideration the cost of administering a patent system.

2.4 *Some Distortions of the Patent System*

Another important question is whether the patent system, the goal of which is supposed to be the encouragement of inventions, can create exactly the opposite effect, that is, hold back innovation. *Stiglitz* examines this problem keeping in mind industrialized countries, and concludes that patents might, in some cases, retard innovation. For him, this depends on how the patent regime is organized; that is, if it creates excessively strong intellectual property rights, it might impede innovation instead of fostering it.[66] *Stiglitz* enumerates some standard situations in which the distortion of the patent system may have such an effect, as follows.

2.4.1 "Leveraging Monopoly Power"

One speaks of leveraging monopoly power when a company uses the dominant power enjoyed in a certain market in order to acquire another market.[67] According to *Stiglitz*, "intellectual property rights generate monopoly power that can be used to leverage 'further monopoly power'."[68] The author mentions the Microsoft case as the most obvious, whereby the company used its monopoly power in operating systems in order

63. Machlup (1958), *An Economic Review of the Patent System*, p. 50.
64. Scherer (2005), "The Economics of the Patent System" in: Scherer (ed.), *Patents—Economics, Policy and Measurement*, Cheltenham (UK), Northampton—MA (USA), p. 15.
65. *Ibid.*
66. Stiglitz (2006), *Making Globalization Work*, London, pp. 109-110.
67. Clarke-Smith (2002), "The Development of the Monopolistic Leveraging Theory and Its Appropriated Role in Antitrust Law," 51 *Cath. U. L. Rev.*, 179-206.
68. Stiglitz (2008), "Economic Foundations of Intellectual Property Rights," *57 Duke L. J.*, 1702.

to obtain a dominant position in the market of text processors and internet browsers.[69] In the United States[70] and in the European Union (EU),[71] for instance, Microsoft suffered defeats before the courts and regulatory organs due to its anticompetitive behavior, but its most important competitor at the time, Netscape, never came back to the market.

2.4.2 "Strategic Patenting"

In many situations, individuals or companies file and obtain patents for inventions they do not intend to develop. They use patents in a speculative manner, only as a way of making money so that those who really want to develop the inventions will have to pay money to the patentee in order to concretize their plans. To illustrate this behavior, *Stiglitz* brings to light the case of the automobile: a very broad patent was granted in the United States for a four-wheeled, self-propelled vehicle. According to him, "the person who received the patent had no intention of developing the automobile; instead, he used it to form a cartel."[72] The broad patent blocked everyone who did not want to work with the patent-driven cartel of the automobile companies. This patent, wrote *Stiglitz*, was challenged before the courts by Henry Ford, who had the idea of producing a low-priced car for the masses and was rich enough to challenge the patent before the courts.

2.4.3 "Patent Thickets"

In practice, more than one company may develop an "invention" at the same time, and often distinct patents are granted for the same invention, while each patent covers a different aspect of it. If you want to develop the invention, you will have to pay license fees to all the patentees, or you pay only one and accept the risk of being sued by the others. It is probable that in this situation, these patents might discourage you from developing the invention you have in mind due to the costs involved. This phenomenon, called "patent thickets," is a very common and long-standing one. *Stiglitz* illustrates this hypothesis with the development of the airplane in the U.S. For him, "patents almost suppressed this important innovation."[73] Although the Wright Brothers obtained some important patents, another innovator, named *Glenn Curtiss*, got similar ones; the airplane was not developed further until the United States government seized all patents related to it in order to develop it.[74]

69. *Ibid.*
70. Brinkley (2000), "U.S. v. Microsoft: The Overview; US Judge says Microsoft Violated Antitrust Laws with Predatory Behavior," *The New York Times*, April 4.
71. In 2004, Microsoft was fined EUR 497 million for abusing its market power in the EU. *See* Stiglitz (2008), "Economic Foundations of Intellectual Property Rights," *57 Duke L. J.*, 1711, fn. 53.
72. *Ibid.*, pp. 1711-1712.
73. *Ibid.*, p. 1712. Along the same lines, *see also* Palmer (1989), "Intellectual Property: A Non-Posnerian Law and Economic Approach," 12 *Hamline L. Rev.*, 261-304.
74. Stiglitz (2008), "Economic Foundations of Intellectual Property Rights," *57 Duke L. J.*, 1712.

2.4.4 Disparity Between Contribution and Return

According to *Stiglitz*, the fundamental problem of the patent system is the "disparity between marginal private and social returns." This problem affects the system's efficiency since the social costs may be higher than the benefits.

2.4.4.1 The Contribution of Having Been the First

Stiglitz refers to the contribution made by an innovator who has an idea a little earlier than others as "marginal social return."[75] The contribution of the race winner might, in some cases, be minimal, compared to the amount of resources invested by all companies together. *Stiglitz* illustrates this problem with the example of the human genome project.[76] In the 1990s, universities and public research institutes around the world joined in the common goal of decoding the human genome, and there was a race between companies to complete the project first. The American company Myriad won the race and was the first to file and receive a patent for having identified the gene for breast cancer. The profits received by the patentee were considerable, although it was not only the party that had invested resources in decoding the human genome. The social benefits were small since only those who were lucky enough to have enough money or a health insurance policy covering this could afford the high prices charged by the company to identify the gene in patients. Furthermore, the firm has been accused of using an out-of-date technique and of blocking its competitors from developing other tests.[77] Even though eventually the American Supreme Court ruled that the Myriad patent was to be revoked[78]—since its object was not patentable—the firm enjoyed a monopoly for almost 20 years in the testing of breast cancer.

2.4.4.2 "Enclosing the Commons"

Stiglitz draws attention to the practice of "enclosing the commons" in the context of patents. His use of the term is the same as that of Boyle,[79] that is, to describe the phenomenon of privatizing something that had been in the public domain.[80] When referring to tangible property, the term was used by *Hardin* as a solution for the problem he described as the "tragedy of the commons,"[81] based on the principle that what is commonly used will be probably overused and destroyed; consequently, "enclosing" common goods avoids their destruction.

75. *Ibid.*, p. 1707.
76. *Ibid.*, p. 1707.
77. Berndt (2012), "Das Geschäft mit Krebsgenen," *Süddeutsche Zeitung*, p. 16, May 30.
78. *See* Kesselheim et al. (2013), "Gene Patenting—The Supreme Court Finally Speaks," 369 *New Eng. J. Med.* 9, August 29, 869-875.
79. Boyle (2008), *The Public Domain—Enclosing the Commons of the Mind*, Yale University Press, New Haven & London, p. 44.
80. Stiglitz (2008), "Economic Foundations of Intellectual Property Rights," 57 *Duke L. J.*, 1708.
81. Hardin (1968), "The Tragedy of the Commons," 162 *Sci., New Series*, 3859, 1243-1248.

However, the concept of "enclosing the commons," when applied to intellectual property, results in a distortion. As a typical example of such enclosing in the patent context, *Stiglitz* mentions biopiracy. He defines this as "the patenting by American and other foreign companies of indigenous medicines, plants, or a variety of indigenous ideas and traditional knowledge."[82] He illustrates the distortion with the basmati rice and turmeric patent. Both of these materials have traditionally been used in India, the first as an agrarian product, and the second as a spice with healing properties, for hundreds of years. Both basmati rice and turmeric were granted patents in the United States. The distortion in both cases consists of the fact that society must pay the patentee for a thing that he did not invent and for which he thus deserves no reward. Someone is granted a patent for a thing that is not the result of his ingenuity. According to *Stiglitz*, the distortion is in the disparity between the minimal, if it exists at all, the contribution made by the patent owner to society and the returns that the patent gives him.

2.5 Benefits and Costs for Developing Countries

In developing countries, domestic companies mostly do not have the resources to finance R & D, and as a result, patents are mostly granted to foreign firms. In Brazil—an upper-middle-income country—for instance, in 2015, circa 90 percent of patent applications were made by nonresidents;[83] that year, the INPI granted patents for 460 residents. Regarding pharmaceutical patents, the imbalance is more blatant. According to *Akkari*, of 101 pharmaceutical patents granted by INPI in 2013, only 3 were granted to Brazilian holders.[84] For comparison, in the U.S., in the same year, 140,969 patents were granted to residents, so that circa one-third of all patents were granted to residents.[85]

This makes it evident that for a developing country, the cost of giving patent monopoly to foreign firms is that this basically serves to restrict the right of local firms to imitate. Local firms lack money to invest in R & D and must pay royalties to use a (foreign) patented technology that, otherwise, they could have freely imitated.[86] For these countries, the benefits of having a patent system might be small, compared to the high social costs they have to pay to use foreign technology. *Scherer*, when commenting on this question, put it in the following way: "Since the amount of domestic inventive activity is modest in underdeveloped countries, one might expect the benefits of a patent system to be particularly small relative to the social costs of granting foreign

82. Stiglitz (2008), "Economic Foundations of Intellectual Property Rights," 57 *Duke L. J.*, 1709.
83. WIPO, *WIPO Statistical Country Profiles*—Brazil.
84. Akkari et al. (2016), "Pharmaceutical Innovation: Differences Between Europe, USA and 'Pharmemerging' Countries," 23 *Gest. Prod.* 2, 375.
85. *See* "WIPO Statistical Country Profiles—United States of America."
86. Correa (2007a), "Analisando tensões entre patentes e o interesse público: rumo a uma agenda para países em desenvolvimento," in: Villares (ed.), *Propriedade Intelectual: tensões entre o capital e a sociedade*, Paz e Terra, São Paulo, pp. 315-316.

patent protection. Indeed, it is somewhat surprising that such countries offer conventional patent rights."[87] *Machlup* attributes many emerging nations' membership of the International Union for the Protection of Industrial Property to pressures from industrialized nations and to prestige motives, suggesting that newly independent nations seem irrationally eager to "have the honor of paying higher prices for imported products."[88]

The scenario has not essentially changed since *Matchup's* description, but there is no longer any reason to speculate as to why almost all developing countries currently grant patents. Since the foundation of the WTO in 1995, when all its 154 members agreed on establishing a patent system, developing countries have been internationally obliged to grant patents for all technologies. This also hinders them from excluding some areas of technology from the scope of patentability in accordance with their economic interests and developmental policies.

In the past, this was exactly what countries in the earlier stages of industrial development would do: they prohibited patents in areas in which they wanted to catch up.[89] "Catching up" is a term used by economists to describe the process by means of which a less industrially developed country tries to reach a more advanced stage of development through successful imitation. De facto, it seems to be the case that all technologically advanced countries today have, at some time, copied the ideas and technologies of more developed countries. *Chang* asks if now industrialized countries, by imposing uniform standards of patentability to developing countries, "are not trying to 'kick away the ladder' by which they have climbed up to the top, by preventing developing countries from adopting policies and institutions that they themselves used."[90] The author uses the ladder metaphor to describe the way earlier industrialized countries, like Britain, tried to convince developing countries of that time, like the United States and Germany, to preach about the benefits of free trade to other nations. *Chang* concludes that, by imposing restrictive patent policies on developing countries, industrialized countries are impeding the "catch-up" of developing countries.[91] According to him, even if the U.S. and most European countries already had a patent system at the time, they were not subject to comparable restrictions to those that are imposed on today's developing countries by the TRIPS Agreement. He argues, for instance, that "these laws accorded only very inadequate protection to the IPR of foreign citizens. In most countries, including Britain (before the 1852 reform), the Netherlands, Austria and France, patenting of imported inventions by their nationals was often explicitly allowed."[92]

87. Scherer (2005), "The Economics of the Patent System", in: Scherer (ed.), *Patents—Economics, Policy and Measurement*, Cheltenham (UK), Northampton—MA (USA), p. 14.
88. Machlup (1968), "Patents," in: *International Encyclopedia of Social Sciences*, Vol. 11, 461-472, Collier-MacMillan, London.
89. UNCTAD-ICTSD (2005), *Resource Book on TRIPS and Development: An Authoritative and Practical Guide to the TRIPS Agreement*, p. 35.
90. Chang (2003), *Kicking Away the Ladder—Development Strategy in Historical Perspective*, Anthem Press, London, p. 10.
91. *Ibid.*, p. 139.
92. *Ibid.*, p. 57.

Moreover, because there was no international law of patents, each country was free to define its patent policy, which permitted it to exclude some inventions from the scope of its patent law. The most obvious example is the case of pharmaceutical and chemical inventions, which were not patentable under the national law of many countries until the 1980s. Other economists also recognize that the standards imposed by the TRIPS Agreement have made it more difficult for developing countries to "catch up."[93] *Stiglitz*, for instance, is concerned about the difficulties developing countries have faced since the enactment of the TRIPS Agreement since they have to pay high prices to obtain access to advanced technologies. As pointed out by *Abbott* in an article published on the occasion of the TRIPS Agreement's 10-year anniversary, highlighted that "the World Bank has estimated a very significant rise in the outflow of patent rents from South to North based on implementation of the TRIPS Agreement."[94] Consequently, it has become more difficult for developing countries to advance successfully.[95]

Stronger patent rights affect differently industrialized and developing countries. While in the case of industrialized countries, the question is whether a patent can retard innovation, in developing countries, the fundamental question is how to find a balance in order to guarantee access to essential patented goods, such as pharmaceuticals, in spite of patent protection.

3 *The Special Case of Pharmaceutical Patents*

Pharmaceuticals concern everyone because they save lives or alleviate suffering. Everyone has, at some point, needed them or will do sooner or later. Since we must pay for pharmaceuticals, their price is directly relevant to everyone. Even those who are lucky enough to have private or public health insurance, which pays for all the medicines they may need, should be concerned that enough money flows through the system in order to finance drug costs, which are becoming more and more expensive. It is estimated that 70 percent of the annual cost increase of drugs is due to expenditure on the newest medicines, those that were introduced fewer than five years previously.[96]

Vogel, remembering that two of the most significant inventions of the twentieth century, namely, the penicillin and the polio vaccine, were not patented, asked: "why is it that the incentives for obtaining patents now are so very different from the time when penicillin and polio vaccine were discovered?" He answers that "patents are necessary for the *now huge* R & D expenditures (...) that will produce more safe and

93. Odakiri/Goto/Sunami/Nelson (2010) *Intellectual Property Rights, Development and Catch-up—An International Comparative Study*, OUP, Oxford, p. 16.
94. Abbott (2005c), "Towards a New Era of Objective Assessment in the Field of TRIPS and Variable Geometry for the Preservation of Multilaterism," 8 *JIEL* 77, 80.
95. *See* Stiglitz (2008), "Economic Foundations of Intellectual Property," *57 Duke L. J.*, 1693-1724.
96. De Joncheere et al. (2003), "Scope of the Problem," in: Dukes et al. (eds.), *Drugs and Money—Prices, Affordability and Cost Containment*, IOS Press Ohmsha, Amsterdam et al., p. 9.

more effective drugs."[97] *Van den Belt and Korthals*, when commenting on Salk's answer about who owns the patent on the polio vaccine, remembered that the Salk Institute today routinely files patents on new vaccines.[98] They called this shift as "a different attitude toward intellectual property" and explained it on historical circumstances. According to them, a major difference of our current times in comparison with the 1950s is "the fact that IP rights have become much more deeply entrenched into our contemporary economic and political system. They are so much taken for granted that a world without them is hardly imaginable anymore for the main corporate actors."[99] *McGillivray*, which also speculated about the reasons why Salk did not patent the polio vaccine, thinks, like *van den Belt*, that the way drug patents are seen today is different from 1954 due to a mentality shift. As stated by him, "our current 'norms' as to drug patents—our post-modern and commodified relations with the world—were yet to be hatched and were not normative values in Salk's day."[100]

Indeed, the costs regarding R & D significantly rose from the 1950s to nowadays. According to the Tufts Center for the Study of Drug Development, the cost of developing a new drug was USD 802 million in 2003, and by 2014 had risen to USD 2,558 million.[101] This figure, however, should be viewed with caution since the Tufts Center is primarily financed by the research-based industries.[102] Furthermore, the reliability of this figure has been questioned by various independent authors and bodies,[103] especially concerning its lack of transparency because it neither clarifies the public sector accounts for health research[104] nor separates marketing costs from development costs.

Not surprisingly, patented medicines are high-priced, not only due to the monopoly that patent protection gives them but also because the person who decides which medicine a patient takes is his or her doctor. If you are sick, you have to take the patented medicine your doctor prescribed without being able to decide for yourself if the prescribed drug is right for you; either you follow the prescription of your doctor,

97. Vogel (2007), *Pharmaceutical Economics and Public Policy*, Binghamton, The Haworth Press, p. 57.
98. Van den Belt / Korthals (2013), "The International Patent System and the Ethics of Global Justice," in: Arapostathis / Dutfield (eds.), *Knowledge Management and Intellectual Property—Concepts, Actors and Practices from the Past to the Present*, Cheltenham, Edgar Elgar, p. 235. The author refers to a TV interview where a reporter asked Dr. Jonas Salk who owned the patent on the infantile paralysis vaccine and he answered: "Well, the people, I would say. There is no patent. Could you patent the sun?"
99. *Ibid.*, p. 249.
100. McGillivray (2017), *Pyrates' of the Lyceum: Big Pharma, Patents, and Academic Freedom in Neoliberal Times*, PhD Thesis, Osgoode Hall Law School of York University, pp. 325-326.
101. Di Masi/Grabowski/Hansen (2016), "Innovation in the Pharmaceutical Industry: New Estimates of R & D Costs," 47 *J. Health Econ.*, 20.
102. Angell (2004), *The Truth About Drug Companies: How They Deceive Us and What to Do About It*, Random House Trade Paperbacks, New York, pp. 41-42.
103. *See*, for instance, *Report of the United Nations Secretary-General's High-Level Panel on Access to Medicines* (2016), p. 35; Dukes (2005), *The Law and Ethics of the Pharmaceutical Industry*, Elsevier Science, Amsterdam et al., p. 239.
104. *Correa*, citing *Burke* and *de Francisco*, affirms that the public sector accounts for around 44 percent of the total funding for health research. *See* Correa (2009), "Intellectual Property Rights and Inequalities in Health Outcomes," in Labonté/Schrecker/Packer/Runnels (eds.) *Globalization and Health—Pathways, Evidence and Policy*, Routledge, New York, p. 266.

or you are deprived of the necessary treatment. In these circumstances, you or your health insurance pays "the highest price that the market will bear"[105] unless neither can afford the cost. That is why pharmaceutical patents affect many more people than any other kind of patent: this is true everywhere in the world, although the effects on the fate of people living in developing countries are more dramatic.

Whether the artificial scarcity produced by patents is desirable for every kind of invention, including pharmaceuticals, is questionable. No one would doubt, for instance, that the social cost of a patented drug that could prevent or cure cancer is much higher than the social cost of a patented smartphone. People who cannot afford a smartphone will have to live with their old mobile phones or without any phones at all, while people who cannot afford the drugs they need will die or suffer pain. This essential distinction has raised the question of whether pharmaceutical inventions should be excluded from patent protection altogether or whether they should be treated in the same way as inventions from other technical fields are. In the past, many countries concerned about the social costs produced by a patent monopoly in the case of pharmaceuticals answered this question with a "yes" by excluding pharmaceutical products and processes from patent protection or by admitting process patents but excluded product patents from patent protection.

In the post-TRIPS era, excluding pharmaceuticals from the scope of patentability is no longer possible, but this does not mean that pharmaceutical inventions should not be treated differently. One size does not fit all. To treat life-saving medicines differently from other technical inventions, with a view to expanding access to them, is consequently reasonable and justified. Because of that, countries must be free enough to individually shape a patent policy flexible enough to guarantee the effectiveness of the right to health and the right to economic development.

This should include, for each country, the right to create a patent regime for pharmaceuticals that considers their exceptional relevance but which, at the same time, does not undermine the patent system. Bearing in mind the question of whether more patents bring more innovation/investment or not, there is no reason a supposed "incentive to innovate" should be more important than other societal goods, such as guaranteeing access to medicines for the poor. On a scale of values, societal goods in the form of access to medicines or access to development cannot be seen as less valuables than patents.

3.1 *Legal Treatment of Pharmaceutical Patents in Some Industrialized Nations*

Most developing countries did not admit patent protection for pharmaceuticals until they were convinced to introduce it as a result of obligations they accepted when acceding to the WTO in the early 1990s. The absence of patent protection for

105. De Joncheere et al. (2003), "Scope of the Problem," in: Dukes et al. (eds.), *Drugs and Money—Prices, Affordability and Cost Containment*, Amsterdam, p. 8.

pharmaceuticals in the developing world has been commonly called "theft of intellectual property" or "piracy" for a long time in many developed countries, especially by those companies with a direct interest.[106]

However, the prohibition of pharmaceutical patents was also common in industrialized nations until some years before the WTO's foundation, as will be showed in what follows.

3.1.1 The United States

In the United States, patent protection for pharmaceutical products and processes has been available since the Patent Act of 1790. Despite having a functioning patent system, the American pharmaceutical industry was not able to develop new medicines until the early years of the twentieth century.[107] According to *Wadlow*, 90 percent of the chemicals and pharmaceuticals consumed in the U.S. when World War I began were imported from Germany, which dominated the chemical sector at the time.[108] Forfeiture or compulsory license of patents, common in many patent laws of the time, was also not available. *Wadlow* notes, however, that when war was declared, a move toward a softening of patent rights was discussed at the time, and suspension of patent protection for the antisyphilitic drug, Salvarsan, was attempted.[109] Although formally no change occurred in patent law, in 1917, the U.S. Government passed the "Trading with Enemy Act," which allowed American firms to manufacture patented inventions produced by companies in enemy territories.[110] Under this law, 6,000 German chemical and pharmaceutical patents were seized as an exceptional wartime measure. According to *Wadlow*, the seized patents were meant to revert to their former patentees when the war ended, but this did not occur with the German chemical and pharmaceutical patents.[111] In March 1918, a second amending Act permitted confiscation and sale of these patents, so that the greater part of these assets was sold in 1919 to the Chemical Foundation, an association of American chemical industries. As *Wadlow* puts it, the sale of the German patents to the Chemical Foundation "set the American chemical industry on the path to independency from Germany and allowed it to compete internationally for the first time."[112]

---

106. *See* Loughlan (2007), "'You Wouldn't Steal a Car': Intellectual Property and the Language of Theft," 29 *Eur. Intell. Prop. Rev.*, 401-405; Sydney Law School Research Paper No. 08/35. About the rhetorical use of the word "piracy" in conjunction with intellectual property *see also* Drahos/Braithwaite (2002), *Information Feudalism—Who Owns the Knowledge Economy*, Routledge, New York, pp. 24-38.
107. Worthen (2004), "American Pharmaceutical Patents from a Historical Perspective," 7 *Int'l J. Pharmaceutical Compounding*, 37-40.
108. Wadlow (2010), "The Great Pharmaceutical Patent Robbery, and the Curious Case of the Chemical Foundation", *I.P.Q.* (3), p. 261.
109. *Ibid.*, p.262.
110. Worthen (2003), "American Pharmaceutical Patents from a Historical Perspective," 7 *Int'l J. Pharmaceutical Compounding*, 37-40.
111. Wadlow (2010), "The Great Pharmaceutical Patent Robbery, and the Curious Case of the Chemical Foundation", *I.P.Q.* (3), p. 272.
112. *Ibid.*, pp. 267-268.

According to *Mowery*, the confiscated German patents were important for the development of the American chemical industry but were not sufficient to support the technology transfer for a competitive industry.[113] The U.S.'s shift from importer to producer country of pharmaceuticals was consolidated after World War II.

3.1.2 Western European Countries

In many European countries, patent protection for pharmaceuticals was not available until the 1970s at the earliest, and some countries introduced such protection in the 1980s. Germany, for instance, introduced patent product protection for pharmaceuticals in 1968.[114] Until then, patent protection in the field of drugs had only been available for pharmaceutical processes.

Switzerland, one of the most innovative countries in the drug sector, introduced patent protection in 1907[115] but excluded pharmaceutical products from patentability until 1977.[116]

In Italy, patent protection for pharmaceuticals was not available until 1978, when a judgment of the Supreme Court declared the legal provision excluding pharmaceuticals from patent protection to be unconstitutional.[117]

In other Western European countries, patent protection for pharmaceuticals was introduced much later. In Spain, it was not available until 1992, when it was introduced as a consequence of Spain's accession to the European Community.[118] In Portugal, patent protection for pharmaceutical substances was not available until 1995 and was introduced as a consequence of Portugal's accession to the European Patent Convention (EPC).[119]

3.2 Legal Treatment of Pharmaceutical Patents in Developing Countries

In many developing countries, including the so-called emerging countries, patent protection has been generally available since the nineteenth century, but either pharmaceuticals or pharmaceutical processes were formerly excluded from the scope of patent protection by law. From the early 1990s, these countries began to change their

113. Mowery (2010), "IPR and US Economic Catch-Up," in: Odagiri et al. (eds.), *Intellectual Property Rights, Development, and Catch-Up*, OUP, Oxford et al., pp. 48-49.
114. Schneider (2008), "Patenting of Pharmaceuticals—Still a Challenge?," 39 *IIC*, 512.
115. Chang (2003), *Kicking Away the Ladder*, p. 58.
116. Boldrin/Levine (2008), "The Pharmaceutical Industry," in: Boldrin/Levine (eds.), *Against Intellectual Monopoly*, CUP, New York et al., p. 216.
117. Schneider (2008), "Patenting of Pharmaceuticals—Still a Challenge?," 39 *IIC*, 512.
118. Boldrin/Levine (2008), "The Pharmaceutical Industry," in: Boldrin/Levine (eds.), *Against Intellectual Monopoly*, Cambridge University Press, New York et al., p. 216
119. EPO, Convention on the Grant of European Patents: Munich, October 5, 1973, UNTC 16208, UNTS 1065-1608; Remédio Marques (2008), "A Patenteabilidade de Substâncias Químicas e Farmacêuticas de Selecção e de Método de Terapia, no Domínio do CPI de 1940—A Dissimulação de Reivindicações de Processo e a Entrada em Vigor do CPI de 1995 e do Acordo TRIPS," in: Remédio Marques (ed.), *Medicamentos versus Patentes—Estudos de Propriedade Industrial*, Coimbra Editora, p. 260.

patent policies by introducing patent protection for pharmaceuticals. In most cases, they did so in order to implement obligations they had assumed when accepting the TRIPS Agreement, which was negotiated within the so-called Uruguay Round, culminating in the creation of the WTO in 1994. This was, for instance, the case of Brazil, Argentina and Egypt. While Brazil introduced patent protection for pharmaceuticals in 1996, Argentina did so in 1995 by passing Law No. 24.481; the Argentinean provision, however, delayed patent protection for pharmaceuticals until 2000, which caused tensions in this country's relations with the U.S.[120] Egypt also introduced patent protection for pharmaceuticals in order to comply with its obligations under TRIPS and did so in 2002.[121] Other Latin American countries, such as Mexico and the Andean Group, had already introduced patent protections for pharmaceuticals before adopting the TRIPS Agreement.[122] Mexico, for instance, did so in 1991, in order to implement obligations that arose from its accession to the North American Free Trade Agreement (NAFTA). China, in its turn, introduced patent protection for pharmaceuticals in 1992, before the WTO was formally created.[123]

3.3 *Importance of Patent Protection for Pharmaceutical Products*

The importance of patent protection as an incentive for the development of pharmaceuticals is often stressed by the pharmaceutical industry,[124] by patent lawyers and by some of the academic community.[125] Basically, these parties advocate that drugs only exist thanks to the patent monopoly incentive. It is also commonly stated that in the case of pharmaceuticals, patent protection is more important than in other fields of technology due to the fact drugs that need more time and money for their development than products of other fields of technology, and, at the same time, they are easier for competitors to copy. Accordingly, capitalists must be encouraged to invest their money in R & D of drugs, and the hope of getting a patent monopoly should be an incentive for making such investments.[126] As discussed above, it is not possible to assess if this hypothesis is right; some empirical surveys carried out in the U.S. suggest that patent protection is seen as more important by managers in the pharmaceutical and chemical industry sector than by those in other industrial sectors. *Mansfield*, for instance, asked 100 American companies to what extent development and commercialization of

120. Bentolila (2002-2003), "Lessons from the United States Trade Policies to Convert a 'Pirate': The Case of Pharmaceutical Patents in Argentina," 5 *Yale J. L. & Tech.*, 59-102.
121. *See* Al-Ali (2008), "The Egyptian Pharmaceutical Industry after TRIPS" 26 *Fordham Int'l L. J.*, 274; El Farag (2008), "TRIPS, TRIPS-PLUS, Developing Countries and Public Health: The Case of Egypt," 5 *J. Int'l Biotechnology L.*, 1-15.
122. Correa (2000b), "Reforming the Intellectual Property Rights System in Latin America," 23 *World Economy*, 851.
123. Ding et al. (2011), "From Imitation to Innovation: A Study of China's Drug R & D and Relevant National Policies," 6 *J. Tech. Mgmt. & Innovation* 2, 6.
124. Lanjouw/Cockburn (2000), *Do Patents Matter? Empirical Evidence After GATT*, NBER, Working Paper 7495.
125. For instance, Straus (2006), "The Impact of the New World Order on Economic Development: The Role of Intellectual Property Rights System," 6 *John Marshall Revue of Intell. Prop. L.*, 1-16.
126. *See* above Chapter 2-A-I-1.3.4.

inventions would decline if patent protection were not available. According to his results, patent protection was considered to be "essential" for the development of more than 30 percent of the inventions only in the pharmaceutical and chemical sector.[127] In the petroleum, machinery and metal products industries, patent protection was considered to be essential for the development of 10-20 percent of inventions. In the remaining fields, patent protection had only limited importance.[128] Although *Mansfield's* survey cannot be seen as proof that patent protection is fundamental for the development of pharmaceuticals, it confirmed that "in a few industries, particularly pharmaceuticals and chemicals, the effects of patent system were reported to be very substantial."[129]

However, the belief that drugs exist only thanks to the patent monopoly incentive seems to be exaggerated. Indeed, in the development history of the pharmaceutical and chemical industry, there were cases in which the pharmaceutical industry flourished in precisely those countries where patent protection was not available for pharmaceuticals. In Germany, for instance, the absence of patent protection for pharmaceuticals until 1968 did not hinder the German pharmaceutical industry from developing to become one of the leading industries in the world. In Brazil, "despite the ban on patents foreign investment in the pharmaceutical sector raised from 113 million US dollars in 1971 to 646 million dollars in 1979, one of the highest growth rates of any industry in Brazil."[130]

On the other hand, it is also not true that the mere granting of pharmaceutical patents can transform national industries. As an example, one can mention *Scherer's* case study on Italy, a country which did not grant pharmaceutical patents until 1978. According to him, no increase in Italian pharmaceutical R & D spending was detected when this was brought in, so "the Italian industry did not succeed in metamorphosing into a more creative generator of important new pharmaceuticals."[131]

4 *Justifying Patents Today*

We live in a time where patent rights have reached an importance in the economy that it had never had before. Currently, the fraction of individual inventors that file patents is minuscule, as they are held mostly by corporations. As observed by *Godt*, patents are now differently used by their holders since they have gained newer functions.[132] As she explained, patents are no longer used only for market exclusivity; they are rather used strategically. Companies that possess a patent portfolio explore them in different fields,

127. Mansfield (1986), "Patents and Innovation: An Empirical Study," 32 *Mgmt. Sci.*, 174.
128. *Ibid.*, p. 174.
129. *Ibid.*, p. 180.
130. Gereffi (1983), *The Pharmaceutical Industry and Dependency in the Third World*, Princeton, p. 229.
131. Scherer (2001), "The Patent System and Innovation in Pharmaceuticals," in: Remiche (ed.), *Pharmaceutical Patents, Innovation and Public Health, Revue Internationale Droit Economique—Special Edition*, De Boeck & Larcier, Bruxelles p. 117.
132. Godt (2008a), "Research Tools—Patents and the Information Market in the Knowledge Based Economy," in: Govaere/Ullrich (eds.), *Intellectual Property, Market Power and the Public Interest*, Peter Lange, Brussels, p. 282.

including the financial sector, as they can be used for obtaining access to credit or for financial markets, or even for being marketed and licensed.[133]

Patents are no longer justified as they did in the past, so that the classical theories that saw patents both as a reward for the inventor and as an incentive to innovation are not more adequate to justify their existence. As *Godt* put it, these classical theories are no longer convincing nowadays for the following reasons: (a) they are based on unconvincing assumptions; (b) they are fixated on legitimating exclusivity, rather than on limiting private autonomy; (c) the interests of competitors and affected third parties are not considered.[134] Consequently, patents are no longer seen as a right granted to the inventor for purposes of reward and incentive, but rather as "information as a commodity," and, therefore, a prerequisite for trade relations.[135]

Other authors see patent law as regulation. *Lemley*, for instance, defined Intellectual Property (IP) rights as "a form of government regulation of the free market designed to serve a useful social end—encouraging innovation and creation."[136] *Ghosh*, in the same way, sees intellectual property as a regulatory tool and calls for a rethinking of its nature. According to him, "rethinking intellectual property law as regulatory sharpens the focus on how the law affects the inventive process and the marketplace and opens the door for a more complete view of the relationship between government and property."[137]

Godt suggested a more modern conception for justifying patents. If patents exist for protecting investments and facilitating the selling of information,[138] they are used within this context as a regulatory tool to promote economic goals; this tool should also regulate the effects that patents produce in social areas in order to find a balance between conflicting interests, such as, for instance, patents and drug access.[139]

II Protecting and Promoting Public Health

1 Drugs and Public Health

Public health, when in connection with medicines, can be thought of using at least two different approaches. The first one is related to pharmacovigilance, and the second one is related to healthcare and, more specifically, to drug access. A pharmacovigilance system has the aim of assessing whether or not a new drug might be considered safe enough to be marketed. It assesses the risks and benefits of a new drug, the effects of which on the human body are unknown. When deciding for or denying a marketing

133. *Ibid.*, pp. 282-283.
134. Godt (2007b), *Eigentum an Information—Patentschutz und allgemeine Eigentumstheorie am Beispiel genetischer Information*, Mohr Siebeck, Tübingen, p. 523.
135. *Ibid.*, p. 416.
136. Lemley (2015), "Faith-Based Intellectual Property," 62 *UCLA L. Rev.*, 1330.
137. Ghosh (2005), "Patent Law and the Assurance Game: Refitting Intellectual Property on the Box of Regulation," 18 *Can. J. L. & Jur.*, 332.
138. *Ibid.*, pp. 557-558.
139. *Ibid.*, p. 446.

license, a pharmacovigilance agency tries to avoid an outcome whereby people suffer or die due to having used a dangerous drug.

In opposition to this idea, a healthcare system aims to promote public health in several ways, for instance, by elaborating preventative public health campaigns in order to inform the population about health risks, or guaranteeing access to medicines for everyone who needs them, so that no sick person suffers or dies precisely because he or she lacks a drug that if it were available, would have alleviated the patient's suffering or prevented his or her death.

In simple words, a pharmacovigilance system assumes that a drug might be dangerous for public health, thereby prohibiting patients from having access to such a risky medicine; a healthcare system, in opposition, assumes that a given drug saves lives and, therefore, that its distribution should be as wide as possible.

2 *Protecting Public Health by Regulating the Efficacy and Safety of Drugs*

2.1 *Short History of the Pharmacovigilance System*

The need for a surveillance system for drugs in Europe, as it is currently understood, emerged in the 1960s as a consequence of the so-called thalidomide disaster.[140] The drug, first launched in Germany with the trade name of "Contergan," was largely prescribed to pregnant women as a sedative for combating morning sickness. Some years after thalidomide was launched, teratogenic effects, such as lack of legs or arms, were observed in thousands of babies whose mothers had taken the drug during pregnancy.[141] In the case of Contergan, the drug had never been tested in pregnant women. Because Thalidomide was sold in many countries, the birth deformation caused by the drug was seen over the globe. In the U.S.—where the pharmaceutical market was already regulated by the Food and Drug Agency (FDA), Contergan did not have the authorization to be marketed due to the diligence of *Frances Oldham Kelsey*, an FDA's officer, who "despite constant pressure from the company, refused to approve the application because of its inadequate evidence."[142]

This scandal made evident the need to regulate the pharmaceutical market and imposed on drug producers the duty of conducting studies, the aims of which were to ensure minimum standards of efficacy and safety of the drugs for human use.

Since the Contergan case, obtaining a license to put a new drug on the market has become a far more bureaucratic process due to the introduction of license proceedings, the aim of which is to evaluate whether the benefits of a drug outweigh its risks.

140. Dieners/Reese (2010), *Handbuch des Pharmarechts—Grundlagen und Praxis*, C.H. Beck, München, p. 11; Feldschreiber (2008), *The Law and Regulation of Medicines*, Oxford University Press, p. 6.
141. For more information about the Contergan case, *see* Beyer (1988), *Grenzen der Arzneimittelhaftung dargestellt am Beispiel des Contergan-Falles*, VVF Verlag, München.
142. FDA (2018), *Frances Oldham Kelsey: Medical Reviewer Famous for Averting a Public Health Tragedy*.

In 1965, the Directive 65/65/EEC of January 26, 1965,[143] which set criteria for all Member Countries of the European Economic Community obliging them to introduce authorization procedures before a medicinal product could be put on the market, was approved at the European level. According to Article 5 of the Directive, authorization should be refused in the following situations: (1) if it was proved that the medicinal product was harmful in normal conditions of use; (2) if it lacked therapeutic efficacy; (3) if its therapeutic efficacy were not sufficiently substantiated by the applicant; or (4) if its quantitative and qualitative composition were not declared.

Before the Contergan case, there had been calls to regulate the pharmaceuticals market in Europe, but the consensus, at the time, was that the costs for the industry of imposing such standards would be too high, which would be undesirable. Even in the U.S.—where since 1938 the law had required a drug's safety to be proved by the applicant before it gained marketing approval (and where thalidomide had not been approved)—the European scandal involving thalidomide had repercussions, and the law was changed so that proof of therapeutic efficacy would also have to be established as a requirement for approval.[144] In Germany, however, it was only in 1976, sometime after the Contergan scandal, that rigid proceedings for obtaining a license to market a drug were put in place.[145]

2.2 Principles

According to the WHO, pharmacovigilance is defined "as the science and activities relating to the detection, assessment, understanding and prevention of adverse effects or any other drug-related problem."[146] Thus, the aim of pharmacovigilance is protecting, as far as possible, public health from any disastrous side effects that a drug might produce. As put by *Härmark*, "regulatory pharmacovigilance is driven by the aim to provide drugs with a positive benefit-harm profile to the public."[147]

This means that in most pharmacovigilance systems in the world, a drug receives a marketing license only if its regulatory authority is convinced, after analyzing the relevant data provided by the applicant, that the benefits of a new drug outweigh its risks. In order to assess this, the drug's developers are required to include in their application proof that they have conducted all the necessary clinical studies, including tests on animals and human subjects. But even after a drug has been launched in the market, it can be withdrawn at any time if there are enough indications that the drug is causing harm to significant numbers of people.

143. *OJ* 22, 9.2.1965, pp. 369-373.
144. Breckenridge et al. (2012), "Thalidomide and its sequelae," 380 *The Lancet*, September, 781-783.
145. Dieners/Reese (2010), *Handbuch des Pharmarechts—Grundlagen und Praxis*, C.H. Beck, Berlin, p. 214.
146. http://www.who.int/medicines/areas/quality_safety/safety_efficacy/pharmvigi/en/index.html (last visited on August 31. 2020).
147. Dae-Hee Härmark (2012), *Web-Based Intensive Monitoring: A Patient-Based Pharmacovigilance Tool*, University Groningen, PhD Thesis, p. 22.

In the following, I briefly show the process a producer of a medicinal product must undergo before that product can receive marketing authorization.

2.3 *Drug Development Process*

Before an application is submitted to authorize a new drug for entry on the market, the drug must be submitted to clinical trials. These tests are divided into four phases, and they may take from 10 to 12 years altogether to be completed.

As a rule, before clinical trials begin, chemical or biological compounds are elected to be tested in the laboratory.

During Phase I (pre-clinic trials), "tests are performed on the lead compound in test tubes (laboratory, in vitro) and on animals (in vivo) to check how they affect the biological systems."[148]

During Phase II (clinic trials), the drug is tested on human subjects, which may be healthy volunteers or on individuals with the target disease. The objective of this phase is to determine its metabolic and pharmacological effects, as well as the maximum tolerated dose. The focus here is to identify possible adverse effects in a small sample. This phase usually takes up to one month.

During Phase III (clinical trials), the drug is tested only in individuals with the target disease. The tests' objective is to evaluate the drug's effectiveness as well to identify its risks and side effects, with the patient's safety in mind. Usually, a group of patients receives a placebo, and another one gets the real drug, neither group being aware of which drug they have been allocated. At the end of the process, results are compared. The aim of which is to obtain additional information about the drug's effectiveness and evaluate the risk-benefit ratio in a broader population from hundreds to thousands of patients, drug-disease interactions are observed, as well as dosage intervals. This phase can take several years to be completed. After this phase has been concluded, the application for market entry is made.

During Phase IV (manufacturing), the drug designated for clinical trials must be manufactured in compliance with current Good Manufacturing Practice following the guidelines of the responsible Drug Agency. As *Ng* puts it, "the emphasis is that drug should be safe, pure, effective, and of consistent quality to ensure that they are fit to be used for their intended functions."[149]

Phase V (marketing application) consists of the application period itself, under which it is necessary to provide the regulatory authorities with documents demonstrating "safety, potency, efficacy and purity of the drug."[150] After the drug has been approved and launched on the market, patient safety will be monitored.

148. Ng (2004), *Drugs—From Discovery to Approval*, John Wiley & Sons, New Jersey, pp. 3-5.
149. *Ibid.*, p. 4.
150. *Ibid.*

3 *Promoting Public Health by Expanding Access to Medicines*

A pharmaceutical product is always involved in a dichotomy: it might save lives, in which case, it represents the cure. But there are also side effects, and in extreme cases, people can even die after getting them. Depending on the situation, pharmaceuticals might be seen either as a boon or a bane.

As seen above, in the context of pharmacovigilance, a drug agency's duty is to accurately verify whether or not a new drug or a generic medicine is safe enough to receive authorization for marketing. If the drug is not safe enough, the agency will prohibit its entrance into the market in order to protect public health.

If, however, the benefits of a drug are recognized by the regulatory body, and the drug is commercialized, one promotes public health by guaranteeing that all those who need a remedy have access to it. This is especially important in the case of life-saving medicines. The question of drug access is not related to drug safety but rather with social justice, which is a question of policy. For achieving that everyone who needs a drug will have access to it, States make use of different instruments, such as price control, public manufacturing of drugs, public health insurance, etc. Similar to the task of protecting public health by checking whether a drug is safe enough for entering into the market, promoting public health is performed by the Ministry of Health directly or by independent agencies.

In Brazil, ANVISA is the federal agency responsible for *protecting* public health within the drug safety process. This is its main mission, but it is not the only one. Due to its expert knowledge, ANVISA also assists the Ministry of Health in *promoting* public health with the question of widening access to medicines, what it does, for instance, by taking part in the patenting process of pharmaceuticals or in the group responsible for monitoring the price of pharmaceuticals.

4 *Relationship Between Patent Protection and Public Health*

As seen in the preceding chapter, patent protection, as a rule, creates an artificial economic scarcity. It makes the patented medicine more expensive, at least during the period the patent protection lasts. The idea of patent protection is to deliberately create this scarcity in order to compensate the capitalists who have invested in developing the pharmaceutical products by giving them high return rates. Thus, patented medicines are usually very expensive.

The relationship between patent protection and public health can be summarized in the following proposition: "The higher a drug's price is, the less likely people will be able to afford it." Therefore, access to medicines will be restricted to people who can pay for it. Poor people who cannot afford a high-priced drug therapy that might save their lives will probably die. Industrialized countries, especially the richest countries of Western Europe, are able to minimize or neutralize the perverse effects of this innovation system through their health systems. In Germany, for example, most patients do not even know how much a drug prescribed by their doctor costs because the drug is directly paid from their health insurance, and therefore, the prices are of direct concern only to the insurance company's budget.

Most developing countries, however, do not have an organized health insurance system. In these countries, most drugs, including high-priced drugs, are directly paid for by those who can afford them; that is, only the rich. As a result of this, it is not surprising that in the developing world, people are more concerned than those

in wealthier countries about the high price of patented medicines: everyone there knows that the more expensive a drug is, the less affordable it will be for the population.

III How Distortions of the Patent System May Affect Public Health and Access to Medicines

1 *Setting the Problem in Context*

As commented in the precedent section, the patent system protects all kinds of technological inventions to the same extent. This means, for instance, that a hypothetical drug able to cure all forms of cancer would deserve the same terms of patent protection as a drug able to prevent hair loss. All that a patent applicant must do is prove that his invention is new, contains an inventive step and is industrially applicable. In the same way, the patent system makes no distinction between breakthrough and improvement inventions; all of them are eligible for 20 years of patent protection. This means that the patenting of an insignificant improvement in the hypothetical anticancer drug of the example above, such as a new form or dosage, would deserve the same patent protection as the drug itself, without consideration of whether the new form brings with it a significant or minor improvement in therapeutic efficacy.

This inherent distortion of the patent system opens the way for exploration by innovator companies. As is usual in every economic sector, entrepreneurs look for strategies to maximize their gains. That the pharmaceutical industry—a sector in which both the costs of developing new drugs and the gains promised by the patent monopoly are so high—adopts a strategic patenting approach, seeking to extend patent life and try to keep generic competitors out of the market is not surprising: these companies do so in order to minimize their expenses in R & D and to maximize their gains from the patent monopoly. In the next section, some concepts surrounding strategic patenting behavior in the field of drugs will be presented.

2 *Some Concepts*

2.1 *Evergreening of Patents (Secondary or Follow-On Patents)*

The name of "evergreening" has been given to a strategic patent behavior on the part of brand-name drug manufacturers, whereby they utilize particular provisions in the legal regime in order to acquire "additional patents of doubtful validity or applicability, in order to delay generic competition."[151] According to *Hemphill* and *Sampat*, "they tend not to be patents that cover the active ingredient, but patents pertaining to ancillary aspects of the drug."[152] Evergreening, however, does not necessarily have to be related to the acquisition of additional patents. In the words of *Faunce* and *Lexchin*, "evergreening is best understood as a social ideal used to refer to the myriad ways in which pharmaceutical patent owners utilize the law and related regulatory processes to extend their high rent-earning intellectual monopoly privileges."[153]

Strategic patent behavior is referred to in different ways by different parties. While originator companies tend to use more neutral expressions, like "secondary patents," generic companies, in their turn, call defensive patents "evergreening." With this expression, they refer to strategies used by originator companies to extend their monopoly over a given product. The term alludes to the kinds of plants that can get through the winter without losing their leaves and, consequently, without having to invest a lot of energy in making new ones.

Different approaches to strategic patent behavior are also present in the literature. *Rathod*, for instance, defines evergreening as "a strategy by which technology producers, using serial secondary patents and other mechanisms, keep their product sales protected for longer periods of time than would *normally* be permissible under the law."[154] *Chalmers* highlights that the practice of evergreening "does not simply refer to extending the original patent, but also includes strategies and practices used to protect a cluster of related, but arguably unoriginal, technologies through the filing of secondary applications."[155] *Darrow*, by contrast, considers criticisms of "evergreening" exaggerated and defines it as "a pejorative term used to refer to the practice of extending the length of patent protection beyond the statutory term of 20 years, most often used in the context of pharmaceutical patents." According to him, "although drug companies do engage in creative strategies to maintain sales levels for as long as possible, criticisms of evergreening are largely overstated."[156] By the same token, *Burton* and *Slope* do not speak of evergreening, but rather of "life-cycle management strategies," the key to which is "to extend patent protection beyond the basic patent term for as long as possible by filing secondary patents which are effective to keep generics off the market."[157]

As stated by *Temermann*, who classifies this practice as an abuse of patent rights, evergreening patents "are hard to challenge since they move along the borderline

151. Hemphill/Sampat (2012), "Evergreening, Patent Challenges, and Effective Market Life of Pharmaceuticals," 31 *J. Health Econ.*, 327.
152. *Ibid.*, p. 328.
153. Faunce/Lexchin (2007), "'Linkage' Pharmaceutical Evergreening in Canada and Australia," 4 *Austl. & N.Z. Health Pol'y*, 4.
154. Rathod (2010), "Evergreening: A Status Check in Selected Countries," 7 *J. Generic Med.*, 227. *See also* Gaudry (2011), "Evergreening: A Common Practice to Protect New Drugs," 29 *Nature Biotechnology*, 876-878.
155. Chalmers (2006), "Evergreen or Deciduous? Australian Trend in Relation to the 'Evergreening' of Patents," 30 *Melb. U. L. Rev.*, 31.
156. Darrow (2010), "Debunking the Evergreening Patent Myth," 131 *Harv. L. Rec.* 6, 131.
157. Burdon/Sloper (2003), "The Art of Using Secondary Patents to Improve Patent Protection," 3 *Int'l J. Med. Marketing*, 213.

between the illegal and illegal, yet they are definitively illegitimate."[158] Such evergreening, however, is far from being a harmless behavior. By doing so, the patentee does not just aim to optimize its patent but to keep generic producers out of the market for longer than 20 years. It is thus anti-competitive.

A common way of optimizing gains is to invest resources in the development of several "secondary patents" surrounding a single active ingredient, the idea of which is to extend the patent life of the "basic patent."[159] Although the granting of secondary patents does not affect the extension of the basic patent—which can be imitated after the basic patent expires—usually, the basic patent is not competitive enough in comparison to the improved patent. Typically, when applying for a patent, the drug originator will at first apply for the basic patent; a few years later, he will apply, for instance, for a patent protecting a second or a further medical indication; afterward, he will apply for an improvement regarding dosage, which would, for instance, affect the way the drug is absorbed by the human organism. So, even when the basic patent and these small improvements are discovered or developed at the same time, patent applicants prefer to apply for the small improvements after the filing of the basic patent. Because the improved product is already on the market, the generic competitor will have, in some cases, to wait until the improved patent expires. Since the improved product has been on the market for years, the generic competitor who introduces into a product covered by the basic patent to the market would probably have less chance to compete. As a consequence, the originator will continue to have a better position in the market, at least for a few years more.

Such strategies are controversial. They can be seen from conflicting economic viewpoints and global-economies perspectives. The pharmaceutical industry, for instance, adopts the view that secondary patents—which they call "incremental innovation"—are as important as the basic patent.[160] Thus, it supports the view that incremental innovation is as important as a "radical innovation." This view is also shared by some scholars.[161] The opposite approach is taken by people concerned with competition law, public health and innovation. Opponents of evergreening argue that strategies aiming to extend the patent term, when successful, may be abusive and may affect both competition and public health. Extension of the patent monopoly is seen as harmful from the point of view of competition law because it may retard the entrance of the generic competitor onto the market after the expiry of a patent. This delay is seen as harmful for public health because the costs of drug therapy are kept high beyond the regular time of patent protection. Both arguments are exacerbated in countries without a developed pharmaceutical industry and depending on generic drug production.

158. Temermann (2011), *The Legal Notion of Abuse of Patent Rights*, NCCR Trade Regulation, Working Paper No. 2011, p. 23.
159. Hutchins (2003), "Extending the Monopoly—How 'Secondary Patents' Can Be Used to Delay or Prevent Competition upon Expiry of the Basic Product Patent," 1 *J. Generic Med.*, 57-71.
160. Thomas (2009), *Patent "Evergreening": Issues on Innovation and Competition*, US Congressional Research Service, November 13. *See also* IFPMA (2006): *Inovação Incremental, Propriedade Intelectual e Interesse Público: Como a Inovação Incremental Leva a Medicamentos Novos Melhores e Mais Seguros.*
161. *See*, for instance, Rayna/Striukova (2009), "The Curse of the First-Mover: When Incremental Innovation Leads to Radical Change," 1 *Int'l J. Collaborative Enterprise*, 4-21.

2.2 *"Patent Thickets" or "Patent Clusters"*

Economists, when examining the phenomena of defensive patenting, focus their view on the effects produced by such patents in the market, especially regarding competition and innovation. The effect is that a single product or technology will be often protected by many patents owned by one or different companies. Thus, if a new player wants to enter the market, she must, at first, fight against "a dense web of overlapping intellectual property rights that a company must hack in order to actually commercialize new technology."[162] Depending on how difficult it is for the new player "to navigate the patent thicket," in the words of *Shapiro*, that new player might give up on entering the market. Economists believe, therefore, that "patent thickets" may inhibit competition and discourage innovation.[163]

In the area of pharmaceuticals, which is characterized by intense patent activity and litigation, the extension of patent protection may be obtained by filing secondary patent applications or divisional applications.[164]

2.3 *"Trivial Patents"*

A "trivial patent" is a patent that protects an invention, the level of inventiveness of which is not considered high enough to deserve a patent; that is, a "minor invention" in the sense that any skilled person would be able to create it with little effort.

The existence of trivial patents indicates a failure in the patent system. In theory, patents should compensate for the necessary costs of R & D of a meaningful invention. Patents do not exist for the sake of good business. If society pays the high price of granting a temporary monopoly to the patent owner, it does so as a form of exchange in return for the patent owner's having assumed the costs and the risk of the R & D of a meaningful invention. This assumes that the invention protected by a patent should not be obvious for a person having ordinary skill in the art.

The problem of patenting trivia is a problem of patent quality, which in turn has to do with how the "inventive step" requirement is assessed. In the last few decades, there has been, in the industrialized countries, a tendency to lower the standards of inventiveness so that trivial patents—often called "improvement patents"—are more often legitimized. *Sears* relates that in the U.S., the American Patent Law Association and other societies representing the patent community began to lobby for a lower standard of patentability as early as the 1940s.[165] Issues related to patent quality have

162. Shapiro (2001), "Navigating the Patent Thicket: Cross Licenses, Patent Pools and Standard-Setting, Innovation Policy and the Economy," in: Jaffe et al. (eds.), *Innovation Policy and the Economy, Vol. 1*, MIT Press, pp. 119-120.
163. Hall/Hermes/von Graevenitz (2016), *Patent Thickets and First-Time Patenting: New Evidence*, CEPR's policy portal.
164. UK Intellectual Property Office (2011), *Patent Thickets, an Overview*, p. 8.
165. Sears (1975), "Tinkering with the Invention Standard: No Solution to the Problems of Patent Quality," 59 *Minn. L. Rev.*, 965.

been discussed for decades in the United States,[166] where the problem is more serious than in Europe. But also, the quality of patent applications in Europe is seen as lower by experts,[167] so the topic has reached the political agenda[168] and the notice of the mass media there.[169]

In the pharmaceutical field, patents of poor quality are often referred to as "me-too drugs";[170] such a drug is very similar to existing drugs but appears later and is not clinically superior.[171] The cause of lower patent quality seems to lay both in the level of the inventive step requirement applied by patent offices and in the increasing number of patent applications.[172]

3 *Practices That Indicate "Evergreening" in the Pharmaceutical Field*

Patents can be obtained if the conditions of patentability are fulfilled, that is, if the invention is new and has an inventive step and industrial application. Whether the invention is a breakthrough one or it represents a small improvement is not relevant in obtaining a patent. In the field of medicine, for instance, a patent can be obtained both for a new chemical entity and for incremental developments made in a known substance, provided that the new developments satisfy the above conditions of patentability.

Pharmaceutical companies tend to apply for multiple patents concerning different aspects of the same substance. They do so not only in the hope of preventing competitors from being the first to apply to get a patent regarding the same development but also in the hope of extending the lifetime of *effective* patent protection.[173] In the words of *Hutchins*, "filing multiple patent applications directed to the active ingredient is typical of the manner in which research-based pharmaceutical companies are able to surround the active ingredient with a web of patents that extend beyond the

166. *See*, for instance, Hall/Harhoff (2004), "Post Grant Reviews in the U.S. Patent System—Design Choices and Expected Impact," 19 *Berkeley Tech. L. J.* 989; Hall, Graham et al. (2003), *Prospects for Improving U.S. Patent Quality via Post-Grant Opposition*, NBER Working Paper 973, pp. 3-5.
167. *See*, for instance, an expert report made by the Scientific Advisory Council of the German Federal Ministry for Economy and Technology: Harhoff/Engel/Möschel (2007), *Patentschutz und Innovation. Gutachten des Wissenschaftlichen Beirats beim Bundesministerium für Wirtschaft und Technologie.*
168. *See*, for instance, a speech given by the former Federal Ministry of Justice in Germany: Zypries (2004), "Hypertrophie der Schutzrechte?," 132 *GRUR*, 977-980.
169. *See*, for instance, an interview given by Mr. Battistelli, a former President of the EPO: "Wir müssen gegen triviale Patente kämpfen," *Süddeutsche Zeitung* (2012), December 13, p. 18.
170. *See* Angell (2000), "The Pharmaceutical Industry—To Whom Is It Accountable?," 342 *New Eng. J. Med.*, 1902-1904, June 22; Angell (2004) *The Truth About the Drug Companies: How They Deceive Us and What To Do About It*, Random House, New York; Stiglitz/Jayadev (2010), "Medicine for Tomorrow: Some Alternative Proposals to Promote Socially Beneficial Research and Development in Pharmaceuticals," 7 *J. Generic Med.*, 221-222.
171. Hollis (2004), *"Me-Too Drugs: Is There a Problem?,"* Paper, December 13.
172. *See* Hall/Harhoff (2004), "Post Grant Reviews in the U.S. Patent System—Design Choices and Expected Impact," 19 *Berkeley Tech. L. J.* 989; Holtz (2008), "Opposition Only After Grant—Any Effects on Inventive Step at the EPO?," *GRUR Int.*, 653-657.
173. For a case study *see* Correa (2001), *Trends in Drug Patenting: Case Studies*, Buenos Aires, Ediciones Corregidor.

expiry of the basic patent."[174] As an example, *Hutchins* cites the case of Pfizer's Lipitor, a cholesterol-lowering drug, the most sold drug worldwide in 2002. He analyzed the U.S. patents listed for Lipitor in the American Food and Drug Agency (FDA) Orange Book and came to the following conclusion: while the U.S. patent which protects the compound atorvastatin was due to expire in 2009, another four U.S. patents protected different chemical and physical forms of the basic compound. Of these four secondary patents, the first one protected an optical isomer of atorvastatin and would expire in 2010; the second one protected a stabilized salt with calcium carbon stabilizer and would expire in 2013; the third one protected a stabilized metal salt formulation and would expire in 2014; the fourth one protected a crystalline form of atorvastatin hydrate and would expire in 2016.[175]

What is the sense of this multiple patenting concerning the same active substance? Ideally, a research-based company that is applying for the basic patent will later try to obtain secondary patents, even if the innovations were developed at the same time as the subject of the first patent. So, when the basic patent expires, the secondary patent carries on. This course of action is driven by the idea that it will probably not be worthwhile for generic competitors to invest resources in the drug protected by the basic patent if an improved form of it is already on the market and, at the same time, is protected by a patent.

3.1 Obtaining Multiple Patenting Regarding the Same Product

3.1.1 Swiss-Type Patent Claims

"Swiss-type claims," according to *Armstrong*, "can mostly basically be described as a variety of 'subsequent medical use' claim, made when someone discovers that a known drug has a previously unknown medical use."[176] They were first recognized in 1984 by the Patent Office of Switzerland, a rich country with one of the most prosperous pharmaceutical industries in the world. As stated by *Armstrong*, this art of patent claim was created for increasing the level of patent protection for drug manufacturers as a reason for the policy. For making the Swiss-type claim understandable, he took the drug aspirin and imagines a situation under which the pharmaceutical company, which had owned the expired patent rights about aspirin—a drug that was originally patented and marketed for easing pain—discovers that aspirin can be used for preventing heart attacks.[177] The author puts himself in the company's place and imagines what he would have to do for obtaining a patent again for aspirin, explaining that there would be the following possibilities of achieving patent protection.

174. Hutchins (2003), "Extending the Monopoly—How 'Secondary Patents' Can Be Used to Delay or Prevent Generic Competition upon Expiry of the Basic Product Patent," 1 *J. Generic Med.*, 58.
175. *Ibid.*, p. 58.
176. Armstrong (2001), "The Arguments of Law, Policy and Practice Against Swiss-Type Patent Claims," in: Frankel/Smith, *Essays on Intellectual Property Law and Policy*, 32 Vic. U. Wellington L. Rev., 203.
177. *Ibid.*, pp. 203-205.

3.1.1.1 Option One and Two: Product Claims over the Drug/ and or Active Chemicals

As clarified by *Armstrong*, the two possible product claims in the aspiring example would try to have a patent granted either over the aspirin medicament or acetylsalicylic themselves. However, these claims would be disallowed because only new products or new uses can be patented.

3.1.1.2 Option Three: Use Claim over the Use of the Drug ("Use of Known Substance X for New Purpose Y")

In *Armstrong*'s words, "the third possibility for our hypothetical aspirin manufacturer is to patent the use of aspirin in treating heart attacks. The use claim avoids the novelty problem encountered by product claims because the patent is over the thing from which novelty derives."[178] Theoretically, it would be possible to have patents over every new use of the drug. However, the Swiss patent law, as many patent laws in the world, prohibits patents on methods of medical treatment. Consequently, a creative solution for obtaining a patent was necessary in such a case.

3.1.1.3 Option Four: Use Claim over the Use of the Active Chemicals (Swiss-Type Claim)

According to *Armstrong*, "for drug manufacturers the unavailability of the above claims poses a conundrum: once the patent on a drug used for a particular purpose expires, they cannot secure a renewed exclusive right to make and sell the drug if a new use is found (...). Their salvation is the Swiss-type claim. It is a purpose-limited use claim that focuses not on the use of the drug, but on the use of the active chemicals to make the drug, side-stepping the prohibition on medical method of treatment patents. Specifically, the patentee claims the exclusive right *to use the relevant active chemicals* in manufacturing a drug *for the new purpose*. A Swiss-type claim in our aspirin example would cover 'the use of acetylsalicylic acids to make aspirin for treating heart attacks'."[179]

This cumbersome solution embraces a very flexible way of interpreting patent law, with the deliberate purpose of making patentable inventions that clearly are not patentable.[180] In other words, the so-called Swiss-type claim is a trick for obtaining a new patent for the same product again. As *Armstrong* stated:

> With alarming success, a drafting trick designed to benefit Switzerland's drug manufacturers has crept into the patent law regimes of several countries. (...) The expansion has been characterized by a frustrating willingness to challenge the

178. *Ibid.*, p. 206.
179. *Ibid.*, p. 208.
180. About this trend *see* Dutfield, (2017), "Healthcare Innovation and Patent Law's 'Pharmaceutical Privilege': Is There a Pharmaceutical Privilege? And If So, Should We Remove It?," 12 *Health Econ. Policy & L.*, 4, 453-470.

received "wisdom" of the EPO Enlarged Board of Appeals, a hesitancy partly attributable to the trend towards regional and international harmonization of intellectual property laws.[181]

That the Swiss-type patent claim was accepted first by the Swiss Patent Office and afterward by other European countries is understandable due to trade policy reasons since the pharmaceutical industry of these countries not only invest large amounts of money in the development of drugs, but they are also the net receivers of patent royalties regarding pharmaceutical products. However, when patent offices of developing countries without an innovative pharmaceutical industry, such as the case of the INPI, accept such patents, there are not trade interests that benefit developing countries. By doing so, patent offices of developing countries help to increase patent royalties of the multinational pharmaceutical companies and, at the same time, to make access to such a drug more difficult.

3.1.2 Selection Patents or Selection Inventions

According to *Grubb*, one refers to "selection patents" when speaking of the patenting of "compounds which, although individually new, fall within an earlier disclosure of a broader group of compounds. The invention then can only be the selection of a particular compound or a relatively small group of compounds from the larger group previously disclosed in broad terms."[182] *Hutchins* clarifies that in many cases, the best strategy might be to delay the application for a patent concerning basic patent compounds. In such cases, research-based pharmaceutical companies will apply for patents for the following types of objects: a generic group of compounds; a narrower, more tightly defined subgroup of more active compounds; individual compounds or individual forms of compounds.[183] According to him, during the research phase, "chemists may find that useful biological activity is associated with a broad class of compounds of quite diverse structures."[184] In this case, the first patent application will cover a broad genus consisting of many thousands of compounds. Depending on how research into this develops, compounds that are shown to be better than others may be the object of a new family of patent applications, which are often referred to as "selection patents."

181. Armstrong (2001), "The Arguments of Law, Policy and Practice Against Swiss-Type Patent Claims," p. 220.
182. Grubb (1999), *Patents for Chemicals, Pharmaceuticals and Biotechnology—Fundamentals of Global Law, Practice and Strategy*, Clarendon Press, Oxford, pp. 196-200.
183. Hutchins (2003), "Extending the Monopoly—How 'Secondary Patents' Can Be Used to Delay or Prevent Generic Competition upon Expiry of the Basic Product Patent," *J. Generic Med.*, 59.
184. *Ibid.*, p. 60.

Although "selection inventions" are accepted by the EPO,[185] their acceptance is controversial in Germany, where the Federal Court of Justice (*Bundesgerichtshof*–BGH) has already ruled that such inventions are not new.[186]

3.1.3 Pharmacologically Active Metabolites

An active metabolite results when a drug is metabolized by the body into a modified form, which continues to produce effects within that body.[187] In such cases, the administered drug is called a pro-drug. According to *Correa*, companies who succeed in synthetically producing a metabolite may obtain a patent seeking to protect that synthetic metabolite. *Correa* and *Hutchins* mention the case of the pro-drug terfenadine.[188] After the expiration of terfenadine's patent, its originator managed to get a patent to cover the active metabolite per se (fexofenadine). Afterward, the originator sued generic competitors, accusing them of "indirect infringement." *Hutchins* relates that the originator, in this case, was unsuccessful in Germany and that in the U.S., the courts decided that the patent covered only metabolites made synthetically, not produced in vivo from terfenadine.[189]

3.1.4 Isomeric Forms

As one might remember from chemistry classes in school, chemical compounds frequently exist in a different isomeric form, which means that such compounds have the same atomic mass but another chemical structure or arrangement of atoms in space. In the latter case, such isomers are called enantiomers or "optical isomers" because they are mirror images of each other. *Hutchins* points out that, in the cases where the active drug compound is a mixture of isomers, one isomer might be found to be more active than others; consequently, the most active isomer may be the basis for a separate patent.[190] As an example of this kind of secondary patent, he again refers to the cholesterol-reducer atorvastatin (Lipitor). According to him, it was an isomer that

185. The literature on selection inventions is abundant in Europe. *See*, for instance, Spangenberg (1997), "The Novelty of 'Selection' Inventions," 28 *IIC*, 808-822; Vivian (1989), "Novelty and Selection Inventions," 20 *IIC*, 303-311.
186. Hansen (2008), "Auswahlerfindungen auf dem Gebiet der Chemie—Brauchen wir einen deutschen Sonderweg?—Anmerkungen nicht nur zur Fluoran-Entscheidung," *GRUR Int.*, 891-899.
187. *See*, for instance, Wang/Huang (2012), "Patent Protection of Pharmacologically Active Metabolites: Theoretical and Technological Analysis on the Jurisprudence of Four Regions," 29 *Santa Clara Computer & High Tech. L. J.*, 492-493.
188. Correa (2007b), *Guidelines for the Examination of Pharmaceutical Patents: Developing a Public Health Perspective* (Working Paper), ICTSD/WHO/UNCTAD, p. 18; Hutchins (2003), "Extending the Monopoly—How 'Secondary Patents' Can Be Used to Delay or Prevent Generic Competition upon Expiry of the Basic Product Patent," 1 *J. Generic Med.*, 61.
189. Hutchins (2003), "Extending the Monopoly—How 'Secondary Patents' Can Be Used to Delay or Prevent Generic Competition upon Expiry of the Basic Product Patent," 1 *J. Generic Med.*, pp. 61-62.
190. *Ibid.*, p. 62.

has given Pfizer an additional year of effective patent protection in the U.S. and up to three additional years outside the U.S.[191]

3.1.5 Polymorphs (Crystalline Forms)

A compound can exist in different crystalline forms and solvates, such as hydrates, which may have different properties (e.g., one form is more stable than another). During the research phase, chemists often try to identify which crystalline form is the most advantageous for a given compound. *Hutchins* notes that this identification "can lead to patents of considerable commercial value that can extend the patent protection for a drug substance beyond the normal 20-year lifetime of a patent."[192] This is because such a patent, when protecting the most stable form, will block generic competitors from selling it. The author refers once more to the case of the cholesterol-reducer Lipitor (Atorvastatin) as an example of this kind of secondary patent. Furthermore, he explains that while "many drug substances are presented in the form of salts, and such salts are often quite stable, this is not always the case" so that "the preparation of more unusual salts having improved properties, such as better solubility or better processability can give rise to new patents."[193]

It is worth noting that obtaining polymorph patents in Europe has become more difficult since 2011. By deciding an opposition filed against Atorvastatin, the Boards of Appeal (BA) of the European Patent Office (EPO) decided "the skilled person in the field of pharmaceutical drug development would have been aware of the fact that instances of polymorphism were commonplace in molecules of interest to the pharmaceutical industry, and have known it to be advisable to screen for polymorphs early on in the drug development process. Moreover, he would be familiar with routine methods of screening. Consequently, in the absence of any technical prejudice and in the absence of any unexpected property, the mere provision of a crystalline form of a known pharmaceutically active compound cannot be regarded as involving an inventive step."[194] Consequently, the patent was revoked.

3.1.6 Process Patents

Another way of extending the effective patent life of a drug is to obtain patents on processes after the expiry of the basic patent. *Hutchins* notes that process patents will usually not keep generic firms out of the market, but this might be possible if the patented process is the only commercially viable process for producing the drug in

191. *Ibid.*
192. *Ibid.*, p. 62. About this strategy (and others) to extend patent rights *see also* Glasgow (2001), "Stretching the Limits of Intellectual Property Rights: Has the Pharmaceutical Industry Gone Too Far?," 41 *IDEA—The J. L. & Tech.*, 250.
193. Hutchins (2003), "Extending the Monopoly—How 'Secondary Patents' Can Be Used to Delay or Prevent Generic Competition upon Expiry of the Basic Product Patent," 1 *J. Generic Med.*, 63.
194. EPO—T 0777/08 (Atorvastatin Polymorphs/ WARNER-LAMBERT of May 24, 2011).

question.[195] As an example of this kind of "evergreening," *Hutchins* cites the case of the "aniline process" for making the antibacterial drug Trimethoprim.

3.1.7 Novel Therapeutic Indications in Connection with "Patent Linkage"

If a new therapeutic indication of the same compound is protected by an additional patent, the generic producer will not be allowed to produce or to market the product protected by the improvement patent. However, depending on the circumstances, a patented new therapeutic indication of an existing drug may also extend the basic patent's effective lifespan. In some countries, however, generic companies cannot obtain authorization for commercializing the patent-expired drug due to so-called regulatory data protection. This is the case when national law dictates that a generic drug only receives marketing authorization if it can be proven that all patents related to a branded product had already expired.

This protection, often called "patent linkage," may prevent generic companies, for a given period of time, from using research data regarding the quality, safety and efficacy of the drug unless they produce that data for themselves. This usually delays competition since the generic company can offer the product at a cheaper price precisely because it does not have to invest heavily in R & D.[196]

The link between regulatory data and patent protection was created in the U.S.,[197] and it has been disseminated in the world through bilateral agreements between the U.S. and other countries, like Canada, Mexico, Australia[198] and China.[199]

3.1.8 Novel Dosage Regimes

As pointed out by *Hutchins*, a drug product is typically launched in the form of a standard tablet, a capsule or an injectable form, but, after the expiration of the basic patent, originators will develop new dosage forms (for instance, in liquid compositions, or chewable or effervescent tablets) and apply for patents regarding such improvements.[200] This may discourage generic competitors from entering the market for fear of patent litigation from the former patent owner.

---

195. Hutchins (2003), "Extending the Monopoly—How 'Secondary Patents' Can Be Used to Delay or Prevent Generic Competition upon Expiry of the Basic Product Patent," 1 *J. Generic Med.*, 64.
196. Tuominen (2009/2010), *Defensive Patent Protection Strategies in the Pharmaceutical Industry—a Response to a Legal Problem?* Master Thesis, College of Europe, Bruges Campus, Law Department.
197. Chen (2012), "Lessons from Generics," 43 *Vanderbilt J. Transnat'l L.*, 1262.
198. Faunce/Lexchin (2007), "'Linkage' Pharmaceutical Evergreening in Canada and Australia," 4 *Austl. & N.Z. Health Pol'y*, 8.
199. Nafis/Srinivasan (2015), "Validity of Patent Linkage Across the Globe," *The Pat. Law.*, 35-37.
200. Hutchins (2003), "Extending the Monopoly—How 'Secondary Patents' Can Be Used to Delay or Prevent Generic Competition upon Expiry of the Basic Product Patent," 1 *J. Generic Med.*, 67.

3.1.9 Combination Therapies

Some patent claims are based on the combination of two or more existing active ingredients, which will indirectly extend their patent life. *Correa* is of the opinion that such inventions are too obvious to deserve a patent. He recommends that such patents are not granted in developing countries unless the combination results in a new and non-obvious "synergy-effect."[201]

3.2 Abuse of the Right to Litigation

In some countries, litigation may also be seen as a facet of "evergreening." This is the case when the mere act of bringing a case before a court legally gives a patentee an extension to his patent rights beyond the expiry of that patent, regardless of the result of the judgment.

The situation can be illustrated in the case of Canada. According to Canadian regulations, when a generic company applies for regulatory approval of a drug related to or compared to a drug listed on the patent register held by the Health Canada Therapeutic Products Directorate, it must at first apply for a "notice of compliance." This notice is only issued if the generic company either agrees to wait until the related patent's expiry before bringing its product onto the market or if it makes an "allegation" that the listed patent is invalid or that its generic drug does not violate the listed patent.[202] If such an "allegation" is made by the generic company that applies for the notice, the owner of the related patent might decide to sue them. If the patent owner decides to sue the generic company, the former will be benefited from an automatic stay of 24 months. During this period, no authorization of marketing can be issued to the generic competitor. Other countries, like the U.S., also have similar provisions.[203] In Brazilian law, this type of provision, which is mostly referred to as a "linkage" in the context of patent rights and regulatory approval, does not exist.

In such cases, one speaks of "strategic litigation" since the only reason for it is to keep generic competitors out of the market for the time period prescribed by law or decided by the court.

4 Consequences of the Abuse of Patent Rights

When a patentee misuses the patent system by using strategies with the aim of extending his patent rights, his aim is to keep generic competitors out of the market in order to enjoy his monopoly rights for more than 20 years. This is a distortion. At least,

201. Correa (2011), "Pharmaceutical Innovation, Incremental Patenting and Compulsory Licensing," *South Center Research Paper* 41, September.
202. Hore (2004), *Patently Absurd—Evergreening of pharmaceutical Patent Protection under the Patented Medicines (Notice of Compliance) Regulations of Canada's Patent Act*, Canadian Generic Pharmaceutical Association.
203. Hore (2000), "A Comparison of United States and Canadian Laws as They Affect Generic Pharmaceutical Market Entry," 55 *Food & Drug L. J.*, 374.

in theory, a patent should be granted in a trade-off, that is, in the hope that society will within a short space of time benefit from the patented invention as a public good after having compensated its inventor with a temporary patent monopoly. In this context, extending that monopoly represents a breach in this balance. On the other hand, the granting of patent rights for "me-too" drugs works rather as an incentive to use the patent system to "promote" minor innovations since the cost of minor improvements is lower than the cost of developing significant inventions, and the profits are proportionally higher.

Furthermore, "me-too" drugs harm the health system both in the developing world and in the industrialized countries. A study conducted in Switzerland between 2000 and 2008 demonstrated that a huge amount of money had been unnecessarily spent on follow-on drugs in cases where replacement with a generic drug would have had the same therapeutic effect.[204] According to this study, the Swiss healthcare system could have saved over EUR 30.3 million if both brand and follow-on drug prescriptions had been replaced by the generic equivalents.

IV Ways of Correcting Abuses and Controlling Quality of Patents

1 Introduction

In the preceding sections, some problems of the patent system were presented, with a focus on pharmaceutical patents. As we have seen, the aim of strategic patenting is the "evergreening" of patents or the creation of "patent thickets" in order to maximize the profits the patent owner can extract from the system. In the first case, evergreen patents will delay the entrance of generic competitors onto the market, whereas in the second case, patents will discourage innovation: instead of fostering it, they slow it down. In the worst case, patents will promote the development of "trivial inventions."

Bearing these problems in mind, it is necessary to develop mechanisms or use existing ones in order to avoid abuses and distortions of the patent system. In the case of "strategic patenting," these mechanisms should be used to identify instances whereby this practice is illegitimate or potentially harmful to society. The challenge patent offices have to meet is to distinguish between normal use and the abuse of the patent system.

In the next section, the instruments of patent law and competition law used to combat misuses of patent rights and improve patent quality will be shortly presented.

204. Vernaz et al. (2013), "Patented Drug Extension Strategies on Healthcare Spending: A Cost-Evaluation Analysis," 10 *PLoS Medicine* 6.

2 *Instruments Within Patent Law*

2.1 *Instruments Concerning Quality of Patents*

2.1.1 Patent Examination System

That patents are not granted before an examination has been carried out by patent offices may nowadays appear to be self-evident. However, the degree of examination changes in time and in terms of regulation goals. In the U.S., for instance, from 1793 to 1836, patents could also be granted merely by registering them. An examination system whereby substantive standards of patentability were tested was only introduced in 1836 after a U.S. Senate Commission had assessed the problems in the quality of the patents that were being granted.[205] Even today, the substantive requirements of patentability are not examined everywhere. As reported by *Correa*, in South Africa, for instance, patents are granted without such examinations.[206]

Another example of a change in time is the case of Great Britain. According to the British Patent Law Amendment of 1852, the only requirements for the granting of patents were registration and the payment of fees. In 1883, the Patent Office began to examine its applications for formal defects and insufficiency of description; in 1905, after it had been established that 40 percent of the patents that had been granted in the U.K. referred to inventions that had already been described, a reform was imposed, stipulating that patents should not be granted without the examination of the requirement of novelty.[207] This change was partially motivated, according to *Khan*, "by the realization that England's early industrial and technological supremacy was threatened by the United States and other nations in Europe."[208] This was an example of regulation for promoting competition.

In the case of Germany, *Khan* reported that at the end of the nineteenth century, "German patent fees were deliberately set high to eliminate protection for trivial inventions, with a renewal system that required payment of 30 marks for the first year, 50 marks for the second year, 100 marks for the third, and 50 marks annually after the third year."[209]

As it happens today, peripheral countries, which are technologically less advanced, could not afford to make such investments in the patent bureaucracy at the end of the nineteenth century. Even if today, most developing countries have a patent office, they used to be underfunded. Their expertise is sometimes the result of years of technical assistance provided by the EPO. As demonstrated by *Drahos*, the EPO's

205. Drahos (2007), *Patent Reform for Innovation and Risk Management: A Separation of Powers Approach*, KEStudies, Vol. 1, p. 2; Kingsland (1948), "The United States Patent Office," 13 *L. & Contemp. Probs.*, 358.
206. Correa (2014), *Patent Examination and Legal Fictions: How Legal Fictions Are Created on Feet of Clay*, South Center, Research Paper 58, p. 4.
207. Khan (2002), "Intellectual Property and Economic Development: Lessons from American and European History," *Commission on Intellectual Property Rights, Study Paper 1a*, National Bureau of Economic Research, p.13.
208. *Ibid.*, p. 13.
209. *Ibid.*, p. 19.

global leadership in this field does not necessarily reflect the development interests of developing countries, whose patent examiners basically grant patents to foreign firms from Europe, the U.S. and Japan.[210]

Brazil, today a major emerging economy, was a country whose economy relied at the end of the nineteenth century exclusively on the export of commodities of low technological value, as many other countries nowadays still do. At the time, Brazil did not have the financial means to invest resources in the improvement of its patent office, so that patents were also granted without examination. Even though the problem of patent quality was not seen as important in the context of Brazil of those times, it is possible to find evidence that patent policy questions were behind patent examination rules. While the early industrialized countries introduced a substantive examination as a general rule for all patent applications, Brazil followed the trend, but in its own way. In 1882, the new Brazilian regulations on patents introduced the requirement to examine a patent application only if the object of the patent were a food, chemical or pharmaceutical invention, which shows that also in these old times, the Brazilian legislator conferred a special treatment for pharmaceutical inventions.[211]

In the post-TRIPS-era, patent examination plays a role more prominent than ever. In times of worldwide harmonized patent law, interpretation of the patentability's requirements is one of the few fields where substantive patent law still left room for flexibility, making it possible that countries shape their examination in accordance with their own interests and realities. Currently, where trivial patents and other problems created by low patentability standards proliferate, it is important, as stated by *Correa*, "stipulating rigorous criteria to assess novelty, inventive step and industrial application."[212]

2.1.2 Patent Opposition System

"Opposition proceedings" refers to the intervention of third parties in the patent grant proceedings before the patent office. Anyone has the right to oppose the granting of a patent. When opposing, the third party must present his or her reasons for the

210. Drahos (2008), "Trust me": Patent Offices in Developing Countries, 34 *AMJLM* 151. *Drahos* comments the technical cooperation given by the EPO to Vietnam with the following words: "An example of this leadership based on technocratic trust come from fieldwork in Vietnam, where over the years the EPO has been active. When examiners in the Vietnamese patent office how to consider a patent application in the pharmaceutical field, they begin by looking at how the EPO has decided the application and what it has said in its search report. They do no confine themselves to the EPO's judgment, as the examiner's decision tree makes clear (...). They may also look at the way in which the USPTO and JPO have treated the application. The decision tree below is the product of years of technical assistance, which includes training visits to beautiful Munich with its designed gardens and wonderful restaurants. It is the story of quiet and steady cultural integration in which examiners of patent offices of the periphery journey to the patent kingdoms of the west to be instructed in systems of apparent technological superiority to their own, systems that continue to influence them once they returned home." (pp. 160-161).
211. Article 3, 2 Paragraph Lei No. 3.129 of October 14, 1882.
212. *See*, for instance, Correa (2012), "Efforts to Raise the Bar in Patent Examination Need to be Supported," *IIC*, 747-750.

objection by a certain deadline, and the Patent Office must examine the matter. Such proceedings may take place before a patent is granted or afterward. In the first case, they are called "pre-grant opposition systems"; in the second, they are called "post-grant opposition systems."

Khan relates that opposition proceedings were introduced in British law as early as 1883.[213] According to her, the British opposition provision foresaw that anyone could oppose the granting of a patent until two months after the publication of the patent specifications. She reports that third parties could oppose if they could demonstrate one of the following three points to the patent office: first, that the idea had been stolen; second, that it had previously been patented in Britain; or third, that the patent specification was different from the description in the provisional patent.[214]

The rationale behind opposition proceedings is that patent offices may fail and, consequently, grant patents for inventions that do not deserve them. Incorrectly issued patents, also known as "bad patents," generate unjustified costs, such as those listed by *Kesan*: "Firms have to pay licenses fees to use the technology, and consumers have to pay higher prices to buy the patentee's products."[215] Although a patent, once granted, can always be challenged in court, the costs of judicial proceedings at this stage are higher, which may deter such challenges.

Considering the expansion of patentable subject matter that has occurred over the last few decades, and which has led to an increased number of patents being issued, with many of them considered to be of a lower "patent quality," patent opposition is gaining more and more importance.[216] According to the Annual Report 2016 of the European Patent Office, which employs the post-grant opposition system, in 2015, 31 percent of opposition cases led to the revocation of the patent.[217]

2.2 *Instruments Concerning Public or National Interest*

2.2.1 Compulsory Licensing

The basic idea of compulsory licensing is a compromise between the patent owner's interests and the *public interest*, which ideally works in the following way: a patentee may be compelled to license to others the right to use the invention for the benefit of public interest, assuming that the patentee will be reasonably compensated for damages.

---

213. Khan (2002), "Intellectual Property and Economic Development: Lessons from American and European History," *Commission on Intellectual Property Rights, Study Paper 1a*, January, p. 13.
214. *Ibid.*, p. 13, fn. 21.
215. Kesan (2009), "Patent Office Oppositions and Patent Invalidation in Court: Complements or Substitutes," in: Takenaka (ed.), *Patent Law and Theory—A Handbook of Contemporary Research*, Edward Elgar, Cheltenham (UK), p. 258.
216. Hall, Graham et al. (2003), *Prospects for Improving U.S. Patent Quality via Post-Grant Opposition*, NBER Working Paper 9731, pp. 3-5.
217. EPO Annual Report 2016, available at https://www.epo.org/about-us/annual-reports-statistics/annual-report/2016/statistics/searches.html#tab4 (last visited on August 31. 2020).

According to *Machlup*, the principle of compulsory licensing was first proposed in 1790 in the United States Senate. It was generally accepted in 1873 at the Patent Congress held at Vienna after patent and free-trade advocates had reached a compromise.[218] Besides compulsory licensing, as *Drahos* highlights, even before, in the United Kingdom, the Crown could make use of a patented invention without the permission of the patent owner.[219] The so-called crown use survived in common law countries, like the UK and the U.S.

In 1883, the principle of compulsory licensing was adopted by the Paris Convention for Industrial Property,[220] although not all contracting parties, including Brazil,[221] implemented this possibility. In 1993, all WTO members accepted compulsory licensing when they approved the Trade-Related Intellectual Property Rights Agreement (TRIPS). Traditionally, however, its use is only accepted in exceptional circumstances, while the essence of public interest was shifted in time.

Although the application of compulsory licensing remains controversial, it has been exceptionally invoked to protect the public interest—either effectively or as a threat—both in the developing and the developed world. In 2001, in the context of the 9/11 attacks, the U.S. Administration threatened to issue a compulsory license in order to enable imports of generic medicines from India, versions of the original Bayer patented drug Cipro.[222] From 2002 to 2004, three African countries that suffered from high rates of HIV/AIDS—Mozambique, Zambia and Zimbabwe—issued compulsory licenses for antiretroviral drugs (ARV Drugs) in order to locally produce them.[223] In 2005, the U.S. administration threatened again to issue compulsory licenses in the context of avian flu if companies producing in the U.S. would not increase the production of avian flu medication.[224] In 2006, Thailand issued a compulsory license for HIV/AIDS medication, and in 2007, it issued a compulsory license for a drug to treat heart disease, becoming the first country to grant compulsory licenses in case of chronic diseases.[225] In 2007, Brazil joined the club of developing countries that issued compulsory licenses against HIV/AIDS patented medicines in order to make them more affordable for those in need.[226] In 2007, Canada became the first country to notify the

218. Machlup (1958), *An Economic Review of the Patent System*, p. 5.
219. Drahos (2007), *Patent Reform for Innovation and Risk Management: A Separation of Powers Approach*, 1 KES Studies, p. 2, fn. 10.
220. Article 5-A-2 PC.
221. *See* Chapter 3, A-3.2.3.3.
222. Moore (2006), "Parallel Trade, Unparallel Laws: An Examination of the Pharmaceutical Parallel Trade Laws of the United States, the European Union and the World Trade Organization," 6 *Rich. J. Global L. & Bus.*, 91; La Croix/Liu (2007), "Patents and Access to Essential Medicines," in: Maskus (ed.) *Intellectual Property, Growth and Trade*, Emerald Group Publishing, Amsterdam, pp. 423-464 (452); Reichman (2009a), "Compulsory Licensing of Patented Pharmaceutical Inventions: Evaluating the Options," 37 *J. L., Med. & Ethics*, 247-263.
223. Musungu/Oh (2006), *The Use of Flexibilities in TRIPS by Developing Countries: Can They Promote Access to Medicines*? South Centre and World Trade Organization, Geneva, p. 33.
224. Böttger (2008), "Zwangslizenzen im Patentrecht—Eine systematische Bewertung der neueren Praxis insbesondere im Bereich der öffentlichen Gesundheit," *GRUR Int.*, 885.
225. Savoie (2007), "Thailand's Test: Compulsory Licenses in an Area of Epidemiologic Transition," 48 *Va. J. Int'l L.*, 238-243.
226. *See*, for instance, Kweitel/Reis (2007), "A Primeira Licença Compulsória de Medicamento na América Latina," 3 *Pontes* 3, ICTSD; Lanzillotti Jannuzzi/Guimarães Vasconcelos (2017), "O

WTO that it would grant a compulsory license for the export of a generic antiretroviral drug to Rwanda, making use of the so-called paragraph 6 Solution of the Doha Declaration, now Article 31*bis* TRIPS.[227] In 2012, a patent court in New Delhi issued a compulsory license authorizing an Indian generic company to produce a German-patented cancer drug.[228]

But it is not only in the developing countries that compulsory licenses based on public interest were granted. As reported by *Godt*,[229] until 2017, the only German judicial ruling after 1945 with respect to compulsory licenses based on public interest had been the "Interferon-Gamma" decision of 1995. In July 2017, the BGH confirmed the grant of a second compulsory license based on public interest,[230] which was issued in 2016 by the German Federal Patent Court (*Bundespatentgericht*–BPatG) in favor of an American company, the object of which was the anti-AIDS drug, Isentress.[231] Both compulsory licenses, however, were not based on public health in order to expand access to medicines, in opposition to the developing countries cases reported above. The "Interferon-Gamma" compulsory license was based on "dependent patents," namely the case of the human immune interferon patent and *Polyferon*. The BPatG granted a compulsory license over the Interferon patent, allowing a third company to use the (dependent) patent in order to develop the drug *Polyferon*.[232] In the second case, an American company, which had obtained the license to market the drug in Germany, first tried to voluntarily obtain a license from the Japanese patent owner in order to enjoy the right of marketing the drug in Germany, in spite of the existence of a valid European patent. After the Japanese company refused to license the patent, the

---

Backlog na Concessão das Patentes e seu Impacto na Utilização de Salvaguardas Legais e no Acesso aos Medicamentos no Brasil," in: Curzel/Nunes (eds.), *Patentes e o Acesso a Antirretrovirais no Brasil—O Desafio da Licença Compulsória*, Editora Appris, Curitiba, pp. 43-72.

227. Cohen-Kohler/Esmail / Perez Cosio (2007), "Canada's Implementation of the Paragraph 6 Decision: Is it Sustainable Public Policy?," 3 *Global Health* 12; Reichman (2009a), "Compulsory Licensing of Patented Pharmaceutical Inventions: Evaluating the Options," 37 *J. L. Med. & Ethics*, 247-263.
228. Einecke (2012), "Streit um teure Medikamente—Fluch und Segen: Preiswerte Zwangslizenzen für wichtige Arzneimittel," *Süddeutsche Zeitung*, 17/18 March, p. 30.
229. Godt (2010), "Differential Pricing of Patent-Protected Pharmaceuticals for Life-Threatening Infectious-Diseases inside Europe—Can Compulsory Licenses Be Employed?," in: Godt (ed.), *Differential Pricing of Pharmaceutical inside Europe—Exploring Compulsory Licenses and Exhaustion for Access to Patented Essential Medicines*, Nomos, Baden-Baden, p. 37.
230. Felmy (2018), "Raltegravir" (Translation of the Decision of the Federal Supreme Court (Bundesgerichtshof) 11 July 2017—Case No. X ZB 2/17, IIC (2018) 49-94-103.
231. *See* Holtorf/Traumann (2017): "BPatG-Entscheidung zur patentrechtlichen Zwangslizenz rechtmäßig," *GRUR-Prax*, 437; Weisser (2017), "Patentrechtliche und kartellrechtliche Zwangslizenz—Unterschiede und Gemeinsamkeiten—‚Isentress'," *Gesellschafts- und Wirtschaftsrecht*, 134-136.
232. Godt (2010), "Differential Pricing of Patent-Protected Pharmaceuticals for Life-Threatening Infectious-Diseases Inside Europe—Can Compulsory Licenses Be Employed?" pp. 37-38; Adrian, *Patentrecht im Spannungsfeld von Innovationschutz und allgemeinen Interesse*, Inaugural Lecture held on January 27, 1996 at the Humboldt University of Berlin.

American company went to the court and started the compulsory licensing proceedings. As reported by *Slowinski*, this compulsory license does not have any practical meaning since the patent was declared as invalid by the EPO in October 2017.[233]

2.2.2 Voluntary Licensing

Another possibility of mitigating the effects of the patent monopoly, especially in the field of pharmaceuticals, is licensing the patent rights by way of a voluntary agreement. As defined by *Amin*, "typically, a voluntary license is where a pharmaceutical company that holds patents on a product (patentee) offers on his own accord a license to a third party (usually a generic producer) to produce, market and distribute the patented product. In exchange, the patentee will usually request a royalty on the net sales made by the licensee as well as impose other restrictions, such as geographical restrictions on where the licensee can sell the product, restrictions on what price the product may be sold at and any other terms or conditions it might insist on."[234]

2.2.3 Forfeiture of Patents

Forfeiture of patents occurs when a patent grant is canceled without compensating the patent owner. This kind of patent revocation was often used in the past as a punishment for the patent owner in cases whereby the patent was designated as "nonworking." This refers to the following situation: if a patent is granted in a country, the related patented invention must necessarily be "worked" (i.e., it must be produced) within the territorial bounds of the country where the patent in question was granted. If a patented invention is merely imported into the country, it is considered to be "nonworking," which means it can be revoked. So, if the patent owner fails to produce the patented invention within a given period of time after the granting of the patent, the patent may be forfeited.

As opposed to a compulsory license, forfeiture does not involve any right to compensation for the patentee. Because of that, it is not seen as an adequate sanction for non-compliance with the local-working requirement. Furthermore, the local-working requirement is not seen as "reasonable" in a globalized economy, where production takes place in the most favorable environment. Notwithstanding, local-working provisions were at one time common in the patent laws of many countries in order to protect the domestic industry. In order to avoid forfeiture on the grounds of

233. Slowinski (2018), "Germany—Comment on the German Federal Supreme Court Decision 'Raltegravir'," 49 *IIC* 125-130, p. 129.
234. Amin (2007), *Voluntary Licenses Practices in the Pharmaceutical Sector: An Acceptable Solution to Improving Access to Affordable Medicines?* Essential Medicines and Health Products Information Portal, World Health Organization resource, p. 3.

local-working provisions, as early as 1925, some of the PC's member countries made efforts to abolish or at least soften local-working provisions in their local laws.[235]

In the current version of the PC, based on its revision in 1967 in Stockholm, forfeiture of patents as a sanction for the importation of the patented invention is forbidden if the imported product was manufactured in any country which is a party to the Convention.[236] Furthermore, according to the Convention, forfeiture of patents may only take place in those cases where the grant of compulsory licenses was not sufficient to prevent or correct abuse of the patent.[237]

The TRIPS Agreement does not contain material provisions concerning the revocation or forfeiture of patents, other than its provision that a judicial review against a revocation or forfeiture's decision must be available.[238] Its Article 27.1, however, requires that patent rights should be available and enjoyable without discrimination as to "whether products are imported or locally produced." Due to this provision, local-working provisions in national law appear not to be compatible with the TRIPS Agreement.

3 *New Developments: Searching for Instruments Outside Patent Law in Order to Deal with Patent Law Problems*

If not earlier, then at the very latest after the TRIPS Agreement—which made evident the inherent tensions between the patent system and the right of access to affordable drugs—patent law became a global political question. As demonstrated by the political scientist *Schneider*, at the European level, it had already become evident that patent law was a major political issue in 1988, when the biopatent directive was drafted.[239] As she puts it, the "need for legislative governance of patent law has been acknowledged, resulting in the insight that patent governance should not be left solely to the patent profession (as a discipline), to patent offices (practices) and to courts (jurisdictions)."[240] According to the *Schneider's* findings, "patent examination and grant is not an 'objective' and 'neutral' act, not merely an execution of law, but a (tacit) policy-making process, significantly contributing to the shaping of technological trajectories."[241]

235. Reichman/Hasenzahl (2003), *Non-Voluntary Licensing of Patented Inventions—Historical Perspective, Legal Framework under TRIPS and an Overview of the Practice in Canada and the US*, UNCTAD-ICTSD Project on IPR and Sustainable Development, Issue Paper no. 5, June, p. 10.
236. Article 5-A (1) PC.
237. Article 5-A (3) PC.
238. Article 32 TRIPS.
239. Schneider (2009), "Can Patent Legislation Make a Difference? Bringing Parliaments and Civil Society into Patent Governance," in: Haunss/Shadlen (eds.), *Politics of Intellectual Property*, Edward Elgar, Cheltenham et al., pp. 129-157.
240. *Ibid.*, p. 151.
241. *Ibid.*, p. 154.

3.1 *Compulsory Licenses of Patents Issued on the Basis of a Violation of Competition Law*

Compulsory licenses may be used as a pure instrument of patent law or as an instrument of competition law. The essential distinction between these lies in the purpose. A compulsory license in patent law waives patent rights based on exceptional circumstances (such as in cases of public interest or to deal with emergencies), where a patentee's monopoly rights should not prevail over more important rights, such as the right to health, for instance. Compulsory licenses in competition law, on the other hand, waive patent rights as a sanction exclusively applied in order to punish anticompetitive behavior by the patentee. Essentially, in the case of a compulsory license in patent law, patent rights are forcibly licensed without any causative relationship between the patentee's conduct and the waiving of his patent rights, while in the case of a compulsory license in competition law, a proven instance of misconduct on the part of the patentee—such as "abuse of his dominant position"—is a prerequisite for this loss of patent rights.

Another important distinction between these forms of the compulsory license is in the remuneration due to the patentee. While in the case of a compulsory license in patent law, the compensation must be "adequate" in competition law, it could be zero, depending on the concrete situation.[242] As it is a punishment, such a compulsory license must discourage the patentee from repeating his anticompetitive behavior, and as such, "adequate compensation" makes no sense.

In practice, compulsory licenses in competition law and patent law may have similar effects, but this does not necessarily have to be the case. While compulsory licenses in the field of competition law have been largely applied to punish anticompetitive behavior in industrialized countries, especially in Western Europe,[243] they are still rare in developing countries. Both forms of the compulsory license of patented medicines may widen access to those medicines. Because of this, some authors have been proposing their use in developing countries.[244]

242. Pires de Carvalho, Nuno (2008), *The TRIPS Regime of Antitrust and Undisclosed Information*, Kluwer Law International, The Hague, p. 142.
243. *Reichman* cites the cases of Italy, where Competition Law authorities issued three compulsory licenses against pharmaceutical companies in 2005, 2006 and 2008. *See* Reichman (2009), "Compulsory Licenses of Patented Pharmaceutical Inventions: Evaluating the Options," 37 *J. L., Med. & Ethics*, 247-263.
244. *See* Pinho de Morais (2016), "Antitrust and Compulsory License in BRICS and Developing Countries," in: Jenny/Katsoulacos (eds.), *Competition Law Enforcement in the BRICS and Developing Countries—Legal and Economic Aspects*, Springer International Publishing Switzerland, pp. 149-167; Flynn (2008), *Using Competition Law to Promote Access to Medicines*, PIJIP, American University Washington College of Law; Mesidor (2013), *Intellectual Property Rights in Competition Law: Compulsory Licensing Issues in Developing Countries*, available at SSRN: https://ssrn.com/abstract=2238796.

3.2 *Identifying Misuse of Patent Rights and Other Strategies: The EU Pharma Sector Inquiry*

In January 2008, the European Commission launched a pharma sector inquiry. Its aim was identifying if there were obstacles created by originator companies in order to both delay entry of generic products in the market ("pay-for-delay deals") and make use of "defensive patenting" in order to block innovative products developed by competitors since there were suggestions, at the time, that competition might be distorted.[245] The final report confirmed such suggestions.[246] Since then, the European Commission has been publishing reports on the monitoring of patent settlements between originator and generic companies in order to potentially identify the agreement which may be harmful to EU consumers.

3.3 *A Peculiar Legal Instrument: ANVISA's Prior Consent (Anuência Prévia)*

In December 1999, the Brazilian patent law was added with a new provision, by which the National Health Surveillance Agency (ANVISA) was given a role in the patent grant proceedings.[247] The amended provision of the Brazilian patent law reads:

> Article 229-C—The granting of patents on pharmaceutical products or processes shall depend on the prior consent of the National Health Surveillance Agency (ANVISA).

As it will be examined later in detail, ANVISA is involved in the granting of patents for pharmaceuticals and has a right to veto their issuance if the granting of that patent would be harmful to public health.

4 **Conclusion**

A functioning patent law system must have adequate instruments with which to find equilibrium between the public interest and the interests of the patent owner, when necessary or desired. In order to satisfy this purpose, the national patent laws of many countries have, traditionally, made use of instruments within the patent law. An example of such instruments is the compulsory license of patent rights. The aim of the

245. European Commission, Competition DG (2008), *Pharmaceutical Sector Inquiry—Preliminary Report.*
246. European Commission, Competition DG (2009), *Pharmaceutical Sector Inquiry—Final Report.*
247. *See* Basso (2006), "Intervention of Health Authorities in Patent Examination: The Brazilian Practice of the Prior Consent," 1 *IJIPM* 1-2, 54-74; Rodrigues Júnior (2005), "Anuência Prévia: integração do direito à saúde aos direitos de propriedade intellectual," *RT* 840, 85-106 (94); Rodrigues Júnior/Murphy (2006), "Brazil's Prior Consent Law: A Dialogue Between Brazil and the United States or Where the TRIPS Agreement Currently Sets the Balance Between the Protection of Pharmaceutical Patents and Access to Medicines"; 16 *Alb. L. J. Science & Technology*, 423-456; Dias Guimarães César (2008), "Flexibilidades do Direito Internacional da Propriedade Intelectual—Reflexões para Amenizar a Crise do Acesso a Medicamentos Essenciais," in: Carvalho (ed.), *Propriedade Intelectual—Estudos em Homenagem à Professora Maristela Basso,* Juruá Editora, Curitiba, pp. 44-75.

compulsory license's mechanism is to deal with emergency situations in a concrete case, whereby the maintenance of exclusive rights for a determined invention may be detrimental to the public interest.

Compulsory licenses, however, should only be used in emergency situations. As such, they are not there to ensure that the patent system works as a whole but to deal with a crisis. A functioning patent law must have an adequate system for patent quality control, which is responsible for preventing the granting of trivial patents, and which, at the same time, guarantees that patents will be issued with the purpose of encouraging innovative inventions. This is, for instance, the aim of opposition patent proceedings, which may take place before a patent is granted (pre-grant proceedings) or afterward (post-grant proceedings).

Godt, who has examined the problem of the expansion of patent law, calls for the necessity of the law to give more importance to access rights, considering that, in the past, patent grants were based on a "compromise between intellectual property rights in favor of the inventor and the interests of society as a collective."[248] According to her, in the past, society was protected both by limitation of patentability and by patent disclosure, but, due to the extension of patent protection and strategic patenting, the balance has shifted in favor of the patentee, so that it is necessary to recover the balance, by granting more access rights to users.[249]

For dealing with the difficulties of conciliation between drug patents and drug accessibility, *di Cataldo* has suggested, among other approaches, improving patent law.[250] As proposed by *Schneider*, this improvement may be achieved with institutional reforms with the aim of politicizing the patent law, which would entail, among others, the participation of experts from other disciplines than patent law or technical areas—in particular, economists, health officers, social and political scientists and ethicists.[251]

Along with the classical instruments of patent law for dealing with situations concerning the public interest and for guaranteeing the quality of patents, mixed instruments have been created in order to deal with new problems. This is the case, for instance, of anticompetitive compulsory licenses, which result from the interface of patent law with competition law. They take the compulsory license of patent law and use it as a sanction with which to punish anticompetitive behavior. Similarly, ANVISA's prior consent mechanism emerged in Brazil in order to deal with problems caused by patent law in the area of drug accessibility.

248. Godt (2008), "Innovationsfreiheit und Innovationsverantwortung post grant," in: Eifert/Hoffmann-Riem (eds.), *Geistiges Eigentum und Innovation—Innovation und Recht I*, Duncker & Humblot, Berlin, p. 366.
249. *Ibid.*, p. 366.
250. di Cataldo (2001), "In Search of Ways to Reconcile Patents with Access to Drugs," in Remiche (ed.), *Pharmaceutical Patents, Innovation and Public Health, Revue Internationale Droit Economique—Special Edition*, De Boeck & Larcier, Bruxelles, p. 164.
251. Schneider (2009), "Can Patent Legislation Make a Difference? Bringing Parliaments and Civil Society into Patent Governance," in Haunss/Shadlen (eds.), *Politics of Intellectual Property*, p. 154.

B INTERNATIONAL LAW, PUBLIC HEALTH AND PATENTS

I International Law: The Discourse on Health as a Human Right and the TRIPS Agreement

At the international level, the right to health, which is included within the right of access to medicines, is regulated by the United Nations human rights system. The most important conventions are, first, the Charter of the United Nations in 1948 and, second, the Covenant on Social, Economic and Cultural Rights (CSECR) of 1966, Article 12 of which expressly guarantees the right to healthcare.

The right to health and other social rights are often referred to as positive human rights because their realization depends on direct action by the state. In other words: The state has a duty to provide sufficient healthcare for all its citizens. While so-called negative human rights are only enjoyed if the state does not do anything to hinder this (for instance, political rights, such as the right to oppose a government), the enjoyment of positive human rights depends on a positive action of the state. The fulfillment of these obligations under the Covenant is not easy for all parties because it depends on the restrictions of each state's budget for healthcare expenses.

Due to the interactions between the health, intellectual property and trade, conflicts arose between obligations assumed under the TRIPS Agreement and the duty to provide sufficient healthcare to citizens. This interaction is well documented[252] and was meanwhile recognized by the WTO and the WIPO.[253] The TRIPS Agreement has a profound impact on several human rights. As stated by *Abbott*, "the area in which concerns have so far been most intense involves the impact of pharmaceutical patents on the rights to life and health. Patents by nature and function increase prices of pharmaceutical products above ordinary competitive-market prices, thereby reducing affordability and access."[254] Notwithstanding, the pharmaceutical industry, sometimes

252. *See*, for instance, Abbott (2006a), "TRIPS and Human Rights: Preliminary Reflexions," in Abbott et al. (eds.), *International Trade and Human Rights—Foundations and Conceptional Issues*, University of Michigan Press, Michigan, p. 153; Anderson (2009), "Unnecessary Deaths and Unnecessary Costs: Getting Patented Drugs to Patients Most in Need," 29 *BCTWLJ*, 85-112; Chapman (2002), "The Human Rights Implications of the Intellectual Property Protection," 5 *JIEL* 4, 861-882; Hestermeyer (2007), *Human Rights and the WTO*, pp. 137-206; Seuba Hernandez (2008), "Human Rights and Intellectual Property Rights," in Correa/Yusuf (eds.), *Intellectual Property and International Trade: The TRIPS Agreement*, Kluwer Law International BV, The Netherlands, pp. 392-394; Rott (2002), *Patentrecht und Sozialpolitik unter dem TRIPS-Abkommen*, Nomos, Baden-Baden, p. 103.

253. *See* WHO/WIPO/WTO (2013), *Promoting Access to Medical Technologies and Innovation—Intersections Between Public Health, Intellectual Property and Trade.* This study was commented by *Abbott*, who highlighted how important is that "WTO and WIPO also acknowledged that the ultimate aim of the innovation and access framework is to improve the life of individuals, and not to generate profits." *See* Abbott (2013), "Review: The Trilateral Study on Health, Intellectual Property, and Trade: The Virtue in Paving a Cleared Roadway," 16 *JIEL* 2, 494-495.

254. Abbott (2006a), "TRIPS and Human Rights: Preliminary Reflexions," in Abbott et al. (eds.), *International Trade and Human Rights—Foundations and Conceptional Issues*, University of Michigan, p. 154.

supported by academic studies,[255] uses to deny that patent protection for pharmaceuticals increases drug prices.

Because the TRIPS Agreement made the satisfaction of the right to health more difficult for the poor, it is widely criticized.[256] The German philosopher *Thomas Pogge*, one of the most incisive critics of the TRIPS Agreement, stated that "the TRIPS Agreement and its imposition are plainly unjust and will, in terms of the magnitude of harm caused, number among the largest human rights violations in history."[257]

As a response to this clash between human rights and patent rights, the Doha Ministerial Declaration of 2001 emerged at the WTO. The Doha Declaration can be viewed, at the same time, as both a human rights instrument and a commercial law instrument.[258] Some authors are of the opinion that the flexibility instruments contained in the TRIPS Agreement provide adequate protection of relevant social rights; consequently, the TRIPS Agreement would not touch the ability of a state to fulfill its obligations under Article 12 of the International Covenant.[259] *Hestermeyer*, however, considers that the TRIPS Agreement's flexibility instruments, while being important tools for providing access to medicines in developing countries, are not able to sufficiently solve the basic conflicts between patent and social rights. Although the standards set by the Human Rights Act should have hierarchical priority over other norms,[260] de facto commercial standards prevail, purely because of the WTO's efficient dispute-settlement mechanism. In his opinion, only an inclusion of human rights within the WTO system would provide an effective solution for this conflict.[261]

255. *See*, for instance, Rozek/Berkowitz (1998), "The Effects of Patent Protection on the Prices of Pharmaceutical Products—Is Intellectual Property Raising the Drug Bill in Developing Countries?" 1 *JWIP* 2, 179-243.
256. *See* Rott (2002), *Patentrecht und Sozialpolitik unter dem TRIPS-Abkommen*, Nomos, Baden-Baden, p. 103; Abbott (2006a), "TRIPS and Human Rights: Preliminary Reflexions," in: Abbott et al. (eds.), *International Trade and Human Rights—Foundations and Conceptional Issues*, University of Michigan, p. 153; Hestermeyer (2007), *Human Rights and the WTO*, pp. 137-206; Seuba Hernandez (2008), "Human Rights and Intellectual Property Rights," in: Correa/Yusuf (eds.), *Intellectual Property and International Trade: The TRIPS Agreement*, Kluwer Law International BV, The Netherlands, pp. 392-394; Van den Belt / Korthals (2013), "The International Patent System and the Ethics of Global Justice," in: Arapostathis / Dutfield (eds.), *Knowledge Management and Intellectual Property—Concepts, Actors and Practices from the Past to the Present*, Cheltenham, Edgar Elgar, pp. 235-251.
257. Pogge (2008), "Access to Medicines," 1(2) *Pub. Health Ethics*, p. 76.
258. Abbott (2006a), "TRIPS and Human Rights: Preliminary Reflexions," in: Abbott et al. (eds.), *International Trade and Human Rights—Foundations and Conceptional Issues*, University of Michigan, p. 153.
259. Kramer (2007), *Patentschutz und Zugang zu Medikamenten. Rechtliche und ökonomische Implikation*, Carl Heymanns, Köln, pp. 89-96.
260. *See*, for instance, Cullet (2004), "Patents and Medicines—The Relationship Between TRIPS and the Human Right to Health," in: Gruskin/Grodin/Marks/Annas (eds.), *Perspectives on Health and Human Rights*, Taylor & Francis, pp. 179-202.
261. Hestermeyer (2007), *Human Rights and the WTO*, p. 207.

II International Patent Law and Minimum Standards of Patent Protection Imposed by the TRIPS Agreement

1 Introductory Remarks

Before the foundation of the WTO in 1995, international conventions on patent law at a multilateral level were administered by the WIPO, a UN agency. The WIPO administered both the Paris Convention for the Protection of Industrial Property of 1883 (the PC), which was at the time the most comprehensive patent multilateral convention and the Patent Cooperation Treaty of 1970 (the PCT), which provides for the filing of international patent applications.

Under the system of the PC, there were neither substantive provisions relating to substantive patent law nor provisions concerning the enforcement of patent rights worldwide. The lack of both elements was seen by many countries, especially by countries that are technology producers, as a serious shortcoming of the international patent system.

First, the lack of minimal substantive requisites regarding patent protection made possible the emergence of significant distinctions between different patent systems around the world, especially where exclusions of the patentable matter were concerned. Some products were considered to be patentable inventions in some countries but not patentable in other countries. This was the case of pharmaceutical inventions, which were in the early 1980s still excluded from patentability by the patent law of many countries, for example, Brazil, China, India, Egypt, Argentina, Republic of Korea and Thailand, etc. Countries which denied patents to pharmaceutical inventions were allowed to do so both on the basis of their internal law—which did not elect pharmaceuticals as patentable subject matter—and of international patent law, which gave those countries the freedom to determine what kind of matter should be patentable. This was seen by the pharmaceutical industry as unfair since their products were freely copied and sold in third countries (mostly developing countries) without any royalties being paid to their developers. Countries that refused to give patents to pharmaceuticals were accused of benefiting as "free riders" from products they had not helped to develop.

Developed countries had been seeking in vain to reform the PC since the 1970s in order to increase the level of intellectual property protection. In 1980, a group of developed countries—as part of an offense to strengthen patent rights—started a movement to reform the PC but did not succeed due to the lack of consensus among developing and developed countries.[262] This topic remained very high on the commercial agenda from that time until the late 1990s. During this period, it was a source of constant tension among developing and developed countries: for many developing countries, denying patent protection for medicines was a matter of public interest, development and sovereignty. For the technology-exporting countries, convincing developing countries to protect pharmaceutical patents was a matter of economic

262. Deere (2009), *The Implementation Game—The TRIPS Agreement and the Global Politics of Intellectual Property Reform in Developing Countries*, OUP, Oxford et al., p. 46.

power enforcement. For instance, the American pharmaceutical industry intensively lobbied the U.S. Government to use its influence in order to impose higher standards of patentability on the developing world.[263] The U.S. used a variety of strategies to convince other countries to provide "adequate patent protection" for its products since it believed that the international intellectual property system of that time threatened its national interests.[264] So it made efforts to increase patent protection worldwide both at the national and at the international level. At the national level, for instance, the US government approved the Trade Act of 1984. This law gave the U.S. Trade Representative's Office (USTR) the power to classify countries according to their level of protection of intellectual property and, consequently, to decide whether their IP policies were considered as "unjustifiable" or "unreasonable" trade practices. If the trade practice of a foreign (developing) country was considered to be "unjustifiable or unreasonable," this country could be excluded from the American Generalized System of Preferences (GSP), which provides for special tariff preferences for goods originating from developing countries. In accordance with this classification, the USTR annually prepares a list called "The Special 301 Report," which puts foreign countries on a "priority watch list," or on a "watch list." At the same time, the U.S. negotiated at the bilateral level in order to attain the "adequate protection" level required by American companies.

Second, the lack of an effective compliance mechanism under the system of the Paris Convention was also seen by technology-exporting countries as a shortcoming within the WIPO system. For these countries, it was not enough for pharmaceutical patents to be available in the countries where they had not been in the past. They also required, in case of conflict, an effective enforcement system to be available to settle disputes.

When it was clear for developed countries that they would not succeed in convincing developing countries to change their patent policy within the WIPO system, they changed their strategy and made the matter a topic of discussion at the General Agreement on Tariffs and Trade (GATT) negotiations for the creation of the WTO.

2 *International Patent Law Before 1996*

The most important provisions of the Paris Convention are those relating to three basic rights: the right to national treatment, the right of priority and the right to take legislative measures to prevent the abuse of patent rights.

263. *See* Gad (2006), "Representational Fairness in WTO Rule-Making—Negotiating, Implementing, and Disputing the TRIPS Pharmaceutical-Related Provisions", *The Brit. Inst. Int'l & Comp. L.* SMU London Forum Initiative, London, pp. 78-92.
264. Chasen Ross/Wasserman (1993), "Trade-Related Aspects of Intellectual Property," in Stewart (ed.), *The GATT Uruguay Round: A Negotiating History (1986-1992) Vol. II: Commentary*, Kluwer Law and Taxation Publishers, p. 2256.

2.1 Right to National Treatment (Articles 2-3 PC)

According to the national treatment principle, each country party to the Convention must grant the same patent protection to nationals of other member countries as it grants to its own nationals. This prevents discrimination against inventors due to their origin but does not impose equality of treatment. If, for instance, an American company had requested a patent for a pharmaceutical invention at the INPI in 1993, the request would have been denied because this kind of invention did not fall into the category of patent matter in Brazil at the time. However, if a Brazilian company had requested a patent for the same invention at the American patent office, the request might have been approved if the substantive requirements of American patent law were fulfilled. Under the PC, it is enough for a country to confer on other member countries the same treatments given to its own nationals since member countries are not obliged to provide reciprocity regarding patent protection.

2.2 Right of Priority (Article 4 PC)

According to this provision, any patent application made in a member country will have a right of priority concerning this invention until 12 months after the filing date. This means that the novelty of an invention is not affected in other member countries during the 12 months starting from the date of the first filing in a member country. Without this provision, inventors seeking patent protection in different countries would have to file patent applications on the same date at different patent offices worldwide. The only thing the applicant must do is to inform the other country's Patent Office of the date it was first filed in the country of origin.

2.3 Independence of Patents (Article 4bis PC)

According to the principle of independence—also known as the territoriality principle of patent protection—patents obtained for the same invention in different countries are considered to be independent of each other. Thus, the amplitude of patent protection varies from country to country in accordance with national law. This provision is to be understood in an unrestricted sense so that (before the TRIPS Agreement) the same invention might obtain 15 years of protection in one country or 20 years in another.

3 International Patent Law and the International Trade System Before the WTO's Foundation

As mentioned before, patent law was not integrated into the international trade law system until the foundation of the WTO in 1994. The topic was included in the international agenda as a result of a proposition by the U.S.[265] during the so-called

265. Stoeva (2010), *New Norms and Knowledge in World Politics –Protecting People, Intellectual Property and the Environment*, Routledge, Oxford, p. 95.

Uruguay Round of the GATT. The developed world took the opportunity to create a new international trade order and to try to correct what they considered to be asymmetries in the national patent laws, irregularities that had been permitted under the WIPO system.

3.1 International Trade Law System (1947-1994)

A formal international trade organization (ITO) did not exist until 1995, although many concrete efforts were made to create such an international agency. The United Nations Monetary and Financial Conference of 1944, which took place in Bretton Woods, Washington, decided to create the following three international economic institutions: the International Monetary Fund (IMF), the World Bank (WB) and the ITO, the latter conceived of as a specialized UN agency.[266] While the IMF and the WB were definitively created, the same did not happen with the ITO. Although the negotiations were concluded and the ITO Charter was approved by some members, it never came into force, mostly because of opposition from the U.S., which did not ratify it.[267] Despite this, there was an international trade system from 1947 until 1995, based on the GATT agreed in 1947 during the ITO negotiations. The GATT of 1947 came into force provisionally in 1948. Because the ITO was never created, the provisory Secretariat created to administer the GATT 1947 became a kind of a de facto international organization, simply known as GATT, with headquarters in Geneva. The system was applicable only to the trading of goods, and its aim was to reduce commercial protectionism among its members by imposing the reduction of duty tariffs.

3.1.1 Principles of GATT 1947

The GATT 1947 is based on two principles: most-favored-nation[268] and national treatment.[269] The principle of the most-favored-nation means that a country cannot discriminate between countries regarding import tariffs so that the treatment conferred on one GATT member must be conferred on all others too. Under the principle of national treatment, also known as the non-discrimination principle, imported and locally produced goods have to be treated equally.

3.1.2 General Exceptions to the Non-discrimination Rule (Article XX GATT)

Under the old GATT, members were already authorized to take measures which might be against GATT principles in the cases foreseen by Article XX GATT, provided that these were not arbitrary or did not take the form of unjustified discrimination, and they

266. Göttsche (2005), "Historische Entwicklung (GATT 1947 und Gründung der WTO)," in: Hilf/Oeter (eds.), *WTO-Recht*, Nomos, Baden-Baden, pp. 71-74.
267. Kaplan (1996), *American Trade Policy 1923-1995*, Greenwood Press, USA, p. 53.
268. Article 1 GATT 1947.
269. Article 3 GATT 1947.

were necessary to protect, for instance, public morals, or human, animal or public health, among other things.

3.1.3 Treaties Other Than the GATT

Over the decades, other trade treaties that focused on an object other than goods were gradually negotiated and concluded under the administration of the GATT Secretariat. However, membership in these was not mandatory for GATT members. Because of this, such treaties were called "plurilateral agreements" in order to distinguish them from the GATT 1947, the only agreement in that system that applied to all GATT members, and was thus a very "multilateral" agreement.

3.2 The GATT Uruguay Round (1986-1994)

By the 1980s, it was clear that this international trade system was not adequate to satisfy the needs of the new international order. On September 20, 1986, at a special conference, the parties to the GATT, aiming to reform the international trade system, launched the Uruguay Round of Multilateral Trade Negotiations in Punta del Este.

3.2.1 Introducing Intellectual Property Rights onto the GATT Agenda

The 1986 agenda was composed of 15 subjects, from tariffs and non-tariff barriers until agriculture, textiles and clothing, antidumping, subsidies, services and intellectual property.[270] The American suggestion of including the topic of IP protection faced strong opposition from developing countries, especially from Brazil and Argentina.[271] These countries countered that the GATT did not have the mandate to deal with the topic of intellectual property, which would have to be treated at the WIPO.[272] Furthermore, developing countries were afraid of an overprotection of intellectual property rights since they were concerned about the impact this would have in terms of the transfer of technology, as well as the price of drugs.[273] As *Drahos* and *Braithwaite* put it, developing countries' resistance to the inclusion of intellectual property was broken through a process of "persuasion and advice."[274] For the 1986 agenda, the

270. GATT (1986), Ministerial Declaration on the Uruguay Round, GATT Document MIN.DEC of September 20, 1986.
271. *See*, for instance, Gervais (2003), *The TRIPS Agreement: Drafting History and Analysis*, 2nd ed., Sweet & Maxwell, London, p. 10; Watal (2001), *Intellectual Property Rights in the WTO and Developing Countries*, Kluwer Law International, The Hague/London/Boston, pp. 19-20.
272. Chasen Ross/Wasserman (1993), "Trade-Related Aspects of Intellectual Property Rights," in: Stewart (ed.), *The GATT Uruguay Round, Vol. II: Commentary*, p. 2263.
273. Gervais (2003), *The TRIPS Agreement: Drafting History and Analysis*, 2nd ed., London, p. 14.
274. Drahos/Braithwaite (2002), *Information Feudalism—Who Owns the Knowledge Economy*, Earthscan, London, p. 111. *See also* Deere-Birkbeck (2010), "Developing Countries in the Global IP Systems Before TRIPS: The Political Context for the TRIPS Negotiations," in Correa (ed.), *Research Handbook on the Protection of Intellectual Property under WTO Rules—Vol. I*, Edward Elgar, Cheltenham (UK), pp. 22-51.

inclusion of TRIPS was approved. According to *Ullrich*, "the real and explicit purpose of the new GATT approach is to force developing countries to adhere to the standards of intellectual property protection which fit the needs of industrialized countries."[275]

3.2.2 TRIPS Negotiations

The negotiations were polarized between developed and developing countries. The latter were concerned that they might be prevented from having access to modern technology due to possible overprotection of intellectual property rights.[276] India, for instance, emphasized that developing countries needed more favorable treatment in the areas of patents and trademarks, whereas Brazil and Korea emphasized that the compulsory license of patents should be permitted.[277] In 1991, a final draft was agreed upon,[278] not without strong criticism on the part of some developing countries, like India.[279] Despite the agreement, some issues concerning TRIPS still remained open. For example, the term during which patent protection would apply was not defined, and further relevant questions were not addressed: these concerned whether patents would need to be available without discrimination on the basis of the place of invention, the field of technology and whether the product object of a patent is imported or locally produced.[280] Another controversial topic concerned transitional periods and the question of provisional protection for existing drugs or those in development.

3.2.2.1 Controversy Concerning Transitional Periods

Developing countries took the approach that they would need a transitional period in which to adapt their domestic laws to TRIPS standards. Furthermore, they thought that they would need yet more time to implement provisions concerning the patentability of inventions that had not previously been patentable under their patent law, such as the case of pharmaceutical inventions. India, for instance, wanted a transitional 10-year delay in the enforcement of TRIPS for inventions deemed to be unpatentable under its law. This approach was strongly opposed to the view of the American delegation,

275. Ullrich (1989), "GATT: Industrial Property Protection, Fair Trade and Development," in: Beier/Schricker (eds.), *GATT or WIPO? New Ways in the International Protection of Intellectual Property*, Munich (IIC Studies - Studies in Industrial Property and Copyright Law, 11), VCH, Weinheim), p. 147.
276. Chasen Ross/Wassermann (1993), "Trade-Related Aspects of Intellectual Property Rights," in Stewart (ed.), *The GATT Uruguay Round: A Negotiating History (1986-1994)*, Vol. II, p. 2267.
277. GATT (1990b), Negotiating Group on Trade-Related Aspects of Intellectual Property, including Trade in Counterfeit Drugs, GATT Doc. No. MTN.GNG/NG11/W71 (May 14, 1990): Communication from Argentina, Brazil, Chile, China, Colombia, Cuba, Egypt, India, Nigeria, Peru, Tanzania and Uruguay.
278. GATT (1991), GATT Uruguay Round—Draft Final Act Embodying the Results of the Uruguay Round of Multilateral Trade Negotiations—GATT Doc. No. MTN.TNC/W/FA (December 20, 1991).
279. *See*, for instance, Dhar/Rao (1992), "Dunkel Draft on TRIPS—Complete Denial of Developing Countries' Interests," *Economic and Political Weekly*, February 8.
280. Chasen Ross/Wassermann, "Trade-Related Aspects of Intellectual Property Rights", in: Stewart (ed.), *The GATT Uruguay Round: A Negotiating History (1986-1992)*, Vol. II, p. 2279.

which required transitional patent protection for pharmaceuticals (the so-called pipeline protection), and which would mean immediate patent protection for existing drugs.[281]

3.2.2.2 The Special Case of the "Mailbox" Provision (Article 70.8 TRIPS) and Its Respective "Exclusive Marketing Rights" (Article 70.9 TRIPS) as a Compromise Solution for the Rejected "Pipeline" Protection

The question of protection for existing drugs was one of the major issues of the negotiations. Some developed nations wanted developing countries to be obliged not only to protect pharmaceutical patents for the future but also to protect existing drugs. In other words, developing countries should protect pharmaceutical inventions that were no longer new, thereby recognizing retroactive patent protection for drugs already patented in other countries but not yet marketed.[282] This kind of provisional protection was called "pipeline protection" in the U.S. as a reference to patented inventions that are either being developed (in the "development pipeline") or waiting for a market license from the regulatory drug agency (the "regulatory pipeline"). The American pharmaceutical industry wanted to ensure that developing countries respected the rights of patented drugs in this "pipeline stage."[283] In this, they had the support of the USTR. In fact, the U.S. delegation presented a draft for the TRIPS Agreement at the time of the multilateral negotiations, under which this kind of retroactive protection was laid down.[284] In their turn, developing countries were strongly opposed to having to provide "pipeline protection" for pharmaceutical patents. They took the approach that such inventions had already fallen within the public domain under the legal regimes they had had prior to the WTO's foundation. Since there was no consensus at this point, the final TRIPS draft of 1992 did not provide for pipeline protection.[285] The U.S. pharmaceutical industry reacted with concern and exerted heavy pressure to modify the final TRIPS draft.[286] Eventually, the U.S. managed to get pipeline protection accepted through smaller or bilateral negotiations, which were running parallel to the Uruguay Round. A successful example of America's efforts to satisfy the interests of its pharmaceutical industry, which sought this transitional protection, was the case of Mexico. The latter country agreed to provide pipeline protection for pharmaceuticals as a condition of becoming a member of the North

281. Gervais (2003), *The TRIPS Agreement: Drafting History and Analysis*, 2nd ed., London, p. 25.
282. Correa (1999), *Intellectual Property Rights, the WTO and Developing Countries—The TRIPS Agreement and Policy Options for Developing Countries*, Zed Books, London, p. 116.
283. Chasen Ross/Wasserman (2003), "Trade-Related Aspects of Intellectual Property Rights," in Stewart (ed.), *The GATT Uruguay Round: A Negotiating History (1986-1992)*, Vol. II, p. 2285.
284. GATT (1990a), Article 26 Draft Agreement on the Trade-Related Aspects of Intellectual Property Rights, Communication from the United States: GATT Doc. No. MTN.GNG/NG11/W/68 (March 29, 1990).
285. GATT (1991), Draft Final Act Embodying the Results of the Uruguay Round of Multilateral Trade Negotiations: GATT Doc. No. MTN.TNC/W/FA (December 20, 1991).
286. Ross/Wasserman (1993), "Trade-Related Aspects of Intellectual Property Rights," in: Stewart (ed.), *The GATT Uruguay Round: A Negotiating History (1986-1992)*, Vol. II, p. 2286.

American Free Trade Area (NAFTA) in 1991.[287] This was also the case of China, which secured "pipeline protection" for American pharmaceutical product patents in its bilateral agreement with the U.S. in January 1992.[288] The U.S. had also managed to obtain pipeline protection in its bilateral agreements with Hungary[289] and Chile.[290] Despite this, pipeline protection did not get through at the GATT multilateral forum. From the perspective of the American pharmaceutical industry, the continued lack of both pipeline protection and provision for transitional protection constituted a "major omission"[291] of the TRIPS Agreement.[292]

At the end of the day, contracting parties reached a compromise solution. Pipeline protection was not accepted, but developing countries agreed to implement a so-called mailbox system for filing patent applications during transitional periods, as provided by Article 70(8) TRIPS. This requires that members who did not confer patent protection for pharmaceutical and agricultural products as of the date the WTO Agreement came into force should introduce a means by which such applications could be filed as if there were a "mailbox" to be opened afterward. So, the novelty of such pharmaceutical and agricultural inventions would be preserved, in spite of delayed patent protection, under the condition that they were filed after the WTO Agreement came into effect. Hence, developing countries that made use of the transitional periods were obliged to apply the criteria of patentability as laid down in the TRIPS Agreement to inventions filed during that time. If the criteria of patentability were met, they would be given patent protection for the remainder of the patent term of 20 years, counted from the filing date. Such patentees would also benefit from exclusive marketing rights for a period of five years if they obtained a marketing license for the product.[293]

The TRIPS mailbox solution, however, did not satisfy the interests of the American pharmaceutical industry.[294] Even after this compromise solution had been

287. Article 1709(4) NAFTA allows "pipeline protection."
288. Ross/Wasserman (1993), "Trade-Related Aspects of Intellectual Property Rights," in: Stewart (ed.), *The GATT Uruguay Round: A Negotiating History (1986-1992)*, Vol. II, p. 2299, fn. 377. *See also* Bodewig (1993), "Volksrepublik China—Erlass einer Verordnung über administrativen Schutz von Arzneimittel," *GRUR Int.*, 581.
289. Ficsor (1995), "Die Einführung des Stoffschutzes im ungarischen Patentrecht," *GRUR Int.*, 1-7.
290. Correa (1994), "Veränderungen im lateinamerikanischen Patentrecht," *GRUR Int.*, 800.
291. Dwyer (1999), "Trade-Related Aspects of Intellectual Property Rights," in Stewart (ed.), *The GATT Uruguay Round: A Negotiating History (1986-1994), Vol. IV: The End Game (Part I)*, pp. 534-535.
292. Clift (2010), "Why IPR Issues Were Brought to GATT: A Historical Perspective on the Origins of TRIPS," in Correa (ed.), *Research Handbook on the Protection of Intellectual Property under WTO Rules*, Edward Elgar, Cheltenham, p. 19.
293. Article 70(9) TRIPS.
294. Ross and Wasserman explain, with basis on a speech given by the USTR Assoc. Gen. Counsel, why pipeline protection was so important for the pharmaceutical industry: "Most of the developed countries would like TRIPs to apply to all existing subject matter, which would include pharmaceuticals in the 'pipeline'. Pipeline protection for pharmaceutical and chemical industries would ensure benefits to these industries ten years after the agreement is signed. For example, if a U.S. Company were to file a patent application on January 1, 1982, and a TRIPs agreement became applicable to a country that previously did not provide protection on January 1, 1994, them that country would have to accept the January 1, 1982 patent application and allow for expiration of the patent on January, 2002. As such, pipeline protection gives an industry the ability to obtain patent protection for the remainder of a patent term, as opposed

reached, the Clinton administration demanded changes in the TRIPS draft: it wanted pipeline protection for pharmaceuticals as well as shorter periods under which transition rules applied for developing countries.[295] So, the U.S. continued to pressurize developing countries to introduce pipeline protection into their new legal patent regimes. It did so through its trade policy, and especially by threatening these countries with the imposition of unilateral trade sanctions. Brazil and Argentina, for instance, continued to face stark American pressure, but they responded to it in different ways. While Brazil introduced pipeline protection for pharmaceuticals in its domestic laws a short while after TRIPS had become mandatory, Argentina still refused to provide for pipeline protection in its legislation.[296]

3.2.3 The Results: The "Grand Bargain"

In 1993, the TRIPS final agreement was complete. In April 1994, the Uruguay Round was successfully concluded,[297] giving birth to the WTO Agreement.[298] As *Ostry* states, the Uruguay Round represented a "Grand Bargain" between developed and developing countries: a deal where developing countries made binding agreements to implement higher standards of intellectual property protection, investment and services, in exchange for more access to the markets of developed nations, by way of limited reductions to import restrictions and export and production subsidies in the area of agriculture, textiles and clothing.[299] It is important to note that the part played by the Global North in this bargain, apart from these reductions to import restrictions, consisted of a non-binding agreement, which would be gradually negotiated within the WTO. Hence, the benefits of trade liberalization for developing countries were minimal, so we might call the developed countries as the "net gainer" in this bargain, which was asymmetric. As *Towse* and *Holzhauer* put it, "it is widely accepted that the US made virtually no concessions in the Uruguay Round negotiations of GATT and imposed upon the world not only the economic interests of its own IP-based industries"

to forcing to forego any protection. *See* Ross/Wasserman (1993), *Trade-Related Aspects of Intellectual Property Rights*, in: Stewart (ed.), *The GATT Uruguay Round: A Negotiating History (1986-1992), Vol. 2: Commentary*, Deventer, p. 2298.

295. Dwyer (1999), "Trade-Related Aspects of Intellectual Property Rights," in Stewart (ed.), *The GATT Uruguay Round: A Negotiating History (1986-1994), Vol. IV: The End Game (Part I)*, p. 518.
296. For a detailed examination of the Argentinian case, *see* Bentolila, "Lessons from the United States Trade Policy to Convert a 'Pirate': The Case of Pharmaceutical Patents in Argentina," 5 *Yale J. L. & Tech.*, 59-102.
297. *GATT* (1994), *Uruguay Round—Marrakesh Declaration of 15 April 1994*, available at https://www.wto.org/english/docs_e/legal_e/marrakesh_decl_e.htm (last visited on August 31, 2020).
298. WTO (1994), Marrakesh Agreement Establishing the World Trade Organization, April 15, 1994, United Nations Treaty Collection (UNTC) I-31874, 1867-1869.
299. Ostry (2009), "The Trade System amidst the Global Financial Crisis," in: Deere-Birkbeck, Carolyn / Meléndez-Ortiz, Ricardo (eds.), *Rebuilding Global Trade: Proposals for a Fairer, More Sustainable Future*, ICTSD, Oxford, pp. 60-61.

but also "a degree of protectionism that is economically and culturally destructive to developing countries."[300]

While the concessions made by developing countries under the TRIPS Agreement were very wide, the WTO Agreement on Agriculture permitted that developed countries maintained their export subsidies for much more time. It was only in 2015—20 years after the conclusion of the Uruguay Round—that WTO members agreed to eliminate export subsidies in the area of agriculture in developed countries during the Ministerial Conference in Nairobi.[301]

4 *Objectives and Principles of the TRIPS Agreement*

As is normal with international treaties, the TRIPS Agreement contains a preamble, where the parties make a statement of the objectives and purposes of the treaty. This declaration of principles serves as a guideline for the interpretation of its relevant provisions, as laid down by the Vienna Convention on the Law of the Treaties (VCLT).[302] What is not so normal is that, in the case of TRIPS, the agreement contains a declaration of objectives not only at the preamble but also in the agreement's body, that is, in its Articles 7 and 8. This fact suggests that the objects and principles laid down in the operative part of the agreement must signify more than those contained in the preamble.

4.1 Preamble

The preamble mirrors the tensions between and differing expectations of developing and developed countries during the negotiations. According to its first sentence, the aim of TRIPS is "to reduce distortions and impediments to international trade," and by participating in it, parties "take into account the need to promote adequate protection of intellectual property rights." To this end, those parties recognized the need for new rules concerning "the provision of adequate standards and principles concerning the availability, scope and use of intellectual property rights." At the same time, they recognized not only that intellectual property rights were private rights but also that public policy objectives are inherent to the protection of intellectual property.

4.2 Promotion of Technological Innovation Versus Transfer and Dissemination of Technology (Article 7 TRIPS)

Article 7 TRIPS emphasizes the need for a balance between the producers and users of technological knowledge by stating that the protection of intellectual property rights

300. Towse/Holzhauer (eds.) (2002), *The Economics of Intellectual Property, Vol I: Introduction and Copyright*, p. XXX.
301. WTO (2015), 10th WTO Ministerial Conference, Nairobi 2015—*Export Competition—Ministerial Decision of 19 December* 2015: WT/MIN (15)/45—WT/L/980.
302. Article 31 Vienna Convention on the Law of the Treaties, done at Vienna on May 23, 1969, entered into force on January 27, 1980, United Nations Treaty Series, V. 1155, p. 331.

should contribute to both the promotion of technological innovation and the transfer and dissemination of technology. Article 7 TRIPS does not contain a norm which imposes a concrete positive or negative obligation on the parties. Consequently, it rather serves as a prime source of the interpretation of the treaty. In the words of *Gervais*, this provision "could be invoked to limit an obligation to protect or enforce a given intellectual property where no promotion of intellectual innovation and/or transfer or dissemination of technology can be proved."[303] It serves to justify the exception of intellectual property rights.

4.3 *Principles Invoked to Protect Public Health and Nutrition and to Deal with the Abuse of Intellectual Property Rights*

Article 8.1 TRIPS stresses that member countries may adopt measures that are necessary to protect public health and nutrition, as well as to protect the public interest in sectors of vital importance to their socio-economic and technological development. As stated by *Rott*, this general provision explicitly clarifies that the TRIPS Agreement does not exist only for protecting the patent holder's interests, but that its purpose is to serve the public good.[304] According to *Rott*, the provision was drafted by a group of developing countries, and its last sentence was added due to the pressure of industrialized countries.[305] The provision's last sentence limits the extension of the exception rule since such measures must be "consistent with the provisions of the agreement." This norm does not allow for any general exception, like Article XX GATT 1947, although its wording is very similar to that clause ("nothing in this agreement shall be constructed to prevent").

There is, however, a decisive difference between Article XX GATT and Article 8 TRIPS.[306] To qualify as a general exception to the rights laid down in the GATT agreement, some conditions must be met (for instance, the exception must be necessary to protect public health and, at the same time, be neither arbitrary nor unjustifiable discrimination). Article 8 TRIPS makes use of similar language, but the conditions under which measures necessary to protect public health can be taken is that such a measure should be consistent with the TRIPS agreement, where in Article XX GATT a consistency with the WTO Agreement is not required. This means that exceptions under TRIPS are narrower than those under the GATT. As already stressed by *Abbott*, this overprotection of intellectual property under the WTO System does not make sense since there is no reason why measures to protect public health, when related to intellectual property, should be more restricted than measures affecting other

303. Gervais (2003), *The TRIPS Agreement: Drafting History and Analysis*, 2nd ed., London, p. 116.
304. Rott (2002), *Patentrecht und Sozialpolitik unter dem TRIPS-Abkommen*, Baden-Baden, Nomos, p. 114.
305. *Ibid.*, pp. 118-119.
306. *See* Frankel (2010), "Applicability of GATT Jurisprudence to the Interpretation of TRIPS," in Correa (ed.), *Research Handbook on the Interpretation and Enforcement of Intellectual Property under WTO Rules, Vol. II*, Edward Elgar, Cheltenham (UK), pp. 14-15.

goods and services.[307] For remedying this contradiction, he suggests that the phrase "provided that such measures are consistent with the TRIPS Agreement" should be deleted.[308]

Notwithstanding, after analyzing in detail Article 8 TRIPS, *Grosse-Ruse Khan* concludes that "the WTO TRIPS balancing objectives support an understanding of the general relationship between IP protection and exceptions to it, as one of balance instead of (universal) role and (minor) exception."[309]

5 *Overview of the Provisions on Patents in the TRIPS Agreement*

The TRIPS Agreement obliges WTO members to adopt minimum standards of patent protection agreed by the parties into their national law. This was, essentially, an obligation assumed by developing countries to reform their patent law in accordance with the minimum standards agreed by TRIPS. Except for a few points, developed countries did not have to substantially modify their national patent law due to obligations assumed by TRIPS since TRIPS reflected the standards of patent law in those developed countries.

These substantive minimum requirements are laid down in Article 27 TRIPS, which defines what constitutes patentable subject matter in its first paragraph (Article 27.1) and what matters might be excluded from patentability from national law in the second and third paragraphs (Article 27.2 and Article 27.3). In this section, only Article 27.1 is going to be examined.

According to the first sentence of Article 27.1, patents should be available for any inventions, whether these are products or processes, in all fields of technology, provided that they are new, involve an inventive step and are capable of industrial application. Exceptions to this rule are provided in the second and third paragraphs.

5.1 *Availability of Patents for Any Inventions, Whether Products or Processes, in All Fields of Technology*

The first rule is that patents must be available for any kind of inventions in all fields of technology. Exclusions are only permitted if they are expressly mentioned by TRIPS as such. This rule is aimed at countries which at the time of the TRIPS negotiations did not provide patent protection for chemical or pharmaceutical inventions.

The clear reference to the duty to protect both product and process patents is also aimed at some of these countries, which had formerly not given patent protection for pharmaceutical or chemical products, for example, but had protected pharmaceutical process patents. Under the pre-TRIPS Brazilian patent law, neither pharmaceutical

307. Abbott (2002a), *WTO TRIPS Agreement and its Implications for Access to Medicines in Developing Countries*—Study Paper 2a, United Kingdom Commission on Intellectual Property Rights, pp. 45-46.
308. *Ibid.*, p. 46.
309. Grosse Ruse-Khan (2009), *Policy Space for Domestic Public Interest Measures under TRIPS*, South Centre Research Paper No. 22, p. 38.

products nor processes could be protected by patents.[310] In India, however, pharmaceutical processes might be protected, although pharmaceutical products were also excluded from patentability. The TRIPS rule thus obliged both countries to change their national patent law.[311]

5.2 *Conditions of Patentability*

Article 27 requires that an invention, to be patentable, must comply with three conditions: (1) it must have an inventive step, (2) it must be new, and (3) it must be capable of industrial application. TRIPS, however, does not provide for definitions of these categories, so that they may vary between different national patent systems. In a traditional approach to patent law, one assumes that patents and the patent law itself are characterized by the neutrality of values. As put by *Lee*, "accordingly, the patent system is loath to impose ex ante value judgements on inventions."[312] As a consequence, such concepts are interpreted in a restricted way, as if they were mere technical requirements.

However, as observed by *Bently and Sherman*, "the task of having to decide the types of subject matter that ought to be patentable invariably generates conflict and uncertainty. This is because patent law finds itself dealing with technologies that it may not yet understand. It is also because the task of having to decide whether to grant property rights in a particular type of invention raises a complex mix of legal, cultural, political and social questions."[313] It follows that what is considered to be new in a national jurisdiction does not have to be so in another. While the categories "novelty" or "inventive step" must be accessed with basis on technology, the interpretation will additionally depend on the legal culture of each jurisdiction, as well on policy considerations.

So, a second medicinal indication of a known substance may be considered to be a new invention in a given jurisdiction, while it might not be considered to be new in another one. How these concepts of novelty and inventiveness are understood is also related to the quality of patents granted in a jurisdiction.[314] This is a matter for WTO members to deal with "within their own legal system or practice."[315]

310. Article 9c, Lei 5.772, of December 21, 2012.
311. Ghose (2006), "TRIPS and India: Crux of the Patent Controversy," in Sengupta et al. (eds.), *Beyond the Transition Phase of the WTO: An Indian Perspective*, Academic Foundation, New Delhi, p. 178.
312. In U.S. patent law, *see*, for instance, Lee (2017), "Towards a Distributive Agenda for U.S. Patent Law," 55 *Hous. L. Rev.* 2, 327-328.
313. Bently/Sherman (2009), *Intellectual Property Law*, OUP, Oxford, p. 392.
314. Mandel (2008), "The Non-Obvious Problem: How the Indeterminate Non-Obviousness Standard Produces Excessive Patent Grants," 42 *UC Davis L. Rev.*, 57-128.
315. Article 1.1 TRIPS.

5.3 *Nondiscrimination (Article 27.1 TRIPS)*

According to Article 27.1 TRIPS Agreement, patents should be available, and patent rights should be enjoyed without discrimination on the basis of the place of invention, the field of technology and whether products are imported or locally produced.

5.3.1 Discrimination as to the Place of the Invention

A patent must be available, and patent rights should be enjoyable without discrimination as to the place of the invention. This rule was aimed at the U.S., which had to modify its substantive patent law by abandoning the "first-to-invent" system and adopting the "first-to-file" system.[316] Under the traditional "first-to-invent" system, deemed to be fairer to the inventor, a patent was given to the person who first created the invention, even if a patent application had already been filed elsewhere by another inventor. However, under U.S. law, the first-to-invent system was only valid for national citizens or enterprises. So, if a non-US citizen created an invention outside of the U.S. and a U.S. citizen afterward filed a patent application at the U.S. patent office, this patent could not be challenged by the inventor, even if she succeeded in proving that she had been the first to invent.

5.3.2 Discrimination as to the Field of Technology

The first sentence of Article 27.1 TRIPS states, as a general rule, that "patents shall be available for any inventions" in all fields of technology, provided that they are new, involve an inventive step and are capable of industrial application. The reason for this general provision was to forbid WTO members from denying patent protection for chemical, pharmaceutical and food patents, as many developing countries still did at the time when the TRIPS Agreement was being negotiated. The second sentence of Article 27.1 TRIPS lays down the exceptions to this general rule. It provides that a patent might not be available for an invention, in any field of technology, in the following cases:

(1) where a developing country has delayed the duty to extend patent protection to products or processes not deemed to be protectable under its national law, for five years from the date that the TRIPS Agreement becomes mandatory for that member (Article 65.4 TRIPS);
(2) where a developing country introduces transitional patent protection for pharmaceutical and agricultural chemical products using a mailbox system (Article 70.8 TRIPS); and
(3) where therapeutic methods are excluded from patent protection, as well as plants and animals other than microorganisms (Article 27.3 TRIPS).

316. Gervais (2003), *The TRIPS Agreement: Drafting History and Analysis*, 2nd ed., London, p. 221.

As *Godt* puts it, Article 27 TRIPS deals exclusively with the explicit exclusion of certain technical areas from patenting (namely, pharmaceuticals), so that Article 27.1 does not prohibit that some areas of technology will be differently regulated due to their specificities.[317]

5.3.3 Discrimination as to Whether Products Are Imported or Locally Produced

According to Article 27.1 of the TRIPS Agreement, patents should be available and patent rights enjoyable without discrimination as to whether products are imported or locally produced. This has to do with the prohibition or forfeiture of patents on the grounds of a lack of local working. Before the TRIPS Agreement, the national law of some countries required that patents should be locally worked as a condition for the enjoyment of patent rights.[318] Under the old Brazilian patent law, for instance, if a patent owner did not produce its patented product in Brazilian territory within four years after the patent was granted, his patent was subjected to "forfeiture"; that is to say, it was canceled.[319] Under the TRIPS Agreement, such a forfeiture provision would represent discrimination in the application of patent rights as to whether products are imported or locally produced.

It is worth noting that the prohibition of forfeiture as a form of discrimination with regard to whether the patented product is imported or locally produced should not be confused with working requirements regarding compulsory licenses since the nondiscrimination principle, as demonstrated by *Lamping et al.*, does not apply to exceptions to patent rights, as in the case of compulsory licenses.[320]

5.3.4 Exceptions to the Principle of Nondiscrimination

5.3.4.1 Transitional Periods (Article 65.4 TRIPS)

According to Article 27.1 TRIPS, the obligation not to discriminate regarding the field of technology, place of invention and whether products are imported or locally produced is waived for 5 or 10 years, where applicable, if a developing country member makes use of the transitional periods.

5.3.4.2 Mailbox (Article 70.8 TRIPS)

Under the mailbox protection system, if a developing country member makes use of the transitional periods, this country is obliged to create a means by which such inventions

317. Godt (2007b), *Eigentum an Information—Patentschutz und allgemeine Eigentumstheorie am Beispiel genetischer Information*, Mohr Siebeck, Tübingen, p. 576.
318. *See* Chapter 3-A-I-3.2.3.2.
319. Article 49(a) Federal Law No. 5.772 of December 21, 1971.
320. *See* Lamping et al. (2014), "Declaration on Patent Protection—Regulatory Sovereignty under TRIPS," 45 *IIC*, 679-698.

could be filed as of the date the WTO Agreement entered into force. Once the transitional periods had ended, these applications should be "opened" and decided by the patent office, and a decision be made according to the minimum standards imposed by TRIPS. These members should provide patent protection in accordance with TRIPS as from the date of the granting of the patent and for the remainder of the patent term of 20 years, counted from the filing date.

Additionally, products in the "mailbox" were to be given exclusive marketing rights for a period of five years, counted from the obtaining of market approval or until a patent application is granted or rejected, whichever period is shorter.

5.3.4.3 Other Exceptions

Article 27.2 and 27.3 TRIPS explicitly lay down other cases of exclusion of patentability, therefore expressly admitting cases in which an invention might not be patentable under national law, even if it is new, has an inventive step and is capable of industrial application. By the same token, Article 30 TRIPS provides for exceptions to the rights conferred by patents. These cases are going to be examined in the next chapter.

5.3.5 Significance of Article 27.1

Article 27.1 is the provision that transformed the global patent system. It is a revolutionary provision because it is the first substantive rule of the international patent system. By providing that patents must be available for any invention, in all fields of technology, contracting parties are no longer free to exclude any fields of technology from the subject matter of patents—as many countries did before the TRIPS era. According to *Carvalho*, this is "the core provision and the reason of being of the whole TRIPS Agreement."[321] It is the successful result of efforts to harmonize patentable subject matter at a global level, which developed countries wished for at the beginning of the Uruguay Round.

Special attention, however, should be given to the extent given to the nondiscrimination provision of Article 27.1 TRIPS. As pointed out by *Lamping et al.*, "Article 27 of the TRIPS Agreement does not prevent states from reasonably differentiating between fields of technology according to the characteristics inherent in the technology at issue and the state public policies pertaining to the sector at issue."[322]

5.4 Patent Rights Conferred by TRIPS (Article 28)

According to Article 28 TRIPS, a patent shall confer on its owner the following exclusive rights: to prevent third parties from engaging in the act of making, using,

321. Pires de Carvalho (2010), *The TRIPS Regime of Patent Rights*, 3rd ed., Kluwer Law International, Alphen aan den Rijn, p. 245.
322. Lamping et al. (2014), "Declaration on Patent Protection—Regulatory Sovereignty under TRIPS," 45 *IIC*, 679-698.

offering for sale, or selling that product, or importing that product for any of the aforementioned purposes, without the owner's consent. By the same token, if the subject matter of a patent is a process, the patent owner should be given the right to prevent third parties from engaging in the act of using that process or from engaging in the acts of using, offering for sale, selling or importing the products obtained directly by that process, without his consent.

It is important to note that the owner's right to prevent third parties from importing products is not limited by Article 6 TRIPS, which states that the exhaustion of patent rights is a topic to be decided by national law.

5.5 *Conditions on Patent Applicants (Article 29)*

The first sentence of Article 29 of TRIPS imposes on patent applicants the duty to disclose the invention "in a manner sufficiently clear and complete for the invention to be carried out by a person skilled in the art." The second sentence of Article 29 of TRIPS allows that national law requires the applicant to indicate the best method for carrying out the invention that is known to the inventor at the filing date.

5.6 *Revocation/Forfeiture (Article 32)*

Revocation of a patent occurs when the patent office, at a second examination, mostly at a superior administrative level, modifies its decision to grant a patent. Forfeiture of a patent occurs in cases regulated by patent law. The most common ground for forfeiture is the failure to pay annual taxes to the patent office. Although the TRIPS Agreement does not regulate cases of revocation or forfeiture, it requires that an opportunity for judicial review of any decision to revoke or forfeit a patent must be available.

5.7 *Minimum 20 Years' Protection (Article 33)*

Article 33 TRIPS imposes a minimum period of 20 years of patent protection counted from the filing date. Members are not entitled to reduce this term, but they are free to give more time than the minimum protection period required by law. The Brazilian patent law, for instance, not only concedes a period of 20 years of patent protection counted from the *filing date* but also guarantees a minimum of 10 years of protection, counted from the *date of the granting* of the patent.[323] This is more than required by the TRIPS Agreement since the Brazilian minimum patent term is counted from the patent grant, while the minimum pattern term in accordance with the TRIPS Agreement is counted from the filing date.

---

323. Article 40, sole paragraph, Law No. 9.279/1996 (LPI).

5.8 Process Patents (Article 34)

Article 34 TRIPS contains a rule of civil proceedings, which creates a presumption in favor of the patentee if the object of the dispute is a process patent. According to this rule, the judge should order the defendant to prove that the process to obtain an identical product is different from the patented process. If the defendant is not able to prove it, the product will be considered to have been obtained by the patented process at least in one of the following two cases: (1) if the product originally obtained by the patentee's new process was new; (2) if there is a substantial likelihood that the identical product was made by the process and the patent owner has been unable, after reasonable efforts have been made by him to do so, to determine the process that was actually used.

III Flexibilities of Patent Rights under the TRIPS Agreement

1 Introductory Remarks

The literature on TRIPS and pharmaceutical patents often uses the term "flexibilities" to refer to legal mechanisms that are able to limit patent rights in certain cases provided for by national law and admitted by international patent law, such as compulsory licenses, exclusions from patentability and other limitations to patentee's rights.[324] Although legal restrictions on the exercise of patent rights have been a known principle of the patent law of many countries since at least the nineteenth century,[325] the use of the term "flexibilities" to designate such a restriction is newer. It appeared during the TRIPS Agreement negotiations, at the time of the Uruguay Round (1986-1994).

Before the TRIPS Agreement, multilateral regulation of patent rights was carried out by the Paris Convention. This Convention did not provide any mandatory standards for protection in the area of patents. Limiting patent rights was reserved for the competence of national law. Therefore, under the Paris Convention, each country was free to decide on how and why these exclusions or limitations should work. Such freedom allowed the coexistence of very different patent regimes among the members of the Paris Convention; these differences were referred to by some of its members as *asymmetries*.[326] One of the declared objectives of the TRIPS Agreement was precisely that of creating some mandatory minimum standards in patent law for all members in

324. About "TRIPS Flexibilities" *see*, for instance, Yamane (2011), *Interpreting TRIPS: Globalization of Intellectual Property Rights and Access to Medicines*, Hart Publishing, Oxford/Portland, pp. 245-248.
325. Dwyer (1993), "Trade-Related Aspects of Intellectual Property Rights," in Stewart (ed.), *The GATT Uruguay Round: A Negotiating History (1986-1994), Vol. IV: The End Game (Part I)*, pp. 465-576.
326. Pires de Carvalho (2010), *The TRIPS Regime of Patent Rights*, 3rd ed., Kluwer Law International, Alphen aan den Rijn, p. 61.

order to minimize such asymmetries.[327] During the negotiations, there was tension between developed countries and developing countries. Developed countries were concerned with "strengthening" the degree of patent protection worldwide, with a focus on the patent owner's rights, whereas developing countries were focused on the rights of the users of, and thus on preserving some degree of "flexibility" in order to guarantee the necessary balance. The latter were concerned that the new agreement might not leave any room for the creation of national patent policies.

Developing countries agreed to the imposition of minimum standards of patent protection, but they did not want to lose their freedom to define their own patent policy. So, they agreed with the introduction of higher standards of patent protection, but, at the same time, they demanded the maintenance of some degree of freedom in the limitation and exclusion of patentable subject matter. Under the context of a negotiation which placed developed and developing countries in opposition to each other, the term "flexibility" started being used by the latter as a counterbalance for the desired strengthening of patent rights. At the end of the day, patent rights were strengthened, but some "flexibility" was maintained. Since then, the word "flexibility" has often been used in this context as a general term to refer to exclusions, exceptions or limitations to patent rights.

However, the term "flexibility" also has a broader meaning. Flexibilities are then understood as the freedom that a member country has to define its patent policy in general, assuming that that policy does not contravene the TRIPS Agreement and that it is in accordance with the principles of the TRIPS Agreement. This includes not only the freedom to define exclusions or limitations to patent rights but also the freedom to establish higher standards of patent protection than those required by TRIPS. In the classification proposed by *Pires de Carvalho*,[328] flexibilities are divided into upward (TRIPS Plus) and downward flexibilities (exceptions and limitations).

Such "flexibilities" are still regulated by both international and national patent law. However, they continue to be a matter of legislative (patent) policy, even if to a smaller degree due to the broader restrictions imposed by the international patent system, according to Article 1.1, first sentence TRIPS. At the present time, a WTO member country still makes its own decisions on how and why these limitations should work, provided it respects its international obligations. By the same token, a country can still decide that it prefers not to limit patent rights at all. Article 1 sentence 2 of TRIPS clearly states that members might (but should not be obliged to) implement in their national law more extensive protection than is required by the TRIPS Agreement. In essence, "flexibility" in this context is a question of patent policy. One country may legislate that some inventions should have their protection time extended, while others might not. Therefore, the flexibility of patent rights has remained a matter of patent

327. Under the letter "b" of the declaration of principles of TRIPS, members recognized the need for new rules and disciplines concerning the provision of *adequate standards* and principles concerning the availability, scope and use of trade-related intellectual property rights.

328. Pires de Carvalho (2010), *The TRIPS Regime of Patent Rights*, 3rd ed., Kluwer Law International, Alphen aan den Rijn, pp. 60-67.

policy within the remit of national law, even if the latter is now more limited by international law than it was before the WTO's foundation.

In the following sections, some of the flexibilities expressly mentioned by the TRIPS Agreement will be briefly examined. They are addressed to national governments, always as a possibility of including them in their national patent law, as an example of the prosecution of national interests.

2 *Flexibilities*

2.1 Parallel Imports

As a rule, a patent confers on its owner exclusive rights to prevent third parties from making, using, offering for sale, selling or importing a patented product if the third parties do not have his authorization to do it.[329] This section concentrates on the exclusive right to prevent a third party from importing a patented product without the consent of the patent owner. The reach of this exclusive right might be more or less extensive, depending on the admission or prohibition of "parallel imports" by national law.

The concept of "parallel imports" is understood to apply to the importing of a patented product in the following circumstances: (1) The patented product "pp" is sold by the patent owner "PO," or with his consent to buyer "B" in country "C"; and (2) afterward, the product "pp" is sold by seller "B" to buyer "R" in country "Y," without the authorization of the patent owner "PO" and the first seller. The import described in point 2 is called a "parallel import." Whether the patent owner "PO" has the exclusive right to prevent that country Y from importing his patented product "P" depends on the legal admission or prohibition of "parallel imports" in national law.

"Parallel imports" are particularly important in the global market of pharmaceuticals because there is, normally, a high level of price variation between different markets worldwide.[330] Therefore, if parallel imports are admitted, money might be saved. If, for instance, a government in a developing country manages to buy a patented product from a seller in a country where it was bought at a cheaper price than it could have been in its own country, it might be an advantage to import it, instead of buying it directly from the patent owner.[331]

The legal admission of parallel imports is a question of the exhaustion of rights. In accordance with the exhaustion principle, a patent owner does not have any rights on a patented product after having put the product into circulation for the first time. Therefore, a patent owner must not prohibit the reselling by other people of a patented

329. Article 28.1(a) TRIPS.
330. Mercurio (2006), "Resolving the Public Health Crisis in the Developing World: Problems and Barriers of Access to Essential Medicines," 5 *Nw. U. J. Int'l Hum. Rts.* 1-40.
331. Moore (2006), "Parallel Trade, Unparallel Laws: An Examination of the Pharmaceutical Parallel Trade Laws of the United States, the European Union and the World Trade Organization," 6 *Rich. J. Global L. & Bus.*, 84; Atik/Lidgard (2007), "Embracing Price Discrimination: TRIPS and the Suppression of Parallel Trade on Pharmaceuticals," 27 *U. Pa. J. Int'l Econ. L.*, 1065.

product that they have sold. Her rights as a patent owner are exhausted with the first sale.

The principle of exhaustion might be valid at the national, supranational or international level, depending on the policy adopted by national law. If a country adopts the principle of national exhaustion, exhaustion only occurs when the first sale happened within the physical boundaries of that country. Therefore, the patent owner is able to prohibit or allow the import of patented products sold by foreign countries so that parallel imports are prohibited in such countries if there is no explicit consent from the patent owner for it. The U.S.[332] and Brazil,[333] for instance, are examples of countries that adopt the principle of national exhaustion. If a country, however, adopts the principle of international exhaustion, exhaustion occurs when the first sale takes place on the global market. Once his product is sold for the first time, independently of where that product was sold, the producer's rights over the patented product are exhausted. Some developing countries, like South Africa or Kenya, adopt the principle of international exhaustion with respect to medicines.[334] The principle of exhaustion might also be adopted at a supranational level, such as in the peculiar case of the EU: exhaustion occurs if a product was sold for the first time in a Member State of the EU, meaning that parallel imports are admitted within the boundaries of these countries. This is so because, in accordance with the case law of the European Court of Justice, the trade of medicinal products is not an exception to the freedom of movement of goods.[335]

Whether parallel imports are allowed or not can be freely decided by national law. This is so because, in accordance with Article 6 TRIPS, the question of the exhaustion of intellectual property rights is not to be dealt with within the international system. As a matter of public policy, it is left to the national legislator's discretion.

Despite the freedom left by TRIPS to national laws to decide about the exhaustion regime, trade disputes occurred in the late 1990s show that the multinational pharmaceutical industry is not disposed to accept this flexibility. A striking example of this is the trade dispute known as "Big Pharma vs. Nelson Mandela." In 1997, the South African government passed a law with the aim of increasing the access of drugs to the population. According to *Hoen*, "provisions included generic substitution of patent of off-patent medicines, transparent pricing for all medicines, and the parallel importation of patented medicines."[336] As a reaction against this, the South African Pharmaceutical Manufacturers Association and 39 multinational pharmaceutical firms sued the government of South Africa, alleging that the South African law violated TRIPS and the South African Constitution. As reported by *Hoen*:

332. United States (2011), U.S. Code Title 35, Patents, § 271 (a).
333. Article 20. LPI.
334. Musungu/Oh (2006), *The Use of Flexibilities in TRIPS by Developing Countries: Can They Promote Access to Medicines?*, South Centre and World Trade Organization, Geneva, p. 48.
335. European Commission (2003), *Commission Communication of Parallel Imports of proprietary medicinal products for which marketing authorizations was granted*, COM (2003) 839 of 30 December 2003.
336. Hoen (2009), *The Global Politics of Pharmaceutical Monopoly Power—Drug Patents, Access, Innovation and the Application of the WTO Doha Declaration on TRIPS and Public Health*, AMB, Universiteit van Amsterdam, p. 21.

> At the start of the litigation, the drug companies could rely on the support of their home governments. For its part, the US had put pressure on South Africa by withholding trade benefits and threatening further trade sanctions, aiming to force the South African government to repeal the Act (Barber 1998; Omnibus Consolidated and Emergency Supplemental Appropriations Act 1999). In 1998, the European Commission joined the US in pressuring South Africa to repeal the legislation (Brittan 1998). AIDS activists effectively highlighted these policies, profoundly embarrassing the-presidential candidate Al Gore, who found himself confronted at election campaign rallies with his personal involvement in the dispute (Barber 1999). As a result of increasing public pressure, the US changed its policies.[337]

2.2 *Exclusion from Patentability (Article 27.2 and 27.3 TRIPS)*

Before TRIPS, providing for exceptions from patentability was considered to be a matter of public policy and was left as a rule to the discretion of national law. Under the current international patent system, exceptions from patentability continue to be a matter of public policy, but they must be in accordance with the TRIPS Agreement. In the following sections, the exceptions to patentability admitted by TRIPS are presented.

2.2.1 Conditional Exclusion of Patentability on the Grounds of *Ordre Public*, Morality or Protection of Public Health

According to Article 27.2 TRIPS, members may exclude from patentability inventions the commercial exploitation of which is prevented by law, if this is necessary to protect: (a) *ordre public*; (b) morality; (c) human, animal or plant life; (d) health; (e) or to avoid serious damage to the environment. So, an exception based on this Article can only be applied to the condition that it is necessary to prevent commercial exploitation of the invention, that is: the product is not allowed to be marketed.[338] Further, mere legal prohibition is not enough to justify the exception. It is necessary that the commercial exploitation of the invention is understood to be a risk to the values cited in Article 27.2.

This condition is not easy to meet. Imagine, for instance, a provision in national law which allows the exclusion from the patentable subject matter of either pharmaceutical product in general or a specific one in order to protect public health with the aim of diffusing such drugs as extensively as possible. In this case, the conditions of Article 27.2 would only be met if: (1) the commercial exploitation of the invention of the medicine is prohibited by law; and (2) the prohibition by law of commercial exploitation is necessary to protect public health.

Article 27.2 would not justify such an exemption since a member cannot refuse a patent on the grounds of morality (which include the protection of public health) and,

337. *Ibid.*
338. *See*, for instance, Watal (2001), *Intellectual Property Rights in the WTO and Developing Countries*, Kluwer Law International, The Hague/London/Boston, pp. 96-98; UNCTAD-ICTSD (2005), *Resource Book on TRIPS and Development*, Cambridge, p. 376.

at the same time, permit its commercial exploitation. What if the intended use is a noncommercial use? Would the refusal to grant a patent be justified? The answer is no because a case of non-commercial use would not satisfy the second condition laid down by Article 27.2; that is, the fact that such an exclusion was not made merely because the exploitation was prohibited by law, but because the prohibition was necessary.

2.2.2 Cases of Unconditional Exclusion of Patentability (Article 27.3 TRIPS)

Article 27.3 TRIPS explicitly refers to another case of possible exclusion of patentability by national law. Unlike the exceptions in Article 27.2, there are no conditions to fulfill. It is enough that national law considers the case not to be eligible for patents.

2.2.2.1 Methods of Medical Treatment (Article 27.3.a TRIPS)

In accordance with Article 27.3.a TRIPS Agreement, members may exclude from patentability diagnostic, therapeutic and surgical methods for the treatment of humans or animals. This exclusion is explained by the existence of this provision in European law, which used to be very common in the national patent law of many European countries in the pre-TRIPS era, as well in Article 53 EPC.[339] Other countries, like the U.S., Australia and New Zealand, do not have such exclusion.[340] Many developing countries also provide for this exception, such as Brazil and India, for instance, but they do so based on concerns of access and not on ethical concerns.[341]

This provision is particularly important for pharmaceutical inventions because they are able to hinder patents that protect new uses of known substances. Such patents, very common in the pharmaceutical field, are granted to protect second or further medical indications of known substances. In Europe, this obstacle to patentability was overcome by the last amendment to the EPC, when Article 53(c) was included to expressly admit that products using these methods and known products which have new therapeutic effects can be patented. Therefore, Article 53(c) EPC is now considered to be an exception to the exception to patentability regarding the non-patentability of diagnostic, therapeutic and surgical methods for the treatments of humans or animals. Prior to this amendment, the obstacle was overcome by a construction known as "Swiss-type patent claims,"[342] according to the following standard: "A claim in the form 'Substance X for use as a medicament' is acceptable, even if X is a known substance, but its use in medicine is not known. Likewise, it is acceptable to have a claim in the form 'Substance X for use in the treatment of disease

339. Visser (2005), "The Exclusion of Medical Methods," in: Kur et al. (eds.), "*... und sie bewegt sich doch! "—Patent Law on the Move, Festschritt für Gert Kolle und Dieter Stauder*, Carl Heymanns, Köln, pp. 469-470.
340. UNCTAD—ICTSD (2005), *Resource Book on TRIPS and Development*, Chapter 20, p. 384.
341. Asif (2013), "Exclusion of Diagnostic, Therapeutic and Surgical Methods from Patentability," 18 *JIPR*, 242-250.
342. *See* above Chapter 2-A.III-3.1.1.

Y', provided that such a claim involves an inventive step over any prior art disclosing the use of X as a medicament."[343]

As stressed by *Watal*, "the TRIPS Agreement is silent about the patentability of new uses of known substances, including second or subsequent therapeutic uses for known pharmaceutical products," therefore patent laws which allow this do so by way of a specific provision.[344] Although TRIPS does not oblige its members to grant patents for new uses or methods of using known products, there is a trend of bilateral agreements between industrialized countries and developing countries, whereby the latter are obliged to grant such patents. This is the case, for instance, of the agreements between the U.S. and countries like Morocco and Bahrain.[345]

2.2.2.2 Biotechnological Clause (Article 27.3.b TRIPS)

According to Article 27.3.b TRIPS, members may exclude from patentability plants and animals other than microorganisms, as well as essentially biological processes for the production of plants and animals other than non-biological and microbiological processes. The second part of the Article 37.3.b provision, however, introduces the duty to provide for the protection of "plant varieties," but this does not have to be necessarily done by means of patents; it can be done by an effective sui generis system.

In this clause, there are two flexibilities allowed to the national legislator: the first one is to exclude patent subject matter from patentability, the second one is the possibility of defining the exact boundaries of the concepts treated in the provision, such as, for instance, the concept of "plants and animals other than microorganisms," as well as the concept of a microorganism itself.

This clause—known as the "biotechnological clause"[346]—was and is still the object of controversy among developed countries and developing countries, considering the different perspectives among them. From the perspective of developed countries—where the biotechnological industries flourish—granting such patents give a trade advantage over their producers. From the developing countries' perspective, however, patents on plants and animals are often related to questions concerning biological diversity and traditional knowledge, and they are afraid that patents may restrict the use of their own natural resources.

This problem can be illustrated in the case of gene patents. Since the advances in gene technology of the early 1990s, it has been widely discussed whether the patenting of genes makes sense or not. As suggested by *Koopman*, the workability of patenting

343. EPO, *Guidelines for Examination*, Part G, Chapter VI, 7.1.
344. *See*, for instance, Abbott (2006b), "The Cycle of Action and Reaction: Developments and Trends in Intellectual Property and Health," in: Roffe et al. (eds.), *Negotiating Health* Earthscan, London / Sterling, p. 30; Watal (2001), *Intellectual Property Rights in the WTO and Developing Countries*, Kluwer Law International, The Hague/London/Boston, pp. 104-105.
345. *See*, for instance, Rangel-Ortiz (2008), "Sensitive Health and Patent Law Issues in Bilateral Trade Agreements Recently Executed by the United States—The Latin American Experience," in: Ghidini/Genovesi (eds.), *Intellectual Property and Market Power, ATRIP Papers 2006-2007*, Eudeba, p. 375.
346. UNCTAD/ICTSD (2005), *TRIPS* and *Development Resource Book*, p. 388.

regimes with regard to life sciences is contested because patenting inventions in these areas might inhibit technological progress.[347] On the other hand, when patents are granted in industrialized nations for biological material found in developing countries, the latter accuse the first countries of "biopiracy." An example of this is the so-called TEFF patent, which is controversial both because of biopiracy and because of being considered a barrier to agrarian research. TEFF is a grain originated from Ethiopia and Eritrea, where it has been produced for thousands of years. TEFF is a special grain because it does not contain gluten and grows in areas up to 3,000 m and is resistant to drought and frost. The process of making flour of TEFF was patented in 2003 in the Netherlands, in 2006 in the United States; in 2007, the European Patent Office granted a patent for TEFF.[348] As reported by *Godt*, it was due to the accusations of "biopiracy" that Ethiopia was pressured to discuss a benefit-sharing agreement on TEFF in accordance with the Convention of Biological Diversity.[349] Besides, she reports the patent conflict on the research of TEFF in Germany, where the Agrarian Chamber of Low Saxony (*Landwirtschaftskammer Niedersachsen*) in vain tried to test the adequacy of TEFF in Germany, without having to pay exclusive patent rights for the Dutch company who had the exclusive patent rights on TEFF.[350]

As reported by *Andersen and Winge*, when the Dutch company went bankrupt in 2009, the whole benefit received by Ethiopia was only EUR 4000 and an interrupted research project.[351] In February 2019, the TEFF-patent was declared invalid by a Dutch court.[352] In August 2019, the Dutch patent owner renounced to the German patent after this one has been challenged by a claim of nullity so that it was declared to be extinct.[353]

2.2.3 Implicit Cases of Exclusion of Patentability

Although TRIPS considerably limits the freedom of national law to provide for exceptions to patentability, the agreement leaves some room for implicit cases of exclusions of patentability. TRIPS, for instance, does not define what "inventions" are. This allows national law room to exclude, for instance, "discoveries" from the patentable subject matter.

---

347. Koopman (2008), "Human Rights Implications of Patenting Biotechnological Knowledge," in Torremans (ed.), *Intellectual Property Rights and Human Rights*, Kluwer Law International, BV, The Netherlands, pp. 551-552.
348. Godt (2012), "Zugang und Vorteilausgleich der Konvention für Biologische Vielfalt—Lehren aus dem TEFF-Fall," in: Bette/Stephan (eds.), Biodiversität, *Geistiges Eigentum und Innovation—Aktuelle Herausforderungen und Kontroversen in der wissensbasierten Bio-Industrie*, Philipps-Universität Marburg, pp. 192-193.
349. *Ibid.*, p. 192.
350. *Ibid.*, pp. 193-194.
351. Andersen/Winge (2012), *The Access and Benefit-Sharing Agreement on Teff Genetic Resources—Facts and Lessons*, FNI Report 6/2012, p. 2.
352. Kluwer Patent Blog (2019), *Teff Patent Declared Invalid, "Great News" for Ethiopia.*
353. beck-aktuell Nachrichten (2019), Nach Nichtigkeitsklage: *Patent für afrikanisches Teff-Mehl in Deutschland erloschen.*

On the other hand, patent rights should be enjoyable for any inventions, with the exception of those mentioned above, whether they are products or processes, and in all fields of technology, provided that:

(1) they are new;
(2) they involve an inventive step;
(3) they are capable of industrial application.

However, TRIPS does not define what is to be understood by the concepts of "novelty," "inventiveness" and "industrial applicability." Thus, it leaves the members room to interpret these in different ways and to define such concepts according to their national law. So, parties can, for instance, provide different definitions for the concepts of "novelty," "inventiveness" or "microorganisms."[354] The question of the patentability of new uses of old inventions is an example of relevant differences concerning definitions between contracting parties. In some countries, new uses for old inventions are considered to be new; for instance, the countries that are parties to the EPC. In other countries, like India,[355] Argentina, Chile and Uruguay, such uses are not considered to be inventions in the sense of patent law.[356] Nevertheless, some regional free-trade agreements oblige their parties to protect new uses with patent rights.[357]

As stated by *Abbott*, it is important that governments of developing countries recognize that the requirements of patentability "are flexible, and may be interpreted restrictively so as to limit the number of patents on pharmaceuticals that are granted."[358] According to him, "development countries might insist that patents be granted only for new drugs that represent major (or breakthrough) developments—significant therapeutic advances—and that patents not be granted for lower-level improvements, for example, for new methods of dosage delivery of existing therapeutic compounds."[359]

2.3 General Exceptions to Rights Conferred by Patents

According to Article 30 TRIPS, members may be provided with limited exceptions to the exclusive rights provided by a patent, provided that:

354. Correa, "Pharmaceutical Inventions: When Is the Granting of a Patent Justified?," 1 *IJIPM* 1-2, 5.
355. Chadha (2007), *WTO, TRIPs and India: Contemporary Issues and Implications for India's Pharmaceuticals Industry,* in: Thakur, Anil Kumar / Sharma, Nageshwar (eds.), *WTO and India*, Deep and Deep Publications, New Delhi, p. 573; Parthasaraty/Goddar (2009), "Patentability of Pharmaceutical Products in India—The Novartis Case," 1 *IIC* 38.
356. Musungu/Oh (2006), *The Use of Flexibilities in TRIPS by Developing Countries: Can they Promote Access to Medicines?* South Centre and World Trade Organization, Geneva, p. 62.
357. Abbott (2004), *The Doha Declaration on the TRIPS Agreement and Public Health and the Contradictory Trend in Bilateral and Regional Free Trade Agreements*, Quaker United Nations Office, Occasional Paper No. 14, p. 10.
358. Abbott (2002a), *WTO TRIPS Agreement and Its Implications for Access to Medicines in Developing Countries,*—Study Paper 2a, United Kingdom Commission on Intellectual Property Rights, p. 46.
359. *Ibid.*, p. 46.

(1) such exceptions are limited;
(2) such exceptions do not conflict to an unreasonable extent with the normal exploitation of the patent; and
(3) such exceptions do not unreasonably prejudice the legitimate interests of the patent owner, taking account of the legitimate interests of third parties.

How Article 30 exceptions should be interpreted was the subject of the WTO Panel Canada—Patent Protection of Pharmaceutical Products.[360] This concerned a dispute regarding two exceptions to the rights conferred by patents in Canadian law: the first of these was the so-called regulatory review exception, which authorized patent owners' competitors to produce a patented medicine before its patent term ended; the second was the so-called stockpiling exception, which authorized patent owners' competitors to stockpile patented drugs produced during a time when the patent in question was still valid, although the right to sell them only emerges when the patent term ends. The panel considered the first case to be in conformity with Article 30 TRIPS, while the second one was not considered to be a limited exception under the terms of that article.

According to the panel's conclusion, "the three conditions are cumulative, each being a separate and independent requirement that must be satisfied."[361] Regarding the first condition, the panel concluded that a "limited exception" must be a very narrow one so that only a "small diminution of the rights in question" is allowed to exist.[362] Regarding the second condition, the panel considered that "exploitation" refers to the commercial activity by which patent owners employ their exclusive patent rights to extract economic value from their patent,[363] while "the normal practice of exploitation by patent owners, as with owners of any other intellectual property right, is to exclude all forms of competition that could detract significantly from the economic returns anticipated from a patent's grant of market exclusivity."[364] Regarding the third condition, the panel rejected the view that "legitimate interests" are essentially "legal interests," concluding that the term "must be defined in the way that it is often used in legal discourse—as a normative claim calling for protection of interests that are 'justifiable' in the sense that they are supported by relevant public policies or other social norms."[365,366]

360. *Canada—Patent Protection of Pharmaceutical Products*, WTO Document WT/DS114/R, March 17, 2000.
361. *Ibid.*, paragraph 7.20.
362. *Ibid.*, paragraph 7.30.
363. *Ibid.*, paragraph 7.54.
364. *Ibid.*, paragraph 7.55.
365. *Ibid.*, paragraph 7.69.
366. For a critical view of the conclusion adopted by the Panel, *see*, for instance, Gad (2008), "TRIPS Dispute Settlement and Developing Countries Interests," in: Correa/Yusuf (eds.), *Intellectual Property and International Trade: The TRIPS Agreement*, Kluwer Law International BV, The Netherlands, pp. 331-383.

As criticized by *Bartelt*, "the Panel followed a strict approach and consequently did not implement Articles 7 and 8, and this was widely criticized."[367]

2.4 *Compulsory License (Article 31 TRIPS)*

The best known "flexibility" regarding patent rights is that which regards so-called compulsory licensing. It concerns a license that a public organ grants to a third company, under certain circumstances, thereby allowing that company to make and to sell a patented product without the patent owner's approval. In the case of medicine, this third company would be legally permitted to manufacture a so-called generic medicine, although the patent protection period had not yet expired. According to *Reichman*, it was "thanks largely to the fortitude and analytical skills of the Indian delegation, the right of governments to grant compulsory licenses on virtually any ground—including public interest, abuse or anti-competitive conduct, or for non-commercial government use, among others—issued stronger and clearer from the TRIPS Agreement than had previously been the case under the Paris Convention."[368]

Justification for a compulsory license is mostly based on public interest, but this is not necessarily the only ground for it.[369] The patent law of most countries authorizes using compulsory licenses in order to protect the public interest.[370] This justifies a cancelation of an exclusive right to make and market in consideration of the general public interest by means of the payment of remuneration to the patent owner. This remuneration, however, is not provided according to his losses. Under Article 31(h) TRIPS, "the right holder shall be paid adequate remuneration in the circumstances of each case, taking into account the economic value of the authorization." The TRIPS agreement does not have any criteria to determine adequate remuneration. In the WHO's guidelines, there are some examples of adequate remuneration. Depending on the methods, royalties vary from less than 1 percent up to 6 percent of the market price.[371] According to *Love*, the guidelines from the 2001 United Nations Development

367. Bartelt (2003), "Compulsory Licenses Pursuant to TRIPS Article 31 in the Light of the Doha Declaration on the TRIPS Agreement and Public Health," 6 *JWIP*, 286-287.
368. Reichman (2010), "Compulsory Licensing of Patented Pharmaceutical Inventions: Evaluating the Options," in Correa (ed.) *Research Handbook on the Protection of IP under WTO Rules*, Edward Elgar, Cheltenham, p. 597.
369. Reichman (2006), *Procuring Essential Medicines under the Amended TRIPS Provisions: The Prospects for Regional Pharmaceutical Supply Centers*, Paper prepared for the Seminar on Intellectual Property Arrangements, UNCTAD, Geneva, Switzerland October 18-20, 2006, p. 6: "In particular, the power of Members to impose compulsory licenses for virtually any grounds survived the Uruguay Round, largely because United States law and practice continues to rely heavily on compulsory licenses of patented inventions for governmental use."
370. Abbott (2005a), "Managing the Hydra: The Herculean task of ensuring access to essential medicines," in: Maskus/Reichman (eds.), *International Public Goods and Transfer of Technology under a Globalized Intellectual Property Regime*, CUP, Cambridge, p. 411.
371. Correa (2007c), *Trade-Related Aspects of Intellectual Property Rights: A Commentary on the TRIPS Agreement*, OUP, Oxford et al., p. 323.

Programme (UNDP) recommend a normal royalty of 4 percent of the generic price, with possible alterations of up to 2 percent.[372]

Compulsory licenses can play a very important role in the question of access to medicines in developing countries. This is so because, in the case of an emergency, poor countries might grant compulsory licenses in order to supply their populations with necessary medicines. But it is not only in developing countries that compulsory licenses are granted. There are numerous examples of compulsory licenses having been granted in industrial countries, even though mostly these licenses were not based on patent legislation but on antitrust legislation.[373] According to *Rosenberg*, compulsory licenses based on antitrust legislation are frequently used in the U.S. as an instrument for correcting competition problems, although, in the medicines market, they are seldom used.[374]

In accordance with Article 31 TRIPS, compulsory licenses may be granted, for instance, in the following cases:

(1) in the case of a "national emergency or other circumstances of extreme urgency";[375]
(2) in case of public non-commercial use;[376]
(3) to remedy anti-competitive practices;[377]
(4) to permit the exploitation of a patent ("the second patent"), which cannot be exploited without infringing another patent ("the first patent").[378]

Article 31 TRIPS provides for certain formal conditions for the grant of compulsory licenses, such as, for instance, the need to try in advance to agree on a compromise solution with the rights holder, except in cases of national emergency or public noncommercial use. Article 31 refers here to the above-named special grounds for granting a compulsory license. Nevertheless, contracting parties' right to grant compulsory licenses based on other grounds is not limited.[379]

In accordance with Article 31(f) TRIPS, products made under compulsory licenses should be "predominantly for the supply of the domestic market." This is not explicitly applicable in the case of anticompetitive compulsory licenses (Article 31(k)

372. Love (2006b), "Four Practical Measures to Enhance Access to Medical Technologies," in: Roffe/Tansey/Vivas-Eugui (eds.), *Negotiating Health*, Earthscan, London, p. 247.
373. Love (2006a), *Letter asking USTR not to interfere with the Thai government decision to issue a government-use license on patents covering the AIDS drug Efavirenz.*
374. Rosenberg (2004), *Patentes de Medicamentos e Comércio Internacional para a Outorga de Licenças Compulsórias*, PhD Thesis, Universidade de São Paulo, pp. 197-198. She cites three cases of compulsory licenses granted in the USA, which were based on antitrust legislation and the objective of which was to correct competition problems in the pharmaceutical market. One of the cited compulsory licenses was granted by the Federal Trade Commission, when the pharmaceutical companies Ciba-Geigy and Sandoz went into fusion in 1997.
375. Article 31(b) TRIPS.
376. Article 31(b) TRIPS.
377. Article 31(k) TRIPS.
378. Article 31(l) TRIPS.
379. Correa (2007c), *Trade-Related Aspects of Intellectual Property Rights: A Commentary on the TRIPS Agreement*, OUP, Oxford et al., p. 14.

TRIPS). The question of whether compulsory licenses based on anti-competition legislation may be granted in order to improve access to medicine for poor people in the developing world is also discussed in the literature.[380] Such licenses require, as an additional requirement, the presence of a violation of competition rights. However, in most developing countries, compulsory licenses based on competition law are not available, either because most of them have no competition law system[381] or because their systems are not mature enough. In the Brazilian case, for instance, legal instruments for granting such compulsory licenses are formally available, but they have never been used.

Provision (f) of Article 31(f) has been especially controversial because it contains a restriction for the least developed countries (LDCs). The problem was that generic medicines produced under compulsory licenses could not be exported to poor countries. Because of this restriction, LDCs were excluded from the benefits of compulsory licensing since they were not able to produce medicines of their own. Only a few developing countries possess a pharmaceutical industry. Most developing countries had tended to import basic medicines at cheap prices from India, which therefore came to be known as the "pharmacy of the poor." The latter country, however, has been bound to TRIPS since 2005, so it is no longer legally allowed to supply other countries with generic versions of patented medicines.

2.5 *The Doha Declaration*

2.5.1 Negotiating History

At the beginning of the new round of negotiation at the WTO in Doha in 2001, developing countries were still avoiding using patent flexibilities negotiated under TRIPS because opposition to their use from industrial countries was frequent.[382] Developing countries were, therefore, afraid of suffering economic sanctions due to the granting of compulsory licenses. The fact that the South African Pharmaceutical Association had sued the South African state in the year 1998 due to the use of parallel imports contributed to this fear.[383] The same is true of the WTO dispute between Brazil and the U.S. about a compulsory license provision contained within Brazilian patent law. *Hoen* reported that the emphasis on public health needs over trade interests given by the WHO in a guide published with recommendations for developing countries regarding TRIPS' implementation "was seen as threat to the commercial sector of the industrialized world."[384] According to her, in 1998, in response to a draft resolution

380. Godt (2007a), "The So-called 'Waiver Compromise' of Doha and Hong Kong: About Contested Concepts of the Nature of the International Intellectual Property System—A Comment," in: Govaere/Ullrich (eds.), *Intellectual Property, Public Policy and International Trade*, Peter Lang, Frankfurt et al., pp. 212-217.
381. *Ibid.*, fn. 67, p. 216.
382. *Ibid.*, fn. 4, p. 202.
383. Oh (2006), "Compulsory Licenses: Recent Experiences in Developing Countries," 1 *IJIPM* 1-2, 23.
384. Hoen (2009), *The Global Politics of Pharmaceutical Monopoly Power*, AMB, p. 17.

prepared by the WHO, the Directorate General for Trade (DG Trade) of the EU concluded: "No priority should be given to health over intellectual property considerations."[385] In the same line, the position supported by the pharmaceutical industry was absolutely opposite to the position supported by governments of developing countries. *Rozek*, for instance, advocated that compulsory license "undermines any regime for protecting IPRs" and that "the AIDS crisis in Africa or other health care problems in the developing world, such as tuberculosis or malaria, will have a greater possibility of being solved by protecting IPRs."[386]

The problematic Article 31(f) TRIPS provision, which made access to medicines in LDCs more difficult, justified the demands to reform TRIPS made by developing countries as part of the Doha Development Agenda negotiations. In June 2001, a group of developing countries presented a draft document to the TRIPS Council, the objective of which was to discuss the relationship between access to medicines and intellectual property. These demands were rejected, for instance, by the U.S., which opposed any flexibilization of patent rights at the beginning of the Doha Round.

This scenario changed after the terrorist attacks of 9/11 in New York when the position defended by the American delegation concerning compulsory licenses became incompatible with the political reaction of the Bush administration concerning bioterrorism. In fact, in September and October 2001, American congresspersons received letters that contained the anthrax bacteria, which infected 22 people and killed 5 of them.[387] At the time, the U.S. administration threatened to issue a compulsory license against the antibiotic Cipro, which was under patent protection. The Bush administration threatened the German company Bayer, which owned the Cipro patent, to issue a compulsory license in order to make possible imports from generic versions of the patented drug from India.[388] The German company and the Bush administration entered negotiations, and, at the end of the day, the company offered a price discount, which was accepted by the U.S. Health and Human Service Department.[389] Although a compulsory license of a patented medicine was avoided, the American position at Doha was seriously weakened. The fact is that in November 2001, the WTO Conference of Ministries had recognized that WTO members had the right to disregard patent rights

385. *Ibid.*
386. Rozek (2000), "The Effect of Compulsory Licensing on Innovation and Access to Health Care," 3 *JWIP* 6, 912.The author was, at the time, the Senior Vice President at National Economic Research Associates, Inc. (NERA).
387. Maggie Fox (2011), "After 9/11, Anthrax Attacks Seemed Too Natural," *National J.*, September 1.
388. Moore (2006), "Parallel Trade, Unparallel Laws: An Examination of the Pharmaceutical Parallel Trade Laws of the United States, the European Union and the World Trade Organization," 6 *Rich. J. Global L. & Bus.*, 91; La Croix/Liu (2007), "Patents and Access to Essential Medicines," in: Maskus (ed.), *Intellectual Property, Growth and Trade*, Maskus (ed.), *Intellectual Property, Growth and Trade*, Emerald Group Publishing Limited, Amsterdam, p. 452.
389. Fleischer-Beck (2002), "The Cipro Dilemma—In the Anthrax Crisis, Tommy Thompson Distorted Patent Law to Save Public Health. Good Move?," *The American Lawyer*, January 2002; Hestermeyer (2007), *Human Rights and the WTO*, p. 16.

to protect public health—and had done so in the document known as Doha Declaration.[390]

2.5.2 The Substantive Provisions of the Declaration on the TRIPS Agreement and Public Health (Doha Declaration)

The core provision of the Doha Declaration is inserted in its paragraph 4, which states:

> 4. We agree that the TRIPS Agreement does not and should not prevent Members from taking measures to protect public health. Accordingly, while reiterating our commitment to the TRIPS Agreement, we affirm that the Agreement can and should be interpreted and implemented in a manner supportive of WTO Members' right to protect public health and, in particular, to promote access to medicines for all.
>
> In this connection, we reaffirm the right of WTO Members to use, to the full, the provisions in the TRIPS Agreement, which provide flexibility for this purpose.[391]

Paragraph 5 exemplifies the considerations one has to have in mind when interpreting the flexibilities ruled on in the TRIPS Agreement. It states, for instance, that these flexibilities include the following:

a) by interpreting the TRIPS Agreement, each provision should be read in the light of the object and purpose of the Agreement as expressed, in particular, in its objectives and principles,[392]
b) the right that each Member has to grant compulsory licenses and the freedom to determine the grounds upon which such licenses are granted,[393]
c) the right that each Member has to determine what constitutes a national emergency or other circumstances of extreme urgency,[394]
d) the freedom that each Member has to establish its own regime for exhaustion of intellectual property rights.[395]

Paragraph 6 of the Doha Declaration also contains a very important provision since it addressed the problem of those WTO members without a pharmaceutical sector, for whom the TRIPS provisions concerning compulsory licenses might not be helpful. According to paragraph 6 of the Doha Declaration, the TRIPS Council should find an "expeditious" solution for this problem. A provisional decision for it was found in 2003 in Cancun.[396] After hard negotiations between the group of developing

390. Hoen (2009), *The Global Politics of Pharmaceutical Monopoly Power—Drug Patents, Access, Innovation and the Application of the WTO Doha Declaration on TRIPS and Public Health*, AMB, Universiteit van Amsterdam, pp. 29-30; Shanker (2002b), "The Vienna Convention on the Law of the Treaties, the Dispute Settlement of the WTO and the Doha Declaration on the TRIPS Agreement," 36 *JWLT*, 759.
391. WTO (2001b), WTO Doc. WT/MIN (01) DEC/2 of November 20, 2001.
392. *Ibid.*, paragraph 5(a).
393. *Ibid.*, paragraph 5(b).
394. *Ibid.*, paragraph 5(c).
395. *Ibid.*, paragraph 5(d).
396. WTO (2003), Implementation of Paragraph 6 of the Doha Declaration on the TRIPS Agreement and Public Health (WTO Doc. WT/L/540 of September 2, 2003).

countries and the group of industrial countries, they reached a compromise of not applying Article 31(f) TRIPS in the case of compulsory licenses of patented medicines, if these are granted in order to combat problems of public health in LDCs. By way of a decision from December 2005, WTO members made this solution permanent, and it became the first amendment to the TRIPS Agreement,[397] by which Article 31*bis* TRIPS was introduced. This amendment came into force in January 2017.[398]

2.5.3 Legal Status and Effects of the Doha Declaration

The first important point of this declaration is the fact that it took the form of an agreement. As suggested by *Abbott*, this should be interpreted as a "decision" of the members under Article IX:1 WTO Agreement.[399] *Correa* shares this opinion by stressing that "the Doha Declaration is a strong political statement that can make it easier for developing countries to adopt measures necessary to ensure access to health care without the fear of being dragged into a legal battle. The Declaration is also a Ministerial decision with legal effects on the Member States and on the WTO bodies, particularly the Dispute Settlement Body and the Council for TRIPS."[400]

If, however, the Doha Declaration is not a formal "decision" in this sense, it must be, at least, a "subsequent agreement" on the method of the application of the Agreement within the meaning of Article 31.3. (a) VCLT.[401]

In this sense, the effects of the Doha Declaration in the interpretation of the TRIPS Agreement are numerous. Due to its nature as an agreement made in order to guide the interpretation of a prior agreement, it must be taken into consideration in every question concerning tensions and the balance of rights of patent owners and the public health. Besides, since the Doha Declaration, the role played by Articles 7 and 8 TRIPS is now more than a mere norm of declaratory content, as stated by the WTO-Dispute Settlement Body (DSB). As *Grosse Ruse-Khan* puts it, "as to its substance, the Declaration places emphasis on Articles 7 and 8 TRIPS as tools for interpretation and implementation of TRIPS tailored to the domestic needs for a balance between incentives for new innovations and their transfer and dissemination to the public."[402]

The view that the Doha Declaration is a "subsequent agreement," and as such, it modified TRIPS interpretation, was for the first time adopted by the WTO panel on

397. WTO (2005), WTO Doc. WT/L/641 8 December 2005, Amendment to the TRIPS Agreement.
398. WTO (2017), WTO: 2017 News Items (January 23, 2017)—TRIPS: WTO IP rules amended to ease poor countries' access to affordable medicines.
399. Abbott (2002), "The Doha Declaration on the TRIPS Agreement and Public Health: Lighting a Dark Corner at the WTO," 5 *JIEL*, 469.
400. Correa (2002), *Implications of the Doha Declaration on the TRIPS Agreement and Public Health*, WHO, *Geneva*, p. 44.
401. *See* Correa (2002), *Implications of the Doha Declaration on the TRIPS Agreement and Public Health*, WHO, Geneva, p. 45; Grosse Ruse-Khan (2008), "Proportionality and Balancing Within the Objectives for Intellectual Property Protection," in: Torremans (ed.), *Intellectual Property and Human Rights (Enhanced Edition of Copyright and Human Rights)*, Kluwer Law International, BV, Alphen aan den Rijn, p. 184.
402. Grosse Ruse-Khan (2008), "Proportionality and Balancing within the Objectives for Intellectual Property Protection," in: Torremans (ed.), *Intellectual Property and Human Rights*, Kluwer Law International, BV, Alphen aan den Rijn, p. 187.

August 28, 2018. In this dispute, the panel decided whether measures concerning restrictions imposed by Australian laws on trademarks and geographical indications regarding tobacco products and their packaging were consistent with the TRIPS Agreement, as reproduced below:

> 7.2407. We note in this respect that the Doha Declaration, adopted by Ministers on 14 November 2001, provides that, "[i]n applying the customary rules of interpretation of public international law, each provision of the TRIPS Agreement shall be read in the light of the object and purpose of the Agreement as expressed, in particular, in its objectives and principles."
>
> 7.2408. While this statement was made in the specific context of a re-affirmation by Members of the flexibilities provided in the TRIPS Agreement in relation to measures taken for the protection of public health, we note that paragraph 5 of the Doha Declaration is formulated in general terms, inviting the interpreter of the TRIPS Agreement to read "each provision of the TRIPS Agreement" in the light of the object and purpose of the Agreement, as expressed in particular in its objectives and principles. As described above, Articles 7 and 8 have central relevance in establishing the objectives and principles that, according to the Doha Declaration, express the object and purpose of the TRIPS Agreement relevant to its interpretation.
>
> 7.2409. This paragraph of the Doha Declaration may, in our view, be considered to constitute a "subsequent agreement" of WTO Members within the meaning of Article 31(3)(a) of the Vienna Convention. As the Appellate Body has clarified: Based on the text of Article 31(3)(a) of the Vienna Convention, we consider that a decision adopted by Members may qualify as a "subsequent agreement between the parties" regarding the interpretation of a covered agreement or the application of its provisions if: (i) the decision is, in a temporal sense, adopted subsequent to the relevant covered agreement; and (ii) the terms and content of the decision express an agreement between Members on the interpretation or application of a provision of WTO law.
>
> 7.2410. In this instance, the instrument at issue is a "declaration" rather than a "decision." However, the Doha Declaration was adopted by a consensus decision of WTO Members, at the highest level, on 14 November 2001 on the occasion of the Fourth Ministerial Conference of the WTO, subsequent to the adoption of the WTO Agreement, Annex 1C of which comprises the TRIPS Agreement. The terms and contents of the decision adopting the Doha Declaration express, in our view, an agreement between Members on the approach to be followed in interpreting the provisions of the TRIPS Agreement. This agreement, rather than reflecting a particular interpretation of a specific provision of the TRIPS Agreement, confirms the manner in which "each provision" of the Agreement must be interpreted, and thus "bears specifically" on the interpretation of each provision of the TRIPS Agreement.
>
> 7.2411. The guidance provided by the Doha Declaration is consistent, as the Declaration itself suggests, with the applicable rules of interpretation, which require a treaty interpreter to take account of the context and object and purpose of the treaty being interpreted, and confirms in our view that

> Articles 7 and 8 of the TRIPS Agreement provide important context for the interpretation of Article 20.[403]

In any case, the Doha Declaration is a very important tool with which to minimize the impact of pharmaceutical patents in the developing world. Its implementation, however, is not automatic, and it is technically difficult. Developing countries must be active and introduce flexibility instruments in their national law, including the possibility of "back-to-back compulsory licenses" according to their individual circumstances.[404]

2.6 *Special Compulsory License System (Article 31bis TRIPS)*

As mentioned above, Article 31*bis,* as well the Annex and the Appendix to the TRIPS Agreement, was added to the TRIPS Agreement by the Amendment originated from paragraph 6 of the Doha Declaration, which came to force in January 2017. By waiving the obligation contained in Article 31(f) TRIPS—which determines as a condition for the grant of compulsory license that the use of the patented product must be predominantly for the supply of the domestic market—Article 31*bis* (1) allows that countries without the capacity to manufacture pharmaceuticals also make use of compulsory licenses. In this scheme, a compulsory license must be issued both by the country that will import the drug, as well by the country which will produce and export the drug for the benefit of the country in need.

According to Article 31*bis* (2), "adequate remuneration" should be paid only by the exporting member to the patent owner when using this special compulsory license mechanism, also known as "back to back compulsory licenses." According to Article 1b of the Annex to the TRIPS Agreement, some countries have agreed not to use the system as importing members,[405] while others have stated that, if they use the system, it would be in no more than situations of national emergency or other circumstances of extreme urgency.[406]

Both importing and exporting members, when using this special compulsory license mechanism, must comply with the requirements determined by the Annex to the TRIPS Agreement, which regulates it in detail. The mechanism has been criticized

403. Australia—Certain Measures Concerning Trademarks, Geographical Indications and other Plain Packaging Requirements applicable to Tobacco Products and Packaging—Report of the Panels, WTO-Document: WT/DS435, WT/DS441/R, WT/DS458/R, WT/DS467/R of June 28, 2018.
404. *See* Timmermans (2006), "Ensuring Access to Medicines in 2005 and Beyond," in: Roffe et al. (eds.), *Negotiating Health—Intellectual Property Rights and Access to Medicines,* Earthscan, USA, pp. 61-62.
405. These countries are the following ones: Australia, Canada, the European Communities with, for the purposes of Article 31*bis* and this Annex, its Member States, Iceland, Japan, New Zealand, Norway, Switzerland, and the United States, in accordance with Article 1b, Footnote 3 Annex to the TRIPS Agreement.
406. *See* WTO (2005), *WTO 2005 Press Release 6 December 2005—Members OK amendment to make health flexibility permanent.* These countries are the following ones: Hong Kong China, Israel, Korea, Kuwait, Macao China, Mexico, Qatar, Singapore, Chinese Taipei, Turkey and United Arab Emirates.

due to the bureaucratic obstacles it imposes for its use, usually seen as unnecessary,[407] was so far only used by Canada and Rwanda.[408] There was a second attempt to use it by India and Nepal, but it failed because Nepal did not formally notify the WTO, so that the Indian company Natco withdrew its compulsory license applications.[409] As reported by *Stirner and Thangaraj*, "attempts by Natco to convince the least developed State to initiate this process remained unsuccessful. The reasons for Nepal's reluctance are not documented."[410]

2.7 Right to Delay Implementation (Article 65 TRIPS)

All WTO members were given a general period of one year following the date of entry into force of the WTO Agreement (January 1, 1995) to implement TRIPS, regardless of whether the member was an industrial or a developing country.[411] As part of the compromise solution, developing countries[412] and former socialist countries,[413] however, were given the right to delay implementation for a further period of four years. Additionally, developing countries could also delay for five more years (until January 1, 2005) the duty to introduce patent protection for products not protectable under their national patent law.[414]

As mentioned above, the right to delay implementation was not absolute during the transitional periods since developing country members were obliged to introduce transitional patent protection for pharmaceutical and agricultural chemical products ("mailbox protection") as of day one.[415] In practice, just a few countries made full use of the transitional periods. India, for instance, did so and defended the view that the duty to introduce mailbox protection was incompatible with the right to delay implementation since it would neutralize it. Because of this position, the U.S. initiated—and won—panel proceedings against India at the WTO.[416]

---

407. *See*, for instance, Urias (2015), *Improving Access to HIV/AIDS Treatment in Brazil—When Are Compulsory Licenses Effective in Price Negotiations?* University of Maastricht, pp. 54-56.
408. *See*, for instance, *Anderson* (2009), "Unnecessary Deaths and Unnecessary Costs: Getting Patented Drugs to Patients Most in Need," *29 BCTWLJ* 85, 105-106.
409. Stirner/Thangaraj (2013), "Learning from Practice: Compulsory License Cases and Access to Medicines," 2 *Pharmaceutical Pat. Analyst* 2, p. 201.
410. *Ibid.*
411. Article 65.1 TRIPS.
412. Article 65.2 TRIPS.
413. Article 65.3 TRIPS.
414. Article 65.4 TRIPS.
415. Article 70.8 TRIPs.
416. WTO (1997), India—Patent Protection for Pharmaceutical and Agricultural Chemical Products—AB-1997-5—Report of the Appellate Body, WTO-Document: WT/DS50/AB R of December 19, 1997.

IV Post-TRIPs Demands, TRIPS-Plus Provisions and the Developing Countries' Right to Use Flexibilities

As seen in the preceding chapters, the TRIPS Agreement imposed higher levels of patent protection on developing countries, but, at the same time, it left room for flexibilities, so that they should still be able to shape a patent policy that fit their necessities, in accordance to their creativity. The reality, however, has shown that developing countries often are pressurized by industrialized countries not to exercise such freedom by accepting or introducing into their internal laws patent standards, which TRIPS does not oblige them to accept.[417]

This is the case of free trade agreements (FTAs), mostly agreed between the U.S. and developing countries, where the weak party renounces such freedoms. For instance, in the bilateral agreements negotiated between the U.S. and Chile, as well as with Australia and Jordan, the latter countries obliged themselves, for instance, to restrict the cases in which a compulsory license may be issued.[418] On the same token, the USTR exercised strong pressure on developing countries in order to persuade them both not to make use of the transitional period[419] or forcing them to introduce pipeline patent protection, as they did, for instance, with Brazil.[420] Other issues focused on by such FTAs include the following: (a) providing for more extensive patent protection (e.g., by imposing the duty to grant patents for new medical uses of known substances); (b) prohibiting the revocation of patents; and (c) restricting parallel importation.[421]

Promoters of TRIPS-plus IP protection have additionally developed other strategies to persuade developing countries not to use TRIPS' flexibilities and to voluntarily introduce stronger patent protection. *Dutfield* calls such rhetoric "the new intellectual property fundamentalism" and provides a summary of this. In his words, these strategies include the following:

417. About the political pressure exerted on governments to limit the use of TRIPS flexibilities, *see*, for instance, UNSGHLPAM (2016), *Report of the United Nations Secretary-General's High Level Panel on Access to Medicines: Promoting Innovation and Access to High Technologies*, pp. 7-9.
418. *See* Abbott (2005b), "The WTO Medicines Decision: World Pharmaceutical Trade and the Protection of Public Health," 99 *Am. J. Int'l L.*, 349-351. Especially concerning Jordan *see* Malkawi (2009), "Patent Protection and the Pharmaceutical Industry in Jordan," 4 *Asian J. WTO and Int'l Health L. & Pol'y*, 93-127.
419. *See*, for instance, Drahos (2002), "Negotiating Intellectual Property Rights: Between Coercion and Dialogue," in: Drahos/Mayne (eds.), *Global Intellectual Property Rights—Knowledge, Access and Development*, Palgrave Macmillan, p. 178.
420. Arslanian/Lyrio (1995), "A Reforma da Lei de Patentes no Brasil e as Pressões Norte-Americanas na Área de Propriedade Intelectual," 4 *Política Externa* 2, 3-12; Cepaluni (2005), "Regimes Internacionais e o Contencioso das Patentes para Medicamentos: Estratégias para Países em Desenvolvimento," 27 *Contexto Internacional* 1, 74.
421. *See*, for instance, Kuanpoth (2008), "Intellectual Property Protection after TRIPS: An Asian Experience," in: Malbon/Lawson (eds.), *Interpreting and Implementing the TRIPS Agreement: Is it Fair?*, Edward Elgar, Cheltenham (UK), p. 74; Muzaka (2009), "Dealing with Public Health and Intellectual Property for Pharmaceuticals at the World Trade Organization," in: MacLean et al. (eds.), *Health for Some—The Political Economy of Global Health Governance*, Palgrave Macmillan, pp. 183-195.

(1) "missionary work", *including the sending of business associations and WIPO experts to developing countries by developed countries' governments, to spread the IP gospel,*
(2) *the* dissemination of propaganda *extoling the virtues of intellectual property, and claiming that IP piracy is inimical to development, that it deters investment, that it is immoral or unfair, or that it supports terrorism activities,*
(3) technical assistance *provided by international organizations, developed countries' governmental agencies and IP offices, business and law associations,*
(4) *latent or overt trade threats and intimidation by rich countries towards poor countries that they accuse of piracy, of having "inadequate" IP systems, or even of openly considering issuing a compulsory license.*[422]

In this context, measures aiming at the greater global alignment of patent rights, such as the WIPO's proposed Substantive Patent Law Treaty (SPLT), are harmful to developing countries.[423] As *Reichman* and *Dreyfuss* suggest, such harmonization efforts would "shrink the remaining flexibilities in the TRIPS Agreement."[424] Consequently, developing countries should continue to resist the SPLT.[425]

C THE BRAZILIAN HEALTH INNOVATION SYSTEM

I National Systems of Innovation

All countries in the world make efforts to achieve or maintain an innovation-driven economic growth, which they do based on what economists call a "national system of innovation." *Mazzucato and Penna*, for instance, wrote that "a broad perspective on the national system of innovation identifies four subsystems: (i) public policy and public funding; (ii) research and education; (iii) the subsystem of production and innovation; and (iv) private finance and private funding. While all subsystems are theoretically of strategic importance, the subsystem of public policy and funding has traditionally led the process of socio-economic development and technical change."[426]

Patent protection, as it is well-known, is included in a major system of innovation. In this section, the Brazilian national health system of innovation will be shortly examined, in order to understand the Brazilian strategy of balancing the need to make affordable medicines for all, and, at the same time, protect pharmaceutical patents, as demanded by the TRIPS Agreement.

---

422. Dutfield (2008), "Knowledge Diplomacy and the New Intellectual Property Fundamentalism," in Malbon (ed.) *Interpreting and Implementing the TRIPS Agreement: Is it Fair?*, Edward Elgar, Cheltenham, pp. 34-35.
423. *See* Barton (2004), "Issues Posed by a World Patent System," 7 *JIEL*, 344.
424. *See* Reichman/Dreyfuss (2007), "Harmonization without Consensus: Critical Reflections on Drafting a Substantive Patent Law Treaty," 57 *Duke L. J.*, 85-130.
425. *See* Reichman (2009b), "Intellectual Property in the Twenty-First Century: Will the Developing Countries Lead or Follow?," 46 *Houston L. Rev.*, 1134.
426. Mazzucato & Penna (2016), *The Brazilian Innovation System: A Mission-Oriented Policy Proposal*, CGEE, Brasília, p. 29.

II Brazilian National Health System of Innovation

1 Country Overview

With circa 211 million inhabitants and covering approximately 8.5 million km^2, Brazil is the biggest and the most populated nation in Latin America. Its Gross Domestic Product (GDP) in 2019 was around USD 1.839 trillion,[427] the largest in Latin America and the ninth largest in the world.[428]

Until the 1950s, the Brazilian economy was based on exports of commodities, such as coffee, sugar, and cotton as the main products. It was during the Vargas Administration (1930-1945) that the country started a public policy of import substitution, which led to a successful industrialization process with a diversified industrial base. This policy continued until the 1980s when it was interrupted due to an economic crisis, which prevented the import substitution efforts from continuing.[429]

Despite being one of the top 10 world economies in terms of GDP, there is still much poverty in Brazil. With a Gross National Income (GNI) per capita of USD 9,130, Brazil is classified as belonging to the group of upper-middle-income countries, along with China, Russia, Turkey, Mexico, among others.[430] This corresponds to the 77th position worldwide.[431] Historically, Brazil has long been known to have one of the more unequal income distributions in the world. In accordance with the Gini coefficient, which measures how income among a population is distributed among a population, in 2017, Brazil was the eighth worst in the world.[432] This position, however, has considerably improved in the last few years, thanks to recent social policies of income distribution to the poor, and as a result, Brazil is classified as a country of "high human development." Nevertheless, 26.5 percent of all Brazilian families were living below the national poverty line in 2016.[433]

According to the United Nations, circa one-quarter of the Brazilian population live in precarious habitations (*favelas*); this amounts to circa 50 million people.[434] The amount of Brazilians who do not have access to a sewage system is very high: according to official national data, in 2017, only 53 percent of the households were connected to such a system.[435]

---

427. The World Bank, *Data by Country*.
428. The World Bank, *Ranking GDP*.
429. Mazzucato & Penna (2016), *The Brazilian Innovation System: A Mission-Oriented Policy Proposal*, Brasília, p. 37.
430. The World Bank, *Data by Country*.
431. The World Bank, *Gross National Income Per Capita 2019*.
432. UNDP (2016), *Human Development Report 2016*, p. 216.
433. The World Bank, *Poverty Headcount Ratio at National Poverty Lines (% of Population)*.
434. O Globo (2011), *Brasil reduziu população das favelas em 16% de 2000 a 2010*, diz relatório da ONU, October 9.
435. Sistema Nacional de Informações sobre Saneamento (SNIS 2017), available at http://www.tratabrasil.org.br/saneamento/principais-estatisticas/no-brasil/esgoto (last visited on May 2, 2019).

2 The Pharmaceutical Industry in Brazil

2.1 Historical Development

The Brazilian pharmaceutical industry started developing in the nineteenth century when the production of drugs was artisanal and took place in small firms called *boticas*.[436] Moved by public health concerns of the time, the federal administration was already involved in the production of pharmaceutical products. It did so by creating several public institutions, the objective of which was research into and production of vaccines and serum. The more renowned of these were the Instituto Butantan (1889) in São Paulo and the Instituto Osvaldo Cruz in Rio de Janeiro (1902), both of which still exist today.[437] As time went by, public laboratories and small firms interacted, resulting in the creation of a relatively innovative industry in the field of biological products, the peak of which occurred in the 1930s.[438]

From the 1940s onward, the modern global pharmaceutical industry, which had just been born in Europe and in the U.S., would become ever more active in Brazil. This presence would cause a decisive shift concerning the dominant position of the domestic industry in Brazil. The market share in pharmaceuticals that was enjoyed by foreign industry pharmaceuticals in the Brazilian market increased from 13.6 percent in 1930 to 33.5 percent in 1940 and to 47.1 percent in 1950.[439] This period—which is referred to in the literature as the "denationalization period"—was marked by two characteristics: first, by the lack of technical capacity of the Brazilian pharmaceutical industry to synthesize drugs from chemical substances; and second, the fact many Brazilian firms were systematically absorbed by U.S. and European pharmaceutical firms.[440] This trend became stronger from the 1950s onward when more representatives of the multinational pharmaceutical industry started to open up subsidiaries in Brazil. They were attracted by a federal policy of the time, the objective of which was to incentivize foreign direct investment (FDI).[441] Since then, the pharmaceutical industry in Brazil has been strongly internationalized. Although necessary, the FDI policies hindered the development of the domestic pharmaceutical industrial industry since "foreign multinationals moved heavily to Brazil, exporting raw materials and setting up low costs manufacturing with imported equipment."[442] According to

436. Queiroz (1993), *Os determinantes da capacitação tecnológica no setor químico-farmacêutico brasileiro*, PhD Thesis, Department of Economics, UNICAMP, p. 105.
437. Urias (2015), *Improving Access to HIV/AIDS Treatment in Brazil—When Are Compulsory Licenses Effective in Price Negotiations?* Doctoral thesis presented to the University of Maastricht, pp. 69-70.
438. Furtado/Urias (2010), *Estudio Sectorial, Sector farmacêutico de Brasil: A Evolução da Indústria Farmacêutica no Brasil: elementos para uma caracterização dos movimentos recentes, com ênfase nas políticas de inovação* (Centro Redes).
439. Queiroz (1993), *Os determinantes da capacitação tecnológica no setor químico-farmacêutico brasileiro*, PhD Thesis, Department of Economics, UNICAMP, p. 106.
440. *Ibid.*, pp. 105-107.
441. Palmeira/Pan (2003), "Cadeia Farmacêutica no Brasil: Avaliação Preliminar e Perspectivas," 18 *BNDES Setorial*, Rio de Janeiro, 12-13.
442. Thach et al. (2014),"Accession to TRIPS and Engagement with the Pharmaceutical Industry," *Ethics & Bus. L. Fac. Publications*, p. 71.

Palmeira and *Pan*, the participation of the international industry in the Brazilian production of pharmaceutical products was equivalent to 14 percent in 1930 but had grown to 35 percent in 1950 and to 73 percent by 1960.[443] Ten years after having abolished patent protection for pharmaceutical products and processes in 1969, the 10 largest national drug companies in Brazil had increased their market share by 10 percent, although this trend, as noted by *Gereffi*, was broken when two of these national firms were acquired by transnational companies.[444] The result was the rudimentary development of the local pharmaceutical industry. As put by *Muzaka*,[445] these developments resulted in two perverse effects, namely, the "marginalization of the Brazilian pharmaceutical companies" and the "damping of dynamism and development effects in the sector."

In 1971, the Brazilian federal administration tried to incentivize domestic manufacture of pharmaceuticals with a policy characterized by the following measures: (a) the creation of the federal agency, Central Authority of Medicines, the Former Brazilian Federal Agency for Development and Procurement of Medicines (Central de Medicamentos—CEME)), the objectives of which were to implement a policy for the development of national technology and procurement of medicines which would favor the national industry;[446] (b) the creation of a National Plan of Drugs (PND), as well as a list composed of essential drugs, which was called (Relação Nacional de Medicamentos Essenciais—RENAME); (c) the imposition of high tariffs for imports of medicines and of reduced tariffs for imports of active pharmaceutical ingredients (APIs); (d) the introduction of medicine price control; (e) the reform of the patent law, which also made processes for the production of pharmaceutical products unpatentable; and (f) funding national production.[447]

Whether this medicine policy could be said to have been successful or not is controversial in the literature. *Loyola* maintains that CEME failed and that this happened due to the strong opposition to it from transnational drug companies, by way of the Brazilian Association of the Pharmaceutical Industry (*Associação Brasileira da Indústria Farmacêutica*—ABIFARMA), as well as lack of interest from the domestic pharmaceutical industry and a lack of support from doctors.[448] *Calixto* and *Siqueira* also wrote that the objectives pursued by the CEME were not reached and that this was the reason why it was abolished in 1998.[449] *Palmeira* and *Pan* share this view, adding that the cause for this failure was the fact that the national industry has not developed the ability to manufacture APIs by itself. These had been continuously imported from

443. *Ibid.*, p. 13.
444. Gereffi (1983), *The Pharmaceutical Industry and Dependency in the Third World*, Princeton, p. 229.
445. Muzaka (2018), "Interrupted Constructions—The Brazilian Health-Industrial Complex in Historical Perspective," 10 *Latin Am. Persp.*
446. Brazil (1971a), Decreto 68.806, June 25, 1971.
447. MoH/MDIC (2007): *Fórum de Competitividade da Cadeia Produtiva Farmacêutica 2003-2006: o desafio a prosseguir*, p. 13.
448. Loyola (2008), "Medicamentos e saúde pública em tempos de AIDS: metamorfoses de uma política dependente," 13 *Ciência e Saúde Coletiva (Suplemento)*, 766.
449. Calixto/Siqueira (2008), "Desenvolvimento de Medicamentos no Brasil: Desafios," 78 *Gazeta Médica da Bahia (Suplemento I)*, 104.

European countries, like Spain and Italy.[450] *Queiroz*, however, shows that measures to technically enable the domestic industry to produce APIs, even if forgotten during the 1970s, had been implemented in the 1980s with relative success; he provides evidence for this partial success with the fact that 61 percent of all APIs used in Brazilian medicines at that time were produced in Brazil.[451] By the same token, a report by the Ministry of Health and the Ministry of Industry, while agreeing that the protectionist policy eventually failed, shows that there were positive results in the meantime. It reported that the domestic production of APIs accounted for 55 percent of all APIs used in medicines produced in Brazil in the late 1980s.[452] According to the cited report, this development could not be maintained after the "abrupt" liberalization of the Brazilian market in the early 1990s, when again, the number of imported APIs grew.

Brazil, like a number of other emerging and developing countries, has the ability to make pharmaceutical products by itself, including the technical capacity to manufacture APIs. However, importing APIs is still cheaper than producing them locally, and therefore this technical capacity is hardly used in Brazil.[453] In 2003, 70 percent of the APIs used to produce medicines in Brazil were imported.[454] By 2010, the dependence on imports to produce drugs had increased to 80 percent.[455] In order to combat these problems and strengthen domestic API production, the current industrial policy for the sector—the PROFARMA program, sponsored by the Brazilian National Development Bank (BNDES)—tries to encourage the local production of raw material, to intensify the competitiveness of the domestic pharmaceutical industry and to encourage R & D of new products.[456] Despite all the efforts that have been made, the pharmaceutical trade

450. Palmeira/Pan (2003), "Cadeia Farmacêutica no Brasil: Avaliação Preliminar e Perspectivas," 18 *BNDES Setorial*, 14.
451. Queiroz, (1993), *Os determinantes da capacitação tecnológica no setor químico-farmacêutico brasileiro*, PhD Thesis, Department of Economics, UNICAMP, p. 135.
452. MoH/MDIC (2007): *Fórum de Competitividade da Cadeia Produtiva Farmacêutica 2003-2006: o desafio a prosseguir*, p. 11.
453. Grangeiro/Teixeira (2007), "Repercussões do acordo de Propriedade Intelectual no Acesso a Medicamentos," in: Villares (ed.), *Propriedade Intelectual: Tensões entre o capital e a sociedade*, São Paulo, pp. 128-130; Milward de Azevedo Meiners (2006), "Patentes Farmacêuticas: um entrave para o acesso a medicamentos?," 5 *Revista de Políticas Públicas e Gestão Governamental* 2, 41.
454. Palmeira/Pan (2003), "Cadeia Farmacêutica no Brasil: Avaliação Preliminar e Perspectivas," 18 *BNDES Setorial*, 18. *See also* Mazzoleni/Martins Costa Póvoa (2010), "Accumulation of Technological Capabilities and Economic Development—Did Brazil's IPR Regime Matter?," in: Odagiri et al. (eds.), *Intellectual Property Rights, Development and Catch-Up—An International Comparative Study*, OUP, Oxford, p. 304.
455. Schüren (2015), *Aufholende Entwicklung in der globalen Ökonomie—Pharmazeutische Innovationssysteme in Indien und Brasilien*, Nomos, Baden-Baden, pp. 221-222.
456. Calliari/Machado Ruiz (2014), "Brazilian Pharmaceutical Industry and Generic Drugs Policy: Impacts on Structure and Innovation and Recent Developments," 41 *Sci. & Pub. Pol'*, 248.

deficit remains very large.[457] By 2015, the dependence on imports to produce medicines had increased to 90 percent.[458]

2.2 *Market Overview*

With a value of circa USD 24.3 billion in 2019, the Brazilian pharmaceutical market is the second largest in the Americas.[459] In 2018, the Brazilian pharmaceutical market was ranked eighth in world sales and was still expanding.[460] The market is highly fragmented, with the presence and rivalry of both multinational and domestic pharmaceutical companies. In 2016, the six major players—two multinational and four domestic companies—enjoyed 27.05 percent of the market share.[461] The remaining market share was divided between more than 500 small firms, including some state-owned laboratories.

A peculiarity of the Brazilian pharmaceutical industry is the existence of a public net of pharmaceutical laboratories, the main goal of which is to produce generic medicines in order to assure the distribution of essential medicines in public hospitals, as well to produce necessary drugs deemed by the private laboratories for not profitable. There are 21 of these public laboratories, both at the federal and state levels.[462] Altogether they produce 101 different APIs, being responsible for 10 percent of the national pharmaceutical production in terms of quantity and for 3 percent of it in terms of value.[463] Most Brazilian state-owned laboratories, with the exception of Farmanguinhos and Vital Brasil, do not engage in the R & D of drugs; they only produce essential drugs that the private market does not produce.[464]

Regarding the kinds of medicines produced in Brazil, three different types of drugs for human use are sold: brand-name drugs, generic drugs (generics) and "similar drugs." The first category is used to refer to drugs which enjoy patent protection and has been offered in the Brazilian market since 1997 when the Brazilian patent act brought in to conform to TRIPS was passed. "Generics" refers to generic versions of brand-name drugs, with the innovator drug as a reference. In order to obtain a license

---

457. Marinho/Varella (2015), "La Protection des Données Générées dans le Cadre du Processus d'Autorization de Mise sur le Marché au Brésil," in: Autenne/Cassiers/Strowel (eds.), *Droit, Économie et Valeurs*, Bruxelles, p. 441; Capanema/Palmeira (2004), *Indústria Farmacêutica Brasileira: Reflexões sobre sua estrutura e potencial de investimento*, p. 191. *See also* MoH/MDIC (2007), *Fórum de Competitividade da Cadeia Produtiva Farmacêutica 2003-2006: o desafio a prosseguir*, pp. 24-25, fn. 128.

458. Almeida Rodrigues et al. (2018), "A Evolução Recente da Indústria Farmacêutica Brasileira nos Limites da Subordinação Econômica," *Physis: Revista de Saúde Coletiva* 28(1).

459. IQVIA MIDAS (2019), Top Ten Pharmaceutical World Markets.

460. *Ibid.*

461. INTERFARMA (2017), Guia 2017—Ranking de fabricantes. This data, however, only includes over-the-counter medicines, which, according to INTERFARMA, make up 59 percent of the market share.

462. Tigre et al. (2016) "Windows of Opportunity and Technological Innovation in the Brazilian Pharmaceutical Industry," 32 *Cadernos de Saúde Pública* 2, 3.

463. Bermudez/Lavra/Oliveira (2006), "A Produção Pública de Medicamentos no Brasil: Uma Visão Geral," 22 *Cadernos de Saúde Pública* 11, 2381.

464. Delgado Bastos (2006), "Laboratórios Farmacêuticos Oficiais e Doenças Negligenciadas: Perspectivas de Política Pública," 13 *Revista do BNDES* 25, 269-298.

for it to be marketed, its producers must prove "bioequivalence" with the innovator drug, according to the high standards of safety and efficacy that have been required by law since 1999.[465] This has not always been the case. Before 1999, generic drugs, in this sense, did not exist. This was so not only due to the lack of patent protection regarding innovator drugs, which also meant that health authorities did not have data on brand-name drugs that were not marketed in Brazil by the patent owner. It was also because standards of efficacy and safety were laxer at the time, and therefore, the requirement of bioequivalence did not exist at all. In the past, there was no obligation to sell drugs under the name of the pharmaceutically active substance, as is now the case. At the time, copied versions of drugs patented elsewhere were usually sold in Brazil under the name of a trademark. These drugs are legally classified as "similar drugs." Today, what distinguishes them from generic drugs is the fact that they must be commercialized under a trade name and the fact that they have not to demonstrate bioequivalence as a requirement for authorization of market entry.

2.3 Research and Development

Historically, the public sector has been the more prominent investor in R & D for health in Brazil. According to *Mello Vianna*, "between 2003 and 2005, Brazil invested USD 481 500 000 in R & D/H (in current American dollars), with an annual average of USD 493 million. The public sector invested around USD 1.1 billion, corresponding to 74.3 percent of the total expenditure in R & D/H."[466] In the period between 2008 and 2011, "the share of public financing of internal R & D activities increased substantially due to federal government policies and measures."[467]

As put by *Tigre*, "a significant share of Brazil's R & D efforts involves public laboratories, which have contributed to the development of the necessary competencies for strengthening the production and innovation base in health."[468]

The private pharmaceutical segment has not made significant investments in R & D of new pharmaceutical products in Brazil. This is true of both multinational and domestic companies. Typically, the former tend to conduct their R & D programs at their headquarters in the central countries in the North, where the availability of highly qualified workers is greater than in emerging countries like Brazil. In their turn, domestic companies tend not to have the financial capacity to support the high costs of investments in R & D. Consequently, they act predominantly in the generics and "similar" drugs area. Investment in the development of new medicines, if it exists in the domestic arena, tends to be concentrated in so-called incremental innovation research—which consists of small improvements in known inventions—or in research into phytotherapeutic products developed from plant extracts obtained from Brazilian

465. Brazil (1999b), *Lei dos Genéricos* (Lei 9.787 of February 10, 1999), DOU, February 11, 1999.
466. Mello Vianna et al. (2009), "Brazil: Financing Resource Flows in Health R & D" in Landriault/Matlin (ed.),—*Monitoring Financial Flows for Health Research 2009—Behind the Global Numbers*, Global Forum for Health Research, Geneva, p. 129.
467. Tigre et al. (2016) "Windows of Opportunity and Technological Innovation in the Brazilian Pharmaceutical Industry," 32 *Cadernos de Saúde Pública* 2, 4.
468. *Ibid.*, p. 5.

flora.[469] According to a study by the Brazilian association of innovative companies ANPEI, the pharmaceutical private sector spent only 0.53 percent of its revenue in R & D in 1998, while the average investment in innovation in all other sectors was 1.33 percent.[470] Even in the case of incremental innovation, Brazilian participation is marginal. A study carried out by *Zalfa*, for instance, found that between January 1995 and December 2007, only 1 percent of the applications filed in Brazil concerning modified release-tablets had been filed by domestic firms.[471] Although the degree of investment has grown in the last years, encouraged by official incentives, the participation of domestic private companies in the research of new drugs is very modest, so that the more significant investor in R & D in the pharmaceutical sector is still the Brazilian State.

3 *Pharmaceutical Production Policies*

Before the TRIPS Agreement, the Brazilian national production of pharmaceuticals was based on imitation, which was only possible because it was free to not grant patents for pharmaceutical patents. Like in India, pharmaceutical technology was acquired by so-called reverse engineering. By this method, chemists deformulate a pharmaceutical formulation with the aim of identifying, quantifying and characterizing the API and then reproduce the formulation as an imitative product. In the Brazilian case, reverse engineering was systematically made, for instance, by FIOCRUZ—as a public pharmaceutical laboratory—in order to produce affordable pharmaceuticals. Besides, one has to mention the creation of CODETEC (*Companhia de Desenvolvimento Tecnológico)* in 1976. The aim of this private company, which was linked to the University of Campinas (UNICAMP), was to help students and professors to create small companies able to generate appropriate technology for the Brazilian conditions.[472] In doing so, by using reverse engineering, it also made pharmaceutical technology available for all public laboratories and for every Brazilian pharmaceutical private company interested in manufacturing them.[473]

With the duty of granting pharmaceutical patents imposed by the TRIPS Agreement, Brazil could suddenly not rely more on imitation as a way of technology acquisition and had to reformulate its drug policy. As we are going to see below in detail, Brazil decided at first for a TRIPS-plus way, in the hope that a stronger patent protection regime would bring more economic growth and technological acquisition in

469. This is the case of "Acheflan," the first hundered percent national drug, launched in 2005. For more information on this, *see* Schüren (2016), *Aufholende Entwicklung in der globalen Ökonomie*, p. 265.
470. Gadelha/Quental/Fialho (2003), "Saúde e inovação: uma abordagem sistêmica das indústrias de saúde," 19 *Cadernos de Saúde Pública* 1, 52.
471. *See* Zalfa (2008), *Comprimidos de liberação modificada: análise dos pedidos de patente depositados no Brasil e da utilização destes na prática do evergreening*, Rio de Janeiro, INCQS/Fiocruz, p. 122.
472. Cerqueira Leite (2008), "CODETEC—Companhia de Desenvolvimento Tecnológico," 7 *Revista Brasileira de Inovação* 2, 484.
473. Schüren (2016), Aufholende Entwicklung in der globalen Ökonomie—Pharmazeutische Innovationssysteme in Indien und Brasilien, Nomos, Baden-Baden, pp. 216-217.

the field of pharmaceuticals. Because of that, it renounced the 10 years' period of grace, and in 1996, prematurely adopted a TRIPS-compatible patent law, making pharmaceutical inventions patentable.

Since the TRIPS Agreement has entered into force, the main form of technology acquisition in the pharmaceutical field in Brazil has been imports from industrialized countries. As highlighted by *Schüren*, the costs of imported medicines rose from USD 900 million in 1996 to USD 6 billion in 2010, making 34 percent of the Brazilian trade deficit in drugs.[474]

As a long-term measure, the federal administration created public-private partnerships in the health sector in 2009, named as "productive development partnerships" (*parcerias de desenvolvimento produtivo*—PDP). Such partnerships involve three partners: a public laboratory, a private laboratory (foreign or national) and a national laboratory able to produce API. Basically, the private company is obliged to make available for one or more public laboratories a pharmaceutical technology considered to be essential or strategic in the health sector. In return, the Ministry of Health is obliged to buy the drug in question exclusively from this private laboratory during an adjusted period. According to *Schüren*, 55 PDPs were agreed upon between 2009 and 2012.[475]

Furthermore, the central public procurement of medicines plays an important role in the health system, mainly because it creates a high demand that can be explored using public policies.[476] *Mazzucato and Penna*, who studied the Brazilian national system of innovation, identified the health sector as a strength. They highlighted that "the industrial policies for the health sector established in the last 15 years have aimed to revamp the sector, strengthening national pharmaceutical firms, and granting universal access to medication and health care, while also enabling the country to produce biological drugs (particularly existing ones with patents that are due to expire), thereby creating a biotech industry."[477]

4 *The Role of the Brazilian Universities*

As stressed by *Suzigan and Motta e Albuquerque*, universities, research institutions and firms, as well the interactions among them, have a key role in the development and success of a national system of innovation.[478] According to them, "health sciences is one of the world-class knowledge in Brazil today, especially in biomedical research for production of serums and vaccines."[479] *Mazzucato and Penna* also concluded that the

474. *Ibid.*, pp. 219-221.
475. *Ibid.*, p. 236.
476. About the importance of public procurement in the Brazilian health system *see* Sorte Junior (2012), "The Production and R&D structure of the Brazilian Pharmaceutical Industry: The Role of Public Procurement and Public Drug Production" in 10 *Global Pub. Health* 7, 1062-1079.
477. Mazzucato/Penna (2016), *The Brazilian Innovation System: A Mission-Oriented Policy Proposal*, Brasília, p. 50.
478. Suzigan/Motta e Albuquerque (2011), "The Underestimated Role of Universities for the Brazilian System of Innovation," 31 *Revista de Economia Política* 1, 3-30.
479. *Ibid.*, p. 19.

core strength of the Brazilian system of innovation is a good infrastructure of science and education, especially in health.[480]

5 *The Main Characteristics of the Brazilian Health Innovation System*

Despite the vast distances between rich and poor, there are four characteristics which make the Brazilian health innovation system unique:

(1) As seen above, it has a long IP history, which started in 1809.
(2) It has a social constitution, which makes possible the development and implementation of persistent public health policies and pharmaceutical production policies.
(3) It has an educated middle class, prospering universities, social permeability, and social inclusion, as well as active participation of civil society.
(4) It has a net public pharma industry based on public laboratories, the goal of which is to meet domestic needs.

As summarized by *Mazzucato and Penna*, "Brazil's health strategy is a well-developed state-led policy that has been able to mobilize a range of public and private actors to develop science and technology-based innovations. Unlike other sectors, the health sector has been able to foster partnerships between different types of public agencies, businesses, and research institutions/universities."[481]

After this short description of the Brazilian health innovation system, it is clear that in contrast to India—another emerging nation with a similar development policy in the health sector—the Brazilian focus is the coverage of the national needs. While India's focus is on the external market, being considered the "pharmacy of the poor," Brazil barely exports drugs.[482] The focus of the Brazilian health innovation system is the coverage of national needs.

D ANVISA'S PRIOR CONSENT AND THE WTO

The question to be examined is whether or not Article 229-C of the Brazilian Patent Law is compatible with Article 27.1 of the TRIPS Agreement. The text of the Brazilian provision is as follows:

> Article 229-C Brazilian Patent Law
>
> "The granting of patents on pharmaceutical products or processes shall depend on the prior consent of the National Health Surveillance Agency (ANVISA)."

480. Mazzucato/Penna (2016), *The Brazilian Innovation System: A Mission-Oriented Policy Proposal*, Brasília, p. 60.
481. Mazzucato/Penna (2016), *The Brazilian Innovation System: A Mission-Oriented Policy Proposal*, Brasília, pp. 54-55.
482. For comparison and analysis of the Indian and the Brazilian system of health innovation, *see* Schüren (2016), *Aufholende Entwicklung in der globalen Ökonomie—Pharmazeutische Innovationssysteme in Indien und Brasilien*, Nomos, Baden-Baden.

In other words: Is the Brazilian rule of prior consent—which requires that the granting of pharmaceutical patents and processes are subjected to ANVISA's prior consent—consistent with the TRIPS provision according to which patent rights should be enjoyable without discrimination as to the field of technology?

To interpret the meaning of the nondiscrimination clause in light of the TRIPS Agreement as a whole, it is necessary to use the customary methods of interpretation of public international law, as codified by the Vienna Convention on the Law of Treaties.[483] With this aim, the pertinent rules contained in the TRIPS Agreement and in the VCLT will be presented. Finally, Article 229-C LPI will be interpreted in light of Article 27 TRIPS.

I Relevant Interpretative Rules Contained in the TRIPS Agreement

1 Preamble

Preambles are common in international treaties; they function as an introduction to the operative part of the treaty. Usually, they set the objectives and expectations of the contracting parties when reaching the agreement. Although they do not have the force of an operative provision, they function as proportionate guidelines for interpretation of their operative clauses. In the TRIPS Agreement's preamble, a tension between different interests and attempts to overcome them and achieve a balance is visible. When TRIPS was negotiated, the bloc of industrialized countries aimed to put an end to free-riding patent rights in the technology field of pharmaceuticals. To achieve this, they made efforts to impose stronger standards of intellectual property rights that would apply to all member countries. In contrast, the bloc of developing countries tried to shape the TRIPS Agreement in a way that would consider intellectual property rights as a matter of public policy and not only of private rights. The preamble resumes such dichotomies and the balance found between the two blocs.

According to the first clause of the TRIPS Agreement's preamble, the end of the treaty was "to reduce distortions to international trade," and to reach this end, it was necessary to "take account the need to promote effective and adequate protection of intellectual property rights." Therefore, as explicitly provided, "promoting effective and adequate protection of intellectual property rights" is a means of achieving the main aim of reducing "distortions to international trade."

In the second clause of the preamble, the parties recognize the need for new rules concerning: (a) the applicability of GATT 1994 and other relevant agreements; (b) adequate standards and principles concerning availability, scope and use of intellectual property rights; (c) the provision of effective means for the enforcement of intellectual property rights, taking into account differences in national legal systems; (d) the provision of effective and expeditious procedures for the prevention and settlement of multilateral disputes; and (e) transitional arrangements.

483. UN (1969), Vienna Convention on the Law of the Treaties (1969), agreed upon in Vienna on May 23; entered into force on January 27, 1980, UNTS 1155, p. 331.

In the third clause, parties recognize the need for a multilateral framework of principles, rules and disciplines dealing with international trade in counterfeit goods.

In the fourth clause, intellectual property rights are recognized by the parties as being private rights. This sentence seems to have been included in the preamble to satisfy the demands of some developing countries parties, which were concerned that governments instead of private companies might respond by infringements of intellectual property rights if the owner fails to enforce his rights.[484]

Clause 5 of the preamble recognizes the "underlying public policy objectives of national systems for protecting IPR, including developmental and technology objectives." According to *Pires de Carvalho*, the reading was borrowed from a text submitted by a group of developing countries during the negotiations on TRIPS.[485] This paragraph should be read together with Article 7 TRIPS.

Clause 6 of the preamble recognizes the "special needs of least developed countries" and gives them "maximum flexibility" regarding the implementation of the substantive provisions of the TRIPS Agreement. This paragraph should be read together with Article 66 TRIPS, which deals with transitional provisions, as well as with Article 4 of the Doha Declaration, which reaffirm the right of member parties "to use, to the full, the provisions of the TRIPS Agreement, which provide flexibility" for the purpose of protecting public health.[486]

2 *Nature and Scope of Obligations (Article 1 TRIPS)*

Article 1.1 of the TRIPS Agreement provides that members should put the provisions of the Agreement into effect. This means that each member country should implement it by issuing national legislation consistent with TRIPS. Most provisions of the TRIPS Agreement are not self-executing since it only provides for a minimal standard of substantive rights. This is evident in the provision contained in Article 1 TRIPS, according to which member countries are "free to implement in their law more extensive protection than is required by this Agreement." Therefore, nothing hinders, for instance, that a member country provides in its legislation that patent rights must be enjoyed for 30 years after the granting of the patent since Article 33 TRIPS provides that the minimum protection time must be 20 years after application for that patent.

More explicitly, sentence 2 of Article 1 TRIPS provides that each member should be free to determine the appropriate method of implementing TRIPS provisions "within their own legal system and practice."

Article 1 TRIPS can play an important role for interpretation purposes since it clarifies that the TRIPS Agreement is neither uniform nor intends to impose a "one-size-fits-all" patent law on all its members.

---

484. Gervais (2003), *The TRIPS Agreement: Drafting History and Analysis*, 2nd ed., London, p. 37.
485. Pires de Carvalho (2010), *The TRIPS Regime of Patent Rights*, 3rd ed., Kluwer Law International, Alphen aan den Rijn, p. 52.
486. WTO (2001b), Declaration on the TRIPS Agreement and Public Health, adopted on November 14, 2001, WTO Document WT/MIN (01)/DEC/2, November 20, 2001.

3 *Objectives (Article 7 TRIPS)*

Article 7 TRIPS sets down the objectives of intellectual property, providing that "the protection of intellectual property should contribute to the promotion of technological innovation," as well as "to the transfer and dissemination of technology," "to the mutual advantage of producers and users of technological knowledge" and "to a balance of rights and obligations."

This provision is not operative and, as such, could be situated in the TRIPS preamble. But the fact that it is situated in the body of the agreement and not in the preamble signals that, as an interpretation tool, it is even more important than those situated in the preamble. Therefore, Article 7 TRIPS is a decisive tool for the interpretation of TRIPS' operative provisions and possible incompatibilities of national laws with them. However, as noted by *Pires de Carvalho*, this provision is not valid for interpreting the agreement as a whole since it refers only to intellectual property rights with technological content, such as patents.[487]

When providing that protecting intellectual property pursues objectives as distinct from each other as those referred to in Article 7, such as "contributing to the promotion of technological innovation" but "in a manner conducive to social and economic welfare, and to a balance of rights and obligations," the text demonstrates the different interests of both developing and developed countries in reaching the TRIPS Agreement. As stated by *Grosse-Ruse Khan*, Article 7 provision "encourages an interpretation and implementation of the IP protection TRIPS provides in a balanced, proportional manner contributing to both social and economic welfare."[488] The challenge, when interpreting the Agreement's operative provisions, is to find the balance desired by all parties.

4 *Principles (Article 8 TRIPS)*

In a similar language to that adopted by Article 7, Article 8 TRIPS provides that "Members may, in formulating or amending their laws and regulations, adopt measures necessary to protect public health and nutrition, and to promote the public interest in sectors of vital importance to their socio-economic development, provided that such measures are consistent with the provisions of the agreement."

This provision serves as an important interpretative tool with which to verify the compatibility of controversial provisions of national law with the TRIPS Agreement. This provision is to be seen as a flexibility tool of intellectual property rights, in the sense that it makes it possible for members to adopt certain "measures," imposing the following conditions for its conformity with the TRIPS Agreement:

487. Pires de Carvalho (2010), *The TRIPS Regime of Patent Rights*, 3rd ed., Kluwer Law International, Alphen aan den Rijn, p. 123.
488. Grosse-Ruse Khan (2017), "The Principle of Integration in WTO/TRIPS Dispute Settlement," in: Cordonier Segger / Weeramantry (eds.), *Sustainable Development Principles in the Decisions of International Courts 1992-2012*, Routledge, London, p. 406.

(1) such measures must be foreseen by laws or regulations;
(2) such measures must be *necessary* to protect public health and nutrition and to promote public interest in areas of vital importance to socio-economic development;
(3) such measures must be consistent with the provisions of the Agreement.

Article 8 TRIPS may justify the use of measures restrictive of intellectual property rights if they satisfy the three conditions above. In other words: it serves as a guide for justifying (or not) the adoption of exceptional measures provided in the national law for protecting some important goods whenever such measures are not expressly provided in other parties of the TRIPS Agreement. In this way, Article 8 will not be useful for justifying the adoption of measures explicitly provided for within the TRIPS Agreement, such as, for instance, the use of compulsory licenses of patent rights in cases of public interest is. Because the TRIPS Agreement already has the explicit operative provision regarding compulsory licenses, the use of such measures is justified by Article 31 of the TRIPS Agreement and not by Article 8.

It is important to note that the decisive condition to be fulfilled is the one contained in the last sentence of Article 8.1, that is, that such measures "must be consistent with the provisions of the TRIPS Agreement." This sentence was introduced in the provision at the end of the Uruguay Round, coming from the industrialized countries.[489] In the case of patent rights, this means that all possible exceptional measures to protect important values, such as public health, must satisfy the conditions put in Article 27 TRIPS. This provision, in its turn, also needs the principles of Article 8 TRIPS to be interpreted.

5 *The Doha Declaration*

As seen above, the "Declaration on the TRIPS Agreement and Public Health" was started by the impulse of a group of developing countries;[490] some of them faced serious public health problems. The group was concerned with the strong opposition suffered by South Africa and Brazil in concretely using instruments of the flexibility of patent rights to deal with problems of public health, such as compulsory licenses and parallel imports, both foreseen by the TRIPS Agreement.[491] In the view of developing countries, both the strong pressure coming from industrialized nations and the multinational pharmaceutical industry against them put at risk the balance found by Member Parties when negotiating the TRIPS Agreement.

The Doha Declaration is composed of seven paragraphs. The first three of them function as a preamble, while the last four paragraphs work as operative provisions. In

489. Rott (2002), *Patentrecht und Sozialpolitik unter dem TRIPS-Abkommen*, Nomos, Baden-Baden, p. 119.
490. Abbott (2002), "The Doha Declaration on the TRIPS Agreement and Public Health: Lighting a Dark Corner at the WTO," 5 *JIEL*, 481.
491. Vandoren (2002), *"Médicaments sans Frontières?* Clarification of the Relationship Between TRIPS and Public Health Resulting from the WTO Doha Ministerial Declaration", 5 *JWIPO* 1, 2-3.

the first three paragraphs, parties recognized "the gravity of the public health problems afflicting many developing countries," while at the same time that they recognized both "that intellectual property protection is important for the development of medicines" and "the concerns about the effects of intellectual property on prices." Moreover, "the need for the WTO-TRIPS Agreement to be part of the wider national and international action to address this problem" is stressed by the parties.

The fourth paragraph is the central provision of the Doha Declaration. According to it, parties agree that "the TRIPS Agreement does not and should not prevent Members from taking measures to protect public health" so that "the Agreement must be interpreted and implemented in a manner supportive of WTO Members' right to protect public health and, in particular, to promote access to medicines for all." In its last sentence, parties "reaffirm of WTO Members to use, to the full, the provisions in the TRIPS Agreement, which provide flexibility for this purpose."

The fifth paragraph clarifies what should be understood by "flexibilities" by giving some examples of them, recognizing that such flexibilities include the following: (a) the provisions of the TRIPS Agreement must be interpreted in accordance with the customary rules of international public law; (b) "each Member has the right to grant compulsory licenses and the freedom to determine the grounds upon which such licenses are granted"; (c) "each Member has the right to determine what constitutes a national emergency or other circumstances of extreme urgency, it being understood that public health crises, including relating to HIV/AIDS, tuberculosis, malaria and other epidemics, can represent a national emergency or other circumstances of extreme urgency"; and (d) each member is free to establish its own regime of the exhaustion of intellectual property rights.

The sixth paragraph deals specifically with problems faced by members with insufficient or no manufacturing capacity in terms of making effective TRIPS provisions concerning compulsory licenses. This point is connected to Article 31 TRIPS, which requires that any use of the subject matter of the patent without the authorization of the right-holder should be authorized predominantly for the supply of the domestic market of the member that, for instance, issued a compulsory license. According to paragraph 6 of the Doha Declaration, the Council for TRIPS was instructed to find an "expeditious" solution to this problem. This provision was implemented in 2003 when WTO members amended the TRIPS Agreement by adding Article 31*bis* to it.[492]

Paragraph 7 of the Doha Declaration postponed until January 1, 2016, the duty of the LDCs to implement TRIPS obligations concerning patent rights and the protection of undisclosed information. In 2015, the WTO Council extended until at least 2033 the right of LDCs to decide for themselves if they wanted to protect pharmaceuticals and clinical trial data or not.[493]

The Doha Declaration is an effort to clarify some provisions of the TRIPS Agreement. As an original source of interpretation, the Doha Declaration is an

492. WTO (2003), Decision of the General Council of August 30, 2003 (WTO Document WT/L/540 and Corr.1).
493. WTO (2015), IP/C/73 Decision of the WTO General Council for TRIPS of November 6, 2015.

important interpretative tool for that Agreement. As put by *Vandoren*, the Doha Declaration "provides a delicate balance between the interests of those who put the issue of the relationship between TRIPS and public health on the agenda of the TRIPS Council, and those whose major preoccupation was to safeguard the TRIPS Agreement."[494] For the purpose of interpreting the compatibility between the Brazilian prior consent rule and the TRIPS Agreement, the most relevant rules are those contained in the fourth and fifth paragraphs of the Doha Declaration.

II Relevant Interpretative Rules Outside the TRIPS Agreement

1 The WTO Dispute Settlement Understanding

A guideline for interpreting WTO Agreements is provided by Article 3.2 of the WTO Dispute Settlement Understanding Agreement (DSU), which foresees that one function of the dispute settlement system is to "clarify existing provisions of those agreements in accordance with customary rules of interpretation of public international law." "Customary rules of interpretation of public international law" should be understood to be the rules compiled in the VCLT, meaning that "both panels and the Appellate Body must be guided by the rules of treaty interpretation set out in the Vienna Convention," as already decided by WTO case law.[495]

2 The Vienna Convention on the Law of the Treaties

The objective of the Convention on the Law of Treaties (VCLT),[496] adopted at Vienna in 1969, was to codify rules of customary law that are universally accepted, therefore serving as a guide for interpreting treaties of international public law.[497]

In the case of the TRIPS Agreement, the Doha Declaration expressly recognizes that "in applying the customary rules of interpretation of public international law, each provision of the TRIPS Agreement should be read in the light of the object and purpose of the Agreement as expressed, in particular, in its objectives and principles."

The Vienna Convention is, therefore, an important tool for the solution of disputes concerning the TRIPS Agreement, even if it was not ratified by all WTO members. Thus, the criteria set down in the UN Vienna Convention for interpreting

494. Vandoren (2002), "*Médicaments sans Frontières?* Clarification of the Relationship Between TRIPS and Public Health Resulting from the WTO Doha Ministerial Declaration," 5 *JWIPO* 1, 11.
495. WTO, *India—Patent Protection for Pharmaceutical and Agricultural Chemical Products* (WT/DS50/AB/BR –December 19, 1997, Appellate Body Report, p. 18, paragraph 46.
496. UN Vienna Convention on the Law of the Treaties (VCLT), adopted in Vienna on May 23, 1969, UNTS 1155, p. 331.
497. *See* preamble VCLT.

treaties should be taken into consideration by the WTO Appellate Body when deciding disputes concerning the TRIPS Agreement.[498]

2.1 *General Rule of Interpretation (Article 31 VCLT)*

According to Article 31.1 Vienna Convention, a treaty should be interpreted in good faith in accordance with the ordinary meaning to be given to the terms of the treaty in its context and in light of its object and purpose.

2.1.1 Good Faith

The first thing to do when interpreting an international treaty's provision is to take into consideration the universally accepted customary principle of good faith. Basically, this means that a provision is to be honestly interpreted in order to achieve a fair result. This serves to discourage interpretations that, for instance, from the beginning, aim to benefit one party.[499]

2.1.2 Ordinary Meaning

The rule that a treaty or a contract's provision is to be interpreted in accordance with its ordinary meaning is also a consequence of the good faith rule. In order to find a fair interpretation, it is necessary that all parties have in mind that the word used in the provision is used in its ordinary meaning. This means that when a treaty does not specify a special or technical definition for a given term, this term will be understood as having its normal meaning.

2.1.3 Context, Object and Purpose

By the same token, the rule that a treaty's provision is to be interpreted according to its original context, object and purpose is also connected with the principle of good faith. This rule calls for a teleological interpretation. It seeks, in the first place, to avoid the predomination of literal interpretations that are disconnected from the context, object and purpose of the treaty.

According to Article 31.2 VCLT, the context and the purpose of a treaty are to be found in the first place in its text, including the preamble and its annexes. In the second place, the Convention expressly establishes two other elements that must be taken into consideration in order to find the context and the purpose of a treaty. These are "any agreement related to the treaty, which was made between all the parties in connection

498. About the VCLT and methods of interpretation for the WTO Agreements, *see* Yamane (2011), *Interpreting TRIPS: Globalization of Intellectual Property Rights and Access to Medicines*, Hart Publishing, Oxford/Portland, pp. 190-208.

499. D'Amato (1995), "Good Faith," in Bernhardt: *Encyclopedia of Public International Law*, Vol. II, Elsevier, Amsterdam, pp. 599-601.

with the conclusion of the treaty" and "any instrument which was made by one or more parties in connection with the conclusion of the treaty and accepted by the other parties as an instrument related to the treaty."

Along with the context of the treaty, Article 31.3 VCLT establishes that the following three elements are also to be taken into account: (1) any subsequent agreement between the parties regarding the interpretation of the treaty or the application of its provisions; (2) any subsequent practice in the application of the treaty which establishes the agreement of the parties regarding its interpretation; and (3) any relevant rules of international law applicable in the relations between the parties.

2.2 *Supplementary Means of Interpretation (Article 32 VCLT)*

In accordance with the Vienna Convention, supplementary means of interpretation might be used in the following three cases: (1) to confirm the meaning resulting from the application of Article 31 VCLT; (2) to determine the meaning when the interpretation according to Article 31 leaves this ambiguous or obscure; or (3) to determine the meaning when the interpretation according to Article 31 leaves the meaning "manifestly absurd" or "unreasonable."

Those supplementary means include, according to Article 32, the preparatory work of the treaty and the circumstances of its conclusion.

III The Meaning of Article 27.1 TRIPS and the Question of the Compatibility of Article 229-C Brazilian Patent Law With It

For examining a possible incompatibility between Article 229-C LPI and Article 27.1 TRIPS, it is necessary to determine the meaning and scope of the latter. To do this, it is necessary to analyze two issues. The first refers to the three substantive conditions of patentability (if the invention is new, involves an inventive step and is capable of industrial application) provided for in Article 27.1 TRIPS, first sentence when one asks the following: Does the treaty allow national legislation to provide for other conditions for patentability other than those three ones? The second question is whether the subjection of pharmaceutical inventions to prior consent by ANVISA—and only such inventions—in the process of obtaining patents constitutes discrimination as to the field of technology, within the sense of Article 27.1 TRIPS, second sentence.

To determine the meaning and scope of Article 27.1 TRIPS, it is first necessary to establish which method of interpretation is to be adopted. Since the Vienna Convention compiles the methods of interpretation of universally accepted public international treaties, and the Convention's application is reinforced by paragraph 5 (a) of the Doha Declaration, by providing that in the interpretation of the flexibilities contained in the TRIPS Agreement, the customary rules of public international law are to be applied, we have to interpret Article 27.1 TRIPS in light of its "object and purpose" and, in particular, its "objectives and principles."

Article 31 of the Vienna Convention provides that a treaty must be interpreted in good faith in accordance with the ordinary meaning given to the terms of the treaty in its context and in light of its object and purpose. In the case of the TRIPS Agreement, its objectives and proposed features are contained in its Articles 7 and 8, as well as in its preamble.

1 *Meaning of Article 27.1 TRIPS, First Sentence*

At first, the question of whether the TRIPS Agreement prohibits WTO member countries from providing in their national law for conditions of patentability other than novelty, inventive step and capability of industrial application will be checked. Second, it will be checked whether ANVISA's prior consent is the fourth hurdle for patentability, and, as such, not admitted by the TRIPS Agreement.

Textually, the first part of Article 27.1 TRIPS only provides that patents shall be available for any inventions, whether products or processes, in all fields of technology, provided that they fulfill the above three conditions. The provision focuses on the obligation to make patents available for any invention; it does not lay down the conditions for obtaining patents. If patents should be available for any inventions, it follows that national law must not exclude from patent protection any invention, whether products or processes, that satisfies the three conditions of patentability, except in the following situations: (1) in the cases of paragraphs 2 and 3 of Article 27, or (2) in the case of developing countries that adopt measures to protect public health and nutrition and to promote the public interest in sectors of vital importance to their socio-economic development, taking into consideration the provisions contained in Articles 7 and 8 of the TRIPS Agreement.

The provision, therefore, does not deal with the topic of "conditions for patentability." It is, rather, concerned with the prohibition of generally excluding from patentability inventions that meet the three cited substantive conditions of patentability.[500] For no other reason, Article 27 is named "patentable subject matter." This interpretation is also supported by the exceptions listed by Article 27.1 TRIPS. All exceptions refer to the permission to exclude the inventions from patentability, as expressly mentioned by Article 27.2 TRIPS (inventions whose commercial exploitation is prohibited for reasons of *ordre public)* and by Article 27.3 TRIPS (diagnostic, therapeutic and surgical methods for the treatment of human or animal health, as well as plants and animals not included in the concept of microorganisms).

Thus, what Article 27.1 TRIPS does is solely to enumerate the three substantive conditions of patentability for the purpose of restricting the patentable subjective matter. Before the enactment of the TRIPS Agreement, every country was free to decide which matter should be excluded from patentability and many countries excluded pharmaceutical inventions from the possibility of being patented. After the enactment of TRIPS, WTO members are prohibited due to Article 27.1 TRIPS from excluding from patentability any invention which, in theory, may meet the three conditions above. It

500. *See* Godt (2007b), *Eigentum an Information—Patentschutz und allgemeine Eigentumstheorie am Beispiel genetischer Information*, Mohr Siebeck, Tübingen, p. 576.

is therefore prohibited from excluding from patentability products of a certain technology, for example, pharmaceutical or chemical inventions. Thus, as its very title ("patentable subject matter") indicates, Article 27 does not restrict the conditions of patentability; it only restricts the possibilities for the exclusion of patentable subject matter.

This interpretation can also be supported by making use of a supplementary means of interpretation, according to Article 32 VCLT. With regard to patents, documents recording the preparatory work of the TRIPS negotiating group during the Uruguay Round show that limiting conditions for patentability was not discussed or even raised by the parties. The discussion was rather focused on the following general topics: (1) the absence of patent law to protect inventions in some countries; (2) exclusions from the patentable subject matter, especially regarding pharmaceuticals, agricultural machinery, cosmetics, biotechnological inventions, lack of protection for plant breeds, etc.; (3) inadequate duration of patent rights; (4) procedural problems with obtaining patent rights; (5) compulsory license and forfeiture of patents; and (6) restrictions on the patent rights of foreigners in order to protect domestic technology.[501]

On the other hand, while Article 27.1 TRIPS clearly prohibits national laws from prohibiting pharmaceutical patents at all (such developing countries did in the pre-TRIPS period), it does not prohibit national law from imposing conditions of patentability other than those that it mentions if the country in question is a developing country and the imposed condition of patentability is necessary to protect public health or to promote public interest in areas of vital importance to socio-economic development, as stated by Articles 7 and 8 of the TRIPS and reinforced by the Doha Declaration. This means that developing countries are not allowed to prohibit pharmaceutical patents, but they are allowed to create flexibilities of patent rights in the sense of the Doha Declaration.

This conclusion is also supported by the context in which TRIPS was negotiated. The purpose of TRIPS was not to harmonize the substantive patent law of the WTO member countries, but only "to reduce distortions and impediments to international trade, taking into account the need to promote effective and adequate protection of intellectual property rights," as stated in its preamble. TRIPS did not intend to regulate in detail the conditions for patentability that each country may impose, but only to set down minimum standards of protection for intellectual property rights.

Therefore, Article 27.1 TRIPS Agreement does not prohibit developing countries from providing for more rigid conditions of patentability, for example, for pharmaceutical inventions, than the ones explicitly mentioned by the TRIPS Agreement (novelty, presence of an inventive step and industrial application), if this is necessary to protect public health, considering the parameters given by the Doha Declaration.[502]

501. GATT (1988a), "Compilation of Written Submissions and Oral Statements," prepared by the Secretariat, GATT Document MTG.GNG/NG11/W12/Rev.1 of February 5, 1988, pp. 15-17.
502. *See also* Godt (2007b), *Eigentum an Information—Patentschutz und allgemeine Eigentumstheorie am Beispiel genetischer Information*, Mohr Siebeck, Tübingen, p. 342.

Consequently, a stricter condition of patentability, such as the case of the Brazilian prior consent, will not represent a "fourth hurdle" for achieving a pharmaceutical patent, but rather a flexibility of patent rights, in the sense of the Doha Declaration, as a necessary measure to protect public health.

2 Meaning of Discrimination in Article 27.1 TRIPS, Second Sentence

Because patents should be available for any inventions and patent rights be enjoyable without discrimination as to the field of technology, the question is whether the requirement of ANVISA's prior consent only for pharmaceutical inventions represents discrimination as to the field of technology and is therefore incompatible with Article 27.1 TRIPS, second sentence.

The key to the answer to this question is in the interpretation of the term "discrimination." To interpret this, it is decisive to establish its ordinary sense, considering the context in which the agreement was done as well as its objectives and purpose. In a broad sense, "discriminating" can be seen as synonymous with "distinguishing or differentiating." In a narrower sense, "discriminate" and "differentiate" do not have the same meaning. Usually, the term "discrimination" is used in a negative connotation, which often refers to distinctions that are "unfair," such as those that occur when different rules are applied to similar cases. For example, if a black student on a university campus is not allowed to use the same bus that his white colleagues do, the rule which imposes such prohibition on the black student is discriminatory because nothing justifies a different treatment on the bus due to his skin color. If, however, black students are benefited by quotas in the admission proceedings at the university, this differential treatment is not understood as discrimination since it is justified by the premise that black students have, as a matter of fact, lower chances of being admitted to the university. Consequently, the quota system which benefits the black student is compensation for his initial position of disadvantage. In both cases, the black student receives a different treatment due to his skin color, but only the first one is discriminatory. In the first case, there is no reason to justify why a black student should use a different bus on the campus. In the second case, the differential treatment is justified by the fact that black and white students do not have the same chances to be admitted to a university. Therefore, when different treatment is applied in such cases, one speaks not of "discriminatory treatment" but of "differential treatment." The point is whether the differential treatment is justified by reasonable grounds or not.

The question, therefore, is whether the term discrimination in Article 27.1 TRIPS should be understood in a broad sense or in a strict sense. In the first case, discrimination would have the same meaning as distinction or differential treatment, without regard to whether or not there were justifiable reasons for differential treatment. In this case, no distinction as to the field of technology would be allowed, except for the types of discriminatory or differential treatment expressly named in Article 27.1 TRIPS, which are the following:

(1) the faculty given to developing countries whose national legislation, before TRIPS, excluded some inventions from certain fields of technology from patent protection to delay the obligation of extending product patent protection for such fields of technology for additional five years (Article 65.4 TRIPS);
(2) the obligation to introduce a transitional patent protection ("mailbox system") in any country which did not make available patent protection for pharmaceutical and agricultural chemical products on the date TRIPS came into force for such inventions (Article 70.8 TRIPS); and
(3) the possibility of excluding from patent protection the following patentable subject matter: (a) diagnostic methods and therapeutic or surgical treatment, and (b) plants and animals not included in the concept of microorganisms (Article 27.3 TRIPS).

Assuming that Article 27.1 TRIPS does not accept any form of differentiation other than those mentioned above, not expressly provided for by TRIPS, any distinction made by national law, regardless of whether it is fair or necessary, would violate the principle of nondiscrimination contained in Article 27.1 TRIPS.

The TRIPS Agreement does not prevent states from differentiating patent treatment according to the technology at issue. As pointed out by *Lamping et al.*, while Article 27.1 of the TRIPS Agreement "prohibits discrimination as to the field of technology, it does not prevent states from treating different situations differently. Differentiation that serves to level the actual conditions of competition across all fields of technology is not discriminatory but rather the opposite. It constitutes a necessary response to the diversity of technologies and, consequently, a *conditio sine qua non* for an intrinsically balanced system of protection that remains neutral in its effects on competition."[503]

The other possibility for interpretation is that Article 27.1 TRIPS distinguishes between differentiation based on reasonable grounds and discrimination, and it prohibits only the latter. This would mean that the cases listed as exceptions by Article 27.1 TRIPS do represent discrimination in its strict sense either as to the availability of patents or to enjoy patent rights. In other words, discrimination is, as a rule, forbidden, but national legislation may discriminate on an exceptional basis, and only in the cases named by Article 27.1 TRIPS. So, by permitting developing countries to delay the obligation to make available patent rights and patent rights enjoyable for pharmaceutical products for 10 years after TRIPS came into force (Article 65.4 TRIPS), the TRIPS Agreement allows discrimination as to the field of technology. In the same way, by imposing the obligation to introduce a transitional patent protection *only* for pharmaceutical and agricultural chemical *products*, it excludes from patentability inventions that might also be protected by transitional patent protection (e.g., pharmaceutical or chemical process patents), therefore treating them in a discriminatory manner as to the field of technology.

503. Lamping et al. (2014), "Declaration on Patent Protection—Regulatory Sovereignty under TRIPS," 45 *IIC*, 679-698.

It cannot be said that the term "discrimination" is used by the TRIPS Agreement in the same sense as distinguishing or differentiating. In the first place, this is because the ordinary sense of the term "discrimination" is not the same as "treating differently," being mostly used to describe situations where differential treatment is not justified. The objective of TRIPS was not to create a uniform patent law for all WTO members but to oblige developing countries to accept higher standards for the protection of intellectual property rights, especially by introducing patent protection for pharmaceutical products and processes.

It should be noted that, in accordance with Article 7 TRIPS, intellectual property rights must be protected in order to contribute the welfare and economic development and a balance between rights and obligations. If Article 27.1 TRIPS is understood to prohibit any *justified* differential treatment in the obtaining and enjoyment of patent rights, the balance between rights and obligations would be affected. This interpretation is also supported by the WTO Panel *Canada—Pharmaceutical Patent Protection*, at which the sense of the term "discrimination was discussed" as follows:

> The primary TRIPS provisions that deal with discrimination, such as the national treatment and most-favored-nation provisions of Article 3 and 4, do not use the term 'discrimination'. They speak in more precise terms. The ordinary meaning of the word 'discriminate' is potentially broader than these more specific definitions. *It certainly extends beyond the concept of differential treatment. It is a normative term, pejorative in connotation, referring to results of the unjustified imposition of differentially disadvantageous treatment. Discrimination may arise from explicitly different treatment, sometimes called 'de jure discrimination', but it may also arise from ostensibly identical treatment which, due to differences in circumstances, produces differentially disadvantageous effects, sometimes called 'de facto discrimination'.* The standards by which the justification for differential treatment is measured are a subject of infinite complexity. 'Discrimination' is a term to be avoided whenever more precise standards are available, and, when employed, it is a term to be interpreted with caution and with care to add no more precision than the concept contains.[504]

Even though the Panel did not directly interpret the term "discrimination," it decided that Article 27.1 TRIPS does not prohibit bona fide exceptions, as follows:

> Article 27 prohibits discrimination only to the place of invention, the field of technology, and whether products are imported or locally produced. *Article 27 does not prohibit bona fide exceptions to deal with problems that may only exist in certain product areas.*[505]

In obtaining patents or enjoying patenting rights, differential treatment as to the field of the technology may be justified by grounds of public policy, as stated by Articles 7 and 8 TRIPS. If such differential treatment "is necessary to protect public health and nutrition, and to promote the public interest in sectors of vital importance" to socio-economic and technological development, it may be considered a bona fide

504. *Canada—Patent Protection of Pharmaceutical Products*, WTO Doc. WT/DS114/R (March 17, 2000), paragraph 7.94.
505. *Ibid.*, paragraph 7.92.

exception. Consequently, such differential treatment will not be considered discriminatory. Therefore, it will be consistent with the TRIPS Agreement. By the way, differential treatment in certain fields of technology is common in the patent law of several WTO members, as the following examples show:

(a) the so-called Bolar exception from the U.S. patent law, which exempts drugs or veterinary biological products from patent infringement if the use of the patented invention is "solely for uses reasonably related to the development and submission of information under a Federal law which regulates the manufacture, use, or sale of drugs";[506]
(b) the possibility of extending patent rights for pharmaceutical inventions for more than five years, as occurs, for instance, in the U.S.[507] and the EU,[508] a privilege given in order to compensate for the time during which the invention was already patented but did not have a license to be marketed, as a way of stimulating the development of innovative medicinal products, and so differentiating pharmaceutical inventions from inventions in other fields of technology;
(c) the requirement of prior informed consent for patenting inventions based on genetic resources or on traditional knowledge that the legislation of some countries, such Brazil,[509] for instance, foresees, following the rules set down by the Convention of Biological Diversity;[510] and
(d) ANVISA's prior consent for pharmaceutical products and processes, under the Brazilian patent law, a measure justified by the need to promote public health and medicines for all.

In all cases above, either a special condition is required for patentability or privilege or restriction is conferred in the enjoyment of patent rights; both apply only to inventions in a certain field of technology. In all these situations, differential treatment is justified by the public, societal or economic interest. The Bolar exception, for instance, by restricting patent rights of the patent holder in favor of producers of generic drugs, makes it possible for the latter to be launched on the market earlier and, therefore, benefits consumers of such drugs, who are able to buy them for a lower price than patented medicines. Similarly, a European supplementary certificate confers additional patent protection on holders of pharmaceutical patents in some countries in order to compensate them for the period that the product could not be marketed

506. Appendice L, Consolidated Patent Law, United States Code, Title 35—Patents U.S.C. § 271(e)(1).
507. *Ibid*.
508. *See* European Communities, Regulation (EC) No. 1610/96 of the European Parliament and the Council of 23 July 1996 concerning the creation of a supplementary protection certificate for plant protection products, OJ, L 198, August 8, 1996, pp. 30-35 and Regulation (EC) No. 469/2009 of the European Parliament and of the Council of May 6, 2009 concerning the supplementary protection certificate for medicinal products, OJ L 152, June 16, 2009, pp. 1-10.
509. Brazil (2015), Lei No. 13.123 of May 20, 2015 (Lei de Acesso ao Patrimônio Genético), DOU, May 21, 2015, Article 9.
510. UN Convention on Biological Diversity, agreed in Rio de Janeiro on June 15, 1992), Article 15.

because it was conducting clinical studies or awaiting authorization from the regulatory body. The justification for such differential treatment is in the economic interest of the state in incentivizing the R & D of innovative drugs.

The interpretation that *discrimination* and a *justified differential treatment*[511] should be differently assessed is reinforced by paragraph 4 of the Doha Declaration on the TRIPS Agreement and Public Health. In accordance with this, "the TRIPS Agreement does not prevent and should not prevent members from taking measures to protect public health." According to the same paragraph 4, the TRIPS Agreement "can and should be interpreted and implemented in a way that supports the rights of WTO members to protect public health and promote access to medicines for all." If one interprets the term discrimination as having the same meaning as a justified differential treatment in the case of pharmaceutical inventions, WTO members would be prevented from taking measures to protect public health. As stated by *Abbott*:

> If specific rules applicable to pharmaceutical or public health patents are necessary to address public health interests, this does not constitute "discrimination" against the field of pharmaceutical technology. It constitutes recognition of legitimate public health interests in differential treatment. Such determinations would be fully consistent with paragraph 4 of the Doha Declaration that expressly acknowledges the need to support access to medicines "for all."[512]

Romandini, who examined the compatibility between ANVISA's prior consent and the TRIPS Agreement, concluded that "Article 27.1 TRIPS does not prohibit differentiation in cases where objective grounds for them exist. If it can be reasonably argued that the participation of ANVISA in the grant procedure in the field of pharmaceutical inventions is necessary because only this agency—in the specific administrative structure of the Brazilian State—has the technical competence or the specific legal skills required to examine all or some of the requirements for protection in that field, the differential treatment might be countered before a WTO Panel as justified."[513]

In the Brazilian case, subordinating the granting of pharmaceutical patents to ANVISA's prior consent is different from excluding pharmaceutical products and processes from the possibility of obtaining patents. Article 229-C LPI does not deal with the exclusion of patentable subject matter; it only provides for a justified different patent examination for pharmaceutical inventions, considering that, in an emerging country like Brazil, the patent impact on access to medicines is stronger. As stated by *Pires de Carvalho,* "nothing in the TRIPS Agreement obliges those WTO Members that have an original system of grants to assign the task of examining patent applications to their patent offices," and therefore, "nothing in the TRIPS Agreement prevents a

511. Dinwoodie und Dreyfuss (2007) suggest that a disparate treatment will be permitted, if a legitimate purpose is demonstrated. *See* "Diversifying without Discriminating: Complying with the Mandates of the TRIPS Agreement," 13 *Mich. Telecomm. Tech. L. Rev.*, 445.
512. Abbott (2002c), *Compulsory Licensing for Public Health Needs: The TRIPS Agenda at the WTO after the Doha Declaration on Public Health*, Quaker United Nations Office (Geneva) (QUNO), p. 50.
513. Romandini (2016), "Flexibilities under TRIPS: An Analysis of the Proposal for Reforming Brazilian Patent Law," 15 *J. Marshall Rev. Intell. Prop. L.*, 205.

country from assigning the examination of patent applications in the pharmaceutical sector to the Ministry of Health."[514]

This textual interpretation is reinforced by Article 1.1 sentence 3 TRIPS. According to this provision, Member States are free to determine the appropriate method of implementing the provisions of the Agreement within their own legal system and practice. In the case of Brazil, the requirement that the National Department of Health makes a preliminary examination of patentability is not new since there was already a similar provision in Decree 16.264 from 1923. According to this old Decree, if a given pharmaceutical invention seemed to be harmful to public health, the National Department of Health should make an examination not only regarding such "harmfulness" but also regarding the novelty of the invention.[515] The participation of the National Department of Health in the patent proceedings was abolished with the advent of the patent law of the year 1945, which eliminated the possibility of patenting pharmaceutical inventions.[516]

In conclusion: the prohibition of discrimination does not prevent that the national law of WTO members contains provisions that foresee a *justified differential treatment* in both obtaining and enjoying patent rights.

3 *Conclusion: Compatibility of Article 229-C LPI with Article 27.1 TRIPS*

Brazilian Patent Law's requirement that the grant of pharmaceutical process and product patents depend on the National Health Surveillance Agency ANVISA's prior consent is compatible with Article 27.1 TRIPS, due to the following reasons: (1) the TRIPS Agreement does not prohibit WTO members from providing in their national law for substantive conditions of patentability other than those provided in Article 27.1 TRIPS, first sentence; and (2) such condition does not constitute discrimination as to the field of technology in the sense of Article 27.1 TRIPS, second sentence.

As seen in the preceding section, the first sentence of Article 27.1 TRIPS does not restrict the possibility that national laws provide for substantive conditions of patentability; it only restricts the possibility of the exclusion of patentable subject matter. Since a pharmaceutical invention, in principle, may fulfill the three requirements of patentability, it follows that WTO members are disallowed to exclude pharmaceutical inventions from the patentable subject matter.

However, this does not mean that the national law may provide for any arbitrary condition of patentability other than novelty, inventive step and industrial application. As demonstrated, in the case of ANVISA's prior consent, the different treatment, consisting of the patent examination carried out by a health authority, is a measure necessary for protecting public health in the sense of the Doha Declaration.

514. Pires de Carvalho (2010), *The TRIPS Regime of Patent Rights*, 3rd ed., Kluwer Law International, Alphen aan den Rijn, p. 276.
515. Brazil (1923), Paragraph 1 of Article 44, Regulamento referred by Decreto 16.264 of December 19, 1923.
516. Brazil (1945), Article 8 Decreto-Lei 7.903 of August 27, 1945.

Therefore, ANVISA's prior consent as a requirement for the grant of pharmaceutical inventions is not discriminatory as to the field of technology since this differential treatment of pharmaceutical patents is justified and fair as a measure necessary to protect public health, in terms of a criterion set down or a value protected by the TRIPS Agreement, considering its purpose, object and principles, as well as the Doha Declaration.

As has already been seen, differential treatment as to the field of the technology is justified on the grounds of public policy, according to Articles 7 and 8 TRIPS Agreement. ANVISA's participation in the patent grant proceedings was introduced in Brazilian law with the aim of protecting public health. According to Article 8 TRIPS Agreement, "Members may, in formulating or amending their laws and regulations, adopt measures necessary to protect public health and nutrition, and to promote public interest in sectors of vital importance to their socio-economic and technological development, provided that they are consistent with the provisions of the agreement."

This interpretation is also supported by the Doha Declaration. According to Article 4 of the Declaration, parties agree that "the TRIPS Agreement does not and should not prevent Members from taking measures to protect public health" so that "the Agreement must be interpreted and implemented in a manner supportive of WTO Members' right to protect public health and, in particular, to promote access to medicines for all." In its last sentence, parties "reaffirm the right of WTO Members to use, to the full, the provisions in the TRIPS Agreement, which provide flexibility for this purpose."

The "one-size-fits-all" approach, by which all types of inventions, without regard to the field of technology, are subject to the same standards of patentability, seems does not fit the meaning that the parties gave to the term "discrimination" when negotiating the TRIPS Agreement. As already highlighted, such an approach is neither compatible with the TRIPS' preamble nor with the principles and objectives clarified in Article 8 TRIPS, according to which members may, in formulating or amending their laws, take appropriate measures to protect public health and nutrition, and to promote the public interest in sectors of vital importance to their socio-economic and technological development.

ANVISA's participation in the granting of patents for pharmaceutical inventions by giving its consent to the patent grant is a measure "taken to protect public health," in the context of a middle-income developing country like Brazil, as part of an effort to balance the conflicting interests of the public health and patent policy. The term discrimination must, in this case, be interpreted with the necessary flexibility.

ANVISA's prior consent is a bona fide *exception* because the differential treatment is justified by the need to protect public health, considering the needs of a developing country. Consequently, this type of differential treatment is not discriminatory; it is rather a necessary measure to deal with problems that only exist with pharmaceutical patents. As seen above,[517] pharmaceutical companies use patent strategies for amortizing their high investment in R & D and maximizing their profits.

517. Chapter 2-A-III-3 ("Practices that indicate 'evergreening' in the pharmaceutical field").

As a developing country without an innovative pharmaceutical industry and with the constitutional duty of promoting drug access for all, it is legitim that Brazil identifies such patent strategies and disallows them by an agency that has the expert knowledge for doing the job.

CHAPTER 3
The Case of Patents and Drugs in Brazil

A WHY WAS IT NECESSARY TO CREATE PRIOR CONSENT IN BRAZIL?

I Development of Brazilian Patent Law

1 National Patent Law Before TRIPS

1.1 Historical Development

Antecedents of patent protection in Brazil can be found during the later years of Portuguese colonial rule (1500-1822). The first general rule passed was the so-called *Alvará* (an edict of the Portuguese King Dom João VI) of 1809, by which machines and inventions could enjoy a usage privilege for a period of 14 years.[1] As explained by *Pires de Carvalho*, the *Alvará* was not a patent law in a modern sense: at its core, it was a tariff law that *also* guaranteed protection for the exclusive use of imported machines and inventions.[2] The *Alvará* was issued only one year after the Portuguese royal family's escape to Rio de Janeiro in the context of the Napoleonic Wars in Europe, by means of which the Portuguese Crown, protected by the English Navy, was based in Brazil from 1808 to 1815. That a Portuguese colony, whose hundred percent agrarian economy was based on slave work, was a pioneer in introducing patent protection is peculiar, considering that patent protection did not exist at the time either in Portugal—where it would later be introduced in 1868[3]—or in other European countries where the industrialization process was much more advanced. Besides, manufacture in

1. Brazil (1809), Alvará de April 28, 1809: Isenta de direitos as matérias primas do uso das fábricas e concede outros favores aos fabricantes e da navegação nacional.
2. Pires de Carvalho (2009), *200 Anos do Sistema Brasileiro de Patentes: o Alvará de 28 de abril de 1809—Comércio, Técnica e Vida*, Lumen Juris, Rio de Janeiro, p. 5.
3. Cruz/Tavares (1986), "As Patentes Brasileiras de 1830 a 1891," 16 *Estudos Econômicos*, 211.

the colonies was still prohibited by law, so that at the time, Brazil did not have any industry to protect. In fact, as explained by *Pires de Carvalho*, patent protection was introduced in Brazil as part of a political bargain between England and Portugal.[4] Under the terms of this bargain, Portugal paid its debt to England by opening Brazilian harbors to English products and, at the same time, guaranteeing patent privileges to English machines.

After Brazil's declaration of independence in 1822—as a constitutional monarchy (1822-1889)—patent protection was confirmed by the first Brazilian constitution (BC) in 1824.[5] Since then, patent protection has been guaranteed in all BCs. The first ordinary patent law was passed in 1830.[6] This was replaced by a new law in 1882, which increased the length of patent protection from 14 to 15 years.[7] As a rule, this law did not foresee a technical examination for patent grants, except in the following situations: (1) if the invention consisted of a pharmaceutical, chemical or food product; and (2) if the invention seemed to be a threat to "public security."[8] It is worth noting that Brazil was included very early in the international patent system. The country signed the Paris Convention in 1883 and ratified it in 1884, being there with one of its 11 original members.

Under the so-called Old Republic (1889-1930), patent legislation was again modified by the *Decreto* 16.264, which created a federal organ in charge of issuing patents (*Diretoria Geral da Propriedade Industrial*).[9] From this point on, the previous examination before the grant became mandatory for all kinds of inventions.[10]

Later, patent legislation was then amended via presidential decree during the civil dictatorship of *Getúlio Vargas*[11] (1930-1945). Time protection of 15 years was maintained, but the decree also provided for another category of industrial property protection—the "model of utility"—which is a kind of a "small patent" with ten years' protection. During the military dictatorship (1964-1985), patent legislation was amended three times, also via decree.[12] At the international level, the Patent Cooperation Treaty was ratified.[13]

The current BC, promulgated in 1988, does not use the word "patents." In referring to patents, the BC uses, instead, the expression "temporary privilege" for

4. Pires de Carvalho (2009), *200 anos do Sistema Brasileiro de Patentes—O Alvará de 28 de abril de 1809—Técnica e Vida*, Lumen Juris, Rio de Janeiro, p. 5.
5. Brazil (1824), Article 179, XXVI Constituição Política do Império do Brasil of March 25, 1824.
6. Danemann (2000), "Die geschichtliche Entwicklung des gewerblichen Rechtschutz in Brasilien," *Mitteilungen der Deutsch-Brasilianischen Juristenvereinigung, Heft* 2, p. 12.
7. Brazil (1882), Lei No. 3.129 of October 14, 1882, originally published in *Coleção das Leis Oficiais do Brasil* on December 31, 1882.
8. *Ibid.*, Article 3, 2nd Paragraph.
9. Brazil (1923), Decreto No. 16.264 of December 19, 1923, Coleção de Leis do Brasil, December 31, 1993, p. 329.
10. *Ibid.*, Article 3, 3rd Paragraph.
11. Brazil (1945), Decreto-Lei 7.903 of August 27, 1945 (Coleção das Leis do Brasil 1945, p. 183).
12. Brazil (1967), Decreto-Lei No. 254 of February 28, 1967 (DOU February 28, 1967, p. 2444); Brazil (1969), Decreto-Lei no. 1005 of October 21, 1969, DOU, Seção I, October 21, 1969, p. 1) and Brazil (1971b), Lei No. 5.772 of December 21,1971 (Código de Propriedade Industrial), DOU, December 31, 1971, Seção I, p. 10897.
13. Brazil (1978), Decreto 81.742, May 31, 1978, DOU, June 1, 1978, p. 8120.

inventors of industrial inventions and establishes that such privilege should take into account "social interests" and "the technological and economic development of the country.'[14] The last legal revision occurred in 1996, in order to make Brazilian patent law compliant with TRIPS. This law and its later amendment of 2001 are going to be examined in the next section.

1.2 Legal Treatment of Pharmaceutical Patents

Pharmaceutical patents have always been eligible for special treatment in Brazilian law. As mentioned before, according to the patent law and regulations of 1882, patents, in general, were granted without a prior examination—except when a patent for food, chemical and pharmaceutical products was requested. Such requests were required to be submitted to a prior examination before the patent could be granted. According to *Borges Barbosa*, such examinations were made by the antecedent of the current National Health Surveillance Agency ANVISA from 1882 onward.[15]

Under the *Decreto* 16.264 from 1923, there was also a certain sensibility in terms of inventions concerning public health, which were submitted to a dual examination. So, if it seemed that an invention might be harmful to public health, it also had to be submitted to an examination by the National Department of Public Health before the Division of Industrial Property decided on the application.[16] The latter would issue a legal opinion about the "harmfulness" and "novelty" of the invention.

Under the civil dictatorship of *Getúlio Vargas* (1930-1945), pharmaceutical product patents were excluded from the normal 15-year patent protection.[17] Process patents on pharmaceutical methods, however, continued to enjoy patent protection.[18] In distinction to the former regulation, the participation of health authorities in the issue of pharmaceutical process patents was no longer provided for.

In 1971, under the military dictatorship of the following decades (1964-1985), process patents were prohibited if their objects were food, pharmaceutical chemical substances or medicines.[19]

Exclusion of pharmaceutical products and processes of patent protection were part of the Brazilian industrial policy adopted for many decades in Brazil—the so-called substitution of importations policy, the goal of which was to support the domestic industry, making it less dependent on exports. The lack of patent protection for pharmaceuticals would trigger a commercial conflict between Brazil and the U.S.

14. Brasil (1988), Constituição da República do Brasil, Article 5 (XXIX), DOU Seção I, October 5, 1988, p. 1.
15. Borges Barbosa (2009a), *O papel da ANVISA na concessão de patentes*. The author concluded this from his analyses of parliamentary debates concerning the Patent Law of 1882.
16. Brazil (1923), Article 44, § 1 Decreto 16.264 of December 19, 1923.
17. Brazil (1945), Article 8, 3 Decreto-Lei 7.903 of August 27, 1945.
18. *Ibid.*, Article 8, sole paragraph.
19. Brazil (1971b), Article 9c, Lei 5.772/1971.

Excursus: Conflict with the U.S. about lack of pharmaceutical patent protection (1986-1990)

In April 1986, the U.S. brought a formal complaint against Brazil at the GATT by asking the Brazilian Ministry of Foreign Affairs for "consultations" about the lack of protection of pharmaceutical patents in Brazil.[20] Previously, the U.S. had already expressed several times concerns about patent law in some developing countries, such as India, Argentina and Mexico, but this measure against Brazil was the first formal initiative.[21]

In June 1987, the Pharmaceutical Manufacturers Association (PMA) pressured the USTR to start complaints against Brazil under "Section 301" proceedings due to the lack of pharmaceutical patent protection in Brazilian law.[22] Brazil was accused by the PMA of copying American pharmaceutical inventions and not paying royalties for them, and therefore, harming the American pharmaceutical industry. According to the PMA, this conduct consisted of denying the "adequate and effective protection" of intellectual property rights, which would justify the USTR in starting investigation proceedings.[23]

Remembering that the GATT negotiations under the Uruguay Round had begun in 1986, it is not difficult to imagine how tense the climate negotiations were for Brazil, which was facing heavy external pressures to change its patent law. Under these circumstances, it is not difficult to understand why Brazil, aligned with India, put up a strong resistance against the American proposal that "new issues," such as intellectual property, services and investment, be introduced to the world-trade-law agenda.[24] In addition, during the first phase of the negotiations, Brazil was explicitly against the granting of patents on pharmaceutical products. At that time, Brazil chose not to change its patent law, first alleging that under the Paris Convention, it was not obliged to protect pharmaceutical patents and second, that it was legitimate to copy medicines if the goal of doing so was to guarantee drug access for the poor.[25]

Trying to find a negotiated solution for the trade conflict unilaterally started by the U.S., Brazil announced that it was inclined, first, to introduce patent protection for pharmaceutical processes and later to introduce patent protection for pharmaceutical substances. This offer, however, was seen by the U.S. as an "inappropriate policy." In July 1988, the U.S. administration announced that it would put Brazil in a "blacklist"

20. Tachinardi (1993), *A Guerra das Patentes: o Conflito Brasil X EUA*, São Paulo, pp. 109-112.
21. Arslanian/Lyrio (1995), "A Reforma das Patentes no Brasil e as Pressões Norte-Americanas na Área de Propriedade Industrial," 4 *Política Externa* 2, 3-12.
22. Harrison (2004), *The Politics of the International Pricing of Prescription Drugs*, Praeger Publishers Westport, p. 107.
23. Tachinardi (1993), *A Guerra das Patentes: o Conflito Brasil X EUA*, São Paulo, p. 111.
24. Arslanian/Lyrio (1995), "A Reforma da Lei de Patentes no Brasil e as Pressões Norte-Americanas na Área de Propriedade Intelectual," 4 Política Externa 2, pp. 3-12; Scholze (2002), *Patentes, Transgênicos e Clonagem—Implicações Jurídicas e Bioéticas*, Fundação Universidade de Brasília, p. 93.
25. Arslanian/Lyrio (1995), "A Reforma da Lei de Patentes no Brasil e as Pressões Norte-Americanas na Área de Propriedade Intelectual," 4 *Política Externa* 2, 3-12.

and impose approximately USD 40 million ad valorem tariff on Brazilian import products.[26]

The Brazilian administration viewed the sanctions as "a surprising and groundless attack."[27] Consequently, it requested consultations in August of that year at the then GATT Council,[28] with the aim of initiating panel proceedings against the U.S. From the Brazilian standpoint, the American retaliations were discriminatory and one-sided, and, therefore, did not comply with the exceptions permitted under Article XX GATT. The American position, on the other hand, defended the imposition of trade sanctions as legitimate since the GATT failed to protect intellectual property.[29] As the parties had not reached an agreement during consultations, Brazil requested a panel in December 1988 against the U.S.[30] Proceedings were then started, and the parties only came to an agreement on the panel's composition in September 1989.[31]

In November 1989, Brazil elected a new administration, which would bring a new turn of events. President *Collor de Mello* was elected on the promise of eliminating the commercial isolation of Brazil and bringing the country into the globalized economy, a promise which included the abandonment of protectionist development policies in the pharmaceutical and informatics sector.[32] In the first month of his mandate, the new president promised the United States it would send Congress a bill to reform the Brazilian patent law. Some days later, the USTR announced that the retaliatory tariffs against Brazil would cease.[33] Subsequently, Brazil withdrew its GATT complaint.[34] On May 1, 1990, the Brazilian presidency submitted a draft law to Congress, the aim of which was to reform Brazilian patent law, especially by introducing patent protection for pharmaceutical substances and processes.[35] From this time on, Brazil changed its position against drug patenting, not only domestically but also within the context of the Uruguay Round negotiations. The former Brazilian position on pharmaceutical patents was now officially considered to have been a brake on economic development.[36] In connection with the new policy, in 1992, Brazil ratified the Stockholm revision of the Paris Convention agreed in 1967.[37]

26. Abbott (1989), "Protecting First World Assets in the Third World: Intellectual Property Negotiations in the GATT Multilateral Framework," 22 *Vand. J. Transnat'l L.*, 709.
27. Tachinardi (1993), *A Guerra das Patentes: o Conflito Brasil X EUA*, São Paulo, p. 133, fn. 2.
28. GATT (1988b), United States—Import Restrictions on Certain Products from Brazil, GATT-Document L/6386/Add.1 (August 24, 1988).
29. Abbott (1989), "Protecting First World Assets in the Third World: Intellectual Property Negotiations in the GATT Multilateral Framework," 22 *Vanderbilt J.Transnat'l L.*, p. 693.
30. GATT (1988c), GATT-Document No. L/6386/Add.1/ (December 7, 1988).
31. GATT (1989), GATT-Document No. C/169 (September 26, 1989).
32. Sallum (2011), "Governo Collor: O Reformismo Liberal e a Nova Orientação da Política Externa Brasileira," 54 *Revista Dados*, 268.
33. Tachinardi (1993), *A guerra das patentes: o Conflito Brasil X EUA*, São Paulo, p. 112.
34. GATT (1990c), GATT-Document C/169/ Add.1 (September 11, 1990).
35. *Projeto de Lei 824, May 8, 1991: Regula direitos e obrigações relativas à propriedade industrial, Diário do Congresso Nacional* (Seção I), May 7, 1991, p. 5406.
36. Arslanian/Lyrio (1995), "A Reforma da Lei de Patentes no Brasil e as Pressões Norte-Americanas na Área de Propriedade Intelectual," 4 *Política Externa* 2, 3-12; Cepaluni (1995), "Regimes Internacionais e o Contencioso das Patentes para Medicamentos: Estratégias para Países em Desenvolvimento," 27 *Contexto Internacional* 1, 74.
37. Brasil (1992), Decreto 635 of August 21, 1992, DOU, January 24, 1992, p. 11434.

Collor's promise to quickly introduce pharmaceutical patent protection, however, could not be kept. In December 1992, he felt compelled to resign after impeachment proceedings had been initiated against him.

The pro-pharmaceutical patent approach consolidated in the following years since the succeeding administration, commanded by the conservative party Brazilian Conservative Party (Partido da Social Democracia Brasileira—PSDB) in coalition with other parties on the right of the political spectrum, under the presidency of *Cardoso*, was convinced that the Brazilian policy for the pharmaceutical sector was no longer appropriate.[38] The bill would become law only in 1996 when the WTO Agreement had already been ratified.

2 *Negotiating History of the New Patent Act (1990-1996)*

Although the pharmaceutical patenting dispute under the GATT was settled with President *Collor's* promise to send a draft bill to Congress, according to which pharmaceutical matter would be patentable, the trade conflict between the two countries was far from being solved in the early 1990s. The USTR canceled its retaliations but maintained Brazil on its "priority watch countries' list," in which countries without "adequate intellectual property protection" were ranked, meaning that Brazil suffered heavy external pressure while the bill was being debated by Congress.

2.1 Câmara dos Deputados (1991-1993)

Willing to keep the promise made to the USTR, President *Collor* requested urgency in the legislative proceedings regarding the draft patent law sent to the Câmara dos Deputados (Lower House at the Brazilian Federal Parliament—CD), the lower house of the Brazilian Parliament.[39] The bill faced such strong opposition that the President sent a message to Congress asking for stopping the urgency's proceedings.[40] As one would expect, the bill was actively discussed: all in all, it received more than 600 amendments from congresspersons. Representatives of different sectors of civil society, such as scientists, professors and representatives of the international and the national industry, the Ministry of Health, the Ministry of Industry, large law firms, the Catholic Church, and so on were also invited to give their views and debate them with Congress members.

The final draft law reflected a certain balance between different sectors of Brazilian society.[41] It provided for patent protection for all fields of technology,[42]

38. Scholze (2002), *Patentes, Transgênicos e clonagem—implicações jurídicas e bioéticas*, Fundação Universidade de Brasília, p. 78.
39. Câmara dos Deputados, Projeto de Lei 824, of May 8, 1991: regula direitos e obrigações relativos à propriedade industrial.
40. Mensagem 218/91, *DCN*, Ata da 71. Sessão, em 6.6.1991 (Seção 1), June 7, 1991, pp. 8924-8925.
41. PL 824-D/91, Mesa Diretora da Câmara dos Deputados, Aprovação da Redação Final oferecida pelo Relator, Dep. Ney Lopes, *DCN*, June 3, 1993, p. 11595.

without excluding pharmaceutical patent protection, but prohibiting the patenting of living beings.[43] The bill provided for a relatively short transitional period of one year but had also decided for an international exhaustion of intellectual property rights,[44] thereby allowing parallel imports. It admitted pipeline protection for pharmaceuticals but required the fulfillment of some conditions: it would be necessary that the medicines had never been either patented or marketed anywhere in the world.[45] Furthermore, pipeline protection could not be claimed if there had been serious preparations for the invention's exploitation in the national territory. The draft law passed at the CD extended the proceedings laid down on pipeline patents to all pending patent applications.[46] This would mean that all pending applications would not have their eligibility for patentability checked by the Patent Office since they would simply be revalidated. Trying to find a balance, the bill also provided for several species of compulsory licenses as safeguards for possible situations of national emergency, including compulsory licenses on the grounds of public interest.[47]

The PMA heavily criticized the draft. It announced that the new Brazilian law was unacceptable, in particular, because its pipeline provision failed to protect drugs already patented in the United States.[48] In May 1993, the USTR started a new offensive against Brazil on the grounds of "inadequate intellectual property protection."[49] Despite this, the CD approved the final draft in June 1993 and sent it to the higher House at the Brazilian Federal Parliament (*Senado Federal*—SF), the higher house of the Brazilian Parliament, to be revised in its second round.

2.2 *SF (1993-1996)*

At the SF, the draft law had to be analyzed by two technical commissions, namely, the Commission for Constitutional and Justice Topics of the Brazilian Parliament (*Comissão de Constituição e Justiça*—CCJ)[50] and the Commission for Economic Topics of the Brazilian Parliament (*Comissão de Assuntos Econômicos*–CAE)[51]. Both had the responsibility of collecting and deciding on amendments, as well as producing a final technical report on the matter. First, the draft law was sent to the CCJ. There, the draft law was again discussed with significant levels of participation from different sectors of civil society, whose representatives had opportunities to present their views to the Senators, either before one or before both parliamentary commissions.[52]

42. Article 8, PL 824-D/91.
43. Article 10. IX and Article 18, III, PL 824-D/91.
44. Article 43, IV, PL 824-D/91, *DCN* June 3, 1993, p. 11595.
45. Article 228, PL 824-D/91.
46. Article 227, PL 824-D/91.
47. Article 68-71, PL 824-D/91.
48. Stewart (1993), *The GATT Uruguay Round: A Negotiating History (1986-1994), Vol. IV: The End Game (Part I)*, p. 497.
49. *Ibid.*, p. 498.
50. "Commission of Constitution and Justice."
51. "Commission of Economic Topics."
52. According to the Senator *Suassuna's* report (*Parecer* Suassuna), this was evident in the public hearing occurred on November 2, 1994 at the CCJ and on June 22, 1994 at the CAE.

Pipeline patent protection for pharmaceuticals, transitional periods and biotechnological inventions were the most discussed topics at the Senate. The Executive Branch—led by President *Cardoso* since January 1, 1995—supported the draft law, as it had passed at the CD. The Executive was also engaged in a quick enactment of the new patent law, without a long period of discussion.[53] Brazilian newspapers of the time reported that President *Cardoso* wanted to have the new patent act enacted before his first official visit to the U.S., which took place in April 1995; the fact that *Cardoso's* government did not manage to do this on time was reported as an "embarrassing" failure for the Executive.[54] The *Cardoso* presidency was especially engaged in the maintenance of the pipeline protection in the draft law, as well in the immediate application of the new patent act; it was also for wider patent protection of biotechnological inventions.[55]

After successive delays,[56] the CCJ approved the technical report made by Senator *Ney Suassuna*, which modified important points of the draft passed at the CD. In the first place, his report rejected pipeline protection for pharmaceutical patents on the grounds that such a retroactive patent protection would violate the principle of novelty as well as national interests. Consequently, all pending patents would have to be examined by the Patent Office in accordance with the patentability criteria set down in the new law.[57] Hence, pipeline protection was replaced by the "mailbox" provision,[58] as well as exclusive marketing rights for five years, following the standards settled by the TRIPS Agreement, which, at that time, had just been incorporated into national law.[59] Transitional periods of one year were maintained,[60] but only after having been pressured by the Executive to do so since the first draft of the CCJ's report provided for a five-year time delay before the law would come into force.[61]

The modifications approved by the CCJ were followed by an animated discussion in civil society; their supporters involved the national pharmaceutical industry,[62] the leftist opposition's senators, newspapers,[63] different NGOs, sectors of scientific communities[64] and the Catholic Church. Among the opponents of the modifications made by the CCJ were the *Cardoso* administration, representatives of the multinational

53. "Senado adia voto sobre patentes," *Folha de São Paulo*, April 17, 1995.
54. Salomon (1995), "Lei de Patentes causa constrangimento," *Folha de São Paulo*, April 19.
55. Freitas (1995), "Derrota Patente," *Folha de São Paulo*, April 13.
56. "Votação do projeto é adiada," *Folha de São Paulo*, April 18, 1995.
57. Senado Federal (1993), Projeto de Lei da Câmara (PLC) No. 115, de 1993, Article 228.
58. Senado Federal (1995), Parecer No. 654, de 1995. Da Comissão de Constituição, Justiça e Cidadania.
59. Brazil (1994b), Decreto 1.355, December 30, 1994, DOU, December 31, 1994.
60. Senado Federal, PLC No. 115, 1993, Article 240.
61. Ulhôa, (1995), "Adiada votação do projeto por mais 15 dias: Relator pediu tempo para analisar as emendas," *Folha de São Paulo*, May 3.
62. Alario (1995), "As patentes e o monopólio da cura," *Folha de São Paulo*, September 13, 1995.
63. "Necessidade Patente," *Folha de São Paulo*, Editorial, May 22, 1995, p. 2.
64. Cerqueira Leite (1995), "Patentes, pirataria e indústria farmacêutica," *Folha de São Paulo*, April 30, p. D-2; Candotti (1995), "As patentes e os cientistas," *Folha de São Paulo*, May 8.

pharmaceutical industry,[65] some large law firms, IP law associations, a number of economists[66] and some sectors of a divided scientific community.

The next step in the legislative proceedings was taken by the CAE. Pressures from the American pharmaceutical industry regarding the lack of pipeline protection in the CCJ's report went on. A few weeks after the approval of the CAE's report, an American delegation of congresspersons came to Brazil in order to transmit the message that a new patent law was "fundamental."[67] The Executive Branch took a position against the amendments made by the CCJ since it seemed to be concerned with the non-approval of pipeline protection.[68] The most discussed topic was, in fact, pipeline protection for pharmaceuticals. Senator *Bezerra* seemed to be concerned with the American threats of trade retaliation.[69]

In order to come back to the unaltered draft, the Executive Branch started concentrating its forces to negotiate this situation at the CAE.[70] When the technical report of the CAE[71] became known in August 1995, it had satisfied almost all the Executive demands. As expected, transitional protection in the form of the "mailbox" system was discarded, being once again replaced by pipeline protection.[72] The pipeline provision was changed again so that such protection would become available for products that had already been patented in other countries,[73] as the PMA had demanded. In response to criticisms that the bill would provide for more patent rights than the minimum standards required by TRIPS, Senator *Bezerra's* report argued first that only with pipeline protection would the positive effects of a new patent policy—such as encouraging the entry of first-line products in Brazil—be able to bring economic and social benefits to the country.[74]

Despite the admission of pipeline protection introduced due to American pressure,[75] *Bezerra's* draft partially satisfied some interests of the national pharmaceutical industry. The draft law exempted national pharmaceutical companies from paying royalties to multinational companies if such royalties were in any way related to inventions that were not patentable under the old law.[76]

---

65. "Senadores rebatem críticas de laboratórios," *Folha de São Paulo,* May 20, 1995.
66. Campos (1995), "Três vícios de comportamento: o Brasil precisa mudar sua cultura, segundo a qual o roubo de uma patente é patriotismo," *Folha de São Paulo,* May 7.
67. Lins da Silva (1995), "Delegação dos EUA visita o Brasil dia 30," *Folha de São Paulo,* May 27.
68. Morais (1995), "Governo quer aprovar nova lei até outubro," *Folha de São Paulo,* June 25.
69. Ulhôa (1995), "Lei de Patentes gera atritos e discussões no PMDB," *Folha de São Paulo,* June 26.
70. "Governo quer votar patentes até setembro: FHC prioriza medida para evitar retaliações comerciais contra exportações do Brasil pelos Estados Unidos," *Folha de São Paulo,* August 2, 1995; Ulhôa (1995), "FHC quer mudanças em projeto de patentes antes de viajar para os Estados Unidos," *Folha de São Paulo,* August 13, 1995.
71. Senado Federal (1995a), "Parecer no. 655, de 1995 da Comissão de Assuntos Econômicos," *Diário do Senado Federal,* Ano L—Suplemento ao No. 007, October 11, pp. 190-239.
72. Senado Federal, Emenda no. 241—CAE: Substitutivo ao PLC no. 115, de 1993, Article 228-229. *Diário do Senado Federal,* Ano L—Suplemento ao No. 007, October 11, 1995, pp. 239-274.
73. Senado Federal (1995a), "Parecer no. 655, de 1995 da Comissão de Assuntos Econômicos," *Diário do Senado Federal,* Ano L—Suplemento ao No. 007, October 11, pp. 190-239.
74. *Ibid.*
75. *See* Figueira Barbosa (1999), *Sobre a Propriedade do Trabalho Intelectual—Uma Perspectiva Crítica,* Rio de Janeiro, Ed. UFRJ, pp. 399-401.
76. Article 232 LPI.

Senator *Bezerra's* report and draft law were approved with the dissenting vote of Senator *Suassuna.*[77] Because of this dissenting vote—which was, again, against pipeline protection—the matter had to be voted on again at the CAE, which meant that the new patent law could only be voted on the next year. This new delay concerned the Executive to such an extent that President *Cardoso* threatened to issue a decree prohibiting national laboratories from producing drugs that were patented outside of Brazil until a new patent law could be approved.[78] The threats never became a reality since the draft meeting Executive demands was approved some weeks later.[79] The draft was sent again to the lower house of the Parliament (CD), where it passed and was enacted on May 14, 1996.[80] President *Cardoso* celebrated the new patent act as a victory of "honesty against stealing and cheating," as he put it in the speech he made after signing the new patent act.[81]

3 National Patent Law Post-TRIPS

3.1 The Problem of the (In) Direct Applicability (Self-Executing) of TRIPS in Brazil

The BC adopted the idea of the monistic system regarding the implementation of treaty obligations so that international agreements are considered to have been incorporated in Brazilian law after being ratified by Congress and enacted by the President, without being necessary that a special implementation act is enacted. However, the question of whether international trade agreements are directly applicable as law or require a special implementation act is controversial. This question, in connection with the ratification of the WTO Agreement and its annexes in December 1994, earned practical relevance. At the time, Brazilian valid patent law provided for a term of protection for patents of 15 years,[82] while Article 33 TRIPS agreement required a minimum term of protection of 20 years. Since TRIPS was fully implemented in Brazil from May 15, 1997, when the New Patent Act (LPI 96) came into force, the question was raised of which norm was applicable for the time between TRIPS' ratification on December 31, 1994, and LPI 96s entering into force on May 15, 1997. The question was first put to the Patent Office (INPI). Many patentees applied for a five-year prolongation of the validity of their patents under the justification that Article 33 TRIPS would be directly applicable.

77. Senado Federal (1995b), "Voto em Separado, Vencido, do Senador Ney Suassuna na Comissão de Assuntos Econômicos, 4.9.1995," *Diário do Senado Federal*, Ano L—Suplemento ao No. 007, October 11, p. 275.
78. "Decreto visa impedir laboratórios de copiar produtos farmacêuticos e agroquímicos," *Folha de São Paulo*, September 12, 1995.
79. "Governo aprova principais exigências: Comissão do Senado diverge apenas em relação à biotecnologia; plenário deve votar projeto em duas semanas," *Folha de São Paulo*, September 28, 1995.
80. Brazil (1996a), "Lei Federal 9.279, de 14.5.1996: Regula direitos e obrigações relativas à propriedade industrial," DOU, May 15, 1996, p. 8353.
81. Cardoso (1996), *Discurso de Solenidade na Sanção da Lei de Patentes*, May 14, 1996.
82. Brazil (1971b), Article 24, Lei No. 5.772 of December 21, 1971.

The Patent Office rejected the above claims on the grounds that only the Old Patent Law (LPI 71) was applicable to the case, which was in force at that time. Numerous lawsuits were filed in court against this decision.

The first rulings were issued in July 1997.[83] For approximately 10 years, case law alternated between one and the other approach. Between 2004 and 2007, the Brazilian Superior Court of Justice (*Superior Tribunal de Justiça*—STJ)[84] ruled that patentees were entitled to get a prolongation of the protection period for 20 years from January 1, 1995.[85] These judgments assumed without further justification and, as a matter of principle, that TRIPS and especially its Article 33 were directly applicable in Brazilian law.[86] The judgments reasoned that, as Brazil had not made use of the transitional periods in accordance with Article 65.2 TRIPS—which allows developing countries to delay TRIPS' implementation—the agreement was completely incorporated into domestic law, so that the patent protection period should be extended to 20 years from January 1, 1995.

In 2008, the STJ was faced with the question again when the court precedents cited above were initially maintained.[87] In the concrete case, the patent had been granted in 1983 with a protection time of 15 years, which would thus expire in 1998. The patentee was of the opinion that TRIPS' incorporation into Brazilian internal law on December 31, 1995 gave him the right to enjoy five more years of patent protection. In 2009, when deciding a plaint under the same case (Du Pont case), the Court reviewed its own position. It ruled, therefore, that TRIPS could not be directly applied to the period before the entry into force of the new patent act in 1997.[88]

In this judgment, the Court recognized that the precedent rulings had falsely assumed as a matter of principle that TRIPS had been directly applicable since its incorporation into Brazilian internal law; this assumption, however, was far from being uncontroversial. Based on the lesson of *Borges Barbosa*[89] and *Basso*[90]—according

83. For instance, 9th Federal Court of First Instance of Rio de Janeiro (in Portuguese: 9ª Vara Federal), Decision 3077/1997, Case No. 97.0003.3260-4, "Zeneca," cited from Franz (2005), *Die Durchsetzung von Immaterialgüterrechten in Argentinien, Brasilien und Mexiko*, Nomos, Baden-Baden, p. 138, fn. 29.
84. Superior Federal Court, the highest Brazilian court for questions not concerning the Constitution. For details, *see* Samtleben, "Föderale Gerichtsverfassung in Brasilien und Argentinien – zwei unterschiedliche Modelle," 66 *RabelsZ*, 259.
85. STJ Recurso Especial No. 423.240-RJ—INPI vs. Gambro AB, March 2, 2004, *Diário da Justiça*, March 15, 2004; STJ Recurso Especial 661.536-RJ—INPI vs. Zeneca Limited, April 7, 2005, *Diário da Justiça* May 30, 2005; STJ Recurso Especial No. 667.025-RJ—Bayer Aktiengesellschaft vs. INPI, December 14, 2006; *Diário da Justiça* February 12, 2007.
86. According to Brazilian law, international agreements are approved by a legislative act from Congress (Decreto Legislativo) and incorporated after that into law by a legal act by the President (decreto presidencial). This gives international agreements the same legal status enjoyed by ordinary law. *See* Rezek (2006), *Direito Internacional Público*, São Paulo, p. 69.
87. Recurso Especial No. 960.728-RJ—E. I. Du Pont de Memours vs. INPI, *Diário da Justiça*, February 25, 2008.
88. Recurso Especial No. 960.728-RJ—E. I. Du Pont de Memours vs. INPI, *Diário da Justiça*, April 15, 2009.
89. Borges Barbosa (2008), *Propriedade intelectual: a aplicação do acordo TRIPS*, Rio de Janeiro, Lumen Juris Editora, p. 18.
90. Basso (2000), "A Data de Aplicação de TRIPS no Brasil," 30 *Revista de Direito Constitucional e Internacional* 8, pp. 13-22.

to which there are self-executing treaties and non-self-executing treaties in Brazilian law—the Court concluded that TRIPS belonged in its proper nature to the category of non-self-executing treaties.[91] Therefore, its incorporation in Brazilian law from January 1, 1995 had only created an obligation for the Brazilian state to implement it within the time limits determined by the treaty. A treaty like TRIPS, which only established minimum standards of protection and gave its member countries the right to decide how they wanted to implement them, was therefore unable to create direct obligations for private parties. The Court also revised the position adopted in its preceding judgments regarding the interpretation of Article 65.2 TRIPS, which provided for a period of grace of four years for developing countries to implement TRIPS. According to the precedents, if the legal act which incorporated TRIPS in Brazilian law was silent regarding the period of grace, this should imply that the right to make use of it was renounced. The court considered that its former interpretation was falsely based on TRIPS' negotiating history, official WTO documents and debates in the Brazilian Senate when the agreement was ratified in 1994. It is worth noting that one of the judges, although denying the complainant the right to have her patent extended, was of the view that TRIPS was also directly applicable for private individuals. Judge *Pargendler*, however, in the concrete case, ruled that patent extension application was to be denied because TRIPS could not be retroactively applied. This would be the case of the complainant's patent, which was granted in 1993. Having had the patent granted before December 31, 1994, when TRIPS was incorporated into Brazilian law, the patentee could not claim for the application of a treaty at a time when it had not yet been ratified.[92]

Setting aside the basic considerations of the STJ in the Du Pont case, it is also worth considering that Article 33 of TRIPS is not about a certain period of time prescribed for patent protection, but only a minimum period.[93] For this reason alone, the possibility of self-executing appears doubtful. On the other hand, in the literature, there are many authors who also assume that Article 33 TRIPS is directly applicable.[94]

The above decisions do not have general effects since they apply only between the petitioner and the respondent. Furthermore, as a rule, lower courts are not bound by rulings from superior courts, except in the case the Brazilian Supreme Court of

91. Recurso Especial No. 960.728-RJ, p. 7.
92. *Ibid.*, p. 21.
93. *See also* the Opinion of the Advocate General at the European Court of Justice in the proceedings C-431/05 of 23.1.2007, paragraphs 89 et seq. In the meantime, the case had already been decided, but the question of direct applicability of Article 33 of TRIPs played no role because the court assumed that the national courts had competence jurisdiction to decide on this issue.
94. For the indirect applicability of TRIPS: Baptista (1996), "A Nova Lei e o TRIPS," *Anais do XVI Seminário Nacional de Propriedade Intelectual (ABPI)*; Basso (2000), "A Data de Aplicação de TRIPS no Brasil," 30 *Revista de Direito Constitucional e Internacional* 8, pp. 18-19; Borges Barbosa (2008), *Propriedade Intelectual—A Aplicação do Acordo TRIPS*, Lumen Juris, Rio de Janeiro, pp. 82 et seq. Another view: Araújo (2003), "A Internalização dos Tratados Internacionais no Direito Brasileiro e o Caso do TRIPS," 62 Revista da ABPI, 3-14; Leonardos (1998), *Dos Prazos de Validade das Patentes em Vista do Acordo TRIPS e da Nova Lei de Propriedade Industrial*; Franz (2002), *Die unmittelbare Anwendbarkeit von TRIPS in Argentinien und Brasilien*, Nomos, Baden-Baden, pp. 136-137; Mitsuuchi Kunisawa (2009a), "Brasilien—Gericht verneint direkte Anwendbarkeit des TRIPS," *GRUR Int.*, 630.

Justice, Constitutional Court (*Supremo Tribunal Federal*—STF) edits a *súmula vinculante*, which is a binding judgment for all courts.[95] How the courts will definitively rule is difficult to predict, particularly because there is no ruling of the STF—the highest court responsible for constitutional matters—on the topic. In the case of Du Pont, the question was brought to the STF, but parties came to an agreement before the case was ruled. How the highest Brazilian court would hypothetically have decided the question cannot be predicted, even though the STF had ruled in 1977, in a majority judgment, that international treaties were directly applicable in Brazilian law.[96] Whether this decision, however, can be a paradigm to the question concerning the applicability of TRIPS is doubtful.

3.2 *The New Industrial Property Law (LPI 96)*

The LPI 96 contains provisions on patents, "models of utility," trademarks and geographic origins as well as grant proceedings. It also has provisions on crimes against industrial property and unfair competition. In this section, some provisions that are relevant for pharmaceutical inventions will be commented on, and the changes regarding the former Patent Law will be highlighted (LPI 71).

3.2.1 What Is an "Invention" According to the New Legal Framework?

As usual in patent laws, LPI 96 first determines which requirements an invention has to fulfill in order to be patentable. Second, it determines what is not considered to be an invention. Third, it determines which inventions cannot be patentable.

3.2.1.1 General Rule

According to Article 8 LPI 96, an invention is patentable if it satisfies the requirements of novelty, inventive step and industrial application. If so, it follows, therefore, the standards set by Article 27.1 TRIPS. Article 11 LPI 96 defines an invention as satisfying the requirement of novelty if it is outside of the state of the art. "State of the art" in its turn, is defined as being everything that had become accessible to the public prior to the filing date of the patent application (Article 11, first paragraph), excepting priority claims guaranteed in international agreements to which Brazil was a party. An invention satisfies the requirement of having an inventive step, according to Article 13, if, from the perspective of a "person having ordinary skill in the art," the invention in

95. In accordance to Article 103-A of the Brazilian Constitution of 1988, the STF may, ex officio or upon request, upon a decision by two thirds of its members, and following reiterated judicial decisions on a constitutional matter, issue a summula (restatement of case law) which, as from publication in the official press, shall have a binding effect upon the lower bodies of the judicial power and the direct and indirect public administration, at the federal, state and local levels, and which may also be reviewed or revoked, as set forth in law.
96. STF Recurso Extraordinário No. 80.004, J. June 4, 1977, DJ December 29, 1977.

question might be considered to be inventive. The requirement of "industrial application" is defined by Article 15 LPI 96 as an invention that can be used or produced in any kind of industry.

As usual, the Brazilian patent law makes use of the category "indefinite legal concepts" to define what an invention is. The law gives the patent examiner some orientation by determining the criteria of "state of the art" and the "person having ordinary skill in the art" but also gives him room enough to decide in accordance with the particularities of the concrete case. In practice, examiners might come to different conclusions when interpreting each of these concepts. In order to reduce this uncertainty and guarantee a certain degree of predictability, a Patent Office usually issues mandatory guidelines as orientation for their examiners.

As we are going to see in the next part, the Patent Office (INPI) and the National Agency of Health Surveillance (ANVISA), in some cases, diverge on the interpretation of novelty and inventive step since the latter tends to adopt more rigid standards of patentability.

3.2.1.2 General Exclusions from the Concept of Invention

Article 10 LPI 96 enumerates what kind of intellectual creations are not considered to be inventions and, therefore, cannot be protected by a patent. Some of them, however, can be protected as other kinds of intellectual property. Under Brazilian patent law, the following cases are excluded from patent protection: (a) discoveries, scientific theories, and mathematical methods; (b) "purely abstract conceptions"; (c) commercial, accounting, financial, educational, advertising, raffling, and inspection schemes, plans, principles or methods; (d) literary, architectural, artistic and scientific works, or any esthetic creation; (e) computer programs per se; (f) presentation of information; (g) rules of games; (h) surgical techniques and methods, as well as therapeutic or diagnostic methods, for application to the human or animal body; (i) parts of or whole of natural living beings and biological materials found in nature, even if isolated therefrom, including the genome or germplasm of any natural living being, and natural biological processes.

In the following, the exceptions that are relevant for pharmaceutical inventions will be commented on.

(a) Discoveries

Discoveries are excluded from patent protection by Article 10(I) LPI 96. Brazilian law does not provide any definition of a "discovery." Usually, a discovery is understood as something that does not result in human activity, nor does it have industrial utility. Therefore, it cannot logically be eligible for patent protection. According to *Borges Barbosa*, however, if a discovery does have industrial utility, it should enjoy patent protection.[97] The INPI also issues discoveries patents if the inventor can demonstrate

97. Borges Barbosa (2011), "As hipóteses de incidência patentária do art. 10 do CPI/96," 4 *REVEL*, 144-167 (146).

the industrial utility of that discovery, and such utility is the result of intellectual work.[98]

(b) Surgical techniques and methods, as well as therapeutic or diagnostic methods, for application to the human or animal body

According to Article 10(VIII), LPI "surgical techniques and methods, as well as therapeutic or diagnostic methods, for application to a human or animal body" are not considered to be an invention or a model of utility.

This exception is justified by the freedom physicians have in choosing how their patients should be treated.[99] In this context, a controversial question is whether or not this provision hinders the patentability of a first or further medical uses of a known product in the name of the therapeutic freedom enjoyed by physicians. The question is essential because, today, most drugs are not based on new molecules or compounds but in new uses of older substances. Frequently, a second or further medical indication of a known drug is later discovered. The antiretroviral drug Zidovudine, known as AZT, for instance, is a notorious case that well illustrates how important the patentability of further uses of a known compound might be. AZT was synthesized at the Michigan Cancer Foundation during the 1960s as an anticancer drug and later abandoned because it did not prove to be effective; in 1983, AZT was tested by the American National Cancer Institute as a possible treatment for AIDS, and in 1987 it was patented in the U.S. as the first drug to treat patients with AIDS.[100] When first launched, AZT was sold for prohibitive prices.[101]

The question is: Does this new use consist of a therapeutic method for application to a human or animal body, and therefore is it not patentable? And how about second and further medical indications of a known pharmaceutical product? Frequently, a pharmaceutical product is patented and launched with a determined medical indication, for instance, for treating the disease "X." If some years after its launch, research conducted by the patentee shows that the same medicament can be successfully used in the treatment of another disease than disease "X," the following question is raised: is this second (and further) medical indication regarding the same medicament patentable?

The answer to these questions depends on what should be understood as a "therapeutic method." Ordinarily, a therapeutic method will be everything that a doctor advises her ill patients to do with the aim of reaching the cure of a disease or an alleviation of its symptoms. According to such definition, surgery, physiotherapy, or drug therapy will be a "therapeutic method" and, as such, unpatentable. From the text

98. Article 1.3 Resolução INPI No.169, July 15, 2016.
99. Basheer/Purohit/Reddy (2010), "Patent Exclusions that Promote Public Health," in: *WIPO Standing Committee on the Law of Patents—Exclusions from Patentability and Exceptions and Limitations to Patentee's Rights* (WIPO-Document No. SCP/15/3, Annex IV), pp. 5-42.
100. Cochrane (2000), "Zidovudine's Patent History," 356 *The Lancet* 9241, November 4, pp. 1611-1612. *See also* Angell (2004), *The Truth about the Drug Companies—How They Deceive Us and What to Do about It*, Random House, New York, pp. 23-27.
101. Chirac et al. (2000), "Aids: Patent's Rights Versus Patient's Rights," 356 *The Lancet* 9228, August 5, 501.

of Article 10(VIII) LPI, it seems evident that no drug with the medical use of a known substance will be patentable under LPI 96.

Regarding uses that are not related to medical indications or therapies, the LPI is silent. Article 10(VIII) LPI is the only provision that refers to uses. As a consequence, it is possible to conclude that other uses, in general, are patentable under the LPI since there are no exceptions applicable to uses other than the ones related to medical therapy.

Part of the Brazilian literature, especially that contributed by patent attorneys, advocates the full acceptance of the European case law construction of "Swiss-type claims" in Brazil, thus supporting patenting on second and further medical indications.[102] INPI's guidelines took over EPO's practice concerning the second and further medical uses.[103] Nevertheless, there has been at least one case in which the INPI refused to grant the patent applied for on the grounds that the claim would consist of a therapeutic method and was therefore not patentable.[104] In this concrete case, the Federal Court in Rio de Janeiro decided as per majority that a patent should not be granted on the grounds that a second medical indication would have patent protection excluded by Brazilian law since a new use of a known drug is considered to be a therapeutic method and as such, is unpatentable under the Brazilian law.[105] The judgment rejected the admissibility of the Swiss-type claim explicitly. One of the judges, however, ruled that patenting second uses would be admitted by Brazilian law, as patentability was only dependent on the existence of novelty and an inventive step. According to her vote, medical uses of known substances would not consist of a therapeutic method, per principle, just because the Swiss-type claim was accepted in Brazil.[106]

Despite the clearness of Article 10(VIII) LPI and the case law, the INPI has been granting patents protecting second or further medical uses.[107] Since the INPI imported EPO's case law, applying it to the Brazilian case without properly considering the

102. *See*, for instance, Mitsuuchi Kunisawa (2009c), "Patenting Pharmaceutical Inventions on Second Medical Use in Brazil," 12 *JWIP*, 297-316; Ahlert/Desiderio (2009), "A Patenteabilidade dos Novos Usos de Substâncias Conhecidas," 100 *Revista da ABPI*; Gusmão/Ferreira (2009), "Novas Aplicações Terapêuticas," 100 *Revista da ABPI*; Trigo de Souza (2008), "Should Brazil Allow Patents on Second Medical Uses?," 93 *Revista da ABPI*, 53-67; Borges Barbosa (2006b), *Reivindicação de Uso e a Questão do Segundo Uso in Usucapião de Patentes e Outros Estudos de Propriedade Intelectual*, Rio de Janeiro; Wolff/Bessa Antunes (2005), "Patentes de Segundo Uso Médico," 74 *Revista da ABPI*, 48-61.

103. INPI (2016), Article 1.29 Resolução INPI No.169, of July 15, 2016 (INPI's Guidelines for Patent Examination); Lanzillotti Jannuzzi et al. (2008), "Especificidades do Patenteamento no Setor Farmacêutico: modalidades e aspectos de proteção de propriedade intelectual," 24 *Cadernos de Saúde Pública*, p. 1213.

104. INPI, PI 9606903-1 Eli Lilly Company, RPI 1663, November 19, 2002.

105. Tribunal Regional Federal da 2a. Região—Instituto Nacional de Propriedade Industrial—INPI vs. Eli Lilly Company, Apelação Cível No. 2005.51.01.507811-1, Judge Azulay Neto, J. September 22, 2009.

106. *Ibid.*, Judge Roriz.

107. INPI file No. PI 9606903-1. In this case, INPI denied patent grant invoking Article 10 (VIII) LPI in 2002, although its guidelines already foresaw the admissibility of Swiss-type patent claims. Interestingly, even if the INPI's technical report did not admit atomitaxine as patentable already in 2002, and the case was definitively ruled by the Court in 2009, INPI did not terminate proceedings. Consequently, the patent is not yet officially denied. The patent request is

Brazilian law, it will be related to how this exception has been treated in European law and case law. This is relevant for understanding the implications of this provision in the patenting of new medical uses of known products in Brazil because while the INPI took over the case law developed by the European Patent Office for justifying the patentability of second and further medical uses, the ANVISA rejected it.[108]

In Europe, the legal exclusion from patentability of therapeutic or diagnostic methods gave rise to two questions: first, in the early 1970s, the question of whether a chemical compound, if used for medical treatment, was also excluded from patent protection, and second, the question of whether the first and the further medical indications would also be excluded from patent protection. In Europe, the statutory provision admitting patents in cases of second and further medical indications of known products is relatively recent. In 1973, when the EPC was agreed upon, the majority of the European delegations were in favor of excluding patent protection for second and further medical uses, while the pharmaceutical industry advocated patent protection to foster R & D in finding new uses of known drugs.[109] In the 1980s, this kind of patenting was not admitted by the EPO; this was regretted by a German patent lawyer of that time:

> Neither the European Patent Office nor the German Patent Office at present grant patents on second use invention. At the Benescience Conference in London in May 1981, regret was expressed that hitherto patent protection for the second use has been refused.[110]

Under the EPC 1973, there is a special provision applicable only to pharmaceutical patents, according to which the exclusion of patentability is not applied to products for use in such therapeutic methods. Article 52(4) EPC 1973 reads (emphasis added):

> Article 52—Patentable Inventions
> (1) European patents shall be granted for any inventions which are susceptible of industrial application, which are new and which involve an inventive step.
> (2) The following in particular shall not be regarded as inventions within the meaning of paragraph 1:
> "..."
> (4) Methods for treatment of the human or animal body by surgery or therapy and diagnostic methods practiced on the human or animal body shall not be regarded as inventions which are susceptible to industrial application within the meaning of paragraph 1. *This provision shall not apply to products, in particular substances or compositions, for use in any of these methods.*
> (5) The provisions of paragraphs 1 to 4 shall not exclude the patentability of any substance or composition, comprised in the state of the art, for use in a

"frozen" and the patent applicant has been paying annually fees since 1996, when it was filed (25 years of patent pendency!). This information is extracted from INPI's online database.

108. Marinho/Varella (2015), "La Protection des Données Générées dans le Cadre du Processus d'Autorization de Mise sur le Marché au Brésil," in: Autenne/Cassiers/Strowel (eds.), *Droit, Économie et Valeurs*, Bruxelles, pp. 443-445.
109. Ventose (2009), "Patent Protection for Second and Further Medical Uses under the European Patent Convention," 6 *SCRIPTed* 1, 62.
110. Suchy (1982), "Patent Protection for a Second Medicinal Use," 13 *IIC*, 471-479.

method referred to in Article 51, paragraph 4, provided that its use for any method referred to in that paragraph is not comprised in the state of the art.

The second sentence of Article 52(4) EPC 1973 was conceived in order to guarantee that chemical compounds used for medical treatment would enjoy compound protection in the pharmaceutical field: this is an exception to one exception. The first medical indication of a known product was also already patentable under Article 54(5) EPC 1973, while second and further medical uses were not recognized as being patentable by law.[111] Such a provision is not present in the Brazilian patent act.

From 1984, the EPO started to admit the patentability of second and further medical indications, but their acceptance remained controversial.[112] Until 2000, when the EPC was amended, this question was decided in Europe by case law, with differing results. *Schneider* cites the *Hydropyridin*[113] ruling of the German Federal Supreme Court (BGH) of 1983 as an example of a judgment for the patentability of second and further medical indications and the *Alfuzosine* ruling[114] of the French Supreme Court (*Cour de Cassation*) of 1993 as a judgment in the opposite direction.[115] In the United Kingdom, many courts did not admit Swiss claims until at least 2008, so that clarity was only reached after the EPC had been amended when British courts aligned its practice to the EPO.[116] *Schneider* highlights the role played by the Enlarged Board of Appeal (EBA) of the European Patent Office (EPO) in shaping the standards of patentability for these cases.[117] When deciding on the patentability of the second and further medical indications, the EBA followed a suggestion made by the Swiss Federal Intellectual Property Office.[118] According to this approach, a claim is patentable if "the use of a substance or composition for the manufacture of a medicament is directed for a specified new and inventive therapeutic application."[119]

According to *Schneider's* analysis, "the so-called Swiss-type claims present a drawback of their own because the use of the compound for the preparation of a medicament is already known for the first medical indication. The problem is, therefore, to substantiate novelty. The EBA solved this problem by analogy to the legal construct for the first medical indication. It construed Article 54(5) EPC 1973 in a manner that the novelty of the manufacturing process was indirectly derivate by the

111. Jaenichen/Meier/Hölder (2009), "Medical Use Claims: EPC 2000 and Its Impact on Prosecution and Enforcement," in: Prinz zu Waldeck and Pyrmont et al. (eds.), *Patent and Technological Progress in a Globalized World*, Berlin / Heidelberg, p. 257.
112. Hansen (1988), "New Problems of the Second Indication," 19 *IIC*, 772-788.
113. *Bundesgerichtshof*, Ruling of September 20, 1983, Case No. X ZB 4/83—"Hydropyridin," available at https://research.wolterskluwer-online.de/document/aadcda0a-d172-4045-95dd-77ca94fc0c9e (last visited on August 31, 2020).
114. *Cour de Cassation, Chambre commerciale*, ruled on October 26, 1993, Case No. 91-17.944, Bulletin 1993 IV No. 354 p. 257, available at https://www.legifrance.gouv.fr/affichJuriJudi.do?idTexte=JURITEXT000007031061 (last visited on August 31, 2020).
115. Schneider (2008), "Patenting of Pharmaceuticals—Still a Challenge?," *IIC* 5, 515.
116. Whitehead/Jackson/Kempner (2008), "Generic Competition and a Pharma Patent Strategies—a Sequel," 3 *JIPLP*, 799-800.
117. Schneider (2008), "Patenting Pharmaceuticals—Still a Challenge," 39 *IIC*, 516.
118. *Ibid.*, p. 516.
119. *Ibid.*, p. 515.

novelty of the specific therapeutic application."[120] This is not seen always as positive in the UK. *MacQueen*, *Waelde* and *Laurie*, pointing out that "a strict application of novelty from within the UK tradition should still impose limits on which medical uses can be claimed for a known substance," criticize both the strong influence from Europe on the British courts and the EPC 2000.[121]

With the revision of the EPC 2000, which came into force in December 2007, the question of the second and further medical indications was statutorily solved: the solution agreed was to transfer Article 52(4) EPC to Article 53 to a new letter c) and introduce a new wording for Article 54 EP, which reads as follows:

> Article 54—Novelty
> (1) An invention shall be considered to be new if it does not form part of the state of the art.
> (2) The state of the art shall be held to comprise everything made available to the public by means of a written or oral description, by use, or in any other way, before the date of filing of the European patent application.
> (3) Additionally, the content of European patent applications as filed, the dates of filing of which are prior to the date referred to in paragraph 2 and which were published on or after that date, shall be considered as comprised in the state of the art.
> (4) Paragraphs 2 and 3 shall not exclude the patentability of any substance or composition, comprised in the state of the art, for use in a method referred to in Article 53(c), provided that its use for any such method is not comprised in the state of the art.
> (5) Paragraphs 2 and 3 shall also not exclude the patentability of any substance or composition referred to in paragraph 4 for any specific use in a method referred to in Article 53(c), provided that such use is not comprised in the state of the art.

This means that since the last revision of the EPC, which came into force on December 13, 2007, the protection introduced via case law by way of "Swiss-type-claims" no longer needs to be used in Europe.[122]

The legal situation in Brazil is different from that in Europe because, in Brazil, there is no such statutory provision making an exception of an exception. The Brazilian LPI, while excluding therapeutic methods of patent protection, does not provide that *despite this exclusion*, first, second and further therapeutic uses of known substances will be patentable. In the LPI, there is not such a legal fiction stipulating that the exception provision concerning therapeutic methods does not apply to products for uses in any of these methods (Article 53, sentence 2 EPC 2000). Neither provides the LPI for an "exception of the exception," thereby admitting patents for the first medical indication (Article 54.4 EPC 2000) nor for the second and further medical indications, as the EPC does (Article 54.5 EPC). If we compare the LPI EPC 1973 and 2000, the

120. *Ibid.*, pp. 515-516.
121. MacQueen/Waelde/Laurie (2008), *Contemporary Intellectual Property—Law and Practice*, OUP, Oxford, pp. 442-444.
122. For a critical analysis of this provision *see* Cockbain/Sterckx (2010), "Purpose-Limited Pharmaceutical Product Claims under the Revised European Patent Convention: A Camouflaged Attack on Generic Substitution?," 1 *I.P.Q.*, 88-107.

following differences are noted:

	Brazilian LPI	*EPC 1973*	*EPC 2000*
General Exclusion of Patentability	Article 10 The following are not considered to be inventions or utility models: VIII. surgical techniques and methods, as well as therapeutic or diagnostic methods, for application to the human or animal body;	Article 52(4) Methods for treatment of the human or animal body by surgery or therapy and diagnostic methods practiced on the human or animal body shall not be regarded as inventions which are susceptible to industrial application within the meaning of paragraph 1. *This provision shall not apply to products, in particular substances or compositions, for use in any of these methods.*	Article 53 European patents shall not be granted in respect of: c) methods for treatment of the human or animal body by surgery or therapy and diagnostic methods practiced on the human or animal body; *this provision shall not apply to products, in particular substances or compositions, for use in any of these methods.*
Related Exception Provision for permitting first medical indications of known substances	None	Article 54(5) The provisions of paragraphs 1 to 4 shall not exclude the patentability of any substance or composition, comprised in the state of the art, for use in a method referred to in Article 51, paragraph 4, provided that its use for any method referred to in that paragraph is not comprised in the state of the art.	Article 54(4) paragraphs 2 and 3 shall not exclude the patentability of any substance or composition, comprised in the state of the art, for use in a method referred to in Article 53(c), provided that its use for any such method is not comprised in the state of the art.

	Brazilian LPI	*EPC 1973*	*EPC 2000*
Related Exception Provision for permitting patenting second and further medical indications	None	None	Article 54(5) paragraphs 2 and 3 shall also not exclude the patentability of any substance or composition referred to in paragraph 4 for any specific use in a method referred to in Article 53(c), provided that such use is not comprised in the state of the art.

As shown in the table above, there is no legal basis in Brazilian law allowing patentability of medical indications of known products, so this question is to be decided by case law. As has happened in Europe, this leaves room for varying interpretations for both the courts and the involved administrative bodies, such as the Patent Office (INPI) and the drugs agency ANVISA. While the INPI absorbed the EPO's practice, ANVISA is of the opinion that patenting of second (and further) medical indications is not permitted by Brazilian law and, therefore, usually denies prior consent to such applications.[123]

The mere transposition from the "European solution" of Swiss-type claims for the problem of patenting second medical indications to Brazilian law—as carried out by the INPI, probably due to the technical assistance it received from EPO[124]—is neither adequate not compatible with Brazilian law. As a result, the line adopted by the INPI is criticized by those concerned with the question of drug access in Brazil.[125] As I showed before, the Brazilian LPI does not have a statutory provision similar to Article 52(4) and 52(5) EPO 1973 or a provision similar to Article 54 EPO 2000. Therefore, there is no legal reason to admit the legality of "Swiss claims" under Brazilian patent law.

Setting aside the legal aspect, there are, of course, policy reasons that justify whether patents involving second medical indications should be available or not. In countries which are the home of big pharmaceutical corporations that develop patented medicines (the net gainers of stronger patent rights), such patents will be

123. *See* Shadlen (2009a), "The Politics of Patents and Drugs in Brazil and Mexico: The Industrial Bases of Health Activism," 42 *Comp. Pol.* 1, 41-58; Abranches da Silva et al. (2010), "Controvérsias sobre a proteção patentária de segundo uso médico de compostos químicos conhecidos," 33 *Química Nova* 8, 1825.

124. Drahos (2008), "Trust Me': Patent Offices in Developing Countries," 34 *Am. J. L. & Med.* 2, 151-174.

125. For instance, Fávaro Arruda Camargo Cerdeira (2005), "Patentes de Medicamentos e Saúde Pública," *RDM* 139, 195.

available due to trade policy reasons. In a country, however, where patented medicines have barely or not at all been developed (the net loser of stronger patent rights), not admitting patentability of second or further medical indications would be the better approach because expanding access to medicines and developing the local pharmaceutical industry is more important than paying high royalties for foreign industries.

(c) The whole or a part of a natural living being and biological materials found in nature

According to Article 10(IX) LPI, "the whole or part of natural living beings and biological materials found in nature, even if isolated therefrom, including the genome or germplasm of any natural living being, and the natural biological processes" are not considered to be an invention. This provision is to be read together with Article 18(II) LPI, which repeats that *natural* living beings are not patentable, except if they consist of a "transgenic microorganism," that is, microorganisms obtained by means of direct human intervention in their genetic composition, a characteristic normally not attainable by the species under natural conditions.[126]

Article 27.3b) TRIPS expressly allows parties to the agreement not to elect plants and animals as a patentable subject matter, but it also provides that microorganisms must be protected. According to *Borges Barbosa*, this exclusion from patentability is not in accordance with international standards and is a peculiarity of the patent law of some Latin American and African countries. In the Brazilian case, this provision reflects the influence and lobby of the Catholic Church—absolutely opposed to any form of "patenting life"—as well of environmentalists concerned with defending Brazilian biodiversity during the time when the bill was being discussed in Congress. This exclusion has been criticized by some authors, who are of the opinion that it is not justified and represents a problem for Brazilian scientists.[127]

Interpreting what exactly should be a "natural living being" and a "microorganism," in the sense of the law, is a complex task. INPI and ANVISA sometimes disagree at this point, the latter considering such an invention as a "natural living being" and, therefore, unpatentable in accordance with Brazilian law, while the Patent Office tends to consider it as a microorganism and, therefore, patentable. In at least 11 cases, the ANVISA denies its prior consent to patent grants precisely based on this distinction.[128]

126. Article 18 LPI: The following are not patentable: II—the whole or a part of living beings, except transgenic microorganisms that satisfy the three requirements of patentability—novelty, inventive step and industrial application—provided for in Article 8 and which are not mere discoveries.

Sole Paragraph—For the purposes of this law, transgenic microorganisms are organisms, except for the whole or a part of plants or animals that express, by means of direct human intervention in their genetic composition, a characteristic normally not attainable by the species under natural conditions.

127. For instance, Borges Barbosa (2011), "As hipóteses de incidência patentária do art. 10 do CPI/96," 4 *REVEL*, 165.

128. *See* below in 3-C-I-2.1.8 and 3-C-I-3.1.2.4.

3.2.2 General Exceptions to Patentability (Article 18 LPI)

3.2.2.1 Inventions Against Morality, Good Morals, Security, Ordre Public and Public Health

As it did in its previous patent laws, Article 18 LPI considers as not patentable those inventions that are contrary to "morality," "*ordre public,*" "security," "good morals," and "public health" as expressly allowed by Article 27.2 TRIPS. At this point, it is important to remember that an invention can only be considered as non-patentable under Article 27.2 TRIPS if prohibiting its commercial use is necessary to protect "*ordre public*" or "morality."[129] Therefore, Article 27.2 TRIPS does not justify a prohibition of patenting in cases where the diffusion of the invention is desired, such as in the case of pharmaceutical inventions.

Article 53(a) EPC also has a morality clause that gained practical importance in 2008, when the EPO refused to grant the patent in the Warf/Thompson case because "uses of human embryos for industrial or commercial purposes" are excluded from patent protection on morality grounds.[130]

The Brazilian morality/*ordre public* provision of Article 18 LPI, in contrast, has not been put into practice so far. *Valle* discusses a case in which the Patent Office (INPI) first refused to grant a patent on the grounds of its being both contrary to morality and that it used mammal embryos, which excluded it from protection by law, but after a review was requested, decided to grant the patent.[131] The invention consisted of a process for obtaining a mammal embryo used in the production of fibrinogen.[132]

Controversially, the possibility of excluding an invention from patent protection based on its being contrary to public health—in the context of Article 18(I) LPI—has been discussed in the context of ANVISA's role in the patent grant proceedings for pharmaceutical products and processes. In this context, some authors[133] and even the Federal Court of Justice of Rio de Janeiro[134] adopted the interpretation that ANVISA's prior consent would be justified by the general public health-clause of Article 18(I) LPI. This interpretation was adopted, at first, by the Brazilian Federal Attorney General

129. UNCTAD-ICTSD (2005), *Resource Book on TRIPS and Development*, Chap. 19, p. 384.
130. EPO, Decision of the Enlarged Board of Appeal dated November 25, 2008, G 2/06, Appellant WISCONSIN ALUMNI RESEARCH FOUNDATION. The full text of the decision can be downloaded at http://www.epo.org/law-practice/case-law-appeals/pdf/g060002ep1.pdf (last visited on August 31, 2020).
131. Valle (2005), "Bioética, Patentes e Experimentação Animal," *Revista Bioética*, March 30, 115-120.
132. INPI, PI1100234-4—"Processos para produzir fibrinogênio de uma descendência transgênica de um mamífero, embrião de um mamífero não humano e mamífero-não-humano-fêmea transgênico"—Applicants: Zymogenetics, Inc., Pharmaceutical Proteins Ltd. (US) and Pharmaceutical Proteins Ltd. (GB).
133. Tojal/Pessôa (2008), "A Anuência Prévia na Concessão de Patentes de Medicamentos e a Regulação Econômica da Indústria Farmacêutica," 8 *RDISAN*, 148-165.
134. TRF 2ª Reg., Ap. Cível 417419—Proc. nº 2004.51.01.517054-0—Novartis vs. ANVISA, January 27, 2010.

(*Advocacia Geral da União*—AGU) in its legal opinion[135] on the legality of ANVISA's prior consent.

ANVISA did not accept AGU's approach until 2017 when it suddenly agreed with INPI's interpretation of Article 229-C LPI 96.[136] In the past, ANVISA had pointed out that it could not base its veto on the general public health clause, specifically because such an examination would require that the drug itself be a risk for patients, which would require an analysis of data regarding safety and efficacy (clinical studies, for instance) which was mostly not available at the time of the granting of the patent.

According to ANVISA's former position, it is not possible to assess whether a drug is harmful to public health before the usual clinical tests regarding safety and efficacy have been carried out. But even if this were possible, it would be necessary to take out of the market a drug that is harmful to public health. This would mean that what ANVISA pursues by denying prior consent to a patent grant would necessarily be that the drug in question will never be commercialized. However, ANVISA's purpose in the patent examination is not to ban a drug from the market but rather to expand access to drugs. If the purpose of ANVISA's prior consent within the patent examination were to ban drugs "harmful to public health" from appearing on the market, the purpose of expanding access to medications would never be reached.

Therefore, I agree with *Borges Barbosa*, for whom AGU's interpretation according to which ANVISA is only allowed to deny prior consent on the basis of the morality/public health clause is false, as is the case law that follows the same line of thinking.[137]

3.2.2.2 Inventions Resulting from the Transformation of the Atomic Nucleus

Article 18(II) LPI excludes from patentability "substances, materials, mixtures, elements or products of any kind, as well as the modification of their physical-chemical properties and the respective processes for obtainment or modification when resulting from the transformation of the atomic nucleus."

This provision, which was already existent in the old Brazilian Patent Law (*Código de Propriedade Industrial*),[138] is rarely commented on in the Brazilian literature. One can say that this exclusion of subject patentable matter is probably motivated by reasons of internal security, to let open the possibility of developing, for instance, nuclear power in civil plants as well nuclear weapons without paying patent royalties. This exclusion of patentable subject matter is expressly allowed by Article 73 TRIPS Agreement.

135. AGU (2010), Parecer No. 337/PGF/EA/2010 approved by the Advogado Geral da União on January 7, 2011.
136. *See* Chapter 3-D-IV-2. ANVISA's change has supposedly to do with the shift to the right occurred in 2016, when President Rousseff was impeached.
137. Borges Barbosa (2014), "Anuência Prévia pela ANVISA: Só Para Proteger a Saúde Pública?," *7PIDCC, Aracaju,* Ano III, Ed. 7, 50-107.
138. Brazil (1971b), Article 9, j, Lei No. 5.772 of December 21, 1971.

3.2.2.3 Living Beings

Article 18(III) LPI excludes from patentability "the whole or part of living beings, except transgenic microorganisms that satisfy the three requirements of patentability—novelty, inventive step and industrial application—provided for in Article 8 and which are not mere discoveries."

Essentially, this provision repeats that of Article 10(IX), which already foresees the whole or a part of a living being, as not patentable with the purpose of making admissible the protection of "transgenic microorganisms," which is mandatory for WTO members due to the provision of Article 27.3b) TRIPS. According to the legal definition,[139] transgenic microorganisms are organisms—not considered as such to be the whole or a part of plants or animals—that have a characteristic normally not present in natural conditions, provided that this was obtained with human intervention.

Whether processes for obtaining a plant or an animal variety are also excluded from patent protection is a controversial matter in Brazil. *Loureiro* answers this question by simply pointing out that such processes must be patentable because the wording of the law does not exclude processes from patentability.[140]

This problem is also relevant in the context of ANVISA's prior consent since there are some cases in which ANVISA refuses to give its consent on the grounds of the prohibition of patents for living beings. In its report on ANVISA's prior consent granted between 2001 and 2006, ANVISA's examiner *Miranda* cites 10 cases in which prior consent was denied because, in ANVISA's view, the invention, if patented, would protect a living being, which is not allowed by law.[141]

3.2.3 Provisions Particularly Relevant for Pharmaceutical Inventions

3.2.3.1 Transitional Patent Protection for Pharmaceuticals, Chemical and Alimentary Products and Processes

(a) Mailbox protection (Article 70.8 TRIPS)

As a developing country, Brazil was obliged to provide for both mailbox protection and exclusive marketing rights between January 1, 1995 and May 14, 1997, when the LPI 96 came into force. At that time, neither a strict law nor a soft law was enacted to regulate this provisional obligation. Notwithstanding, the Patent Office received

139. Article 18 LPI sole paragraph.
140. de Andrade Vieira Loureiro (1999), *A Lei de Propriedade Industrial Comentada*, Lejus, São Paulo, pp. 73-74.
141. Miranda (2008), *Avaliação da análise dos pedidos de patentes farmacêuticas feita pela ANVISA no cumprimento do mandato legal da anuência prévia*, Fundação Osvaldo Cruz, Rio de Janeiro, p. 64.

applications based on Article 70.8 TRIPS.[142] According to *Basso*, INPI applied de facto mailbox provision from January 1, 1995 until May 14, 1996.[143] However, after approval of the LPI 96, all pending applications were only to be decided in accordance with the pipeline mechanism,[144] which was much more favorable to patent holders than the mailbox provision since, under the pipeline provision, the novelty was not to be examined at all.

Because the transitional protection provided by the "pipeline protection" was much broader than the one given by so-called exclusive marketing rights, the Brazilian patent law complied with TRIPS.

(b) Pipeline patent protection (Articles 230-231 LPI)

By admitting this transitional form of protection, the new legal regime recognized as being patentable inventions for which patents were already granted in other countries at a time when such inventions were not patentable in Brazil.[145] This included the time before the WTO Agreement entered into force.

(i) Object of the pipeline protection: product and process patents

According to Article 230 LPI, both product and process patents could be protected by the "pipeline" system, provided that the subject matter to which the product or process related was not patentable before the TRIPS Agreement came into force. The scope of the protection was more extensive than that of the pipeline protection proposed by the U.S. during the TRIPS negotiations since the latter[146] required transitional protection for products, but not for processes.

(ii) Conditions of grant

According to Article 230 LPI, a pipeline patent would be granted if the following conditions were satisfied: (1) the invention had not been marketed anywhere in the world, either directly by the patent owner or with his express consent; (2) no "serious and effective" preparations for the invention's exploitation had been made in Brazil by any third person; (3) the object of pipeline protection did not fall within the matter that

142. Borges Barbosa (2009b), *Direitos Exclusivos de Comercialização: um instituto inexistente no direito brasileiro*, p. 59, available at: http://denisbarbosa.addr.com/emr.pdf (last visited on August 31, 2020).
143. *See* Basso (2005), "TRIPS e os Exclusive Marketing Rights (EMRs)—Aplicação, Observância e Efeitos do Article 70.9 no Brasil," in: Basso/Prado/Zaitz (eds.), *Direito do Comércio Internacional*, p. 401.
144. Article 229 LPI in its original wording, that is, before the amendment made in December 1999: "The provisions of this Law shall apply to pending applications, except as regards patentability of substances, materials or products obtained by chemical means or processes, and alimentary or chemical-pharmaceutical substances, material, mixtures or products or medications of any kind, as well as the respective processes for obtaining or modifying them, which shall only be patentable under the conditions established by Articles 230 and 231."
145. *See* Chapter 3-A-I-2.1.
146. GATT (1990a), Article 26 Draft Agreement on the Trade-Related Aspects of Intellectual Property Rights, Communication from the United States: GATT Doc. No. MTN.GNG/NG11/W/68 (March 29, 1990).

was considered not to be an invention in Brazil in accordance with Article 10 LPI, nor unpatentable according to Article 18 LPI; and (4) a patent had been granted in the country of origin.[147] Once these conditions were present, the patent should be granted in Brazil, as it had been granted in its country of origin.[148]

(iii) Summary proceedings

Applicants had to file their pipeline applications at the latest one year after the new law came into force (i.e., before May 14, 1997), and they had to indicate the date of the first filing abroad.[149] Afterward, the Patent Office had to publish such applications, which remained dormant for a period of 90 days. Within this time, third parties were given the opportunity to present objections with respect to whether the object of the application had been already marketed elsewhere. Once this period of time was gone, the Patent Office had to test whether the matter was patentable under the new law. If an application fulfilled the conditions required under Article 230 LPI, a pipeline patent would be granted for the time of patent protection remaining in the country where the first application was filed, counted from the date the application was made in Brazil.

(iv) Pending applications

Pipeline provisions should also be applied to all pending applications at the time of the enactment of the new law if the invention filed regarded matter related to pharmaceutical, chemical and alimentary substances and processes. Consequently, the special conditions and proceedings laid down for pipeline protection were also applicable to pending applications filed before the coming into force of the LPI.[150] Making pipeline proceedings available for all pending applications was very beneficial to patent applicants since, under the mailbox system, they would have to show that their invention was new, inventive and had an industrial application. Under the pipeline proceedings, a new substantial examination would not be made by the Patent Office in Brazil. Besides, patent applicants who had a pending application that had been submitted to the INPI were allowed to abandon this application and file a pipeline application.[151]

(v) Time of protection

The time of protection was the period of protection remaining in the country where the first application had been filed.[152] For instance, let us assume an application for a pharmaceutical product or process was filed in the U.S. on January 13, 1992, and a patent was granted there on December 1, 1994, for the time of 17 years, that is, until December 2011. Suppose that on November 13, 1996, a pipeline application was

147. Article 230 LPI.
148. Article 230.3 LPI.
149. Article 230.1 LPI.
150. Article 229 LPI in its original wording.
151. Article 230.5 LPI.
152. Article 230.4 LPI.

applied for in Brazil and that in December 1999, the INPI decided to accept the application. This invention would enjoy 11 years of pipeline patent protection in Brazil.

(vi) Controversy over pipeline patent protection

Pipeline patent protection is very controversial in Brazil. From the start, the literature has discussed whether such a form of patent protection is compatible with the BC. *Borges Barbosa* was of the opinion that pipeline protection would be incompatible with the prohibition of retroactivity of the law since such patents protected inventions that belonged to the public domain before 1996.[153] The other school of thought—mostly composed of members of the Brazilian patent community—supports the view that pipeline patents are in accordance with the BC.[154] In April 2009, a complaint of unconstitutionality against Articles 230 and 231 LPI was initiated by the Prosecutor General of Brazil (*Procurador Geral da República*) at the Supreme Court of Brazil (STF). In August 2020[155]—more than 11 years after the case having been initiated—the Supreme Court had not yet judged it.[156]

3.2.3.2 Compulsory Licensing (Articles 68-71 LPI)

Compulsory licenses of patents are often equated with expropriation, and sometimes they are treated as if they would belong to the same category of rights. However, both institutes are very distinct with regard to essential aspects. Because of that, even if both are institutions of administrative law, they are submitted to very different legal regimes.

First, they are so different because expropriation and compulsory licenses have different objects. While the object of an expropriation is tangible property rights (*propriedade*)—which is an institute of civil law, and as such, submitted to the Brazilian Civil Code (*Código Civil Brasileiro*)[157]—the object of compulsory licenses is "intellectual property rights," such as patents, trademarks, copyrights, geographical

153. Borges Barbosa (2013), *Sempre as Inconstitucionalidades das Patentes Pipeline: Uma Visão Renovada*, July 2013. *See also* Avelãs Nunes et. al. (2009), "A Inconstitucionalidade das Patentes 'Pipeline' Brasileiras (Artigos 230° e 231° do Código da Propriedade Industrial de 1996," *REVEL—Edição Especial "Patentes Pipeline,"* 4-73 (November); Grau-Kuntz (2009), "Sobre a Controvertida Questão das Patentes 'Pipeline'," *REVEL—Edição Especial "Patentes Pipeline,"* 82-95; Silveira (2009), "Apontamentos Relativos à Questão do Pipeline," *REVEL—Edição Especial "Patentes Pipeline,"* 74-81.
154. *See*, for instance, Bacelar Ahlert/de Bessa Antunes (2007), "Pipeline e Constituição: de que Inconstitucionalidade Falamos?," *Revista da IBPI* 87, 45-68; Gomes Canotilho/Machado (2008), *A Questão da Constitucionalidade das Patentes "Pipeline" à Luz da Constituição Federal Brasileira de 1988*, Editora Almedina, Coimbra.
155. *See* ADI 4234, information available at http://www.stf.jus.br/portal/processo/verProcessoAndamento.asp?incidente=12879 (last visited on August 23, 2020).
156. *Lunardi* and *Dimoulis*, both Law Professors, respectively, at the UNESP and the FGV, strongly criticize the grave STF's omission in Dimoulis/Lunardi (2017), *O custo social da inércia do STF: Réquiem da ADI 4234*, available at http://www.unesp.br/portal#!/noticia/28330/artigo-o-custo-social-da-inercia-do-stf-requiem-da-adi-4234/ (last visited on August 31, 2020).
157. Law No. 10.406 of January 10, 2002, DOU January 11, 2002.

indications, etc. Although IP rights are called "property," this denomination is deceptive. Because of their different legal nature, IP rights are not submitted to the Civil Code regime, but they are regulated by laws foreseeing a special regime for them. For instance, patents and trademarks are dealt with by the LPI, while copyrights are treated by the Copyright Law (*Lei dos Direitos Autorais*).[158] With regard to patents, the essential distinction is in their origin. Tangible property arises as a rule either from a deal between two individuals (e.g., a sale agreement) or by succession. Exceptionally, the tangible property will arise from usucapion, but the tangible property will never arise from an administrative act. Patent rights, however, are par excellence generated by an administrative act which is issued after complex and extensive proceedings. Unlike tangible property rights, patent rights can never be primarily originated between private persons since their existence will always depend on a request and the grant by the INPI.

Second, while expropriation of a tangible property requires that the good to be expropriated will be declared by the State as being of "public usefulness" (*bem de utilidade pública*),[159] a compulsory license requires either "public interest"—which is much more than the mere "public usefulness"—or an inadequate or abusive exploration of the patent.

Third, the compulsory license of patents and expropriation have very different proceedings. First, while expropriation proceedings will always start ex officio, compulsory licenses can be initiated both by a competitor's request or ex officio.

Compulsory licenses were first introduced in Brazil in 1945. At that time, there were only two reasons for the granting of compulsory licenses: one was the non-use of a patent for a period lasting two years after the granting of that patent; the other was the interruption of its use.[160] The LPI 1971 introduced an additional reason for granting a compulsory license, namely the public interest. As it is to be expected from a legal mechanism whose purpose is that it be used in an exceptional situation, the Brazilian experience with compulsory licenses is limited. When the LPI was approved in 1996, two compulsory licenses had already been granted.[161] The first time was in 1977; this case was based on the public interest and concerned the patent protecting the foot and mouth disease vaccine.[162] The second compulsory license was granted in 1984, based on the "local-working" provision.[163] Its object was also a chemical product, and its owner was an American company. The compulsory license was applied for by a Brazilian company from the Patent Office (INPI), which granted it.[164]

158. Law No. 9.610 of February 19, 1998, DOU February 20, 1998.
159. Article 2 Decreto-Lei 3.365, June 27, 1941, DOU July 18, 1941.
160. Brazil (1945), Articles 53-63 Decreto-Lei 7.903, August 27, 1945, DOU, September 29, 1945.
161. Faria (2006), "Licença Compulsória como Alternativa para a Garantia do Acesso Universal a Antirretrovirais no Brasil," 85 *Revista da ABPI*, 32.
162. Patent No. 71.767, RPI November 29, 1977, p. 152, cited from Guise Rosina (2007), *Comércio Internacional, Patentes e Saúde Pública*, Master Thesis, Universidade Federal de Santa Catarina, p. 96.
163. Patent No. 71.07076, RPI May 29, 1984, p. 86, cited from Guise Rosina (2007), *ibid.*, p. 96.
164. Nortox Agroquímica S/A vs. Monsanto: PI7107076, RPI 710 29.5.1984, S. 86, DIRCO/1649/83, cited from Borges Barbosa (1983), *Nota sobre a licença compulsória Monsanto de 1983*, p. 1.

The original patent owner sued the INPI and the Brazilian company afterward, but the decision on the compulsory license was upheld by the Courts.[165]

The LPI 1996, mirroring the TRIPS Agreement, expanded the possibilities for granting compulsory licenses. According to Articles 68 and 71 LPI, the following cases justify the granting of compulsory licenses:

(1) national emergency or public interest (Article 71);
(2) non-utilization or insufficient utilization of the domestic patent ("local working");
(3) dependent patents; and
(4) restraint of competition and abuse of patent rights (antitrust compulsory licenses).

The proceedings of compulsory licensing on the grounds of national emergency or public interest were not regulated by the LPI 96. This was regulated later by a proper decree, which will be examined in the section concerning the first reform of the patent law, which occurred in 1999.[166] The other cases are examined here.

(a) Non-utilization or insufficient utilization of the domestic patent ("local working")

According to Article 68.1 LPI—the "local-working" provision—a compulsory license may be justified in two cases:

(1) non-exploitation of the object of the patent within the Brazilian territory in terms of failure to manufacture or incomplete manufacture of the product, or also failure to make full use of the patented process, except for cases where this is not economically feasible when importation shall be permitted; or
(2) commercialization that does not satisfy the market's needs.

However, the compulsory license must not be granted in the following cases:

(1) if the patent owner justifies the non-exploitation with legitimate reasons;
(2) if the patent owner proves that serious and effective preparations for the patent's exploitation have been made; and
(3) if the patent owner justifies the failure to manufacture as being by reason of an obstacle of a legal nature.

The procedure for obtaining this type of compulsory license is different from the one concerning the grant of a compulsory license based on public interest. The procedure is not initiated ex officio. It is necessary that an interested party makes a

165. Borges Barbosa (1983), *Nota sobre a licença compulsória Monsanto de 1983*; Levy/Licks (2003), *O Requisito de Fabricação Completa do Objeto de uma Patente no Território Nacional*, p. 6.
166. *See* Chapter 3, Part B, Section 4.3.

request for a compulsory license to be granted. This request shall be submitted to the patent office. Article 68(5) LPI requires that a time period of three years from the granting of the patent has passed; otherwise, the application is inadmissible. The request must include, according to Article 73 LPI, an offer concerning the conditions of license. The patent owner shall be heard by the patent office. He is given a period of 60 days in which to make a statement about the request. If this period expires without a statement from the patent owner, the compulsory license is to be issued in accordance with the conditions offered by the applicant.[167] If the patent owner makes a statement concerning the compulsory license, the Patent Office must make a decision about the compulsory license within 60 days.[168]

This provision of the Brazilian Patent Act caused a second commercial patent conflict between Brazil and the U.S., which challenged it in a panel at the WTO, accusing the Brazilian local working provision of being incompatible with the TRIPS Agreement. In June 2000, the U.S. requested consultations with the WTO regarding the provisions of the Brazilian patent law concerning the "local-working requirement."[169] In their view, the local-working provision discriminated between products made in Brazil and products made elsewhere by submitting the latter to compulsory licenses. This would be incompatible with the prohibition of discrimination within the terms of Article 27.1 of the TRIPS Agreement.[170]

The Brazilian government took the view that the local-working requirement was not contrary to TRIPS due to Article 5 of the Paris Convention,[171] a position which was also supported by the literature.[172] As no agreement could be reached, a panel was installed.[173] In addition, Brazil requested consultations with respect to an alleged non-conformity of the U.S. patent law with TRIPS. Brazil argued that also the U.S. patent law provides for a kind of "local working" because patents that have been developed with public money must be produced in the United States.[174]

167. Article 73.1 LPI.
168. Article 73.2 LPI.
169. WTO (2000), Brazil—Measures Affecting Patenting Protection (WTO Document WT/DS199/1).
170. For a detailed analysis of the conflict, *see* Shanker (2002a), "Brazil, the Pharmaceutical Industry and the WTO," 5 *JWIP*, 53-104.
171. Nogueira Viana (2002), "Intellectual Property Rights, the World Trade Organization and Public Health: the Brazilian Perspective," 17 *Conn. J. Int'l L.*, 312.
172. For the compatibility of Local Working with TRIPS: Basso et al. (2001), "A Lei de Patentes e as Regras da Organização Mundial do Comércio," 55 *Revista da ABPI*, 35-40; Beltrame (2011), "Lei de Propriedade Industrial do Brasil em Discussão na OMC," 55 *Revista da ABPI*, 31-34; Santos Cruz (2006), "A Licença Compulsória como Instrumento de Adequação da Patente à sua Função Social," 80 *Revista da ABPI*, 45-55. Other view: Levy/Licks (2003), *O Requisito da Fabricação Completa do Objeto de uma Patente no Território Nacional*; Hey (2003), *Licença Obrigatória de Patentes—Entender Antes de Aplicar*, Interfarma, p. 38.
173. WTO (2000), WTO Doc. WT/DS199/1, Brazil—Measures Affecting Patent Protection of June 8, 2000.
174. Shanker (2002a), "Brazil, the Pharmaceutical Industry and the WTO," 5 *JWIP*, pp. 92-94.

The dispute was not decided by the panel since the parties found a compromise: the Brazilian government promised to consult the U.S. before applying its "local-working provision."[175] This agreement was largely perceived in Brazil as a "victory."[176] In any case, to date, the local-working provision has never been used in Brazil.

(b) Dependent patents

Under Article 70 LPI 96, a compulsory license may be granted in the case of dependent patents. This is the case when the following elements are present:

(1) A patent is "dependent" on another patent;
(2) the subject of the dependent patent constitutes a substantial technical advance in relation to the earlier patent; and
(3) the patent owner makes no agreement with the dependent patent's owner concerning the use of the earlier patent.

According to Article 70.1 LPI, a patent is considered to be a dependent patent when its use depends on an older patent. To date, a compulsory license on this basis has never been granted in Brazil.

(c) Restraint of competition and abusive exercise of patent rights (compulsory license of antitrust law's nature)

Compulsory licenses of antitrust law were introduced in 1994 by an antitrust act (AL 94) that was approved at that time.[177] Under Article 24(IV-b) AL 94, Administrative Counsel for the Economic Defense, Brazilian Antitrust Authorities (Conselho Administrativo de Defesa Econômica—CADE) may *recommend* that compulsory licensing of patents is issued as an additional penalty in serious cases of antitrust violation. In 2011, a new antitrust law was passed (AL 2011), and the provision on the compulsory license was maintained under Article 38(IV-a) with the proviso, however, that the infraction was connected with the use of intellectual property rights.[178] The hypothesis of the application is determined by the LPI 96. In accordance with Article 68 LPI 96, a patent owner might have the patent licensed on a compulsory basis if he exercises his rights in an abusive manner or in an abuse of economic power, proving that the abusive conduct is declared as such by an administrative or judicial decision.

The procedure for antitrust licenses might have two or three stages: first, there are the administrative proceedings at the CADE, which is competent to determine if the conduct constitutes an anti-competitive act and, in such a case, to recommend that a compulsory license is issued as a penalty; second, administrative proceedings follow at

175. WTO (2001a), WTO Doc. WT/DS199/4 G/L454 IP/D/23/Add.1 of July 19, 2001.
176. Oliveira/Moreno (2007), "Negociações Comerciais Internacionais e a Democracia: o Contencioso Brasil x EUA das Patentes Farmacêuticas na OMC," 50 *DADOS—Revista de Ciências Sociais*, p. 198.
177. Brasil (1994a), Lei No. 8.884 of June 11, 1994, DOU, June 13, 1994, p. 8437.
178. Brasil (2011b), Lei No. 12.529 of November 30, 2011, DOU, Seção I, December 1, 2011, p. 1.

the INPI, which is competent to issue a compulsory license, provided that no judicial remedy is applied against the advice of the antitrust authority.

In 1999, the Ministry of Health ordered the Cartel Authority (CADE) to give its legal opinion on the question of how to apply this instrument because antitrust law is silent on the procedure for the granting of such compulsory licenses.[179] The legal authority concluded that a compulsory license may be recommended by CADE whenever the conditions imposed by Article 21 (AL 1994) are fulfilled.[180] This provision does not define anticompetitive behavior but gives 24 examples of such behavior. In addition, the abuse should have something to do with the patent itself.

For the purposes of this kind of compulsory license proceedings, anticompetitive behavior is determined only by the CADE. This body determines whether the conduct in question constitutes an abuse of patent rights and decides whether to recommend the compulsory license or not. The patent office's role is only to grant compulsory licenses and decide on the amount of compensation to be paid.[181]

Rosenberg and other Brazilian authors consider antitrust compulsory license as an adequate and effective instrument for reducing drug prices so that they might also play a role in improving access to medicines.[182] They have to date[183] never been applied in Brazil, neither with reference to a drug nor to another product.[184] In March 2020, however, the CADE opened a formal investigation to address possible anticompetitive practices of pharmaceutical companies and other firms acting in the healthcare sector in the context of the coronavirus (COVID-19) pandemic.[185]

In Europe, on the other hand, punishing anticompetitive behavior due to abuse of a dominant position (such as, for instance, the so-called pay for delay settlements agreed between the brand company and the generic competitor) may be punished with the imposition of high fines.

---

179. Rosenberg (2004), *Patentes de Medicamentos e Comércio Internacional: Os Parâmetros do TRIPS e do Direito Concorrencial para a Outorga de Licenças Compulsórias*, PhD Thesis, Universidade de São Paulo, p. 207.
180. CADE: Consulta 31/99 (Resolução CADE 18/98), cited from Rosenberg (2007), *Patentes de Medicamentos e Comércio Internacional: Os Parâmetros do TRIPS e do Direito Concorrencial para a Outorga de Licenças Compulsórias*, fn. 605.
181. Vaz e Dias (2001), "Licença Compulsória de Patentes e o Direito Antitruste," 54 *Revista da ABPI*, 7.
182. Rosenberg (2004), *Patentes de Medicamentos e Comércio Internacional: Os Parâmetros do TRIPS e do Direito Concorrencial para a Outorga de Licenças Compulsórias*, PhD Thesis, p. 241; Amaral Júnior (2006), "O Acordo TRIPS, a Licença Compulsória e os Países em Desenvolvimento," *Revista do Tribunal Regional Federal—3ª Região*, 115; Salomão Filho (2007), "Razoabilidade e Legalidade do Licenciamento Compulsório do Ponto de Vista Concorrencial," in: Basso/Salomão/Calixto/Polido/César (eds.), *Direitos de Propriedade Intelectual e Saúde Pública—O Acesso Universal aos Medicamentos Antirretrovirais no Brasil*, São Paulo, pp. 165-166.
183. August 2020.
184. *See* Rosenberg (2004), *Patentes de Medicamentos e Comércio Internacional: Os Parâmetros do TRIPS e do Direito Concorrencial para a Outorga de Licenças Compulsórias*, PhD Thesis, p. 207.
185. CADE (2020), Despacho SG Instauração de Procedimento Preparatório No. 19/2020, Case No. 08700.001354/2020-48, available at http://www.cade.gov.br/noticias/cade-abre-investigacao-no-setor-de-produtos-medicos-farmaceuticos (last visited on August 23, 2020).

3.2.3.3 Exceptions to Rights Conferred by a Patent

As provided by Article 42 LPI, a patent confers on its owner the right to prevent any other party from—without his consent—producing, using, offering for sale, selling or importing a patented product or a product directly obtained by the patented process. The Brazilian patent law admits some limited exceptions to these exclusive rights, which are briefly presented below.

(a) "Private use" exception

Article 43(I) LPI foresees that the exclusive rights conferred by a patent do not extend to acts carried out by unauthorized third parties if such acts are done in a private way and without commercial purpose, and provided that these acts do not cause an economic loss for the patentee. Brazilian literature does not mention any practical case regarding the application of this provision. *Loureiro* imagines as characterizing this exception in the case of a non-authorized person who produces a patented product only for her domestic use;[186] *Borges Barbosa* imagines an artisan who produces the patented invention in his private studio as a mere hobby.[187] Both authors emphasize that the decisive element in this exception is the lack of an economic aspect to such use.

(b) Research exception or experimental use

Under Article 43(II) LPI, third parties are allowed—without the authorization of the patent owner—to make use of the patented product or process for experimental purposes, provided that these are connected with scientific or technological studies or research. In common with the exception regarding the "private use" exception, this unauthorized use should not have any commercial purpose. In contrast to it, however, this unauthorized use may be public.

(c) Individual prescription exception

According to Article 43(III) LPI, the preparation of medicines for individual cases in accordance with a medical prescription carried out by a qualified professional does not affect any existing patent rights. In Brazil, pharmacies that engage in this are called *farmácias de manipulação*. Usually, such pharmacies are small businesses with their own laboratories.

In practice, this exemption has not been relevant. In the first place, this is because most active ingredients used in Brazil are not produced locally, meaning that these types of small pharmacies also have to import from third countries. However, there are practical difficulties associated with importing active ingredients in small quantities. In order to circumvent such difficulties, they tend to buy the active ingredients from larger import firms, a fact which supports the view that such importing does not violate

186. De Andrade Vieira Loureiro (1999), *Comentários à Lei de Propriedade Industrial*, São Paulo, p. 109.
187. Borges Barbosa (2002), *Limites do direito de patente, exaustão, fair usage e importação paralela*.

patent rights since it is done only to sell the patented product for the purpose of individual preparations in small pharmacies. This interpretation has been rejected at least twice by the Court of Justice of São Paulo, which ruled that the individual preparation exception must be restrictively interpreted; therefore, it cannot be extended to import firms.[188] The case law on this topic, however, is still hesitant. The Federal Court of Rio de Janeiro ruled—per majority—in a case involving the same parties that this exception must be extended to import firms in order to make them viable.[189] In the concrete case, however, the import of the patented active ingredient was suspended by ANVISA on regulatory grounds.[190]

(d) Exhaustion regime and parallel imports

Under Article 42, in combination with Article 43(IV) LPI, the patent owner is granted the exclusive right to make, to sell and to import his product, unless the product was not directly marketed, by the patentee or with his consent, in the internal market. In the Brazilian literature, the dominant opinion is that the LPI adopted the principle of national exhaustion so that parallel imports of patented products are not generally allowed.[191] There has been at least one decision by the São Paulo Court of Second Instance in this direction.[192]

According to *Scholze*, the principle of national exhaustion was not foreseen in the first patent bill, which had been discussed for five years in Congress.[193] This author writes that, in the beginning, the Executive Branch was convinced that local production should be promoted, but, at the same time, that parallel imports should also be generally allowed. *Scholze* relates that by the time the question was being debated at the Congress, the Executive Branch noted that it would be difficult to conciliate the promotion of local production if, at the same time, parallel imports were admitted, and

188. TJSP—Agravo de Instrumento (AI) No. 994.08.019492-0. SP Farma Ltda. vs. Sanofi Aventis, J. May 19, 2010.
189. TRF2—Agravo de Instrumento 2008.02.01.015342-7, SP Farma Ltda. vs. Sanofi Aventis and INPI, Ruling Date October 15, 2008, DJ October 17, 2008.
190. TRF-2, AI No. 0015342-78.2008.4.02.0000 (TRF2 2008.02.01.015342-7), SP Farma Ltda. vs. Sanofi Aventis, Ruling Date March 31, 2009, DJ June 19, 2009, p. 195.
191. Guise Rosina (2006), *Comércio Internacional, Patentes e Saúde Pública*, Master Thesis, Universidade Federal de Santa Catarina, p. 87; Scholze (2001), "Fabricação Local, Licença Compulsória e Importação Paralela na Lei de Propriedade Industrial," 54 *Revista da ABPI*, 11-12; Rosenberg (2004), *As Patentes de Medicamentos e Comércio Internacional: Os Parâmetros do TRIPS e do Direito Concorrencial para a Outorga de Licenças Compulsórias*, PhD Thesis, Universidade de São Paulo, p. 226; Vargas (2006), *O Direito da Propriedade Intelectual face ao Direito de Acesso a Medicamentos*, Master Thesis, Universidade de São Paulo, p. 113. Villagra Marques (2001), *A Questão da Importação Paralela no Comércio Internacional*, writes that the very few existing court decisions on the topic also assume that the Brazilian law adopted the regime of national exhaustion. However, she does not mention any single decision.
192. TJSP, Ap. 90.43257.15.2006.8.26.0000. Gamma Comércio Importação Ltda. vs. Abbot GmbH e Co KG, J. December 14, 2006. In the concrete case, the Court prohibited the respondent to import the patented active ingredient sibutramine (used in drugs against obesity), due to lack of authorization of the patent owner, but the question of national or international exhaustion is not explicitly discussed.
193. Scholze (2001), "Fabricação Local, Licença Compulsória e Importação Paralela na Lei de Propriedade Industrial," 54 *Revista da ABPI*, 10.

it, therefore, started to support national exhaustion. A consensual solution was then achieved by adopting the principle of national exhaustion as a rule, but, at the same time, admitting exceptions from it. The consensual solution provided by the LPI would be connecting the questions of "local working," compulsory licensing and parallel imports to each other so that the last two would exceptionally function as a kind of sanction for lack of "local working."[194]

Consequently, there are cases where the law, exceptionally, allows imports of a patented product into the domestic market without the patent owner's approval. This, however, is only allowed in conjunction with a lack of local production of the patented product, and in two cases: namely: (1) after the grant of a compulsory license;[195] or (2) if the patentee, instead of locally manufacturing the patented product in Brazil, imports it into the Brazilian internal market because otherwise, local production would be economically not viable.[196]

Fonseca da Silva[197] is of the opinion—followed at least by one ruling of São Paulo's Court of Second Instance[198]—that there is one more legal prevision of parallel imports. In his interpretation of Article 43(IV) LPI, parallel imports would also be legally possible when a patented product is introduced to the internal market directly by the patentee or with his consent. This would mean, for instance, that, if a certain amount of the drug Y legally reaches the internal market, any other party would consequently be also allowed to import the medicament Y. I think, however, that this is incorrect because exhaustion would only apply to the concrete units of the medicament Y that were, in fact, introduced to the Brazilian market. If the patent owner, for instance, directly imported 1,000 units of the medicament Y into Brazil, exhaustion would occur only in the case of these 1,000 units. On this basis, third parties are not allowed to import another 1,000 units of the medicament Y because the exclusive rights regarding these would not be exhausted. In order to do so, third parties would require authorization from the patentee.[199] As a consequence, parallel imports are only admitted in Brazilian law if they have been either preceded by a compulsory license or if the patent was only "worked" through importing.

194. For a critical view of this legal solution and the need for change, *see* Barros e Castro (2003), *Em Pauta—o Projeto de Lei nº. 139 e a Propriedade Industrial no Brasil.*
195. Article 68(I) LPI.
196. Article 68, § 1°. LPI.
197. Fonseca da Silva (2002), "Importação Paralela de Medicamentos," 39 *Revista de Informação Legislativa* 154, 35.
198. Tribunal de Justiça de São Paulo (TJSP), Apelação No. 0272901-70.2009.8.26.0000. Galena Química e Farmacêutica Ltda. vs. Pharmaspecial Especialidades Químicas e Farmacêuticas Ltda., Ruling date June 7, 2011. In this concrete case, however, the patented product had been introduced to the Brazilian market without the authorization of the patentee. The product was legally bought on the international market and then introduced to Brazil. The Court, in a technical mistake, did not make a distinction between international and national exhaustion.
199. Patrocínio (2006), "O Princípio da Exaustão dos Direitos de Propriedade Intelectual e a Importação Paralela," 84 *Revista da ABPI*, 47-52 (51).

(i) Parallel imports based on a compulsory license

According to the LPI's wording, only compulsory licenses based either on the omission of the domestic exploitation of the patent[200] or on the abusive exercise of patent rights[201] are able to justify a general permission of parallel imports.[202] One requirement for issuing a compulsory license in the case of non-local working is that the patented product is not domestically manufactured within three years after the patent grant. If, during compulsory licensing proceedings, the patentee proves that production on the domestic market is uneconomical, a compulsory license will not be granted, but the patent owner will be punished with the authorization of parallel imports. It is worth noting that, also, in this case, imports are only admitted if they originate from an authorized supplier.[203] Therefore, imports of a generic drug as a sanction for lack of local working are not permitted.[204]

(ii) Parallel imports based on exclusive exploitation via imports

Under Article 68(4) LPI, third parties may also import the patented product without the authorization of the patentee if the patentee does not produce the patented invention in the Brazilian market but instead imports it from overseas. The literature discusses whether this would be an unjustified different treatment in comparison to the case of a compulsory license since the latter requires that the patent has not been worked for at least three years since it was granted. If the patent owner does not work the patent for three years—which means that he neither locally produces the patented product nor imports it from abroad—no one is allowed to import the product of a third party until compulsory licensing proceedings start. If, however, the patentee, instead of doing nothing, uses his patent only by importing his patented product from overseas, third parties may also import the product.

(iii) The exhaustion question at the MERCOSUR (Common Market of the South)

The issue of the exhaustion of patent rights is neither treated in the contract that created the MERCOSUL in 1991[205] nor in the later Protocol on Harmonization of

200. Article 68(I) LPI.
201. Article 68 § 4 LPI.
202. For parallel imports and the case of compulsory licenses based on public interest or national emergency, *see* Section 4.3 of this chapter.
203. Article 68(I), second sentence LPI.
204. Scholze (2001), "Fabricação Local, Licença Compulsória e Importação Paralela na Lei de Propriedade Industrial," 54 *Revista da ABPI*, 11.
205. MERCOSUR (1991), Tratado para la Constitución de un Mercado Comun (Tratado de Asunción), March 26, 1991.

Intellectual Property.[206] Whether a special regime of exhaustion valid only for member countries will be developed or not remains to be seen.[207]

(e) "Living-material" exception

In Brazilian patent law, there are two special exception rules concerning patent rights related to "living material," that is, microorganisms (the only kind of living material which is patentable under Brazilian law).

Article 43(V) LPI sets forth that third parties may use the patented product related to the living material in question, without having an economic interest, as an initial source of variation or propagation with which to obtain other products. Article 43(VI) LPI determines that third parties may use, place in circulation, or market a patented product that has been legally introduced into commerce by the patent owner (or the holder of a license), provided that the patented product is not used for commercial multiplication or propagation of the living material in question.

3.2.3.4 Minimum 10-Years' Term of Patent Protection after Patent Grant

Following the standard set by Article 33 of the TRIPS Agreement, Article 40 LPI provides for a patent term of 20 years from the filing date. The Brazilian LPI goes further than TRIPS, and, in a TRIPS-plus provision, it provides that the patent term should not be less than 10 years for an invention patent, beginning on the date the patent is *granted*, unless the INPI has been prevented from examining the merits of the application by a proven pending judicial dispute or for reasons of force majeure.

A patent is considered to be pending between the data of publication—which occurs 18 months after filing—and the data of granting of the patent. Article 44 LPI reads:

> The patent holder is assured the right to obtain indemnification for improper exploitation of the object of his patent, including that which occurs between the date of publication and the date of granting of the patent.

This provision guarantees the patentee a minimum patent term of 10 years after the grant, not including the backlog time of patents pending. In 2015, the backlog in the INPI varied from 8 to 11 years.[208] Regarding pharmaceutical patents, INPI takes 12 to 14 years to examine patent applications.[209] In practice, this provision guarantees that,

206. MERCOSUR (1995) Protocolo de Armonización de Normas sobre Propiedad Intelectual en el MERCOSUR, en materia de Marcas, Indicaciones de Procedencia y Denominaciones de Orígen. Asunción, August 5, 1995.
207. Fekete (1997), "Importações Paralelas: A Implementação do Princípio da Exaustão de Direitos no Mercosul, diante do Contexto de Globalização," *Revista da ABPI—Anais do XVII Seminário Nacional de Propriedade Industrial*, pp. 76-102.
208. Gouveia (2007), "Inovação e Patentes: o tempo de maturação no Brasil," 3 *Inovação UNIEMP* 3, 24-25; Rodrigues Alves (2015), "País demora 11 anos para aprovar patentes," *O Estado de São Paulo*, May 24, 2015.
209. Sampat/Shadlen (2017), *Secondary Pharmaceutical Patenting: A Global Perspective*, NBER Working Paper No. 23114, p. 30.

in Brazil, a patent term of 28 to 30 years is de facto enjoyed by the patentees. This is so because the non-authorized use of a pending patent may give rise to damages.

In August 2019, a study conducted by the Federal University of Rio de Janeiro confirmed that drugs enjoy in Brazil, on average, 23 years of patent protection. The study found that since 1997, the INPI has granted 683 pharmaceutical patents; therefrom 630 (92 percent) were benefited with a patent protection time longer than 20 years. According to *Paranhos*, the economist who coordinated the study, there are cases in which the patent protection reaches 28 years. The study figured that this legal patent extension costs 3.8 billion Brazilian *real* (or circa USD 1 billion) for the Brazilian Public Healthcare System (*Sistema Universal de Saúde*—SUS).[210]

3.3 Important Topics That the LPI 96 Does Not Deal With

Two important topics regarding the patentable subject matter are not dealt with by the LPI 96. The first one concerns patenting a new medical use of a known substance; the other one refers to the so-called selection inventions. In consequence, it is possible to grant or to deny patentability to such inventions, depending on how the concepts of novelty and inventiveness are interpreted. Because the LPI 96 does not have any special provision concerning the patentability of second medical indications and invention selections,[211] there is the flexibility to accept them or not. INPI, which adopts a pro-patent policy, tends to consider both kinds of inventions as patentable. In spite of this, the question of the patentability of such inventions in Brazil is an open question because it has not yet been the object of judgments from higher Brazilian Courts.

II Patent Grant Proceedings

In this section, the normal course of patent proceedings in Brazil will be presented. First, some basic principles of administration law in Brazil will be presented since they are applicable to all administrative processes—and then the ordinary patent proceedings, applicable to all inventions, will be discussed.

1 Basic Principles of Administrative Law in Brazil

In Brazilian Administrative Law, every administrative decision can be challenged at any time via judicial remedy, even if the administrative proceedings (internal review process) has not yet ended. This means that an administrative decision issued, for instance, by the INPI, can be brought to a judicial court at any time. So, the applicant

210. Paranhos (2020), "Public Health System Increasing Costs due to the Extension of Drug Patente Terms," Webinar Knowledge Network for Innovation and Access to Medicines, Global Health Centre.
211. About selection inventions in Brazilian law, *see* Borges Barbosa (2009c), *Nota sobre as reivindicações de seleção no direito brasileiro.*

decides whether she wants to challenge the administrative decision via an administrative remedy or by bringing the case to the courts. The same is valid for any ANVISA's decision. If ANVISA, for instance, refuses to give its consent to patent grant, the applicant has the choice of challenging the decision via either an administrative or a judicial remedy. Usually, bringing the case before a judicial court prior to the end of the administrative process results in a considerable delay in obtaining a final administrative decision since the latter must wait until a final judicial decision supervenes.

2 *Brazilian Judicial System*

In some countries, patent cases, when brought to justice, are decided by specialized courts. This is, for instance, the case in Germany, where the patent office's decisions are decided by the BPatG[212] (Superior Federal Court of Patents). In Brazil, there is no specialized court for patent questions, so patent cases are decided by the "Common Justice," that is to say, the Courts of Justice, which decide on general matters.

Basically, the judicial branch is separated into two levels in Brazil, each one with different competencies and independently organized. One level is run by the Member States of the Brazilian federation, the so-called Justiça dos Estados. The other one is administered by the federal authorities, the competence of which is determined by the Federal Constitution.[213] The competence of the judiciary of the federal states is defined in a supplementary way, so every matter that does not lie within the competence of the federal courts is to be decided by the courts of the Member States. As a rule, all cases in which a federal entity takes part—such as the Patent Office and the Health Agency—are to be decided by the federal courts. In practice, this means that a decision issued by INPI or ANVISA would be challenged before the Federal Court of First Instance (*Justiça Federal*). Appellations are judged by the Federal Court of Second Instance (*Tribunal Regional Federal—TRF*). Judgments by the TRF can be challenged before the Federal Superior Court of Justice (STJ). If there is a question of constitutional relevance in the case, it might be possible, depending on the circumstances of the case, to challenge the STJ's ruling before the Constitutional Federal Court of Justice (STF).

3 *Ordinary Patent Proceedings*

3.1 *First Administrative Instance*

Patent proceedings must follow the formal procedure determined by LPI.[214] A patent application is filed either online or via mail, or in person at the patent office's main headquarters, in the former Brazilian capital city of Rio de Janeiro, or in one of its regional offices. The application must satisfy the formal requirements set down by Article 19 LPI, such as to request, description and specifications, claims and proof that

212. Patentgesetz, § 65.
213. Constituição da República Federativa do Brasil, Article 109.
214. *See* Articles 19-39 LPI.

the relevant taxes have been paid. These requirements are summarily checked within the ambit of a formal preliminary examination.[215] After that, the application is kept secret for 18 months either from the date of filing in Brazil or from the date it was first filed in another country member to the PC, when the right of priority is applicable, after which it is published. From this moment on, every interested third party may submit objections, including documents and data—called *subsídios*[216]—to assist this examination. This is not to be confused with the regular opposition proceedings as they are known in the patent law of other countries.

The applicant (or other interested parties) must request a patent examination within a period of 36 months of the date of filing; otherwise, her application will be dismissed.[217] Within this period, the patent applicant is allowed to change her request.[218] However, the patent application may be reinstated if the applicant so requests, within 60 days of the date it was dismissed.[219] This provision was already present in the former Brazilian patent law, although, under the old regime, the penalty for not requesting patent examination within 60 days deadline was that the invention entered the public domain.[220] Today, however, the provision does not have any reason that justifies its existence, so that it should be abolished in order to avoid unnecessary administrative costs.

After that, the patent examiner carries out the technical examination, which contains a report of the examiner's prior art and an opinion with respect to the application's patentability, the appropriateness of the claims, and the technical requirements of the application.[221] When the examiner's decision is for the non-patentability of the application or the incompatibility of the claim requested, or makes some demand, the applicant is required to submit any comments within a period of 90 days.[222] If there is no response to this demand, the application is definitively dismissed.

Decisions are published in the official press vehicle *Revista de Propriedade Industrial* (*RPI*). Once the examination has been concluded—which currently takes circa 11 years after the filing date[223]—a decision should be issued either approving or rejecting the patent application.[224] The patent is then granted after taxes are paid.[225]

215. Article 20 LPI.
216. Article 31 LPI.
217. Article 33 LPI.
218. Article 32 LPI.
219. Article 33 Sole paragraph LPI.
220. Domingues (1980), *Direito Industrial Patentes*, Rio de Janeiro, Forense, p. 198.
221. Article 35 LPI.
222. Article 36 LPI.
223. Lancillotti Jannuzzi/Guimarães Vasconcelos (2017), "O Backlog na Concessão das Patentes e seu Impacto na Utilização de Salvaguardas Legais e no Acesso aos Medicamentos no Brasil," in: Curzel/Nunes (eds.), *Patentes e o Acesso a Antirretrovirais no Brasil*, Editora Appris, Curitiba, p. 65.
224. Article 37 LPI.
225. Article 38 LPI.

3.2 *Second Administrative Instance*

The INPI does not have an organized Board of Appellations for remedies against decisions issued in the first instance by a patent examiner. According to the LPI, all decisions of the Patent Office, except in special cases expressly determined by law, may be administratively challenged via the adequate legal remedy (*recurso*) within 60 days. Only the President of the Patent Office is competent to decide about such legal remedies,[226] but the President can, in practice, delegate this power to a commission designed for it. Therefore, the INPI does not have an independent technical board, the function of which is to review the decisions of patent examiners. In this respect, the LPI 96 maintained the system that had been introduced by the LPI 71, which had abolished the previously existing Board of Appeals of the INPI (*Conselho de Recursos da Propriedade Industrial*).[227]

3.3 *No Provision for Opposition Proceedings*

As mentioned before, the new Brazilian patent law removed pre-grant opposition.[228] This does not mean that in the Brazilian system, third parties are not allowed to bring their considerations to the examiner: see the above-mentioned *subsídios*, which they might use to oppose a patent grant. However, at least in the LPI, there is no provision that obliges the examiner to take this "assistance" into consideration.

III The LPI 96: A "TRIPS-Plus" Patent Law

As shown in the preceding sections, the LPI 96 not only implemented the minimum patent protection standards set by the TRIPS Agreement but deliberately opted to introduce, in some aspects, a more extensive patent protection than the one required by TRIPS. This is severely criticized, for instance, by *Figueira Barbosa*, who sees it as a weakening of the public interest and the system of intellectual property protection itself weakened.[229]

The most evident "TRIPS-plus" provision is the one concerning the admission of retroactive patent protection for existing drugs via the pipeline system, instead of an adoption of the "mailbox system"; this should be seen alongside with the waiving of a delayed introduction for pharmaceutical patents, which were de facto introduced in 1996. As stated by *Sundaram*, "the net result was that pipeline patents based on foreign

226. Article 212 LPI.
227. Domingues (1980), *Direito Industrial—Patentes*, Editora Forense, pp. 126-127.
228. In the same line, Borges Barbosa (2004b), *Falta de busca de anterioridades como causa de nulidade da patente*, p. 4; Ahlert/Goulart (2005), "The Enforcement of Patent Rights in Brazil," in: Heath/Petit (eds.), *Patent Enforcement Worldwide: A Survey of 15 Countries. Essays in Honor of Dieter Stauder*, Hart Publishing, Oxford et al., p. 450.
229. Figueira Barbosa (2001), "Preços na Indústria Farmacêutica: Abusos e Salvaguardas em Propriedade Industrial: A Questão Brasileira Atual," in: Picavelli/Aranha (eds.), *Política de Patentes em Saúde Humana*, pp. 114-116.

patents for pharmaceutical and chemical compounds were automatically granted, waiving the novelty requirement."[230]

The *Cardoso* government's decision to protect patents that had been granted or filed before the WTO Agreement came into force, despite the lack of international obligation to provide for retroactive patent protection, can be attributed to the following four reasons.

The first reason was the international pressure for retroactive patent protection. Brazil had been subject to strong American pressure since the late 1980s when it suffered punitive trade measures on the grounds of not granting patents for pharmaceuticals. According to Senator *Suassuna*, when the parties came to an agreement ending the conflict at the GATT in 1992, President *Collor* informally promised the U.S. that Brazil would retroactively protect pharmaceutical patents within the new patent law. Senator *Suassuna* afterward stated that both President *Franco* and President *Cardoso* wanted to keep the informal promise made by their predecessor *Collor* to the U.S.[231]

The second reason for the admission of pipeline patents was *Cardoso*'s administration's commitment to market-friendlier economy policies. The *Cardoso* presidency was committed to improving the global image of a "modern Brazil," an image that did not fit with a country that did not recognize patent rights for pharmaceuticals. Similarly to President *Collor*, *Cardoso* had also been elected on the promise to make the Brazilian economy more efficient and more "modern." The shift in the Brazilian position regarding pharmaceutical and chemical patents took place during the short period of *Collor's* presidency.[232] Afterward, it was strongly supported by *Cardoso*, who was the Foreign Minister of the administration, who succeeded President *Collor*. In this position, he promised American President *Bill Clinton* to make efforts to accelerate the enactment of the new patent act in Congress in 1994.[233] Before taking office as President, he also announced his intention to approximate Brazil to the developed world, again, by promising to accelerate the enactment of the new patent act, which had been going through Congress since 1991.[234] So, *Cardoso's* administration was

---

230. *Sundaram* (2014), "Brazil's Implementation of TRIPS Flexibilities: Ambitious Missions, Early Implementation, and the Plans for Reform," 23 *Info. & Communications Tech. L.* 2, 98.
231. Suassuna (1995), Speech made by Senator *Ney Suassuna* at the tribune of the Federal Senate on December 12, 1995, when he tried to convince his colleagues that the retroactive patent protection desired by the USA and sponsored by the Executive Branch was against the national interest. *See also Sundaram* (2014), "Brazil's Implementation of TRIPS Flexibilities: Ambitious Missions, Early Implementation, and the Plans for Reform," 23 *Info. & Communications Tech. L.* 2, 96.
232. 1990-1992.
233. Salomon (1995), "Lei de Patentes causa constrangimento," *Folha de São Paulo*, 19.4.1995: "No início do governo de Bill Clinton, ainda no cargo de Ministro das Relações Exteriores de Itamar Franco, FHC tomou a iniciativa de garantir às autoridades norte-americanas o apoio ao reconhecimento de patentes de produtos químicos e farmacêuticos, além de micro-organismos produzidos em laboratórios."
234. "O Itamaraty abre as portas: Entra em crise na diplomacia a era dos 'barbudinhos,' embaixadores ligados à corrente terceiro-mundista...," *Folha de São Paulo*, December 18, 1994, pp. 4-6; "Três projetos são definidos: Líderes dos partidos da coligação que elegeu o presidente Fernando Henrique Cardoso decidiram tentar votar, ainda este ano, três projetos considerados essenciais para iniciar o governo," *Folha de São Paulo*, November 2, 1994, pp. 1-4.

convinced that strengthening intellectual property rights was the right thing to do. *Massard da Fonseca*, after having culled hundreds of government documents and interviewed 47 key actors, also concluded that "patent protection was aligned with the government's agenda of opening the economy to international trade and investment."[235]

A third important factor was the fact that the old policy, based on the substitution of importations, did not bring good results in the field of the pharmaceutical industry since the national industry had a low level of technical development if compared with other countries which had adopted the same policy, like India.[236] Even if the Brazilian pharmaceutical industry engaged itself in both the lobby against pipeline protection and the defense of the full use of the transitional periods, its position was weak.[237] At the time, it was seen as an industry that had enjoyed the protection of the law on a nationalistic basis, but it had not been able to develop in a satisfactory way.[238] In addition, representatives of other national industries, especially those who had already suffered U.S. trade sanctions in the late 1980s, such as the paper and electronic products sectors, did not want to suffer losses again, so that they supported the government's position that patent rights would have to be strengthened. This weak position of the national pharmaceutical industry might also have played a role in the shaping of the new patent regime in Brazil.

A fourth important factor for the approval of a TRIPS-plus patent law was the lack of discussion regarding the question of how patents affect the prices of medicines. As *Massard da Fonseca* observed, "at the same time the Patent Bill was approved by the Congress, a bill granting universal access to AIDS medicines was enacted. However, there is no record that this very new and very engaged activism participated or understood the relevance of the contest on patent protection."[239]

As seen above, another nocive provision to public interest was Article 44 provision; however, its effects were not perceived at the time the LPI was amended.[240]

In any case, if it is true that the first Brazilian TRIPS-compliant patent law preferred not to make use of the transitory flexibilities admitted by TRIPS, the same cannot be said regarding permanent flexibility instruments of patent rights. As seen

235. Massard da Fonseca / Bastos (2016), "Implementing Intellectual Property of Pharmaceuticals in Middle-Income Countries: A Case-Study of Patent Regulation in Brazil," 41 *J. Health Pol. Pol' & L.* 3, 435.
236. *See* Hasenclever/Paranhos (2014), *The Development of the Pharmaceutical Industry in Brazil and India: Technological Capability and Industrial Development*, Economics Innovation Research Group, Economics Institute, Federal University of Rio de Janeiro; Guennifi/Ramani (2011), *Catching up in Pharmaceuticals: A Comparative Study Between India and Brazil*, UNU Merit Working Paper Series 2010-19, version from October 14, 2011.
237. Ranzani (2006), *O descompasso entre o interno e o externo numa era de interdependência: o caso do acesso a Medicamentos para HIV/AIDS no Brasil*, Master Thesis, Fundação Getúlio Vargas, São Paulo, p. 77.
238. As seen above (*see* Chapter 3-A-I-3.2.3.4), the real reason the Brazilian pharmaceutical industry did not reach a higher development in spite of the prohibition of pharmaceutical product patents was a spillover effect of the FDI policies implemented at the time.
239. Massard da Fonseca/Bastos (2016), "Implementing Intellectual Property of Pharmaceuticals in Middle-Income Countries: A Case-Study of Patent Regulation in Brazil," 41 *J. Health Pol., Pol'y & L.* 3, 435.
240. *See* Chapter 3-A-I-3.2.3.4.

above, the new law did not forget to regulate compulsory licenses, bearing in mind possible cases of national emergency or public interest, which could occur at any time, and not only during the grace period.

IV The Brazilian Policy on Access to Medicines

1 Public Health System (SUS)

The present public health system in Brazil emerged from the democratic constitution approved in 1988 as a result of the demands of the so-called sanitary movement.[241] Before 1988, the Brazilian public health system was financed by taxes on wages, which were paid by employers, employees and the federal government. Therefore, the system was not accessible to people who did not pay taxes into the social security system, meaning that the latter had to rely on philanthropy in order to have medical assistance. Because so many people were excluded, the system was heavily criticized, especially by the sanitary movement, which campaigned for a health system that could guarantee everyone in Brazil the right to healthcare.[242] In response to these demands, the BC of 1988 created the basis for a universal system, which is supposed to include all citizens, regardless of whether or not they pay taxes. This was the first BC to enshrine social rights, such as the right to health.

Healthcare is provided by both the public and private sectors in Brazil. The public health system is called the Sistema Único de Saúde—SUS (in English: Unified Health System). It has the duty to provide healthcare for everyone, including those who are privately insured. This is so because services provided by the SUS have to be "universal," as mandated by the BC.[243] However, there is an enormous gap between law and reality since the system is not able to satisfy the healthcare demands of the population on the grounds of a lack of financial resources. As a result of its precarious service, the SUS is mostly used by the poor, except in the case of pharmaceutical assistance, when people pay for expensive drugs and afterward sue the state to compensate them.

The way SUS is financed is peculiar because it does not have a reliable source of funding. Inspired by the English model, SUS is not allowed to charge its users any fees. This means that the Brazilian public health system is not financed by contributions paid on a regular basis by its users or the administration, nor its resources are complemented by official health funds. Its expenses are integrally covered by the "annual social security budget," which comes from federal, state and municipal taxes and social contributions in general. The result is that the system is precariously financed. In 2010, for instance, the public purse was responsible for 47 percent of all

241. On the formation of the SUS *see* Mello e Souza (2005), *The Power of the Weak: Advocacy Networks, Ideational Change and the Global Politics of Pharmaceutical Patent Rights*, PhD Thesis, Stanford University, pp. 177-182.
242. Paiva/Teixeira (2014), "Reforma Sanitária e Criação do Sistema Único de Saúde: Notas sobre Contextos e Autores," 21 *História, Ciências, Saúde*, 15-35.
243. Constituição da República Federativa do Brasil, Article 196.

healthcare costs in Brazil, which corresponded to 9 percent of Brazilian GNP; the remaining fraction of health expenses in Brazil were paid with private resources.[244] While 25 percent of the population is privately insured, the remaining 75 percent depends completely on the SUS.[245]

As a rule, drug costs are neither covered by private insurance nor by the public health system, except in cases of hospital treatment, in which drug costs must be paid either by the public health system or the patient's private insurance. There is a second exception regarding essential medicines, but it applies only to the public health system. Such costs must be paid by the state in every case, including patients that are not hospitalized. An "essential medicine" is defined in numerous clauses in the RENAME list. Basically, the situation regarding drug financing in Brazil does not differ from that in other developing countries: drug costs must mostly be paid by the patient, in a way usually classified by health experts as an "out-of-pocket" basis.[246] This is true of those who are privately insured, as well as those who have to rely on the public health system. Since the first group can mostly pay drug costs by themselves, the problem of access to medicines is suffered by the poor, who cannot afford the high priced medicines.[247] The gravity of the situation is illustrated by the fact that in the year 2000, 60 percent of all medicines produced in Brazil were used by only a small segment of the population (23 percent).[248]

2 *The Constitutional Right to Health and the Court's Understanding of the Right to Access Medicine*

According to Article 196 BC, the provision of healthcare is a duty of the state and that care is the right of each citizen. This right is to be realized by means of social and economic policies, the aims of which are to reduce the risk of illness and promote universal and equal access to services for health. The constitutional right to health was regulated by ordinary law in 1990.[249]

After the Constitution's approval, a discussion on the legal nature of the right to health started. The question was whether the right to health should be classified as a basic right or as a social right. Some authors were of the view that the right to health could not be considered a basic right so much as a civil right because its exercise cannot be assured without positive activity on the part of the state since it will always be

244. Ocké-Reis (2015), "Gasto Privado em Saúde Pública no Brasil," 31 *Cadernos de Saúde Pública*, 1351-1353.
245. Barros/Bertoldi (2008), "Out-of-Pocket Expenditure in a Population Covered by the Family Health Program in Brazil," 37 *Int'l J. Epidemiology*, 758-765.
246. Cohen (2000), *Public Policies in the Pharmaceutical Sector: A Case Study of Brazil*, LCSHD Paper Series 54, Department of Human Development, The World Bank.
247. According to Calixto/Jarbas (2008), "Desenvolvimento de Medicamentos no Brasil: Desafios," 78 *Gazeta Médica da Bahia*, 100, 50 percent of the Brazilian people do not have access to medicines.
248. Cosendey et al. (2000), "Assistência farmacêutica na atenção básica de saúde: a experiência de três estados brasileiros," 16 *Cadernos de Saúde Pública*, 171-182.
249. Brasil (1990), Lei 8.080, September 19, 1990, DOU, September 20, 1990, p. 18055.

dependent on the availability of financial resources.[250] Others are of the opinion that there is no distinction between basic and social rights since the exercise of both is to be assured in any case by the state, irrespective of the availability of financial resources.[251] This view was later the basis of numerous individual lawsuits against the state. Claimants argued that the state had a duty to make any medicine available for all patients and that the only requirement for that should be the existence of medical prescription.[252]

The defendant that is the Brazilian state, also under pressure due to the scarcity of public funds, countered that the right to health could only be effective by means of a rational medicine policy. This view was legally based on the second sentence of Article 196 BC, which states that the right to health is to be realized by means of a social and economic policy. Therefore, the individual right would be limited by the financial capacity of the state to implement it, which is not infinite.

The Brazilian state pleaded that the right to medical care could only be secured under the framework of the medicines policy developed by the Federal Ministry of Health. One of its objects was promoting access to "essential medicines" for the population.[253] Decisive for this policy is the official list of medicines that the Brazilian Health Ministry considers to be essential for the population: this list, called RENAME, is known as "the SUS list." To decide what an essential medicine is, public health experts follow the criteria set by the WHO while considering local epidemiological characteristics, for instance, which illnesses most frequently affect the population or are of strategic interest on other grounds. Every drug added to the list must be available at no charge for everyone who lives in Brazil. The Federal Administration is in charge of procuring these drugs, while the state and the city administration share the responsibility of distributing them for the ones who need it.

This policy has been regularly challenged by the courts since it was brought in. Many people who need prescribed drugs, not on the SUS list (RENAME), go to court and claim that the refusal of the state to pay for them is not compatible with their constitutional right to health. According to this logic, the state should have to pay for the costs of every prescribed drug, irrespective of whether or not it is on the RENAME. This view has tended to prevail. According to a study that analyzed 144 judgments by the State Court of São Paulo, the state was in all cases ordered to obtain for the individual patient a drug that was not on the RENAME.[254] These judgments are so common that, in some cases, the state has been obliged to import very expensive drugs, even if the drug had no marketing authorization in Brazil.[255] Surprisingly, this view has

250. For a deep analyze of the social health and its concretization in Brazil *see* Sarlet (2002), "Soziale Grundrechte in Brasilien: Probleme ihrer Verwirklichung unter dem Druck der Globalisierung," *Zeitschrift für internationales Arbeits- und Sozialrecht,* 12.
251. Mazur (2015), *Durchsetzung von Leistungsansprüchen aus sozialen Grundrechten in Brasilien und in Deutschland,* Shaker Verlag, Aachen, pp. 265-266.
252. Carvalho (2007), *O Acesso a Medicamentos e as Patentes Farmacêuticas junto à Ordem Jurídica Brasileira,* § 1, Editora Atlas, Curitiba.
253. Portaria MS/GM No. 3.916, October 30, 1998, DOU, November 10, 1998, p. 18.
254. Duran Ferreira et al. (2004), *O Judiciário e as Políticas de Saúde no Brasil: o Caso AIDS,* § 3.3, Universidade de São Paulo.
255. *Ibid.,* fn. 48, Universidade de São Paulo.

also prevailed in the highest courts in the decisions relating to several concrete cases. The Supreme Court, for instance, commanded the City of Aracaju to pay for the expensive drug interferon for a sick patient to whom had been prescribed the medication but did not have the money to pay for it.[256]

In Brazilian case law, it is almost a consensus that the realization of the right to health must take priority regardless of the availability of resources. In practice, this means that everyone who individually sues the state in order to obtain free drugs, not on the SUS list (RENAME), irrespective of the cost of that medication, wins. As it is forced to pay for these individuals' medication, the state must use money that it could otherwise have directed into the financing of "essential medicines" in general. Consequently, it has less money available to collectively finance the system. However, it is clear that not all existing drugs and therapies could be admitted to the RENAME since the Brazilian state does not have limitless resources to pay for the high prices of new medicines and therapies. What is at stake is the question of the health system's priorities in a developing country, where the majority of the population relies on official medical assistance. However, members of that majority do not have the financial resources to cover lawyer's fees, so they cannot sue in order to gain access to the prescribed drug for free.

At the end of the day, these well-intentioned judgments worsen health inequalities in Brazil.[257] *Ferraz* cites, for instance, the case of the State of São Paulo, which in 2008 expended BRL 400 million (almost USD 200 million) only to comply with court orders benefiting 35,000 people; according to him, this was the same amount of money that the Federal Ministry of Health had announced would finance a vaccination program which would benefit 3.2 million children, but this program was not fully implemented due to the limitations of the health budget.[258]

In an attempt to stop the courts from intervening in how the health budget for free drugs is to be distributed, the federal administration managed to get approval in 2011 for a law, the target of which was to impose some limits on such judgments.[259] This law provides a definition for "integral pharmaceutical assistance," limiting this to therapies registered on the SUS list, the RENAME, or in other administrative norms.[260] Furthermore, the law expressly forbade the public administration to pay for therapies that had

256. Supremo Tribunal Federal, Josivaldo Tavares dos Santos vs. Município de Aracaju, SS 3962/SE- Sergipe (DJ April 15, 2010).
257. *See* Badim Marques/Gandolfi Dallari (2007), "Garantia do Direito Social à Assistência Farmacêutica no Estado de São Paulo," 41 *Revista de Saúde Pública*, 105; Ferraz (2007), "Direito à Saúde, Escassez e o Judiciário," *O Estado de S. Paulo*, August 10, 2007; Guise Rosina/Wang/De Campos (2010), "Access to Medicines: Pharmaceutical Patents and the Right to Health," in: Shaver (ed.), *Access to Knowledge in Brazil—New Research on Intellectual Property, Innovation and Development*, Bloomsbury Academic, New York, pp. 177-178.
258. Ferraz (2009), "The Right to Health in the Courts of Brazil: Worsening Health Inequalities?," 11 *Health & Hum. Rts. J.* 2, 33-45.
259. Brazil (2011a), Lei 12.401, April 28, 2011, DOU, April 29, 2011.
260. *Ibid.*, Article 19-M.

no marketing license in Brazil.[261] At the same time, the law made the process of adding drugs to RENAME more democratic.[262] Unfortunately, this change did not produce results since the lower courts, despite the new law, continued to decide the question in the same way. As a result, the State expenses for buying the drugs it is obliged to do due to court rulings continue arising.[263] In 2018, the STJ ruled that the State has the duty to pay for drugs not included in the SUS list if the following conditions are fulfilled: (1) a doctor must prescribe the drug and attest that the medicines included in the list do not have the same therapeutic efficacy; (2) the patient lacks money for paying the drug; (3) ANVISA issued an authorization to market the drug in question in Brazil.[264]

The question of whether the Brazilian state is duty-bound to make all drugs or therapies that are not included on the SUS list universally available for free, irrespective of their cost, was on March 2020 discussed by a judgment on the part of the Federal Supreme Court (STF).[265] It was expected that this judgment, which was pending since 2007, should definitively solve the controversy.[266] In the concrete case, the Brazilian state of Rio Grande do Norte had lodged an extraordinary appeal to the Supreme Court against the local court's ruling, which obliged it to make the drug Sildenafil available for the plaintiff in the treatment of pulmonary hypertension. On the course of proceedings, the medication was included on the SUS list, but the STF decided not to stop proceedings given the existence of 42,000 suitcases discussing the same question. Like the STJ's ruling of 2018, the STF rejected the remedy per majority and ruled that the State has the duty to pay for drugs not included on the SUS list, provided that some cumulative requirements are fulfilled. Among the conditions proposed by the judges were the following ones: (1) the patient cannot afford the treatment; (2) the drug in question was not included on the SUS list due to the existence of an express decision of the Ministry of Health denying its inclusion on the list; (3) nonavailability of an equivalent drug on the SUS list; (4) the drug effectiveness must be proven according to the postulates of evidence-based medicine; (5) the federal administration must be part of the suitcase as a respondent. Since, however, the STF did not yet agree on the way these requirements will look, this judgment is not yet finished so that the question remains open.

261. *Ibid.*, Article 19-T.
262. *Ibid.*, Article 19-Q and 19-R.
263. In 2016, the Federal Ministry of Health expended BRL 1.3 billion with drugs bought due to court rulings. *See* Sulpino Vieira (2018), "Evolução no gasto com medicamentos do sistema único de saúde no período de 2010 a 2016," *IPEA -Texto para Discussão 2356*, p. 24.
264. STJ—Recurso Especial 1.657.156-RJ (2017/0025629-7), Estado do Rio de Janeiro vs. Fatima Theresa Estheves dos Santos Oliveira (DJe May 4, 2018).
265. Recurso Extraordinário 566471, Estado do Rio Grande do Norte vs. Carmelita Anunciada de Souza, Ata de Julgamento No. 5 of March 5, 2020 (DJe March 17, 2020). The STF continue to judge the case on August 21, 2020 but the judgment was interrupted seven days later, after three judges having diverged on how the requirements for the duty of the State to provide medicines outside the SUS list should look like. *See* STF's website: http://portal.stf.jus.br/processos/detalhe.asp?incidente=2565078 (August 30, 2020).
266. In this cause the court recognized the existence of a general interest (*Repercussão Geral—Tema 6*) in accordance with Article 102.3 of the Brazilian Constitution. This means that the judgment's effects arise out of the individual case, as soon as the judgment finishes.

3 *AIDS in Brazil*

3.1 *History and Development of AIDS/HIV in Brazil*

The first Brazilian AIDS case was reported in 1982 in São Paulo state. At around this time, the first AIDS NGOs were founded in São Paulo. The first official response to the epidemic took place in 1983 when the government of the State of São Paulo created a local AIDS program. In 1985, after other states had launched their own campaigns against the spread of the disease, the federal administration created a national AIDS program (PNA—Programa Nacional da AIDS),[267] the implementation of which started two years later.

The legal and political background of that time influenced the contours of the national program. The new BC was under discussion, particularly once the military dictatorship had ended. According to the draft constitution, the provision of guaranteed healthcare for all citizens would be a duty of the state. The new Brazilian health system (SUS) was designed at this time. According to *Marques*, there was a convergence between the basic ideas of the National AIDS Program and the Brazilian health system as a whole, which might have contributed to the later success of the AIDS program.[268]

3.2 *Brazilian National AIDS/HIV Program*

The Brazilian National AIDS Program gained international attention for three reasons: the first of these was the fact that it was based on the domestic production of ARV Drugs—at a time when patent protection was not available for pharmaceutical products. The second was the fact that (elsewhere, high-priced) drugs were distributed for free to sick people. This was considered peculiar, as it happened in a developing country.

However, at the time of the program's creation, the distribution of ARV Drugs for free was not part of it. At that time, the program was based both on the defense of the rights of people affected by HIV/AIDS, as well on preventive measures, like free distribution of condoms and preventive public information campaigns, the goal of which was to enlighten the population on the forms of AIDS transmission.

In 1992, Brazil asked the WB for a loan to support its fight against the spread of AIDS. During the negotiations for the terms of this loan, the WB demanded that the free distribution of AZT should stop since public health expenses were not seen as a priority for a developing country.[269] In 1993, the first loan was approved, and the Brazilian national AIDS program received USD 160 million in the framework of a so-called Brazil

267. MoH (1985), Portaria No. 236 of February 5, 1985, DOU Seção I, May 6, 1985, p. 6856.
268. Da Costa Marques (2002), "Saúde e Poder: a emergência política da AIDS/HIV no Brasil," 9 *Histórias, Ciências, Saúde—Manguinhos* (Suplemento), p. 54.
269. Berkman et al. (2005), "A Critical Analysis of the Brazilian Response to HIV/AIDS: Lessons Learned for Controlling and Mitigating the Epidemic in Developing Countries," 95 *Am. J. Pub. Health*, 1162-1172.

AIDS I Project. To get this loan, the Brazilian federal government had to participate with USD 90 million of its own resources but would not have to halt its growing expenses in public health. The program was further financed by the WB: The AIDS Project I was followed by the AIDS Projects II and III (1998-2006).

As of 1994, public producers of pharmaceuticals in Brazil started making the medicine azidothymidine (AZT) as a generic medicine and distributing it for free to AIDS patients.[270] But this was only an experimental initiative authorized by the federal administration. The systematic distribution of ARV Drugs would start later. In any case, Brazil was the first developing country to do it.

According to *Nunn*, the duty to distribute ARV Drugs for free was introduced to the Brazilian AIDS policy as the result of the actions of one man, namely, the former President *José Sarney*.[271] In 1996, as a senator, he sent a draft law to Congress, which would have a huge impact on the public health system. Without further ado, the draft law obliged the public health system, SUS, to cover the full costs of antiretroviral therapy on a universal basis for everyone living with HIV/AIDS in Brazil.[272] The draft bill passed quickly through Congress, even without the support of *Cardoso's* administration.[273] In this way, Brazil became the first developing country to have a legal duty to finance very expensive medicines: In a middle-income country like Brazil, this was seen as incompatible with its scarce resources.

This law, known as "Lei Sarney" (Sarney's Law), was in no way supported by the WB, the view of which was that such a policy was neither sustainable nor affordable for a developing country.[274] Because Brazil refused to stop this policy, the WB imposed the following condition for financing the next project: the borrowed money must not be used to pay for ARV Drugs.[275] The condition was accepted: In 1998, a loan of USD 165 million, with a government contribution of USD 135 million, was approved. As a result, in order to continue its policy of providing free ARV treatment for everyone who needed it, Brazil had to make use of its own resources. This would later oblige health policymakers to be creative not only in applying these scarce resources but in maintaining a policy based on the public production of generic medicines. Although, until 1996, all drugs could be freely copied and produced by the local pharmaceutical industry, after that time, things would have to change due to the introduction of patent protection for pharmaceuticals.

Despite all the measures, in 1997, there were few reasons to celebrate. Since the first cases had been reported, the epidemic had spread strongly and steadily: in 1997

270. Orsi et al. (2003), "Intellectual Property Rights, Anti-Aids Policy and Generic Drugs—Lessons from the Brazilian Public Health Program," in: Moatti, Coriat, Souteyrand, Barnett, Dumoulin, Flori, (eds.), *Economics of AIDS and Access to HIV/AIDS Care in Developing Countries Issues and Challenges*, Paris, Agence Nationale de Recherches sur le Sida et les Hépatites Virales, p. 125.
271. Nunn (2009), *The Politics and History of Aids Treatment in Brazil*, New York, Springer, pp. 87-88.
272. Brasil (1996b), Lei 9.313, November 13, 1996, DOU, Seção I, November 14, 1996, p. 23725.
273. Nunn (2009), *The Politics and History of Aids Treatment in Brazil*, New York, pp. 87-88.
274. The World Bank (2004), *Brazil—First and Second AIDS and STD Control Projects (English)*, Washington, DC: World Bank, p. 6.
275. *Ibid.*

alone, 23,500 new cases were reported. In 1999, approximately 120,000 people died of AIDS, and it became one of the main causes of death for people between 20 and 49 years old.[276] The WB's projection in 1994 that the number of AIDS sufferers in Brazil would reach 1.2 million people by the year 2000 seemed to be coming true.[277] However, this prediction did not eventuate. In 2000, there were in Brazil 540 million people living with AIDS; that is, half of the WB's estimate. At this point, the mortality rate had dropped by 60 percent, the quality of life of patients had been improved, and the rate of new AIDS cases had stabilized.[278] The annual cost of antiretroviral therapy of USD 7,858 per person per year in 1997 fell to USD 4,137 per person in 2001, which was three times cheaper[279] than in the United States.

Because of the short time period between the universal distribution of ARV Drugs and its positive results, the Brazilian AIDS policy became world-famous and was seen as a "role model" for other developing countries.[280]

The Brazilian AIDS policy consisted of the following elements:

(i) participation of NGOs specialized in fighting against AIDS and the prejudice in all parts of the program, which played a decisive role in the AIDS program due to the following three reasons: (1) their high grade of professionalism, (2) their role as mediator among the press, the public administration, people with AIDS and the general community, (3) their active work both in collaboration with national government agencies, as well as their presence as observers in the international AIDS scene;[281]
(ii) preventive campaign in all media;
(iii) distribution of condoms in public hospitals in the country;
(iv) possibility of having free AIDS tests in public hospitals;
(v) free antiretroviral therapy for all and continuous monitoring of patients;
(vii) manufacturing of generic ARVs by public pharmaceutical laboratories;
(viii) procurement of large quantities of patented ARV drugs by the federal administration directly from international pharmaceutical companies.

276. Calcagnotto/Wogart (2006), "Brazil Fight's Against AIDS and Its Implications for Global Health Governance," 8 *World Health and Population*, 4-19.
277. Lazzarini (2003), "Making Access to Pharmaceuticals a Reality: Legal Options under TRIPS and the Case of Brazil," 6 *Yale Hum. Rts. & Dev. L. J.*, 128.
278. *Ibid.*, p. 129.
279. *Ibid.*
280. UNAIDS (2003), Press Release September 1, 2004: *Brazil and UNAIDS joint forces in the global fight against AIDS*. The literature also cites Brazil as a model for other developing countries, as for instance, Cohen (2007), "Brazil's Historical Approach to Intellectual Property Law: The Pharmaceutical Sector," in: Ashiya (ed.), *TRIPS and the Pharmaceutical Industry—Impact on Developing Countries*, The Icfai University Press, Hyderabad, p. 71; Nair (2008), "Compromising TRIPS: Brazil's Approach to Tackle the HIV/AIDS Imbroglio," 13 *JIPR*, 456-463; Okie (2006), "Fighting HIV—Lessons from Brazil", 354 *New Eng. J. Med.* 1977-1981, May 11, 2006; Quintanilha Marques et al. (2005), "Brazil's AIDS Controversy: Antiretroviral Drugs, Breaking Patents, and Compulsory License," 60 *Food & Drug L. J.*, 471-477.
281. On the role played by NGOs within the Brazilian AIDS program, *see* Mello e Souza (2005), *The Power of the Weak: Advocacy Networks, Ideational Change and the Global Politics of Pharmaceutical Patent Rights*, PhD Thesis, Stanford University, pp. 182-191.

Furthermore, in the Brazilian AIDS policy, the following strategies have been used:

(i) continuous negotiations between the Ministry of Health and international pharmaceutical companies regarding prices of ARV drugs;
(ii) constant threats by the Ministry of Health to grant a compulsory license for ARV drugs;
(iii) the inclusion of ANVISA in the patent grant proceedings, with the aim of widening access to medicines;
(iv) from 2009, a partnership between three pharmaceutical laboratories, the aim of which was to transfer technology in order to locally produce a drug: these were namely: (a) a foreign pharmaceutical company, which dominates the technology in question; (b) a Brazilian private company; and (c) a public pharmaceutical laboratory.[282]

Although using the existing structure of public pharmaceutical laboratories to produce ARV drugs was important to guarantee access to free antiretroviral therapy, this was not enough in itself. Patients also needed the so-called second-line ARV drugs, which, however, enjoyed patent protection, and consequently, could not freely be copied by the public pharmaceutical laboratories. The strategy that the Ministry of Health adopted was that of buying patented drugs in large quantities. In doing so, the Ministry of Health started negotiating prices of new drugs with the patent owner and threatening to issue compulsory licenses if the patentee did not voluntarily reduce its prices.[283]

It is worth noting that the possibility of convincing patent holders to agree with voluntarily licensing their patent rights—by which, for instance, a public pharmaceutical laboratory would be authorized to produce itself a patented drug—was never used by the Brazilian Ministry of Health.

All in all, the Brazilian AIDS policy was viewed as a success.[284] The WHO saw the Brazilian example as a model for action to combat AIDS, and other developing countries, such as Namibia, Uganda and Ethiopia, considered producing ARV drugs for themselves.[285] However, as pointed out by *Malich and Marion*, replicating Brazilian success is unlikely for other developing countries due to some historical factors that

282. *See* Schüren (2015), *Aufholende Entwicklung in der globalen Ökonomie—Pharmazeutische Innovationssysteme in Indien und Brasilien*, Nomos, Baden Baden, pp. 232-233; Coriat/Hasenclever/Paranhos/Zaire (2017), "Tratamentos Antirretrovirais de Terceira Linha: Estratégias para Gerir um Custo Significativo no Brasil," in: Curzel/Nunes (eds.), *Patentes e o Acesso a Antirretrovirais no Brasil*, Editora Appris, Curitiba, pp. 94-95.
283. Cohen/Lybecker (2005), "Aids Policy and Pharmaceutical Patents: Brazil's Strategy to Safeguard Public Health," 28 *The World Economy* 2, 222.
284. Gad (2006), *Representational Fairness in WTO Rule-Making—Negotiating, Implementing and Disputing the TRIPS Pharmaceutical-Related Provisions*, The British Institute of International and Comparative Law, SMU London Forum Initiative, London pp. 210-211; Hein/Kohlmorgen (2005), "Global Health Governance: Conflicts on Global Social Rights," *7 GIGA Working Papers*, August, p. 31; Wogart (2006), "Multiple Interfaces of Big Pharma and the Change of Global Health Governance in the Face of HIV/AIDS," 24 *GIGA Working Paper*, p. 20.
285. Cohen/Lybecker (2005), "Aids Policy and Pharmaceutical Patents: Brazil's Strategy to Safeguard Public Health," 28 *The World Economy* 2, 225.

made the Brazilian case unique, namely: (1) government commitment to public health and indigenous production capacity; (2) emergence of a civil society coalition; (3) creation of a functional independent regulatory agency; (4) the use of compulsory licenses; and (5) international harmonization of quality assurance and clinical standards.[286]

4 *National Medicines Policy*

After the new patent act had passed, it was clear that a new medicine policy was necessary to satisfy new demands and problems. First, it was felt that access to essential drugs must be expanded. This was done by promoting both generic medicines and by introducing a system of control of the price of patented medicines. Second, it was felt to be urgent to ensure the population had access to secure, high-quality and effective medicines. This was done by reforming the public health surveillance system. The principles and objectives of the new medicines policy were resumed in a soft law norm of the Ministry of Health, the *Portaria* No. 3916/GM.[287]

4.1 *Reforming the Public Health Surveillance System: The Creation of the National Health Surveillance Agency (ANVISA)*

Under the system prior to 1999, the administration of public health surveillance was carried out by a secretariat in the federal health ministry. This secretariat worked directly under the orders of the ministry, without having its own budget. This was seen as a deficiency in the system. Since the early 1990s, there had been a growing consensus in Brazil that the public health surveillance system should be structurally reformed, especially by giving it financial and administrative autonomy. Executive agencies with administrative and financial autonomy are called in Brazil *autarquia* and must be created by law. According to the view of health experts, giving the public health surveillance secretariat the status of an *autarquia* was a necessary measure that would be able to produce a more efficient system. Otherwise, that system would continue to rely exclusively on the decisions made by the ministry of health. At the same time, the so-called regulatory agencies (in Portuguese: *agências reguladoras*) were created in Brazilian law, inspired by the American experience. This form of an administrative agency is deemed to be a special regime agency (in Portuguese: *autarquia de regime especial*) since it differs in some aspects from the ordinary federal agencies or *autarquias*). For instance, such an agency must usually have a director with a set mandate of four years, irrespective of changes in government.

The National Public Health Surveillance Agency (ANVISA) was created by an executive decree, the *Medida Provisória* (MP) 1791, which was sent to Congress on

286. Malich/Marion (2015), "Increasing Access to Medicines—Leveraging Brazil's Experience," 2 *CIGI Graduate Fellows Series*, 3.
287. MoH (1998), Portaria No. 3916/GM (Política Nacional de Medicamentos), October 30, 1998, DOU 215-E, Seção I, November 10, 1998, pp. 18-22 (revoked by PRC-2 MS/GM, DOU, October 3, 2017, Suplemento, p. 61).

December 30, 1998 and converted into an ordinary law in the last days of January 1999.[288] ANVISA was created in the political context of intensification of trade in the international arena; in the domestic context, it was brought into being in order to be able to deal with urgent problems that the former Public Health Surveillance Secretariat had not been able to solve.[289] One of these urgencies was the difficulty of harmonization between the duty to grant pharmaceutical patents and, at the same time, the duty to make medicines affordable for all. According to *Figueira Barbosa*—a former INPI director who happened to be the first director of the intellectual property unit at ANVISA—from the Ministry of Health's point of view, the INPI was at the time taking a position that was extremely favorable to patent holders, and which put the success of the Brazilian access-to-medicines policy at risk.[290]

ANVISA's primary goal is twofold, that is, protecting and promoting public health. The reformulation of the public health surveillance system through the creation of this independent National Health Surveillance Agency was the first step toward a better quality control for medicines that were produced and marketed in Brazil, and, at the same time, to deal with the question of expanding access to medicines.

ANVISA's main responsibility is defining the national health surveillance system.[291] For doing it, it regulates the market entrance of products, services, and technologies related to health[292] and executes the policies related to products that present a risk to health.[293] ANVISA is, for instance, responsible for both drug registration[294] and for establishing rules concerning clinic trials.

In November 2016, ANVISA was accepted as a new regulatory member of the International Council on Harmonization of Technical Requirements for Registration of Pharmaceuticals for Human Use (ICH).[295] The ICH—which currently has 17 members—was founded by the FDA, the EC and Japan in 1990.[296]

4.2 *Expanding Access to Medicines*

4.2.1 Adoption of a List of "Essential" and "Strategic" Medicines

The problem of the scarcity of financial resources with which to maintain the ambitious universal Brazilian public health system was addressed by the national medicines

288. Brasil (1999a), Lei 9.782, of January 26, 1999.
289. Piovesan/Lavra (2007), "Institutional Change and Political Decision-Making in the Creation of the Brazilian National Health Surveillance Agency," 23 *Cadernos de Saúde Pública*, 1373-1383.
290. *Figueira Barbosa*, in an interview kindly granted to the author in his office at the FIOCRUZ on March 17, 2009.
291. Brasil (1999a), Article 2 (II) and Article 7 Lei 9.782/1999.
292. *Ibid.*, Article 2 (III) and Article 7 Lei 9.782/1999.
293. *Ibid.*, Article 2 (IV) and Article 7 Lei 9.782/1999.
294. The drug registration process is regulated by Article 16-24-B of Law No. 6.360 of November 23, 1976.
295. Huynh-Ba/Beumer Sassi (2018), "ANVISA: An Introduction to a New Regulatory Member with Many Challenges," *AAPS Open*, p. 1.
296. Information extracted from ICH's website, available at https://www.ich.org/page/members-observers (last visited on August 31, 2020).

policy inaugurated in 1998. As reported above, this policy assumed a government duty to provide medical care; it also assumed that financial resources were limited, and therefore, the duty to provide medicinal care must also be limited. According to the policy, the government must provide all essential medicines free of charge. Essential medicines, according to the WHO, are those that satisfy the priority health care needs of the population.[297] According to the WHO's criteria, they are selected based on disease prevalence and public health relevance, evidence of clinical efficacy, comparative costs and cost-effectiveness.[298] In the case of Brazil, they are enumerated by the Ministry of Health (MoH) in the abovementioned list called RENAME and updated every two years or more. Until 2012, the selection of medicines in the list was made with basis on the WHO's criteria when the criteria changed. For *Aragão Figueiredo*, since 2012, "RENAME is no longer a list of essential medicines, but has become a list for financing pharmaceutical care."[299] All drugs included in this list are to be bought in bulk by the state and distributed for free to those who need them. The list also includes some medicines which are not considered to be essential but are considered to be of strategic importance for epidemiological reasons.[300]

The list plays a key role in the shaping of the medicines policy, the objective of which is both to reduce the price of medicines bought in bulk by the state and to encourage the production of drugs made in state laboratories, thereby expanding access to medicines to as many people as possible.

4.2.2 Generic Medicines

The national medicines policy defined the promotion of generic medicines as a means to make pharmaceutical drugs more accessible to the poor. According to the purpose of this policy,[301] not only should the production of generic medicines be encouraged but also the quality of generic medicines in Brazil should be improved. This policy was implemented in February 1999 through Law 9.787,[302] known as the Generic Medicines' Law, which determined the criteria for improving the quality control of generic medicines as well as setting up a regime of preferences in the frames of the public administration.

297. WHO, Essential Medicines and Health Products, "Definition of Essential Medicines," available at https://www.who.int/medicines/services/essmedicines_def/en/ (last seen on August 31, 2020).
298. *Ibid.*
299. Aragão Figueiredo et al. (2014), "Seleção de Medicamentos Essenciais e a Carga de Doença no Brasil," 30 *Cad. Saúde Pública* (11), p. 2344, Rio de Janeiro.
300. RENAME 2020, last updated in November 2019 by Portaria MoH 3047 of November 28, 2019, DOU, Seção I, November 28, 2019, p. 334.
301. For an analysis of the Brazilian policy of generic medicines *see* Massard da Fonseca (2012), *Reforming Pharmaceutical Regulation: A Case Study of Generic Drugs in Brazil,* PhD Thesis, University of Edinburgh.
302. Brasil (1999b), Lei 9.787 of February 2, 1999, DOU Seção I, February 11, 1999, p. 1.

5 *Controlling Prices*

After an intermittent period of no state control,[303] drug prices again started to be systematically controlled by the federal administration. In December 2000, President *Cardoso* issued MP 2.063,[304] which provided for a price-calculation formula and created an administrative body, the *Câmara de Medicamentos* (Chamber of Medicines), the aim of which was to approve price rises for medicines.[305] This MP was reissued four times,[306] until Congress converted it into Law 10.213 in March 2001.[307]

Currently, the topic is dealt with by Law 10.742/2003, which replaced the Chamber of Medicines by the *Câmara de Regulação do Mercado de Medicamentos* (CMED),[308] a body consisting of the Ministry of Health, Ministry of the Interior (*Casa Civil*), Ministry of Justice and Ministry of Finances. CMED's executive secretariat is exercised by ANVISA. More than simply approve price rises, CMED's function is to regulate the drug market, considering the drug policies regarding access. CMED is also responsible for stipulating the price a new medicine should be commercialized in Brazil. Therefore, a drug must fulfill two requirements for being marketed in Brazil, namely: (1) approval after registration proceedings, and (2) respect the price stipulated by CMED.

6 *Using Compulsory Licensing on the Grounds of Public Health*

The next step taken in the policy of promoting generic medicines was to start using compulsory licenses, the aim of which was to reduce the price of patented medicines bought by the federal administration.

According to Article 71 LPI, an ex officio compulsory license could be granted in cases of national emergence or public interest declared as such by an act of the federal executive authorities and provided that the patent holder or his licensee does not fulfill such a need. In October of 1999, the President, together with the Minister of Health and the Minister of Trade and Industry, edited Decree No. 3.201.[309] This decree (Decree about Compulsory Licensing—DCL) defined the cases under which a compulsory license under Article 71 LPI could ex officio be granted.

303. Câmara/ Godoy/Oliveira (2004), *O Controle de Preços na Indústria Farmacêutica do Brasil*, UFRGS, Porto Alegre.
304. Medida Provisória 2.063, 18.12.2000, DOU, December 19, 2000.
305. About the role played by CMED *see* Gava (2008), "Vendem-se vidas," 21 *Revista Brasileira de Direito Público*, 93-111.
306. Medida Provisória 2.130-1, December 27, 2000, DOU, December 28, 2000, p. 73, which was overruled by the MP 2.130.2, December 28, 2000, DOU, December 29, 2000. p. 22. The latter was overruled by the MP 2.138-3, January 26, 2001, DOU, January 27, 2001, p. 60, which was overruled and reissued by the MP 2.138-4, February 23, 2001, DOU, February 27, 2001.
307. Brazil (2001b), Lei 10.213, March 27, 2001, DOU, Seção I, March 28, 2001, p. 1. This law was later overruled by Lei 10.742, October 6, 2003 (cited as Brazil 2003b).
308. Brazil (2003b), Article 5-6 Law 10.742 of October 6, 2003.
309. Brasil (1999c), Decreto No. 3.201, of October 6, 1999, DOU, December 22, 1999, later altered by Decreto No. 4.830 of September 4, 2003, DOU, September 5, 2003.

6.1 *Field of Coverage of Decree 3.201*

According to the original wording of Article 1 DCL, the grant of compulsory licenses on the grounds of both public interest or national emergency was, first, restricted to non-commercial public use; second, the existence of such an emergency situation must be declared by the government; third, it must be provided that the patent holder or his licensee could not satisfy the needs of either the public interest or such a national emergency.

6.2 *Cases of National Emergency and Public Interest*

Neither the LPI nor the DCL gives a definition of national emergency or the public interest. A national emergency is understood to be a condition of impending danger to the public, even if this exists only in a part of the national territory.[310] However, the decree does not define what an "impending danger to the public" (*perigo público*) is supposed to be. It also does not provide any example of a situation of national emergency, suggesting that the public administration is free to declare a situation as such, as far as this is not considered to be an arbitrary or abusive use of that decision-making power. To date, a compulsory license has never been granted on the grounds of a national emergency in Brazil.

Regarding the public interest, the decree provides examples of situations considered to befall within it. This includes those facts, among others, related to *public health*, nutrition and the protection of the environment, as well as those of primordial importance to the technological or social and economic development of the country.

Bandeira de Mello provides a public interest concept. According to him, this is a category opposed to the category of private and individual interests, that is, the private interests of each one. It follows that "public interest" constitutes the interest of the collectivity, but, at the same time, it is not the sum of individual interests. Therefore, for *Bandeira de Mello*, public interest should be understood as the interest resulting from the set of interests that individuals personally have when considered in their quality as members of society and by the mere fact of being members of the society.[311] It is, therefore, an indefinite legal concept that must be adequately interpreted by the applicants of law.[312]

Souza da Silva studied the case law of the STJ and identified that the Court interpreted the sense of "public interest" in three different ways. According to her analysis, the STJ interprets "public interest" sometimes as coincident with individual

310. Brasil (1999c), Article 2, § 1 DCL.
311. Bandeira de Mello (2004), *Curso de Direito Administrativo*, Malheiros Editores, São Paulo, pp. 50-53.
312. Gabardo/Moura Rezende (2017), "O conceito de interesse público no direito administrativo brasileiro," 115 *Revista Brasileira de Estudos Políticos*, 274-276.

rights, other times as equivalent to the state right and other times as equivalent to social rights.[313]

6.3 *Competent Authority*

By contrast to other kinds of compulsory license,[314] which are granted by the patent office, as a result of administrative proceedings requested by someone legitimately interested in having the patent licensed (Article 68 paragraph 2 LPI), compulsory licenses on the grounds of public interest or national emergency are not allowed to be granted by the patent office. According to Article 3 DCL, the situation of "national emergency" or "public interest" must be declared as such by a federal administrative act of the minister of state responsible for the subject matter in question. However, whether a situation is to be considered a national emergency or a matter of public interest depends on the wide discretionary power of the responsible minister of state. In such a case, the law allows the Minister to declare the situation of national emergency or public interest as such, but it does not oblige him to do so since this is a political decision.

6.4 *Proceedings*

Compulsory licensing proceedings on the grounds of public interest are made in three phases. First, the situation of national emergency or public interest under Article 3 DCL must be declared as such by an administrative act of the responsible minister. This federal administrative act must be published in the *Federal Official Gazette*. Second, it is necessary that the incapability of the patent holder or his licensee to satisfy the special needs arising from that situation of public interest or national emergency will be assessed. Third, the compulsory license will be granted by the "public authority" (poder público),[315] having also to be immediately published in the *Federal Official Gazette*.[316] The patent office's participation in the proceedings is limited to the purposes of entering a record of the compulsory license that has been granted in the patent register (Article 14 DCL).

Regarding compulsory licenses of patented medicines, the Ministry of Health is the competent Ministry to declare a situation of public interest or national emergency. It does not have the legal duty to declare it, but it might do so. Once the MoH does this, the "public authority" might or not grant a compulsory license for a patented medicine ex officio. This shows that the grant proceedings of compulsory licenses comprise a political element in both phases. In the case of a compulsory license on the grounds of

313. Souza da Silva (2009), *O Interesse Público na Jurisprudência do STJ: Uma Abordagem sobre a Fixação de Conteúdos Normativos pelo Raciocínio Judiciário*, Master Thesis, Universidade Federal Fluminense, pp. 82-101.
314. Article 68 LPI.
315. In the case of the unique compulsory license so far granted in Brazil, the "public authority" who signed the act granting it was the Brazilian President at the time, Mr. Luiz Inácio Lula da Silva.
316. Article 4 DCL.

public interest, the administration acts in an area of discretion. Therefore, both decisions may judicially be checked as far as this is possible for a discretionary decision: for example, with a view to procedural errors, arbitrariness or abusiveness.

6.5 *Requirements of the Compulsory License Grants Act*

Under Article 5 DCL, at least the following requirements must be present in the administrative act that grants such a compulsory license: (1) the term of the license and the possibility of renewal; (2) the conditions offered by the public administration, particularly regarding the compensation of the titleholder; and (3) the obligation of the titleholder, if needed, to transmit necessary and sufficient information for the effective reproduction of the patented object. Moreover, the second paragraph of Article 5 DCL provides for the determination of the compensation to which the patent holder is entitled, taking into consideration the relevant market and economic circumstances, the price of similar products and the economic value of the authorization. In the case that the situation of national emergency or public interest characterizes extreme urgency, the compulsory license can produce full effects without having to comply with such requirements in advance.[317]

A further requirement is that the exploitation of a compulsorily licensed patent must be made either directly by the Brazilian Federation or by third parties contracted by the administration (Article 9 DCL). Importation is allowed, but only in a case whereby the product placed on the domestic market might not suffice for the situation of national emergency or the manufacture of the object of the patent is found to be unfeasible.

6.6 *Threats to Grant Compulsory Licenses as Part of the Medicines Policy (1999-2007)*

Once the legal instrument which regulated compulsory licenses on the grounds of public interest had been approved, in 1999, the Ministry of Health began a strategy to negotiate prices of drugs with the theoretical option of threatening to issue compulsory licenses. The aim of this policy was to obtain price reductions of patented medicines bought in bulk by the MoH, and it was used in the framework of price negotiations of antiretroviral medicines between the Federal MoH and international pharmaceutical companies. If a company refused to lower its prices, MoH threatens to grant a compulsory license of the patent on the grounds of public interest.[318] The first time the MoH threatened to do this was in 2001, during price negotiations for the antiretroviral medicine Nelfinavir.[319] At the time, the company which had patent rights over Nelfinavir offered a 40 percent discount in prices, but it did it after nine months of

317. Article 7 DCL.
318. Bastos/Massard da Fonseca (2017), "Licenciamento Compulsório do Efavirenz no Brasil: Um Mecanismo Sui-Generis ou Aplicável a Outros Produtos?," in: Curzel/Nunes (eds.): *Patentes e o Acesso a Antirretrovirais no Brasil*, Editora Appris, Curitiba, p. 138.
319. *See* Nunn (2009), *The Politics and History of AIDS Treatment in Brazil*, New York, p. 128.

negotiation and only after the Ministry of Health had taken the first step toward issuing a compulsory license on the grounds of public health, by declaring the antiretroviral Nelfinavir to be of public interest.[320] This policy was so successful that other laboratories also reduced the prices of their ARV medicines so that the individual cost of ARV therapy declined from USD 6,240 in 1997 to USD 2,210 in 2001.[321]

Brazil was successful with this tactic, at least until 2005. Between 1997 and 2001, the absolute cost of antiretroviral therapy diminished, despite the constant increase in the number of patients being treated. The Ministry of Health estimated that USD 1.1 million had been saved.[322] This success can be explained by the fact that the government's threat to grant a compulsory license seemed credible. In 2001, for instance, the company Merck, after long negotiations with the Ministry of Health, conceded discounts of 65 and 59 percent in the prices of two drugs.[323] Efavirenz, produced by Merck, for instance, had its price reduced by 73 percent, the price of *Abbott's* lopinavir/ritonavir was reduced by 53.3 percent, and that of *Roche's* Nelfinavir was reduced by 73.8 percent.[324]

This trend only lasted until 2003. As demonstrated by *Nunn and others,* "total HAART costs in Brazil declined from US$ 204 million in 2001 to US$ 162 million in 2003, before rising by around 20 percent in 2004 and then more than doubling in 2005 to US$ 414 million. Patented ARVs accounted for between 60 percent and 70 percent of total costs from 2001 to 2003 but then jumped to 80 percent of total costs in 2004 and 2005."[325] In 2007, patented drugs were responsible for 79 percent of all spending on antiretroviral therapy, as 7 of the 15 drugs of the anti-AIDS cocktails had be purchased directly from the patent holders.[326] This indicated that by 2005 the mere threatening to issue a compulsory license, without concretizing it, seemed no longer to work.

As reported by the literature, these developments raised concerns over the Brazilian government's ability to continue with its AIDS program because of the consequences of the 1996 patent-law reform.[327] According to *Chamas,* "government expenditure for its access policy was around US$ 34 million in 1996 and has grown

320. Kweitel/Reis (2007), "A Primeira Licença Compulsória de Medicamento na América Latina," 3 *Pontes* 3, ICTSD.
321. Loyola (2008), "Medicamentos e saúde pública em tempos de AIDS: metamorfoses de uma política dependente," 13 *Ciência e Saúde Coletiva (Suplemento),* 763-778.
322. Cohen/Lybecker (2005), "Aids Policy and Pharmaceutical Patents: Brazil's Strategy to Safeguard Public Health," 28 *The World Economy* 2, 218.
323. *Ibid.*, p. 220.
324. Benoliel/Salama (2010), "Pharmaceutical Patent Bargains: The Brazilian Experience," 18 *Cardozo J. Intell. & Competition L.* 3, 659.
325. Nunn et al. (2007), "Evolution of Antiretroviral Drug Costs in Brazil in the Context of Free and Universal Access to AIDS Treatment," 4 *PLoS Medicine,* 11, e305, 1804-1817.
326. *Ibid.*
327. Mazzoleni/Martins Costa Póvoa (2010), "Accumulation of Technological Capabilities and Economic Development—Did Brazil's IPR Regime Matter?," in: Odagiri et al. (eds.), *Intellectual Property Rights, Development and Catch-Up—An International Comparative Study,* OUP, Oxford et al., p. 303; César/Polido (2008), *Proteção patentária de Medicamentos na interface com o direito à saúde: sustentabilidade do programa brasileiro de acesso universal às terapias antirretrovirais,* IDCID, São Paulo, p. 113.

steadily to US$ 332 million in 2000."[328] The Brazilian policy strategy no longer seemed to be working well. Brazil was obtaining fewer and fewer discounts in its price negotiations with international pharmaceutical companies.[329] In fact, between 2002 and 2006, threats to grant compulsory licenses were becoming less and less credible because, as of 2006, the Brazilian threats were never followed upon.[330] In 2005, the federal administration reached an agreement concerning the ARV drug Kaletra (lopinavir/ritonavir) with the American company, *Abbott*, which was seen as contrary to the public interest.[331] In accordance with this deal, Abbot agreed to be paid with a price of USD 1,380 per patient per year until 2011, while the Brazilian government obligated itself not to issue a compulsory license for lopinavir/ritonavir for this time.[332]

6.7 The Efavirenz Case: The First and So Far, Only Brazilian Compulsory License on the Grounds of Public Health

In May 2007, Brazil issued a compulsory license on the grounds of public health for the first time, the object of which was the drug Efavirenz, an anti-AIDS drug patented by Merck.[333] Efavirenz was seen as a threat to public finances due to the high number of patients treated by the program, which had increased from 2,500 patients in 1999 to 75,000 patients in 2007.[334] The total treatment cost for Efavirenz was estimated at USD 42.9 million per year.[335] Before the Minister of Health issued the compulsory license, he declared by decree the public interest in the anti-AIDS drug Efavirenz.[336] The following reasons were given by the Minister of Health to justify the compulsory license:

- Health is a fundamental human right.
- Right to the treatment of endemic diseases is a fundamental human right.
- Protection of intellectual property must observe the social rights enshrined in the BC.

328. Chamas/Carvalho/Salles Filho (2007), "Current Issues of IP Management in Health and Agriculture in Brazil," in: Krattiger/Mahoney/Nelsen et al. (eds.), *Intellectual Property Management in Health and Agriculture Innovation,* MIHR et al., Oxford et al., 1569.
329. Mello e Souza (2017), "O Licenciamento Compulsório como Estratégia para Promover Acesso a Medicamentos Essenciais: o Caso do Brasil," in: Curzel/Nunes (eds.), *Patentes e o Acesso a Antirretrovirais no Brasil,* Editora Appris, Curitiba, p. 117.
330. Bjornberg (2006), "Brazil's Recent Threat on Abbott's Patent: Resolution or Retaliation?," 27 *Nw. J. L. & Bus.*, 211.
331. Cassier/Correa (2007), "Intellectual Property and Public Health: Copying of HIV/AIDS Drugs by Brazilian Public and Private Pharmaceutical Laboratories," 1 *RECIIS—Electronic Journal of Communication, Information and Innovation in Health,* 84.
332. Sundaram (2014), "Brazil's Implementation of TRIPS Flexibilities: Ambitious Missions, Early Implementation, and the Plans for Reform," 23 *Info. & Communications Tech. L.* 2, 100.
333. Brazil (2007), Decreto No. 6.108 of May 4, 2007, DOU, May 7, 2007.
334. Mitsuuchi Kunisawa (2015), *The TRIPS Agreement Implementation in Brazil—Patents in the Pharmaceutical Area,* Nomos, Baden Baden, p. 162.
335. D 'Almeida et. al (2008)., "New Antiretroviral Treatments and Post-2005 TRIPS Constraints: First Moves Towards IP Flexibilization in Developing Countries," in: Coriat (ed.), *The Political Economy of HIV/AIDS in Developing Countries,* Cheltenham, Edward Elgar, p. 42.
336. Portaria No. 886, of April 24, 2007, DOU, April 25, 2007.

- The Brazilian state must provide universal and free access to basic drugs, with anti-AIDS drugs legally classified as a basic drug according to Law 9 313 from November 13, 1996.
- The drug Efavirenz is essential for the Brazilian anti-AIDS program, but its price was so high that the continuation of the anti-AIDS program could not be guaranteed.

As seen above, according to Article 31(f) TRIPS Agreement, when a compulsory license on the grounds of public interest is issued, the patentee must be paid with an "adequate remuneration," taking account of the economic value of the authorization. In the case of the Brazilian compulsory license, the decree set in favor of the patentee 1.5 percent of the production costs of the drug; for the drug that was not to be produced by the Ministry of Health, the decree set as a compensation for the patentee 1.5 percent of the selling prices of the medicine.[337]

As recounted by *Mitsuuchi Kunisawa*, Brazilian official laboratories did not immediately start producing Efavirenz by themselves, as at first, the federal administration imported the drug from Indian laboratories,[338] which charged USD 0.4270 and USD 0.4430 per tablet.[339] This price represented 39.9 percent of the final offer made by Merck in April 2007, when it offered a price of USD 1.10 per tablet, an 84 percent reduction of its initial price of USD 6.96 price in 2000.[340] In 2009, the state-owned laboratory Farmanguinhos delivered the first batch of nationally manufactured Efavirenz.[341] By 2011—four years after the compulsory license was issued—Farmanguinhos was able to supply a hundred percent of the Efavirenz required by the Brazilian Ministry of Health.[342]

According to *Rodrigues*, procuring the generic version of Efavirenz allowed the Ministry of Health to reduce the annual cost of treating patients using the 600-mg tablet by 71.35 percent and by 65.6 percent in the case of patients using the 200-mg capsule version. All in all, according to this author, Efavirenz's compulsory license was brought to the Ministry of Health, an estimated USD 30.6 million saving in drug costs.[343] On the other hand, the compulsory license of Efavirenz also revealed the incapacity of Brazil at that time to quickly and cheaply produce ARV Drugs, largely due

337. Brazil (2007), Article 2° Decreto No. 6.108, of May 4, 2007.
338. Although Brazil at the first moment imported Efavirenz from Indian laboratories, this compulsory license was internationally justified by Article 31*bis* TRIPS, and not by Article 31*bis*. This was an ordinary compulsory license, and not a back-to-back one. India was allowed to produce and export Efavirenz because this drug was not patented there. So, India did not have to issue a compulsory license in order to export Efavirenz to Brazil.
339. Mitsuuchi Kunisawa (2015), *The TRIPS Agreement Implementation in Brazil—Patents in the Pharmaceutical Area*, Nomos, Baden-Baden, pp. 164-165.
340. *Ibid.*, pp. 162-163.
341. Nogueira (2009), "Coquetel Antiaids- Farmanguinhos entrega 1° lote de Efavirenz Nacional," *Folha de São Paulo*, February 17.
342. Mitsuuchi Kunisawa (2015), *The TRIPS Agreement Implementation in Brazil—Patents in the Pharmaceutical Area*, Nomos, Baden-Baden, p. 165.
343. *See* Abbott (2011), *Trends in Local Production of Medicines and Related Technology Transfer*, WHO Department of Public Health, FSU College of Law, Public Law Research Paper No. 569, p. 56; Rodrigues/Soler (2009), "Licença compulsória do Efavirenz no Brasil em 2007: contextualização"; 26 *Revista Panamericana de Salud Publica* 6, 553-559.

to its dependence on Indian laborers to import API.[344] Such dependency might have weakened the position of the Brazilian Ministry of Health in the negotiations for the purchase of antiretrovirals.[345]

V Reasons for Creating ANVISA's Prior Consent

1 Clash Between the New Patent Policy and the National Medicines Policy

That the Federal Ministry of Health, as the main buyer of medicines in Brazil, would suffer an enormous financial impact as a result of the post-TRIPS patent law of 1996 from its very beginning was predictable. The reason for this was the previous Brazilian policy on access to medicine. As already seen, at that time, the policy had been based both on the procurement of non-patented medicines and in the production of non-patented medicines by official pharmaceutical laboratories. This policy was only possible because, until 1996, drug patents were forbidden in Brazil. Therefore, since medicines became patentable, the Ministry of Health would have to spend much more money than before on procuring medicines since it would have to start buying patented brands or licensing.

However, what no one seems to have predicted was that the financial impact of LPI 96 would be so immediate. In 1999—that is, just two years after it came into force—LPI 96 was amended with the purpose of reducing drug prices and extending access to medicines. Such an early amendment suggests that the Federal Ministry of Health was surprised by the enormous financial impact of the new patent law and the crisis so that it had to handle it quickly. The reasons for this urgent need to amend the LPI, from the viewpoint of the Ministry of Health, was the cumulative impact of the new LPI with the so-called Sarney's Law, which had been approved on November 1996, that is, only six months after the LPI came into effect.[346] While Sarney's Law ensured the right to free and universal access to drugs for AIDS treatment, by obliging the Ministry of Health to buy these and distribute them to everyone who needed them, the LPI meant that the Ministry of Health had to pay much more for the patented drugs it was now obliged to buy directly from the patent holder or from a generic company (if the patent holder agreed with licensing his patent rights).

It is important to note that, until November 1996, the public administration was not obliged by law to distribute drugs for AIDS treatment for free. Even if AIDS medication was de facto distributed for free, the Ministry of Health did this first on a voluntary basis, and, second, it procured only non-patented medicines or medicines produced by state laboratories. According to *Nunn*, "the combination of these two laws

344. Mello e Souza (2011), *O Acordo Sobre os Aspectos dos Direitos de Propriedade Intelectual Relacionados ao Comércio (TRIPS): Implicações e Possibilidades para a Saúde Pública no Brasil*, IPEA—Texto para Discussão 1615.
345. *See* Milward de Azevedo Meiners (2007), "Patentes farmacêuticas e saúde pública: desafios à política brasileira de acesso ao tratamento antirretroviral," 24 *Cadernos de Saúde Pública* 7, 1474-1478.
346. Nunn (2009), *The Politics and History of AIDS Treatment in Brazil*, New York, p. 91.

led to a rapid spike in the cost of AIDS treatment and created a serious fiscal dilemma for Brazil that political actors in the executive branch of government would have to resolve."[347]

The impact of these two laws on public costs was abrupt due to the pipeline mechanism—which, along with the decision of not taking advantage of the 10 years transition-period—anticipated the effects of patent protection's introduction in Brazil. As seen before, the Brazilian pipeline mechanism allowed the protection of pharmaceutical inventions for which patents had been filed outside of Brazil at a time when patent protection for pharmaceutical inventions was not yet available in Brazil. In fact, all requests to grant pharmaceutical patents that had been filed outside of Brazil beyond the priority period of 12 months and before the TRIPS Agreement entered into force, despite the new LPI, could not be seen as new in Brazil. Consequently, they would remain unpatentable there. It was precisely to prevent this state of non-patentability that the pipeline mechanism was introduced since, under this exceptional form of patent protection, the usual conditions of patentability (being new and having an inventive step) would not be examined by the INPI. The introduction of this retroactive patent protection made patentable some pharmaceutical inventions that were already in the Brazilian public domain. Therefore, many pharmaceutical products that could theoretically have been freely copied and produced in Brazil until 1996 suddenly lost their unpatentable status. On the other hand, because the Patent Office did not have to examine the novelty and the presence of an inventive step, many pipeline patents were quickly granted.

The impact of pipeline patents on the Ministry of Health budget is clear when one observes, for example, how rapidly the cost of acquiring ARV Drugs increased. According to the Ministry of Health, in 1996, the annual costs for procuring such medicines amounted to circa USD 35 million.[348] In 1997, those costs were nearly seven times higher and amounted to circa USD 240 million. In 1998, the cost of antiretroviral therapy was nearly twice that of the year before. In 1999, the year when ANVISA's prior consent was created, the cost reached circa USD 632 million. In short, it is possible to say that only three years after the new LPI had entered into force, the cost to the Ministry of Health of acquiring ARV Drugs had increased 18 times.

Hasenclever observes that, on the whole, 1,182 requests for pipeline patents were filed at the INPI during the period they were admissible. According to her, many of them resulted in the granting of patents that strongly affected the public health system.[349] This was, according to her, the case for the following ARV Drugs: Efavirenz, Lopinavir/Ritonavir, Abacavir, Nelfinavir and Amprenavir, as well as the cancer drug Imatinib (commercially known as Glivec or Gleevec). It is worth noting that the

347. *Ibid.*
348. Chequer (1999) *Terapia Anti-retroviral e saúde pública—Um balanço da experiência brasileira*, Brazil, Ministério da Saúde; Guise Rosina/Wang/De Campos (2010), "Access to Medicines: Pharmaceutical Patents and the Right to Health," in: Shaver (ed.), *Access to Knowledge in Brazil—New Research on Intellectual Property, Innovation and Development*, Bloomsbury, pp. 184-186.
349. Hasenclever et al. (2010), "O Instituto das Patentes Pipeline e o Acesso a Medicamentos: Aspectos Econômicos e Jurídicos Deletérios à Economia da Saúde," 11 *RDISAN* 2, 164-188.

Efavirenz patent—which was the first object of a compulsory license based on public interest issued in Brazil—was granted in 1999 as a pipeline patent.[350] After analyzing data provided by the Ministry of Health, *Hasenclever* noted that the federal administration spent about USD 705 million on acquiring ARV Drugs protected by pipeline patents in the period from 2001 to 2006. She compared the minimum prices of these drugs on the international market with the prices paid for them by the Brazilian MoH and calculated that the hypothetical damage suffered to the MoH's budget as a result of the introduction of pipeline patents—only taking the ARV Drugs into consideration—should be about USD 420 million to USD 519 million.[351] Between 2009 and 2010, it is estimated that Brazil paid between 704 percent and 5,622 percent more for drugs patented under the pipeline mechanism.[352]

This abrupt increase in drug costs created an enormous problem for the MoH. Pressed between the legal obligations to respect pharmaceutical patents and to guarantee access to medicines for the population, the MoH started to view the patent office's role in the granting of pharmaceutical patents more critically. As mentioned before, from the Ministry of Health's point of view, the INPI was at the time taking a position that was extremely favorable to patent holders, and which put the success of the Brazilian access-to-medicines policy at risk.[353] It seems that many Ministry of Health technicians thought that pharmaceutical patents were being granted by the INPI without the necessary rigidity, probably due to the fact that the INPI lacked both experience in the matter and familiarity with lobbyists of the international pharmaceutical industry.[354] As shown by *Drahos*, patent offices in developing countries tend to assume pro-patent positions; this does not happen by chance, and it is rather the result of years of technical assistance and technocratic support provided by the EPO, the United States Patent and Trademark Office (USPTO) and the JPO to developing countries.[355]

According to *Gonzalo Vecina*, ANVISA's president at the time that prior consent was introduced in the Brazilian law,[356] the idea was that involving health officers in the patent grant process would correct the problem mentioned above since ANVISA not only had experience regarding medicines but also knew how to deal with lobbyists of the international pharmaceutical industry since its officials were already familiar with them. He reported that prior to the reform, the Brazilian Ministry of Industry and Trade

350. *See* Chapter 3-A-IV-6.7.
351. Hasenclever et al. (2010), "O Instituto das Patentes Pipeline e o Acesso a Medicamentos: Aspectos Econômicos e Jurídicos Deletérios à Economia da Saúde," 11 *RDISAN* 2, 177.
352. Chaves/Scopel (2016), "Initiatives to Challenge Patent Barriers and Their Relationship with the Price of Medicines Procured by the Brazilian Unified National Health System," 32 *Cadernos de Saúde Pública* 11, 6.
353. *Figueira Barbosa*, in an interview kindly granted to the author in his office at the FIOCRUZ on March 17, 2009.
354. According to *Figueira Barbosa*, many officers at the Ministry of Health did not trust the INPI at the time und suspected that INPI officers might have taken bribes from the international pharmaceutical industry, and, in return, adopted a pro-patent holder position in their examinations.
355. Drahos (2008), "'Trust Me': Patent Offices in Developing Countries," 34 *Am. J. L. & Med.* 151, 163.
356. *Vecina*, interview kindly given to the author in São Paulo on March 24, 2009.

(MDIC) and the INPI were informed about the proposal to introduce ANVISA as a second patent examination body and that they strongly opposed it. This is also confirmed by *Schüren.*[357]

Hence, the prior consent mechanism arose because the Ministry of Health, at the end of the 1990s, felt that it was necessary to monitor the job the INPI was doing regarding the examination of pharmaceutical patents. The purpose of prior consent was to put an end to a patent policy that was exaggeratedly pro-patent holder and which might threaten the population's access to essential medicines.[358] According to *Massard da Fonseca,* the idea of putting ANVISA to review INPI's examination "was sponsored by the Minister of Health because several denouncers of local pharmaceutical firms have argued that the Patent Office was influenced by and biased toward innovator companies."[359]

2 Discontentment with the INPI's Performance

At the time of the enactment of the patent act of 1996, the INPI was ill-equipped to deal with the flood of pipeline-patent applications for which it would soon be responsible. The Patent Office, which had been created in the early 1970s as the successor of the old *Departamento Nacional de Propriedade Intelectual (DNPI)*, was a poorly resourced federal agency staffed by a few officers, none of whom had experience in the fields of chemicals or pharmaceuticals since these matters had not been patentable under the old law. Some examiners were hired as an emergency, but these measures were not enough to meet the new demands placed on the office by the immediate efficacy of the pipeline provision. Even nearly 20 years after the new patent law came into force, the so-called patent backlog (the average working time the Patent Office needs for a decision on a patent application) for examining pharmaceutical patents is circa 12 to 14 years.[360] Moreover, the INPI lacked credibility. This was so manifest that, in 1999, the INPI's President declared to the Brazilian Parliament, when he was speaking to a parliamentary investigative committee about medicines, that he had been invited to take the INPI presidency as part of a mission to recover its credibility.[361] According to the final report of the Câmara dos Deputados, his testimony indicated that the INPI was in a situation of "chaos, disorganization, omission or ineptitude."[362] Above all, the

357. Schüren (2016), *Aufholende Entwicklung in der globalen Ökonomie—Pharmazeutische Innovationssysteme in Indien und Brasilien*, p. 272.
358. Vecina (2009): interview.
359. *Massard da Fonseca / Bastos* (2016), "Implementing Intellectual Property of Pharmaceuticals in Middle-Income Countries: A Case-Study of Patent Regulation in Brazil," 41 *J. Health Pol., Pol'y & L. 3*, 440.
360. Sampat/Shadlen (2017), *Secondary Pharmaceutical Patenting: A Global Perspective*, NBER Working Paper No. 23114, p. 30.
361. Câmara dos Deputados (1999), CPI Medicamentos, transcription of two interviews from December 14, 1999, p. 6 and p. 58.
362. Câmara dos Deputados (2000), CPI Medicamentos, Final Report from May 30, 2000, pp.160-161.

national pharmaceutical industry felt that the INPI did not have enough independence to do its work and mistrusted it.[363]

The INPI, which did not have any experience concerning pharmaceutical patents, suddenly started granting patents in a very undifferentiated way. As *Figueira Barbosa* puts it, at the time, "no one trusted the INPI."[364] Also, for *Borges Barbosa*, INPI acted as an "entreguista."[365] As *Drahos* reported, behind INPI's pro-patent policy was also the fact that local law firms had funded the training of patent examiners.[366]

By introducing ANVISA in the patent examination, the government's intent was to control INPI's examination process, which was deemed to be of low quality.[367]

VI Conclusion

The impact of the new patent law on medicines policy was almost immediate due to the Brazilian renunciation of the option to make full use of the period of grace and its adoption of the pipeline patents. As we have already seen, many pharmaceutical inventions which belonged to the public domain under the former law suddenly became patentable on the grounds of the introduction of retroactive patent protection ("pipeline patents"). Furthermore, by voluntarily anticipating its obligations under the TRIPS Agreement by seven years, the impact of the new Brazilian Patent Law (LPI) on the medicines policy became rapidly visible. Because generic medicines can only be legally produced either in the case of a lack of patent protection for pharmaceuticals or after the patent's expiration, a medicines policy based only on the promotion of generic medicines and which did not explore the flexibilities of the TRIPS Agreement would have made more sense if it had been implemented under the old patent law, that is, before 1996.

The fact that this medicines policy was introduced *after* the coming into force of the LPI suggests that patent policy and medicines policy in the late 1990s were not dealt with in a joined-up manner by the federal government.[368] This was confirmed by *Vecina*, the first President of ANVISA when he was interviewed by the author in Brazil.[369] It seems that only in 1999 did it become clear to the federal administration that the success of the medicines policy might be inhibited by the patent policy adopted

363. *Vecina*, interview at the Hospital Sírio-Libanês, São Paulo on March 24, 2009; an anonymous representative of the pharmaceutical industry in a short interview in a coffee break in the Economic Forum Brazil-Germany in Cologne, Germany on August 25, 2008.
364. Figueira Barbosa, interview on March 17, 2009 in Rio de Janeiro, Farmanguinhos.
365. Borges Barbosa, interview on March 16, 2009.The word "entreguista" is used in Brazilian Portuguese for characterizing people who do not care about national development interests and advocate, as a general principle, privatization of public property. "Entreguistas" may receive bribes in exchange of performing *entreguistas* policies, but it does not have to.
366. Drahos (2010), "Joining the Patent Office Conga Line," in: Drahos, Peter (ed.), *The Global Governance of Knowledge—Patent Offices and Their Clients*, CUP, Cambridge et al., p. 249.
367. Schulz (2004), "The TRIPS Agreement and Intellectual Property Protection in Brazil," in: *Intellectual Property Rights in Global Trade Framework: IP Trends in Developing Countries, ASIL Proceedings, CUP, Cambridge* 98,100-103 (103).
368. Aith (2001), "Brasil cedeu direitos à droga fora de acordo de propriedade: Patente de remédio antiaids revela erro estratégico do país," *Folha de São Paulo*, March 11, 2001.
369. Vecina (2009), interview at the Hospital Sírio-Libanês, São Paulo.

by the LPI. It was especially clear that a medicines policy based on the promotion of domestic production of generics would have to consider the connection between the patent and the medicines policy. The only solution the Ministry of Health could see for this imbroglio was to look for flexibilities in the TRIPS agreements and in the LPI in order to put these into practice. However, aside from the provision concerning compulsory license, the original text of the LPI, as approved in 1996, did not leave much room for the flexibilities of patent rights.

On the other hand, once Brazil had adopted transitional patent protection via the pipeline system and chosen not to make use of the right to delay ordinary patent protection for pharmaceuticals—flexibilities that would have postponed the impact of the new patent law on medicines policy—it was soon obvious that the problem needed a long-term solution. This would have to be a creative one, considering the strict framework of the TRIPS Agreement. Moreover, at the time, the public health system SUS was compelled, as a result of pressure from civil society, to provide medicines to the poor at no charge, without considering if they were patented or not.[370] Within a few years, the federal administration came under increasing pressure as it was obliged to cover the cost of expensive drug therapies.

There was also financial pressure from the legislative system. This was the case of the abovementioned "Sarney's Law," which obliged the public health system to cover the costs of the expensive ARV therapy for everyone who required it. The Brazilian judiciary also increasingly decided in favor of the public health system's obligation to cover the costs of all drugs, not just antiretrovirals. As a consequence, public expenses for the distribution of medicines grew higher each year.[371] Pressurized on every side to procure patented medicines at high prices, the Ministry of Health was compelled to find a creative way to make such medicines cheaper.

From the viewpoint of the Ministry of Health, it was necessary to change LPI 96 with the purpose of creating a national medicines policy able to expand the flexibilities of patent rights since it was now clear to the federal administration that an instrument, such as a compulsory license, was not enough in itself to reach an equilibrium between its policies on patents and on access to medicines. Compulsory licenses, as an instrument to be used in emergencies, serve to correct severe problems caused by patents; they cannot prevent such problems from happening in the first place. Such a substantial shift in the LPI was not easy to reach, first, because this was not desired, for instance, by the Ministry of Industry and Commerce for political motives other than those of the MoH, and, second because LPI 96 had been strongly supported by President *Cardoso* himself. That the MoH succeeded in making this change was due to personal reasons more than anything else: At the time, the Minister for Health was the economist *José Serra*, both a powerful politician under the conservative party PSDB and a personal friend of President *Cardoso*, as well as a prospective candidate in the

370. Nunn (2009), *The Politics and History of Aids Treatment in Brazil*, New York, p. 91.
371. *Ibid.*

presidential elections of 2002.[372] Given these circumstances, he managed to amend the LPI by weakening patent rights in some circumstances related to public health.

In its original 1996 version, the only legal mechanism available under the Brazilian LPI to deal with the problem of the conflict between the patents policy and the policy regarding access to medicines was that of granting compulsory licenses on the grounds of public health. In order to increase patent flexibilities under Brazilian law, an amendment was made to the LPI, which is going to be the subject of the next section.

B CONTENTS OF THE AMENDMENT TO THE PATENT LAW (LAW 10.196/2001)

I Legislative History

On December 13, 1999, the Ministry of Health[373] sent the President of Brazil a draft proposal for the amendment of the patent law via an executive decree called an "*MP*," which was in 2001 converted into Law 10.196.[374] The proposal—also subscribed to by three other ministers, namely the Minister of Development, Industry and Foreign Trade, the Minister of Foreign Affairs and the Minister of Planning—was immediately implemented by President *Cardoso*, becoming MP No. 2.006.[375]

Until its eventual conversion into law, this "MP" took an unusual path. The MP 2.006, like any other MP, had legal force from the day of its publication. On December 30, 1999, President *Cardoso* issued MP 2.014,[376] which regulated the same matter, thereby overruling MP 2.006.

At the time, if an MP were not converted into law by Congress 30 days up from its issue, the MP would lose its "force of law."[377] In order to avoid the abrogation of MP

372. During the first term of *Cardoso's* Presidency (1998-2002), *Serra* had been Minister of Planning and Budget, until he had to leave because of conflicts with the Minister for the Economy. These internal conflicts were caused by the critical position taken by Serra regarding the policies recommended by the IMF/BID at the time, which the Minister for the Economy had embraced. To avoid such conflicts, *Serra* was made head of the Ministry of Health.
373. Mensagem No. 1.290. de 1999-CN/E.M. I No. 92, of December 13, 1999, *Diário do Congresso Nacional*, January 28, 2000. pp. 3195-3202.
374. According to Article 62 of the Brazilian Constitution, the President of the Republic is authorized, in cases of "relevance and urgency," to send the Congress a decree which has the force of a law. This presidential decree, called *medida provisória* (in English: provisional measure), enjoys the status of a law from the moment that it is issued. After being published, it has "force of law" for 60 days. Congress must deliberate over it with that time period. If it is approved, the decree (MP) is converted into law; if, however, Congress rejects it, the acts carried out during its period of validity will remain in effect, except if the Congress issues a norm ruling it differently. If Congress neither approves nor rejects it, the MP has its "law's efficacy" extended for 60 more days, and it must be voted for under an urgency regime. In such a case, Congress is not allowed to deliberate on other matter until it has considered the MP edited by the President.
375. Brasil (1999d), Medida Provisória 2.006, of December 14, 1999. DOU of December 15, 1999.
376. Medida Provisória 2.014, of December 30, 1999, DOU, December 31, 1999, p. 7, Seção 1.
377. Article 62 Constituição do Brasil. Parágrafo único. As medidas provisórias perderão eficácia, desde a edição, se não forem convertidas em lei no prazo de 30 dias, a partir de sua publicação, devendo o Congresso Nacional disciplinar as relações jurídicas dela decorrentes. (Abrogated on September 11, 2001 by the Emenda Constitucional 32).

2.014, President *Cardoso* used the legal artifice of issuing the MP 2.014-2,[378] the content of which, however, was the same as that of the expiring MP 2.014. The reissue of the "new" MP one day before the original MP was due to expire served to extend the "law's efficacy" of the expired MP 2.014. Thus, near to its expiry date, President *Cardoso* issued MP 2.014-2, which had the same content as MP 2.014-1. When MP 2.014-2's expiration was imminent since Congress again had not deliberated on the matter, the President edited MP 2.014-3,[379] repeating the content of MP 2.014-2. This attempt to amend the LPI via MP became a game of cat and mouse between the Executive and the Legislative Branch, with the Presidency reissuing the same MP every month of the year 2000[380] and the Congress steadily resisted deliberating on it. By reissuing the MP for the 15th and last time, in January 2001, the Executive Branch won the game. Thus, Congress converted MP 2.105-15 into law in February 2001; that is, it became Law 10.196.[381] Although the changes made to the LPI in the repeated MPs issued by the President formally had "force of law," in practice, they were not applied until they had been converted into law, given the legal uncertainties.

II Content of the Reform

1 *Limiting the Possibility of the LPI's Retroactivity (Article 229 LPI)*

According to the original wording of Article 229 LPI, the new patent law was to be applied to pending patent applications, except for cases of chemical or pharmaceutical products or processes, which would *only* be protected under the pipeline mechanism.[382] This provision caused two problems that, apparently, were only perceived a short time before the TRIPS Agreement came into force for developing countries (on January 1, 2000). The point was that, at that time, there were circa 2000 pending applications for pharmaceutical patents in Brazil that had been filed under the old law, and for which no application under the pipeline mechanism had been filed.[383] The first problem affected pending applications that had been filed before December 31, 1994,[384]

378. Medida Provisória 2.014-2, of January 28, 2000, DOU, January 29, 2000.
379. Medida Provisória 2.014-3, of February 25, 2000, DOU, February 28, 2000.
380. Medida Provisória 2.014-4, of March 28, 2000 (DOU, March 29, 2000), followed by MP 2.014-5, de 27.4.2000 (DOU, April 28, 2000), followed by MP 2.014-6, of May 26, 2000 (DOU, May 28, 2000), followed by MP 2.014-7, of June 26, 2000 (DOU, June 27, 2000), followed by e MP 2.014-8, of July 26, 2000 (DOU, July 27, 2000), followed by MP 2.014-9, of August 25, 2000 (DOU, August 26, 2000), followed by MP 2.014-10, of September 22, 2000 (DOU, September 25, 2000), followed by MP 2.014-11, of October 24, 2000 (DOU, October 25, 2000), followed by MP 2.014-12, of November 23, 2000 (DOU, November 24, 2000), followed by the MP 2.014-13, of December 21, 2000 (DOU, December 22, 2000), followed by MP 2.105-14, of December 27, 2000 (DOU, December 28, 2000), followed by the MP 2.105-15, of January 26, 2001 (DOU, January 27, 2001—Special edition).
381. Brazil (2001a), Lei No. 10.196, of February 14, 2001, DOU, February 15, 2001.
382. Articles 230-231 LPI.
383. "Medida provisória de dezembro indefere pedidos de registro," *Folha de São Paulo* (Cotidiano), February 21, 2000.
384. Pharmaceutical companies started filing pharmaceutical patent applications in Brazil in 1992, when it was expected that President *Collor* would have success in approving a new patent law.

the date TRIPS came into effect internationally; the second problem affected pending applications that had been filed between January 1, 1995 and May 14, 1997, the date on which the new LPI came into force in Brazil.

To understand the problem, one has to have in mind the duty under Article 70.7 TRIPS—according to which applications that are pending on the date that TRIPS comes into effect for the member country in question should be allowed to be amended so as to claim any enhanced protection. If Article 70.7 TRIPS were directly applicable (i.e., self-executing), consequently, all pending applications would have to be decided in accordance with the new patent law.

Applying the new LPI for pending pharmaceutical applications filed before December 31, 1994, however, could come with the following problematic consequence: some medicines that had already been produced as generic drugs in Brazil might suddenly become patentable so that many laboratories in Brazil might have to stop producing them or to pay compensation to the patent owner. Consequently, if nothing was done until January 1, 2000 and Article 70.7 TRIPS were respected, many inventions that belonged to the public domain would probably be privatized.

The problem concerning pharmaceutical applications filed between May 15, 1997 and January 1, 2000 had to do with conformity to TRIPS of Article 229 LPI. Considering that the deadline for filing pipeline patents had expired on May 15, 1997, it was questionable whether it would be compatible with TRIPS to apply, from January 1, 2000, the old patent law to all pending applications that had not been converted into "pipeline applications." This problem arose because the Brazilian LPI originally did not cover the mailbox provision due to an erroneous assumption that it was not obliged to provide for it because it had pipeline provision (this, however, had nothing to do with the pipeline provision, which was not an obligation under the TRIPS Agreement). Consequently, if Article 229 LPI were not changed, all pending applications filed between January 1, 1995 and May 14, 1997, the object of which were pharmaceutical inventions, would have to be denied because the old law, which applied to them, prohibited pharmaceutical patents.

The fact that, at the end of 1999, the INPI would not be able to decide all pending patent applications filed before December 31, 1994, was seen as a significant failure on the part of the INPI.[385] It should have been a simple administrative matter to refuse such applications, based purely on the fact that the applicable law prohibited pharmaceutical patents. Had INPI timely decided the applications for pharmaceutical patents that had been filed before December 31, 1994, the problem concerning pending applications and the public domain would never have arisen. Consequently, the legislator would not have had to change the LPI in order to correct INPI's mistake.

Two weeks before TRIPS came into force in Brazil, that is, on January 1, 2000, MP 2006 clarified how the law should be applied in terms of pending applications by giving a new wording to Article 229 LPI.[386] Thereby all pending patent applications should be decided, as a rule, in accordance with the patentability criteria established by the new

385. Brazil, Câmara dos Deputados (2000), *Relatório da CPI-Medicamentos*, p. 161.
386. "Medida provisória de dezembro indefere pedidos de registro," *Folha de São Paulo* (Cotidiano), February 21, 2000.

law. If, however, the following three conditions were present, they should be, exceptionally, decided in accordance with the patentability criteria established by the old law: (1) they involved products or processes obtained by chemical means or processes and alimentary and chemical-pharmaceutical substances, matter, mixtures or products and medicaments of any type; and (2) they had been filed before the coming into force of the WTO Agreement, that is before December 31, 1994; and (3) no application for patent protection under the pipeline mechanism had been filed.[387]

2 *Introduction of Article 229 Parágrafo Único LPI (Mailbox Provision—Article 70.8 TRIPS)*

When the LPI introduced transitional protection for pharmaceutical patent applications in the "pipeline form" in 1996, it was assumed that this provision would be enough to fulfill the requirements of TRIPS concerning transitional protection. After all, parties to the treaty were only obliged to introduce the "mailbox" protection, which conferred much less protection than the "pipeline." Eventually, this assumption was perceived to have been a mistake. In fact, not every application filed before the new law came into force could be converted into a pipeline application for a number of different reasons. For instance, a requirement for getting pipeline protection was that the patent had already been granted in another WTO country.

The amendment of 1999 changed the wording of Article 229, sole paragraph, in order to introduce the mailbox provision, following the parameters given by Article 70.8 TRIPS. Its aim was to regulate the legal situation of agricultural and pharmaceutical product patents applied for between January 1, 1995 and May 14, 1997, that is, the time between the WTO Agreement's coming into effect internationally and the publication of the LPI. Pharmaceutical and agricultural patent applications filed during this time enjoyed transitional patent protection provided by the "mailbox." Therefore, for such applications, the criteria for patentability laid down by the new patent act are to be applied. However, patent protection is provided as from the granting of the patent and for the remainder of the patent term, counted from the filing date in Brazil or from the priority date, if this is available and has been claimed.

This provision was introduced in order to guarantee provisional patent protection for pending applications that had been filed after the entry into force of the WTO Agreement, but before the approval of the Brazilian TRIPS-compliant patent law, and which had not been the object of a "pipeline application." With this provision, the legal vacuum mentioned before was filled and thus, the risk of having to apply the new law to the old applications disappeared.

387. Brasil (2001a), Article 1, Law 10.196, of February 14, 2001, which gave a new wording to Article 229 LPI.

3 *Introduction of Article 229-A LPI*

The amendment excluded process patents filed under the old law from being decided in accordance with the new law since TRIPS did not provide for any transitory protection for such patents.[388] In accordance with the amendment, patent protection should be denied for all pending applications of pharmaceutical processes patents, which had been filed before December 31, 1994.

Article 229-A was introduced to exclude pending process-patent applications filed between January 1, 1995 and May 14, 1997 from any transitional patent protection. By doing so, the amendment reduced patent protection to the minimum level demanded by the international trade law, as TRIPS did not demand any form of transitional protection for *process* patents for the developing world, but only for products protected by agricultural or pharmaceutical patents. In other words, the amendment eliminated patent protection for cases whereby the LPI allowed more rights than Article 70.8 TRIPS demanded, as was the case of process patents. With the amendment, not only was pipeline protection for pending process applications eliminated, but it was also excluded by the newly introduced mailbox protection,[389] which was applicable only for *product* applications filed between January 1, 1995 and May 14, 1997.

Considering that the original LPI's wording provided for pipeline patent protection for both products and processes when TRIPS did not impose any form of transitional protection for process patents, the amendment sought to balance the equation by means of LPI's original wording: on the one hand, it introduced the mailbox mechanism for pending product patents not converted into the pipeline; on the other hand, it eliminated the (TRIPS-plus) protection for process applications given by the original LPI.

4 *Introduction of Article 229-B LPI*

The purpose of Article 229-B was only to regulate the processing time of pending applications filed between January 1, 1995 and May 14, 1997, the object of which were pharmaceutical and agricultural chemical products. According to the newly introduced Article 229-B, such applications were to be decided by December 31, 2004, under the patentability criteria of the new law, if no pipeline application were pending.

The reason for this deadline might be found under Article 70.7 TRIPS and Article 32 LPI. The first of these imposes that pending applications at the time of application of the Agreement in the country shall be allowed to be amended to claim any enhanced protection. The latter prohibits any amendments after the applicant has requested the examination of his application. As TRIPS was internationally applicable in Brazil from January 1, 2000 or 2005, depending on what subject patent matter is treated, it may be that the legislator wanted to avoid the possibility that applicants might deliberately

388. *See* Article 70.8 TRIPS.
389. Article 229, sole paragraph LPI.

delay the course of their applications in order to be benefited with the chance of amending them. By stating that pending applications filed during the transition time should be decided by December 31, 2004, the new law avoided the possibility of potential applicants amending their applications in order to claim enhanced protection.

5 Creating ANVISA's *Anuência Prévia* (Article 229-C LPI) and Its Purpose

As seen above, the Brazilian patent law (LPI 96) was amended. It introduced ANVISA's participation in the patent grant proceedings with the novel Article 229-C, which stipulated in a few words that the granting of patents for pharmaceutical products and processes should depend on the prior consent (*anuência prévia*) of the National Health Surveillance Agency, ANVISA.

According to *Figueira Barbosa*, the MP 2.006 primarily aimed only at defining a transition regime applicable to pending applications filed before the entry into force of the WTO Agreement, which, otherwise, would have had to enjoy full patent protection just because of their status as pending applications on January 1, 2000.[390] *Figueira Barbosa* reported that the Health Authority ANVISA's inclusion in the patent grant proceedings was conceived of by Minister *Serra*, who was very concerned with the high prices charged by the pharmaceutical industry and took the opportunity of urgently amending the patent law via decree. *Figueira Barbosa* is not the only voice to attribute the creation of ANVISA's prior consent mechanism to Minister *Serra's* activity in the Ministry of Health. *Jorge Raimundo*, INTERFARMA's (Associação da Indústria Farmacêutica de Pesquisa) representative in Brazil, for instance, pejoratively declared to me that the "peculiar" idea of including a health authority in the patent grant proceedings came from Minister *Serra*" and that "its purpose was to lower the price of medicines and to favor the generics industry."[391]

According to the official purpose of the new mechanism, found in the justifications of the draft text for a provisional measure sent by the MoH to the President, ANVISA's prior consent would inaugurate a system of patent grants based on cooperation between the Patent Authority, INPI, and the Regulatory Authority, ANVISA. Its aim should be to guarantee "the best technical standards" in the granting of pharmaceutical patents, which would be "similar to the proceedings applied by the most advanced systems of patent control and of sanitary vigilance working in industrialized countries."[392] It is possible that the patent law of other countries might have served as inspiration for the creation of the prior consent mechanism. *Romandini*, in his analysis of ANVISA's prior consent, wrote that in the past, both Italian and the U.S. law foresaw

390. Interview given on March 17, 2009, Farmanguinhos, Rio de Janeiro. According to his own statement, *Figueira Barbosa* is the one who wrote MP 2.006's text.
391. Raimundo, INTERFARMA's representative: Interview given in his private office in Rio de Janeiro on March 16, 2009. For him, the introduction of ANVISA's prior consent mechanism represents a "barrier to economic growth" and is therefore "deplorable."
392. Mensagem 1.290 of 1999-CN—E.M.I. 92, Item 8, *Diário do Congresso Nacional*, January 28, 2000, 3197.

the participation of the Health's authority in the patent proceedings. He reported that "in Italy, if the Patent Office held that the invention might be harmful to health, it had to ask—up until 1979—the Public Health Agency for an opinion. If the latter concluded that the invention was harmful, the Patent Office had to reject the application."[393] According to him, in the U.S., "some inventions were excluded from patent protection for lack of utility when they were held to be dangerous for public health."[394] However, as stressed by the Italian commentator, these systems were abandoned because "the specification of a patent application does not contain the data necessary to assess whether or not the invention is safe."[395] Even if these data were available, assessing safety within the patent proceedings would create unnecessary costs since, at this stage, it is not possible to anticipate whether the invention will be commercialized since most patents are not explored.

The Brazilian prior consent mechanism, however, has a decisive distinction in comparison to the old Italian and U.S. systems. What makes ANVISA's prior consent different is its purpose, considering that it was introduced to expand access to medicines, not to check drug safety and prohibit them. While the idea of involving a health authority in patent proceedings is not new, a systematical peer system based on the cooperation of a sanitary vigilance body with the purpose of considering the effects of the patent in the access to drugs is rather original. As seen before, during the investigation conducted by the Parliamentary Commission of Inquiry on Medicines (*CPI dos Medicamentos*),[396] INPI's performance in the patent grant of pharmaceutical products in 1999 was seen as disastrous.[397]

As the official justification indicates, one reason that motivated the legislator to create ANVISA's prior consent must have been the problem of patent quality in the field of pharmaceutical inventions. "Patent quality" is a catch-all formula, which includes a rejection of lax approval, which hampers all sorts of public goods, such as competition, public health, food security, etc.

Involving two different government bodies in complex administrative proceedings is, in fact, something ordinary in administrative law. This is often done within administrative cases concerning environmental issues. In Brazil, for instance, the competent authority for issuing an environmental license must obtain a prior consent of the federal environment agency IBAMA if the project in question foresees that an important biome will be suppressed, like the Atlantic forest.[398]

Furthermore, the idea of putting a health authority in the patent examination was not new in Brazil. As mentioned before, the requirement that the National Department of Health (ANVISA's predecessor) makes a preliminary examination of patentability

---

393. Romandini (2016), "Flexibilities under TRIPS: An Analysis of the Proposal for Reforming Brazilian Patent Law," 15 *J. Marshall Rev. Intell. Prop. L.*, 207.
394. *Ibid.*, p. 208.
395. *Ibid.*, p. 208.
396. Câmara dos Deputados (2000), CPI Medicamentos, Final Report from May 30, 2000, pp.160-161.
397. For a critical analysis of the Brazilian Patent Office *see* Drahos (2010), "Joining the Patent Office Conga Line," in: Drahos, Peter (ed.), *The Global Governance of Knowledge—Patent Offices and Their Clients*, CUP, Cambridge et al., pp. 242-256.
398. Article 14 of Federal Law (Lei Federal) No. 11.428 of December 22, 2006.

already existed in a similar provision in Decree 16.264 from 1923. According to this old Decree, if a given pharmaceutical invention seemed to be harmful to public health, the National Department of Health should make an examination not only regarding such "harmfulness" but also regarding the novelty of the invention.[399] Therefore, under the old Brazilian system, the health authority's participation was not limited to questions of drug safety.

According to *Figueira Barbosa*, making the patent grant dependent on ANVISA's consent was intended to serve both to control the patent office[400] and, at the same time, help the further development of the Brazilian national generics industry. When I interviewed *Borges Barbosa*, he maintained that Article 229-C had been created in order to find a balance between public policies and to correct INPI's exaggeratedly pro-patent policy.[401] Most important, it was to serve as a safeguard to guarantee that every Brazilian citizen would have access to medicines.[402]

However, the function which ANVISA's prior consent really serves is concerned with the public policy regarding access to medicines. The central point in the idea of ANVISA's prior consent is that precisely the authority whose primary function is to guarantee the efficacy and safety of medicines should also have responsibility concerning access to medicines. In other words: ANVISA should officially ensure that everyone has access to the medicines they need, and the way ANVISA does this is by participating in the patent grant proceedings. Since the question of pharmaceutical patents affects the question of access to medicines, it makes sense that they are decided together. By involving the Health Authority, ANVISA, in the pharmaceutical patent grant proceedings, the legislator gives it a new function regarding access to medicines, one that is as important as its function of guaranteeing that only effective and safe medicines are authorized to be marketed.[403]

6 *Giving the INPI More Structure (Article 2 MP)*

At the same time that the amendment imposed on the Patent Office the duty to submit its work for review by the health regulatory authority, Article 2 MP 2.006 also provided for the improvement of the INPI's structure, which had been neglected for decades. Article 2 MP allowed urgent hiring of qualified personnel at the Patent Office since, in

399. Brazil (1923), Paragraph 1 of Article 44, Regulamento referred by Decreto 16.264 of December 19, 1923.
400. Figueira Barbosa: "Ninguém confiava mais no INPI! Na época, o sentimento era de que o INPI, realmente, precisava ser vigiado" (interview given to me on March 17, 2009).
401. *Borges Barbosa* also declared in the interview he gave to me that INPI had granted too many patents in the past due to pressure from pharmaceutical transnational companies. In his words: "Eu acho que a introdução do Artigo 229-C foi exatamente para tentar um reequilíbrio de políticas públicas para corrigir a política entreguista do INPI" (Interview given on March 16, 2009 in his law firm in Rio de Janeiro).
402. *See* Fonseca Mendes/Constantino de Oliveira/Amorim Pinheiro (2014), "Anuência Prévia da ANVISA: a evolução da regulamentação de uma política de estado," 4 *Revista Brasileira de Políticas Públicas* 2, 157-172.
403. *See also* Drahos (2008), "'Trust Me': Patent Offices in Developing Countries," 34 *Am. J. L & Med.* 151, 168.

Brazil, hiring civil servants is a long process, as demanded by law. This illustrates the twofold concerns of the policymakers: if from one perspective, the amendment introduced another authority to the patent grant proceeding, indicating that the INPI was seen as not doing a good job, from another, it also provided the INPI with more material resources, so that it also worked to improving patent quality by strengthening the INPI.

7 *Introducing the Regulatory Exception ("Early Working")*

When the MP 2.014 was edited for the eighth time, in June 2000,[404] it did not just repeat its preceding content but instead took the opportunity to create a new provision. In this way, the regulatory exception, also known as the "Bolar exception" or "early working," was introduced into patent law. This exception was introduced after the WTO Panel report issued within the proceedings initiated by the European Communities (EC) against Canada, to which Brazil was attached as a third party.[405] In that case, the issue was the Canadian patent law, which permitted third parties to manufacture and store patented medicines before the date on which the patent's term expires. The EC complained that such permission was incompatible with TRIPS, even considering that the drug was intended to be sold as a generic medicine after the brand drug will not be protected anymore by patent rights. According to Canada, both the regulatory and the "stockpiling" are allowed by Article 30 TRIPS. The EC took the view that the conditions set by Article 30 TRIPS would not be fulfilled because the Canadian legislation would be neither "limited" nor "normal." According to the WTO panel, the regulatory exception was considered to be "normal," and thus, should be considered an exception to the rights conferred by patents. The "stockpiling" exception, however, in the panel's interpretation of Article 30 TRIPS, was not considered to be in conflict with a "normal" exploitation of patents.

According to the new Article 43 VII LPI, the protection given by patent rights should not prevent non-authorized third parties from performing acts regarding patented inventions if such acts are aimed exclusively at the production of information, data and test results directed to obtain a marketing license, so as to allow the exploitation and commercialization of the patented product before a patent expires.

III Repercussions

Negative reactions against the amendment, which introduced ANVISA's prior consent, came both at the international and at the domestic level. Pharmaceutical Research and Manufacturers of America (PhRMA) argued that ANVISA's prior consent is not consistent with the TRIPS Agreement because this would violate the prohibition of

404. Medida Provisória 2.014-7, June 26, 2000, DOU, June 27, 2000.
405. *Canada—Patent Protection of Pharmaceutical Products*—Complaint by the European Communities and their Member States—Report of the Panel (WTO/Doc WT/DS114/R), March 17, 2000.

discrimination in accordance with the field of technology (Article 27.1 TRIPS).[406] According to comments published in Brazilian newspapers at the time, the U.S. administration requested the Brazilian federal administration to abrogate not only the amendment but also the federal decree regulating compulsory licenses on the basis of public interest.[407] The first President of ANVISA, *Gonzalo Vecina*, confirmed that a U.S. delegation came to Brasília in early 2000 especially to exert pressure against the amendment.[408]

At the domestic level, one of the first voices to criticize the Amendment was that of the Brazilian Association for Intellectual Property (Associação Brasileira de Propriedade Intelectual—ABPI), an association of the classical "patent community," which included representatives of the multinational innovative industry, lawyers[409] and engineers, as well as lobbyists for stronger intellectual property rights.[410] The ABPI strongly condemned the amendment to the patent law in all its points. Regarding ANVISA's prior consent, ABPI called this a measure of "extreme violence," which would, in any case, be incompatible with both the BC and Article 27 TRIPS Agreement.[411]

After the MP had become law, INTERFARMA, an association which represents the interests of the multinational pharmaceutical industry in Brazil,[412] hired a law firm specializing in intellectual property in order to produce a report which would be widely circulated by the association in the following years, as a manifesto against ANVISA's prior consent.[413] At the same time, legal articles started appearing in daily newspapers as well in academic publications where INTERFARMA's position concerning ANVISA's prior consent was more widely propagated.[414] Since then, ANVISA's participation in

---

406. Cohen (2007), *Brazil's Historical Approach to Intellectual Property Law: The Pharmaceutical Sector*, LCSHD Paper Series 54, The World Bank, p. 71.
407. Vasconcelos (2000), "Mudanças na lei desagradam múltis," *Folha de S. Paulo*, February 21; Nanci (2005a), "Concessão de patentes não é assunto da ANVISA, dizem especialistas," *Consultor Jurídico*, March 8, 2005.
408. *Vecina* was the first President of ANVISA.
409. Licks (2001), "A Falta de Transparência no Direito de Patentes," *Gazeta Mercantil*, São Paulo, August 8.
410. *Shadlen* also described how associations representing transnational firms, as well local IP attorneys and association of patent agents and patent lawyers support stronger patent rights and are the loudest opponents of the pre-TRIPS regime. *See* Shadlen (2009b), *Reforming and Reinforcing the Revolution: The Post-TRIPS Politics of Patents in Latin America*, Working Paper 09-02, Global Development and Environment Institute.
411. ABPI (2000), "Resolução da APBI nº 2," Item 5 of January 27, 2000.
412. About the multinational pharmaceutical companies lobbying in the Brazilian Parliament *see* Passos (2016), "O Complexo 'Fármaco-Político" in: Berron / González, *A Privatização da Democracia—Um catálogo da captura corporativa no Brasil*, pp. 109-122.
413. Momsen Leonardos and Cia, Manifestação da INTERFARMA—O Regime da Anuência Prévia da ANVISA para Concessão de Patentes de Invenção, Instituído pelo Artigo 229-C introduzido na Lei 9.279/96 e suas Consequências para as Obrigações Internacionais Assumidas pelo Brasil com os demais Países-Membros da Organização Mundial do Comércio—OMC—Uma Violação Tripla aos Artigos 27 e 62 do TRIPS (unpublished). No date. Given by hand to the author by Raimundo, INTERFARMA's Consultive President, when interviewed at his office in Rio de Janeiro, March 16, 2009.
414. For instance Licks (2001), "A falta de transparência no direito de patentes," *Gazeta Mercantil*, August 8, 2001; Leonardos/Licks (2002), "A Exegese do Article 229-C da Lei de Propriedade Industrial após a Edição das Medidas Provisórias 2.006, de 15/12/99 e 2.014, de 21/12/2000 e

the patent grant proceedings has been continuously repudiated by INTERFARMA.[415] At the same line, also patent lawyers criticize ANVISA's veto right to pharmaceutical patents.

On the other hand, the introduction of ANVISA's prior consent was seen as positive by some scholars[416] and by NGOs involved with patient's rights,[417] as well as by associations representing the pharmaceutical local industry, such as ABIFINA and ALANAC; the latter supported the amendment, which they saw as an incentive to the development of the local generics industry.[418] PROGENERICOS, an association representing the generic pharmaceutical industry, including international companies, was of the view that ANVISA's work important for combatting against misuses and prolongation of patent rights beyond the patent term of 20 years.[419] However, the Brazilian pharmaceutical industry's support to ANVISA's prior consent seems to be disappearing, possibly due to its own interest in obtaining incremental patents, as hypothesized by *Shadlen*.[420]

IV Conclusion

All in all, an amendment of the new patent law, the initiative for which came from the Ministry of Health, only 3.5 years after that law had come into force, indicates that the Ministry of Health had not been prepared enough for the immediate impact of the new patent law in the procurement of medicines. In fact, both forgoing the full use of the transitional periods and introducing pipeline protection made the change in the Brazilian legal patent regime too abrupt. This development, often criticized by some

a Promulgação da Lei N° 10.196, de 14/02/2001," 61 *Revista da ABPI*, 57-68. *See also* Biase Guimarães (2008), *Direito à Saúde e Propriedade Intelectual de Medicamentos no Brasil—A Anuência Prévia da Agência Nacional de Vigilância Sanitária*, PhD Thesis, IMS—UERJ, pp. 43-46, which collects several arguments published in Brazil by the patent community against ANVISA's prior consent.

415. INTERFARMA rejects ANVISA's participation in the patent grant and repeatedly complaints about it. *See*, for instance, ABPI (2002), *Aplicação equivocada da legislação de patentes preocupa a indústria farmacêutica, Boletim da ABPI N° 28* (2002). The same rejection, in a more vehement way, was declared by INTERFARMA's Vice-President and Brazilian Director of Boehringer Ingelheim do Brasil, *Volker Bargon*, in his presentation for the panel "Indústria Química e Farmacêutica: Desenvolvimento de Produtos com Novas Matérias Primas" at the Annual German-Brazilian Economic Meeting, which took place in Cologne on August 25, 2008 and the author participated.
416. *See*, for instance, Basso (2006), "Intervention of Health Authorities in Patent Examination: The Brazilian Practice of the Prior Consent," 1 *IJIPM* 1-2, 54-75; Drahos (2008), "Regulating Patenting Offices: Countering Pharmaceutical Homogen," 5 *ScriptEd* 3, 512-513; Rodrigues Júnior (2005), "Anuência Prévia: Integração do direito à saúde aos direitos de propriedade intelectual," 94 *RT* No. 840, 84-106.
417. *See* Shadlen (2012), "The Politics of Pharmaceutical Patent Examination in Brazil," in: Burlamaqui/Castro/Kattel (eds.), *Knowledge Governance: Reasserting Public Interest*, Anthem Press, London/New York, pp. 139-162.
418. Vasconcelos (2000), "Mudanças na Lei desagradam múltis," *Folha de São Paulo*, February 21, 2000.
419. Lobo, technical manager at PRO-GENERICOS, in interview given on March, 27 in São Paulo.
420. Shadlen (2011b), "The Political Contradictions of Incremental Innovations: Lessons from Pharmaceutical Patent Examination in Brazil," 39 *Pol. & Soc'y* 2, 163.

scholars[421] in Brazil, ended up having a positive effect, from the point of view of patient rights: it "forced" the Ministry of Health's bureaucrats to react and find a creative solution to harmonize patent rights and the right of access to medicines. This was done by means of the conception of ANVISA's prior consent to the granting of patents in the field of medicines.

On the other hand, the fact that ANVISA's prior consent has been introduced into the LPI through a presidential decree has not contributed to give it legitimacy at the INPI. In fact, according to one INPI examiner, ANVISA "was inserted in the patent grant proceedings in a very surprising way for both sides—without any discussion or preparations."[422] This vision seems to be exaggerated, considering that according to *Vecina*, who was the first ANVISA's president, the Ministry of Health discussed the law amendment with the Ministry of Trade and Industry intensively.[423]

Bearing in mind policy and regulatory considerations, the creative idea of getting health experts to cooperate with patent offices makes sense, and it has been admired by some commentators outside Brazil. *Yu*, citing *Drahos*, advocates that this idea should also be used in the developed countries.[424] Indeed, health experts are in a better position to make assessments about drugs in a broader context in which health, access to medicines and innovation are interrelated.

C THE IMPLEMENTATION OF ANVISA'S PRIOR CONSENT PROCEDURE

I Historical Development

1 The First Period (2001-2003): Confusing Times

In March 2001, ANVISA created an intellectual property unit named Coordenação de Propriedade Intelectual da ANVISA—(COOPI).[425] The unit was installed on an empty floor in the old building of the Patent Office (INPI) in Rio de Janeiro. The team was at that time composed of 15 recently hired examiners, most of them biologists, chemists or pharmacists.[426] From June 2001, INPI started sending the patent files regarding pharmaceutical applications to ANVISA for review examination.

From the beginning, the INPI had reservations about ANVISA's inclusion in the job of examining patents. As it had not taken part in the administrative discussions regarding the amendment to the patent law, it seems that the Patent Office felt

421. For instance, Lopes dos Santos (2010), *Sustentabilidade do Programa DST/AIDS: Análise da Capacidade de Oferta e Preços dos Medicamentos Antivirais*, pp. 15-16, 36, Universidade Federal do Rio de Janeiro.
422. An INPI examiner, wishing to remain anonymous: interview given on March 16, 2009.
423. Vecina, in interview given in São Paulo on March 24, 2009.
424. Yu (2008), "Access to Medicines, BRICS Alliances, and Collective Action," 34 *American J. L. & Med.*, 345-394 (378).
425. ANVISA examiner I: interview given on March 9, 2009.
426. *Ibid.*

surprised and unfairly excluded from the decision-making process.[427] Moreover, some of the first ANVISA examiners had worked at the Patent Office before as temporary staff. All of this, allied with the physical installation of ANVISA's unit in the old Patent Office building, seemed to have helped from the very beginning to create rivalries and a lack of inclination on the Patent Office's side to cooperate with ANVISA in the job of examining patents.

In addition, neither the law nor an administrative regulation had established how exactly ANVISA should exercise its mandate, and especially on which criteria a veto or a sanction for or against patentability should be based. Consequently, the role that ANVISA should play in the patent grant proceedings was not clear for either ANVISA or the INPI.[428] According to one ANVISA's examiner interviewed by the author, the initial work was carried out almost without orientation, with some limited instances of advice directly coming from *Serra*, the Minister of Health.[429] According to *Figueira Barbosa*, the first head of the ANVISA Intellectual Property Division and a former Patent Office head officer, at first, there was not much to do since all files coming to ANVISA concerned pipeline applications, for which no examination was needed to be carried out; the team then corrected translation mistakes and other formal errors contained in the examination reports coming from the Patent Office.[430] Also, ANVISA Examiner IV and the INPI Examiner I confirmed in their interviews that in the first years of the arrangement, ANVISA's re-examination tasks were limited to the correction of translation mistakes. This kind of cooperation was disliked by the Patent Office, which understandably did not see a positive contribution in such a task.[431] The INPI's examiner I interviewed reported that in 2003 when the new federal government was elected, the COOPI had no manager for several months, so the work was not well organized. According to her, it was only from September 2003 that the cases and ANVISA's role in the patent system started to be discussed internally.

2 *The Second Period (2003-2012): Rivalry's Times Between ANVISA and the INPI*

From September 2003, ANVISA began to conduct a substantive patent examination. From 2003 to June 2012, ANVISA steadily denied its consent based on reasons of patent law. The agency acted as if it were a patent opposition division, with the particularity that all pharmaceutical patent applications must be *ex lege* examined again. This situation was viewed by the Patent Office with discomfort[432] because ANVISA's

427. An INPI examiner from the Chemical Division: interview given on March 16, 2009, INPI, Rio de Janeiro. This information, however, is controversial. According to *Vecina*, INPI was informed about the project of introducing ANVISA as a second patent body.
428. ANVISA examiner I, speaking for the ANVISA and an INPI examiner, speaking for the INPI.
429. ANVISA examiner II: interview given on March 9, 2009, São Pedro-SP.
430. Figueira Barbosa, interview given on March 17, 2009 in Rio de Janeiro, Farmanguinhos.
431. ANVISA exanaminer II: interview given on March 9, 2009, São Pedro-SP and INPI examiner: interview given on March 16, 2009 in Rio de Janeiro, INPI.
432. An INPI examiner: interview given on March 16, 2009 in Rio de Janeiro, INPI.

inclusion might suggest that the INPI's personnel do not have the capacity to decide cases of drug patenting[433] or were unable to resist corruption.

This climate of rivalry between both federal agencies made it difficult for the cooperation desired by law to materialize. As reported by *Shadlen*, in most of the cases in which ANVISA did not give its consent, INPI simply stopped proceedings so that neither a positive nor a negative decision was enacted.[434] In some cases, the patent applicant challenged ANVISA's denial of prior consent before the courts. But, in those cases in which ANVISA's denial of prior consent was not challenged, the patent status remained unresolved since INPI decided to neither grant the patent nor deny it.[435] In such cases, proceedings simply stopped.

Until 2017, INPI and ANVISA disagreed about both the substantive and procedural aspects ANVISA had to take into account to justify its decision on prior consent. According to INPI's view, shared by some authors,[436] ANVISA was only entitled to consider health matters concerning the safety and efficacy of drugs, not patent matters, since INPI maintained that it would be the only agency responsible for patents themselves.[437] ANVISA, however, argued that it would be impossible to consider the safety and efficacy of a drug during patent proceedings since such data is only available after clinical studies are finished, which happens during a later phase when a license to market the drug is to be issued;[438] ANVISA took the view that it should instead carry out a substantive patent examination, bearing in mind the potentially harmful effects that patents may have on public health since the high price of patented medicines affects their availability to the population. Consequently, as a basis for deciding on prior consent, ANVISA carried out a second examination on the substantive conditions of patentability, after a first report had already been made by the INPI. In doing so,

433. Borges Barbosa (2006a) related, about a National Aids Program's conference that was held in 2005, where both ANVISA and INPI officers were invited to take part in a table of discussion, at which the INPI officers were criticized by other participants and decided to leave the conference. It is reported that one participant had declared that the Patent Office did not have personnel with the capacity to produce technical report concerning pharmaceutical products (Borgers Barbosa (2006a), "A Proibição, pela ANVISA, de Reivindicações de Uso Farmacêutico," in: Borges Barbosa (ed.), *Usucapião de Patentes*, p. 718, fn. 12.

434. *See* Shadlen (2012), "Pharmaceutical Patent Examination in Brazil," in: Burlamaqui/Castro/Kattel (eds.), *Knowledge Governance—Reasserting the Public Interest*, Anthem Press, London/New York, pp. 139-161. This has also been confirmed by Borges Barbosa: "Toda vez que a ANVISA nega a anuência, o INPI não decide. Esse é um efeito perverso da anuência prévia da ANVISA, porque gera uma 'patente de fato', pois ninguém entra no mercado. Assim, prorroga-se o efeito prático da patente." (Interview given on March 9, 2009.)

435. This was confirmed by the INPI's Examiner I in my interview, with the following words: "Se o pedido não for anuído pela ANVISA, ele vai para a diretoria do INPI e o processso *fica parado*. O processo fica parado por falta de previsão legal sobre o que deve ser feito nos casos em que ANVISA nega a anuência."

436. For instance, Sichel (2013), "A Anuência Prévia, pela ANVISA—patentes farmacêuticas," *Revista Eletrônica do IBPI* 8, 56-66; Mueller/Moreira Taketsuma Costa (2014), "Should ANVISA be Permitted to Reject Pharmaceutical Patent Applications in Brazil?," 24 *Expert Opinion on Therapeutic Pat.*, 1-4.

437. *See* Shadlen (2012), "The Politics of Pharmaceutical Patent Examination in Brazil," in: Burlamaqui et al. (eds.), *Knowledge Governance: Reasserting Public Interest*, Anthem Press, London/New York, p. 146.

438. ANVISA's Officer I: Interview given in Brasília, March 17, 2009.

ANVISA used more rigorous criteria to assess the conditions of patentability (novelty, inventive step and industrial application) of the invention in question, justifying such rigor with the direct impact caused by a patent on the price of the drug.[439] As it was to be expected, ANVISA sometimes came to the conclusion that an invention that had been found to be patentable by the Patent Office did not deserve a patent. Based on this second examination of the conditions of patentability, prior consent to grant a patent was then denied by ANVISA. The INPI, however, did not agree with ANVISA's approach and maintained that by following it, ANVISA would illegally invade its own exclusive competence to decide on patent matters.[440]

Furthermore, ANVISA and INPI had different views concerning the procedural rules ANVISA's participation in the patent proceedings should follow, which caused serious difficulties in the patent proceedings of pharmaceutical patents. One such difficulty concerns the timing of when the INPI should send patent files to ANVISA so that the latter can examine the case and gives or not give its consent to the granting of the patent. Another difficulty concerns how communication between ANVISA and the patentee should be conducted, whether directly or intermediated by the INPI; a third problem concerns what the INPI has to do after ANVISA returns patent files to its office, with or without its consent, to grant the patent, especially in the last case. The INPI and ANVISA, however, were at first able to agree only regarding the first point, so their conflict has created serious problems in the implementation of the prior consent mechanism, as shown below.

From the earliest days of the arrangement until June 2012, the procedure was as follows: ANVISA was called upon (by the INPI) to give an opinion about prior consent after INPI's technical report had been officially published, which normally occurs a short time before proceedings end. During that time, at first, the INPI did its job as usual and, afterward, sent proceedings files to ANVISA. If ANVISA gave its consent for the patent grant, INPI continued with the proceedings by granting the patent. If, however, ANVISA had a query for the INPI, for instance, requesting the patentee for clarification, INPI often used to do nothing, so that the patent applicant was not notified that ANVISA had requested any information; consequently, the application became "frozen."[441] In the same way, when ANVISA denied prior consent, the INPI would also do nothing, so that the applicant was never formally notified that ANVISA had not given its consent to grant the patent. Also, in this case, the INPI's interruption of the procedure meant that the patent application simply became "frozen." In other words, proceedings remained in legal limbo because the patent application in question had been neither granted nor denied.[442]

439. Mitsuuchi Kunisawa (2015), *The TRIPS Agreement Implementation in Brazil—Patents in the Pharmaceutical Area*, Nomos, Baden-Baden, p. 106.
440. About the conflict between INPI and ANVISA *see* Shadlen (2011a), "The Rise and Fall of 'Prior Consent' in Brazil," 3 *WIPO J.*, 110.
441. Abreu (2017), "Prospecção tecnológica aplicada na otimização da concessão de patentes no Brasil," p. 115; Shadlen (2012), "Pharmaceutical Patent Examination in Brazil," in: Burlamaqui et al. (eds.), *Knowledge Governance—Reasserting the Public Interest*, Anthem Press, London/NewYork, pp. 139-161.
442. This was reported, for instance, by ANVISA's officer II, interviewed on March 12, 2009.

The first procedural question, which refers to the time when ANVISA should give its consent to patent grant, does not seem to be a problem: both cooperation partners agreed that at first, INPI should carry out this examination, and ANVISA should do it afterward. From June 2012, when this workflow was inverted, the cooperation partners INPI and ANVISA apparently continued to agree on this question.

The second procedural question, which refers to how ANVISA communicates with the patentee, is a more problematic point. As mentioned above, at first, ANVISA did not communicate directly with the patentee; instead, it used the INPI as an intermediary authority. In these cases, however, the INPI tended not to notify patentees of ANVISA's requests. In order to solve this problem, ANVISA made use of its normative power by approving a decree which regulated the internal application's flow in the agency.[443] Therewith, ANVISA stopped using the INPI as an intermediary between the patentee and the agency, so that any communication from ANVISA to the patentee was made via the Official Journal, without using the Patent Office.

The third procedural question, which is also the most serious one, refers to what the INPI has to do in those cases in which ANVISA denies prior consent. An agreement about this question was only reached in April 2017 by the INPI and ANVISA.[444]

Due to the incompatible approaches adopted by these agencies on the question of what ANVISA was allowed to examine in order to justify its decision concerning prior consent and how to do it, a legal battle between both agencies began. The conflict between the views maintained by the Medicines Agency and the Patent Office concerning ANVISA's role in the granting of pharmaceutical patents was also reflected in the respective legal offices of the two agencies. The first divergence between these legal offices (*Procuradoria da União*) dates from 2002, and it concerned patent pipeline applications. The INPI at first took the view that for pipeline proceedings, ANVISA should not be involved, while ANVISA believed that in these types of proceedings, its participation was also necessary.[445] Until August 2000, INPI stipulated that ANVISA should only carry out its examination for the regular patent applications, but not for pipeline applications, and therefore, 257 pipeline patents were issued without ANVISA's prior consent.[446] In the literature, there are also authors supporting the view that ANVISA's participation in the patent examination would be transitory. According to this interpretation, ANVISA should give prior consent only for applications concerning pipeline patents, in which case, it would help the Patent Office verify one of its requisites of patentability, namely, whether the patented product was or was not available in the market.[447]

Because under the organization of the Brazilian state, the Federal Union is represented by a central body of public lawyers the AGU ANVISA's legal office brought this controversial question to the AGU. ANVISA wanted the AGU to enact a

443. ANVISA (2008), Resolução da Diretoria Colegiada—RDC No. 45, of June 23, 2008.
444. *See* Chapter 3: D-IV-2 (pp. 295-297).
445. ANVISA's Officer I: Interview given in Brasília, March 17, 2009.
446. Licks/Leonardo (2002), "A Exegese do Article 229-C da Lei de Propriedade Industrial após a Edição das Medidas Provisórias 2.006, de 15/12/99 e 2.014, de 21/12/2000, e a Promulgação da Lei N° 10.196, de 14/02/2001," 61 *Revista da ABPI*, 58-59.
447. *Ibid.*, p. 62.

legal opinion, a so-called *parecer*, in order to unify the interpretation of the federal administration on the question.[448] In 2006, the AGU issued the *Parecer* N° AGU/MP-09/2006, according to which all patent applications, including pipeline applications, should be sent to ANVISA in order to obtain consent for the patent grant.[449] The *parecer*, however, did not limit its analysis to the question of pipeline applications but instead gave its interpretation about how ANVISA's prior consent was to be exercised in general. AGU's conclusion was that ANVISA should not examine the requirements of patentability because this was an exclusive task of the Patent Office. Therefore, ANVISA must not deny its consent on the basis of patent law, but only on the basis of health law, within the sense of Article 27.2 TRIPS.[450]

In 2008, the INPI formally requested the Brazilian Attorney General (AGU) to issue a legal opinion on this question. The first legal opinion was issued in 2009.[451] According to this, ANVISA must not deny its prior consent based on patent requirements; instead, it would only be allowed to deny it with a basis on the sanitary control of the production and marketing of products and services harmful to public health. ANVISA asked for reconsideration, arguing that evaluating whether a pharmaceutical invention might present problems in the field of public health law during the patent application would be impossible during the patent application period.[452]

AGU's opinion, however, was maintained.[453] Notwithstanding, ANVISA continued to make prior-consent report examinations a requirement of patentability.[454] In January 2011, AGU's opinion was approved by AGU's head, the *Advogado Geral da União*,[455] signifying that it might become binding for all federal administrative agencies. This created a new political dispute between both federal agencies, with ANVISA supported by NGOs and the INPI by the private sector, represented by IP lawyers.[456] ANVISA, however, continued to base its analyses on the grounds of the requirements of patentability, alleging that the AGU's *parecer* was not binding, as long as it had not been approved by the President of the Republic.[457] The President has, in fact, never approved the *parecer*.

448. ANVISA's Officer I: Interview, Brasília, March 17, 2009.
449. Fernandes de Moura (2011), "Patentes de Medicamentos e a Discussão a Respeito da Interpretação do Article 229-C da Lei 9.279/96," XV *Revista CEJ* 53, 80-87.
450. ANVISA's Officer I: Interview given in Brasília, March 17, 2009.
451. AGU (2009), Parecer No. 210/PGF/AE/2009 of October 16, 2009.
452. Fernandes de Moura (2011), "Patentes de Medicamentos e a Discussão a Respeito da Interpretação do Article 229-C da Lei 9.279/96," XV *Revista CEJ* 53, 80; Corrêa/Guimarães (2012), "Propriedade Intelectual e Saúde Pública: o Papel da Agência Nacional de Vigilância Sanitária no Patenteamento Farmacêutico no Brasil," 6 *RECIIS—Electronic Journal of Communication, Information and Innovation in Health*, 3; ANVISA's Officer I: Interview given in Brasília, March 17, 2009.
453. AGU (2010), Parecer No. 337/PGF/EA of March 4, 2010.
454. ANVISA's examiner I: declaration given in a personal e-mail to the author, of February 11, 2010.
455. The then General Unions's Attorney, Dr. Luis Inácio Lucena Adams, approved Parecer No. 337/PGG/EA, of March 4, 2009 on January 7, 2011.
456. Formenti (2001), "AGU restringe poder da ANVISA na concessão de patente de medicamento," *O Estado de São Paulo*, January 24.
457. ANVISA's examiner I: declaration given in a personal e-mail to the author, of December 15, 2011.

At that time, INPI supported the opinion that in cases where ANVISA denied prior consent, the Patent Office was neither authorized to grant the patent nor to deny it because there was no legal norm that ruled how to proceed in this case. In other words, the INPI took the view that even though the INPI was no longer legally entitled to grant a pharmaceutical patent without ANVISA's prior consent, the Patent Office was not allowed to deny the patent in this case.[458] In these cases, the Patent Office stopped proceedings. According to an INPI officer, the patent law did not provide for how the INPI should act in cases in which ANVISA did not give its consent; the law just prohibited the granting of a pharmaceutical patent without ANVISA's consent. Consequently, the INPI's position was that the patent should neither be granted nor be rejected.[459]

The approach taken by the INPI was extremely formal. Such an approach might be justified by Brazilian administrative law, which imposes as a general principle that the public administration is only allowed to do something if there is a law that regulates this performance (*princípio da legalidade administrativa*). However, as a public authority, the main function of which is to execute norms concerning industrial property,[460] the INPI has the autonomy to issue procedural rules concerning the entire patent proceedings. This means that if there is no law in a strict sense that rules how to proceed in a case where ANVISA's prior consent is denied, the INPI has the duty to issue such a norm in order to guarantee that the LPI is correctly applied.

De facto, INPI does not need a law in a strict sense to rule patent procedural questions. If the INPI wanted to cooperate with ANVISA, it could have issued an administrative norm, the aim of which would be to implement ANVISA 's prior consent. As mentioned above, as the body responsible for the patent proceedings, INPI has the power to regulate procedural details via soft law. Nothing would hinder the INPI from issuing a norm ruling what procedures are to be followed in cases in which prior consent is denied. But instead of issuing such a norm, the patent authority simply did nothing and alleged it was not allowed to do anything because of the lack of a law.

In doing this, the INPI undermined the prior consent mechanism. With this conduct, the INPI made Article 229-C-provision inoperative, making things even worse for public health than they would be in the absence of ANVISA's prior consent, in an arrangement that Barbosa called "a perverse effect of ANVISA's prior consent mechanism."[461] This is so because an undefined (legal) situation in which a patent application is neither issued nor denied does not help to expand access to medicines, considering that a mere patent application also produces legal effects de facto. An example of such an effect is that a possible competitor who started producing an invention the patent of which had been requested at the Patent Office, but not yet

458. An INPI examiner from the Chemical Division of the INPI, interviewed on March 16, 2009, Rio de Janeiro.
459. An INPI examiner from the Chemical Division of the INPI, interviewed on March 16, 2009, Rio de Janeiro. *See also* article published in the Brazilian press, "O INPI possui 102 pedidos de patente negados que, se publicados, abririam caminho para a produção de novos genéricos no país," *O Estado de São Paulo*, May 17, 2010.
460. Brazil (1970), Article 2°, Lei No. 5.648 of December 11, 1970, DOU, December 14, 1970.
461. Borges Barbosa (2009), interview at his law firm in Rio de Janeiro, on March 16, 2009.

decided, might be required to pay the patentee compensation for damages. The longer a patent application needs to be decided, the longer the pharmaceutical invention protected by the (pending) application will need to be able to be marketed as a cheaper generic drug.

II The GTI's Suggestions to Solve the Conflict Between the INPI and ANVISA

As reported above, the lack of agreement between ANVISA and the INPI concerning ANVISA's prior consent implementation caused chaos in the proceedings of pharmaceutical patents in Brazil. The reason for the confusion was the INPI's behavior because it always stopped the proceedings in cases where ANVISA had denied prior consent. As a reaction to this dysfunctionality, the federal administration intervened in order to establish better compliance with Article 229-C LPI. In 2011, an Interministerial Committee (Brazilian Interministerial Working Group (*Grupo de Trabalho Interministerial*—GTI)) was created with the aim of harmonizing and rethinking proceedings concerning prior consent.[462] The group was composed of representatives of ANVISA, the INPI and the Ministry of Health, as well as those from the Ministry of Development, Industry and Commerce. In order to solve this conflict at the administrative level, the Federal Administration gave the GTI the task of studying the problem and suggesting a solution for it, bearing in mind the following objectives: (1) to promote cooperation between ANVISA and the INPI; (2) to make viable an interaction between policies concerning innovation and access to medicines; (3) to make the intellectual property approach and the public health approach compatible with each other, keeping the Doha Declaration in mind; and (4) to create a workflow for prior consent which should be observed by the INPI and ANVISA.[463]

With respect to the question of the procedural workflow between the two agencies concerning prior consent (i.e., who does what, and when?), GTI's report suggested the following workflow for the cooperation between INPI and ANVISA:

> Phase 1: The INPI makes the initial formal examination of the patent application.
> Phase 2: Once the request is approved by means of a formal examination, the INPI identifies the type of product and process and send ANVISA requests relating to pharmaceutical products and processes.
> Phase 3: ANVISA carries out a technical examination of the patent application and publishes the respective report concerning prior consent to the patent request in the Official Journal.
> Phase 4: Once it has published its opinion, ANVISA sends the patent files back to the INPI.

462. MoH/MDIC/AGU (2011), Portaria Interministerial MS/MDIC/AGU No. 1956 of August 16, 2011, DOU, August 17, 2011.
463. MoH/MDIC/AGU (2012), Portaria Interministerial No. 1065 MS/MDIC/AGU of May 24, 2012, DOU, May 25, 2012.

Phase 5a: If prior consent is given by ANVISA, the INPI proceeds with a technical examination of the patent application and publishes its decision to grant the patent or dismiss the request.
Phase 5b: If ANVISA denies prior consent, the INPI dismisses (*arquiva*) the patent application and officially publishes this decision.[464]

From June 2012, the INPI and ANVISA started following the recommendation of the GTI's final report, so that the workflow was inverted (i.e., ANVISA decides about prior consent first; the INPI writes its technical report afterward). Since then, ANVISA's analysis regarding prior consent has been decided prior to the INPI's analysis.

With respect to the other points the GTI had to address, its final report[465] generally concluded that ANVISA's analysis regarding prior consent should consider the impact of a pharmaceutical product or process in the light of public health, considering its scientific knowledge. On the other hand, the GTI also concluded that ANVISA's activity concerning pharmaceutical patent examination should be linked with Article 18(I) LPI. This provision excludes from patentability "anything contrary to morals, standards of respectability and public security, order and health." Therefore, according to the GTI, ANVISA should carry out its job whilst bearing in mind that the prohibition of patentability must be based on the fact that inventions contrary to "morality," "public order" and "public health" are not patentable. The provision of Article 18 LPI, however, must be consistent with Article 27.2 TRIPS Agreement. According to this provision, the prohibition of exploitation is a requirement for excluding patentability. Consequently, if a patent grant is hindered with the basis on Article 18 LPI, the product for which the patent was denied will not be put on the market.

Therefore, invoking Article 18 LPI as a motivation for ANVISA's denial of prior consent is a mistake since ANVISA's prior consent was created in order to expand access to medicines. Because Article 18 LPI must be consistent with Article 27.2 TRIPS, it is not possible to prohibit patenting of an invention on the basis of Article 18 LPI and, at the same time, except that this prohibition will contribute to widening access to medicines since a drug prohibited from commercialization will not reach anyone who may need it.

Besides, the problem of the legal competences of both agencies (who does what and how?) was not adequately addressed by the GTI. Its final report did not clarify, for instance, the question of whether ANVISA is allowed to decide about prior consent based on reasons of patent law or not, as had been discussed in the courts. The GTI apparently concludes that each federal authority should make decisions bearing in mind its own competence given by law (i.e., the INPI should make its decisions based on patent law, and ANVISA should decide about prior consent based on public health law, keeping in mind the need to satisfy the criterion of access to medicines for all), although such competences cannot be so easy and discretely distinguished when dealing with access to medicines.

464. Portaria Interministerial MS/MDIC/AGU No. 1065/12, pp. 7-9.
465. Portaria Interministerial No. 1065 MS/MDIC/AGU of May 24, 2012, DOU, May 25, 2012.

In short, the GTI failed in that it could find neither an adequate nor a correct solution for the conflict between ANVISA and the INPI. Consequently, it is no wonder that the GTI's solution, in practice, changed nothing: ANVISA continued to deny prior consent on the grounds of patent law, and the INPI continued to ignore this.

III Reaction of ANVISA

According to the conclusion presented by the Interministerial Committee, ANVISA's participation should take place in accordance with the needs of the public healthcare system, SUS. This indicates that ANVISA's participation in the patent proceedings is justified by the need to expand access to drugs within that system. Following this final report and a public consultation carried out by the MoH, in April 2013, ANVISA introduced an administrative norm (Resolução da Diretoria Colegiada—RDC 20[466]), which sets down the substantive criteria for its examination, as well as the new workflow for doing it. According to RDC 20, ANVISA should deny prior consent for pharmaceutical patents and products if the patent requested is considered "contrary to public health," which would apply to patent grants in the following situations:[467]

(1) if the product or process described in the patent request will be "a risk for health"; or
(2) if the product or process described in the patent request will be of interest for drug or pharmaceutical assistance policies within the public health system SUS and, at the same time, will not satisfy the conditions of patentability given by the Patent Law.

After setting down in which cases ANVISA is authorized to deny prior consent, RDC-ANVISA No. 20 defines how the situations described under I and II are to be read. So, it establishes that "the risk to health will be present when the pharmaceutical product either comprises a substance, the use of which was prohibited within the country or the pharmaceutical process results in such a prohibited substance."[468]

RDC-ANVISA No. 20 also clarifies the cases in which a pharmaceutical product or process will be considered of "interest to drug policies or pharmaceutical assistance policies within the public health service (SUS)." Accordingly, pharmaceutical products or processes are considered as such when they "comprise" or "result" in substances listed in RENAME, as well as when they "comprise" or "result" in substances pertaining to the medical indication registered under RENAME. The question of which medicines are listed as "strategic" depends on the criteria adopted for this by the MoH. Originally, the RENAME list was considered a part of the national medicines policy; it used to be updated annually and contained the names of all pharmaceutical products considered to be essential or strategic for the SUS. In 2013, the MoH defined as being

466. ANVISA (2013), Resolução—RDC ANVISA 20 of April 10, 2013, DOU, April 15, 2013, p. 68.
467. ANVISA (2013), Article 4.1.II, Resolução-RDC ANVISA 45 of June 23, 2008, according to the reading given by Resolução-RDC ANVISA 20 of April 10, 2013, DOU, April 15, 2013, p. 68.
468. *Ibid.*, Article 4 (2-I).

strategic for the SUS those pharmaceutical products that satisfy criteria of "high social significance," such as medication for neglected diseases, products of high technological value and biotechnological products.[469]

It is worth mentioning that a substance may be considered of interest to the medicines policy—in the context of ANVISA's prior consent—even if it is not listed as such in the MoH's annual lists. When the object of the invention's patent request is not contained in the MoH's list, it is enough if the substance in question is related to the following types of drugs: I—antiviral and antiretroviral drugs; II—drugs needed to treat neglected diseases; III—drugs needed to treat degenerative diseases, such as Alzheimer's or Parkinson's; IV —immunosuppressive drugs; V—drugs needed to treat mental illness, such as antipsychotics or anticonvulsants; VI—products obtained by biological routes; VII—vaccines and serums; VIII—blood products; and IX—oncology products.[470]

Notwithstanding the conclusion presented by the GTI, the conflict between the INPI and ANVISA, however, was not solved until 2017, under the auspices of the

469. *See* MoH (2013), Portaria MS 3.089, of December 11, 2013, DOU, December 13, 2013, p. 52. According to Article 3rd, pharmaceutical products which satisfy criteria of high social significance are divided into the following categories:

I— Group 1: Antiviral and antiretroviral drugs used in the treatment of viral diseases and STD/AIDS;
II— Group 2: Neglected diseases, which deals with products for high-magnitude diseases, such as chagas, leprosy, malaria, leishmaniasis, tuberculosis, dengue, schistosomiasis, filariasis, spotted fever and systemic mycoses;
III— Group 3: Chronic noncommunicable diseases (NCDs), which deals with products for disease, such as degenerative diseases and mental illnesses;
IV— Group 4: Products obtained by biological routes, which deals with high-tech products, such as recombinant DNA routes and monoclonal antibodies, enzymes, hormones and proteins;
V— Group 5: Vaccines and serums, which applies to vaccines and serums considered strategic for the National Immunization Program (NIP) or which have significant importance for public health and are the focus of targeted measures and initiatives to increase local production, innovation and technology transfer;
VI— Group 6: Blood products, which deals with all blood products purchased by the SUS which are strategic to meet the demands of public health and promotion of local production;
VII— Group 7: Medicines and supplies for the resulting disease therapy needed in the event of a nuclear accident;
VIII— Group 8: Oncology products prioritized by SUS, which deals with strategic products used in cancer treatments and which are not provided for in the other groups mentioned in this article; IX—Group 9: Herbal medicines, which deals with strategic products for promoting the National Program for Medicinal Plants and Herbal Medicines, provided for by Ministerial Decree No. 2,960 / MS / CCPR / MAP / MCT / MinC / MDA / MDS / MDIC / MIN / MMA of December 9, 2008; and
X— Group 10: Antibiotics, which deals with strategic antibiotic products for the SUS that have high imports of active pharmaceutical ingredients and the drug itself.

Currently, the addition of drugs to the RENAME list is governed by MoH (2019), Portaria No. 3.047 of November 28, 2019, and by MoH (2017b), PRC-5, of September 28, 2017, DOU, October 3, 2017.

470. *See* MoH Portaria de Consolidação No. 2 (PRC-2): Articles 12, 13, 14 DOU-Suplemento October 3, 2017, p. 61.

conservative presidency of Mr. *Temer*,[471] when ANVISA suddenly gave up on its position and agreed that the INPI alone should have the last word about the patentability of pharmaceutical inventions in Brazil.

IV Controversy on the Applicability of Article 229-C in the Brazilian Jurisprudence

The following explores some case law on ANVISA's prior consent by instance courts before ANVISA and the INPI reached the agreement of 2017, as well as one case that took place afterward. So far, there has been no definitive decision upon the question since the highest Brazilian courts, the STJ and the STF, have not yet decided the question.

1 Report of Judgments

1.1 Valganciclovir (Valcyte) Case

The first judicial dispute concerning ANVISA's prior consent was brought to the courts by a Swiss company in 2004. Its object was patenting an antiretroviral medicine called Valganciclovir. The patent application was filed at the INPI in 1995.[472] After the Patent Office issued a first report for the patentability in May 2003, the file was sent to ANVISA, which denied prior consent. In its view, the compound valganciclovir was already disclosed in the form of the Markush formula in EP 0375329. Consequently, it would not satisfy the patentability conditions of novelty and inventive step, in such a way as to be obvious in light of the prior art. Due to ANVISA's refusal to grant prior consent, the patentee sued INPI before a federal court in Rio de Janeiro, requesting that the court oblige the INPI to continue proceedings and to grant the patent applied for, notwithstanding ANVISA's lack of prior consent. The plaintiff argued that ANVISA was not allowed to deny prior consent based on the grounds of patent law, but it must base it only on the grounds of public health and that Article 229-C LPI would not be applicable without a federal norm detailing the workflow of this cooperation. ANVISA, which had been called by the court to take part in the proceedings, counterargued with the following points: (a) Article 229-C LPI would be auto-applicable so that it would not need to wait for a special norm to be applied; (b) Article 229-C LPI invests ANVISA with the power to examine patents in coordination with the Patent Office; (c) the criteria ANVISA uses to examine a drug's risk for public health should not be mixed with questions of patent law or with access to medicines; (d) ANVISA could not consent to the patent grant because the invention would not satisfy the requirements of novelty. Furthermore, the judgment would be void on the grounds of having violated the

471. Mr. Temer became the President of Brazil after succeeding in a legal maneuver to impeach President Rousseff in August 2016.
472. INPI File No. PI9503468-4, filed by F. Hoffmann-La Roche AG on July 27, 1995.

procedural right of ANVISA to examine its allegations with the making of an expert report.

The Court of First Instance ruled on the dispute in November 2004. This judgment declared ANVISA's veto to be unconstitutional due to two reasons: (1) ANVISA would not be competent to decide about conditions of patentability; (2) because, by requesting a technical proof, ANVISA had indirectly "confessed" its technical inability to test patents.[473]

The Court of Second Instance (*Tribunal Regional Federal da Segunda Região*), however, did not rule on the substantive question on discussion and declared this judgment void in December 2007.[474] Consequently, the case came back to the Federal Court of First Instance to be judged again.

In June of 2015, the case was judged by the Court of First Instance, after the court had accepted a request from ANVISA, which wanted the testimony of an expert's report.[475] According to the judgment, the expert's report itself, in a first examination, concluded that valganciclovir did not have an inventive step, but, on a second examination, the expert changed their opinion and concluded that in regard to 12 of the 13 claims, valganciclovir was new and had an inventive step, maintaining that only one claim would not be new. According to the expert, however, ANVISA's opinion that the invention in question would not be new was also technically possible, being a question of interpretation of the concepts of relative and absolute novelty. It is interesting to note that during the proceedings, the INPI twice changed its technical report regarding valganciclovir's patentability. At the end of the day, the INPI then concluded that valganciclovir was new and did contain an inventive step regarding the 13 claims requested.

Regarding the preliminary questions, the judgment ruled, first, that ANVISA might and should examine the conditions of patentability; second, that this decision must not be discretionary; and third, that the INPI was not allowed to grant a pharmaceutical patent without ANVISA's prior consent. Subsequently, the judgment examined whether the drug Valganciclovir satisfied the conditions of patentability. In doing so, it first clarified that Valganciclovir was to be viewed in the category of "invention selection" and that the invention in question had been anticipated before by a broad Markush formula. Regarding novelty, the judgment did not follow ANVISA's opinion and ruled that Valganciclovir was new; with respect to the presence of an inventive step, however, the judgment followed ANVISA and ruled that for a person skilled in the art, Valganciclovir would be an obvious technical solution, bearing in mind the prior art contained in the antecessor European document EP375329. Furthermore, the judgment ruled that the invention had not been described in sufficient detail in the application to obtain a patent, even though this shortcoming was corrected

473. Justiça Federal do Rio de Janeiro, 37ª Vara Federal, Case No. 2004.51.01.506840-0 (F. Hoffmann-La Roche AG vs. ANVISA and INPI), DJe November 22, 2004, p. 89.
474. Tribunal Regional Federal da 2ª Região (TRF-2), Apelação Cível No. 2004.51.01.506840-0. Judgment of December 11, 2007, published in the Official Journal on December 13, 2007.
475. 13a Vara Federal Rio de Janeiro, Case No. 0506840-58.2004.4.02.5101, F. Hoffmann La Roche AG vs. INPI and ANVISA, Federal Judge Marcia Maria Nunes de Barros, DOU, July 16, 2015.

during the court case.[476] The patentee and the INPI appealed to the Court of Second Instance (Federal Court of Second Instance, 2nd District (*Tribunal Regional Federal da 2a Região*—TRF-2)), which ruled the case in December 2017.[477] TRF-2 upheld the decision of the lower Court, thereby maintaining the non-patentability of Valganciclovir. It is worth noting that, while the Court did not recognize the invention as patentable, it did not accept that ANVISA is allowed to check patentability requirements, stressing that ANVISA should only check questions of drug safety. With regard to this point, the court's reasoning is not convincing. As discussed above, ANVISA's prior consent examination cannot take into consideration drug safety criteria[478] because the reason for being of its participation is the need of promoting drug access. The judgment became final on July 11, 2019.

1.2 Docetaxel Case

The controversy around the case of the anticancer drug Docetaxel was brought to the Brazilian courts in 2004 after ANVISA had denied its prior consent to the patent grant. The patent application was filed by a French multinational pharmaceutical company in 1995, under the old patent law.[479] In this case, the Patent Office issued a technical report on the patentability of the invention after the applicant had made changes in her request.[480] The files were then sent to ANVISA, which denied prior consent. According to ANVISA, the object of the application was a process patent, and this kind of patent did not fall within the category of the eligible patent subject matter under the old Brazilian patent law, which was applicable in this case.[481] In response, the company sued both ANVISA and the INPI, requesting that the court declare ANVISA's report void and, consequently, oblige the INPI to grant the patent.[482]

The first instance gave the plaintiff an interim measure that declared ANVISA's report void and obliged the INPI to grant the patent.[483] This interim measure, however, was vetoed by the superior instance,[484] so that the INPI canceled its preceding

476. This judgment was criticized by the Brazilian patent community. *See*, for instance, Mueller (2015), "13th Federal District Court of Rio de Janeiro Holds that ANVISA Can Examine Patentability Requirements of Patent Applications Claiming Pharmaceutical Inventions," *The National L. Rev.*, June 26.
477. TRF-2, Apelação Cível No. 2004.51.01.506840-0. Judgment of December 14, 2017, published in the Official Journal on January 22, 2018.
478. *See* Chapter 3-B-II-5.
479. INPI File No. PI 9508789-3, filed by Rhone-Poulenc Rorer S.A (later succeed by Aventis Pharma S/A) on July 7, 1995.
480. RPI 1626, April 29, 2003.
481. I have not had direct access to this ANVISA report, but its content is copied in the ruling of the Federal Court of Second Instance (TRF-2) in the Apelação em Mandado de Segurança No. 2004.51.01.513854-1 of July 15, 2008, Judgment published in the Official Journal (*DOE*) on July 31, 2008, pp. 252-257.
482. Justiça Federal do Rio de Janeiro, 38ª Vara Federal, Aventis Pharma S/A vs. ANVISA and INPI (Case No. 2004.51.01.513854-1).
483. RPI 1771, December, 17, 2004.
484. Tribunal Regional Federal da 2a Região (TRF-2), Aventis Pharma S/A vs. ANVISA and INPI (Suspensão de Liminar em Agravo Interno No. 2004.02.014281-3) ruled on July 7, 2005.

decision.[485] Some months later, the INPI changed its technical report and concluded that the invention did not deserve a patent.[486] At this time, the French multinational company requested termination of the proceedings, but the court did not accept it and ruled on the case, deciding that ANVISA's participation in the procedure was in conformity with the law.[487] The French company appealed against this decision, but the ruling of the first instance was maintained by the Federal Court of Second Instance (TRF-2).[488] The patentee then lodged an extraordinary appeal against this judgment to the highest Brazilian federal courts in the year 2008.[489]

In September 2019, the Superior Tribunal de Justiça (STJ) upheld the TRF-2's ruling.[490] However, the Court did not rule whether ANVISA is authorized to reassess the standard requirements of patentability and whether this would be against Article 27.1 TRIPS Agreement since the special appeal (*Recurso Especial*) was not admitted for judgment by formal reasons. This ruling became final on February 2020, after the court had judged a legal remedy against the decision of non-admission, which had been lodged by the French pharmaceutical company.[491]

In May 2020, the Supremo Tribunal Federal (STF) rejected the extraordinary appeal (*Recurso Extraordinário*) and upheld the TRF-2' ruling.[492] The STF did not admit the appeal for judgment because there was no question of constitutional law to be decided in the case. This ruling became final in August 2020 after the STF had rejected a legal remedy lodged by AVENTIS against the decision of nonadmission.[493]

In the meantime, other companies started to produce the drug in the form of a generic medicine.[494] This was the case, for instance, of a Brazilian company that was forbidden by the State Court of São Paulo to produce the drug in 2005.[495] At this time, the Brazilian company had just made the winning bid in a public tender in order to procure the anticancer drug to the State of São Paulo, but then it was hindered from

485. RPI 1779 of February 11, 2005.
486. RPI 1835 of March 7, 2006.
487. 38thVara Federal do Rio de Janeiro (Federal Court of First Instance), Aventis Pharma S/A vs. ANVISA and the INPI (Mandado de Segurança), Ruling of September 5, 2005.
488. Tribunal Regional Federal da 2a Região (TRF-2), Aventis Pharma S/A vs. ANVISA and INPI (Case Number 2004.51.01.513854 1), ruled on July 15, 2008.
489. Superior Tribunal de Justiça (STJ) Recurso Especial No. 1.192.940 and Supremo Tribunal Federal (STF), Recurso Extraordinário No. 627.558, Aventis Pharma S/A vs. ANVISA/INPI. Under the Brazilian system of legal remedies for the STF and the STJ, a condition for the STF to decide the extraordinary appeal is that the STJ has before definitively ruled against the plaintiff.
490. Superior Tribunal de Justiça (STJ) Recurso Especial No. 1.192.940, ruled on September 9, 2019, DJe/STJ 2755, September 17, 2019.
491. Superior Tribunal de Justiça (STJ) AgInt no Agravo em Recurso Especial No. 1.273.074-RJ (2018/0076338-4), ruled on December 17, 2019, DJe/STJ, December 19, 2019. The decision became final on February 26, 2020.
492. Supremo Tribunal Federal, Recurso Extraordinário No. 627.558, ruled on May 12, 2020, DJe/STF 119, May 14, 2020.
493. Supremo Tribunal Federal, Segundo Agravo no Recurso Extraordinário No. 627.558, DJe/STF 210, August 25, 2020.
494. Nanci (2005b), "Eurofarma briga para produzir remédio contra câncer," *Conjur*, July 9.
495. Tribunal de Justiça do Estado de São Paulo (TJSP), Agravo de Instrumento No. 380.600.4/6-00 e380.600.4/8-01, Aventis Pharma S/A and Aventis Pharma Ltda. vs. Quiral Química do Brasil S/A, judged on March 9, 2005.

selling it. The French multinational company raised prices by 70 percent and sued the State of São Paulo, in order to oblige the state to suspend the tender, on the grounds that only the French company would be authorized to produce the drug in Brazil; this result was obtained by an interim measure.[496] Eventually, the highest federal Brazilian court (STF) suspended this ruling and guaranteed the State of São Paulo the right to buy the drug from the Brazilian company.[497] This ruling, however, did not approach the question of the legality of ANVISA's participation in the patent proceedings. The decision was made only to avoid a loss to public health and public finances.[498]

1.3 Penciclovir Case

The court battle around the drug penciclovir—an agent used in the treatment of Hepatitis B—started in 2004. The plaintiff, a multinational Swiss company, had filed two patent applications, the first one under the old patent law (a product patent)[499] and the second one as a pipeline patent.[500] In 2002, the Patent Office issued its technical report concluding that both inventions were patentable.[501] In 2004, ANVISA denied prior consent to both requests. As a result, the patent applicant sued ANVISA, claiming that the Patent Office should continue proceedings and grant the patents.[502] According to the report made by the Federal Court of First Instance on the ruling,[503] ANVISA based its veto on the fact that none of the inventions fulfilled the requisite condition of novelty. According to this report, the Patent Office changed its opinion concerning the ordinary patent application but maintained its opinion on the pipeline application. The latter was justified on the special regime of pipeline patents, under which no substantive requirements of patentability should be proved.

The Court of First Instance rejected both demands brought by the pharmaceutical company. With regard to the ordinary patent application, the judgment did so on the grounds of "lack of legal interest" from the plaintiff, considering that the Patent Office had changed its report in the course of the court proceedings. With regard to the

496. Court of the First Instance of the State of São Paulo, 12a Vara da Fazenda Pública do Estado de São Paulo, Case Number 288.053.04.6560-2, Aventis Pharma S/A vs. Fazenda do Estado de São Paulo.
497. Supremo Tribunal Federal (STF), Suspensão de Liminar 64, Estado de São Paulo vs. Tribunal de Justiça do Estado de São Paulo and Aventis Pharma S/A, with participation of Quiral Química do Brasil S/A and Dr. Reddy's Farmacêutica do Brasil Ltda, DJ No. 118 of June 22, 2005.
498. Under Brazilian law, the public administration has the privilege of obtaining a judicial interim measure suspended only on the grounds of public interest or a loss in the public finances disregard the matter subject of the case.
499. INPI File No. PI 9507494-5, filed by Novartis International Pharmaceutical Ltd. (BM) on October 21, 1995.
500. INPI File No. PI 1100076-7, filed by Novartis International Pharmaceutical Ltd. (BM) on December 31, 1996.
501. RPI 1656 of October 1, 2002 and RPI 1665, of December 3, 2002.
502. Federal Court of First Instance in Rio de Janeiro, 35a Vara Federal, Case Number 2004.51.01.517054-0. Novartis International Pharmaceutical vs. Instituto Nacional de Propriedade Industrial (INPI) and Agência Nacional de Vigilância Sanitária (ANVISA).
503. The case was judged in the first instance on November 27, 2007, Diário Oficial da Justiça, November 30, 2017.

pipeline patent, the court rejected the demand by deciding that Article 229-C LPI does not need regulation to be applied. In the judge's words, "ANVISA is allowed to check the patentability of inventions in a coordinated action with the Patent Office" in order that pharmaceutical patent applications can be proved with "double care." The judgment justified this special procedure in the social interest and in that of public health. With respect to the pipeline patent application, the judge incidentally decided that also in this exceptional case of retroactive protection, the substantive requirements of patentability should be examined by the Patent Office, and therefore, justified ANVISA's points.

The plaintiff appealed to the Federal Court of Second Instance (TRF-2), which decided the case in 2010.[504] The Court ruled, per majority, that although ANVISA's participation in the patent grant proceedings was in conformity with the BC, ANVISA was not authorized to check the substantive requirements of patentability again. ANVISA's role was rather to verify whether, from the point of view of public health, an obstacle to patenting is present. In the words of the majority's vote, ANVISA should anticipate its administrative role as the authority responsible for giving a license to market the medicine, pronouncing in advance if the drug represents a risk to health. This point of the judgment is not convincing since ANVISA's participation in the patent grant proceedings is not based on "security" but on "access." As a consequence, the Court concluded that, by proofing the substantive requirements of patentability, ANVISA had acted outside of its legal competence. The ruling, however, was not unanimous. One of the judges decided in favor of ANVISA. First, the divergent vote was of the view that the pipeline provision of the LPI did not conform to the BC due to the constitutional prohibition of the retroactivity of law if it is an *ato jurídico perfeito*.[505] This would be the case for inventions that became protectable by means of pipeline patents with the LPI; that is because, as at the time such inventions already belonged to the public domain, they could not be affected by the new law. Second, the divergent vote took the view that Article 229-C LPI was directly applicable so that a regulatory presidential decree would not be necessary in order to apply Article 229-C LPI. Third and last, ANVISA would be allowed to prove the substantive requirements of patentability on the grounds of its expertise.

Due to the divergent vote, ANVISA submitted a legal remedy to the same court, which maintained its previous judgment. In 2013, ANVISA lodged a special recourse to the STJ and has been waiting for its judgment ever since.[506]

504. Tribunal Regional Federal da 2ª. Região (TRF-2), Apelação Cível No. 2004.51.01.517054-0, judged on April 27, 2010, DOU, May 7, 2010.
505. In Brazilian intertemporal law, the expression "ato jurídico perfeito" refers to legal acts that, carried out under the former law, are not affected by the new law because they were "perfect" at the time the new law came into the world.
506. STJ, Recurso Especial No. 1543826 / RJ (2015/0173736-6). The case was scheduled to be ruled on March 20, 2020, but the judgment was cancelled due to the COVID-19 lockdown.

1.4 Leishmaniasis Case

The leishmaniasis case was born from an application claiming a patent for a new process to obtain a known drug used to treat leishmaniasis, by which side effects would be reduced, comparing to the process used at the time.[507] This was a pipeline patent application, and the original proceedings originated from Germany, where the application was first filed in 1991.[508] The judicial dispute in Brazil concerning this application started in 2005 when ANVISA denied prior consent to a patent grant. The controversy, however, had already started earlier. During the proceedings at the Patent Office, the Brazilian Association of National Laboratories (ALANAC) opposed the patent grant by means of presenting *subsídios* to the INPI's report. It argued that the process of obtaining the drug was already known and was even used in Brazil in cancer therapies.[509] According to *Biase Guimarães*, the Patent Office rejected ALANAC's points, taking the view that when dealing with pipeline patents, substantive requisites of patentability do not have to be examined.[510] Afterward, ANVISA denied prior consent due to lack of novelty, having stressed that the claimed patent would protect a second medical indication, which would be harmful to public health.[511]

The patent applicant challenged ANVISA's report at the Federal Court of First Instance, demanding that it be declared void and that the Patent Office be forced to continue proceedings and issue the letter of patent. The Court of First Instance ruled in favor of the plaintiff.[512]

ANVISA appealed. The Federal Court of Second Instance (TRF-2) inverted the judgment and decided that the patent should not be granted.[513] Notwithstanding, the Court confirmed its view that ANVISA did not have legal competence to prove substantive requisites of patentability and should base its veto only on reasons of public health. At the same time, the Court was of the view that also, in the case of pipeline applications, the substantive requirements of patentability should be examined. Because the Patent Office had only revalidated the foreign patent, without

507. *See* INPI File No. PP 1100133-0 at the INPI. According to the website of the Brazilian Patent Office, the patent application was filed on May 25, 1992 by Asta Medica AG, being the application of 1997 converted to a pipeline application. In 2004, the patent applicant was succeeded by Zeutauros AG and by the Max Planck Gesellschaft zur Förderung der Wissenschaft e.V.
508. DPMA Register, File No. 4132344, information available at https://register.dpma.de/DPMAregister/pat/st27?AKZ=41323440 (August 25, 2020).
509. Biase Guimarães (2008), *Direito à Saúde e Propriedade Intelectual de Medicamentos no Brasil—A Anuência Prévia da Agência Nacional de Vigilância Sanitária*, IMS, UERJ, PhD Thesis, pp. 77-78.
510. *Ibid.*, p. 78.
511. *Ibid.*, p. 79.
512. Federal Court of First Instance in Rio de Janeiro, 35a Vara Federal, Case No. 2005.51.01.500.427-9, Max Planck Gesellschaft zur Förderung der Wissenschaft e.V. and Zeutaurus AG vs. Instituto Nacional de Propriedade Industrial (INPI) and Agência Nacional de Vigilância Sanitária (ANVISA). Judgment published in the *D.O.E.R.J.* of December 10, 2007, Ano XXXIIII, No. 228, Secão II—Federal, p. 26.
513. Tribunal Regional Federal da 2ª. Região (TRF-2), Apelação Cível No. 2005.51.01.500.427-9, ruled on May 25, 2010.

checking these requirements, and, especially, without examining whether the invention was new, a patent should not be granted. Thus, the Federal Court of Second Instance judged that the INPI was not allowed to issue a patent without making such an examination.

The Federal Prosecutor Office (*Ministério Público Federal*—MPF) appealed to the STJ, claiming that all the proceedings should be considered void from the beginning, on the grounds that the MPF had not been called to participate in the case. The STJ, however, dismissed the MPF's appeal in 2017[514] so that TRF-2's judgment became final, and the administrative proceedings at the INPI should continue.

In December 2017, the INPI issued a technical report for the patentability of the invention,[515] but the patent was afterward not granted. The INPI terminated proceedings in 2020 based on the lack of payment of annual fees by the applicant.[516] However, the INPI should have also based its decision on termination on the fact that the patent applicant did not prove that the patent was issued in Germany (it was a pipeline application originated from Germany, and the LPI requires that a patent grant in Brazil would presuppose a prior patent grant in Germany). Such a condition would be impossible for the applicant to meet since, in Germany, the patent application terminated in 2004, when the application was refused after examination.[517]

1.5 Isobutylgaba Case

The judicial controversy around the patenting of the substance Isobutylgaba began in 2009. The patent application was filed in 1997 as an ordinary application.[518] The object of the application was the use of the substance in pain-relief therapy. At first, the INPI held that the invention was patentable.[519] ANVISA, however, denied prior consent and justified its decision based on the view that the use of the substance consisted of a method of treatment, and as such, would not be patentable under Brazilian law.[520] After having unsuccessful challenged ANVISA's report under the administrative instance, the patent applicant brought the case to the Federal Court of First Instance of Brasília.[521] During court proceedings, however, the Patent Office changed its earlier report and decided that the invention would not be patentable, and justified its new opinion on the basis of ANVISA's grounds for denying prior consent.[522] According to the INPI's website, the applicant administratively disputed the validity of this report. In

514. STJ, Recurso Especial No. 1448295(2014/0083382-8—04/04/2017), DOU April 4, 2017.
515. RPI 2451, Relatório de Exame Técnico PP1100133-0 of December 18, 2017.
516. RPI 2589 of August 18, 2020. Código 23.3: *Arquivado por falta de pagamento da retribuição referente a expedição da carta patente.*
517. DPMA Register, File No. 4132344, information available at https://register.dpma.de/DPMAregister/pat/st27?AKZ=41323440 (August 25, 2020).
518. INPI File No. 9710536-8, filed by Warner-Lambert Company LLC on July 16, 1997.
519. *See* Chapter 3: D-IV.2 (pp. 295-297).
520. ANVISA Parecer No. 163/04 of June 18, 2004 (PI 9710536-8), application filed by Warner Lambert Company on June 24, 1996.
521. Case No. 2009.34.00.020302-1, 20a Vara Federal da Seção Judiciária do Distrito Federal.
522. RPI No. 2081, of November 23, 2010.

August 2013, the INPI decided to maintain that the invention was not patentable.[523] In 2015, the Federal Court of First Instance decided to nonsuit the case.[524] This decision was grounded on a procedural question consistent with the proceedings' purpose, namely, the fact that the plaintiff had required that ANVISA's decision not to grant prior consent should be void so that the INPI would be obliged to grant the patent, irrespective of ANVISA's prior consent. However, because the INPI changed its decision, dismissing the patent request, there was no reason for the judicial proceedings to continue. Consequently, the question of the grounds on which ANVISA had denied prior consent became irrelevant because only the INPI is allowed to decide on the substantive requirements of patentability. Since the INPI had decided not to grant the patent, there was no procedural reason to continue the proceedings and declare ANVISA's decision void. In 2016, the plaintiff appealed to the Federal Court of the Second Instance, but until August 2020, the case was not yet decided.[525]

1.6 Gleevec Case

First of all, it is important to note that the judicial controversy around Gleevec in Brazil does not refer to its API imatinib, which enjoyed patent protection in Brazil from the year 2001 to 2012, as a pipeline patent.[526] In the case in question, the patent was requested for the protection of an improvement patent, consisting of the administering of only one high-dosage capsule containing imatinib to the leukemia patient, instead of more capsules several times per day. ANVISA denied prior consent, concluding that the invention lacked both novelty and an inventive step.[527] Besides, ANVISA also pointed out that some claims should not be protected by patent because they have the nature of the therapeutic method, and consequently, their protection by patent under Brazilian law would not be possible.

After ANVISA's veto, the patent applicant brought the case to a federal district court in Brasilia, alleging that the issue of a patent for his compound would not be against the interests of public health; hence, prior consent should be issued. The court issued a provisional injunction ordering that ANVISA immediately issued prior consent in the case.[528] ANVISA then granted prior consent.[529] Afterward, patent proceedings continued at the INPI, which eventually rejected the patent based on the fact that the

523. RPI No. 226, of September 3, 2013.
524. This case was judged on April 6, 2015 and published on April 15, 2015, according to the Court's website.
525. TRF-1 case number 0020188-19.2009.4.01.3400. Laboratories Pfizer Ltda. and Warner Lambert Company LCC vs. ANVISA, INPI, and PRO-GENERICOS.
526. Patent Application No. PP1100739-7, patent granted on June 6, 2000 and expired on April 3, 2012.
527. Parecer ANVISA 733/13/COOPI/GADIP/ANVISA of November 14, 2013, Patent Applicant: Novartis AG, Patent Application No. PI 0309528-2.
528. Federal District Court from Brasília, 4th Section (Vara Federal da Seção Judiciária de Brasília), Case No. 5466-07.2014.4.01.3400, DOU, August 29, 2014.
529. Resolução ANVISA No. 3.389, of September 2, 2014, DOU Seção I, No. 169, September 3, 2014, p. 60.

invention lacked both novelty and an inventive step.[530] The patent applicant administratively appealed against the decision. In February 2017, the INPI's administrative board maintained its anterior decision by ruling that the invention in question lacked inventiveness.[531]

1.7 Gilead Case

The controversy around the Gilead's case, known as the "Sofosbuvir case,"[532] began in 2017, after ANVISA's denial to issue prior consent to the patent grant. The object of the application—which had been filed in 2004 by Gilead[533]—was the use of the substance in the treatment of viral infections, including hepatitis C and other diseases. In February 2015, the INPI sent the proceedings to ANVISA, which in December 2016 denied prior consent.[534] ANVISA justified the lack of prior consent based on the view that the use of the substance did not satisfy the requirements of novelty and inventive step, as well it did not enough describe the invention so that the invention would not be reproducible by a person skilled in the art.[535]

The patent applicant challenged ANVISA's report and brought the case to the Federal Court of First Instance of Brasília,[536] alleging that ANVISA was solely allowed to deny prior consent if the invention were a danger to human health. Even though the view that ANVISA's prior consent should be justified on safety reasons is flawed, as demonstrated above,[537] the Court ruled, by means of a provisional injunction (*liminar em mandado de segurança*) that ANVISA was obliged to grant prior consent.[538] Surprisingly, instead of pleading in Court that the ruling was impossible to be complied with and appealing to the Court of Second Instance—as ANVISA has done so far in such cases—ANVISA simply accepted the provisional injunction and, therefore, granted prior consent without motivation.[539] This political shift—occurred during the conservative Presidency of Mr. *Temer*—suggests that the Ministry of Health for the present will no longer make efforts to support ANVISA's prior consent.

The INPI, which at a first moment, agreed with ANVISA regarding the non-patentability, after hearing Gilead, concluded that the invention was patentable. Interestingly, neither ANVISA nor Farmanguinhos (which was participating in the proceedings as an assistant and which required the non-recognition of patentability)

530. PI 0309528-2, Relatório de Exame Técnico, RPI 2355, February 23, 2016.
531. RPI 2419, May 16, 2017.
532. The Brazilian mass media referred to Gilead's patent request as "Sofosbuvir's patent." However, according to *Bermudez*, this patent does not cover the compound Sofosbuvir itself, but only an intermediary compound used by Gilead during the process of obtaining Sofosbuvir. *See* Bermudez (2018), *Patente: Sofosbuvir entre o comércio e o direito à cura*, Centro de Estudos Estratégicos da Fiocruz.
533. INPI File No. PI0410846-9, filed by Gilead Pharmasset LLC (US) on April 4, 2004.
534. Parecer Técnico No. 754/16/COOPI/GGMED/ANVISA of December 8, 2016.
535. *Ibid.*
536. Mandado de Segurança No.1002316-90.2017.4.01.3400, 5ª. Vara Federal da Seção Judiciária do Distrito Federal.
537. Resolução ANVISA RE No. 1341 of May 19, 2017, DOU-Seção 1 of May 22, 2017, p. 35.
538. Relatório de Exame Técnico INPI in PI041846-9 of September 13, 2018.
539. RPI 2489 of September 18, 2018.

challenged INPI's decision. This confirms a political shift regarding patents and access to drugs within the Ministry of Health. The patent was finally granted in favor of Gilead in January 2019.[540]

It is worth noting that the federal pharmaceutical laboratory Farmanguinhos took part in the patent proceedings as an assistant (*subsidiária*) because it had developed the generic drug Sofosbuvir in partnership with a Brazilian private laboratory, for which they obtained the authorization for marketing the drug in July 2018.[541] Sovaldi, which is commercialized by Gilead, is a brand name of Sofosbuvir.

2 *Evaluation*

The examination of the seven cases above reveals, first, that the flawed idea of obliging ANVISA to carry out prior consent examination based on criteria of drug safety came from the Brazilian courts, which followed the view supported by multinational pharmaceutical companies.

Second, it reveals that the reasons given by ANVISA for denying prior consent were based both on the Brazilian transitional provisions of patent law or in its interpretation of the patentability requirements. Curiously, these cases discussed higher standards of patentability developed in industrial nations in favor of their own pharmaceutical industry (such as invention selections, Markush-Formel, improvement patents and therapeutic methods), but that is still controversial even in these developed countries.

Third, it reveals that in four cases (Docetaxel, Penciclovir, Isobutylgaba, Gleevec), the Patent Office changed its technical report due to ANVISA's examination. In these cases, the INPI first issued a report for the patentability, but during the court proceedings, it altered their reports and adopted ANVISA's view.

D ANVISA'S EXAMINATION: WHAT DOES IT CHECK AND ACCORDING TO WHICH CRITERIA?

I The Empirical Study

1 *Method and Content*

Initially, my intention was to investigate upon which criteria ANVISA based its decisions concerning prior consent and to what extent they differed from those used by the Patent Office in its technical reports. For doing that, I planned to compare a sample of 100 technical reports (*parecer*) from ANVISA with the INPI's technical reports. Because my focus was on investigating why prior consent had been denied—and not how often it had been denied—I tried to get access to technical reports for cases for

540. RPI 2506 of January 15, 2019.
541. Farmanguinhos—Instituto de Tecnologia em Fármacos (2018), Farmanguinhos obtém registro do antiviral sofosbuvir, usado contra hepatite C, available at https://www.far.fiocruz.br/2018/07/farmanguinhos-obtem-registro-do-antiviral-sofosbuvir/ (last visited on August 31, 2020).

which I knew that ANVISA had denied its consent for patent grant. I made my selection from a list published at the time by the Patent Office, which identified 62 cases in which prior consent had been denied,[542] as well from a list published on ANVISA's website, which detailed whether prior consent had been granted or not, or whether ANVISA had asked the applicant for clarification.

Obtaining access to the reports was, at the time, a time-consuming task. All in all, I needed to wait for 14 months just to obtain access to the reports. In January 2008, I asked ANVISA how to gain access to its technical reports concerning the predefined 100 cases.[543] According to ANVISA's answer, such data should be consulted at the Patent Office. After checking that the reports had neither been published in the INPI's official publications[544] nor been made available on the INPI's website, I asked the INPI to send me copies of the reports by ordinary or electronic mail.[545] I received no answer from the Patent Office and was informed by phone that I would only obtain access to the reports if I personally requested this at the headquarters of the Patent Office, where the files are publicly available for everyone to access.[546] On February 3, 2009, I made a request by fax to view the desired 100 proceedings files, announcing that I would be there in person between March 9 and 16, 2009.[547] When I arrived at the "copy department" in the Patent Office, it seemed that my request had never been processed. And despite my presence, I was not given access to the files. In fact, I only obtained access to the copies of the reports nine months after my request had been made.[548] However, the INPI only sent me reports for 77 cases. As a result, I limited my study to the analysis of these 77 ANVISA reports, which became the basis of this work.

2 *Cases Decided under the Old Workflow*

All 77 analyzed cases were filed at the INPI between 1995 and 1998. In all of them, ANVISA's first report concerning prior consent was given between 2003 and 2009, within six months of the files having being sent to it by the INPI.

Of the 77 analyzed cases, 14 were of the type "pipeline application," and 63 were ordinary applications. The kind of pharmaceutical invention involved was also varied

542. INPI (2008), "*Pedidos de patentes não anuídos pela ANVISA, excluídos os que foram indeferidos ou arquivados definitivamente pelo INPI,*" Situation on December 9, RPI 1982 December 30, 2008.
543. E-Mail from January 29, 2008 to propriedade.intelectual@anvisa.gov.br.
544. *Revista do INPI.*
545. E-Mail sent by the author on August 20, 2008 to patente@inpi.gov.br.
546. Thanks to the financial support of the Max Planck Institute for Intellectual Property in Munich, I was able to travel to the Brazilian Patent Office, the INPI, where I requested the copies. Since May 3, 2011, INPI's technical reports have been available in its databank, known as "e-parecer"; however, this only includes those that have been published in the *Revista do INPI* since that date.
547. Fax sent to the INPI at February 3, 2009 from the Max Planck Institute for Intellectual Property in Munich.
548. Fortunately, the accessibility of INPI's documents has considerably improved. Today, it is possible for members of the public to download ANVISA's examination's reports from the research data base on the INPI's website.

in nature: some of them were antiretroviral[549] or anticancer[550] drugs, but there were also other types of pharmaceutical inventions, such as, for instance, ophthalmological,[551] neurological[552] or tropical-disease-therapy inventions,[553] and, surprisingly, a dental gel[554] and an anti-caries gum.[555]

As summarized by Table 1, in 46 of the 77 cases, ANVISA denied its consent to the patent grant; in 19 cases, ANVISA gave its consent after having asked for clarifications or a change in the application, while in the other 12 cases, ANVISA gave its consent without hearing the patent applicant.

Table 1 Prior Consent—Sample of 77 ANVISA's Reports (2003-2009)

Denied	*Granted after Hearing the Applicant*	*Granted after Corrections of Translation and Orthography Mistakes*	*Immediately Granted*
46	10	9	12

Source: own elaboration.

2.1 Criteria Used by ANVISA

2.1.1 Correction of Translation and Formal Mistakes

Three of ANVISA's reports concerning pipeline applications demanded corrections of translation mistakes. In one case, ANVISA listed 30 such mistakes while stressing that they would not have an impact on public health and suggesting that prior consent would be given;[556] in another case, the examiner listed minor formal errors, such as lack of page numbering or of an officer's signature, as well as demands that inaccurately translated terms should be improved, or even that typing errors should be corrected,[557] as a condition of granting prior consent. In three cases, despite ANVISA's

549. For example, PI 9509925-5 (Rega Institute), PI 9507615-8 (Pharmacia & Up John Company), PI 9611838-5 (Uniroyal), PI 1100663-3 (Abbott); PI 9508664-1 (GSF GmbH).
550. For example, PI 9611647-1 (Tulane Educational Fund), PI 9608082-5 (Zeneca Ltd.), PI 1100769 (Hoechst AG), PI 9508151-8 (Merck), PI 9710686-0 (Octamer Inc).
551. *See*, for instance, PI 9604878 (Dr. Gerhard Mann).
552. *See*, for instance, PI 9508019-8 (Genentech).
553. *See*, for instance, PI 9611455-0 (Corixa Corp).
554. *See*, for instance, PI 9707368-7 (Colgate-Palmolive).
555. PI 9711339-5 (ADA Foundation).
556. Parecer ANVISA 220/04 of July 16, 2004, PI 1100784-2, Quadrant Holdings Cambridge Limited, filed on May 12, 1997.
557. (1) Parecer ANVISA and Carta-Exigência COOPI No. 52/01, of September 5, 2001, PI 1101020-7, filed by Claude Nofre and Jean-Marie Tinti on May 14, 1997. ANVISA's report requested that the word "intesções" be corrected to "intenções" (pp. 239-241); (2) Parecer 030/06/COOPI/ANVISA of March 21, 2006 (PI 9611790-7), filed by Pierre Fabre Medicament on November 27, 1996.

examiner having demanded corrections of translation mistakes, prior consent was issued by the director.[558]

In two cases concerning ordinary patent applications, ANVISA's technical report identified a failure to meet substantive requirements for patentability while also demanding the correction of formal and translation mistakes, while stressing that the latter would not have relevance for public health.[559]

2.1.2 State of the Art, Lack of Novelty

In 13 cases in which ANVISA denied prior consent to a patent grant, its report was based on a lack of novelty. Usually, ANVISA decided this either as a result of having carried out a new search regarding the state of the art[560] or based on the fact that its (ANVISA's) interpretation of the term "novelty" did not coincide with the INPI's view.[561] In some reports, ANVISA's decision was based on a mixture of both criteria.[562] In one such case, ANVISA's examiner carried out a new search concerning the state of the art and came to the conclusion that the invention had already been anticipated by the publication of an academic article some years before the patent was filed.[563] In another case, for instance, ANVISA denied prior consent because it, unlike the INPI, considered that the invention lacked novelty because it consisted of a well-known salt.[564] In this case, INPI changed the conclusions of its technical report after ANVISA's

558. Parecer ANVISA of July 19, 1997, PI 1100122-4, Genentech, Inc., filed on December 11, 1996; Parecer ANVISA of May 7, 2003, PI 1100147-0 filed by Warner-Lambert Company on September 12, 1994; "Parecer Técnico de Anuência" 031/08/COOPI/GGMED/ANVISA, of February 8, 2008 (PI 9804055-3), application filed by Gerhard Gergely on October 27, 1997.
559. (1) Parecer ANVISA 134/03 of December 15, 2003 (PI 9507930.0), application filed on December 5, 1996 by H. Lundbeck; (2) Parecer ANVISA of August 27, 2002 (PI 9500380-0), filed by Pfizer, Inc; (3) Parecer ANVISA098/06/COOPI/ANVISA of November 9, 2006 (PI 9509286-2), application filed by Flamel Technologies on October 18, 1995.
560. (1) Parecer ANVISA 027/07/COOPI/ANVISA of March 7, 2007 (PP 1100756-7), application filed on May 12, 1997 by Takeda Pharmaceutical Co. Ltd.; (2) Parecer ANVISA 108/08/COOPI/GGMED of May 26, 2008 (PI 9612750-3), application filed by IDEA AG on October 17, 1996.
561. Parecer ANVISA 118/04 of August 6, 2004 (PP 1100533-5), application filed on May 13, 1997 by John Wyeth & Brother Ltd.
562. (1) Parecer ANVISA 134/03 of December 15, 2003 (PI 9507930.0), application filed on December 5, 1996 by H. Lundbeck. In this case, a patent was neither granted, nor it was expressly denied. Despite this, the proceedings at the INPI were stopped, apparently for procedural reasons. After the applicant had presented an administrative remedy against the ANVISA decision not to grant consent, the Patent Office demanded a response from the patent applicant. Under the Brazilian patent proceedings system, if the patent applicant does not respond within 90 days, proceedings must stop and cannot be restarted; (2) Parecer ANVISA 164/03, of December 15, 2003 (PI 9711411-1), application filed on March 24, 1999 by Knoll AG; (3) Parecer ANVISA 026/04 of January 30, 2004 (PI 9510422-4), application filed on June 27,1996 by Astra Aktiebolag; (4) Parecer ANVISA 165/04 of December 15, 2003 (PI 9508384-7), application filed on June 28, 1995 by Bayer AG; (5) Parecer ANVISA 004/04 of January 16, 2004 (PI 9601909-3), application filed on July 3, 1996 by AnormMED Inc.
563. Parecer 084/07/COOPI/ANVISA of June 6, 2007 IP (PI 1100266-2), application filed on April 14, 1997 by Ajinomoto Co.
564. *Parecer* ANVISA 197/04 of August 6, 2004, PI 9709807-8, application filed on June 12, 1997 by Pierre Fabre Medicaments.

report and decided that the invention did not, in fact, deserve a patent.[565] In another case, the object of which was a drug to treat arthrosis, ANVISA, also denied prior consent based on a lack of novelty, considering that the invention was already protected for an older patent.[566]

2.1.3 Therapeutic and Surgical Methods

Three of the analyzed reports which denied prior consent did so because the patent claim was seen as a method for treatment of the human body, and therefore not patentable. One of them, for instance, had for its object a method for treating cancer. According to ANVISA's report, at first, the INPI was also of the opinion that the invention should not be patented, but after the applicant had made changes in the application, the INPI's examiner saw the request as a patentable invention. ANVISA, however, argued that the object of the application was still a therapeutic method, as the applicant had just replaced the word "method" with the word "use."[567] In this case, the INPI again changed its opinion after ANVISA's produced its report and issued a technical report concluding that the application was, in fact, not patentable.[568] Against it, the applicant lodged an administrative appeal, but the INPI maintained its decision.[569]

The third case in which ANVISA denied prior consent based on the prohibition of patenting therapeutic methods was within an application seeking a patent for a combination of two ARV Drugs.[570] In this case, the patent applicant wanted a patent for a combination of two different antiretrovirals, one of which was ritonavir, with the other having been created from three different ARV Drugs. According to ANVISA's report, a simple combination of two known antiretrovirals did not result in a new compound. Moreover, ANVISA also based its opinion on a new search for a prior art, as a result of which it concluded that the effects of a combination of two ARV Drugs in the treatment of HIV/AIDS were already known in the academic community before the filing of the first patent application.

2.1.4 State of the Art, Lack of Inventive Step

In four reports, ANVISA denied prior consent to a patent grant because it could not assess the presence of an inventive step in the invention. For instance, regarding the patenting of the microorganism *Lactobacillus plantarum*, ANVISA's report, based on a new search concerning the state of the art, concluded that some academic articles had

565. *Revista de Propriedade Industrial* 1931, January 8, 2008.
566. *Parecer* ANVISA No. 004/04 of January 16, 2004 (PI 901909-3), application filed on July 13, 1995 by AnorMED Inc.
567. *Parecer* ANVISA 105/04 of April 11, 2004 (PI 9710686-0), application filed on May 30, 1997 by Octamer, Inc.
568. *Revista de Propriedade Industrial* 1975 (November 11, 2008).
569. RPI No. 2096 (March 9, 2011).
570. *Parecer Técnico* No. 100/03 of November 17, 2003 (PI 9608284-4), application filed on May 7, 1997 by Abbott Laboratories.

already anticipated the invention, in the sense that the effects observed in the new compound could have been predicted by an expert, meaning that it lacked an inventive step.[571] Similarly, in two other cases, ANVISA denied prior consent to the patenting of a cancer drug, based on a new search it conducted regarding the state of the art and from which it concluded that these inventions were obvious, too.[572] On the same basis, ANVISA denied prior consent to a dietetic compound, the aim of which would be to stimulate the intestinal flora and which was to be used as a supplementary food product.[573] Similarly, ANVISA denied prior consent to patents for anti-caries chewing gums, candies, gels and toothpaste, claiming that the inventions were obvious given the state of the art.[574]

2.1.5 Lack of Sufficient Description of the Invention/Scope of the Invention Too Broad

In eight reports, ANVISA denied prior consent to a patent grant because the invention was not sufficiently described so that the information presented in the application could not have been used by an expert to reproduce the invention; therefore, a patent grant would violate Article 25 LPI. In two reports, the application's object was a combination of substances for use in cancer treatment.[575] In two other cases, where the object of application was the patenting of a protein, ANVISA's report denied prior consent and justified the decision on the basis that the inventions claimed were not sufficiently described in the application.[576] In a case involving patenting of eye drops for dry eyes,[577] as well as in a case involving a drug for the treatment of amyloidosis,[578] ANVISA denied prior consent because it was of the opinion that the patent claims were

571. Parecer ANVISA 022/07/COOPI/ANVISA of February 8, 2007 (PI 9608284-4), application filed on May 8, 1996 by PROBI AB.
572. (1) Parecer ANVISA 101/06 COOPI/ANVISA of November 6, 2006 (PI 9508151-8), application filed on June 7, 1995 by Merck & Co., Inc; (2) Parecer ANVISA 109/07/COOPI/GGMED/ANVISA, of August 15, 2007 (PI 9601276-5), application filed on April 6, 1995 by F. Hoffman-La Roche AG.
573. Parecer No. 092/07/COOPI/ANVISA of June 22, 2007 (PI 9706554-4), application filed on June 3, 1997 by Renata Maria Anna Cavaliere Vesely.
574. Parecer Técnico de Ciência N° 048/08/COOPI/GGMED/ANVISA, of March 7, 2008 (PI 9711339-5), application filed by the American Dental Association on August 19, 1997.
575. For instance, Parecer ANVISA 091/94 of March 26, 2004 (PI 1101065-7), application filed on May 14,1997 by Dr. Gerhard Ohlenschläger und Gernot Treusch and Parecer 018/08/COOPI/GGMED/ANVISA, of February 19, 2008 (PI 9609137-1), application filed by Alza Corporation on June 5, 1995.
576. (1) Parecer ANVISA 062/08/COOPI/GGMED/ANVISA of March 20, 2008 (PI 9507618-2), application filed on May 5, 1995 by Institut Gustave Roussy, Institut National de la Santé et de la Recherche Medicale et Applied Research Systems Ars Holding; (2) Parecer ANVISA 025/07/COOPI/ANVISA of February 9, 2007 (PI 1101002-9), application filed on May 14, 1997 by Amgen Boulder, Inc.
577. Parecer 197/08/COOPI/GGMED/ANVISA of September 12, 1998 (PI 960878-6), application filed by Dr. Gerhard Mann Chem. Pharm. Fabrik GmbH on December 20, 1996.
578. Parecer 111/06/COOPI/ANVISA of January 26, 2007 (PI 9607197-4), application filed on March 15, 1996 by Queens University at Kingston, succeeded by Neurochem (International) Limited.

not sufficiently described. With the same reasoning, ANVISA denied prior consent for patenting to a gastric drug[579] and to an anti-HIV drug.[580]

In another case, where the object of the patent was a drug that would be used to treat cancer and viral infections, ANVISA considered the scope of the claim to be too broad and asked the patent applicant to alter its request in order to restrict the application. Because the patent applicant did not do so, prior consent was denied.[581] In August 2020, the Patent Office has finally issued a technical report on this application. According to this report, which considered ANVISA's lack of prior consent as "assistance" (*subsídios*), the patent should be granted despite ANVISA's disapproval. The reason for that was that the arguments carried out by ANVISA would not be applicable to pipeline patents due to Article 230.3 LPI, which exempts pipeline patents of satisfying conditions concerning Articles 24 and 25 LPI.[582] Therefore, the patent should be granted with validity until November 12, 2013,[583] applying the criteria laid down by Article 230.4 LPI.

In one case involving patenting of an anticancer drug, ANVISA first denied prior consent on the grounds of insufficient description of the claim.[584] However, after the applicant had changed the claims in the sense ANVISA demanded, prior consent was granted.[585]

In another case, the objective of which was the patenting of a compound inductor of growth hormone, ANVISA, also denied prior consent based on a lack of sufficient description of all claims. In this case, the claimed invention was based on a Markush formula, and ANVISA demanded that all possible compounds be individually described.[586] The same demand was made by ANVISA in another case, the objective of

579. Parecer 006/07/COOPI/ANVISA of January 26, 2007 (PI 9610153-9), application filed on August 21, 1996 by Pfizer Research and Development Company, N. V. S/A. The same approach was followed in the Parecer No. 047/07/COOPI/ANVISA of April 3, 2007 (PI 9510533-6), application filed on December 4, 1995.
580. Parecer No. 074/04 of April 5, 2004 (PI 9509925-5), application filed on November 29, 1995 by Rega Institute (US)The application was "frozen" until November, 28, 2017, when it was terminated by shelving (*arquivamento*) due to lack of payment of annual fees, RPI 2447.
581. Parecer 137/06/COOPI/ANVISA of December 14, 2006 (PP 1100769-9), filed by Hoechst AG on May 12, 1997.
582. INPI, Relatório de Exame Técnico of August 11, 2020, RPI 2589 of August 18, 2020.
583. It is worth noting that the patent protection intended to be granted in 2020 refers to a protection time that is already expired (November 12, 2013).
584. "Parecer Técnico de Formulação de Exigência a Pedido de Patente de Produtos e Processos Farmacêuticos" No. 072/07/COOPI/GGMED/ANVISA of July 10, 2007 (PI 9611647-1), filed on November 14, 1996 by the Administrators of the Tulane Educational Fund, maintained by both "Parecer Técnico de Não Anuência a Pedido de Patentes de Produtos e Processos Farmacêuticos" N° 069/08/COOPI/GGMED/ANVISA of March 20, 2008 and "Parecer Técnico de Não Anuência" 277/08/COOPI/GGMED/ANVISA of November 19, 2008.
585. "Parecer Técnico de Retratação de Decisão que Negou Anuência" No. 057/09/COOPI/GGMED/ANVISA of February 10, 2009.
586. "Parecer Técnico de Formulação de Exigência" No. 073/08/COOPI/GGMED/ANVISA of April 11, 2008 (PI 9606845-0), application filed on November 26, 1996 by Novo Nordisk A/S. ANVISA also denied prior consent based on identical reasons in a case filed by Wyeth Corporation, the objective of which was the patenting of a compound to treat menopause (PI 9701895-3).

which was the patenting of an anti-inflammatory drug.[587] In the first case, the applicant did not change his claims; thus, prior consent was not given. In the second case, the applicant changed his claim, and prior consent was then given.[588]

2.1.6 Selection Inventions (Lack of Inventive Step and Novelty)

In eight cases, ANVISA denied prior consent because it did not see as patentable chemical compounds known as "selection inventions." This term in the patent law literature refers to compounds considered to be new, although they were previously known. In these cases, the condition of novelty should not be assessed in an absolute way. A condition for the patent would be the fact that a given compound had not previously been individually described, although it had been included before in an earlier disclosure of a broader group of compounds. According to *Grubb*, in such cases, "the invention then can only be the selection of a particular compound or a relatively small group of compounds from the larger group previously discovered in broad terms."[589] In the cases studied, ANVISA did not consider such inventions as patentable. In one case, for instance, ANVISA was of the opinion that the earlier disclosure of a broader class of compounds would make it an obvious step for an expert to find compounds that, although individually new, fall within the broad category described as "invention selections."[590] The same approach was taken in another case,[591] where the INPI did, in fact, alter its technical report after ANVISA's refusal to grant prior consent. The decision, however, was later changed again by the INPI after a legal remedy has been lodged by the applicant, after which INPI decided the invention was indeed new.[592] In this case, ANVISA maintained its refusal to give prior consent to the patent grant.[593] The patent was granted in 2018.[594] In another case of "selection inventions," ANVISA denied prior consent for the patenting of a compound that was an optical isomer of a compound previously known in another form, considering that this isomer could not be considered to be new.[595]

In two cases involving selection inventions, the objects of which were patents for an antiretroviral drug, ANVISA also denied prior consent. In one case, the applicant

587. "Parecer Técnico de Formulação de Exigência" No. 085/08//COOPI/GGMED/ANVISA of April 17, 2008 (PI 9806870-9), application filed by Glaxo Group Limited on July 12, 1999.
588. "Parecer Técnico de Anuência" 175/08/COOPI/GGMED/ANVISA of August 27, 1998.
589. Grubb (1999), *Patents for Chemicals, Pharmaceuticals and Biotechnology—Fundamentals of Global Law, Practice and Strategy*, Clarendon Press, Oxford, p. 196.
590. Parecer ANVISA of April 2, 2003 (PI 9611234-4), application filed on April 27, 1998 by Astra Aktiebolag, confirmed by Parecer ANVISA 87/03 of October 1, 2003, Parecer ANVISA 82/04 of March 18, 2004 and Parecer ANVISA 252/04 of November 18, 2004.
591. Parecer (Ofício) nº 158/05/COOPI/ANVISA of July 15, 2005 (PI 9509819-4), application filed by Janssen Pharmaceutica N.V. on November 24, 1994.
592. INPI's decision DIRPA/CGPAT 1/ DIQUIM II (PI 9509819-4) of July 9, 2007.
593. Parecer 145/07/COOPU/GGMED/ANVISA of December 18, 2007, maintained by Parecer No. 180/08/COOPI/GGMED/ANVISA, of September 12, 1998.
594. RPI 2471 of May, 15, 2018.
595. Parecer ANVISA of August 27, 2002 (PI 9500380-0), application filed on January 30, 1995 by Pfizer, Inc. and Carta de Exigência COPI No. 028/02 of August 29, 2002, confirmed by Parecer ANVISA 028/03 of September 22, 2003.

applied for a patent for a composition that would be useful to combat the virus's dissemination in the organism.[596] In the other case, the object of patenting was the anti-HIV drug tipranavir. According to ANVISA's report in both cases, prior consent could not be given since the compound had already been anticipated by the so-called Markush formula—a general formula which permits an expert to easily find all compounds pertaining in a collection of chemicals with a similar structure. While the Patent Office (INPI) recognized novelty and an inventive step in these kinds of compounds, ANVISA did not.[597] This case had enormous repercussions in Brazil at the time since the company holding the patent rights over the antiretroviral drug announced that it would not apply for a marketing license due to the fact that its inventor rights were not being respected.[598] There were other ANVISA reports denying prior consent based on the rejection of selection inventions due to their anticipation by the Markush formula.[599] The same approach was adopted by ANVISA in a pipeline application claiming the patenting of a compound claimed to be useful in the treatment of diseases of the nervous system, as well as in a case involving an anticancer drug.[600] However, because the compound had already been disclosed by means of a Markush formula, ANVISA denied prior consent since it did not see anything new or inventive in the compound in question.[601]

In most reports I analyzed, the Patent Office considered "invention selections" as patentable, while ANVISA mostly did not. In one case, ANVISA reconsidered its initial decision to deny prior consent after an administrative remedy was attempted by the applicant.[602] The question is still open in Brazil, although there are already some court decisions that do not recognize selection patents as patentable. In the Valcyte case above commented, the Court of Second Instance (TRF-2) ruled that "selection inventions," while fulfilling the requirements of novelty and industrial applicability, do not satisfy the requirement of inventiveness.[603] In 2009, a case such as those mentioned

596. Parecer No. 074/07/COOPI/ANVISA of May 25, 2007 (PI9611838-5), application filed by Uniroyal Chemical Company on November 15, 1996.
597. Parecer ANVISA 041/06/COOPI/ANVISA of May 5, 2006 (PI 9507615-8), application filed by Pharmacia & Up John Company, maintained by Parecer 128/06/COOPI/ANVISA of December 28, 2006, Parecer 084/08/COOPI/GGMED/ANVISA of April 10, 2008 and Parecer 499/2008 of November 28, 2008.
598. *Boehringer não lançará medicamento no Brasil* (2008), o Estado de São Paulo, November 4, 2008.
599. For instance, Parecer No. 139/04 of August 4, 2004 (PI 1100690-0), application filed by Chugai Seiyaku Kaisha on May 8, 1997, and "Parecer Técnico de Não Anuência" 317/08/COOPI/GGMED/ANVISA of December 9, 2008 (PI 9710372-1), application filed by Merck Frosst Canada & Co on July 8, 1997.
600. Parecer No. 228/04 of August 27, 2004 (PI 96088082-5), application filed on April 23, 1996 by Zeneca Limited. The latter was followed by "Parecer Técnico de Não Anuência" 146/08/COOPI/GGMED/ANVISA of July 16, 2008, which upheld the denial of prior consent.
601. Parecer ANVISA 118/04 of August 6, 2004 (PI 1100533-5), application filed on May 13, 1997 by John Wieth & Brother Limited.
602. Parecer ANVISA No. 54/07/COOPI/ANVISA of April 18, 2007 (PI 9611871-7), application filed on November 22, 1996 by ARPIDA AG, maintained by "Parecer Técnico de Não Anuência" No. 033/08/COOPI/GGMED/ANVISA of March 3, 1998. According to a publication made in the Brazilian *Official Journal*, prior consent was given after an administrative remedy was tried by the applicant (Resolução ANVISA No. 5.719 of December, 17, 2009).
603. *See* 3- C-IV-1.1., pp. 255-257.

above was brought to the courts by an applicant, who asked the court to force the Patent Office to grant the patent despite ANVISA's refusal to grant prior consent.[604] ANVISA's decision not to grant prior consent was declared to be void by the Court of First Instance, which, however, did not analyze the question of whether selection patents should be patentable in Brazil or not.[605]

2.1.7 Second Medical Indication

In five cases, ANVISA denied prior consent because the invention to be patented consisted of a second medical indication. In one case, the examiner used reasons of public health instead as the basis for denying prior consent.[606] According to ANVISA's report, prior consent should be refused because this kind of patent protection would be too broad and harmful to the social interest since the second patent would hinder competitors from producing the drug for the second illness to be treated, and therefore it would impede the population's access to that medicine.[607] While it cites reasons of public health for its denial of prior consent, the report also refers to Article 10. I LPI as being the legal basis for denying prior consent. This provision is the one that excludes discoveries from patent protection. Similarly, ANVISA denied prior consent to a compound that was to be used in Alzheimer's therapy, with the same reasoning.[608]

In another case, whereby the applicant wanted to protect a new use of the compound efaroxan in the treatment of Huntington's disease, ANVISA's report denied prior consent with the same motivation.[609] In this case, after ANVISA's decision, the Patent Office reviewed its own report and denied the patent grant.

In another case, where the applicant wanted to protect a known compound—the first medical use of which was in identifying diseases of the digestive system and in the treatment of disturbances of the nervous system—for a second and new use, namely,

604. Seção Judiciária do Distrito Federal, 6ª Vara Federal, Case No. 0020407-32.2009.4.01.3400, Astra Zeneca do Brasil Ltda. and Astrazeneca UK Limited vs. ANVISA and INPI.
605. Judgment of June 16, 2017.
606. Parecer ANVISA 164/03 of December 15, 2003 (PI 9711411-1), application filed on March 24, 1999 by Knoll AG.
607. In original from the Portuguese: "O pedido em questão também reivindica o uso dos compostos arilciclobutilalquilamina para a manufatura de um medicamento para profilaxia e/ou tratamento de hiperlipidemia, hipercolesteromia ou hipertrigliceridemia. Caracterizando, portanto, o segundo uso médico destes compostos. Sob a ótica da proteção à saúde pública, esta agência entende que a concessão de uma proteção indevida pode prejudicar o acesso do público a medicamentos, seja pela não disponibilidade do medicamento no mercado ou pela prática de preços incompatíveis com o poder aquisitivo da população. Neste sentido, a proteção de pedidos relativos ao segundo uso médico é considerada ampla e prejudicial aos interesses sociais, uma vez que tal proteção proporcionaria ao detentor da patente o direito de impedir que terceiros comercializem medicamentos à base daquele composto ativo para o tratamento da doença descrita na patente, mesmo que tais medicamentos sejam provenientes de inovações tecnológicas posteriores, independentemente de apresentarem composições diferentes ou propriedades melhoradas." From Parecer ANVISA 164/03, of December 15, 2003 (PI 9711411-1), application filed on March 24, 1999 by Knoll AG, pp. 57-58.
608. Parecer ANVISA No. 163/03 of December 15, 2003 (PI9710693-3), application filed on December 23, 1998 by Cephalon Inc.
609. Parecer ANVISA 092/94 of March 19, 2004 (PI 9711059-0), application filed on August 12, 1996 by Pierre Fabre Medicament.

to treat sexual dysfunction. In its first report, ANVISA denied prior consent, on the basis that the discovery of further medical uses of a known compound could not be considered as being new or having an inventive step.[610] In its second report on the same case, however, ANVISA avoided justifying its lack of prior consent with reference to the question of second or further medical indications; instead, it concentrated on the lack of inventive step in the invention.[611]

In another patent application, the aim of which was the patenting of a painkiller compound, ANVISA at first justified its refusal to grant prior consent on the basis of the general assumption that patenting second medical uses of known drugs would be against the interests of public health.[612] In a letter addressed to the Patent Office, ANVISA noted that the case had jointly discussed by both agencies and that both came to the conclusion that a patent could not be granted because it lacked an inventive step.[613] In a second report, ANVISA maintained its view that the invention was not new and added some reasons of a procedural nature to support its refusal to give of prior consent.[614] The patent applicant challenged ANVISA's reports before the Federal Court of Brasília.[615] However, before the case was decided, INPI altered its technical report and rejected the patent on the basis of the prohibition of patenting therapeutic methods and violation of Article 8 LPI.[616]

2.1.8 Living Beings

In two reports I examined, ANVISA denied prior consent based on Article 10. IX LPI. In one case, the object of the patent consisted of a DNA sequence, which was considered to be a "biological material found in nature," a kind of patenting that is prohibited by Brazilian law.[617] In the other case, the object of patenting consisted of a protein, which, according to ANVISA's report, could also be found in nature, and therefore was unpatentable.[618] Both applications were of the "pipeline" type.

2.1.9 Former Patent Law

In one report, ANVISA denied prior consent to patenting of a dental gel and justified it on the basis of Article 229-A LPI, which was introduced with the Patent Law Reform of

610. Parecer ANVISA 149/03 of December 8, 2003 (PI 1100547-5), application filed by Cesar Roberto Dias Nahoum on May 13, 1997.
611. Parecer ANVISA 075/05/COOPI/ANVISA of August 11, 2005.
612. Parecer No. 163/04 of June 18, 2004 (PI 9710536-8), application filed by Warner Lambert Company on June 24, 1996.
613. Ofício No. 101/05 of April 8, 2005 from ANVISA to INPI.
614. "Parecer Técnico de Ciência" No. 295/08/COOPI/GGMED/ANVISA, of December 1, 2008.
615. Case 2009.34.00.020302-1, 20a Vara Federal da Seção Judiciária do Distrito Federal.
616. Revista de Propriedade Industrial 2081, November 23, 2010.
617. Parecer ANVISA 113/04 of April 19, 2004 (PI 1101009-6), application filed by Biopharm Gesellschaft zur Biotechnologischen Entwicklungen von Pharmaka MBH on May 14, 1997. Moreover, ANVISA considered some claims of this application too broad. After an objection of the applicant, the report's findings were maintained by Parecer 126/08/COOPI/GGMED/ANVISA, issued on June 12, 2008.
618. Parecer ANVISA 135/07/COOPI/GGMED/ANVISA of November 7, 2007 (PI 1100689-7), application filed on May 8, 1997 by Sanofi Aventis. After an objection by the applicant, report's finding was maintained by Parecer 098/08/COOPU/GGMED/ANVISA of May 13, 2008.

2001. According to this provision, patent applications concerning patenting of pharmaceutical processes filed up until the date on which the LPI came into force, in May 1997, should be rejected and be decided under the regime of the old law.[619] Similarly, ANVISA refused to grant prior consent to a patent Chagas disease diagnosis kit for the same reason.[620]

2.1.10 Formal Procedural Criteria of the Patent Law

In two reports I examined, ANVISA denied prior consent based on procedural grounds. In one of them, ANVISA denied prior consent to the patent grant of medicine for the treatment of diabetes.[621] In this case, some claims were extemporaneously changed, which, according to ANVISA, was not allowed under Article 32 of the patent law. In the other one, the patent application consisted of a division of a pipeline patent application into two distinct patents.[622] ANVISA believed accepting the division of a pipeline patent several years after the expiration of the period in which this was allowed would be against Article 230 LPI.[623]

2.1.11 Prior Consent Given after Hearing the Applicant

In twelve cases, ANVISA gave prior consent to a patent grant after the first issuing report recommending changes in the claim.[624] It did so, for instance, in a case regarding a diagnosis method for Chagas disease. In that case, ANVISA stated, in its first technical report, that some claims were not enough described and other claims involved protein combinations existing in nature, the patentability of which as forbidden by Brazilian law.[625] Similarly, ANVISA granted prior consent to a patent for a compound able to inhibit protein aging after the applicant had altered its claims, giving up those which, according to ANVISA, did not fulfill the requirement of novelty.[626] In some cases,

619. Parecer Técnico de Ciência para Não-Anuência No. 050/08/COOPI/GGMED/ANVISA of March 7, 2008 (PI 9707368-7), application filed by Colgate-Palmolive Co. on February 5, 2008.
620. Parecer No. 118/06/COOPI/ANVISA of December 20, 2006 (PI 9603267-7), application filed by Universidade Federal de São Paulo on August 2, 1996.
621. Parecer Técnico de Ciência para Não-Anuência 131/07/COOPI/GGMED/ANVISA of October 18, 2007 (PI 9503036-0), application filed by Eli Lilly and Company on June 30, 1995.
622. Parecer No. 127/06/COOPI/ANVISA of December 26, 2006 (PI 1101197, divided from PI 1100278-6), application originally filed on April 16, 1997 by Novartis AG.
623. The opinion was also maintained after the applicant had entered an administrative remedy against it by Parecer No. 503/2008, Expediente No. 894145/08-9 of December 3, 2008.
624. Parecer Técnico de Anuência No. 005/008/COOPI/GGMED/ANVISA of June 11, 2008, (PI 9611455-0) of May 30, 2007, application filed on June 14, 1996 by Corixa Corporation.
625. Parecer No. 076/07/COOPI/ANVISA (PI 9611455-0) of May 30, 2007, application filed on June 14, 1996 by Corixa Corporation and Parecer 087/06/COOPI/ANVISA of September 28, 2006 (PI 9603619-2), application filed on August 30, 1996 by Hoffman-La Roche.
626. "Parecer Técnico de Formulação de Exigência" No. 159(07/COOPI/GGMED/ANVISA of December 20, 2007 (PI 9607598-8), application filed on January 18, 1996 by Alteon Inc., followed by "Parecer Técnico de Anuência" No. 190/08/COOPI/ANVISA of September 10, 2008, which gave prior consent.

ANVISA demanded some minor alterations as a condition for granting prior consent, such as adjustments in the claim's descriptions.[627]

In the reports analyzed in this work, ANVISA refused to give prior consent to patent grants based on the grounds shown in the table below.

Table 2 Reason for Denying Prior Consent/Legal Basis (2003-2009)

Motivation	*Quantity of Cases*	*Text Reference*
State-of-the-art search/ Lack of novelty (Article 8 LPI)	13	Page 270
Therapeutic methods (Article 10, VIII LPI)	3	Page 270
State of the Art / Lack of inventive step (Article 8 LPI)	4	Page 271
Lack of sufficient description/ Scope of the patent too broad (Article 24 LPI)	8	Page 272
Selection inventions (Article 8 LPI)	8	Page 274
Second medical indication	5	Page 276
Living beings	2	Page 278
Article 229-A LPI	1	Page 278
Formal reasons	2	Page 278
Sum	46	

Source: own elaboration.

2.2 *Standard of ANVISA's Technical Reports*

The majority of the reports I analyzed followed a common standard pattern. First, they summarized the patent claim. Then, the examiner verified whether the claimed invention fulfilled the legal conditions of patentability according to the patent law, theoretically grounding its reexamination on the same legal basis used by the Patent Office. Often the report details the results of a new search regarding the state of the art, which serves to prove that the invention had already been anticipated by an academic publication or by an older patented invention. Afterward, it concludes that the claimed invention does not fulfill the conditions of patent law. Reasons for public health, consisting of the necessity of extending access to medicines, were not used as a basis for the denial of prior consent.

After analyzing the case under the light of patent law and denying prior consent on the grounds that the invention lacks either novelty or inventive activity, most reports include a warning, of a general and abstract nature, of the risk that an "undue

627. Parecer No. 064/06/COOPI/ANVISA of August 17, 2006 (PI 9711338-7), application filed by Bayer AG on August 7, 1997.

patent grant might ultimately lead to damage to the social interest with a risk to public health and to the technical development of the country" and that "this damage might take the form of restricting both population's access to medicines to which an undue monopoly is granted and population's access to the benefits originated from technical advances already described in the state of the art."[628] Finally, prior consent is denied on the grounds of a reanalysis of the requirements of patent law, along with the observation that "ANVISA's mission is to protect and promote public health."

2.3 *Interpreting the Findings*

The findings of this study show that concerning the first period (2003-2012), ANVISA checks the same constituent elements for qualifying for a patent that ordinary patent offices around the world do.

As the findings showed, ANVISA's patent examination was similar to the examination made by the INPI since both agencies checked the same requirements of patentability. Therefore, ANVISA does not use a "fourth requirement" for assessing patentability but uses the same criteria that every Patent Office around the world does.

The similarity, however, is only formal since ANVISA interprets the requirements of patentability differently than the INPI does. What makes ANVISA's examination different is that it possesses an "impact sensibility-knowledge" in the field of medicines, which gives it another understanding of the patentability requirements. Therefore, no double examination is carried out.

As seen in the empirical study, ANVISA's approach resulted in a more stringent examination of the requirements for patentability. Therefore, fewer pharmaceutical patents will be granted.

3 *Cases Decided under the GTI's Workflow*

From June 2012 until July 2016, ANVISA denied prior consent in 205 cases, according to the official data published on its website.[629] From these cases, only 62 were definitively decided by ANVISA and sent back to the INPI.[630] All 62 cases were filed at

628. In the original (Portuguese): "Cabe ressaltar que a concessão indevida de uma patente pode significar em última instância, prejuízo ao interesse social com risco à saúde pública e ao desenvolvimento tecnológico do país. Este prejuízo pode ser materializado pela restrição do acesso da população aos medicamentos aos quais é garantido o monopólio indevido e aos benefícios advindos dos avanços tecnológicos já descritos no estado da técnica, premissas dos artigos 5° e 6° da Constituição Federal de 1988, e artigo 2° da Lei n° 9.279/86." Parecer Técnico de Não Anuência N° 014/COOPI/MED/ANVISA of March 24, 2008, PI n° 9607197-4.
629. *See* ANVISA—Report of cases sent to ANVISA as of May 24, 2012 according to the new workflow (last updated on July 14, 2016): http://portal.anvisa.gov.br/documents/33828/0/PIs+novo+fluxo+-+08+07+2016.pdf/44b68c67-42eb-4802-8795-75e9c199a39b (last visited on August 25, 2020).
630. *See* ANVISA—Report of cases whithout ANVISA's prior consent, updated on October 24, 2014: http://portal.anvisa.gov.br/documents/33836/2820971/PIs%2Bn%C3%A3o%2Banu%C3%ADdos%2B-%2Bfluxo%2Bnovo.pdf/382135f5-c67b-461f-a18e-9b7682c0fff3 (last visited on August 25, 2020).

the INPI between 1997 and 2003. In all of them, ANVISA's first report concerning prior consent was given within six months of the files having been sent from the INPI. The data confirms a backlog period at the INPI itself of 10 to 15 years.

I examined 60 of the 62 technical reports that were listed on ANVISA's website in March 2016.[631] In all of them, ANVISA denied consent motivated by the existence of "contrariness to public health," as foreseen by the GTI's workflow.[632] According to the latter, an invention may be considered contrary to public health in two different situations:[633] first, if a pharmaceutical product or process should represent a "risk for health." This would be the case if the invention results in or involves a substance, the use of which is forbidden in Brazil. The second situation occurs if a pharmaceutical product or process is of interest in the context of medicines policy or of pharmaceutical assistance within the SUS, and, at the same time, does not satisfy the conditions of patentability.

The therapeutic purposes of the pharmaceutical inventions, which were the object of ANVISA's report, were varied. Many of them were developed to treat illnesses, such as cancer (17 cases), Alzheimer (7 cases) and other serious diseases, such as hepatitis, tuberculosis, AIDS, Parkinson, diabetes and arthritis.

3.1 *Criteria Used by ANVISA to Deny Prior Consent*

3.1.1 "Risk to Health"

Remembering that the presence of "risk to health" is assessed by checking whether the invention involves or results in a substance that is forbidden in Brazil, ANVISA denied prior consent on the grounds of a "risk to health" in two cases, both involving the use of tetrahydrocannabinol, the main psychoactive constituent of cannabis. In one case, the invention was directed to pharmaceutical compositions containing water-soluble pro-drugs of propofol and methods of administering the pro-drug to induce a generalized anesthetic state in an amount sufficient to cause loss of consciousness.[634] Due to the fact that one of the claims involved tetrahydrocannabinol (THC), ANVISA asked the patentee to exclude this claim from his request.[635] Because there was no reaction from the patentee, ANVISA consequently denied prior consent. According to the report, as THC was prohibited in Brazil, its presence in the invention would be "a risk to health."[636]

631. Three of the 62 reports were not available on the INPI's online database at the time of research (March 2016).
632. ANVISA (2013), Resolução (RDC) ANVISA No. 21, April 10, 2013, Article 4, § 1°.
633. *Ibid.*, Article 4.
634. PI 0308857-0. EISAI Inc. (applicant).
635. Parecer Técnico de Exigência 245/13/COOPI/ANVISA of June 17, 2013.
636. Parecer Técnico de Não-Anuência. 058/2014/COOPI/GADIP/ANVISA of February 6, 2014.

In the second case, the object of the invention, cannabis oil,[637] was seen by ANVISA as a "risk to health" simply because tetrahydrocannabinol was prohibited in Brazil.[638] Therefore, its object would be contrary to public health.

3.1.2 Invention Considered to Be of Interest to Medicines Policies

In the remaining cases, contrariness to public health was based on the fact that the pharmaceutical invention was considered to be of interest to medicines or pharmaceutical assistance policies within the SUS and, at the same time, did not satisfy the conditions of patentability.

In all the reports, such interest was assessed by verifying whether the object of the invention was related to the therapeutic aims enumerated in a list of strategic medicinal products produced by the Ministry of Health.[639] If so, ANVISA examined the conditions of patentability, and prior consent was given or denied depending on this review.

3.1.2.1 Lack of Novelty

Lack of novelty was the most frequent reason given by ANVISA to justify lack of prior consent, namely in 23 cases. Under the old workflow, lack of novelty was mostly motivated by the fact that the invention in question had been anticipated by an older application, which was found in a new search regarding the state of the art. This was the case, for instance, of a drug developed to treat asthma, arthritis and other diseases,[640] as well as the case of another one developed to treat Alzheimer's and Parkinson's disease.[641] In another eight cases, ANVISA decided that the invention should not be patented because its formula was already known from a so-called Markush formula (selection inventions).[642]

637. PI 0311867-3, LTS Lohmann Therapie-Systeme AG (applicant).

638. Parecer Técnico de Não Anuência 559/13/COOPI/GADIP/ANVISA of September 25, 2013.

639. Portaria MS/GM 1284, of May 26, 2010. This norm was later abrogated by Portaria PRT GM 3089 of December 12, 2013.

640. Parecer Técnico de Não Anuência 220/2013/COOPI/DIP/ANVISA of July 5, 2013, Patent Application PI 005616-2, Patent Applicant F. Hoffmann-La Roche. According to ANVISA, this invention had been anticipated in the patent application PI 0000908-3.

641. Parecer Técnico de Não Anuência 547/13/COOPI/GADIP/ANVISA of September 24, 2013, Patent Applicant Sanofi-Aventis. According to ANVISA, this invention had been anticipated in the patent application no. PI 9612686-8.

642. (1) Parecer Técnico de Ciência para Não Anuência No. 014/13/COOPI/GADIP/ANVISA of February 18, 2013, Patent Applicant F. Hoffmann-La Roche AG, Patent Application No. PI00056162; (2) Parecer Técnico de Não Anuência No. 676/13/COOPI/GADIP/ANVISA of October 14, 2013, Patent Applicant F. Hoffmann-La Roche AG (Patent application No. PI 0112695-4); (3) Parecer Técnico de Exigência No. 346/13/COOPI/GADIP/ANVISA of August 6, 2013, Patent Applicant Astrazeneca AG (Patent Application No. PI 02112620); (4) Parecer Técnico de Exigência No. 358/13/COOPI/GADIP/ANVISA of August 13, 2013, Patent Applicant Cancer Research Technology Ltd (Patent Application No. PI 0215986-4); (5) Parecer Técnico de Ciência ou Exigência No. 262/13/COOPI/GADIP/ANVISA of June 24, 2013, Patent Applicant Sanofi Aventis (Patent Application No. PI 0306707-6); (6) Parecer Técnico de Formulação de Exigência No. 134/13/COOPI/GADIP/ANVISA of May 20, 2013, Patent Applicant Merck Frosst

In some cases, ANVISA found that patent claims lacked novelty, but that this was not true to all of the claims requested. In such cases, ANVISA asked the patentee to change her request by suppressing the claims ANVISA opined would not be new. If, as often occurred in such cases, the patentee did not reply, ANVISA would deny prior consent, justifying this with the reasoning that the patent could be detrimental to public health. This was the case, for instance, of a cancer drug,[643] as well as in the case of a hepatitis drug.[644] In a case concerning a rhinitis drug, however, the patentee suppressed some claims ANVISA considered to be unpatentable, but not all of those claims; consequently, ANVISA upheld its first opinion and denied prior consent.[645]

It is worth noting that in most cases in which lack of novelty was indicated by ANVISA as the reason for denying prior consent, this was not the sole reason for its decision. Lack of novelty was usually indicated alongside other shortages, such as lack of an inventive step, exception of therapeutic method or insufficient description of the invention.[646]

3.1.2.2 Lack of an Inventive Step

Lack of an inventive step was given as a reason, among others, for denying prior consent in 14 cases. As in the case of lack of novelty, this was usually just one of many reasons why prior consent was denied. Among the few cases in which lack of an inventive step was indicated as the only hindrance to patentability was, for instance, an antibiotic drug developed by a Brazilian university. According to ANVISA, such a request could not deserve a patent because "identifying optimal conditions for cultivating *Chromobacterium violaceum*" would be an obvious solution for a person having ordinary skill in the art.[647] Lack of an inventive step was the reason given by ANVISA for its denial of prior consent in a case involving an antiretroviral drug in which the patent applicant—a Brazilian company—had developed a way to improve its solubility in water; this improvement was also seen as an obvious solution for a person

Canada Ltd (Patent Application No. PI 0307050-6); (7) Parecer Técnico de Ciência para Não Anuência No. 228/13/COOPI/GADIP/ANVISA of June 11, 2013, Patent Applicant Schering AG (PI 0307723-3); (8) Parecer Técnico de Exigência No. 296/13/COOPI/GADIP/ANVISA of July 10, 2013, Patent Applicant Sanofi Aventis and Mitsubishi Pharma Corporation (Patent Application No. PI 03081095).

643. Parecer Técnico de Exigência (Technical Opinion of Demand) No. 234/13/COOPI/ANVISA of June 13, 2013, Patent applicant Ipsen Pharma S.A.S, Patent application No. PI0215336-0, which was followed by Parecer Técnico de Não-Anuência (Technical Opinion of Negative of Prior Consent) No. 685/13/COOPI/GADIP/ANVISA, of October 17, 2013.
644. Parecer Técnico de Não Anuência No. 101/14/COOPI/GADIP/ANVISA of March 7, 2014, Patent Applicant Yang Sheng Tang Company Limited, Patent Application No. PI0014390-1.
645. Parecer Técnico de Exigência No. 134/13/COOPI/GADIP/ANVISA of May 20, 2013, Patent Applicant: Merck Frost Canada Ltd, Patent Application No. PI 0307050-6, followed by Parecer Técnico de Não Anuência No. 435/13/COOPI/GADIP/ANVISA of August 27, 2013.
646. Parecer Técnico de Não Anuência No. 726/13/COOPI/GADIP/ANVISA of November 7, 2013, Patent Applicant Yang Sheng Tang Company Limited, Patent Application No. PI0014390-1.
647. Parecer Técnico de Ciência ou Exigência No. 760/13/COOPI/ANVISA, December 3, 2013, Patent Applicant Universidade Estadual de Campinas—UNICAMP, Patent Application No. PI0100199-0. followed by Parecer Técnico de Não Anuência No. 193/14/COOPI/GAP/DIP/ANVISA of April 1, 2014.

having ordinary skill in the art, and therefore not deserving of a patent.[648] In another case, the object of which was a method of treating Alzheimer's disease, ANVISA, also denied prior consent on the grounds of lack of an inventive step. That case concerned a compound that could be manipulated into producing antibodies that worked against proteins considered to be favorable to Alzheimer's disease.[649] According to ANVISA's opinion, it was not possible to see a technological advance in this, due to the fact that in an older patent application, the same strategy to cause an immunological reaction in the human body had already been described. Similarly, prior consent was denied in a case involving a drug useful against andropause and in hormone replacement therapy for men. For ANVISA, producing the compounds described in that application would be an obvious step for a person having ordinary skill in the art, considering the existence of older applications that described drugs producing similar reactions in the human body.[650] Lack of an inventive step was also given as a reason for refusing prior consent in a case of therapeutic combinations involving compounds used for the treatment of respiratory diseases like asthma. In that case, ANVISA's examiner agreed that an unexpected effect in relation to the "state of the art" was described in the application, but because this unexpected effect was not proved, he did not recognize the presence of an inventive step.[651]

As in the cases where lack of novelty was invoked by ANVISA in order to deny prior consent, in most cases, lack of an inventive step was not ANVISA's only reason for denying that consent. Lack of an inventive step was mostly cited along with a lack of novelty, exception as a therapeutic method or an insufficient description of the invention.

3.1.2.3 Therapeutic Method

As seen above,[652] Brazilian patent law does not consider "surgical techniques or methods, as well as therapeutic or diagnostic methods, for application to human or animal body" to be inventions. In 19 of 60 cases analyzed, "therapeutic method" was cited by ANVISA as a hindrance to patentability.

ANVISA denied prior consent, for instance, to a process developed by a Brazilian university, the object of which was to extract, purify and apply an antibiotic pigment produced by *Chromobacterium violaceum* in order to use it to treat tuberculosis and other diseases.[653]

---

648. Parecer Técnico de Ciência No. 342/13/COOPI/ANVISA of August 7, 2013, Patent Applicant: Cristália Produtos Químicos Farmacêuticos Ltda., Patent Application No. 0302424-5.
649. Parecer Técnico de Ciência No. 274/13/COOPI/ANVISA of June 28, 2013, Patent Application No. PI0108566-2.
650. Parecer Técnico de Não Anuência No. 295/13/COOPI//GADIP/ANVISA of July 10, 2013, Patent Applicant Schering AG, Patent Application No. PI0206653-0.
651. Parecer Técnico de Ciência No. 345/13/COOPI/GADIP/ANVISA, of July 5, 2013, Patent Applicant Boehringer Ingelheim, Patent Application No. 0207883-0.
652. *See* Chapter-3-A-I-3.2.1.2(b).
653. Parecer Técnico de Ciência No. 271/13/COOPI/GADIP/ANVISA, of June 27, 2013, Patent Applicant UNICAMP—Universidade Estadual de Campinas, Patent Application No. PI0101346-7.

In at least three cases, ANVISA's examiner stated in just one sentence that the claim consisted of a therapeutic method and that therefore the invention in question was not patentable. In the first case, the invention in question was a drug to treat muscle degeneration;[654] the second case had as its object a drug for the treatment of cancer, diabetes and Alzheimer's disease;[655] while in the third case, the invention in question was a drug to treat cancer and Alzheimer's disease.[656]

The question of the so-called Swiss-type patent claim was discussed in two of the 19 cases. In both of them, ANVISA denied prior consent based on the fact that the Brazilian patent law does not accept the patentability of therapeutic methods.[657] In the first case, the invention in question was a drug to treat menopause symptoms; in the second case, it was a drug developed to treat cancer.

3.1.2.4 Living Beings

As seen earlier, the LPI excludes from a patentable subject matter "the whole or part of living beings, except transgenic microorganisms that satisfy the three requirements of patentability and which are not discoveries."[658] Based on this provision, ANVISA denied prior consent in eight of 60 cases analyzed. This was the case, for instance, of a patent application, the object of which was some particles of the virus parainfluenza, which contained a mutation that was to be used to produce vaccines against the influenza virus.[659] According to ANVISA, such an invention could not be patented under Brazilian law, even if the mutation in the virus was introduced through human intervention. The reason for this, according to ANVISA, was that the patent applicant would not have been able to show that such a mutation could happen naturally. In most cases, prior consent was denied based on the presence of other hindrances to patentability, such as lack of an inventive step, lack of novelty, or consisting of a therapeutic method. The latter was also, for instance, the case of the "*Chromobacterium violaceum,*" which ANVISA saw as a natural pigment synthesized by bacteria, and, consequently, not patentable under Brazilian law.[660]

654. Parecer Técnico de Ciência No. 716/13/COOP/GADIP/ANVISA, of November 1, 2013, Patent Applicant Novartis AG, Patent Application No. 0213970-7.
655. Parecer Técnico de Exigência No. 473/13/COOPI/GADIP/ANVISA, of September 11, 2013, Patent Applicant Astrazeneca AB, Patent Application No. PI 0214605-3.
656. Parecer Técnico de Formulação de Exigências No. 719/13/COOPI/GADIP/ANVISA of November 4, 2013, Patent Applicant: Wyeth, Patent Application No. 0214767-0.
657. 1) Parecer Técnico de Ciência No. 477/13/COOPI/GADIP/ANVISA of September 13, 2013, Patent Applicant Barr Laboratories Inc (Patent Application No. PI 03090329; 2) Parecer Técnico de Não Anuência 093/14/COOPI/GADIP/ANVISA of February 25, 2014, Patent Applicant Aeterna Zentaris GmbH (Patent Application No. PI 03130480-7).
658. *See* Chapter 3-A-I-3.2.2.3.
659. Parecer Técnico de Não Anuência No. 036/14/COOPI/GADIP/ANVISA, of January 27, 2014, Patent Applicant; Government of USA, Patent Application No. 0011159-7.
660. Parecer Técnico de Ciência No. 271/13/COOPI/GADIP/ANVISA, of June 27, 2013, Patent Applicant UNICAMP—Universidade Estadual de Campinas, Patent Application No. PI0101346-7.

3.1.2.5 Insufficient or Imprecise Description

According to Article 24 Brazilian Patent Law, the specifications of the patent application shall clearly and sufficiently describe its object, so as to permit its reproduction by a person having ordinary skill in the art, and shall indicate, when applicable, the best way of doing it. In 28 of 60 examined cases, ANVISA denied prior consent based on the absence of such a precise description of the patent's object. This was, for instance, the case of an application requesting a patent to protect a drug for the treatment of cancer, the object of which, according to ANVISA, did not describe the basic characteristics of its API.[661] Similarly, in a case involving an antimalarial medication, ANVISA denied prior consent based on the fact that a significant portion of the claimed compounds was not be described in the specifications of the patent application.[662]

3.1.2.6 Claim Too Broad

According to Article 25 of the Brazilian patent law, patent claims shall be substantiated in their specifications and clearly and precisely define the subject matter that would be the object of the patent's protection. This demand has to do with the scope of patent protection so that no one is prohibited from doing or producing anything other than the patented invention itself. The aim is to avoid issuing a patent which, for instance, prohibits someone from doing something that is de facto not protected by the patented invention. The reports on cases whereby ANVISA denied prior consent on this basis show that ANVISA often asked the patent applicant to change his or her request regarding the specifications of the patent. Whenever the patent applicant did not follow this recommendation, ANVISA denied prior consent.[663] In other cases, for instance, in an application involving a cancer drug, ANVISA was of the opinion that some compounds should be excluded from the claims, as these were based on a Markush structure, which would be outside the protection scope of the independent claim.[664] Similarly, ANVISA denied prior consent in a case involving vaccines against herpes.[665] The reason for not granting prior consent, in this case, was a lack of information

661. Parecer Técnico de Não Anuência No. 708/13/COOPI/GADIP/ANVISA, of October 31, 2013, Patent Applicant: The Scripps Research Institute/Lexingen Pharmaceuticals Corporation, Patent Application No. PI 0008161-2.
662. Parecer Técnico de Não Anuência No. 554/13/COOPI/GADIP/ANVISA, of September 24, 2013, Patent Applicant: Centre National de La Recherche Cientifique, Patent Application No. PI 0109885-3.
663. For instance, Parecer Técnico de Não Anuência No. 726/13/COOPI/GADIP/ANVISA, of November 7, 2013, Patent Applicant: Yang Sheng Tang Company Limited, Patent Application No. PI 0014390-1, as well Parecer Técnico de Exigência No. 558/13/COOPI/GADIP/ANVISA, of September 25, 2013, PI 0015320-6, Patent Applicant: Albany Molecular Research, Inc., Patent Application No. PI 15320-6.
664. Parecer Técnico de Não Anuência No. 367/13/COOPI/GADIP/ANVISA, of August 15, 2013. Patent Applicant F. Hoffmann-La Roche AG, Patent Application No. PI 0009887-6.
665. Parecer Técnico de Não Anuência No. 563/13/COOPI/GADIP/ANVISA, of November 25, 2013, Patent Applicant: Smith Kline Beecham Biologicals S.A., Patent Application No. PI 0014171-2.

relating to which virus strains the compound was based on; consequently, the object of the patent was too broad. Another patent application, the object of which was 4 trillion compounds to act against digestive problems, also had prior consent denied based on the fact that these claims were made in too broad a way.[666]

Similar to the reasons described above, in most cases, a too broad patent scope was not given as the sole factor in why ANVISA did not give prior consent. For instance, in a case involving antigens useful in the treatment of infections caused by streptococcus, ANVISA denied prior consent for the following reasons: lack of novelty and exclusion from patentability due to the fact that the object of the patent had been classified as a therapeutic method and as consisting of living beings.[667]

3.1.2.7 Presentation of Information

According to Article 10(VI) Brazilian Patent Law, the presentation of information is excluded from the patentable subject matter. Of all the cases analyzed, there was just one in which ANVISA denied prior consent based on this reason. In this case, the object of the application consisted of different methods for producing antibodies. According to ANVISA, however, it was not possible to identify if an invention had been concretized; consequently, the request did not deserve a patent as it consisted of the mere presentation of information.[668]

3.2 Standard of ANVISA's Examination under the GTI's Workflow

All the analyzed reports followed a common pattern. First, patent claims were summarized. Then, the examiner verified whether the patent request was of interest to the policies relating to medicines or pharmaceutical assistance within the SUS by checking whether its object was listed in the relevant rules set out by the Ministry of Health. If the answer to this was affirmative, ANVISA examined whether the patent application fulfilled the requirements of patentability (novelty, inventive step, industrial applicability), as well as checking that the object of the patent application did not fall into the category of excluded patent subject matter. In all the reports analyzed, ANVISA denied prior consent to patent grants based on the grounds given in the table below.

666. Parecer Técnico de Exigência No. xxx/13/COOPI/GADIP/ANVISA, of November 14, 2013, Patent Applicant: Eli Lilly and Company, Patent Application No. PI0111562-6.
667. Parecer Técnico de Ciência No. 698/13/COOPI/GADIP/ANVISA, of October 25, 2013, Patent Applicant: ID Biomedical Corporation, Patent Application No. PI0112497-8.
668. Parecer Técnico de Ciência No. 236/13/COOPI/GADIP/ANVISA, of November 13, 2013, Patent Applicant: Abbott Laboratories, Patent Application No. PI0112026-3.

Table 3 Reasons for ANVISA to Deny Prior Consent/Legal Basis (2012-2015)

Motivation	*Quantity of Cases*	*Text Reference*
1) Risk to health—RtH (Article 18, II LPI)	2	Page 282
2) Lack of novelty—LoN—State of the art (Article 8 LPI)	15	Page 283
3) Lack of novelty—LoN—Selection Inventions (Article 8 LPI)	8	Page 283, Fn. 1171
4) Lack of inventive step—LoIS (Article 8 LPI)	14	Page 284
5) Therapeutic method—TM (Article 10. VIII LPI)	19	Page 285
6) Living beings—LB (Article 10. IX LPI)	8	Page 286
7) Lack of sufficient description—LoSD (Article 24 LPI)	28	Page 287
9) Scope of patent too broad—SoPtB (Article 25 LPI)	8	Page 287
9) Presentation of information—PoI (Article 10. VI LPI)	1	Page 288
10) Non-compliance with ANVISA's requests (NCoAR)	44	Page 289
SUM[669]	60	

Source: own elaboration.

Table 4 Cases Analyzed under the GTI's Workflow: Reasons for ANVISA to Deny Prior Consent (2012-2016)

	1) LoN	*2) LoIS*	*3) TM*	*4) LB*	*5) LoSD*	*6) RtH*	*7) SoPtB*	*8) PoI*	*9) NCoAR*
PI00056162	X								X
PI00081612					X				X
PI00098876							X		X
PI00111597				X					
PI00141712							X		X
PI00142360							X		
PI00143901	X	X	X	X	X				X

669. ANVISA can indicate one or more reasons for denying prior consent. "Lack of sufficient description," for instance, is often combined with another reason.

	1) LoN	*2) LoIS*	*3) TM*	*4) LB*	*5) LoSD*	*6) RtH*	*7) SoPtB*	*8) PoI*	*9) NCoAR*
PI00146870	X	X							
PI00153206					X				X
PI00169218	X								X
PI01001990		X							X
PI01013467			X	X					
PI01085662		X							X
PI01098853					X				X
PI01115626			X	X	X		X		X
PI01120263					X			X	X
PI01124978	X		X	X			X		X
PI01126954	X	X	X						X
PI01172530		X		X	X				X
PI02066530		X							X
PI01162292					X				X
PI02078830		X							
PI02110725	X								
PI02112620	X	X	X		X				X
PI02125986	X			X					X
PI02128098	X		X	X	X				X
PI02133296		X	X						X
PI02139324		X	X		X		X		X
PI02139707	X		X						X
PI02142457	X	X							X
PI02146053	X	X	X		X				X
PI02147670			X		X				X
PI02151570					X		X		X
PI02153360	X								X
PI02159350	X		X		X		X		
PI02159864			X		X		X		X
PI03024245		X							X
PI03067076	X				X				
PI03070506	X						X		
PI03074617	X		X						X
PI03077233	X				X				
PI03081060					X				X

	1) LoN	*2) LoIS*	*3) TM*	*4) LB*	*5) LoSD*	*6) RtH*	*7) SoPtB*	*8) PoI*	*9) NCoAR*
PI03081095	X				X				X
PI03088570						X			X
PI03090329			X		X				X
PI03091171	X	X	X						
PI03096645	X		X				X		X
PI03100189			X				X		X
PI03113299	X	X			X				X
PI03118673						X			
PI03130444	X	X			X				X
PI03130487	X		X		X				
PI03131629	X	X							
PI03141128			X				X		X
PI03147975			X						X
PI03154319	X	X			X				
PI03175189					X				X
PI04033167	X	X							X
PI98078585	X	X			X				X
PI99175002			X		X				

Source: own elaboration.

After analyzing the case from the perspective of patent law and denying prior consent on the grounds that the invention lacked, for instance, novelty or evidence of inventive activity, all the reports in question concluded that granting the patent application in question would be contrary to public health since to grant a patent for an invention that did not deserve one would reduce access to medicines for all.

It is worth noting that in circa 75 percent of all cases, ANVISA denied prior consent after giving the patent applicant a chance to respond. In all those cases, the patent applicant did nothing, and, consequently, ANVISA denied the patent grant.

3.3 *Interpreting the Findings*

As my research showed, ANVISA checked whether a pharmaceutical product or process claimed as an invention is seen as a "risk to health." If so, ANVISA denied prior consent to patent grant.

Examining the presence of "risk to health," however, is rather a constituent element for the examination of drug safety, which takes place within pharmacovigilance proceedings. If the health authority finds out that a drug, whether patented or not, represents a risk for health, this product will have denied authorization to be marketed in order to protect public health.

Drug safety, therefore, is a condition that must be proved to obtain approval to market the drug. This question, however, is not relevant for the patent grant, since at this stage of drug development, no one knows whether it will be someday marketed or not. As is known, most of the patented inventions are never commercialized.[670] Therefore, requiring that drug safety—which is assessed within clinical tests that are timely and costly expensive—will be a condition for patentability is not reasonable.

As seen above, ANVISA checked the presence of a risk to health by simply verifying whether the invention for which the patent is requested is prohibited or not in Brazil. If a risk to health is not present and the pharmaceutical product or process is of interest to SUS, ANVISA checked the ordinary requirements of patentability.

The effects of assessing drug safety within the patent examination proceedings will depend on how the term “risk to public health” is understood. There are two possibilities of doing so, namely:

(1) If the safety requirement is earnestly assessed, ANVISA must request that expensive and time-consuming clinical studies proving the drug safety will be provided by the patent applicant. Therefore, if the patent applicant does not present such data, ANVISA must deny prior consent. This would signify that ANVISA would have to deny prior consent to all pharmaceutical patent applications since data concerning drug safety, as a rule, is not available before the patent grant.
(2) If the safety requirement is assessed by verifying whether the invention in question involves a substance that is forbidden in Brazil, ANVISA must virtually grant prior consent to all patent applications.

In the first case, ANVISA’s prior consent would be neither reasonable nor in accordance with Article 27.1 TRIPS since it would mean, in practice, a ban on pharmaceutical patents. In the second case, ANVISA’s prior consent will be useless.

With respect to the assessment of the ordinary requirements of patentability, the same conclusions drawn regarding the data concerning the first period are also valid for the second period.

II How Often Has ANVISA Denied Prior Consent?

1 From 2001 to 2010

On examining ANVISA’s data, reproduced in the table below, one sees, at first glance, that 9.7 percent of the pharmaceutical patents applied for in Brazil failed to obtain ANVISA’s prior consent between June 2001 and July 2010.

670. Sichelman (2010), “Commercializing Patents,” 62 *Stan. L. Rev.* 2, p. 341.

Table 5 Status of Patent Applications at ANVISA (June 2001-July 2010)

Situation	*Number of Cases*	*Percentage Rate %*
Prior consent granted	1,100	74.3
Awaiting response from the applicant	17	1.1
Work in progress	63	4.3
Decision in review	8	0.3
Patent grant rejected by the INPI as a result of ANVISA's examination	22[671]	1.5
The INPI stops proceedings as a result of ANVISA's examination	57	3.9
No prior consent is granted	143	9.7
Others	70	4.7
Total	1,480	100

Source: ANVISA: http://portal.anvisa.gov.br/wps/wcm/connect/df1c670047458e62976fd73fbc4c6735/julho+2010.pdf?MOD=AJPERES (last visited on February 14, 2016; as of October 2017, no longer available online).

When we look more closely at the table above, we see that the rate of applications that did not get ANVISA's prior consent is slightly higher than 9.7 percent. For the grouping of "patent grant rejected by INPI as a result of ANVISA's examination," we presume prior consent was also denied for these cases. Furthermore, we assume that for the category "the INPI stops proceedings as a result of ANVISA's examination," ANVISA also denied prior consent. This is so because, as a rule, whenever ANVISA refused to grant prior consent, the INPI would stop proceedings.

2 *From June 2012 to July 2016*

From June 2012, patent file proceedings began to be processed according to the workflow proposed by the GTI. From this time, ANVISA no longer carried out a patent reexamination since it began work before the INPI had produced its technical report about the patentability of the invention. From June 2012 to July 2016, ANVISA denied prior consent in 9 percent of all cases—including those cases that were not definitively decided—as shown in the following table.

671. It is worth noting that these figures may change from year to year. In 2009, the results were different. *Lima, Paranaguá et al.* highlight that according to ANVISA's available data for the period up until 2009, of 1,346 cases analyzed by ANVISA, the INPI denied a patent grant after ANVISA's examination in 90 cases. *See* Lima/Paranaguá et al. (2013), *A Revisão da Lei de Patentes: Inovação em Prol da Competitividade Nacional*, Câmara dos Deputados—Centro de Estudos e Debates Estratégicos, pp. 158-160.

Table 6 Status of Patent Applications at ANVISA (July 2012-July 2016)

Situation	*Number of Cases*	*Percentage Rate %*
Prior consent granted	1,702	74.5
Prior consent granted after a judgment review	10	0.5
Cases definitively shelved by the INPI	137	6.0
Prior consent not granted/Denial of prior consent maintained	207	9.0
ANVISA is waiting for the patentee's response to its demands	87	3.8
Decision in administrative revision	69	3.0
Uncompleted request	33	1.5
The publication of the decision to grant a patent is declared void	21	0.9
Analysis suspended	17	0.8
Total number of cases decided[672]	2,283	100

Source: ANVISA: http://portal.anvisa.gov.br/wps/wcm/connect/df1c670047458e62976fd73fbc4c6735/julho+2010.pdf?MOD=AJPERES (last visited on February 14, 2016; as of October 2017, no longer available online).

III How Effectively Has ANVISA Influenced the Granting of Patents for Medicines and Has Improved Access to Medicines?

1 Period under the Old Workflow (1999-2012)

The data collected in the empirical study shows that in all 46 cases in which ANVISA denied prior consent to grant a patent, the patent was, in fact, afterward not granted by the Patent Office. This suggests, at a first look, that ANVISA's influence in the granting of patents for medicines in the studied period of 2001-2009 was significant. However, if it is true that the INPI did not grant any of those 46 patents without ANVISA's prior consent, it is also true that the INPI did not reject these patent requests. If the collaboration between ANVISA and the Patent Office had worked, this would have been expected to happen. Instead, the Patent Office stopped proceedings in all 46 cases.

672. According to data published by ANVISA, 4,625 patent application files were forwarded to ANVISA between June 2012 and July 2016. From this total number of 4,625 cases, 1,810 cases (i.e., 39 percent of the total number) had not been assessed by ANVISA by July 2016. Besides, ANVISA sent 532 cases (i.e., 11 percent of the total number) back to the INPI without assessing them, since their referral was unfounded, presumably because they did not fulfill the conditions of being of interest to medicine policies. Table 3, however, did not consider cases that had not yet been decided, or cases that ANVISA sent back to the INPI without having assessed them.

In other words: the requested patent was neither granted nor denied, and as a result, proceedings are still pending in all these cases.[673]

In such an uncertain situation, potential competitors able to produce the drug after a patent's expiration will be cautious enough to wait until the end of the patent proceedings before starting to produce the generic drug. Otherwise, the generic competitor would risk being sued by the original patent applicant, whose request had been filed but not yet decided. From the viewpoint of the patent applicant, such a delay in the granting of a patent is surely not positive. However, he is safeguarded by Brazilian law, according to which patent owners must enjoy patent protection for at least 10 years from the date on which the patent is issued. On the part of the patent applicant, there will always be the hope that the INPI issues the patent someday, even if patent grant proceedings take decades to be concluded.

In all the 46 cases in which ANVISA denied prior consent to a patent grant, INPI boycotted ANVISA's job, and as a result, the granting of that patent was avoided or delayed. Therefore, due to the lack of cooperation between ANVISA and the INPI, ANVISA's prior consent mechanism did not function normally.

2 *Period under the GTI's Workflow (June 2012-July 2016)*

According to the workflow proposed by the interministerial committee, when ANVISA denies prior consent, the INPI should dismiss/shelve the patent application, with this decision being published by means of the official medium (phase 5b). Based on the data published by ANVISA on its website in January 2016,[674] one can see that from June 2012 to January 2016, ANVISA denied prior consent in 62 patent applications, considering only the applications that were definitively decided by ANVISA. Of these, patent proceedings were dismissed by the INPI in 52 cases. However, these dismissals were not based on the lack of prior consent. In these 52 cases, the patentee stopped paying patent annual fees after having been notified that ANVISA had denied prior consent. In the remaining 10 cases in which prior consent was denied, the INPI did not dismiss the request, but, in distinction to the other 51 cases, the patentee continued to pay patent annual fees after prior consent had been denied.[675] In such cases, according to data published on the INPI's website, the INPI again did nothing, leaving the patent request in an indefinite legal status ("frozen"), as it did under the old workflow.

Under the GTI's workflow, ANVISA's review regarding prior consent is carried out before the Patent Office writes its technical report. If ANVISA gives prior consent, patent proceedings continue, and the Patent Office must carry out a patent examination again. If ANVISA does not give prior consent, the INPI should archive proceedings. As

673. Sampat/Shadlen (2017), *Secondary Pharmaceutical Patenting: A Global Perspective*, NBER Working Paper No. 23114, p. 3.

674. http://portal.anvisa.gov.br/wps/wcm/connect/f0118c8045f3c482a688a67ffa9843d8/PIs + n %C3%A3o + anu%C3%ADdos + - + fluxo + novo.pdf?MOD = AJPERES (last visited on January 30, 2016: as of August 2017 this is no longer available online).

675. Data held in the INPI's patent search database.

a rule, the Brazilian Patent Act uses the word *arquivamento* for cases where proceedings end without the Patent Office grants a patent.[676] This is the case, for instance, when the Patent Office concludes that the patent should not be granted. Proceedings also terminate when the patent applicant does not require the examination to be carried out or when the patent owner does not pay annual fees, which can occur before or after a substantive examination is carried out. In those cases, patent proceedings might be restarted if a request is made in time by the involved party.

Considering only applications that were definitively decided on by ANVISA between June 2012 and July 2016, ANVISA denied prior consent in 62 cases. Of those, the INPI did not follow ANVISA's veto in any case. Under the GTI's workflow, INPI was supposed to archive patent applications for which ANVISA's prior consent had been denied. Instead, INPI archived 52 of the 62 patent applications, but not as a consequence of ANVISA's veto; this was done as a consequence of the lack of payment of annual fees.[677] This suggests that in circa 83 percent of all cases in which prior consent was definitively denied, the patent applicant apparently lost interest in obtaining the patent. A possible reason for such a sudden loss of interest on the part of the patentee might be the huge backlog at the INPI since, in nearly all these cases, patent applications had been filed circa 15 to 20 years earlier.

In the remaining 10 cases, in spite of the lack of ANVISA's prior consent, proceedings are still formally active, but they have not been decided upon by the INPI. As had happened under the old workflow, the Patent Office simply stopped proceedings in all these 10 cases, without concluding them, so that the requested patent was neither granted nor denied.

3 *Concluding Remarks*

The data collected show that in the period between 2012 and 2016, the cooperation between ANVISA and INPI did not work since the INPI continued to act as it had done under the old workflow; namely, it did not terminate proceedings when ANVISA denied prior consent.[678] This means, in practice, that in all cases in which ANVISA denied prior consent and the patent applicant did not withdraw his or her application

676. For instance, Article 21 LPI (proceedings are archived, when formal conditions are not satisfied), Article 26 LPI (proceedings are archived, when the patentee requests a division of his application, but does not satisfy the applicable formal requirements), Article 33 LPI (proceedings are archived if the patentee does not ask for a substantive examination until 36 months after the application), Article 36 LPI (proceedings are archived if the patentee does not satisfy the demands made by the patent examiner, Article 38 and Article 86 LPI (proceedings are archived if the patentee does not pay patent fees).
677. According to Article 84 Brazilian Patent Law, patent applicants are subject to payment of an annual fee from the beginning of the third year after the filing date. If these annual fees are not paid, the patent application must be shelved (cf. Article 86 PI).
678. Guise Rosina/Wang/De Campos (2010), "Access to Medicines: Pharmaceutical Patents and the Right to Health," in: Shaver (ed.), *Access to Knowledge in Brazil—New Research on Intellectual Property, Innovation and Development*, Bloomsbury, pp. 192-193.

(by not paying annual fees), the granting of the patent was de facto (not de jure) hindered.[679]

Despite this, as the case law analysis revealed, in four cases where ANVISA denied prior consent, INPI changed its view after ANVISA's examination view about the requirements of patentability and rejected the patent.[680] This was, for instance, the case of the oncologic drug Docetaxel, where the patent rejection allowed that the State of São Paulo saved money by buying the more affordable generic drug instead of the patented drug, which was then distributed for free for the population.[681] Furthermore, according to *Lima & Paranaguá*, there were 90 cases in which the INPI had first concluded that the patentability requirements were present, but changed its opinion after ANVISA's examination, and finally rejected the patent.[682] This indicates that despite the lack of cooperation between both agencies, drug access was improved in Brazil due to ANVISA's participation in the patent grant proceedings.

IV Managing the Dispute Between ANVISA and the INPI

1 *Why Was There a Lack of Cooperation Between ANVISA and the INPI for Such a Long Period?*

From the beginning, some factors combined to play a role in making cooperation between ANVISA and the INPI difficult. First of all, when ANVISA was included in the pharmaceutical patent examination, no one knew how coordination between the two agencies should happen since this topic was not regulated by law. ANVISA did nothing at first and waited for a federal regulation that weirdly never came, although the Presidency of the Republic has the constitutional competence for issuing decrees regulating federal laws.[683]

Second, when ANVISA finally decided to implement prior consent by itself, it did not do so in a constructive way. As reported above, ANVISA used to make the correction of translation or orthography mistakes made by patentees and not improved by INPI a condition of issuing prior consent. Third, the less the federal administration did in order to settle the conflict of attributions between the INPI and ANVISA, the more the INPI and ANVISA persisted in their unilateral approaches. In fact, the federal administration did nothing to solve the conflict between the agencies until at least

679. About the legal insecurity and the "de facto monopoly" created by the INPI's inertia *see* Lima/Paranaguá et al. (2013), *A Revisão da Lei de Patentes: Inovação em Prol da Competitividade Nacional*, Câmara dos Deputados, p. 159; Dias de Oliveira/Khater Covesi (2015), "Estratégias para Adiar o Acesso aos Medicamentos no Brasil," in: Villardi, Vieira and Carvalho (eds.), *Prêmio GTPI Jacques Bouchara de Produção Acadêmica voltada para o Ativismo*, pp. 55-84.
680. *See* Chapter 3-C-IV-3.
681. *See* Chapter 3-C-IV-1.1.
682. Lima/Paranaguá et al. (2013), *A Revisão da Lei de Patentes: Inovação em Prol da Competitividade Nacional*, Câmara dos Deputados, p. 160. According to the author, his source for this figure (90 cases) was ANVISA.
683. Article 84, IV, BC.

August 2011, when it created an interministerial group to study the case and solve the problem.

In practice, both agencies have been only able to work together when ANVISA has had the same opinion as to the INPI concerning patentability. In such a case, after ANVISA gives its prior consent, the INPI grants the patent. If instead, ANVISA has a different opinion than that of the INPI and refuses to give prior consent, the INPI halts proceedings without deciding the patent application. Only in a few cases did the INPI change its opinion and decide not to grant the patent.

From 2001 until 2017, ANVISA's vetoes of patent grants were neutralized by the INPI's decision to stop proceedings; as a result, the application remained ongoing. By delaying a decision over the patentability of an invention, the INPI also delayed a possible launching of generics into the market. Considering that a generic competitor will only start producing after a patent expires (or is not granted at all), then later, a patent is issued, and later the corresponding generic drug will be produced. The delay caused by the INPI in not terminating proceedings in those cases where prior consent has been denied is more harmful to patients than for patentees since the latter are protected by Article 40 LPI. This provision guarantees a minimum of 10 years' patent protection for every invention, counted from the time the patent is granted.[684] The existence of this provision might explain why only a few cases were brought to the Brazilian courts, despite the clear illegality of INPI's failure to decide.

As mentioned above, from June 2012, when the GTI's workflow started to be applied, the situation changed. In the majority of cases (51 of 61) in which ANVISA's prior consent was denied, patent proceedings were terminated. This, however, occurred not as a consequence of the INPI's decision to dismiss the case in question but because the patent applicant lost interest in the patent and stopped paying fees. If, however, in such a case, the applicant continues to pay fees, the INPI does exactly what it did under the old workflow, namely, let the application "freeze." As *Shadlen* puts it, "INPI is explicit in its strategy of 'completely rejecting' ANVISA's participation in patent examination, and as such has sought to minimize the latter's role de facto."[685]

Even though the GTI's workflow was introduced as a result of concerted work by the INPI, ANVISA, and other partners from the interministerial group, the conflict of attributions between ANVISA and the INPI remained unsolved since the INPI continued to sabotage ANVISA's work.

Considering that ANVISA's prior consent mechanism was introduced in the Cardoso administration (1996-2002) and its role in the patent proceedings was supported by the left administrations of Mr. Lula da Silva (2003-2010) and Ms. Rousseff (2011-2016), it is difficult to understand why the three of these Presidents passively watched the INPI's sabotage of ANVISA's work during the long period of 16 years. Such a political omission is peculiar since the President of the Republic not only has the power to issue decrees in order to regulate federal laws, but it is the only one who is entitled to lead the federal administration in accordance with Article 84, II of the BC. In

684. Article 40, sole paragraph LPI.
685. Shadlen (2011b), "The Political Contradictions of Incremental Innovations: Lessons from Pharmaceutical Patent Examination in Brazil," 39 *Pol. & Soc'y* 2, 152.

the case of ANVISA's prior consent, three Presidents of the Republic were not able to issue a decree to regulate Article 229-C, nor were they able to lead the federal administration by settling the unreasonable dispute between INPI and ANVISA in order to make effective their public health policy on access to medicines.

By not solving the conflict of attributions between ANVISA and the INPI in the sense of public health—as the Brazilian government did between 2001 and 2016 at the international forum—the three Brazilian Presidents showed a lack of leadership in the domestic arena. None of them were able to force the INPI to coordinate with health experts. This might be explained by the fact that the three mentioned Presidents governed in a coalition with conservative parties mostly aligned with a neoliberal agenda in which there is no place for a public health policy that would flexibilize patent rights.

2 *The 2017 Solution: ANVISA's Veto Power Comes to an End*

In March 2017—during the interim presidency of Mr. *Temer* (2016-2018), which assumed office in a coalition built by parties of the right spectrum, after the impeachment of Ms. *Rousseff*—ANVISA and the INPI announced that they had reached an agreement about how Article 229-C LPI should be implemented.[686] At this point, a political shift to the right was being implemented in the federal administration, which adopted a neoliberal agenda.

In April 2017, this agreement was formalized through an administration regulation signed by both agencies (*Portaria conjunta*).[687] In August 2017, ANVISA issued the RDC No. 168 in order to internally regulate the prior consent workflow in accordance with the agreement with the INPI.[688] According to these regulations, ANVISA will continue to examine pharmaceutical patents "in the light of public health."

However, the extent of its examination has been greatly reduced since ANVISA is only allowed to deny prior consent when a pharmaceutical product or process presents a "risk to health."[689] To be considered to present such a risk, a pharmaceutical product will have to contain or to result in a substance, the use of which is forbidden in Brazil.[690] In any other case where the patent is considered to be of interest for medicines policy within the SUS, ANVISA will continue to raise concerns against patentability,[691] but the INPI will no longer be obliged to act on ANVISA's advice. If the

686. Formenti (2017), "ANVISA e INPI chegam a Acordo sobre Patentes de Medicamentos," *O Estado de São Paulo*, March 15.
687. ANVISA/INPI (2017), Portaria conjunta ANVISA/ INPI No. 1, of April 12, 2017, DOU, Seção I, April 13, 2017, p. 63.
688. ANVISA (2017), Resolução da Diretoria Colegiada (RDC) ANVISA No. 168, of August 8, 2017, DOU, Seção I, August 10, 2017, p. 52.
689. ANVISA/INPI (2017), Portaria conjunta ANVISA/ INPI No.1-2017, Article 4.
690. *Ibid.*, Article 4, § 2. *See also* ANVISA (2017) RDC No. 168, of August 8, 2017.
691. *Ibid.*, Article 5.

Patent Office disagrees with ANVISA's view, it only has to explain why it sees the issue differently, appointing the reasons why the INPI does not agree with ANVISA's view.[692]

In practice, ANVISA no longer has any right of veto against the issue of pharmaceutical patents, but its voice will continue to be heard in all cases concerning pharmaceutical patents. ANVISA's right of veto will only exist in a case whereby an invention uses a substance that is forbidden in Brazil. In these cases, a "risk to health" will be present, and ANVISA may block the patent from being issued.

As one sees, the conflict of attributions between ANVISA and the INPI was settled in a few months after the interim President, Mr. *Temer,* had been put in office. This solution—which is incorrect as regards content, as it will be demonstrated in the next chapter—weakened ANVISA's prior consent mechanism and made the INPI stronger. This is coherent with the *Temer* administration, which was characterized by implementing neoliberal policies in a short time period, as demanded by the Brazilian and transnational financial elite.[693] Flexibilization of patent rights in favor of public health was, from this point, not more present in the agenda of the federal administration.

692. ANVISA/INPI (2017), Portaria conjunta ANVISA/ INPI No. 1-2017, Article 6 and ANVISA 2018), Orientação de Serviço No. 51/ DIARE/ANVISA, of July 5, 2018.
693. *See*, for instance, Souza (2019), "A Elite do Atraso—Da escravidão a Bolsonaro," p. 248.

CHAPTER 4

Integrating Pharmacological Superior Expertise in the Patent Examination for Public Health Policies Interests

A CRITIQUE OF THE 2017 SOLUTION

In the public health context of access to medicines, ANVISA's mission in its activity related to patents is to promote access to medicines for all, assuming that the drug in question, if marketed, would save lives, considering threats to health based on population health analysis. This is the sense and purpose of ANVISA's prior consent. Regarding this point, the 2017 Solution brought about one improvement by establishing that ANVISA should only examine pharmaceutical patents that are of interest to the public health system or relevance to pharmaceutical policies. Thereby, more pertinence to public health law was introduced in the patent examination. This is a positive development, but it is not enough to make ANVISA's prior consent an effective instrument for promoting access to medicines, in the sense of the Doha Declaration.

The shortcoming of the 2017 Solution is that it allows ANVISA to veto pharmaceutical patents only in the case where there is a risk to public health, taking in mind the concept of public health in the context of drug safety. This does not make sense because ANVISA's participation in the patent grant proceedings must not be seen in the public health context of drug safety (pharmaco-vigilance safety) but in the public health context of access to medicines (pharmaco-supply safety).

This mistake was already made in 2012 by the GTI when it created a new workflow of patent examination between ANVISA and the INPI, and the 2017 Solution repeated it.[1] As seen above, in 2012, the GTI concluded that a drug patent may be seen

1. Originally, the mistake was made by the AGU when it opined that ANVISA was not allowed to examine requirements of patentability because this function does not have pertinence with ANVISA's attributions (AGU, 2010—Parecer PGF/AE/337/2011).

as "contrary to public health" based merely on the fact that the invention uses a substance prohibited in Brazil. This is the case, for instance, for patents involving marijuana and other illegal drugs. Even if a patent might be refused on the grounds of "morality," denying prior consent on the grounds of such a prohibition is a mere moral judgment that has nothing to do with access to medicines or even with public health. ANVISA does not protect public health when it denies granting prior consent for an invention because it uses a prohibited drug. After all, an illegal drug used as a narcotic can also have a medical use, such as morphine and marijuana, for instance. If someone discovers that such a drug may have therapeutic efficacy, one could prohibit the patent grant for moral reasons, but not on the grounds of public health.

In the context of drug safety, ANVISA's mission is to check and to guarantee that drugs allowed to be marketed are safe enough for use by the population, after weighing up the potential risks and benefits associated with those drugs. As discussed above, "risk to public health" is neither related to the public health context of access to medicines nor to patents. As a result, it cannot be mixed with the question of drug access. Therefore, the issue of drug safety, the analysis of which is necessary for deciding whether the drug will be commercialized or not, has nothing to do with ANVISA's prior consent in the context of patent grant. In practice, ANVISA can deny prior consent for the patenting of a given pharmaceutical invention that is considered to be trivial ("me-too drugs"), and later, deny authorization to the marketing of this drug in Brazil as a generic drug if its producer was not able to demonstrate that the administration of the drug in the human body does not represent a risk to public health. If ANVISA denies prior consent, this does not mean that this drug will never be brought to the Brazilian market. Inversely, ANVISA can give prior consent for the patent grant, and later, in the context of sanitary vigilance, not authorize that this drug to be marketed in Brazil.

Consequently, the 2017 Solution did not interpret Article 229-C accurately. By reducing ANVISA's veto power to the grant of pharmaceutical patents in the situations where a "risk to public health" is present, as the 2017 decision did, it completely hollows out ANVISA's work; apart from that, such an analysis is de facto impossible to be done since, within patent grant proceedings, neither is data and studies concerning drug safety available nor are they object of the patent proceedings.[2]

B HOW ARTICLE 229-C LPI HAS BEEN INTERPRETED

ANVISA's participation in patent grant proceedings was hotly discussed from the outset. The question of how ANVISA should cooperate with the Patent Office in the granting of pharmaceutical patents was also differently understood by different parties. In the following, it will be summarized how the application of ANVISA's prior consent provision has been interpreted in Brazil.

2. In the same line *see Romandini* (2016), "Flexibilities under TRIPS: An Analysis of the Proposal for Reforming Brazilian Patent Law," 15 *J. Marshall Rev. Intell. Prop. L.*, 208.

I Patent Community's View: ANVISA as Controller of the Granting of Pipeline Patents

One interpretation of Article 229-C was made by the Brazilian Association of Intellectual Property (ABPI), an entity that represents the interests of the Brazilian patent community, composed of multinational industries based in Brazil and patent lawyers who mostly represent them. From the beginning, the ABPI supported the view that ANVISA should in no way examine matters concerning formal or substantive requirements of patentability since nothing in the Patent Law would authorize ANVISA to do so.[3] Moreover, ANVISA's analysis should be restricted to assessing whether a patent grant would be "harmful to public health," in the sense of Article 18 LPI.

Later, the ABPI supported the view that ANVISA's analysis should be restricted to the examination of pipeline patents instead of pharmaceutical patents in general. ANVISA's role would be to check whether the object of the pipeline application was commercialized in Brazil. This view was founded in the fact that the prior consent provision is situated in the last chapter of the law, called "transitional provisions."[4] For ABPI, this interpretation was necessary to make Article 229-C LPI compatible with Article 27.1 TRIPS, according to which all inventions which satisfy the substantive requirements of patentability should be patentable. An additional requirement that patenting of pharmaceutical inventions obtain "prior consent" from a third agency would create a fourth requisite of patentability applicable only to pharmaceutical inventions, which would, therefore, discriminate against such inventions.[5]

This interpretation—which was only supported by the multinational pharmaceutical industries based in Brazil and their Brazilian lawyers—is not correct. As demonstrated above,[6] there is no discrimination when a country, invoking the Doha Declaration, takes measures that are necessary to protect public health.

II ANVISA's Interpretation of Article 229-C LPI: Acting as an Ordinary Patent Division

From at least 2003 until April 2017, ANVISA checked the substantive requisites of patentability as if it were a Patent Division at the Patent Office. As seen in the empirical part, ANVISA used the criteria established by the Patent Law so that it examined whether an invention is new, has an inventive step and is commercially applicable. According to this interpretation, ANVISA is only authorized to make a patent examination following the LPI's requirements of patentability, without considering criteria other than those.

3. ABPI Resolução No. 16—Pedido de patente para produtos e processos farmacêuticos, of September 12, 2001.
4. ABPI Resolução No. 63—Alerta técnico da ANVISA, October 21, 2004.
5. Trigo de Souza (2008), "Should Brazil Allow Patents on Second Medical Uses?," 93 *Revista da ABPI*, 53-67.
6. *See* Chapter 2-D.

As seen in the empirical part of this work, ANVISA interpreted the requirements of novelty and inventiveness, in some cases (for instance, the cases involving a second medical indication) in a different manner the INPI did. The mere fact that ANVISA examined patent requirements a second time was often criticized by the opponents of ANVISA's prior consent as a "wasting of time." In their view, there would be no reason to redo a patent examination already done.[7] This view assumes the following points: (1) patent requirements can only be interpreted in one way. (2) If ANVISA concludes that the invention is new and has an inventive step, such as the INPI did, this means that ANVISA rightly worked, but its work of redoing the examination was useless since INPI did this work before. (3) If ANVISA concludes that a pharmaceutical invention does not fulfill the requirements of novelty or of having an inventive step, in opposition to INPI's conclusion, this means that ANVISA wrongly interpreted patent requirements, since only the INPI would have the authority to decide about the patent grant.

None of the three points above are justified. First of all, patent requirements can be interpreted in different ways, either lax or more rigorously. When a patent grant is revoked, either within patent opposition administrative proceedings or by a judicial court, this is as a rule based on a different evaluation of the criteria of novelty, inventiveness or commercial applicability. As seen above, WTO Members are free to interpret the requirements of patentability since the TRIPS Agreement does not define the requirements of novelty, inventiveness and commercial application.[8] As *Plomer* puts it, "it is well accepted that the absence of a uniform definition is one of the 'flexibilities' enjoyed by WTO Members to implement Article 27 in their national laws reflect their economic and social priorities."[9]

Second, ANVISA and this is the core argument, reexamined the patent requirements on the basis of its superior pharmacology expertise (or rather examined them prior to the INPI, according to the GTI's workflow). As clarified by *Figueira Barbosa*, this superior expertise is originated from its knowledge of the pharmaceuticals, which have more or less chance of entering the market. It should not be a surprise that ANVISA's interpretation of the patent requirements was, in some cases, different from INPI's interpretation. After all, the legislator did not create ANVISA's prior consent aiming that ANVISA will do the same that INPI does. The legislator wanted that ANVISA, based on its superior pharmacology expertise, makes a different interpretation of the patent's requirements, as a counterpart to INPI's patent-friendly view. ANVISA's mandate, according to Article 229-C, is authorizing or not the grant of a pharmaceutical patent. For doing it, it must do something different than the INPI does. If ANVISA's interpretation would never be different from INPI's interpretation, there would be no reason for ANVISA's work, which would be useless.

Third, the point that only the INPI would have the legal authority to decide on patents is also not justified since there is no hierarchy between ordinary laws in Brazil. Article 229-C LPI was introduced by an ordinary law that changed another older

7. This is, for instance, the position of *Raimundo*, INTERFARMA's representative.
8. *See* the Chapter 2—III—2.2.3, which examines the flexibilities of patent rights under the TRIPS Agreement.
9. Plomer (2019), "The EPO as a Patent Law-Maker in Europe," 25 *Eur. L. J.*, 68.

ordinary law. It gave ANVISA the veto power to authorize or not the grant of pharmaceutical patents. From the moment this law was approved, INPI had to share its authority to grant pharmaceutical patents with ANVISA. Furthermore, as stressed by *Basso*, INPI's competence for granting patents is not based on the Constitution, but on the ordinary law, so that there is no incompatibility in sharing the competence between INPI and ANVISA.[10] On the other hand, the fact that ANVISA does the examination does not violate the WTO-Law. This is so because Article 27 TRIPS does not determine that patent examination must be carried by a Patent Office. Therefore, each WTO Member has the discretion to decide how the examination process is organized.

Until the 2017 Solution, ANVISA maintained that its examination of patent applications concerning pharmaceutical inventions would avoid the issue of unsuitable patents. In this way, ANVISA indirectly protects public health by improving access to medicines. Some judgments also supported this view.[11]

III ANVISA as an Instance of "Public Health" Within the Meaning of Article 18, I LPI (2017 Solution)

Another view present in the Brazilian literature[12] and case law[13] is that ANVISA should not act as a pure patent revision department but as a "public health instance" in the sense of Article 18 LPI. The solution agreed in 2017 between ANVISA and INPI followed this view, as the inter-ministerial group charged with finding a solution to the conflict between ANVISA and the INPI in 2012 also did. According to this view, ANVISA should make its examination using criteria other than those used by the Patent Office for its review. In other words, ANVISA must use "criteria of public health" to make its decision on the prior consent to a patent grant. Those who have this view justify ANVISA's veto when a patent "contrary to public health" should be prohibited, as stated in Article 18(I) LPI. This is the case when the invention itself, instead of the patent effect, is harmful to public health (pharmaco-vigilance safety).

This view assumes that ANVISA's participation in the patent grant proceedings is only justified if its objective is the protection of public health, similar to what is ordinarily considered to be the role of the National Health Surveillance Agency, that is: verifying whether or not the benefits of a new drug outweigh its risks. If the result is positive, the new drug is approved to be marketed; if the result is negative, the new drug does not receive approval to be marketed.

10. Basso (2008), "Intervention of Health Authorities in Patent Examination: the Brazilian Practice of Prior Consent," in: Casella et. al. (eds.), *Direito Internacional, Humanismo e Globalidade—Guido Fernando Silva Soares—Amicorum Discipulorum Liber*, Ed. Atlas, São Paulo, p. 77.
11. For instance, 13ª Vara Federal Rio de Janeiro, Pro Genericos vs. AstraZeneca AB and INPI, Case Number 00802461-54.2011.4.02.5101, *Caderno Judicial JFRJ*, June 10, 2015, pp. 387-410.
12. Tojal/Pessôa (2008), "A Anuência Prévia na Concessão de Patentes de Medicamentos e a Regulação Econômica da Indústria Farmacêutica," 8 *RDISAN*, 148-165.
13. For instance, TRF-1, Apelação Cível No. 2009.34.00937369-9/DF, Judgment September 22, 2014.

Assuming that ANVISA's participation in patent proceedings is necessary to expand access to medicines, it is essential to note that "protecting public health" within patent proceedings cannot and should not be understood as a question bound to the issue of pharmaco-vigilance safety. Instead, its participation is based on the need to provide pharmaco-supply safety.

Believing that ANVISA should base its prior consent on criteria related to pharmaco-vigilance safety is a common mistake found both in the literature and case law in Brazil. *Fernandes de Moura* is one of the few voices in the Brazilian literature that rejects this interpretation for the reason that it would make ANVISA's role useless in the patent proceedings.[14] Instead, he suggests that ANVISA continues to examine requirements of patentability in the light of public health while highlighting the impact of the granting of patents on the public health system. At the same time, he thinks that ANVISA's role should be limited to helping the INPI, to whom ANVISA should submit its analysis without having the last word on the possibility of patenting pharmaceuticals.

Some judicial rulings forced ANVISA to grant prior consent, just because ANVISA had not justified its refusal to grant prior consent based on "harm to public health" in the context of pharmaco-vigilance safety.[15] These rulings are not accurate because they do not distinguish between the case of "harm to public health" caused by limitations to drug access (such as patents) and the case of "harm to public health" caused by a lack of drug safety. In the first case, ANVISA's task is to expand access to drugs by limiting the granting of patents (pharmaco-supply safety), while in the second case, ANVISA's task is to prevent a drug from going on the market (pharmaco-vigilance safety).

ANVISA's prior consent, however, must be understood in the context of the Doha Declaration on the TRIPS Agreement and Public Health. It is a flexible instrument of patent rights, the objective of which is to deal with grave problems of public health existing in developing countries. In that context, the term "public health" cannot be understood as having any connection with drug safety, as Article 1 of the Declaration shows when it states that:

> We recognize the gravity of the public health problems afflicting many developing and least-developed countries, especially those resulting from HIV/AIDS, tuberculosis, malaria, and other epidemics.

More explicitly, Article 4 of the Doha Declaration states that "the TRIPS Agreement can and should be interpreted in a manner supportive of WTO Members' *right to protect public health, and, in particular, to promote access to medicines for all.*"

Notwithstanding, the 2017 Decision agreed by INPI and ANVISA consolidated this mistake by stating that ANVISA is only allowed to exercise its veto power to a pharmaceutical patent grant if a "risk to health"—considering this a risk related to drug safety—is present.

---

14. Fernandes de Moura (2011), "Patentes de Medicamentos e a Discussão a Respeito do Artigo 229-C da Lei 9.279/96," XIV *Revista CEJ* 53, 80-87. *See also* Borges Barbosa (2014), *Anuência Prévia pela ANVISA: Só para Proteger a Saúde Pública?*, PIDCC, Aracaju, Ano III, Ed. 7, pp. 50-107.
15. This was, for instance, the case of the drug Gleevec.

C THE AUTHOR'S VIEWPOINT

I Examination of the Patentability's Requirements as the Chore of ANVISA's Prior Consent

As demonstrated in the empirical part of this work, ANVISA examined both substantive requirements of patentability, such as novelty, inventiveness and commercial application, as well as formal conditions of patentability, such as the presence of sufficient description of the invention. Furthermore, ANVISA evaluated whether the invention for which the patent was requested was unpatentable under the Brazilian patent law.

While in most cases, ANVISA agreed to patent grant following INPI's report, in some cases, ANVISA did not agree with the grant of the patent. As showed in the empirical part, ANVISA justified its disagreement on the following points:

(1) the requirement of novelty was interpreted in a more rigorous way than the INPI did;[16]
(2) some patent requests were interpreted as consisting of therapeutic and surgical methods, which are not patentable under the Brazilian Patent Law;[17]
(3) the requirement of inventive step was interpreted in a more rigorous way than the INPI did;[18]
(4) the description of the invention contained in the patent request was considered not to be sufficient for making a person skilled in the art to reproduce the invention;[19]
(5) the so-called selection inventions were interpreted as unpatentable since they were known before broadly disclosed, and as a result, they do not satisfy the requirement of novelty; and[20]
(6) second or further medical uses of a known substance were considered to be unpatentable; therefore, it interpreted them as being mere discoveries, which are not patentable under the Brazilian patent law.[21]

The empirical work shows that while ANVISA, in theory, did the same work as the INPI, it did so differently that the INPI refused to adopt ANVISA's view. While ANVISA checked the same requirements of patentability as the INPI, it differently interpreted the requirements of patentability.

16. *See* Chapter 3-D-III-2.1.2.
17. *See* Chapter 3-D-III-2.1.3.
18. *See* Chapter 3-D-III-2.1.4.
19. *See* Chapter 3-D-III-2.1.5.
20. *See* Chapter 3-D-III-2.1.6.
21. *See* Chapter 3 -D-III-2.1.7.

II What Does Differ ANVISA's Report from the INPI's and What Is the Use of It?

1 *Finding the Right Balance Between Innovation Policy and Health Policy*

The existence of conflicting views about the patentability of pharmaceutical inventions between ANVISA and the INPI reflects the conflict between two federal bodies charged with executing different policies. While the INPI is the federal body charged with executing a patent policy, ANVISA—as a body linked to the Ministry of Health—is primarily concerned with the negative impact that patents can have on drug access since patents restrict access by making drugs more expensive.

ANVISA's prior consent's opponents and supporters often tend to have polarized views, which can be summarized in the following contrapositive sentences: *no patents mean more access/fewer patents mean more access/more patents mean more innovation.* As is known, this contraposition is one-dimensional. Patents serve public interest in technological development, which also includes the field of health. It is wished that access to medicines, in general, will be promoted, which also includes access to new medicines. Notwithstanding, whether patents serve the public interest or not will depend on the right tailoring of patent rights since too much patent protection may harm the public interest, considering the interests of developing countries. As *Caroll* puts it, "to promote progress, intellectual property law must strike a balance, providing sufficient incentives to innovation without unduly stifling the efforts of follow-on innovators or the liberties of end-users."[22] Therefore, patent rights must be limited.

In the case of ANVISA's and INPI's patent examination, the pivotal question is how the balance among public health policy, patent policy, and industrial policy is to be achieved. Like other economies of the world, Brazil has to take policy decisions considering different public interests, having to weigh what interest in which case should predominate. For emerging or developing economies, like Brazil, it is important both to achieve industrial catch up and, at the same time, guarantee drug access to their populations.

As seen above, the requirements of patentability can be differently interpreted, such as ANVISA and INPI did. One can interpret the novelty and the inventiveness requirements in a broader or at a narrower way since neither the TRIPS Agreement nor the Brazilian LPI determines how such requirements are to be interpreted. WTO Members are free to decide how they will deal with the interpretation of these categories. In doing that, they may take different approaches. The most common approach is the one taken by the Members of the EPC; these countries leave these categories open for the interpretation of their patent offices. Other countries, like India, determine by law how novelty is to be interpreted in the case of pharmaceutical

22. Carroll (2009), "One Size Does Not Fit All: a Framework for Tailoring Intellectual Property Rights," 70 *Ohio St. L. J.* 6, 1368.

inventions, which is binding for the patent examiner.[23] The Brazilian approach is the third one since the Brazilian patent law leaves the interpretation of the patent requirements to both the Patent Office (INPI) and the National Health Surveillance Agency (ANVISA), which obliges that, at the end of the day, the grant of a pharmaceutical patent takes into consideration both reasons of innovation policy and reasons of public health policies, such as the question of access to drugs. This makes the grant of a pharmaceutical patent a complex administrative act.

Why had the Brazilian legislator chosen such a complex system? If only the question of access to drugs were important for Brazil, the patent law could have determined that the requirements of novelty and inventive step are *always* to be interpreted with rigidity. At the same token, the legislator could expressly have prohibited both "selection patents" or patents on second medical uses. In this situation, INPI would have to apply the law and deny patent in those requests. Such a global solution, however, seemed not to be desired for the legislator, considering the complexities of the Brazilian economy and the different interests and demands of its distinct sectors.

The legislator, when integrating ANVISA in the patent proceedings, preferred a "tailored solution" instead of a "global solution" regarding pharmaceutical patents. Therefore, instead of imposing INPI, the duty to interpret the requirements of patentability rigidly, it gave ANVISA the competence to veto (or not) the pharmaceutical patent after having assessed the requirements of patentability in the concrete case. For doing that, ANVISA must assess whether the pharmaceutical patent, if granted, would have a negative impact on drug access, considering the priorities of the Brazilian national health system (SUS).

By introducing ANVISA in the patent grant proceedings, the Brazilian national legislator gave ANVISA the power to decide in which cases the right to affordable medicines, when in conflict with the right to obtain pharmaceutical patents, will prevail, under the circumstances of the concrete case. This is how Brazil implements the Doha Declaration on the TRIPS Agreement and Public Health.

2 *Pharmacological Expert Knowledge*

A second differential in the patent examination made by ANVISA in comparison to INPI's examination is the fact that it is conducted by people who have expert knowledge regarding pharmaceuticals and pharmaceutical corporations. This pharmacological expert knowledge is different from a mere chemical expert knowledge since it brings an "impact sensibility," which affects the interpretation of the patent requirements.

23. The Indian patent law excludes patentability of new forms of known substances unless this new form results in the enhancement of the known efficacy of that substance. Furthermore, it created a legal fiction whereby "salts, esters, ethers, polymorphs, metabolites, pure form, particle size isomers, mixtures of isomers, complexes, combination and other derivatives of known substances shall be considered to be the same substance." For a comprehensive study of the Indian case, *see* Chatterjee (2019), *Evergreening—Voraussetzungen der Patentfähigkeit im deutschen, europäischen und indischen Patentrecht*, Nomos, Baden-Baden.

As evidenced in the empirical part of this work, this impact knowledge brings a different stance on the assessment of the patent requirements ("novelty," "inventive step," "disclosure," "second medical indication"). This impact-related knowledge informs the evaluation of patentability requirements, which are not simple technical test steps, but normative categories. As *Godt* explained, referring to *Henk van den Belt's* research, patentability's requirements are not clear-cut requirements but general normative terms open to interpretation.[24] In the same line, *Plomer* wrote that the patentability requirements are not "pure technical requirements but hybrid criteria which require an evaluation of the technical aspects of the claim and the application of a legal threshold which must be met for the patent to be granted."[25]

3 *INPI Versus ANVISA: A Conflict Within the Patent Community?*

3.1 *The Conception of "Epistemic Community" and "Legal Epistemic Community"*

According to the conception provided by *Haas*, "an epistemic community is a network of professionals with recognized expertise and competence in a particular domain and an authoritative claim to policy-relevant knowledge within that domain or issue-area."[26] In consonance to his definition, an epistemic community is built by professionals which have in common the following distinctions: (1) they share a set of normative and principled beliefs; (2) they share causal beliefs; (3) they share notions of validity; and (4) they share a common policy enterprise.

Drahos and van Waarden used the *Haas* theory of the "epistemic community" to characterize a community of lawyers, which they identified as a "special epistemic community." According to *Drahos and van Waarden*, a "legal epistemic community" is different from other expert communities because lawyers "are strongly institutionalized politically and at the front of the policy-making."[27] Due to the role lawyers play in society, the community also has interests which may have consequences for the development of the law and the profession.

Schneider transposed the definition of epistemic communities developed by *Haas* in her analysis of the European patent system and concluded that the epistemic patent community—composed both by patent lawyers, natural scientists, and engineers with an additional legal qualification—fulfills the characteristics set out in the definition of Haas in the following way:

24. Godt (2007b), *Eigentum an Information—Patentschutz und allgemeine Eigentumstheorie am Beispiel genetischer Information*, Mohr Siebeck, Tübingen, p. 131.
25. Plomer (2019), "The EPO as a Patent Law-Maker in Europe," 25 *Eur. L. J.*, 65.
26. Haas (1992), "Introduction: Epistemic Communities and International Policy Coordination," 46 *Int'l Org.* (1), 3.
27. Drahos/van Waarden (2002), "Courts and (Epistemic) Communities in the Convergence of Competition Policy," 9 *J. Eur. Pub. Pol'y* 6, 930.

(1) The normative and principled beliefs shared by the patent community are the dogmas of patent law as follows: (a) technological neutrality, (b) innovations-friendliness, (c) uniformity ("one size fits all"), and (d) the existence of a correlation between the quantity of patents granted and the innovation capacity of a country.[28]

(2) The causal beliefs shared by the patent community are related to the dogmas mentioned above. According to *Schneider*'s critique, it primarily consists of the assumption that the patent law contributes all the time positively to the development of technology and the innovation capacity of a country.[29]

Regarding the peculiarities of the patent community, because it is a legal community, *Schneider* highlights the fact that patent lawyers represent their clients—since representation is essentially the main occupation of attorneys—and that this representation has consequences in the way that patent attorneys see patent law, considering their own interests.[30] The way patent attorneys use to interpret requirements of patentability coincides with the most favorable interpretation of patent law for patent applicants. Not coincidently, the dogmas of patent law, especially the principle of neutrality of technologies, are also supported by multinational pharmaceutical companies.[31]

Finally, *Schneider* accentuates that the experts that are part of the patent epistemic community see themselves as the ones who have a monopoly on interpreting patent law. Consequently, the patent community is "hermetically closed" for other disciplines, other branches of law or perspectives, where this closeness is apparent since the community admits the entrance of non-experts if they share the same view of patent law supported by the community, such as, for instance, patent applicants do.[32] Another peculiarity of the patent legal community is its increasing internationalization, which has been not only pushed on since the TRIPS Agreement but also by agreements of cooperation among patent offices in the world.

Godt, finally, adds that professionals of an epistemic legal community, in contrast with scientists, "are expected to find consensus," which exacerbates the conflict when they are in debate with experts of other branches.[33]

28. Schneider (2010), "Das Europäische Patentsystem—Wandel von Governance durch Parlamente und Zivilgesellschaft," pp. 194-197.
29. *Ibid.*, pp. 197-198.
30. *Ibid.*, pp. 199-203.
31. See, for instance, Novartis (2017), "Novartis Position on Intellectual Property," p. 2.
32. Schneider (2010), "Das Europäische Patentsystem—Wandel von Governance durch Parlamente und Zivilgesellschaft," p. 217.
33. Godt (2016), "Experts and Politics in Patent Policy: The Final Report of the Expert Group on the Development and Implications of Patent Law in the Field of Biotechnology and Genetic Engineering of the European Commission, 17 May 2016," *IIC* 47, 976-977.

3.2 *The Conflict INPI Versus ANVISA as a Conflict Between Two Different Patent Communities*

In Brazil, it is possible to identify two different patent communities. The first Brazilian patent community is primarily composed of patent attorneys and professionals of the natural sciences who work for law firms that represent multinational companies, their staff of experts, these companies themselves, the ABPI, as well INPI's patent examiners. This patent community, which is patent-friendly, does not differ from the classical western community, as described by *Schneider*. However, differently than in Europe, the pharmaceutical industry's view is overrepresented in the Brazilian legal specialized literature. *Heath*, a Member of the EPO's Board of Appeals, when visiting Brazil in 2007, was surprised because he did not find in the Brazilian patent-specialized literature any commentaries to the LPI other than the one written and published by the law firm *Dannemann Siemsen*, whose content often reflects biased perspectives in benefit of patent owners, which are the clientele of this law firm.[34] As typical for such an epistemic community, their members see ANVISA's participation in the patent grant proceedings as a "foreign body," which the patent system should expel. They see themselves as the only ones that are legitimate to interpret patent law and do not accept other perspectives.

The second Brazilian patent community sees intellectual property more critically and is composed of the following experts: (1) public health physicians (*médicos sanitaristas*); (2) economists, mostly professors or civil servants concerned with the Brazilian economic development who tend to support the Brazilian patent policy existing before the TRIPS Agreement; (3) researchers in the field of public health, chemistry, biology, and pharmacy who work for public organizations, mostly public pharma laboratories; (4) patent lawyers who represent national companies, especially pharmaceutical companies; (5) associations representing interests of those national industries; (6) ANVISA's patent examiners; and (7) NGO's concerned with the question of drug access.

3.3 *Consequences*

As seen above, INPI and ANVISA are not part of the same "epistemic patent community."

As the results of the empirical analysis showed, such affiliation plays a role in the way INPI and ANVISA interpret the requirements of patentability: while the INPI makes mostly a pro-patent examination, ANVISA's interpretation of the requirements of patentability is mostly pro-patient.

34. Heath (2007), "Os limites dos direitos patentários em termos temporais, geográficos e de conteúdo," in: Beas Rodrigues/Polido, *Propriedade Intelectual—Novos Paradigmas Internacionais, Conflitos e Desafios*, Rio de Janeiro, Elsevier, p. 19. By now, other Commentaries to the LPI were published, such as, for instance, the one written by *Santa Cruz/Guterres* (2016) and *Borges Barbosa/Borges Barbosa* (2018).

As shown by *Schneider*, patent law should not be interpreted alone by a small community, the interests of which are mostly coincident with the interests of the patent applicants.[35] Other actors must take part in the patent proceedings in order to make it more democratic. The Brazilian system of integrating the National Health Surveillance Agency ANVISA in the patent grant proceedings brings additional expert knowledge to the assessment of patent law. This is important for the interpretation of the patentability requirements.

It would be naïve to say that checking patentability requirements is just "technical." In the case of ANVISA's prior consent, we see interpretation through the lenses of a developing country with the specificities of Brazil, that is, a country with both big national private laboratories and state-owned laboratories, the objective of which is the public production for covering national needs.

4 *The Regulatory Function of Patents*

As written by *Godt*, with the TRIPS Agreement, a regulatory understanding of the patent protection became more accepted.[36] According to her analysis, TRIPS did more than simply set a minimum standard for intellectual property protection. While TRIPS raised worldwide the level of patent protection in the sense of the developed countries, it also recognized a minimum standard of national regulatory sovereignty. Thereby, the TRIPS Agreement obliges its Member States to coordinate their patent policy with protection policies in the field of health, environment and national development. *Godt* observes furthermore that patents currently cannot more be seen as mere incentives to invent, but rather as a condition for the exchange of information.[37] According to her, this opening of patent law for economic regulation also means that patent law must be opened for social regulation.

Eisenberg, when analyzing biopharmaceutical innovations, saw a necessity of recognizing that the role of patents in the innovation process is changing due to the interaction of the patent system with other legal regulations of drugs.[38] Due to that, she suggested already in 2001 that the FDA, instead of the PTO, should rather be responsible for granting patent rights to pharmaceutical inventions, with the following words:

> Although this functional allocation marks a departure from tradition and arguably involves the FDA in economic regulation lying outside its core scientific competence, there is some logic to using FDA regulation rather than patents to confer market exclusivity. The pharmaceutical industry's need for market exclusivity is driven in part by the costs of regulatory burdens that do not apply to innovation in other industries. The Hatchman-Waxman Act attempts to adjust the patent term for pharmaceutical inventions to account for this regulatory burden, but it

35. Schneider (2010), "Das Europäische Patentsystem—Wandel von Governance durch Parlamente und Zivilgesellschaft," pp. 666-668.
36. Godt (2007b), *Eigentum an Information*, p. 562.
37. *Ibid.*, p. 446.
38. Eisenberg (2001), "The Shifting Functional Balance of Patents and Drug Regulation," 19 *Health Aff.* 4, 121.

> necessarily involves the FDA alongside the PTO in administering these provisions and it might be simpler and more elegant to concentrate industry-specific rules in the agency that is specialized in the oversight of the pharmaceutical industry.[39]

When the Brazilian legislator created ANVISA's prior consent mechanism, it wanted to regulate the impact of the post TRIPS intellectual property system in the field of drug access in order to find a balance.

In theory, accepting the premise that patents are justified because they are an important instrument of fostering innovation and protecting investments does not imply that all kinds of innovations should be promoted in the same way since what is needed is a balance among patent protection and other more important social goods, such as public health interests in the case of drug access. However, this premise is not simply transportable for developing countries whose economies are not based on high technological products. No country is obliged to foster all kinds of innovations, irrespective of its degree of industrial development. Each country is free, for instance, to foster incremental or radical innovations or to build a patent system where patents are easier or more difficult to obtain, following its policy goals. In other words, each country is free to decide whether it wants to foster "weak" or "strong" patents, "trivial" or "meaningful" patents, and so on. Decisions about patent policy for individual countries are to be made by themselves. As reported in this work, in the field of pharmaceuticals, the Brazilian patent law has decided in favor of a patent policy where trivial patents are hampered, provided that the public health system would be disproportionally affected by a possible patent.

In this sense, the Brazilian prior consent mechanism does not make patents unavailable for pharmaceuticals; it rather prevents the rewarding of the patent incentive to innovations that are merely "trivial" or to inventions that are otherwise harmful to the public interest, in the sense of the Doha Declaration. Therefore, Brazilian ANVISA's prior consent mechanism is a regulatory mechanism to reduce the impact of the new intellectual property regime imposed by TRIPS, under the perspective of an emerging economy which, in general, is not able to develop innovative medicines by itself.

III Conclusion: ANVISA's Prior Consent as a "Raising the Bar" Reform to the Patentability of Pharmaceutical Inventions in Benefit of Access Rights

As evidenced in the empirical analysis, ANVISA's examination raised the bar to patentability requirements, while the INPI used to apply lower standards to the requirements of patentability. ANVISA infused a different stock of expert knowledge regarding pharmaceutical markets. Consequently, when analyzing the same requirements of patentability, ANVISA and INPI came to different conclusions.

ANVISA's participation in the patent examination of pharmaceutical inventions, whilst protecting public health, at the same time also regulates patent quality. If an

39. *Ibid.*, p. 123.

ANVISA officer examines the patentability of a pharmaceutical invention, the examination of such patents will be more accurate than others. As *Hilty* puts it when discussing the problem of patent quality in Europe, "applications that are likely to incur more social costs should be examined more accurately than others."[40]

ANVISA's prior consent is a flexibility to the system patent protection in the sense of the Doha Declaration. In comparison with compulsory licenses, it is a preventative mechanism, the advantage of which is that it avoids the high political and economic costs of removing patents that have already been granted. Nevertheless, ANVISA's prior consent is also an instrument for the regulation of patent quality. As *Drahos* puts it, "it links patentability criteria in the area of pharmaceuticals to the goal of welfare-enhancing innovation in the health sector."[41]

On the other hand, as seen in the empirical part of this work, ANVISA, making use of its expert knowledge in pharmaceuticals, made a patent examination of high quality. It was a more rigid examination of the patentability requirements, which is a question of interpretation. Therefore, ANVISA's patent examination is neither arbitrary nor considers criteria other than the standard requirements of patentability.

As seen above, in practice, the INPI undermined ANVISA's prior consent mechanism. By doing so, it hindered that ANVISA's patient-friendlier interpretation of the requirements of patentability had prevailed. Had the prior consent mechanism been successful, it would have resulted in quantitatively fewer pharmaceutical patents.

Summing up: This "raised bar" to standard patentability requirements is in line with Brazil's legitimate policy under the flexibilities of the TRIPS Agreements. As demonstrated above, this minus to patent availability is TRIPS-conform.

The result is a different balance decision. This is what the legislator aimed at when introduced ANVISA's participation in the patent proceedings. It was the government's failure of leadership to enforce this legislative intent vis-à-vis INPI that hindered this instrument from functioning.

40. Hilty (2009), "The Role of Patent Quality in Europe," in: Drexl et al. (eds.), *Technology and Competition, Technologie et Concurrence—Contribution in Honour of Hans Ullrich*, Larciers, Bruxelles, p. 105.
41. Drahos (2008), "'Trust Me': Patent Offices in Developing Countries," 34 *Am. J. L. & Med.*, 151, 169-170.

CHAPTER 5

Lessons for the Future

One of the aims of this work was to assess whether ANVISA's prior consent violates Article 27.1 TRIPS Agreement. The legal analysis carried out (Chapter 2: D) demonstrated that this is not the case. The differential treatment for pharmaceutical inventions is a justified measure in a double sense. First, it reacts to the different functioning of patents in markets of emerging economies. Second, it reacts to the specific needs of an emerging country with regard to protecting public health: ANVISA's prior consent represents a bona fide exception, in light of Articles 7 and 8 of the TRIPS Agreement and reinforced by the Doha Declaration, as part of an effort to balance conflicting interests of the public health and patent policy.

Another aim of this work was to verify how ANVISA, in practice, used its veto power in the granting of pharmaceutical patents. This was done by examining 147 reports ANVISA issued as a basis for its decisions. According to the results of the empirical study carried out (Chapter 3: D), ANVISA in the first period (2003-2012) checked the same constituent elements for qualifying for a patent that patent offices around the world ordinarily do, namely, the presence of novelty, inventive step and industrial applicability. From 2012 to 2016, ANVISA also checked whether the patent, if granted, would represent a "risk to health." However, ANVISA interpreted "risk to health" as a requirement for drug safety, which takes place within pharmacovigilance proceedings. From 2017 until the present, ANVISA has only been authorized to deny prior consent to patent grant on the grounds of drug safety. In the cases where the invention for which the patent was filed is of interest for the public health system SUS, ANVISA checks the ordinary conditions of patentability, based on which it recommends to INPI to grant or to deny the patent.

While ANVISA, at first sight, did the same work as the INPI (Chapter 4: C-II.1), it did it differently so that the INPI refused to adopt ANVISA's view. However, while ANVISA examined the same requirements of patentability as the INPI, on second sight, they performed their task in a very different manner, recurring to a different body of knowledge.

ANVISA did so due to its pharmaceutical expert knowledge, which brought an "impact sensibility" to the patent examination so that the negative impact of patent rights on access to medicines can be mitigated (Chapter 4: C-II.2). This opens the patent law for a perspective different than the one supported by the chemically narrowed perspective of the classical patent community to which the INPI belongs (Chapter 4: C-II-3) and, therefore, gives it more legitimacy. Consequently, the present thesis has shown that ANVISA's participation in the patent proceedings is an example of modern horizontal policy integration, incorporating public health policy into an industrial policy decision.

Notwithstanding, the implementation of ANVISA's prior consent did not meet the early expectations. The Agency was blocked by a lack of internal consensus between government agencies. At that time, the federal government consisted of a coalition of progressive and conservative parties (Chapter 3: B-C). In the international arena, the Ministry of Foreign Affairs supported ANVISA's prior consent, invoking the TRIPS Agreement and the Doha Declaration for legitimating it. Domestically, the situation was different. While the Ministry of Development, Industry, and Commerce doubted that ANVISA's prior consent was an adequate measure for promoting innovation in Brazil, the Ministry of Health advocated for its validity. The Ministry of Health did so, pressured by the immense costs caused, on the one hand, by the constitutional duty to distribute essential and strategic medicines for all, and on the other hand, by the interference of the courts, which forced the government to buy expensive medicines not considered to be essential or strategic by its health experts (Chapter 3: A-IV.2).

Outside the federal administration, ANVISA's prior consent was opposed as a legal instrument by both representatives of the multinational pharmaceutical companies and by the domestic sector, which used to support liberal market economies (Chapter 3: B-III). The importance of the legal discussion around the alleged incompatibility of Article 229-C LPI with the TRIPS Agreement has been overstated since it was dominated by the classical patent community, the view of which was, in part, followed by the Brazilian courts (Chapter 3: C-IV). Influenced by the discussion on the supposed "fourth hurdle" to patentability, ANVISA reacted defensively by limiting itself to assess the three standard requirements of patentability.

All of this, along with the INPI's boycott and successive failure of the executive branch in forcing the INPI to change its practices (Chapter 3: D-IV), weakened ANVISA's prior consent mechanism. Its implementation, which hesitatingly begun, developed in an unassertive way. As a result, ANVISA missed the opportunity to define the task entrusted to the agency. Instead of doing its "homework" as ministerial administration, which is to program its task by administrative guidelines, it justified the lack of prior consent on grounds like trivial inventions, second medical indication or evergreening (Chapter 3-D-I-.2.1.). By doing so, ANVISA simply reiterated the critical patent debate which unfolded at the same time in the industrial countries and failed to develop a model for patent examination in emerging economies.

With the 2017 solution, ANVISA's right to veto the patent grant was completely emptied since it is only allowed to deny prior consent in the cases where a "risk to health" in the sense of pharmacovigilance safety is present. This, however, does not have anything to do with the right to affordable drugs and with intellectual property questions since the later ones are related to pharmaco-supply safety (Chapter 4: A).

For making ANVISA's prior consent effective in the future, the 2017 Solution must be abrogated. Instead of that, a new internal regulation should replace it to establish, in the first place, that ANVISA's decision must be binding to INPI in all cases. Second, it should explain that what ANVISA checks is not drug safety (pharmacovigilance safety) but drug access (pharmaco-supply safety).

In addition, it is necessary that the requirement of "public health" in the sense it has in pharmacovigilance, will be removed from ANVISA's prior consent mechanism and replaced by a requirement to enhance drug access since ANVISA's participation at the patent grant proceedings was introduced as a measure for safeguarding access to affordable drugs for all, in the sense of the Doha Declaration. The political goal of "secure access" can be programmed by an economic extrapolation, which rests on complementary expert knowledge about pharmaceutical markets in Brazil. Since this is a projection, the decision must rest on the modeling of the economic discipline. This take would follow the "more economic approach" in interpreting antitrust laws.[1]

However, the drug safety-approach is not the only problem of the current Brazilian practice of ANVISA's prior consent. Although ANVISA's examination of the standard patentability requirements is compatible with Article 27.1 TRIPS, the analysis of the Brazilian experience reveals that such an approach was not effective in dealing with the difficult task of balancing patent rights with the right of access to affordable medicines. Therefore, the question is not whether ANVISA's prior consent is in conformity with the TRIPS Agreement, but the efficiency of the Brazilian mechanism in granting drug access.

Due to its expert knowledge about pharmaceuticals and the pharmaceutical market, ANVISA did a good job of reassessing the requirements of patentability. However, by limiting its role in accessing requirements of patentability, ANVISA's examination was predominantly perceived as an invasion of INPI's competencies, which stimulated rivalry between both agencies. This could have been avoided if the Ministry of Health had interpreted Article 229-C LPI under the premise that ANVISA's role was to guarantee "pharmaco-supply safety" instead of "pharmacovigilance safety."

This interpretation of Article 229-C LPI should be oriented by the possible effects that a pharmaceutical patent, if granted, would produce in the Brazilian public health system. Ideally, ANVISA would analyze the possible effects of the patent grant in the individual case, in cooperation with economists, who would make prognoses regarding the patent impact at the Ministry of Health's budget. For carrying out this examination, ANVISA could develop a "more economic approach" in the sense that this idea has in European competition law. Concretely, ANVISA would have to verify

1. *See*, for example, Drexl (2008), "Is There a 'More Economic Approach' to Intellectual Property and Competition Law?", in: Drexl (ed.), *Research Handbook on Intellectual Property and Competition Law*, Edward Elgar, Cheltenham, UK; Northampton, MA, pp. 27-53; Lademann (2011), "Zur Methodologie des more economic approach im Kartellrecht," in: Bechthold et al. (eds.), *Recht, Ordnung und Wettbewerb—Festschrift zum 70. Geburtstag von Werhard Möschel*, Baden-Baden, pp. 381-394.

whether the patent grant would signify a "threat to the national supply of essential or strategic medicines."

Therefore, ANVISA's examination would be based on its expert knowledge about drugs and the pharmaceutical sector in coordination with economists of the Ministry of Health. Based on the results of this examination, ANVISA would give (or not) prior consent to patent grant.

On this line, ANVISA's prior consent should be seen as a flexibility instrument of patent rights, in the sense that it serves to protect public health and to promote access to medicines for all, in the spirit of the Doha Declaration on the TRIPS Agreement and Public Health, by way of bringing in a special body of extra specialists' knowledge.

Notwithstanding the shortcomings observed in the Brazilian experience of prior consent, given the difficulties in implementing that system, the involvement of other public authorities in patent examination is an idea that offers itself to be followed by other emerging countries to enhance access to life-saving drugs.

By introducing a health authority to decide about the patentability of drugs important for the public health system of an emerging country, Brazil puts in practice the idea of regulatory patent law since its patent policy institutions (ANVISA and INPI) consider and weigh conflicting interests. By doing so, it secures a proper balance of interests in the patent system.

Bibliography

Abbott, Frederick M. (1989), "Protecting First World Assets in the Third World: Intellectual Property Negotiations in the GATT", 22 *Vanderbilt Journal of Transnational Law*, 689-745.

Abbott, Frederick M. (2002a), *WTO TRIPS Agreement and its Implications for Access to Medicines in Developing Countries*, Study Paper 2a, United Kingdom Commission on Intellectual Property Rights, 2002, available at https://papers.ssrn.com/sol3/papers.cfm?abstract_id=1924420 (last visited on August 31, 2020).

Abbott, Frederick M. (2002b), "The Doha Declaration on the TRIPS Agreement and Public Health: Lighting a Dark Corner at the WTO", 5 *Journal of International Economic Law*, 469-505.

Abbott, Frederick M. (2002c), *Compulsory Licensing for Public Health Needs: The TRIPS Agenda at the WTO after the Doha Declaration on Public Health*, Quaker United Nations Office (Geneva) (QUNO), Occasional Paper 9, February 2002, available at https://papers.ssrn.com/sol3/papers.cfm?abstract_id=1977304 (last visited on August 310, 2018).

Abbott, Frederick M. (2004), The Doha Declaration on the TRIPS Agreement and Public Health and the Contradictory Trend in Bilateral and Regional Free Trade Agreements, Quaker United Nations Office (Geneva), Occasional Paper No. 14.

Abbott, Frederick M. (2005a), "Managing the Hydra: The Herculean Task of Ensuring Access to Essential Medicines", in: Maskus, Keith E / Reichman, Jerome H. (eds.), *International Public Goods and Transfer of Technology under a Globalized Intellectual Property Regime*, CUP, Cambridge et al., 393-424.

Abbott, Frederick M. (2005b), "The WTO Medicines Decision: World Pharmaceutical Trade and the Protection of Public Health", 99 *American Journal of International Law*, 317-358.

Abbott, Frederick M. (2005c), "Toward a New Era of Objective Assessment in the Field of TRIPS and Variable Geometry for the Preservation of Multilateralism", 8 *Journal of International Economic Law* 77.

Abbott, Frederick M. (2006a), "TRIPS and Human Rights: Preliminary Reflections", in: Abbott, Frederick M. / Breining-Kaufmann, Christine / Cottier, Thomas (eds.),

International Trade and Human Rights—Foundations and Conceptual Issues, World Trade Forum Vol. 5, University of Michigan Press, Michigan 145-169.

Abbott, Frederick M. (2006b), "The Cycle of Action and Reaction: Developments and Trends in Intellectual Property and Health", in: Roffe, Pedro / Tansey, Geoff / Vivas-Eugui, David (eds.), *Negotiating Health—Intellectual Property and Access to Medicines*, Earthscan, London / Sterling, 27-40.

Abbott, Frederick M. (2008), "Intellectual Property Rights in World Trade", in: Abbott, Frederick M. / Cottier, Thomas / Gurry, Thomas (eds.), *International Intellectual Property in an Integrated World Economy*, Wolters Kluwer, Gaithersburg, 187-199-.

Abbott, Frederick M. (2011), Trends in Local Production of Medicines and Related Technology Transfer, WHO Department of Public Health, FSU College of Law, Public Law Research Paper No. 569, available at http://digicollection.org/hss/documents/s19063en/s19063en.pdf (last visited on October 25, 2018).

Abbott, Frederick M. (2013), "Review: The Trilateral Study on Health, Intellectual Property, and Trade: The Virtue in Paving a Cleared Roadway", 16(2) *Journal of International Economic Law*, 494-495.

Abbott, Frederick M. / Reichman, Jerome H. (2007), "The Doha Rounds Public Health Legacy: Strategies for the Production and Diffusion of Patented Medicines under the Amended TRIPS Provisions", 10 *Journal of International Economic Law*, 921-987.

ABPI (2002), "Aplicação equivocada da legislação de patentes preocupa a indústria farmacêutica", *Boletim da ABPI* No. 28.

Abranches da Silva, Maria L. et al. (2010), "Controvérsias sobre a proteção patentária de segundo uso médico de compostos químicos conhecidos", 33 *Química Nova* 8, 1821-1826.

Abreu, Jussanã Cristina de (2017), "Prospecção tecnológica aplicada na otimização da concessão de patentes no Brasil", doctoral thesis presented to the Institute of Economics of the Federal University of Rio de Janeiro—UFRJ, available at www.ie.ufrj.br/images/defesas/jussana_cristina_de_abreu__94a6d.pdf (last visited on June 15, 2019).

Adrian, Johann (1996), *Patentrecht im Spannungsfeld von Innovationschutz und allgemeinem Interesse*, Inaugural Lecture on January 27, 1996 at the Humboldt University of Berlin, available at http://edoc.hu-berlin.de/humboldt-vl/adrian-johann/PDF/Adrian.pdf (last visited on October 21, 2017).

AGU (2009), *Parecer nº 210/PGF/AE/2009 of October 16, 2009*, available at http://www.agu.gov.br/page/content/detail/id_conteudo/102324 (last visited on November 2, 2017).

AGU (2010), *Parecer No. 337/PGF/EA/2010, approved by the Advogado Geral da União in January 7, 2011*, available at http://www.agu.gov.br/sistemas/site/TemplateImagemTextoThumb.aspx?idConteudo = 153676&id_site = 3 (last visited on November 11, 2017).

Ahlert, Ivan B. / Desiderio, Mauricio T. (2009), "A Patenteabilidade dos Novos Usos de Substâncias Conhecidas", 100 *Revista da ABPI*, May-June, 23-31.

Aith (2001), "Brasil cedeu direitos à droga fora de acordo de propriedade: Patente de remédio antiaids revela erro estratégico do país", *Folha de São Paulo,* March 11, 2001.

Al-Ali, Nermien (2003), "The Egyptian Pharmaceutical Industry After TRIPS", 26 *Fordham International Law Journal,* 274-314.

Alario, Dante J. (1995), "As patentes e o monopólio da cura", *Folha de São Paulo,* August 13, 1995.

Akers, Darnita York / Ecers, Sencer (2009), "The TRIPS Agreement and Its Effects on the R & D Spending of US-Owned Multinational Countries in Developing Countries", 43 *Journal of World Trade,* 1173-1192.

Akkari, Alessandra C. S. / Munhoz, Igor P. / Tomioka, Jorge / Fernandes dos Santos, Neusa M. / Fernandes dos Santos, Roberto, (2016), "Pharmaceutical Innovation: Differences Between Europe, USA and 'Pharmemerging' Countries", 23 *Gestão e Produção.* 2, São Carlos, 365-380.

Almeida Rodrigues, Paulo Henrique / Dorneles Ferreira da Costa, Roberta / Kiss, Katalina (2018), "A Evolução Recente da Indústria Farmacêutica Brasileira nos Limites da Subordinação Econômica", *Physis: Revista de Saúde Coletiva, Rio de Janeiro,* 28(1), e280104, 201.

Amaral Júnior, Alberto (2006), "O Acordo TRIPS, a Licença Compulsória e os Países em Desenvolvimento", 79 *Revista do Tribunal Regional Federal—3ª Região,* 99-116.

Amin, Tahir (2007), *Voluntary Licenses Practices in the Pharmaceutical Sector: An Acceptable Solution to Improving Access to Affordable Medicines?,* Essential Medicines and Health Products Information Portal–A World Health Organization Resource, available at https://apps.who.int/medicinedocs/documents/s19793en/s19793en.pdf (last visited on July 12, 2018).

Andersen, Regine / Winge, Tone (2012), *The Access and Benefit-Sharing Agreement on Teff Genetic Resources—Facts and Lessons,* FNI Report 6/2012, available at https://www.fni.no/getfile.php/131843-1469869194/Filer/Publikasjoner/FNI-R0612.pdf (last visited on October 7, 2018).

Anderson, Erin M. (2009), "Unnecessary Deaths and Unnecessary Costs: Getting Patented Drugs to Patients Most in Need", 29 *Boston College Third World Law Journal, 85-112.*

Andrade Vieira Loureiro, Luiz Guilherme (1999), *A Lei de Propriedade Industrial Comentada,* Lejus, São Paulo.

Angell, Marcia (2000), "The Pharmaceutical Industrial—To Whom It Is Accountable?", 342 *New England Journal of Medicine,* 1902-1904, June 22.

Angell, Marcia (2004), *The Truth About the Drug Companies—How They Deceive Us and What to Do About It,* Ramdon House, New York.

Aragão Figueiredo, Tatiana/Mendes de Andrade Schramm, Joyce/ Edais Pepe, Vera Lúcia (2014), "Seleção de Medicamentos Essenciais e a Carga de Doença no Brasil", 30 *Cad. Saúde Pública* (11), p. 2344-2356, Rio de Janeiro.

Araújo, Nádia de (2003), "A Internalização dos Tratados Internacionais no Direito Brasileiro e o Caso do TRIPS", 62 *Revista da ABPI,* 3-14.

Armstrong, Daniel (2001), "The Arguments of Law, Policy and Practice Against Swiss-Type Patent Claims", in Frankel, Susy / Smith, Tim (eds.), *Essays on Intellectual Property Law and Policy, Victoria University of Wellington Law Review,* 201-254.

Arslanian, Regis / Lyrio, Mauricio M. (1995), "A Reforma das Patentes no Brasil e as Pressões Norte-Americanas na Área de Propriedade Industrial", 4 *Política Externa* 2, 3-12.

Asif, E. (2013), "Exclusion of Diagnostic, Therapeutic and Surgical Methods from Patentability", 18 *Journal of Intellectual Property Rights,* 242-250, available at http://nopr.niscair.res.in/bitstream/123456789/18370/1/JIPR%2018(3)%2024 2-250.pdf (last visited on September 15, 2017).

Atik, Jeffery / Lidgard, Hans H. (2006), "Embracing Price Discrimination: TRIPS and the Suppression of Parallel Trade on Pharmaceuticals", 27 *University of Pennsylvania Journal of International Economic Law* 1043-1076.

Avelãs Nunes, António José / Remédio Marques, João Paulo F. / Coutinho de Abreu, João Manuel / Cunha, Luís Pedro (2009), A Inconstitucionalidade das Patentes "Pipeline" Brasileiras (Artigos 230° e 231° do Código da Propriedade Industrial de 1996), *REVEL—Edição Especial "Patentes Pipeline"*, 4-73, available at https://ibpieuropa.org/?media_dl=278 (last visited on October 21, 2017).

Bacelar Ahlert, Ivan / de Bessa Antunes, Paulo (2007), "Pipeline e Constituição: de que Inconstitucionalidade Falamos", 87 *Revista da ABPI,* 45-68.

Badim Marques, Silvia / Gandolfi Dallari, Sueli (2007), "Garantia do Direito Social à Assistência Farmacêutica no Estado de São Paulo", 41 *Revista de Saúde Pública,* 101-107.

Bandeira de Mello, Celso Antônio (2004), *Curso de Direito Administrativo,* Malheiros Editores, São Paulo.

Baptista, Luís Olavo (1996), "A Nova Lei e o TRIPS", Anais do XVI Seminário Nacional de Propriedade Intelectual—ABPI, 14-19.

Barros, Aluísio J. / Bertoldi, Andrea D. (2008), "Out-of-Pocket Expenditure in a Population Covered by the Family Health Program in Brazil", 37 *International Journal of Epidemiology* 4, 758-765.

Barros e Castro, Marco Túlio (2003), "Em Pauta—o Projeto de Lei n°. 139 e a Propriedade Industrial no Brasil", *Consultor Jurídico,* 8 December, available at https://www.conjur.com.br/2003-dez-08/projeto_lei_139_propriedade_industrial_brasil (last visited on October 21, 2017).

Bartelt, Sandra (2003), "Compulsory Licenses Pursuant to TRIPS Article 31 in the Light of the Doha Declaration on the TRIPS Agreement and Public Health", 6 *The Journal of World Intellectual Property,* 283-310.

Barton, John (2004), "Issues posed by a World Patent System", 7 *Journal of International Economic Law,* 341-357.

Bartsch, Sonja / Kohlmorgen, Lars (2007), *The Role of Southern Actors in Global Governance: The Fight Against HIV/AIDS,* GIGA Research Program, Working Paper 46, available at https://www.giga-hamburg.de/de/system/files/publications/wp46_bartsch-kohlmorgen.pdf (last visited on October 21, 2017).

Basheer, Shamnad / Purohit, Shashwat / Reddy, Prashant (2010), *Patent Exclusions that Promote Public Health*, Annex IV of WIPO Standing Committee on the Law of Patents—Exclusions from Patentability and Exceptions and Limitations to Patentee's Rights (WIPO-Document No. SCP/15/3), available at http://www.wipo.int /edocs/mdocs/scp/en/scp_15/scp_15_3-annex4.pdf (last visited on October 21, 2017).

Basso, Maristela (2000), "A Data de Aplicação de TRIPS no Brasil", 30 *Revista de Direito Constitucional e Internacional* 8, 13-22.

Basso, Maristela (2005), "TRIPS e os Exclusive Marketing Rights (EMRs)—Aplicação, Observância e Efeitos do Art. 70.9 no Brasil", in: Basso, Maristela / Prado, Maurício A. / Zaitz, Daniela (eds.), *Direito do Comércio Internacional: Pragmática, Diversidade e Inovação: Estudos em Homenagem ao Prof. Luiz Olavo Baptista*, Juruá, Curitiba, 395-416.

Basso, Maristela (2006), "Intervention of Health Authorities in Patent Examination: The Brazilian Practice of the Prior Consent", 1 *International Journal of Intellectual Property Management* 1-2, 54-75.

Basso, Maristela (2008), "Intervention of Health Authorities in Patent Examination: the Brazilian Practice of Prior Consent" in: Casella et. al. (eds), *Direito Internacional, Humanismo e Globalidade—Guido Fernando Silva Soares—Amicorum Discipulorum Liber*, Ed. Atlas, São Paulo, 62-85.

Basso, Maristela /Estrela, Ângela /Floh, Fabio (2001), "A Lei de Patentes e as Regras da Organização Mundial do Comércio", 55 *Revista da ABPI*, 35-40.

Bastos, Francisco Inácio / Massard da Fonseca, Elize (2017), "Licenciamento Compulsório do Efavirenz no Brasil: Um Mecanismo Sui-Generis ou Aplicável a Outros Produtos?", in: Curzel, Rosana / Nunes, João (eds.), *Patentes e o Acesso a Antirretrovirais no Brasil—O Desafio da Licença Compulsória*, Editora Appris, Curitiba, 135-162.

beck-aktuell Nachrichten (2019), *Nach Nichtigkeitsklage: Patent für afrikanisches Teff-Mehl in Deutschland erloschen*, available at https://rsw.beck.de/aktuell/ meldung/nach-nichtigkeitsklage-patent-fuer-afrikanisches-teff-mehl-in-deutsch land-erloschen, August 6, 2019 (last visited on August 12, 2019).

Beltrame, Priscila A. (2011), "Lei de Propriedade Industrial do Brasil em Discussão na OMC", 55 *Revista da ABPI*, 31-34.

Benoliel, Daniel / Salama, Bruno (2010), "Pharmaceutical Patent Bargains: The Brazilian Experience", 18 *Cardozo Journal of Intellectual and Competition Law* 3, 633-682.

Bently, Lionel. / Sherman, Brad (2009), *Intellectual Property Law*, Oxford University Press, New York, 3rd edition.

Bentolila, Hernan L. (2003), "Lessons from the United States Trade Policies to Convert a 'Pirate': The Case of Pharmaceutical Patents in Argentina", 5 *Yale Journal of Law and Technology*, 59-102.

Berkman, Alan / Garcia, Jonathan / Munoz-Laboy, Miguel / Paiva, Vera / Parker, Richard (2005), "A Critical Analysis of the Brazilian Response to HIV/AIDS:

Lessons Learned for Controlling and Mitigating the Epidemic in Developing Countries", 95 *American Journal of Public Health* 1162-1172.

Bermudez, Sérgio (2018), *Patente: Sofosbuvir entre o comércio e o direito à cura, Centro de Estudos Estratégicos da Fiocruz,* available at https://cee.fiocruz.br/?q=Patente-sofosbuvir-entre-o-com%C3%A9rcio-e-o-direito-%C3%A0-cura%E2%80%93por-Jorge-Bermudez (last visited on July 22, 2019).

Bermudez, Jorge / Andrade de Oliveira, Egléubia / Labra, Maria E. (2006), "A Produção Pública de Medicamentos no Brasil: Uma Visão Geral", 22 *Cadernos de Saúde Pública*, 11, 2379-2389.

Beyer, Christian (1988), *Grenzen der Arzneimittelhaftung dargestellt am Beispiel des Contergan-Falles*, VVF Verlag, München.

Biase Guimarães, Eduardo Ribas de (2008), *Direito à Saúde e Propriedade Intelectual de Medicamentos no Brasil—A Anuência Prévia da Agência Nacional de Vigilância Sanitária*, IMS, UERJ, PhD Thesis, available at https://bvssp.icict.fiocruz.br/lildbi/docsonline/get.php?id=1376 (last visited on October 31, 2017).

Bjornberg, Jennifer (2006), "Brazil's Recent Threat on Abbott's Patent: Resolution or Retaliation?", 27 *Northwestern Journal of International Law and Business*, 199-226.

Bodewig, Theo (1993), "Volksrepublik China—Erlass einer Verordnung über administrativen Schutz von Arzneimitteln", *Gewerblicher Rechtschutz and Urheberrecht—Internationaler Teil*, 581.

Boldrin, Michele / Levine, David K. (2007), "Intellectual Property and the Efficient Allocation of Social Surplus from Innovations", in: Porrini, Donatella / Ramello, Giovanni (eds.), *Property Rights Dynamics: A Law and Economic Perspective*, Routledge, London, 93-115.

Boldrin, Michele / Levine, David K. (2008), "The Pharmaceutical Industry", in: Boldrin; Michele / Levin, David K. (eds.), *Against Intellectual Monopoly*, CUP, New York et al., 212-242.

Borges Barbosa, Denis (1983), *Nota sobre a licença compulsória Monsanto de 1983*, available at http://denisbarbosa.addr.com/monsanto.doc (last visited on October 21, 2017).

Borges Barbosa, Denis (2002), *Limites do direito de patente, exaustão, fair usage e importação paralela*, available at http://denisbarbosa.addr.com/103.rtf (last visited on October 21, 2017).

Borges Barbosa, Denis (2004a), *A inconstitucionalidade da anuência da ANVISA no procedimento de concessão de patentes como manifestação discricionária da Administração Federal*, available at http://www.denisbarbosa.addr.com/anuencia.doc (last visited on October 21, 2017).

Borges Barbosa, Denis (2004b), *Falta de busca de anterioridades como causa de nulidade da patente*, available at http://denisbarbosa.addr.com/falta.doc (last visited on November 14, 2017).

Borges Barbosa, Denis (2006a), "A proibição, pela ANVISA, de Reivindicações de Uso Farmacêutico", in: Borges Barbosa, Denis (ed.), *Usucapião de Patentes e Outros Estudos de Propriedade Intelectual*, Lumen Juris, Rio de Janeiro, 715-747.

Borges Barbosa, Denis (2006b), "Reivindicação de Uso e a Questão do Segundo Uso", in: Borges Barbosa, Denis (ed.), *Usucapião de Patentes e Outros Estudos de Propriedade Intelectual*, Lumen Juris, Rio de Janeiro, 681-715.

Borges Barbosa, Denis (2008), *Propriedade intelectual: a aplicação do acordo TRIPS*, Rio de Janeiro, Lumen Juris, Rio de Janeiro.

Borges Barbosa, Denis (2009a), *O papel da ANVISA na concessão de patentes*, available at http://denisbarbosa.addr.com/papelanvisa.pdf (last visited on October 21, 2017).

Borges Barbosa, Denis (2009b), *Direitos Exclusivos de Comercialização: um instituto inexistente no direito brasileiro*, available at denisbarbosa.addr.com/emr.pdf (last visited on October 21, 2017).

Borges Barbosa, Denis (2009c), *Nota sobre as reivindicações de seleção no direito brasileiro*, available at http://denisbarbosa.addr.com/selectio.pdf (last visited on October 8, 2017).

Borges Barbosa, Denis (2010), "*O papel da ANVISA e o acórdão do TRF de 27-04-2010*", in: Borges Barbosa's Blog: http://denisbarbosa.blogspot.com/2010/06/o-papel-da-anvisa-e-o-acordao-do-2trf.html (last visited on October 21, 2017).

Borges Barbosa, Denis (2011), "As hipóteses de incidência patentária do art. 10 do CPI/96", 4 *REVEL*, 144-167, available at https://ibpieuropa.org/?media_dl=283 (last visited on October 21, 2017).

Borges Barbosa, Denis (2013), *Sempre as Inconstitucionalidades das Patentes Pipeline: Uma Visão Renovada*, available at http://www.denisbarbosa.addr.com/arquivos/200/propriedade/sempre_inconst_patentes_pipeline.pdf (last visited on October 15, 2017).

Borges Barbosa, Denis (2013a), "Patents and the Emerging Markets of Latin America" in: Abbott, Frederick M. / Correa, Carlos M./ Drahos, Peter (eds.), *Emerging Markets and the World Patent Order*, Edward Elgar, Cheltenham (UK), Northampton—MA (USA), p. 140.

Borges Barbosa, Denis (2014), "Anuência Prévia pela ANVISA: Só Para Proteger a Saúde Pública?", in: Borges Barbosa, Denis (ed.), *Ensaios e Estudos de Propriedade Intelectual 2014-2015*, Edição do Instituto Brasileiro de Propriedade Intelectual, 201-218 available at *Borges Barbosa, Denis* (last visited on October 21, 2017).

Borges Barbosa, Pedro Marcos N. / Borges Barbosa, Denis (2018), *Código da Propriedade Industrial conforme os Tribunais. Patentes*, Vol. I, Lumen juris, Rio de Janeiro.

Böttger, Fabian (2008), "Zwangslizenzen im Patentrecht—Eine systematische Bewertung der neueren Praxis insbesondere im Bereich der öffentlichen Gesundheit", *Gewerblicher Rechtschutz and Urheberrecht—Internationaler Teil*, 881-891.

Boyle, James (2008), *The Public Domain—Enclosing the Commons of the Mind*, Yale University Press, New Haven & London, available at http://thepublicdomain.org/thepublicdomain1.pdf.

Branstetter, Lee G. (2004), "Do Stronger Patents Induce More Local Innovation?", 7 *Journal of International Economic Law* 359-370.

Breckenridge, Alasdair / Duff, Gordon/Emanuel, Michael / Rawlins, Michael (2012), "Thalidomide and its sequelae", 380 *The Lancet*, September 1, 781-783.

Brinkley, Joel (2000), "U.S. vs. Microsoft: The Overview: U.S. Judge says Microsoft violated antitrust laws with predatory behavior", *The New York Times,* April 4, 2000, available at http://www.nytimes.com/2000/04/04/business/us-vs-microsoft-overview-us-judge-says-microsoft-violated-antitrust-laws-with.html (last visited on November 3, 2017).

Burdon, Michael / Sloper, Kristie (2003), "The Art of Using Secondary Patents to Improve Patent Protection", 3 *Journal of Medical Marketing: Device, Diagnostic and Pharmaceutical Marketing,* 226-238.

Calcagnotto, Gilberto / Wogart, Jan Peter (2006), "Brazil Fight's Against AIDS and Its Implications for Global Health Governance", 8 *World Health and Population,* 4-19.

Calixto, João B. / Siqueira Junior, Jarbas M. (2008), "Desenvolvimento de Medicamentos no Brasil: Desafios", 78 *Gazeta Médica da Bahia* 1, 98-106.

Calliari, Thiago / Machado Ruiz, Ricardo (2014), "Brazilian Pharmaceutical Industry and Generic Drugs Policy: Impacts on Structure and Innovation and Recent Developments", 41 *Science and Public Policy,* 245-256.

Câmara dos Deputados (1999), *CPI Medicamentos,* Transcription of two interviews from December 14, 1999, available at http://www2.camara.leg.br/atividade-legislativa/comissoes/comissoes-temporarias/parlamentar-de-inquerito/51-legislatura/cpimedic/notas/cpimed_nt141299m.pdf, (last visited on December 4, 2015).

Câmara dos Deputados (2000), CPI Medicamentos, Final Report from May 30, 2000, available at http://www2.camara.leg.br/atividade-legislativa/comissoes/comissoes-temporarias/parlamentar-de-inquerito/51-legislatura/cpimedic/relatfinal.html, pp. 160-161 (last visited on December 4, 2015).

Câmara, Marcia R.G. / Godoy, Marcia R. / Oliveira, André L.R. (2004), Porto Alegre: UFRGS, *O Controle de Preços na Indústria Farmacêutica do Brasil,* available at http://www.academia.edu/3178611/O_Controle_de_Pre%C3%A7os_na_Ind%C3%BAstria_Farmac%C3%AAutica_no_Brasil (last visited on October 21, 2017).

Campos, Roberto (1995), "Três vícios de comportamento: o Brasil precisa mudar sua cultura, segundo a qual o roubo de uma patente é patriotismo", *Folha de São Paulo,* May 7, 1995.

Candotti, Elio (1995) "As patentes e os cientistas", *Folha de São Paulo, May 8,* 1995.

Capanema, Luciana Xavier de Lemos / Palmeira, Pedro Lins Filho (2004), *Fármacos: indústria Farmacêutica Brasileira: Reflexões sobre sua estrutura e potencial de investimento,* available at http://www.bndes.gov.br/SiteBNDES/export/sites/default/bndes_pt/Galerias/Arquivos/conhecimento/liv_perspectivas/06.pdf (last visited on October 21, 2017).

Cardoso, Fernando H. (1996), *Discurso de Solenidade na Sanção da Lei de Patentes,* May 14, 1996, available at http://www.biblioteca.presidencia.gov.br/presidencia/ex-presidentes/fernando-henrique-cardoso/discursos/1o-mandato/1996-1/76%20-%20/view (last visited on November 2, 2017).

Carroll, Michael W. (2009), "One Size Does Not Fit All: A Framework for Tailoring Intellectual Property Rights", 70 *Ohio State Law Journal* 6, 1361-1434.

Carvalho, Patrícia Luciane de (2007), *O Acesso a Medicamentos e as Patentes Farmacêuticas junto à Ordem Jurídica Brasileira*, Editora Atlas, Curitiba.

Cassier, Maurice / Correa, Marilena (2007), "Intellectual Property and Public Health: Copying of HIV/AIDS Drugs by Brazilian Public and Private Pharmaceutical Laboratories", 1 *RECIIS—Electronic Journal of Communication, Information and Innovation in Health*, 83-90.

Cepaluni, Gabriel (2005), "Regimes Internacionais e o Contencioso das Patentes para Medicamentos: Estratégias para Países em Desenvolvimento", 27 *Contexto Internacional*, 51-99.

Cerqueira Leite, Rogério C. (1995), "Patentes, pirataria e indústria farmacêutica", *Folha de São Paulo*, April 30, 1995. D-2.

Cerqueira Leite, Rogério C. (2008), "CODETEC—Companhia de Desenvolvimento Tecnológico", *Revista Brasileira de Inovação* 7(2), 483-489.

César, Priscilla / Polido, Fabrício (2007), "Proteção patentária de Medicamentos na interface com o direito à saúde: sustentabilidade do programa brasileiro de acesso universal às terapias antirretrovirais," in: Basso, Maristela / Salomão Filho, Calixto / Polido, Fabrício / César, Priscilla (eds.), *Direitos de Propriedade Intelectual & Saúde Pública: O acesso universal aos medicamentos antirretrovirais no Brasil*, IDCID, São Paulo, 3-114.

Chadha, Vikram (2007), "WTO, TRIPs and India: Contemporary Issues and Implications for India's Pharmaceuticals Industry", in: Thakur, Anil Kumar / Sharma, Nageshwar (eds.), *WTO and India*, Deep and Deep Publications, New Delhi, 569-582.

Chalmers, Robert (2006), "Evergreen or Deciduous? Australian Trend in Relation to the 'Evergreening' of Patents", 30 *Melbourne University Law Review*, 29-61.

Chamas, Claudia Inês / Carvalho, Sergio M. Paulino de / Salles-Filho, Sergio (2007), "Current Issues of IP Management in Health and Agriculture in Brazil", in: Krattiger, Mahoney, Nelsen et al. (eds.), *Intellectual Property Management in Health and Agriculture Innovation*, MIHR, PIPRA, Osvaldo Cruz Foundation and bioDevelopments-International Institute, Oxford, Davis, Rio, Ithaka, 1563-1575.

Chang, Ha Joon (2003), *Kicking Away the Ladder—Development Strategy in Historical Perspective*, Anthem Press, London.

Chapman, Audrey R. (2002), "The Human Rights Implications of the Intellectual Property Protection", 5 *Journal of International Economic Law* 4, 861-882.

Chasen Ross, Julie / Wasserman, Jessica A. (1993), "Trade-Related Aspects of Intellectual Property", in: Stewart, Terence P. (ed.), *The GATT Uruguay Round: A Negotiating History (1986-1992), Vol. 2: Commentary*, Kluwer Law and Taxation Publishers, Deventer, 2242-2334.

Chatterjee, David (2019), *Evergreening—Voraussetzungen der Patentfähigkeit im deutschen, europäischen und indischen Patentrecht*, Nomos, Baden-Baden.

Chaves, Gabriela Costa / Scopel, Carolinne T. (2016), "Initiatives to Challenge Patent Barriers and Their Relationship with the Price of Medicines Procured by the Brazilian Unified National Health System", 32 *Cadernos de Saúde Pública* 11, 1-11.

Chen, Molly F. M. (2012), "Lessons from Generics", 43 *Vanderbilt Journal of Transnational Law,* 1262-1281.

Chequer, Pedro (1999), *Terapia antirretroviral e saúde pública—Um balanço da experiência brasileira,* Brazil, MoH, available at http://bvsms.saude.gov.br/bvs/publicacoes/terapia.pdf (last visited on October 21, 2017).

Chirac, Pierre. / von Schoen-Angerer, Tido / Kasper, Toby / Ford, Nathan. (2000), "Aids: Patent's Rights Versus Patient's Rights", 356 *The Lancet* 9228, p. 501, August 5.

Clarke-Smith, Jennifer M. (2002), "The Development of the Monopolistic Leveraging Theory and Its Appropriated Role in Antitrust Law", 51 *Catholic University Law Review* 179-206, available at http://scholarship.law.edu/cgi/viewcontent.cgi?article=1304&context=lawreview (last visited on October 22, 2017).

Clift, Charles (2010), "Why IPR Issues Were Brought to GATT: A Historical Perspective on the Origins of TRIPS", in: Correa, Carlos M. (ed.), *Research Handbook on the Protection of Intellectual Property under WTO Rules*, Edward Elgar, Cheltenham (UK), Northampton MA, 3-21.

Cochrane, James M. T. (2000), "Zidovudine's Patent History", 356 *The Lancet* 9228, 1611-1612, November 4.

Cockbain, Julian/Sterckx, Sigrid (2010), "Purpose-Limited Pharmaceutical Product Claims under the Revised European Patent Convention: A Camouflaged Attack on Generic Substitution?", *Intellectual Property Quarterly.*, 88-107.

Cohen, Jillian Clare (2000), *Public Policies in the Pharmaceutical Sector: A Case Study of Brazil,* LCSHD Paper Series 54, Department of Human Development, The World Bank.

Cohen, Jillian Clare (2007), "Brazil's Historical Approach to Intellectual Property Law: The Pharmaceutical Sector", in: Ashiya, Manish (ed.), *TRIPS and Pharmaceutical Industry—Impact on Developing Countries*, The Icfai University Press, Hyderabad, 59-74.

Cohen, Jillian Clare / Lybecker, Kristina M. (2005), "Aids Policy and Pharmaceutical Patents: Brazil's Strategy to Safeguard Public Health", 28 *The World Economy* 2, 211-230.

Cohen-Kohler, Jillian C. / Esmail, Laura C. / Perez Cosio, Andre (2007), "Canada's Implementation of the Paragraph 6 Decision: Is it Sustainable Public Policy?", 3 *Global Health* 12, available at https://www.ncbi.nlm.nih.gov/pmc/articles/PMC2180169/ (last visited on October 28, 2017).

Coriat, Benjamin / Hasenclever, Lia / Paranhos, Julia / Zaire, Carla (2017), "Tratamentos Antirretrovirais de Terceira Linha: Estratégias para Gerir um Custo Significativo no Brasil", in: Curzel, Rosana / Nunes, João (eds.), *Patentes e o Acesso a Antirretrovirais no Brasil,* Editora Appris, Curitiba, 73-104.

Cornish, William (2003), *Intellectual Property—Omnipresent, Distracting, Irrelevant?* Oxford University Press, Oxford.

Correa, Carlos M. (1994), "Veränderungen im lateinamerikanischen Patentrecht", *Gewerblicher Rechtschutz and Urheberrecht—Internationaler Teil,* 799-807.

Correa, Carlos M. (1999), *Intellectual Property Rights, the WTO and Developing Countries—The TRIPS Agreement and Policy Options for Developing Countries,* London, Zed Books.

Correa, Carlos M. (2000a), *Integrating Public Health Concerns into Patent Legislation in Developing Countries*, South Centre, Geneva.

Correa, Carlos M. (2000b), "Reforming the Intellectual Property Rights System in Latin America", *23 World Economy*, 851-872.

Correa, Carlos M. (2001), *Trends in Drug Patenting: Case Studies*, Ediciones Corregidor, Buenos Aires.

Correa, Carlos M. (2002), *Implications of the Doha Declaration on the TRIPS Agreement and Public Health*, World Health Organization, Geneva, available at http://www.who.int/medicines/areas/policy/WHO_EDM_PAR_2002.3.pdf (last visited on October 21, 2017).

Correa, Carlos M. (2003), *International Developments in the Area of Intellectual Property Rights*, ICTSD-UNCTAD Dialogue, 2. Bellagio Series on Development and Intellectual Property, 18-21/9.

Correa, Carlos M. (2006), "Pharmaceutical Inventions: When Is the Granting of a Patent Justified?", 1 *International Journal of Intellectual Property Management* 1-2, 4-21.

Correa, Carlos M. (2007a), "Analisando tensões entre patentes e o interesse público: rumo a uma agenda para países em desenvolvimento", in: Villares, Fábio (ed.), *Propriedade Intelectual: tensões entre o capital e a sociedade*, Paz e Terra, São Paulo, 306-333.

Correa, Carlos M. (2007b), *Guidelines for the Examination of Pharmaceutical Patents: Developing a Public Health Perspective*, Working Paper ICTSD/WHO/UNCTAD.

Correa, Carlos M. (2007c), *Trade Related Aspects of Intellectual Property Rights: A Commentary on the TRIPS Agreement*, OUP, Oxford et al.

Correa, Carlos M. (2009), "Intellectual Property Rights and Inequalities in Health Outcomes", in: Labonté, Ronald / Schrecker, Ted / Packer, Corinne / Runnels, Vivien (eds.), *Globalization and Health—Pathways, Evidence and Policy*, Routledge, New York et al., 263-288.

Correa, Carlos M. (2011), *Pharmaceutical Innovation, Incremental Patenting and Compulsory Licensing*, Research Paper 41South Centre, available at http://apps.who.int/medicinedocs/documents/s21395en/s21395en.pdf (last visited on October 21, 2017).

Correa, Carlos M. (2012), "Efforts to Raise the Bar in Patent Examination Need to Be Supported", *International Review of Intellectual Property and Competition Law*, 747-750.

Correa, Carlos M. (2014), Patent Examination and Legal Fictions: How Legal Fictions are Created on Feet of Clay", South Center, Research Paper 58, available at https://www.southcentre.int/wp-content/uploads/2014/12/RP58_Patent-Examination-Legal-Fictions-rev2_EN.pdf (last visited on August 5, 2019).

Correa, Carlos M. (2015), *Intellectual Property: How Much Room Is Left for Industrial Policy?*, UNCTAD Discussion Papers No. 233, available at http://unctad.org/en/PublicationsLibrary/osgdp20155_en.pdf (last visited on October 21, 2017).

Corrêa, Marilena / Guimarães, Eduardo (2012), "Propriedade Intelectual e Saúde Pública: o Papel da Agência Nacional de Vigilância Sanitária no Patenteamento Farmacêutico no Brasil", 6 *RECIIS—Electronic Journal of Communication, Information and Innovation in Health* 3.

Cosendey, Maria A. E. / Zepeda Bermudas, Jorge A. / de Almeida dos Reis, André L. / da Silva, Haine Felipe / Oliveira, Maria A. /Luiza, Vera L. (2000), "Assistência farmacêutica na atenção básica de saúde: a experiência de três estados brasileiros", 16 *Cadernos de Saúde Pública*, 171-182.

Costa Marques, Maria Cristina da (2002), "Saúde e Poder: a emergência política da AIDS/HIV no Brasil", 9 *Histórias, Ciências, Saúde—Manguinhos* (Suplemento), 42-65.

Cruz, Hélio N. da / Tavares, Martus A. R. (1986), "As Patentes Brasileiras de 1830 a 1891", 16 *Estudos Econômicos*, Faculdade de Economia da Universidade de São Paulo- São Paulo, 205-225.

Cullet, Phillipe (2004), "Patents and Medicines—The Relationship Between TRIPS and the Human Right to Health", in: Gruskin, Sofia / Grodin, Michael A. / Marks, Stephen P. / Annas, George J. (eds.), *Perspectives on Health and Human Rights*, Taylor & Francis, New York, 179-202.

Dae-Hee Härmark, Linda Veronica (2012), *Web-Based Intensive Monitoring: A Patient-Based Pharmacovigilance Tool*, PhD Thesis, University of Groningen, available at http://citeseerx.ist.psu.edu/viewdoc/download;jsessionid=EFB9CE89F3CAE9C48B7F8FF4085A44D1?doi=10.1.1.475.7815&rep=rep1&type=pdf (last visited on July 15, 2019).

D'Almeida, Cristina / Hasenclever, Lia / Krikorian, Gaelle / Orsi, Fabienne / Sweet, Cassandra / Coriat, Benjamin (2008), "New Antiretroviral Treatments and Post-2005 TRIPS Constraints: First Moves Towards IP Flexibilization in Developing Countries" in Coriat, Benjamin (ed.), *The Political Economy of HIV/AIDS in Developing Countries*, Cheltenham, Edward Elgar, pp. 25-49.

D'Amato, Anthony (1995), "Good Faith", in Bernhardt, Rudolf (ed.): Encyclopedia of Public International Law (consolidated library edition / published under the auspices of the Max Planck Institute for Comparative Public Law and International Law), Vol. II, North-Holland, Amsterdam et al., 599-601.

Danemann, Gert E. (2000), "Die geschichtliche Entwicklung des gewerblichen Rechtschutzes in Brasilien", *Mitteilungen der Deutsch-Brasilianischen Juristenvereinigung*, Heft 2, 17-22.

Darrow, Jonathan J. (2010), "Debunking the Evergreening Patent Myth", 131 *Harvard Law Record* 6, available at http://papers.ssrn.com/sol3/papers.cfm?abstract_id=2050696 (last visited on October 21, 2017).

Davi, Paul A. (2001), *A Tragedy of the Public Knowledge "Commons"? Global Science, Intellectual Property and the Digital Technology Boomerang*, UNU-MERIT Research Memoranda. UNU-MERIT, available at http://collections.unu.edu/view/UNU:1084 (last visited on October 19, 2017).

Deere, Carolyn (2009), *The Implementation Game—The TRIPS Agreement and the Global Politics of Intellectual Property Reform in Developing Countries*, OUP, Oxford et al.

Deere-Birkbeck, Carolyn (2010), "Developing Countries in the Global IP Systems Before TRIPS: The Political Context for the TRIPS Negotiations", in: Correa, Carlos M. (ed.), *Research Handbook on the Protection of Intellectual Property under WTO Rules, Vol. I*, Edward Elgar, Cheltenham (UK); Northampton MA, 22-51.

Delgado Bastos, Valéria (2006), "Laboratórios Farmacêuticos Oficiais e Doenças Negligenciadas: Perspectivas de Políticas Pública", 25 *Revista do BNDES*, 269-298.

Dias de Oliveira, Ana C. / Khater Covesi, Letícia (2015), "Estratégias para Adiar o Acesso aos Medicamentos no Brasil", in: Villardi / Vieira / Carvalho (eds.), *Prêmio GTPI Jacques Bouchara de Produção Acadêmica voltada para o Ativismo*, 55-84, available at https://www.ime.usp.br/images/arquivos/imagens/destaques/premio_GTPI_grafica.pdf (last visited on October 21, 2017).

Dias Guimarães César, Priscilla Maria (2008), "Flexibilidades do Direito Internacional da Propriedade Intelectual—Reflexões para Amenizar a Crise do Acesso a Medicamentos Essenciais", in: Carvalho, Patrícia L. (ed.), *Propriedade Intelectual—Estudos em Homenagem à Professora Maristela Basso*, Juruá Editora, Curitiba, 44-75.

di Cataldo, Vicenzo (2001), "In Search of Ways to Reconcile Patents with Access to Drugs", in: Remiche, Bernard (ed.), *Pharmaceutical Patents, Innovation and Public Health, Revue Internationale Droit Economic—Special Edition*, De Boeck & Larcier, Bruxelles, 163-167.

Dieners, Peter / Reese, Ulrich (2010), *Handbuch des Pharmarechts—Grundlagen und Praxis*, C.H. Beck, München.

Di Masi, Joseph / Grabowski, Henry / Hansen, Ronald (2016), "Innovation in the Pharmaceutical Industry: New Estimates of R & D Costs", 47 *Journal of Health Economics*, 20-33.

Dimoulis, Dimitri / Lunardi, Soraya (2017), *O custo social da inércia do STF: Réquiem da ADI 4234*, available at http://www.unesp.br/portal#!/noticia/28330/artigo-o-custo-social-da-inercia-do-stf-requiem-da-adi-4234/ (last visited on October 18, 2017).

Dinwoodie, Graeme B. / Dreyfuss, Rochelle C. (2007), "Diversifying Without Discriminating: Complying with the Mandates of the TRIPS Agreement", 13 *Michigan Telecommunication Technology Law Review*, 445-456.

Ding, Jingxi / Xue, Yajiong / Liang, Huigang / Shao, Hong / Chen, Jongfa (2011), "From Imitation to Innovation: A Study of China's Drug R & D and Relevant National Policies", 6 *Journal of Technology Management and Innovation* 2, 1-12.

Domingues, Douglas Gabriel (1980), *Direito Industrial—Patentes*, Forense, Rio de Janeiro.

Dose, Giovanni / Stiglitz, Joseph (2013), *The Role of Intellectual Property Rights in the Development Process, with Some Lessons from Developed Countries: An Introduction*, LEM Working Papers Series, No. 2013/23, available at http://www.lem.sssup.it/WPLem/files/2013-23.pdf (last visited on November 3, 2017).

Drahos, Michaela / van Waarden, Frans (2002), "Courts and (Epistemic) Communities in the Convergence of Competition Policy", 9 *Journal of European Public Policy* 6, 913-934.

Drahos, Peter (1999), "Intellectual Property and Human Rights", *Intellectual Property Quarterly*, 349-371.

Drahos, Peter (2002), "Negotiating Intellectual Property Rights: Between Coercion and Dialogue", in: Drahos, Peter / Mayne, Ruth (eds.), *Global Intellectual Property*

Rights: Knowledge, Access and Development, Palgrave Macmillan, Basingstoke / New York, 161-182.

Drahos, Peter (2007), "Patent Reform for Innovation and Risk Management: a Separation of Powers Approach", 1 *KEStudies*, available at https://www.anu.edu.au/fellows/pdrahos/articles/pdfs/2007patentreformforinnovriskmgmt.pdf (last visited on November 10, 2017).

Drahos, Peter (2008), "'Trust Me': Patent Offices in Developing Countries", 34 *American Journal of Law & Medicine* 2, 151-174.

Drahos, Peter (2008), "Regulating Patenting Offices: Countering Pharmaceutical Hegemony", 5 *ScriptEd* 3, 501-514.

Drahos, Peter (2010), "Joining the Patent Office Conga Line", in: Drahos, Peter (ed.), *The Global Governance of Knowledge—Patent Offices and their Clients*, CUP, Cambridge et al., pp. 242-256.

Drahos, Peter / Braithwaite, John (2002), *Information Feudalism—Who Owns the Knowledge Economy?* Earthscan Publications, London.

Drexl, Josef (2008), "Is There a 'More Economic Approach' to Intellectual Property and Competition Law?", in: Josef Drexl (ed.), *Research Handbook on Intellectual Property and Competition Law*, Edward Elgar, Cheltenham, UK; Northampton, MA, pp. 27-53.

Dukes, Graham (2005), *The Law and Ethics of the Pharmaceutical Industry*, Elsevier Science, Amsterdam et al.

Duran Ferreira, Camila et al. (2004), *O Judiciário e as Políticas de Saúde no Brasil: o Caso AIDS*, Universidade de São Paulo. Prêmio IPEA-Caixa 2004, Brasília.

Dutfield, Graham (2008), "Knowledge Diplomacy and the New Intellectual Property Fundamentalism", in: Malbon, Justin / Lawson, Charles (eds.), *Interpreting and Implementing the TRIPS Agreement—Is it Fair?* Edward Elgar, Cheltenham, (UK), 31-44.

Dutfield, Graham (2017), "Healthcare Innovation and Patent Law's 'Pharmaceutical Privilege': Is There a Pharmaceutical Privilege? And If So, Should We Remove It?", 12 *Health Economics, Policy and Law*, 4, 453-470.

Dwyer, Amy (1999), "Trade-Related Aspects of Intellectual Property Rights", in: Stewart, Davi P. (ed.), *The GATT Uruguay Round: A Negotiating History (1986-1994), Vol. IV: The End Game (Part I)*, Kluwer Law International, Cambridge, MA, 463-773.

Eisenberg, Rebecca S. (2001), "The Shifting Functional Balance of Patents and Drug Regulation", 19 *Health Affairs* 4, 119-135.

El Farag, Mohamed Salem Abou (2008), "TRIPS, TRIPS-PLUS, Developing Countries and Public Health: The Case of Egypt", 5 *Journal of International Biotechnology Law*, 1-15.

Einecke, Helga (2012), "Streit um teure Medikamente—Fluch und Segen: Preiswerte Zwangslizenzen für wichtige Arzneimittel", *Süddeutsche Zeitung*, March 17-18, p. 30.

EPO, Annual Report 2016, available at https://www.epo.org/about-us/annual-reports-statistics/annual-report/2016/statistics/searches.html#tab4 (last visited on October 4, 2017).

EPO, Guidelines for Examination, available at http://www.epo.org/law-practice/legal-texts/html/guidelines/e/g_vi_7_1.htm (last visited on October 28, 2017).

European Commission (2003), *Commission Communication of Parallel Imports of proprietary medicinal products for which marketing authorizations was granted*, COM (2003) 839 of 30 December 2003.

European Commission, Competition DG (2008), Pharmaceutical Sector Inquiry—Preliminary Report, available at http://ec.europa.eu/competition/sectors/pharmaceuticals/inquiry/preliminary_report.pdf (last visited on July 26, 2018).

European Commission, Competition DG (2009), Pharmaceutical Sector Inquiry—Final Report, available at http://ec.europa.eu/competition/sectors/pharmaceuticals/inquiry/staff_working_paper_part1.pdf (last visited on July 26, 2018).

Falcone, Bruno (2005), "Questões controversas sobre patentes farmacêuticas no Brasil", in: de Carvalho, Patricia L. (ed.), *Propriedade intelectual: estudos em homenagem à Prof. Maristela Basso*, Juruá, Curitiba, 209-235.

Faria, Jacqueline B. (2006), "Licença Compulsória como Alternativa para a Garantia do Acesso Universal a Antirretrovirais no Brasil", 85 *Revista da ABPI*, 27-37.

Fávaro Arruda, Gustavo / de Camargo Cerdeira, Pablo (2005), "Patentes de Medicamentos e Saúde Pública", 139 *Revista de Direito Mercantil*, 189-201.

FDA (2018), *Frances Oldham Kelsey: Medical Reviewer Famous for Averting a Public Health Tragedy*, available at https://www.fda.gov/about-fda/virtual-exhibits-fda-history/frances-oldham-kelsey-medical-reviewer-famous-averting-public-health-tragedy (last visited August 19, 2018).

Feldschreiber, Peter (2008), *The Law and Regulation of Medicines*, Oxford University Press, Oxford.

Fekete, Elizabete (1997), "Importações Paralelas: A Implementação do Princípio da Exaustão de Direitos no Mercosul, diante do Contexto de Globalização", Revista da ABPI—Anais do XVII Seminário Nacional de Propriedade Industrial, pp. 76-102.

Fernandes de Moura, Humberto (2011), "Patentes de Medicamentos e a Discussão a Respeito da Interpretação do Art. 229-C da Lei 9.279/96", XV *Revista CEJ* 53, 80-87, available at http://www.jf.jus.br/ojs2/index.php/revcej/article/view/1537/1487 (last visited on October 21, 2017).

Ferraz, Octavio L. Motta (2007), "Direito à Saúde, Escassez e o Judiciário", *O Estado de S. Paulo*, August 10, 2007.

Ferraz, Octavio L. Motta (2009), "The Right to Health in the Courts of Brazil: Worsening Health Inequalities?", 11 *Health and Human Rights Journal* 2, 33-45.

Fialho, Beatriz de Castro / Gadelha, Carlos Augusto Grabois / Quental, Cristiane (2003), "Saúde e inovação: uma abordagem sistêmica das indústrias de saúde", 19 *Cadernos de Saúde Pública* 1, 47-59.

Ficsor, Miháli Zoltán (1995), "Die Einführung des Stoffschutzes im ungarischen Patentrecht", *Gewerblicher Rechtschutz and Urheberrecht—Internationaler Teil*, 1-7.

Figueira Barbosa, Antonio Luiz (1999), *Sobre a Propriedade do Trabalho Intelectual—Uma Perspectiva Crítica*, Ed. UFRJ, Rio de Janeiro, 399-418.

Figueira Barbosa, Antonio Luiz (2001), "Preços na Indústria Farmacêutica: Abusos e Salvaguardas em Propriedade Industrial. A Questão Brasileira Atual", in: Picavelli, Márcia F. S. / Aranha, Marcio I. (eds.), *Política de Patentes em Saúde Humana*, Editora Atlas, São Paulo, 89-129.

Figueira Barbosa, Antonio Luiz (2005), Patentes: *Crítica à racionalidade, em busca da racionalidade*, Caderno de Estudos Avançados, Instituto Oswaldo Cruz, No. 1.

Figueira Barbosa, Antonio Luiz (2005), "Patentes farmacêuticas e o papel da ANVISA", *Boletim Eletrônico da Sociedade Brasileira de Química*, No. 555, available at http://www.sbq.org.br/publicacoes/beletronico/bienio0406/boletim555.htm (last visited on December 21, 2017).

Fleischer-Beck, Matt (2002), "The Cipro Dilemma—In the Anthrax Crisis, Tommy Thompson Distorted Patent Law to Save Public Health. Good Move?," *The American Lawyer*, January, available at http://www.cptech.org/ip/health/cl/cipro/americanlawyer012002.html (last visited on November 3, 2017).

Flynn, Sean M. (2008), *Using Competition Law to Promote Access to Medicines*, PIJIP, American University Washington College of Law, available at https://www.researchgate.net/publication/49251150_Using_Competition_Law_to_Promote_Access_to_Knowledge (last visited on October 18, 2017).

Fonseca da Silva, Antonio Carlos (2002), "Importação Paralela de Medicamentos," 39 *Revista de Informação Legislativa* 154, 31-40, available at http://www2.senado.leg.br/bdsf/handle/id/769 (last visited on October 21, 2017).

Fonseca Mendes, Dany Rafael / Constantino de Oliveira, Miguel Angelo / Amorim Pinheiro, Adalberto (2014), "Anuência Prévia da ANVISA: a evolução da regulamentação de uma política de estado", 4 *Revista Brasileira de Políticas Públicas* 2, 157-172.

Forman, Lisa (2007), "Trade Rules, Intellectual Property, and the Right to Health", 21 *Ethics and International Affairs*, 337-357.

Formenti, Ligia (2011), "AGU restringe poder da ANVISA na concessão de patente de medicamento", *O Estado de São Paulo*, January 24, 2011, available at http://www.estadao.com.br/noticias/impresso,agu-restringe-poder-da-anvisa-na-concessao-de-patente-de-medicamenro,670238,0.htm (last visited on November 3, 2017).

Formenti, Ligia (2017), "ANVISA e INPI chegam a Acordo sobre Patentes de Medicamentos", *O Estado de São Paulo*, March 15, 2017, available at http://economia.estadao.com.br/noticias/geral,anvisa-e-inpi-chegam-a-acordo-sobre-patentes-de-medicamentos,70001699653 (last visited on November 3, 2017).

Fox, Maggie (2011), "After 9/11, Anthrax Attacks Seemed Too Natural", *National Journal*, September 1, 2011, available at http://www.nti.org/gsn/article/after-9 11-anthrax-attacks-seemed-too-natural/ (last visited on November 2, 2017).

Frankel, Susy (2010), "Applicability of GATT Jurisprudence to the Interpretation of TRIPS", in: Correa, Carlos (ed.), *Research Handbook on the Interpretation and Enforcement of Intellectual Property under WTO Rules, Vol. II*, Edward Elgar, Cheltenham (UK), 3-23.

Franz, Martin (2005), *Die Durchsetzung von Immaterialgüterrechten in Argentinien, Brasilien und Mexiko—Eine Untersuchung vor dem Hintergrund des TRIPS-Übereinkommens*, Nomos, Baden-Baden.

Freitas, Jânio de. (1995), "Derrota Patente", *Folha de São Paulo*, April 13, 1995.

Furtado, João / Urias, Eduardo (2010), "A Evolução da Indústria Farmacêutica no Brasil: elementos para uma caracterização dos movimentos recentes, com ênfase nas políticas de inovação", Estudio Sectorial, Sector farmacéutico de Brasil: (Centro Redes), Argentina—Uruguay, available at: https://idl-bnc-idrc.dspacedirect.org/bitstream/handle/10625/45331/131797.pdf (last visited on October 20, 2018).

Gabardo, Emerson / Moura Rezende, Maurício Corrêa de (2017), "O conceito de interesse público no direito administrativo brasileiro", 115 *Revista Brasileira de Estudos Políticos*, 267-318.

Gad, Mohamed Omar (2006), *Representational Fairness in WTO Rule-Making—Negotiating, Implementing and Disputing the TRIPS Pharmaceutical-Related Provisions*, The British Institute of International and Comparative Law, SMU Dedman School of Law - London Forum Initiative, London.

Gad, Mohamed Omar (2008), "TRIPS Dispute Settlement and Developing Countries Interests", in: Correa, Carlos M. / Abdulqaqi, Yusuf A. (eds.), *Intellectual Property and International Trade: The TRIPS Agreement*, Kluwer Law International BV, The Netherlands, 331-383.

GATT (1986), *GATT Multilateral Trade Negotiations—The Uruguay Round—Group of Negotiations on Goods: "Ministerial Declaration on the Uruguay Round"*, GATT Document MIN.DEC (September 20, 1986), available at http://www.jus.uio.no/lm/wto.gatt.ministerial.declaration.uruguay.round.1986/portrait.pdf (last visited on November 11, 2017).

GATT (1988a), *GATT Multilateral Trade Negotiations—The Uruguay Round—Group of Negotiations on Goods: "Compilation of Written Submissions and Oral Statements"*, prepared by the Secretariat, GATT Document MTG.GNG/NG11/W12/Rev.1 (February 5, 1988).

GATT (1988b), *United States—Import Restrictions on Certain Products from Brazil, Request by Brazil*, GATT-Document L/6386 (August 24, 1988).

GATT (1988c), *Council—United States—Import Restrictions on Certain Products from Brazil—Recourse to Article XXIII:2 by Brazil—Communication from Brazil*, GATT-Document L/6386/Add.1/ (December 7, 1988).

GATT (1989), *Council—United States—Import Restrictions on Certain Products from Brazil—Recourse to Article XXIII:2 by Brazil—Note by the Chairman*, GATT Document C/169 (September 26, 1989).

GATT (1990a), *GATT Multilateral Trade Negotiations—Uruguay Round—Group of Negotiations on Goods (GATT)—Negotiating Group on Trade-Related Aspects of Intellectual Property Rights, Including Trade in Counterfeit Goods—Draft Agreement on Trade-Related Aspects of Intellectual Property Rights*, GATT Document MTN.GNG/NG11/W/68 (March 29, 1990).

GATT (1990b) *GATT Multilateral Trade Negotiations—The Uruguay Round—Negotiating Group on Trade-Related Aspects of Intellectual Property,*

Including Trade in Counterfeit Drugs, Communication from Argentina, Brazil, Chile, China, Colombia, Cuba, Egypt, India, Nigeria, Peru, Tanzania and Uruguay, GATT Document MTN.GNG/NG11/W71 (May 14, 1990).

GATT (1990c), *Council—United States—Import Restrictions on Certain Products from Brazil—Recourse to Article XXIII:2 by Brazil—Communication from Brazil,* GATT Document C/169/Add.1 (September 11, 1990).

GATT (1991), *GATT Uruguay Round—Draft Final Act Embodying the Results of the Uruguay Round of Multilateral Trade Negotiations,* GATT Document MTN.TNC/W/FA (December 20, 1991).

GATT (1994), *Uruguay Round—Marrakesh Declaration of 15 April 1994,* available at https://www.wto.org/english/docs_e/legal_e/marrakesh_decl_e.htm (last visited on September 22, 2018).

Gaudry, Kate S. (2011), "Evergreening: A Common Practice to Protect New Drugs", 29 *Nature Biotechnology*, 876-878.

Gava, Rodrigo (2008), "Vendem-se vidas (Globalização e intervenção estatal no acesso a medicamentos: algumas perspectivas itinerantes sobre o 'Acordo TRIPS' da OMC e a 'Resolução nº 4/2006' da CMED/ANVISA em face das patentes da indústria farmacêutica)", 21 *Revista Brasileira de Direito Público*, 75-112.

Gereffi, Gary (1983), *The Pharmaceutical Industry and Dependency in the Third World,* Princeton University Press, Princeton, New Jersey.

Gervais, Daniel (2003), *The TRIPS Agreement: Drafting History and Analysis,* 2nd ed., Sweet & Maxwell, London.

Ghose, Subhodip (2006), *"TRIPS and India: Crux of the Patent Controversy",* in: Sengupta, Dipankar / Chakraborty, Debashis / Banerjee, Pritam (eds.), *Beyond the Transition Phase of the WTO: An Indian Perspective,* Academic Foundation, New Delhi, 167-211.

Ghosh, Shuba (2005), "Patent Law and the Assurance Game: Refitting Intellectual Property on the Box of Regulation", 18 *Canadian Journal of Law and Jurisprudence*, 307-332.

Glasgow, Lara J. (2001), "Stretching the Limits of Intellectual Property Rights: Has the Pharmaceutical Industry Gone Too Far?", 41 *IDEA—The Journal of Law and Technology* 227-258.

Godt, Christine (2007a), "The So-called 'Waiver Compromise' of Doha and Hong Kong: About Contested Concepts of the Nature of the International Intellectual Property System—A Comment", in: Govaere, Inge / Ullrich, Hans (eds.), *Intellectual Property, Public Policy and International Trade,* Peter Lang, Frankfurt et al., 201-228.

Godt, Christine (2007b), Eigentum an Information—Patentschutz und allgemeine Eigentumstheorie am Beispiel genetischer Information, Mohr Siebeck, Tübingen.

Godt, Christine (2008a), "Research Tools—Patents and the Information Market in the Knowledge Based Economy", in: Govaere/Ullrich (eds.), *Intellectual Property, Market Power and the Public Interest,* Peter Lange, Brussels, 275-298.

Godt, Christine (2008b), "Innovationsfreiheit und Innovationsverantwortung: Geistiges Eigentum und öffentliche Ziele post grant", in: Eifert, Martin / Hoffmann-Riem, Wolfgang (eds.), *Geistiges Eigentum und Innovation—Innovation und Recht I*, Duncker & Humblot, Berlin, 363-377.

Godt, Christine (2010), "Differential Pricing of Patent Protected Pharmaceuticals inside Europe—Can Compulsory Licenses be Employed", in: Godt, Christine (ed.), *Differential Pricing of Pharmaceuticals inside Europe—Exploring Compulsory Licenses and Exhaustion for Access to Patented Essential Medicines*, Nomos, Baden-Baden, 37-73.

Godt, Christine (2012), "Zugang und Vorteilausgleich gemäß der Konvention für Biologische Vielfalt—Lehren aus dem TEFF-Fall", in: Bette, Kristina / Stephan, Michael (eds.), *Biodiversität, Geistiges Eigentum und Innovation—Aktuelle Herausforderung und Kontroversen in der wissensbasierten Bio-Industrie*, Phillips-Universität Marburg, Technologie- und Innovationsmanagement, 189-210.

Godt, Christine (2016), "Experts and Politics in Patent Policy: The Final Report of the Expert Group on the Development and Implications of Patent Law in the Field of Biotechnology and Genetic Engineering of the European Commission, 17 May 2016", 47 *International Review of Intellectual Property and Competition Law*, 960-980.

Gomes Canotilho, J.J. / Machado, Jônatas (2008), *A Questão da Constitucionalidade das Patentes "Pipeline" à Luz da Constituição Federal Brasileira de 1988*, Ed. Almedina, Coimbra.

Göttsche, Götz J. (2005), "Historische Entwicklung (GATT 1947 und Gründung der WTO)", in: Hilf, Meinhard / Oeter, Stefan (eds.), *WTO-Recht*, Nomos, Baden-Baden, 59-76.

Goulart (2004), "ANVISA e INPI tentam uniformizar pareceres", *Valor Econômico, Legislação e Tributos*, December 22, 2004.

Goulart, Joaquim Eugênio / Ahlert, Ivan B. (2005), "The Enforcement of Patent Rights in Brazil", in: Heath, Christopher and Petit, Laurence (eds.), *Patent Enforcement Worldwide: A Survey of 15 Countries. Essays in Honor of Dieter Stauder*, Hart Publishing, Oxford and Portland, 449-464.

Gouveia, Flávia (2007), "Inovação e Patentes: o tempo de maturação no Brasil", 3 *Inovação UNIEMP* 3, 24-25.

Grangeiro, Alexandre / Teixeira, Paulo Roberto (2007), "Repercussões do acordo de Propriedade Intelectual no Acesso a Medicamento", in: Villares, Fábio (ed.), *Propriedade Intelectual: Tensões entre o capital e a sociedade*, Ed. Paz e Terra, São Paulo, 115-139.

Grau-Kuntz, Karin (2009), "Sobre a Controvertida Questão das Patentes 'Pipeline'", *REVEL—Edição Especial "Patentes Pipeline"*, 82-95, available at https://www.ibpieuropa.org/?media_dl=278 (last visited on October 21, 2017).

Grimes, Warren S. (2005), "Counterproductive Incentives for Innovation?—Exclusionary Conduct in the Sale of an IP Product", 36 *International Review of Intellectual Property and Competition Law*, 214-225.

Grosse Ruse-Khan, Henning (2008), "Proportionality and Balancing within the Objectives for Intellectual Property Protection", in: Torremans, Paul L.C. (ed.),

Intellectual Property and Human Rights (Enhanced Edition of Copyright and Human Rights), Kluwer Law International, BV, Alphen aan den Rijn, 161-194.

Grosse Ruse-Khan, Henning (2009), *Policy Space for Domestic Public Interest Measures under TRIPS* (July 21, 2009). South Centre Research Paper No. 22. Available at SSRN: https://ssrn.com/abstract=1542542 or http://dx.doi.org/10.2139/ssrn.1542542 (last visited on June 25, 2019).

Grosse-Ruse Khan, Henning (2017), "The Principle of Integration in WTO/TRIPS Dispute Settlement" in: Cordonier Segger / Weeramantry (eds.), *Sustainable Development Principles in the Decisions of International Courts 1992-2012*, Routledge, London, 398-424.

Grubb, Philip W. (1999), *Patents for Chemicals, Pharmaceuticals and Biotechnology—Fundamentals of Global Law, Practice and Strategy*, Clarendon Press, Oxford.

Guennifi, Samira / Ramani, Shyama V. (2011), *Catching Up in Pharmaceuticals: A Comparative Study Between India and Brazil*, UNU Merit Working Paper Series 2010-19, Version from October 14, 2011, available at https://hal.archives-ouvertes.fr/hal-00632439/document (last visited on October 20, 2017).

Guise Rosina, Monica Steffen (2006), *Comércio Internacional, Patentes e Saúde Pública*, Master Thesis, Universidade Federal de Santa Catarina (May 2006), available at http://repositorio.ufsc.br/xmlui/handle/123456789/88622 (last visited on October 20, 2017).

Guise Rosina, Monica Steffen / Wang, Daniel /de Campos, Cristina (2010), "Access to Medicines: Pharmaceutical Patents and the Right to Health", in: Shaver, Lea (ed.), *Access to Knowledge in Brazil—New Research on Intellectual Property, Innovation and Development*, Bloomsbury Academic, New York, 165-213.

Guise Rosina, Mónica Steffen / de Oliveira Novaes, Adalina (2014), "Brazil and the Case of Patents and Access to Medicines. A Material Condition?", in: Dreyfuss, Rochelle C. / Rodríguez-Garavito, César (eds.), *Balancing Wealth and Health. The Battle over Intellectual Property and Access to Medicines in Latin America*, Oxford University Press, Oxford pp. 89-110.

Gusmão, José Roberto / Ferreira, Katia Jane (2009), "Novas Aplicações Terapêuticas", 100 *Revista da ABPI*, 43-50.

Haas, Peter M. (1992), "Introduction: Epistemic Communities and International Policy Coordination", 46 *International Organization* (1), 1-35.

Halbert, Debora J. (2005), "Moral Discourses: South Africa's Intellectual Property Fight for Access to AIDS Medication", in: Halbert, Deborah J. (ed.), *Resisting Intellectual Property*, Routledge, London & New York, 87-111.

Halbert, Debora J. (2006), *The World Intellectual Property Organization: Changing Narratives on Intellectual Property*, Paper presented at the International Studies Association Conference, San Diego, California, available at http://regulation.upf.edu/bath-06/1_Halbert.pdf (last visited on October 21, 2017).

Hall, Bronwyn H. / Graham, Stuart J. H. / Harhoff, Dietmar / Mowery, David C. (2003), *Prospects for Improving U.S. Patent Quality via Post-Grant Opposition*, NBER

Working Paper Series, Working Paper 9731 National Bureau of Economic Research (May), available at http://www.nber.org/papers/w9731 (last visited on October 21, 2017).

Hall, Bronwyn H. / Harhoff, Dietmar (2004), "Post Grant Reviews in the U.S. Patent System—Design Choices and Expected Impact", 19 *Berkeley Technology Law Journal*, 989-1015.

Hall, Bronwyn / Hermes, Christian / von Graevenitz, Georg (2016), *Patent Thickets and First-Time Patenting*: New Evidence, April 23, CEPR's Policy Portal, available at http://voxeu.org/article/patent-thickets-and-first-time-patenting-new-evidence (last visited on October 21, 2017).

Hansen, B. (1988), "New Problems of the Second Indication", 19 *International Review of Intellectual Property and Competition Law*, 772-788.

Hansen, B (2008) "Auswahlerfindungen auf dem Gebiet der Chemie—Brauchen wir einen deutschen Sonderweg?—Anmerkungen nicht nur zur Fluoran-Entscheidung", *Gewerblicher Rechtschutz and Urheberrecht—Internationaler Teil*, 891-899.

Hardin, Garrit (1968), "The Tragedy of the Commons", *162 Science 3859 New Series*, 1243-1248.

Harhoff, Dietmar / Engel, Christoph / Möschel, Wernhard (2007), *Patentschutz und Innovation Gutachten des Wissenschaftlichen Beirats beim Bundesministerium für Wirtschaft und Technologie*, available at https://www.bmwi.de/Redaktion/DE/Publikationen/Ministerium/Veroeffentlichung-Wissenschaftlicher-Beirat/patentschutz-und-innovation.html (last visited on October 26, 2017).

Harnisch, Sandy (2006), *Die Zwangslizenz im südafrikanischen und deutschen Patentrecht—ein Rechtsvergleich unter besonderer Berücksichtigung der Arzneimittelerfindungen*, BWV, Berlin.

Harrison, Christopher Scott (2004), *The Politics of the International Pricing of Prescription Drugs*, Praeger Publishers, Westport.

Hasenclever, Lia / Lopes, Rodrigo / Costa Chaves, Gabriela / Reis, Renata / Vieira Fogaça, Marcela (2010), "O Instituto das Patentes Pipeline e o Acesso a Medicamentos: Aspectos Econômicos e Jurídicos Deletérios à Economia da Saúde", *11 Revista de Direito Sanitário* 2, 164-188.

Hasenclever, Lia / Paranhos, Julia (2014), *The Development of the Pharmaceutical Industry in Brazil and India: Technological Capability and Industrial Development*, Economics Innovation Research Group, Economics Institute, Federal University of Rio de Janeiro April 29, available at https://www.researchgate.net/publication/228859162_The_development_of_the_pharmaceutical_industry_in_Brazil_and_India_technological_capability_and_industrial_development (last visited on September 30, 2017).

Heath, Christopher (2007), "Os limites dos direitos patentários em termos temporais, geográficos e de conteúdo" in: Beas Rodrigues/Polido, *Propriedade Intelectual—Novos Paradigmas Internacionais, Conflitos e Desafios*, Rio de Janeiro, Elsevier, pp. 19-41.

Hein, Wolfgang / Kohlmorgen, Lars (2005), *Global Health Governance: Conflicts on Global Social Rights*, GIGA Working Paper 7, Hamburg, available at https://www

.giga-hamburg.de/de/publication/global-health-governance-conflicts-on-global-social-rights-0 (last visited on October 15, 2017).

Hemphill, C. Scott / Sampat, Bhaven N. (2012), "Evergreening, Patent Challenges, and Effective Market Life of Pharmaceuticals", 31 *Journal of Health Economics*, 327-339.

Herrmann, Christoph (2002), "TRIPS, Patentschutz für Medikamente und staatliche Gesundheitspolitik: Hinreichende Flexibilität?," *Europäische Zeitschrift für Wirtschaftsrecht*, 37-43.

Herrlich, Christoph (2005), *Internationale Menschenrechte als Korrektiv des Welthandelsrechts—Eine Vertragskonkurrenz im Spannungsfeld von Pharmapatentschutz und dem Zugang zu Medikamenten*, LIT Verlag, Berlin.

Hestermeyer, Holger (2007), *Human Rights and the WTO—The Case of Patents and Access to Medicines*, OUP, Oxford et al.

Hey, Raul (2003), "Licença Obrigatória de Patentes—Entender Antes de Aplicar", 66 *Revista da ABPI*, 3-11.

Hilty, Reto M. (2009), "The Role of Patent Quality in Europe", in: Drexl, Josef / Hilty, Reto M. / Boy, Lawrence / Godt, Christine / Remiche, Bernard (eds.), *Technology and Competition, Technologie et Concurrence—Contributions in Honour of/ Mélanges en L'honneur de Hans Ullrich*, Larciers, Bruxelles, 91-121.

't Hoen, Ellen F.M. (2009), *The Global Politics of Pharmaceutical Monopoly Power—Drug patents, access, innovation and the application of the WTO Doha Declaration on TRIPS and Public Health*, AMB, Universiteit van Amsterdam, available at https://www.msfaccess.org/sites/default/files/MSF_assets/Access/Docs/ACCESS_book_GlobalPolitics_tHoen_ENG_2009.pdf (last visited on October13, 2017).

Hollis, Aidam (2004), *Me-Too Drugs: Is There a Problem?*, published December 13, Paper available at http://www.who.int/intellectualproperty/topics/ip/MetooDrugs_Hollis1.pdf, (last visited on October 13, 2017).

Holtorf, Marc L. / Traumann, Julia (2017), "BPatG-Entscheidung zur patentrechtlichen Zwangslizenz rechtmäßig", *GRUR-Prax*, 437.

Holtz, Catarina (2008), "Opposition Only After Grant—Any Effects on Inventive Step at the EPO", *German Journal of International Intellectual Property Law*, 653-657.

Hore, Edward (2000), "A Comparison of United States and Canadian Laws as They Affect Generic Pharmaceutical Market Entry", 55 *Food and Drug Law Journal*, 373-388.

Hore, Edward (2004), *Patently Absurd—Evergreening of Pharmaceutical Patent Protection under the Patented Medicines (Notice of Compliance) Regulations of Canada's Patent Act*, available at http://www.hazzardandhore.com/docs/papers/patently_absurd_04.pdf (last visited on October 21, 2017).

Hutchins, Mike (2003), "Extending the Monopoly—How 'Secondary Patents' Can Be Used to Delay or Prevent Competition upon Expiry of the Basic Product Patent", 1 *Journal of Generic Medicines*, 57-71.

Huynh-Ba, Kim / Beumer Sassi, Alexandra (2018), "ANVISA: An Introduction to a New Regulatory Member with Many Challenges", 4 *American Association of Pharmaceutical Scientists Open 9*.

IFPMA (2006), *Inovação Incremental, Propriedade Intelectual e Interesse Público: Como a Inovação Incremental Leva a Medicamentos Novos Melhores e Mais Seguros,* (Brazilian edition, Institutional Propaganda), Geneva.

INTERFARMA (2017),—*Guia 2017—Ranking de fabricantes,* available at https://www.interfarma.org.br/guia/guia-2017/dados-do-setor#ranking-de-fabricantes (last visited November 13, 2017).

IQVIA MIDAS (2018), *Top Ten Pharmaceutical World Markets,* available at *https://www.iqvia.com/-/media/iqvia/pdfs/canada-location-site/2018-trends/top10 world widesales_en_18.pdf?la = en&hash = 5EF58E3BF8D12DCE503E70616939D52624 C73A75* (last visited on September 4, 2019).

Jaenichen, Hans-Rainer / Meier, Jürgen / Hölder, Niels (2008), "Medical Use Claims: EPC 2000 and its Impact on Prosecution and Enforcement", in: Prinz zu Waldeck und Pyrmont, Wolrad / Adelmann, Martin J. / Brauneis, Robert / Drexl, Josef / Nack, Ralph (eds.), *Patent and Technological Progress in a Globalized World—Liber Amicorum Joseph Straus*, Springer Verlag, Berlin / Heidelberg, 254-274.

Joncheere, Kees de / Haaijer-Ruskamp, Flora M. / Rietveld, Ad. H. / Dukes, Maurice.Nelson.Graham. (2003), "Scope of the Problem", in: Dukes, Maurice.Nelson.Graham et al. (eds.), *Drugs and Money—Prices, Affordability and Cost Containment*, IOS Press Ohmsha, Amsterdam et al., 7-13, available at https://www.euro.who.int/__data/assets/pdf_file/0011/96446/e79122.pdf (last visited on October 19, 2020).

Kaplan, Edward S. (1996), *American Trade Policy 1923-1995*, Greenwood Press, USA.

Kesan, Jay P. (2009), "Patent Office Oppositions and Patent Invalidation in Court: Complements or Substitutes?", in: Takenaka, Toshiko (ed.), *Patent Law and Theory—A Handbook of Contemporary Research*, Edward Elgar, Cheltenham (UK), 246-270.

Kesselheim, Aaron S. / Cook-Degan, Robert M. / Winnickoff, Davi E. / Mello, Michelle M. (2013), "Gene Patenting—The Supreme Court Finally Speaks", 369 *New England Journal of Medicine* 9, August 29, 869-875, available at https://www.ncbi.nlm.nih.gov/pmc/articles/PMC3777541/ (last visited on November 5, 2017).

Khan, B. Zorina (2002), "Intellectual Property and Economic Development: Lessons from American and European History", *Commission on Intellectual Property Rights, Study paper 1a*, National Bureau of Economic Research, available at http://www.iprcommission.org/papers/pdfs/study_papers/sp1a_khan_study.pdf (last visited on November 5, 2017).

Kingsland, Lawrence C. (1948), "The United States Patent Office", 13 *Law and Contemporary Problems*, 354-367.

Knoblich, Ruth (2017), *Die globale Regulierung geistiger Eigentumsrechte. Interessen, Strategien und Einfluss Brasiliens, Indiens und Chinas*, Springer VS, Wiesbaden.

Koopman, Jerry (2008), "Human Rights Implications of Patenting Biotechnological Knowledge", in: Torremans, Paul L.C. (ed.), *Intellectual Property and Human Rights (Enhanced Edition of Copyright and Human Rights)*, Kluwer Law International, BV, The Netherlands, 533-583).

Kluwer Patent Blog (2019), *Teff Patent Declared Invalid, "Great News" for Ethiopia*, available at http://patentblog.kluweriplaw.com/2019/02/12/teff-patents-declared-invalid-great-news-for-ethiopia/, February 12, 2019 (last visited on August 10, 2019).

Kramer, Birgit (2007), *Patentschutz und Zugang zu Medikamenten. Rechtliche und ökonomische Implikation*, Carl Heymanns, Köln.

Kuanpoth, Jakkrit (2008), "Intellectual Property Protection after TRIPS: An Asian Experience", in: Malbon, Justin / Lawson, Charles (eds.), *Interpreting and Implementing the TRIPS Agreement—Is it Fair?* Edward Elgar, Cheltenham (UK), 71-96.

Kweitel, Juana/ Reis, Renata (2007), "A Primeira Licença Compulsória de Medicamento na América Latina", *Pontes*, Vol. 3, No. 3, ICTSD, available at http://www.ictsd.org/bridges-news/pontes/news/a-primeira-licen%C3%A7a-compuls%C3%B3ria-de-medicamento-na-am%C3%A9rica-latina (last visited on November 3, 2017).

La Croix, Summer / Liu, Ming (2007), "Patents and Access to Essential Medicines", in: Keith E. Maskus (ed.), *Intellectual Property, Growth and Trade*, Emerald Group Publishing Limited, Amsterdam, 423-464.

Lademann, Rainer P. (2011), "Zur Methodologie des more economic approach im Kartellrecht", in: Bechthold, S. / Jickeli, J. / Rohe, M. (eds.), *Recht, Ordnung und Wettbewerb—Festschrift zum 70. Geburtstag von Werhard Möschel*, Baden-Baden, pp. 381-394.

Lamping, Mathias / Hilty, Reto / Burk, Dan / Correa, Carlos M. / Drahos, Peter / Gopalakrishnan, N.S / Ruse-Khan, Henning / Kur, Annette / van Overwalle, Geertrui / Reichman, Jerome H. / Ullrich, Hans (2014), "Declaration on Patent Protection—Regulatory Sovereignty under TRIPS", 45 *International Review of Intellectual Property and Competition Law*, 679-698.

Lang, Markus (2014), "The Anti-patent Movement Revisited: Politics and Professionalism in Nineteenth-century Germany", in: Müller, Dietmar / Siegrist, Hannes (eds.), *Professionen, Eigentum und Staat: Europäische Entwicklungen im Vergleich—19. und 20. Jahrhundert*, Wallstein, Göttingen, 230-249.

Lanjouw, Jean O. / Cockburn, Iain (2000), *Do Patents Matter? Empirical Evidence After GATT*, NBER, Working Paper 7495, available at http://www.nber.org/papers/w7495.pdf (last visited on October 15, 2017).

Lanzilotti Jannuzzi, Anna Haydée / Guimarães Vasconcelos, Alexandre / Gomes de Souza, Cristina (2008), "Especificidades do Patenteamento no Setor Farmacêutico: modalidades e aspectos de proteção de propriedade intelectual", *24 Cadernos de Saúde Pública*, 1205-1218.

Lanzillotti Jannuzzi, Anna Haydée / Guimarães Vasconcelos, Alexandre (2017), "O Backlog na Concessão das Patentes e seu Impacto na Utilização de Salvaguardas Legais e no Acesso aos Medicamentos no Brasil", in: Curzel, Rosana / Nunes, João (eds.), *Patentes e o Acesso a Antirretrovirais no Brasil—O Desafio da Licença Compulsória*, Editora Appris, Curitiba, 43-72.

Lazzarini, Zita (2003), "Making Access to Pharmaceuticals a Reality: Legal Options under TRIPS and the Case of Brazil", 6 *Yale Human Rights and Development Law Journal*, 103-138.

Lee; Peter (2017), "Towards a Distributive Agenda for U.S. Patent Law", 55 *Houston Law Review* 2, 321-375.

Lemley, Mark A. (2015), "Faith-Based Intellectual Property", 62 *UCLA Law Review*, 1328-1346.

Leonardos, Gustavo S. (1998), "Dos Prazos de Validade das Patentes em Vista do Acordo TRIPS e da Nova Lei de Propriedade Industrial", 87 *Revista dos Tribunais* 758, 89-105.

Leonardos, Luiz / Lick, Otto (2002), "A Exegese do Art. 229-C da Lei de Propriedade Industrial após a Edição das Medidas Provisórias 2.006, de 15/12/99 e 2.014, de 21/12/2000, e a Promulgação da Lei Nº 10.196, de 14/02/2001", 61 *Revista da ABPI*, 57-68.

Levy, Marcos / Licks, Otto (2003), *O Requisito de Fabricação Completa do Objeto de uma Patente no Território Nacional*, Interfarma, São Paulo.

Lewis, Tracy / Reichman, Jerome H. (2005), "Using Liability Rules to Stimulate Local Innovation in Developing Countries: Application to Traditional Knowledge", in: Maskus, Keith E. / Reichman, Jerome H. (eds.), *International Public Goods and Transfer of a Technology under a Globalized Intellectual Property Regime*, CUP, Cambridge et al., 337-366.

Liebig, Klaus (2006), *Auswirkungen des internationalen Patentregimes auf die Medikamentenproduktion und den Zugang zu Medikamenten in LDCs*, Deutsches Institut für Entwicklungspolitik, Bonn.

Licks, Otto (2001), "A falta de transparência no direito de patentes", *Gazeta Mercantil*, August 8, 2001.

Lima, Newton /Paranaguá, Pedro et al. (2013), *A Revisão da Lei de Patentes: Inovação em Prol da Competitividade Nacional*, Câmara dos Deputados—Centro de Estudos e Debates Estratégicos, available at https://www2.camara.leg.br/a-camara/estruturaadm/altosestudos/temas/seminarios/lancamento-patentes-9-10-13/a-revisao-da-lei-de-patentes (last visited on November 17, 2018).

Lopes dos Santos, Rodrigo S. (2010), *Sustentabilidade do Programa DST/AIDS: Análise da Capacidade de Oferta e Preços dos Medicamentos Antivirais*, Master Thesis, Universidade Federal do Rio de Janeiro, available at http://www.dominiopublico.gov.br/pesquisa/DetalheObraForm.do?select_action=&co_obra=180704 (last visited on October 20, 2018).

Loughlan, Patricia Louise (2008), "'You Wouldn't Steal a Car': Intellectual Property and the Language of Theft", 29 *European Intellectual Property Review*, 401-405 / Sydney Law School Research Paper No. 08/35, available at https://papers.ssrn.com/sol3/papers.cfm?abstract_id=1120585 (last visited on October 21, 2017).

Love, James (2006a), "Letter Asking USTR Not to Interfere with the Thai Government Decision to Issue a Government-Use License on Patents Covering the AIDS Drug Efavirenz", *Third World Resurgence* 196, Malaysia, 25-27, available at http://www.cptech.org/ip/health/c/thailand/ustr12dec2006thailand.html (last visited on October 20, 2017).

Love, James (2006b), "Four Practical Measures to Enhance Access to Medical Technologies", in: Roffe, Pedro / Tansey, Geoff / Vivas-Eugui, David (eds.), *Negotiating Health—Intellectual Property and Access to Medicines*, Earthscan. Dondon / Sterling, 241-256.

Loyola, Maria Andréa (2008), "Medicamentos e saúde pública em tempos de AIDS: metamorfoses de uma política dependente", 13 *Ciência e Saúde Coletiva (Suplemento)*, 763-778.

Machlup, Fritz (1958), *An Economic Review of the Patent System—Study of the Subcommittee on Patents, Trademarks and Copyrights of the Committee on the Judiciary*, United States Senate, 85th Congress, 2d Session, Study n° 15, United States Govenrment Printing Office, Washington

Machlup, Fritz (1968) "Patents", in: *International Encyclopedia of Social Sciences*, Vol. 11, 461-472, Collier-MacMillan, London.

Machlup, Fritz / Penrose, Edith T. (1950), "The Patent Controversy in the 19th Century", *X the Journal of Economic History*, 1-29.

MacQueen, Hector / Waelde, Charlotte / Laurie, Hector (2008), *Contemporary Intellectual Property—Law and Policy*, OUP, Oxford et al.

Malich, Erika / Marion, Sarah (2015), "Increasing Access to Medicines—Leveraging Brazil's Experience", 2 *Policy Brief CIGI Graduate Fellows Series*, 1-7.

Malkawi, Bashar H. (2009), "Patent Protection and the Pharmaceutical Industry in Jordan", 4 *Asian Journal of WTO and International Health Law and Policy*, 93-127.

Mandel, Gregory (2008), "The Non-Obvious Problem: How the Indeterminate Non-Obviousness Standard Produces Excessive Patent Grants", 42 *UC Davis Law Review*, 57-128, available at http://lawreview.law.ucdavis.edu/issues/42/1/articles/42-1_Mandel.pdf (last visited on October 21, 2017).

Mansfield, Edwin (1996), "Patents and Innovation: An Empirical Study", 32 *Management Science*, 173-181.

Marinho, Maria Edelvacy / Varella, Marcelo (2015), "La Protection des Données Générées dans le Cadre du Processus d'Autorization de Mise sur le Marché au Brésil", in: Autenne, d'Alexia / Cassiers, Vincent / Strowel, Alain (eds.), *Droit, Économie et Valeurs—Hommage à Bernard Remiche*, Larcier, Bruxelles, 439-451.

Maskus, Keith E. / Reichman, Jerome H. (2004), "The Globalization of Private Knowledge Goods and the Privatization of Global Public Goods", *7 Journal of International Economic Law*, 279-318.

Massard da Fonseca, Elize (2012), *Reforming Pharmaceutical Regulation: A Case Study of Generic Drugs in Brazil*, PhD Thesis, University of Edinburgh.

Massard da Fonseca, Elize / Bastos, Francisco I. (2016), "Implementing Intellectual Property of Pharmaceuticals in Middle-Income Countries: A Case-Study of Patent Regulation in Brazil", 41 *Journal of Health Politics, Policy and Law* 3, 423-450.

Mazur, Szymon (2015), *Durchsetzung von Leistungsansprüchen aus sozialen Grundrechten in Brasilien und in Deutschland*, Shaker Verlag, Aachen.

Mazzoleni, Roberto / Nelson, Richard (1998), "The Benefits and Costs of Strong Patent Protection: A Contribution to the Current Debate", *27 Research Policy*, 273-284.

Mazzoleni, Roberto / Martins Costa Póvoa, Luciano (2010), "Accumulation of Technological Capabilities and Economic Development—Did Brazil's IPR Regime Matter?", in: Odagiri, Hiroyuki / Goto, Akira / Sunami, Atsushi / Nelson, Richard R. (eds.), *Intellectual Property Rights, Development and Catch-Up—An International Comparative Study*, OUP, Oxford et al. 280-314.

Mazzucato, Mariana / Penna, Caetano (2016), *The Brazilian Innovation System: A Mission-Oriented Policy Proposal*, Centro de Gestão e Estudos Estratégicos, Brasília.

McCalman, Phillip (2001), "Reaping What You Sow: An Empirical Analysis of International Patent Harmonization", 55 *Journal of International Economics*, 161-186.

McGillivray, James (2017), *"'Pyrates' of the Lyceum: Big Pharma, Patents, and Academic Freedom in Neoliberal Times"*, PhD Thesis, Osgoode Hall Law School of York University, available at https://digitalcommons.osgoode.yorku.ca/cgi/viewcontent.cgi?article=1030&context=phd (last visited on April 29, 2019).

Mello e Souza, André de (2005), *The Power of the Weak: Advocacy Networks, Ideational Change and the Global Politics of Pharmaceutical Patent Rights*, PhD Thesis, Stanford University, UMI Dissertation Services.

Mello e Souza, André de (2011), O Acordo Sobre os Aspectos dos Direitos de Propriedade Intelectual Relacionados ao Comércio (TRIPS): Implicações e Possibilidades para a Saúde Pública no Brasil, IPEA—Texto para Discussão 1615.

Mello e Souza, André de (2017), "O Licenciamento Compulsório como Estratégia para Promover Acesso a Medicamentos Essenciais: o Caso do Brasil", in: Curzel, Rosana / Nunes, João (eds.), *Patentes e o Acesso a Antirretrovirais no Brasil—O Desafio da Licença Compulsória*, Editora Juruá, Curitiba, 107-133.

Mello Vianna, Cid Manso / Caetano, Rosângela / Mendes da Silva, Rondinelli / Autran Sampaio, Mariana M. / Rodrigues, Rodolfo R. D. (2009), "Brazil: Financing Resource Flows in Health R & D" in Landriault, Erik / Matlin, Stephen A. (ed.), *—Monitoring Financial Flows for Health Research 2009—Behind the Global Numbers*, Global Forum for Health Research, Geneva, 129-135.

Mercurio, Bryan (2006), "Resolving the Public Health Crisis in the Developing World: Problems and Barriers of Access to Essential Medicines", 5 *Northwestern University Journal of International Human Rights*, 1-40.

Merges, Robert P. (1994), "Of Property Rules, Coase, and Intellectual Property", 94 *Columbia Law Review*, 2655-2673.

Merges, Robert P. (2005), "A Transactional View of Property Rights", *20 Berkeley Technology Law Journal*, 1477-1520.

Mesidor, Marie D. (2013), *Intellectual Property Rights in Competition Law: Compulsory Licensing Issues in Developing Countries*, available at https://papers.ssrn.com/sol3/papers.cfm?abstract_id=2238796.

Milward de Azevedo Meiners, Constance Marie (2007), "Patentes Farmacêuticas: um entrave para o acesso a medicamentos?", 5 *Revista de Políticas Públicas e Gestão Governamental* 2, 27-49.

Milward de Azevedo Meiners, Constance Marie (2008), "Patentes farmacêuticas e saúde pública: desafios à política brasileira de acesso ao tratamento antirretroviral", 24 *Cadernos de Saúde Pública* 7, 1474-1478.

Miranda, Helen (2008), *Avaliação da análise dos pedidos de patentes farmacêuticas feita pela ANVISA no cumprimento do mandato legal da anuência prévia*, Master Thesis, Fundação Osvaldo Cruz (Escola Nacional de Saúde Pública Sérgio Arouca), Rio de Janeiro.

Mitsuuchi Kunisawa, Viviane Yumy (2009a), "Brasilien—Gericht verneint direkte Anwendbarkeit des TRIPS", *Gewerblicher Rechtschutz and Urheberrecht—Internationaler Teil*, 630.

Mitsuuchi Kunisawa, Viviane Yumy (2009b) "Brasilien: Aktuelle Entwicklungen hinsichtlich der Rolle der nationalen Gesundheitsbehörde ANVISA im Erteilungsverfahren für pharmazeutische Patente", *Gewerblicher Rechtschutz and Urheberrecht—Internationaler Teil*, 88-89.

Mitsuuchi Kunisawa, Viviane Yumy (2009c) "Patenting Pharmaceutical Inventions on Second Medical Use in Brazil", 12(4) *The Journal of World Intellectual Property*, 297-316.

Mitsuuchi Kunisawa, Viviane Yumy (2015), *The TRIPS Agreement Implementation in Brazil—Patents in the Pharmaceutical Area*, Nomos, Baden-Baden.

MoH/MDIC (2007), Fórum de Competitividade da Cadeia Produtiva Farmacêutica 2003-2006: o desafio a prosseguir, available at http://bvsms.saude.gov.br/bvs/publicacoes/forum_competitividade_cadeia_farmac_2003a2006_1ed.pdf (Last visited on November 2, 2017).

MoH/MDIC/AGU (2011), Portaria Interministerial MS/MDIC/AGU n° 1956 of August 16, 2011, *DOU* August 17, 2011, p. 72, available at http://bvsms.saude.gov.br/bvs/saudelegis/gm/2011/pri1956_16_08_2011.html (last visited on November 2, 2017).

MoH/MDIC/AGU (2012), Portaria Interministerial (PRI) MS/MDIC/AGU No. 1.065, of May 24, 2012: Torna público o relatório final apresentado pelo Grupo de Trabalho Interministerial constituído pela PRI No. 1956 MS/MDIC/AGU, *DOU* Seção I, May 25, 2012, p. 35, available at http://bvsms.saude.gov.br/bvs/saudelegis/gm/2012/anexo/anexo_pri1065_24_05_2012.html.pdf (last visited on November 2, 2017).

Momsen Leonardos & Cia, Manifestação da INTERFARMA—O Regime da Anuência Prévia da ANVISA para Concessão de Patentes de Invenção, Instituído pelo Artigo 229-C introduzido na Lei 9.279/96 e suas Consequências para as Obrigações Internacionais Assumidas pelo Brasil com os demais Países-Membros da Organização Mundial do Comércio—OMC—Uma Violação Tripla aos Artigos 27 e 62 do TRIPS (Given by hand to the author by Raimundo, INTERFARMA's Consultive President, when interviewed at his office in Rio de Janeiro), unpublished.

Moore, Julia (2006), "Parallel Trade, Unparallel Laws: An Examination of the Pharmaceutical Parallel Trade Laws of the United States, the European Union and the World Trade Organization", 6 *Richmond Journal of Global Law and Business*, 77-93.

Mowery, David C. (2010), "IPR and US Economic Catch-Up", in: Odagiri, Hiroyuki / Goto, Akira / Sunami, Atsushi / Nelson, Richard R. (eds.), *Intellectual Property*

Rights, Development, and Catch-Up—an International Comparative Study, OUP, Oxford et al., 31-62.

Mueller, Lisa L. (2015), "13th Federal District Court of Rio de Janeiro Holds That ANVISA Can Examine Patentability Requirements of Patent Applications Claiming Pharmaceutical Inventions", *The National Law Review*, June 26, available at https://www.natlawreview.com/article/13th-federal-district-court-rio-de-janeiro-holds-anvisa-can-examine-patentability-re (last visited on January 17, 2018).

Mueller, Lisa L. / Moreira Taketsuma Costa, Silvia (2014), "Should ANVISA Be Permitted to Reject Pharmaceutical Patent Applications in Brazil?", *24 Expert Opinion on Therapeutic Patents*, 1-4, available at http://www.tandfonline.com/doi/full/10.1517/13543776.2014.854773 (last visited on January 21, 2018).

Musungu, Sisule F. / Oh, Cecilia (2006), *The Use of Flexibilities in TRIPS by Developing Countries: Can They Promote Access to Medicines?* Geneva: South Centre and World Health Organization.

Muzaka, Valbona (2009), "Dealing with Public Health and Intellectual Property for Pharmaceuticals at the World Trade Organization", in: MacLean, Sandra J. / Brown, Sherri A. / Fourie, Pieter (eds.), *Health for Some—The Political Economy of Global Health Governance*, Palgrave MacMillan, London, pp. 183-195.

Muzaka, Valbona (2018), "Interrupted Constructions—The Brazilian Health-Industrial Complex in Historical Perspective", *Latin America Perspective*, 1-24.

Nair, Mohan D. (2008), "Compromising TRIPS: Brazil's Approach to Tackle the HIV/AIDS Imbroglio", 13 *Journal of Intellectual Property Rights*, 456-463.

Nafis, Soya/Srinivasan, Divya (2015), "Validity of Patent Linkage across the Globe", *The Patent Lawyer*, 35-37, available at https://www.lexorbis.com/wp-content/uploads/2015/10/Patent-Lawyer-as-published.pdf (last visited on October 22, 2017).

Nanci, Luciana (2005a), "Concessão de patentes não é assunto da ANVISA, dizem especialistas", *Consultor Jurídico*, March 8, 2005, available at https://www.conjur.com.br/2005-mar-08/atuacao_anvisa_ilegal_afirmam_especialistas (last visited on November 3, 2017).

Nanci, Luciana (2005b), "Eurofarma briga para produzir remédio contra câncer", *Conjur* July 9, available at http://www.conjur.com.br/2005-jul-09/eurofarma_briga_produzir_remedio_cancer (last visited on November 3, 2017).

Ng, Rick (2004), *Drugs—From Discovery to Approval*, John Wiley & Sons, New Jersey.

Nogueira Viana, José M. (2002), "Intellectual Property Rights, the World Trade Organization and Public Health: the Brazilian Perspective", 17 *Connecticut Journal of International Law*, 311-317.

Novartis (2017), "Novartis Position on Intellectual Property", available at https://www.novartis.com/sites/www.novartis.com/files/novartis-intellectual-property-position.pdf (last visited on July 15, 2019).

Nunn, Amy (2009), *The Politics and History of Aids Treatment in Brazil*, Springer, New York.

Nunn, Amy / Fonseca, Elize M. / Bastos, Francisco I. / Gruskin, Sofia / Salomon, Joshua A. (2007), "Evolution of Antiretroviral Drug Costs in Brazil in the Context of Free and Universal Access to AIDS Treatment", 4 *PLoS Medicine 11*, e305, 1804-1817.

Ocké-Reis, Carlos Octávio (2015), "Gasto Privado em Saúde Pública no Brasil", 31 *Cadernos de Saúde Pública*, 1351-1353, available at http://www.scielo.br/pdf/csp/v31n7/0102-311X-csp-31-7-1351.pdf (last visited on October 21, 2017).

Odagiri, Hiroyuki / Goto, Akira / Sunami, Atsushi / Nelson, Richard R. (2010), "Introduction", in: Odagiri, Hiroyuki / Goto, Akira / Sunami, Atsushi / Nelson, Richard R. (eds.), *Intellectual Property Rights, Development, and Catch-Up—an International Comparative Study*, OUP, Oxford et al., 1-27.

Odermatt, Jed (2009), "Investigating New Models of Pharmaceutical Innovation to Protect the Human Right to Health", 40 *International Review of Intellectual Property and Competition Law*, 173-181.

Oh, Cecilia (2006), "Compulsory Licenses: Recent Experiences in Developing Countries", 1 *International Journal of Intellectual Property Management* 1-2, 22-36.

Okie, Susan (2006), "Fighting HIV—Lessons from Brazil", 354 *New England Journal of Medicine* 1977-1981, May 11, 2006.

Oliveira, Marcelo F. / Moreno, Fernanda F. (2007), "Negociações Comerciais Internacionais e a Democracia: o Contencioso Brasil x EUA das Patentes Farmacêuticas na OMC", 50 *DADOS—Revista de Ciências Sociais*, 189-220.

Orsi, Fabienne / Hasenclever, Lia / Fialho, Beatriz / Tigre, Paulo / Coriat, Benjamin (2003), "Intellectual Property Rights, Anti-AIDS Policy and Generic Drugs: Lessons from the Brazilian Public Health Program" in: Moatti, Jean-Paul, Coriat, Benjamin, Souteyrand, Yves, Barnett, Tony, Dumoulin, Jerome and Flori, Yves-Antoine (eds.), *Economics of AIDS and Access to HIV/AIDS Care in Developing Countries Issues and Challenges*, Paris: Agence Nationale de Recherches sur le Sida et les Hépatites Virales, 109-35.

Ostry, Sylvia (2009), "The Trade System Amidst the Global Financial Crisis", in: Deere-Birkbeck, Carolyn / Meléndez-Ortiz, Ricardo (eds.), *Rebuilding Global Trade: Proposals for a Fairer, More Sustainable Future*, ICTSD, Oxford, pp. 60-61.

Paiva, Carlos Henrique Assunção / Teixeira, Luiz Antonio (2014), "Reforma Sanitária e Criação do Sistema Único de Saúde: Notas sobre Contextos e Autores", 21 *História, Ciências, Saúde*, 15-35, available at http://www.scielo.br/pdf/hcsm/v21n1/0104-5970-hcsm-21-1-00015.pdf (last visited on October 22, 2017).

Palmeira, Pedro Lins Filho/ Pan, Simon Shi Koo (2003), "Cadeia Farmacêutica no Brasil: Avaliação Preliminar e Perspectivas", *BNDES Setorial 18*, Rio de Janeiro, pp. 3-22, available at http://www.bndes.gov.br/SiteBNDES/export/sites/default/bndes_pt/Galerias/Arquivos/conhecimento/bnset/set1801.pdf (last visited on October 21, 2017).

Palmer, Tom G. (1989), "Intellectual Property: A Non-Posnerian Law and Economic Approach", 12 *Hamline Law Review*, 261-304.

Paranhos, Julia (2020), "Public Health System Increasing Costs due to the Extension of Drug Patent Terms", Webinar Knowledge Network for Innovation and Access to Medicines, Global Health Centre—Extending monopolies: evidence from Brazil and Europe on the impact on innovation and access to medicines, 25th June

2020, available at https://www.graduateinstitute.ch/sites/internet/files/2020-06/presentation-juliaparanhos.pdf (last visited on August 23, 2020).

Parthasaraty, R. / Goddar, Heinz (2009), "Patentability of Pharmaceutical Products in India—The Novartis Case", 1 *International Review of Intellectual Property and Competition Law* 38, 38-45.

Passos, Najla (2016), "O Complexo Fármaco-político", in: Bérron, Gustavo / Gonzalez, Luz (eds.), *A Privatização da Democracia: Um Catálogo da Captura Corporativa no Brasil*, 109-122, available at http://www.vigencia.org/wp-content/uploads/2016/08/Vige%CC%82ncia_Cata%CC%81logo_FINAL-1.pdf (last visited on October 22, 2017).

Patrocínio, Daniel Moreira do (2006), "O Princípio da Exaustão dos Direitos de Propriedade Intelectual e a Importação Paralela", 84 *Revista da ABPI*, 47-52.

Penrose, Edith Tilton (1951), *The Economics of the International Patent System*, The John Hopkins Press, Baltimore.

Peritz, Rudolph J. R. (2008), *Draft Patents and Progress: The Incentive Conundrum*, Paper presented at the ATRIP Conference Session: Free Access to Use: What We Learned in the Past Fifty Years? Max Planck Institute, Munich, July 21, 2008.

Pinho de Morais, Rafael (2016), "Antitrust and Compulsory License in BRICS and Developing Countries", in: Jenny, Frederic / Katsoulacos, Yannis (eds.), *Competition Law Enforcement in the BRICS and Developing Countries—Legal and Economic Aspects*, Springer International Publishing Switzerland, 149-167.

Piovesan, Márcia Franke/Lavra, Maria E. (2007), "Institutional Change and Political Decision-Making in the Creation of the Brazilian National Health Surveillance Agency", 23 *Cadernos de Saúde Pública* 6, 1373-1383.

Pires de Carvalho, Nuno (2001), "The Primary Function of Patents", *Journal of Law, Technology and Policy*, 25-74.

Pires de Carvalho, Nuno (2008), *The TRIPS Regime of Antitrust and Undisclosed Information*, Kluwer Law International, The Hague.

Pires de Carvalho, Nuno (2009), *200 anos do Sistema Brasileiro de Patentes—O Alvará de 28 de abril de 1809—Técnica e Vida, Lumen Juris, Rio de Janeiro.*

Pires de Carvalho, Nuno (2010), *The TRIPS Regime of Patent Rights*, 3rd ed., Kluwer Law International, Alphen aan den Rijn.

Pogge, Thomas (2008), "Access to Medicines",1 *Public Health Ethics* 2, 73-82.

Plomer, Aurora (2019), "The EPO as a patent law-maker in Europe", 25 *European Law Journal*, 57-74.

Pretorius, Willem (2002), "TRIPS and Developing Countries: How Level Is the Playing Field?" in Drahos, Peter/Mayne, Ruth, *Global Intellectual Property Rights—Knowledge, Access and Development*, Pallgrave Macmillan, Chippenham, Wiltshire, 183-197.

Queiroz, Sergio Robles Reis de (1993), *Os determinantes da capacitação tecnológica no setor químico-farmacêutico brasileiro*, PhD Thesis, Department of Economics, UNICAMP, 1993, UNICAMP's digital library, available at http://repositorio.unicamp.br/handle/REPOSIP/285374?mode=full (last visited on October 22, 2017).

Quintanilha Marques, Ubirajara Regis / Santos Guimarães, Valeska / Sternberg, Caitlin (2005), "Brazil's AIDS Controversy: Antiretroviral Drugs, Breaking Patents, and Compulsory License", 60 *Food and Drug Law Journal*, 471-477.

Rayna, Thierry / Striukova, Ludmilla (2009), "The Curse of the First-Mover: When Incremental Innovation Leads to Radical Change", 1 *International. Journal of Collaborative Enterprise*, 4-21.

Rangel-Ortiz, Horacio (2008), "Sensitive Health and Patent Law Issues in Bilateral Trade Agreements Recently Executed by the United States—The Latin American Experience", in: Ghidini, Gustavo / Genovesi, Luis Mariano (eds.), *Intellectual Property and Market Power—ATRIP Papers 2006-2007*, Eudeba, 367-382.

Ranzani, Caroline (2006), *O descompasso entre o interno e o externo numa era de interdependência: o caso do acesso a Medicamentos para HIV/AIDS no Brasil*, Master Thesis FGV—Fundação Getúlio Vargas, São Paulo.

Rathod, Sandeep Kanak (2010), "Evergreening: A Status Check in Selected Countries", 7 *Journal of Generic Medicines* 3, 227-242.

Reichman, Jerome H. (1994), "Legal Hybrids between the Patent and Copyright Paradigms", 94 *Columbia Law Review*, 2432-2558.

Reichman, Jerome H. (1996), "From Free Riders to Fair Followers: Global Competition under the TRIPS Agreement", 29 *New York University Journal of International Law and Politics*, 423-456.

Reichman, Jerome H. (2006), *Procuring Essential Medicines under the Amended TRIPS Provisions: The Prospects for Regional Pharmaceutical Supply Centers*, Paper prepared for the Seminar on Intellectual Property Arrangements: Implications for Developing Countries Productive Capabilities in the Supply of Essential MedicinesUNCTAD, Geneva, Switzerland October 18-20, 2006, available at https://www.researchgate.net/publication/265399247_PROCURING_ESSENTIAL_MEDICINES_UNDER_THE_AMENDED_TRIPS_PROVISIONS_THE_PROSPECTS_FOR_REGIONAL_PHARMACEUTICAL_SUPPLY_CENTERS (last visited on October 22, 2017).

Reichman, Jerome H. (2009a), "Compulsory Licensing of Patented Pharmaceutical Inventions: Evaluating the Options", 37 *Journal of Law, Medicine and Ethics*, 247-263.

Reichman, Jerome H. (2009b), "Intellectual Property in the Twenty-First Century: Will the Developing Countries Lead or Follow?", 46 *Houston Law Review* 4, 1115-1185.

Reichman, Jerome H. / Dreyfuss, Rochelle Cooper (2007), "Harmonization Without Consensus: Critical Reflections on Drafting a Substantive Patent Law Treaty", 57 *Duke Law Journal*, 85-130.

Reichman, Jerome H. / Hasenzahl, Catherine (2003), *Non Voluntary Licensing of Patented Inventions: Historical Perspective, Legal Framework under TRIPS and an Overview of the Practice in Canada and the US*, UNCTAD-ICTSD Project on IPR and Sustainable Development, Issue Paper No. 5, available at https://www.ictsd.org/pubs/ictsd_series/iprs/CS_reichman_hasenzahl.pdf (last visited on October 22, 2017).

Remédio Marques, João Paulo F. (2008), "A Patenteabilidade de Substâncias Químicas e Farmacêuticas de Selecção e de Método de Terapia, no Domínio do CPI de 1940—A Dissimulação de Reivindicações de Processo e a Entrada em Vigor do CPI de 1995 e do Acordo TRIPS", in: Remédio Marques, João Paulo F. (ed.), *Medicamentos versus Patentes—Estudos de Propriedade Industrial*, Coimbra Editora, 259-376.

Rezek, Francisco (2006), *Direito Internacional Público—Curso Elementar*, Editora Saraiva, São Paulo.

Ridder, Claudia (2004), *Die Bedeutung von Zwangslizenzen im Rahmen des TRIPS-Abkommens unter besonderer Berücksichtigung des Spannungsverhältnisses zwischen patentrechtlichen Vorgaben und gesundheitlichen Erfordernissen*, Verlag Recht und Wirtschaft, Düsseldorf.

Robinson, Joan (1956), *The Accumulation of Capital*, London: Macmillan.

Rodrigues Alves (2015), "País demora 11 anos para aprovar patentes", O Estado de São Paulo, May 24, 2015.

Rodrigues Júnior, Edson Beas (2005), "Anuência Prévia: Integração do direito à saúde aos direitos de propriedade intelectual", *RT* No. 840, 84-106.

Rodrigues Júnior, Edson Beas / Murphy, Bryan (2006), "Brazil's Prior Consent Law: A Dialogue Between Brazil and the United States over Where the TRIPS Agreement Currently Sets the Balance Between the Protection of Pharmaceutical Patents and Access to Medicines", 16 *Albany Law Journal of Science and Technology*, 423-456.

Rodrigues, William C.V. / Soler, Orenzio (2009), "Licença compulsória do Efavirenz no Brasil em 2007: contextualização", 26 *Revista Panamericana de Salud Publica* 6, 553-559.

Romandini, Roberto (2016), "Flexibilities under TRIPS: An Analysis of the Proposal for Reforming Brazilian Patent Law", 15 *The John Marshall Review of. Intellectual-Property. Law*, 150-212.

Rosenberg, Barbara (2004), *Patentes de Medicamentos e Comércio Internacional para a Outorga de Licenças Compulsórias*, PhD Thesis, Universidade de São Paulo.

Rosman, Eduardo Colonna (2004), "O Limite Normativo da Agência Nacional de Vigilância Sanitária (ANVISA)", 71 *Revista da ABPI*, 34-37.

Rosman, Suzel Whitaker de Assumpção Mattos / Rosman, Eduardo Colonna (2005), "'Segundo Uso'—Remédios Jurídicos contra a ANVISA", 74 *Revista da ABPI*, 62-70.

Rott, Peter (2002), *Patentrecht und Sozialpolitik unter dem TRIPS-Abkommen*, Nomos, Baden-Baden.

Rozek, Richard P. / Berkowitz, Ruth (1998), "The Effects of Patent Protection on the Prices of Pharmaceutical Products—Is Intellectual Property Raising the Drug Bill in Developing Countries?" 1 *The Journal of World Intellectual Property* 2, 179-243.

Rozek, Richard P. (2000), "The Effect of Compulsory Licensing on Innovation and Access to Health Care", 3 *The Journal of World Intellectual Property* 6, 889-917.

Salomão Filho, Calixto (2007), "Razoabilidade e Legalidade do Licenciamento Compulsório do Ponto de Vista Concorrencial", in: Basso, Maristela / Salomão Filho, Calixto / Polido, Fabrício/César, Priscilla (eds.), *Direitos de Propriedade*

Intelectual e Saúde Pública—O Acesso Universal aos Medicamentos Antirretrovirais no Brasil, IDCID, São Paulo, 147-166, available at http://www.researchgate.net/publication/280319087_Direitos_de_Propriedade_Intelectual_e_Saude_Publica_o_acesso_universal_aos_medicamentos_anti-retrovirais_no_Brasil (last visited on October 22, 2017).

Sallum Jr., Brasilio (2011), "Governo Collor: O Reformismo Liberal e a Nova Orientação da Política Externa Brasileira," 54 *Revista Dados*, 259-288, available at http://www.scielo.br/pdf/dados/v54n2/v54n2a02.pdf (last visited on October 22, 2017).

Sampat, Bhaven N. / Shadlen, Kenneth C. (2017), *Secondary Pharmaceutical Patenting: A Global Perspective*, NBER Working Paper N. 23114, available at https://www.nber.org/papers/w23114 (last visited on August 12, 2019).

Samtleben, Jürgen (2002), "Föderale Gerichtsverfassung in Brasilien und Argentinien—zwei unterschiedliche Modelle", 66 *RabelsZ*, 250-267.

Santa Cruz, André / Martins Guterres, Thiago (2016), *Comentários à Lei de Propriedade Industrial*, Juspodivm, Salvador.

Santos Cruz, Adriana Alves dos (2006), "A Licença Compulsória como Instrumento de Adequação da Patente à sua Função Social", 80 *Revista da ABPI*, 45-55.

Sarlet, Ingo Wolfgang (2002), "Soziale Grundrechte in Brasilien: Probleme ihrer Verwirklichung unter dem Druck der Globalisierung", *Zeitschrift für internationales Arbeits- und Sozialrecht*, 1-21.

Savoie, Brent (2007), "Thailand's Test: Compulsory Licenses in an Area of Epidemiologic Transition", *48 Virginia Journal of International Law*, 211-248.

Scherer, Frederic M. (2001), "The Patent System and Innovation in Pharmaceuticals", in: Remiche, Bernard (ed.), *Revue Internationale Droit Economic—Special Edition: Pharmaceutical Patents, Innovation and Public Health*, De Boeck & Larcier, Bruxelles, 107-120.

Scherer, Frederic M. (2005), "The Economics of the Patent System," in: Scherer, Frederic M. (ed.), *Patents: Economics, Policy and Measurement*, Edward Elgar, Cheltenham (UK), Northampton—MA (USA), 3-22.

Scherer, Frederic M. /Watal, Jayashree (2002), "Post-TRIPS Options for Access to Patented Medicines in Developing Nations", 5(4) *Journal of International Economic Law*, 913-939.

Schneider, Dieter R. (2008), "Patenting of Pharmaceuticals—Still a Challenge?", 39 *International Review of Intellectual Property and Competition Law*, 511-525.

Schneider, Ingrid (2009), "Can Patent Legislation Make a Difference? Bringing Parliaments and Civil Society into Patent Governance", in: Haunss, Sebastian / Shadlen, Kenneth C. (eds.), *Politics of Intellectual Property—Contestation over the Ownership, Use, and Control of Knowledge and Information*, Edward Elgar, Cheltenham (UK), 129-157.

Schneider, Ingrid (2010), "Das Europäische Patentsystem—Wandel von Governance durch Parlamente und Zivilgesellschaft", Campus Verlag, Frankfurt am Main /New York.

Scholze, Simone H.C., (2001), "Fabricação Local, Licença Compulsória e Importação Paralela na Lei de Propriedade Industrial", 54 *Revista da ABPI*, 9-12.

Scholze, Simone H.C (2002), *Patentes, Transgênicos e Clonagem—Implicações Jurídicas e Bioéticas*, Brasília, Fundação Universidade de Brasília.

Schrader, Christian (2012), "Wir müssen gegen Triviale Patente kämpfen—Der Präsident des Europäischen Patentamts, Benoît Battistelli, zur umstrittenen Bonuszahlung für die Mitarbeiter seiner Behörde, zu der steigenden Zahl von Patenterteilungen und der Frage, ob Patente überhaupt die Innovationskraft der Wirtschaft steigern," *Süddeutsche Zeitung*, December 13, 2012.

Schulz, Claudia (2004), "The TRIPS Agreement and Intellectual Property Protection in Brazil", in: Abbott, Frederick and Chien Hale, Elizabeth (eds.), *Intellectual Property Rights in Global Trade Framework: IP Trends in Developing Countries, 98 Proceedings of the Annual Meeting of the American Society of International Law*, Cambridge University Press, Cambridge, 100-103.

Schüren, Verena (2015), *Aufholende Entwicklung in der globalen Ökonomie—Pharmazeutische Innovationssysteme in Indien und Brasilien*, Nomos, Baden-Baden.

Sears, Mary Helen (1975), "Tinkering with the Invention Standard: No Solution to Problems of Patent Quality", 59 *Minnesota Law Review*, 965-990.

Senado Federal (1995a), "Parecer No. 655 of 1995, Comissão de Assuntos Econômicos (Senator Fernando Bezerra)", *Diário do Senado Federal*, Ano L—Suplemento ao No. 007, October 11, 1995, pp. 190-239.

Senado Federal (1995b)—"Voto em Separado, Vencido, do Senador Ney Suassuna na Comissão de Assuntos Econômicos", *Diário do Senado Federal*, Ano L—Suplemento ao No. 007, October 11, 1995, pp. 275-288.

Seuba Hernandes, Xavier (2008), "Human Rights and Intellectual Property Rights", in: Correa, Carlos M. / Yusuf, Abdulqawi A. (eds.), *Intellectual Property and International Trade: The TRIPS Agreement*, Kluwer Law International BV, The Netherlands, 387-419.

Shadlen, Kenneth C. (2009a), "The Politics of Patents and Drugs in Brazil and Mexico: The Industrial Bases of Health Policies", 42 *Comparative Politics* 1, 41-58, available at http://eprints.lse.ac.uk/27051/1/politics_of_patents_and_drugs_in_Brazil_and_Mexico_(LSERO).pdf (last visited on October 22, 2017).

Shadlen, Kenneth C. (2009b) *Reforming and Reinforcing the Revolution: The Post-TRIPS Politics of Patents in Latin America*, Global Development and Environment Institute—Working Paper 09-02, April 2009, available at https://ideas.repec.org/p/dae/daepap/09-02.html (last visited on September 22, 2017).

Shadlen, Kenneth C. (2011a), "The Rise and Fall of 'Prior Consent' in Brazil," 3 *WIPO Journal*, 103-112, available at http://www.wipo.int/edocs/pubdocs/en/intproperty/wipo_journal/wipo_journal_3_1.pdf (last visited on September 22, 2017).

Shadlen, Kenneth C. (2011b), "The Political Contradictions of Incremental Innovations: Lessons from Pharmaceutical Patent Examination in Brazil", 39 *Politics & Society 2*, 143-174.

Shadlen, Kenneth C. (2012), "The Politics of Pharmaceutical Patent Examination in Brazil", in: Burlamaqui, Leonardo / Castro, Ana Célia / Kattel, Rainer (eds.),

Knowledge Governance: Reasserting Public Interest, Anthem Press, London / New York, 139-162.

Shanker, Daya (2002a), "Brazil, the Pharmaceutical Industry and the WTO", 5 *The Journal of World Intellectual Property*, 53-104.

Shanker, Daya (2002b), "The Vienna Convention on the Law of the Treaties, the Dispute Settlement System of the WTO and the Doha Declaration on the TRIPS Agreement", 36 *Journal of World Trade*, 721-772.

Shapiro, Carl (2001), "Navigating the Patent Thicket: Cross Licenses, Patent Pools and Standard-Setting", in: Jaffe, Adam B. / Lerner, Josh / Stern, Scott (eds.), *Innovation Policy and the Economy*, Vol. 1, NBER, MTI Press, 119-150, available at www.nber.org/chapters/c10778.pdf (last visited on October 22, 2017).

Sichel, Ricardo Luiz (2013), "A Anuência Prévia, pela ANVISA—patentes farmacêuticas", 8 *REVEL*, 56-66, available at https://ibpieuropa.org/?media_dl=379 (last visited on October 22, 2017).

Sichelman, Ted (2010), "Commercializing Patents", 62 *Stanford Law Review* 2, 341-414.

Silveira, Newton (2009), "Apontamentos Relativos à Questão do Pipeline", *REVEL—Edição Especial "Patentes Pipeline"*, 74-81.

Slowinski, Peter R. (2018), "Germany—Comment on the German Federal Supreme Court Decision 'Raltegravir'", 49 *International Review of Intellectual Property and Competition Law*, 125-130.

Sorte Junior, Waldemiro Francisco (2012), "The Production and R&D Structure of the Brazilian Pharmaceutical Industry: The Role of Public Procurement and Public Drug Production", 10 *Global Public Health* 7, 1062-1079.

Souza, Jessé (2019), *A Elite do Atraso—Da Escravidão a Bolsonaro*, Estação Brasil, Rio de Janeiro, 248-259.

Souza da Silva, Shyrley (2009), *O Interesse Público na Jurisprudência do STJ: Uma Abordagem sobre a Fixação de Conteúdos Normativos pelo Raciocínio Judiciário*, Master Thesis presented to the Universidade Federal Fluminense, available at http://dominiopublico.mec.gov.br/download/teste/arqs/cp127626.pdf (last visited July 8, 2019).

Spangenberg, Reinhard (1997), "The Novelty of 'Selection' Inventions", 28 *International Review of Intellectual Property and Competition Law*, 808-822.

Stiglitz, Joseph E. (2006), *Making Globalization Work*, Allen Lane / Penguin Books, London.

Stiglitz, Joseph E. (2008), "Economic Foundations of Intellectual Property Rights", 57 *Duke Law Journal*, 1693-1724.

Stiglitz, Joseph E. / Jayadev, Arjun (2010), "Medicine for Tomorrow: Some Alternative Proposals to Promote Socially Beneficial Research and Development in Pharmaceuticals", 7 *Journal of Generic Medicines*, 217-226.

Stirner, Beatrice / Thangaraj, Harry (2013), "Learning from Practice: Compulsory License Cases and Access to Medicines", 2 *Pharmaceutical Patent Analyst* 2, 195.213.

Stoeva, Preslava (2010), *New Norms and Knowledge in World Politics—Protecting People, Intellectual Property and the Environment*, Routledge, Oxford.

Straus, Joseph (2006), "The Impact of the New World Order on Economic Development: The Role of Intellectual Property Rights System", 6 *John Marshall Revue of Intellectual Property Law*, 1-16.

Straus, Joseph (2008), "Is There a Global Warming of Patents?",11 *The Journal of World Intellectual Property* 58-62.

Suassuna, Ney (1995), Speech Given at the Tribune of the Brazilian Federal Senate on December 12, 1995, DSF December 13, 1995, p. 5547, available at: http://www25.senado.leg.br/web/atividade/pronunciamentos/-/p/texto/178806 (last visited November 2, 2017).

Suchy, Herbert (1982), "Patent Protection for a Second Medicinal Use", 13 *International Review of Intellectual Property and Competition Law*, 471-479.

Sulpino Vieira, Fabíola (2018), "Evolução no gasto com medicamentos do sistema único de saúde no período de 2010 a 2016", *IPEA -Texto para Discussão 2356*, available at *http://repositorio.ipea.gov.br/bitstream/11058/8250/1/TD_2356.pdf* (last visited on July 8, 2019).

Sundaram, Jae (2014), "Brazil's Implementation of TRIPS Flexibilities: Ambitious Missions, Early Implementation, and the Plans for Reform", 23 *Information and Communications Technology Law* 2, 81-116.

Suzigan, Wilson / Motta e Albuquerque, Eduardo da (2011), "The Underestimated Role of Universities for the Brazilian System of Innovation", 31 *Revista de Economia Política* 1, 3-30.

Tachinardi, Maria Helena (1993), *A Guerra das Patentes: o Conflito Brasil x EUA*, Editora Paz e Terra, São Paulo.

Temermann, Michelangelo (2011), *The Legal Notion of Abuse of Patent Rights*, NCCR Trade Regulation—Swiss National Centre of Competence in Research, Working Paper No. 2011/23.

Thach, Sharon V. / Marsnik, Susan J. /Rizzo, Anne-Marie (2014), "Accession to TRIPS and Engagement with the Pharmaceutical Industry", *Ethics and Business Law Faculty Publications*, 67-80.

The World Bank, Data by Country, available at: http://data.worldbank.org/country/brazil (last visited on November 2, 2017).

The World Bank, Ranking GDP, available at http://databank.worldbank.org/data/download/GDP.pdf (last visited on August 17, 2019).

The World Bank, Gross National Income Per Capita 2018, available at http://databank.worldbank.org/data/download/GNIPC.pdf (last visited August 17, 2019).

The World Bank, Poverty Headcount Ratio at National Poverty Lines (% of population), available at http://data.worldbank.org/country/brazil (last visited on April 12, 2019).

The World Bank (2004), *Project of Performance Assessment Report: Brazil: First and Second AIDS and STD Control Project,* Report N° 28819 of April 27, 2004, Washington, DC, available at http://documents.worldbank.org/curated/en/963411468744108959/Brazil-First-and-Second-AIDS-and-STD-Control-Projects (last visited on January 8, 2018).

Thomas, John R. (2009), *Patent "Evergreening": Issues on Innovation and Competition*, US Congressional Research Service, November 13, available at https://www.

ipmall.info/sites/default/files/hosted_resources/crs/R40917_091113.pdf (last visited on October 22, 2017).

Tigre; Paulo B. / Nascimento, Caio V. M. França / Costa, Laís S. (2016) "Windows of Opportunity and Technological Innovation in the Brazilian Pharmaceutical Industry", 32 *Cadernos de Saúde Pública* 2, 1-9.

Timmermans, Karin (2006), "Ensuring Access to Medicines in 2005 and Beyond", in: Roffe, Pedro / Tansey, Geoff / Vivas-Eugui, David (eds.), *Negotiating Health—Intellectual Property and Access to Medicines*, Earthscan, London / Sterling, 41-63.

Tojal, Sebastião Botto de Barros / Pessôa, Rodrigues Patrícia (2008), "A Anuência Prévia na Concessão de Patentes de Medicamentos e a Regulação Econômica da Indústria Farmacêutica", 8 *Revista de Direito Sanitário*, 148-165.

Towse, Ruth / Holzhauer, Rudi (eds.) (2002), *The Economics of Intellectual Property, Vol. I: Introduction and Copyright*, Edward Elgar, Cheltenham (UK).

Tuominen, Nicoleta (2010), *Defensive Patent Protection Strategies in the Pharmaceutical Industry—a Response to a legal problem?*, Master Thesis, College of Europe, Bruges Campus, Law Department, available at http://www.mayerbrown.com/public_docs/Thesis_Nicoleta_Tuominen.pdf (last visited on October 22, 2017).

Trigo de Souza, Marcela (2008), "Should Brazil allow Patents on Second Medical Uses?", 93 *Revista da ABPI*, 53-67.

UK Intellectual Property Office (2011), *Patent Thickets, an Overview,* available at https://www.gov.uk/government/publications/patent-thickets (last visited on November 8, 2017).

Ullrich, Hans (1989), "GATT: Industrial Property Protection, Fair Trade and Development", in: Beier, Friedrich-Karl / Schricker, Gerhard (eds.): *GATT or WIPO? New Ways in the International Protection of Intellectual Property*, Max Planck Institute for Foreign and International Patent, Copyright, and Competition Law, Munich(IIC Studies - Studies in Industrial Property and Copyright Law, 11), VCH, Weinheim),128-159.

UNAIDS (2004), *Brazil and UNAIDS Joint Forces Against AIDS (Press Release)*, available at http://data.unaids.org/Media/Press-Releases02/pr_brazil_01sep04_en.pdf (last visited on October 28, 2017).

UNCTAD-ICTSD (2005), *Resource Book on TRIPS and Development: An Authoritative and Practical Guide to the TRIPS Agreement*, available at https://unctad.org/en/PublicationsLibrary/ictsd2005d1_en.pdf (last visited on October 28, 2017).

UNDP (2016), *Human Development Report 2016,* available at http://hdr.undp.org/en/2016-report/download (last visited on October 29, 2017).

UN Office of the High Commissioner (1986), General Assembly, Declaration on the Right to Development, Document No. A/RES/41/128, December 4, 1986, available at https://www.ohchr.org/EN/ProfessionalInterest/Pages/RightToDevelopment.aspx (last visited on August 12, 2019).

UNSGHLPAM (2016), *Report of the United Nations Secretary-General's High-Level Panel on Access to Medicines: Promoting Innovation and Access to High Technologies,* available at http://www.unsgaccessmeds.org/final-report (last visited on November 3, 2017).

Urias, Eduardo Muniz Pereira (2015), *Improving Access to HIV/AIDS Treatment in Brazil—When Are Compulsory Licenses Effective in Price Negotiations?*, PhD Thesis presented to the University of Maastricht, available at http://www.merit.unu.edu/training/theses/urias.pdf (last visited on August 15, 2019).

Valle, Silvio (2005), "Bióetica, Patentes e Experimentação Animal", 30 *Revista Bioética*, March 30, 115-120, available at http://revistabioetica.cfm.org.br/index.php/revista_bioetica/article/viewFile/128/130 (last visited on October 22, 2017).

Van den Belt, Henk / Korthals, Michiel (2013), "The International Patent System and the Ethics of Global Justice" in Arapostathis / Dutfield (eds.), *Knowledge Management and Intellectual Property—Concepts, Actors and Practices from the Past to the Present*, Cheltenham, Edgar Elgar, 235-251.

Vandoren, Paul (2002), "*Médicaments sans Frontières?* Clarification of the Relationship Between TRIPS and Public Health Resulting from the WTO Doha Ministerial Declaration", 5 *The Journal of World Intellectual Property* 1, 5-14.

Vargas, Fabio Aristimunho (2006), *O Direito da Propriedade Intelectual face ao Direito de Acesso a Medicamentos*, Master Thesis: Universidade de São Paulo, Law Faculty.

Vaz e Dias, José C. (2001), "Licença Compulsória de Patentes e o Direito Antitruste", 54 *Revista da ABPI*, 3-8.

Ventose, Eddy D. (2009), "Patent Protection for Second and Further Medical Uses Under the European Patent Convention", 6 *SCRIPTed – A Journal of Law, Technology and Society* 1, 57-74.

Vernaz, Nathalie / Haller, Guy / Girardin, François et al. (2013), "Patented Drug Extension Strategies on Healthcare Spending: A Cost-Evaluation Analysis", 10 *Public Library of Science Medicine* 6.

Villagra Marques, Claudia S. (2001), *A Questão da Importação Paralela no Comércio Internacional*, published in the law firm's website "Villagra Marques Advogados", available at http://www.villagramarques.com.br/artigos/importacao_paralela.doc (last visited on October 22, 2017).

Visser, Derk (2005), "The Exclusion of Medical Methods", in: Kur, Annette / Luginbühl, Stefan / Waage, Eskil (eds.), "*... und sie bewegt sich doch!" – Patent Law on the Move, Festschrift für Gert Kolle und Dieter Stauder*, Carl Heymanns, Köln, 469-486.

Vivian, Michael F. (1989), "Novelty and Selection Inventions", 20 *International Review of Intellectual Property and Competition Law*, 303-311.

Von Kraack, Christian (2006), *TRIPs oder Patentschutz weltweit—Zwangslizenzen, Erschöpfung, Parallelimporte*, Duncker & Humblot, Berlin.

Vogel, Ronald (2007), *Pharmaceutical Economics and Public Policy*, Binghamton, The Haworth Press.

Wadlow, Christopher (2010), "The Great Pharmaceutical Patent Robbery, and the Curious Case of the Chemical Foundation", 3 *Intellectual Property Quartely*, 256-292, also available at http://works.bepress.com/cgi/viewcontent.cgi?filename=0&article=1029&context=christopher_wadlow&type=additional (last visited on October 22, 2020).

Wang, Richard Li-Dar / Huang, Pei-Chen (2012), "Patent Protection of Pharmacologically Active Metabolites: Theoretical and Technological analyze on the Jurisprudence of Four Regions", 29 *Santa Clara Computer and High Technology Law Journal*, 489-521.

Watal, Jayashree (2001), *Intellectual Property Rights in the WTO and Developing Countries*, Kluwer Law International, The Hague / London / Boston.

Weisser, Johannes (2017), "Patentrechtliche und kartellrechtliche Zwangslizenz—Unterschiede und Gemeinsamkeiten—'Isentress'", *Gesellschafts- und Wirtschaftsrecht*, 134-136.

Whitehead, Brian / Jackson, Stuart / Kempner, Richard (2008), "Generic Competition and Pharma Patent Strategies—a Sequel", 3 *Journal of Intellectual Property Law & Practice*, 799-800.

WIPO /WHO/ WTO (2013), *Promoting Access to Medical Technologies and Innovation—Intersections Between Public Health, Intellectual Property and Trade*, available at https://www.wipo.int/edocs/pubdocs/en/global_challenges/628/wipo_pub_628.pdf (last visited on August 15, 2019).

Wit, Severin de (2014), "Challenges in Public and Private Domains will Shape the Future of Intellectual Property", 3 *National Taipei University of Technology Journal of Intellectual Property Law and Management*, 21-33.

Wogart, Jan Peter (2006), Multiple Interfaces of Big Pharma and the Change of Global Health Governance in the Face of HIV/AIDS, *Giga Working Paper* No. 24, June, available at https://www.giga-hamburg.de/en/publication/multiple-interfaces-of-big-pharma-and-the-change-of-global-health-governance-in-the-face (last visited on October 22, 2017).

Wolff, Maria Thereza / de Bessa Antunes, Paulo (2005), "Patentes de Segundo Uso Médico", 74 *Revista da ABPI*, 48-61.

Worthen, Dennis B. (2003), "American Pharmaceutical Patents from a Historical Perspective", 7 *International Journal of Pharmaceutical Compounding*, 37-40.

WHO—Essential Medicines and Health Products—Pharmacovigilance, available at https://www.who.int/medicines/areas/quality_safety/safety_efficacy/pharmvigi/en/ (last visited on August 14, 2019).

WTO (2000), *Brazil—Measures Affecting Patenting Protection, Request for Consultation by the United States*, WTO Document WT/DS199/1 (June 8, 2000).

WTO (2001a), *Brazil—Measures Affecting Patent Protection—Notification of Mutually Agreed Solution*, WTO Document WT/DS199/4 G/L454 IP/D/23/Add.1 (July 19, 2001).

WTO (2001b), *Doha WTO Ministerial Declaration on the TRIPS Agreement and Public Health—Adopted on 14 November 2001*, WTO Document WT/MIN (01) DEC/2 (November 20, 2001).

WTO (2003), *General Council—Implementation of Paragraph 6 of the Doha Declaration on the TRIPS Agreement and Public Health—Decision of the General Council of 30 August 2003*, WTO Document WT/L/540 and Corr. 1 (September 1, 2003).

WTO (2005), *WTO 2005 Press Release 6 December 2005—Members OK Amendment to Make Health Flexibility Permanent*, available at https://www.wto.org/english/news_e/pres05_e/pr426_e.htm (last visited on August 13, 2019).

WTO (2015), *Tenth WTO Ministerial Conference, Nairobi, 2015—Export Competition Ministerial Decision of 19 December 2015*, WTO Document WT/ MIN (15)/45 — WT/L/980.

WTO (2017), WTO: 2017 News Items (23 January 2017)—*TRIPS: WTO IP Rules Amended to Ease Poor Countries' Access to Affordable Medicines*, available at https://www.wto.org/english/news_e/news17_e/trip_23jan17_e.htm (last visited on November 12, 2017.

Yamane, Hiroko (2011), *Interpreting TRIPS: Globalization of Intellectual Property Rights and Access to Medicines*, Hart Publishing, Oxford/Portland.

Yu, Peter K. (2008), "Access to Medicines, BRICS Alliances, and Collective Action", 34 *American Journal of Law and Medicine*, 345-394.

Zalfa, Viviane Mega de Andrade (2008), *Comprimidos de liberação modificada: análise dos pedidos de patente depositados no Brasil e da utilização destes na prática do evergreening*, Master Thesis INCQS/Fiocruz, Rio de Janeiro.

Zypries, Brigitte (2004), "Hypertrophie der Schutzrechte?", 132 *GRUR*, 977-980.

Legal Materials

ANVISA (2008), Resolução da Diretoria Colegiada (RDC) ANVISA No. 45 of June 20, 2008: Dispõe sobre o procedimento administrativo relativo à prévia anuência da ANVISA para a concessão de patentes para produtos e processos farmacêuticos, DOU Seção I, June 24, 2008, p. 67.

ANVISA (2013), Resolução da Diretoria Colegiada (RDC) ANVISA No. 21 of April 10, 2013: Altera a Resolução—RDC nº 45, de 23 de junho de 2008, que dispõe sobre o procedimento administrativo relativo à prévia anuência da ANVISA para a concessão de patentes para produtos e processos farmacêuticos, DOU Seção I, April 15, 2013, p. 68.

ANVISA (2017), Resolução da Diretoria Colegiada (RDC) ANVISA No. 168 of August 8, 2017: Dispõe sobre o procedimento administrativo relativo à prévia anuência da ANVISA para a concessão de patentes para produtos e processos farmacêuticos, regulamentado pela Portaria Conjunta ANVISA-INPI n° 01, de 12 de abril de 2017, DOU Seção I, August 10, 2017, p. 52.

ANVISA (2018), Orientação de Serviço 51/DIARE/ANVISA of July 5, 2018: detalha os parâmetros para o exame de pedidos de patente de produtos e processos farmacêuticos à luz da saúde pública, available at http://portal.anvisa.gov.br/documents/33828/0/OS + 51-2018 + - + publicada.pdf/295bdf2b-353b-4998-a31 e-67731b2652ca (last visited on July 7, 2019).

ANVISA/INPI (2017), Portaria Conjunta 1 of April 12, 2017: Regulamenta os procedimentos para a aplicação do artigo 229-C da Lei nº 9.279, de 14 de maio de 1996, acrescido pela Lei nº 10.196, de 14 de fevereiro de 2001, e dá outras providências, DOU, April 13, 2017, available at http://www.in.gov.br/materia/-/asset_publisher/Kujrw0TZC2Mb/content/id/20163436 (last visited on May 18, 2019).

Brazil (1809), Alvará de 28 de Abril de 1809: Isenta de direitos às matérias primaz do uso das fábricas e concede outros favores aos fabricantes e da navegação nacional), Collecção das Leis do Brasil 1809, Bibliotheca da Camara dos Deputados, Rio de Janeiro, Imprensa Nacional (1891), pp. 45-48, available at http://www2.camara.leg.br/atividade-legislativa/legislacao/publicacoes/doimperio/colecao1.html (last visited on October 30, 2017).

Brazil (1824), *Constituição Política do Império do Brazil,* Collecção das Leis do Império do Brazil of March 25, 1824, Bibliotheca da Camara dos Deputados, Rio de Janeiro, Imprensa Nacional (1886) available at http://www2.camara.leg.br/atividade-legislativa/legislacao/publicacoes/doimperio/colecao2.html (last visited on October 30, 2017).

Brazil (1882), *Lei nº 3.129 of October 14, 1882: Regula a concessão de patentes aos autores de invenção ou descoberta industrial,* Coleção das Leis do Império do Brasil 1882, Parte I—Tomo XXIX—Parte II—Tomo XLX, Rio de Janeiro, Tipografia Nacional, pp. 82-87, available at http://www2.camara.leg.br/atividade-legislativa/legislacao/publicacoes/doimperio/colecao8.html (last visited on October 30, 2017).

Brazil (1923), Decreto nº 16.264 of December 19, 1923: *Crea a Diretoria Geral da Propriedade Industrial, Coleção das Leis da República dos Estados Unidos do Brasil de 1923*—Actos do Poder Executivo, Vol. III, 1ª Parte, March 31, 1993, p. 329, available at http://www2.camara.leg.br/atividade-legislativa/legislacao/publicacoes/republica/colecao4.html (last visited on October 30, 2017).

Brazil (1945), Decreto-Lei 7.903 of August 27, 1945: *Código da Propriedade Industrial, República dos Estados Unidos do Brasil*—Coleção das Leis de 1945—Atos do Poder Executivo, Imprensa Nacional 1945, Rio de Janeiro, p. 184, available at http://www2.camara.leg.br/atividade-legislativa/legislacao/publicacoes/republica/colecao6.html (last visited on October 30, 2017).

Brazil (1967), Decreto-Lei 254 of February 28, 1967: *Código da Propriedade Industrial,* DOU, February 28, 1967, p. 2444, available at http://www.planalto.gov.br/ccivil_03/decreto-lei/1965-1988/Del0254.htm (last visited on October 31, 2017).

Brazil (1969), Decreto-Lei 1.005 of October 21, 1969: *Código da Propriedade Industrial,* DOU Seção I, October 21, 1969, p. 1, available at http://www.planalto.gov.br/ccivil_03/decreto-lei/1965-1988/Del1005.htm (last visited on October 31, 2017).

Brazil (1970), Lei No. 5.648 of December 11, 1970: *Cria o Instituto Nacional da Propriedade Industrial e dá outras providências,* DOU, December 14, 1970, available at http://www.planalto.gov.br/ccivil_03/leis/L5648.htm (last visited on October 31, 2017).

Brazil (1971a), Decreto 68.806 of June 25, 1971: *Institui a Central de Medicamentos (CEME),* available at http://www.planalto.gov.br/ccivil_03/decreto/1970-1979/D68806.htm (last visited on October 31, 2017).

Brazil (1971b), Lei nº 5.772 of December 21, 1971 (CPI 71): *Institui o Código da Propriedade Industrial e dá outras providências,* DOU, December 31, 1971, Seção I, p. 10897, available at http://www.planalto.gov.br/ccivil_03/Leis/L5772.htm (last visited on October 31, 2017).

Brazil (1978), Decreto 81.742 of May 31, 1978: *Promulga o Tratado de Cooperação em Matéria de Patentes (PCT),* DOU, June 1, 1978, p. 8120, available at http://www

2.camara.leg.br/legin/fed/decret/1970-1979/decreto-81742-31-maio-1978-430903-publicacaooriginal-1-pe.html (last visited on October 31, 2017).

Brazil (1988), *Constituição da República do Brasil*, DOU Seção I, October 5, 1988, p. 1, available at http://www2.camara.leg.br/legin/fed/consti/1988/constituicao-1988-5-outubro-1988-322142-normaatualizada-pl.html (last visited on October 31, 2017).

Brazil (1990), Lei 8.080 of September 19, 1990 (Lei Orgânica da Saúde): Dispõe sobre as condições para promoção, proteção e recuperação da saúde, a organização e o funcionamento dos serviços correspondentes e dá outras providências, DOU, September 20, 1990, p. 18055, available at http://www2.camara.leg.br/legin/fed/lei/1990/lei-8080-19-setembro-1990-365093-normaatualizada-pl.html (last visited on October 31, 2017).

Brazil (1992), Decreto 635 of August 21, 1992: *Promulga a Convenção de Paris para a Proteção da Propriedade Industrial, revista em Estocolmo a 14 de julho de 1967*, DOU, January 24, 1992, p. 11434, available at http://www2.camara.leg.br/legin/fed/decret/1992/decreto-635-21-agosto-1992-449103-publicacaooriginal-1-pe.html (last visited on October 31, 2017).

Brazil (1994a), Lei No. 8.884 of June 11, 1994 (Lei Antitruste / Lei da Defesa da Concorrência): Transforma o Conselho Administrativo de Defesa Econômica—CADE em Autarquia, dispõe sobre a prevenção e a repressão às infrações contra a ordem econômica e dá outras providências, June 13, 1994, p. 8437, available at http://www2.camara.leg.br/legin/fed/lei/1994/lei-8884-11-junho-1994-349808-norma-pl.html (last visited on October 31, 2017).

Brazil (1994b), Decreto Legislativo 1.355 of December 30, 1994: *Promulga a Ata Final que Incorpora os Resultados da Rodada Uruguai de Negociações Comerciais Multilaterais do GATT*, DOU Seção I, December 31, 1994, p. 21394, available at http://www2.camara.leg.br/legin/fed/decret/1994/decreto-1355-30-dezembro-1994-449684-publicacaooriginal-1-pe.html (last visited on October 31, 2017).

Brazil (1996a), Lei 9.279 of May 14 (LPI), 1996: *Regula direitos e obrigações relativas à propriedade industrial*, DOU, May 15, 1996, p. 8353, available at http://www2.camara.leg.br/legin/fed/lei/1996/lei-9279-14-maio-1996-374644-norma-pl.html (last visited on October 31, 2017).

Brazil (1996b), Lei No. 9.313 of November 13, 1996 (Sarney Law): *Dispõe sobre a distribuição gratuita de medicamentos aos portadores do HIV e doentes de AIDS*, DOU Seção I, November 14, 1996, p. 23725, available at http://www2.camara.leg.br/legin/fed/lei/1996/lei-9313-13-novembro-1996-349070-publicacaooriginal-1-pl.html (last visited on October 31, 2017).

Brazil (1999a), Lei No. 9.782 of January 26, 1999 (Lei do Sistema Nacional de Vigilância Sanitária): *Define o Sistema Nacional de Vigilância Sanitária, cria a Agência Nacional de Vigilância Sanitária, e dá outras providências*, DOU Seção I, January 27, 1999, p. 1, available at http://www2.camara.leg.br/legin/fed/lei/1999/lei-9782-26-janeiro-1999-344896-publicacaooriginal-1-pl.html (last visited on October 31, 2017).

Brazil (1999b), Lei 9.787 of February 10, 1999 (Lei dos Medicamentos Genéricos): Altera a Lei nº 6.360, de 23 de setembro de 1976, que dispõe sobre a vigilância sanitária, estabelece o medicamento genérico, dispõe sobre a utilização de nomes genéricos em produtos farmacêuticos e dá outras providências, DOU, February 11, 1999, p. 1, available at http://www2.camara.leg.br/legin/fed/lei/1999/lei-9787-10-fevereiro-1999-351613-norma-pl.html (last visited on October 31, 2017).

Brazil (1999c), Decreto 3.201, of October 6, 1999 (DCL): Dispõe sobre a concessão de ofício de licença compulsória, nos casos de emergência nacional e de interesse público de que trata o art. 71 da Lei nº 9.279 de 14.5.1996, DOU Seção I, October 7, 1999, p. 17, available at http://www2.camara.leg.br/legin/fed/decret/1999/decreto-3201-6-outubro-1999-369245-normaatualizada-pe.html (last visited on October 31, 2017).

Brazil (1999d), Medida Provisória (MP) 2.006 of December 14, 1999: Altera e acresce dispositivos à Lei Nº 9.279, de 14 de Maio de 1996, que regula direitos e obrigações relativos à propriedade industrial, e dá outras providências, DOU, December 15, 1999, available at http://www.planalto.gov.br/ccivil_03/MP/Antigas/2006.htm (last visited on October 31, 2017).

Brazil (2001a), Lei 10.196 of February 14, 2001: Altera e acresce dispositivos à Lei n° 9.279, de 14 de maio de 1996, que regula direitos e obrigações relativos à propriedade industrial, e dá outras providências, DOU, February 16, 2001, p. 4, available at http://www2.camara.leg.br/legin/fed/lei/2001/lei-10196-14-fevereiro-2001-372495-publicacaooriginal-1-pl.html (last visited on October 31, 2017).

Brazil (2001b), Lei 10.213 of March 27, 2001: Define normas de regulação para o setor de medicamentos, institui a Fórmula Paramétrica de Reajuste de Preços de Medicamentos—FPR, cria a Câmara de Medicamentos e dá outras providências, DOU Seção I, March 28, 2001, p. 1., available at http://www2.camara.leg.br/legin/fed/lei/2001/lei-10213-27-marco-2001-367183-publicacaooriginal-1-pl.html (last visited on October 31, 2017).

Brazil (2003a), Decreto 4.830 of September 4, 2003: Dá nova redação aos arts. 1°, 2°, 9°, 5° e 10° do Decreto 3.201, de 6.10.1999, que dispõe sobre a concessão, de ofício, de licença compulsória nos casos de emergência nacional e de interesse público de que trata o art. 71 da Lei nº 9.279 de 14.5.1996, DOU September 5, 2003, p. 1, available at http://www2.camara.leg.br/legin/fed/decret/2003/decreto-4830-4-setembro-2003-473483-publicacaooriginal-1-pe.html (last visited on October 31, 2017).

Brazil (2003b), Lei 10.742 of October 6, 2003: Define normas de regulação para o setor farmacêutico, cria a Câmara de Regulação do Mercado de Medicamentos—CMED e altera a Lei nº 6.360, de 23 de setembro de 1976, e dá outras providências, DOU Seção I, October 7, 2003, p. 1, available at http://www2.camara.leg.br/legin/fed/lei/2003/lei-10742-6-outubro-2003-497717-normaatualizada-pl.html (last visited on November 1, 2017).

Brazil (2007), Decreto 6.108 of May 4, 2007: *Concede licença compulsória, por interesse público, de patentes referentes ao Efavirenz, para fins de uso público não-comercial*, DOU May 7, 2007, p. 2, available at http://www2.camara.leg.br/legin/fed/decret/2007/decreto-6108-4-maio-2007-553667-normaatualizada-pe.html (last visited on November 1, 2017).

Brazil (2011a), Lei 12.401 of April 28, 2011: Altera a Lei nº 8.080, de 19 de setembro de 1990, para dispor sobre a assistência terapêutica e a incorporação de tecnologia em saúde no âmbito do Sistema Único de Saúde, DOU Seção I, April 29, 2011, p. 1, available at http://www2.camara.leg.br/legin/fed/lei/2011/lei-12401-28-abril-2011-610586-publicacaooriginal-132349-pl.html (last visited on November 1, 2017).

Brazil (2011b), Lei No. 12.529 of November 30, 2011 (Lei Antitruste): Estrutura o Sistema Brasileiro de Defesa da Concorrência; dispõe sobre a prevenção e repressão às infrações contra a ordem econômica; altera a Lei nº 8.137, de 27 de dezembro de 1990, o Decreto-Lei nº 3.689, de 3 de outubro de 1941—Código de Processo Penal, e a Lei nº 7.347, de 24 de julho de 1985; revoga dispositivos da Lei nº 8.884, de 11 de junho de 1994, e a Lei nº 9.781, de 19 de janeiro de 1999; e dá outras providências, DOU, December 1, 2011, Seção I, p.1., available at http://www2.camara.leg.br/legin/fed/lei/2011/lei-12529-30-novembro-2011-611850-normaatualizada-pl.html (last visited on November 1, 2017).

Brazil (2015), Lei No. 13.123 of May 20, 2015 (Lei do Acesso ao Patrimônio Genético; Marco da Biodiversidade): Regulamenta o inciso II do § 1º e o § 4º do art. 225 da Constituição Federal, o Artigo 1, a alínea j do Artigo 8, a alínea c do Artigo 10, o Artigo 15 e os §§ 3º e 4º do Artigo 16 da Convenção sobre Diversidade Biológica, promulgada pelo Decreto nº 2.519, de 16 de março de 1998; dispõe sobre o acesso ao patrimônio genético, sobre a proteção e o acesso ao conhecimento tradicional associado e sobre a repartição de benefícios para conservação e uso sustentável da biodiversidade; revoga a Medida Provisória nº 2.186-16, de 23 de agosto de 2001; e dá outras providências, DOU Seção I, May 21,2015, p. 1, available at http://www2.camara.leg.br/legin/fed/lei/2015/lei-13123-20-maio-2015-780834-publicacaooriginal-146991-pl.html (last visited on November 1, 2017).

EPO, Convention on the Grant of European Patents (European Patent Convention): Munich, October 5, 1973, UNTC 16208, UNTS 1065-1608.

European Communities, Regulation (EC) No. 1610/96 of the European Parliament and the Council of 23 July 1996 concerning the creation of a supplementary protection certificate for plant protection products, OJ, L 198, August 8, 1996, pp. 30-35.

European Communities, Communication from the Commission—Commission Communication of Parallel Imports of proprietary medicinal products for which marketing authorizations have already been granted, COM (2003) 839 of 30 December 2003, available at http://eur-lex.europa.eu/LexUriServ/LexUriServ.do?uri=COM:2003:0839:FIN:en:PDF (last visited on November 12, 2017).

European Communities, Regulation (EC) 469/2009 of the European Parliament and of the Council of 6 May 2009 concerning the supplementary protection certificate for medicinal products, OJ, L 152, June 16, 2009, pp. 1-10.

INPI (2016), Resolução 169 of July 15, 2016 (Guidelines for Patent Examination), available at http://www.inpi.gov.br/menu-servicos/patente/legislacao-patente-1 (last visited on November 1, 2017).

MERCOSUR (1991), Treaty establishing a Common Market (Asunción Treaty) between the Argentine Republic, the Federative Republic of Brazil, the Republic of Paraguay and the Eastern Republic of Uruguay, Asunción: March 26, 1991, UNTC 37341, UNTS Vol. 2140.

MERCOSUR (1995), Protocol on harmonization of norms on intellectual property in Mercosur, in matter of trademarks, indications of sources and appellations of origin, Asunción: August 5, 1995, UNTC 37341, UNTS Vol. 2145.

MoH (1985), Portaria nº 236 of 2 May 1985: Estabelece as Diretrizes para o Programa de Controle da Síndrome de Imunodeficiência Adquirida, SIDA ou AIDS, no âmbito do Território Nacional, DOU Seção I, May 6, 1985. p. 6856 (abrogated by PRC-2 MS/GM, DO October 3, 2017, Suplemento, p. 61).

MoH (1998), *Portaria No. 3.916/GM—Política Nacional de Medicamentos*, October 30, 1998, DOU 215-E Seção 1, pp. 18-22, November 10, 1998 (abrogated by PRC-2 MS/GM, DOU, October 3, 2017, Suplemento, p. 61).

MoH (2013), Portaria No. 3.089 of December 11, 2013, DOU Seção I, December 13, 2013, p. 153 (abrogated by Portaria MS 2531 of November 13, 2014, p. 102).

MoH (2019), Portaria No. 3.047 of November 28, 2019: Estabelece a Relação Nacional de Medicamentos Essenciais: RENAME 2020 no âmbito do Sistema Único de Saúde (SUS) por meio da atualização do elenco de medicamentos e insumos da Relação Nacional de Medicamentos Essenciais, DOU Seção I, November 29, 2019, p. 334, available at https://bvsms.saude.gov.br/bvs/publicacoes/relacao_medicamentos_rename_2020.pdf (last visited on August, 24, 2020).

MoH (2017b), Portaria de Consolidação MS/GM No. 2 (PRC-2): *Consolidação das normas sobre as políticas nacionais de saúde do Sistema Único de Saúde*, DOU-Suplemento, October 3, 2017, p. 61, available at http://bvsms.saude.gov.br/bvs/saudelegis/gm/2017/prc0002_03_10_2017.html (last visited on November 2, 2017).

NAFTA (1992), North American Free Trade Agreement, available at https://www.nafta-sec-alena.org/Home/Texts-of-the-Agreement/North-American-Free-Trade-Agreement (last visited on November 11, 2017).

UN (1969), Vienna Convention on the Law of the Treaties, Vienna: May 23, 1969, UNTC 18232, UNTS Vol. 1155, p. 331.

UN (1992), Convention on the Biological Diversity, Rio de Janeiro June 5, 1992, UNTC 30619, UNTS Vol. 1760, p. 79.

United States (2011), Code Title 35, Patents, § 271 (a), available at https://www.gpo.gov/fdsys/granule/USCODE-2011-title35/USCODE-2011-title35-partIII-chap28-sec271 (last visited on March 15, 2018).

WHO (2020), Statement on the second meeting of the International Health Regulations (2005) Emergency Committee regarding the outbreak of novel coronavirus (2019-nCoV) of January 30, 2020, available at https://www.who.int/news-room/detail/30-01-2020-statement-on-the-second-meeting-of-the-international-health-regulations-(2005)-emergency-committee-regarding-the-outbreak-of-novel-coronavirus-(2019-ncov) (last visited on August 15, 2020).

WTO (1994), Marrakesh Agreement establishing the World Trade Organization from April 15, 1994, UNTC I—31874, 1867-1869.

WTO (2005), WTO Doc. WT/L/641 8 December 2005, Amendment to the TRIPS Agreement, available at https://www.wto.org/english/tratop_e/trips_e/wtl641_e.htm (last visited on August 31, 2017).

WTO (2015), IP/C/73 Decision of the WTO General Council for TRIPS of November 6, 2015.

Table of Cases

WTO

WTO (1997) India—Patent Protection for Pharmaceutical and Agricultural Chemical Products—AB-1997-5—Report of the Appellate Body, WTO-Document WT/DS50/AB R (December 19, 1997), 98

WTO (2000a), Canada—Patent Protection of Pharmaceutical Products—Panel Report, WTO Document WT/DS114/R (March 17, 2000), 89

WTO (2018) Australia—Certain Measures Concerning Trademarks, Geographical Indications and other Plain Packaging Requirements applicable to Tobacco Products and Packaging—Report of the Panels, WTO-Document: WT/DS435, WT/DS441/R, WT/DS458/R, WT/DS467/R of June 28, 2018, 97

Supremo Tribunal Federal (STF)

Ação Direta de Insconstitucionalidade (ADI) No. 4234 (Procurador Geral da República vs. Congresso Nacional / Presidente da República), http://www.stf.jus.br/portal/processo/verProcessoAndamento.asp?incidente = 12879 (last visited on August 23, 2020), 156

Recurso Extraordinário (RE) No. 80.004/SE (Belmiro da Silveira Góes vs. Sebastião Leão Trindade), Ruling Date: June 4, 1977,DJ December 29, 1977, p. 9433 / *83 RTJ 3*, p. 809, available at http://redir.stf.jus.br/paginadorpub/paginador.jsp?docTP = AC&docID = 175365 (last visited on November 1, 2017), 141

Suspensão de Segurança (SS) No. 3962 /SE (Josivaldo Tavares dos Santos vs. Município de Aracaju) Ruling date: April 9, 2010, DJ April 15, 2010), available athttp://www.stf.jus.br/portal/diarioJustica/verDiarioProcesso.asp?numDj = 66&dataPublicacaoDj = 15/04/2010&incidente = 3698911&codCapitulo = 6&numMateria = 49&codMateria = 7 (last visited on November 1, 2017), 176

Recurso Extraordinário (RE) No. 566.471/RN (Estado do Rio Grande do Norte vs. Carmelita Anunciada de Souza), Ata de Julgamento No.5 of March 5, 2020, DJe March 17, 2020, 177

Superior Tribunal de Justiça (STJ)

Tribunal Regional Federal da 2ª. Região (TRF-2).

Tribunal de Justiça do Estado de São Paulo (Court of Second Instance)

Courts of First Instance

Personal Interviews

ANVISA's Examiner I (2009, March 9), interviewed in São Pedro, Brazil, 209, 219
ANVISA's Examiner II (2009, March 9), interviewed in São Pedro, Brazil, 210
ANVISA's Officer I (2009, March 17), interviewed in Brasília, 211
ANVISA's Officer II (2009, March 12), interviewed in Rio de Janeiro on March 12, 212
Borges Barbosa, Denis (2009, March 16), interviewed in his law firm in Rio de Janeiro, 196
Figueira Barbosa, Antonio Luiz (2009, March 17), interviewed at the FIOCRUZ, Rio de Janeiro, 215
INPI's Examiner (2009, March 16), interviewed at INPI, Rio de Janeiro, 210
Lobo, Luciano, PRO-GENERICOS's technical manager (2009, March 27), interviewed in São Paulo, 208
Raimundo, Jorge, INTERFARMA's representative (2009, March 16), interviewed in his office in Rio de Janeiro on March 16, 203
Vecina, Gonzalo, first ANVISA's President (2009, March 24): interviewed at the Hospital Sírio-Libanês in São Paulo, 196

List of Cited ANVISA's Reports on Prior Consent Within Patent Proceedings at the INPI

Old Workflow (1999 -2012)

1) PP 1100266-2—Ajinomoto Co., Inc (JP), 233
2) PP 1100663-3 A2—Abbvie Inc. (US), 232
3) PP 1100756-7—Takeda Pharmaceutical Company Ltd (JP), 233
4) PP 1100769-9—Hoechst AC (DE), 232
5) PI 9508019-8—Genentech Inc. (US), 232
6) PI 9508151-8—Merck & Co., Inc. (US), 232
7) PI 9601276-5—Hoffmann-La Roche AG (CH), 241
8) PI 9604878-6—Gerhard Mann Chem.-Pharm. Fabrik GmbH (DE), 232
9) PI 9607197-4—Bellus Health (International) Limited (CH), 235
10) PI 9609137-1—Alza Corporation (US), 235
11) PI 9610153-9—Novartis International Pharmaceutical Ltd. (BM), 235
12) PI 9611647-1—Administrators of the Tulane Educational Fund. (US), 232
13) PI 9611871-7—Arpida AG (CH), 238
14) PI 9701895-3—Wyeth (US). 236
15) PI 9706554-4—Renata Maria Anna CavaliereVesely (IT) / Claudio de Simone (IT), 235
16) PI 9707368-7—Colgate-Palmolive Co. (US),232
17) PI 9710536-8—Warner-Lambert Co. LLC (US), 227
18) PI 9710693-3—Cephalon Inc. (US), 239
19) PI 9711339-5—ADA Foundation (US), 232
20) PI 9608082-5—Astrazeneca UK Ltd. (GB), 232
21) PI 9710372-1—Merck Canada Inc. (CA), 238
22) PI 9603267-7—UNIFESP—Universidade Federal de São Paulo (BR), 241
23) PI 9601909-3—AnormMED Inc. (CA), 234
24) PI 9510533-6—Hoffmann-La Roche AG (CH), 235

25) PI 9509925-5—Rega Institute (BE), 232
26) PI 9603619-2—Hoffmann-La Roche AG (CH), 241
27) PI 9606845-0—Novo Nordisk A/S (DK), 236
28) PI 9607598-8—AlteonInc (US) / The Picower Institute for Medical Research (US), 241
29) PI 9611838-5—Uniroyal Chemical Company Inc. (US) / Chemtura Canada Co. (CA), 232
30) PI 9612750-3—IDEA AG (DE), 233
31) PI 9711338-7—Bayer AG (DE), 241
32) PI 9804055-3—Dr. Gerhard Gergely (AT), 233
33) PI 9806870-9—Glaxo Group Ltd. (GB), 236
34) PI 1100784-2—Quadrant Drug Delivery Ltd. (GB), 232
35) PP 1100122-4—Genentech Inc. (US), 233
36) PP 1100147-0—Warner-Lambert Co. LLC (US), 233
37) PP 1101020-7—Claude Nofre (FR) / Jean-Marie Tinti (FR), 232
38) PP 1101065-7—Gerhard Ohlenschlager (DE) / Gernot Treusch (DE), 235
41) PI 9507930-0—H. Lundbeck A/S (DK), 233
42) PI 9508384-7—Bayer AG (DE), 233
45) PI 9510422-4—Astra Aktiebolag (SE), 233
51) PI 9611234-4—Astra Aktiebolag (SE), 237
52) PI 9611455-0—Corixa Corp. (US), 232
53) PI 9611790-7—Pierre Fabre Medicament (FR), 233
58) PI 9709807-8—Pierre Fabre Medicament (FR), 233
59) PI 9710686-0—Octamer Inc. (US), 232
60) PI 9711059-0—Pierre Fabre Medicament (FR), 239
61) PI 9711148-1—Yamonouchi Europe B.V. (NL), 239
62) PI 9711411-1—Abbott GmbH & Co. KG (DE), 233
64) PI 9509819-4—Janssen Pharmaceutica N.V. (BE), 237
65) PI 9608284-4—Probi AB (SE), 235.
66) PI 9508664-1—GSF—Forschungszentrum Fuer Umwelt und Gesundheit, GmbH (DE), 232
67) PI 9507618-2—Institut Gustave Roussy (FR) / Institut National de La Sante Et de La Recherche Medicale (Inserm) (FR) / Laboratoires Serono S.A. (CH), 235
68) PI 9507615-8—Pharmacia & Up John Company (US), 232
69) PI 9503036-0—Eli Lilly and Co. (US), 241
70) PI 9500380-0—Pfizer Inc. (US), 233
71) PP 1101197-1—Novartis AG (CH), 241
72) PP 1101009-6—Biopharm Gesellschaft Zur Biotechnologischen Entwicklung Von Pharmaka Mbh (DE), 240
74) PP 1100690-0—Chugai Seiyaku Kabushiki Kaisha (JP), 238
75) PP 1100689-7—Sanofi-Aventis (FR), 240
76) PP 1100547-5—César Roberto Dias Nahoum (BR), 239
77) PP 1100533-5—John Wyeth & Brother Limited (GB), 238

GTI's Workflow (2012-2016)

1) PI 0005616-2—F. Hoffmann La Roche AG (CH), 251
2) PI 0008161-2—The Scripps Research Institute (US) / Lexigen Pharmaceuticals Corporation (US), 251
3) PI 0009887-6—F. Hoffmann-La Roche AG (FR),251
4) PI 0011159-7—The Government of the United States of America as Represented Bby the Department of Health and Human Services (US), 251
5) PI 0014171-2—Smeethkline Beecham Biologicals S.A. (BE), 251
6) PI 0014236-0—University of Iowa Research Foundation (US) / Coley Pharmaceutical GmbH (DE), 251
7) PI 0014390-1—Beijing Wanta Biological Pharmacy Enterprise Co. Ltd. (CN), 251
8) PI 0014687-0—Daiichi Sankyo Co. Ltd. (JP), 251
9) PI 0015320-6—Albany Molecular Research Inc. (US),251
10) PI 0016921-8—Sanofi-Aventis (FR),251
11) PI 0100199-0—Unicamp (BR), 251
12) PI 0101346-7—Unicamp (BR),251
13) PI 0108566-2—H. Lundbeck A/S (DK), 246
14) PI 0109885-3—Centre National de La Recherche Scientifique (FR), 251
15) PI 0111562-6—Eli Lilly and Co. (US), 251
16) PI 0112026-3—Abbott Laboratories (US),250
17) PI 0112497-8—ID Biomedical (CA), 250
18) PI 0112695-4—F. Hoffmann-La Roche AG (CH),245
19) PI 0116229-2—The Procter & Gamble Company (US), 252
22) PI 0117253-0—NeuTec Pharma Ltd. (GB), 252
23) PI 0206653-0—Schering AG (DE), 247
24) PI 0207883-0—Boehringer Ingelheim Pharma GmbH & Co. KG (DE), 247
25) PI 0211072-5—Astrazeneca UK Ltd. (GB),252
26) PI 0211262-0—AstraZeneca AB (SE), 245
27) PI 0212598-6—Bionorica AG (DE), 252
28) PI 0212809-8—Wyeth (US), 252
29) PI 0213329-6—Indena S.P.A (IT), 252
30) PI 0213932-4—Novartis AG (CH), 252
31) PI 0213970-7—Novartis AG (CH), 247
32) PI 0214245-7—F. Hoffmann-La Roche AG (CH), 252
33) PI 0214605-3—Astrazeneca AB (SE), 248
34) PI 0214767-0—Wyeth (US), 248
35) PI 0215157-0—The Procter & Gamble Company (US), 252
36) PI 0215336-0—Ipsen Pharma S.A.S. (FR).
37) PI 0215935-0—Wyeth (US), 252
38) PI 0215986-4—Cancer Research Technology Limited (GB), 245
39) PI 0302424-5—Cristália Produtos Químicos Farmacêuticos Ltda. (BR), 246
40) PI 0306707-6—Sanofi-Aventis (FR), 245
41) PI 0307050-6—Merck Frosst Canada (CA), 245

Index

D

E

Q

R

S

www.ingramcontent.com/pod-product-compliance
Ingram Content Group UK Ltd.
Pitfield, Milton Keynes, MK11 3LW, UK
UKHW020233290926
15470UKWH00002B/511

9 789403 528823